Test Bank

for

Stewart's

Calculus
Early Transcendentals

Fifth Edition

THOMSON

BROOKS/COLE

Australia • Canada • Mexico • Singapore • Spain • United Kingdom • United States

Printed in the United States of America
1 2 3 4 5 6 7   08 07 06 05 04

Printer: Thomson/West

ISBN: 0-534-39336-5

For more information about our products,
contact us at:
Thomson Learning Academic Resource Center
1-800-423-0563

For permission to use material from this text or product, submit a request online at
http://www.thomsonrights.com.
Any additional questions about permissions can be submitted by email to **thomsonrights@thomson.com.**

Thomson Brooks/Cole
10 Davis Drive
Belmont, CA 94002-3098
USA

Asia
Thomson Learning
5 Shenton Way #01-01
UIC Building
Singapore 068808

Australia/New Zealand
Thomson Learning
102 Dodds Street
Southbank, Victoria 3006
Australia

Canada
Nelson
1120 Birchmount Road
Toronto, Ontario M1K 5G4
Canada

Europe/Middle East/South Africa
Thomson Learning
High Holborn House
50/51 Bedford Row
London WC1R 4LR
United Kingdom

Latin America
Thomson Learning
Seneca, 53
Colonia Polanco
11560 Mexico D.F.
Mexico

Spain/Portugal
Paraninfo
Calle/Magallanes, 25
28015 Madrid, Spain

Table of Contents

Chapter 5
Test Form A- Free Response
Test Form B- Free Response
Test Form C- Multiple Choice
Test Form D- Multiple Choice
Test Form E- Mixed (Free Response/Multiple Choice)
Test Form F- Mixed (Free Response/Multiple Choice)
Test Form G- Mixed (Free Response/Multiple Choice)
Test Form H- Mixed (Free Response/Multiple Choice)

Chapter 6
Test Form A- Free Response
Test Form B- Free Response
Test Form C- Multiple Choice
Test Form D- Multiple Choice
Test Form E- Mixed (Free Response/Multiple Choice)
Test Form F- Mixed (Free Response/Multiple Choice)
Test Form G- Mixed (Free Response/Multiple Choice)
Test Form H- Mixed (Free Response/Multiple Choice)

Chapter 7
Test Form A- Free Response
Test Form B- Free Response
Test Form C- Multiple Choice
Test Form D- Multiple Choice
Test Form E- Mixed (Free Response/Multiple Choice)
Test Form F- Mixed (Free Response/Multiple Choice)
Test Form G- Mixed (Free Response/Multiple Choice)
Test Form H- Mixed (Free Response/Multiple Choice)

Chapter 8
Test Form A- Free Response
Test Form B- Free Response
Test Form C- Multiple Choice
Test Form D- Multiple Choice
Test Form E- Mixed (Free Response/Multiple Choice)
Test Form F- Mixed (Free Response/Multiple Choice)
Test Form G- Mixed (Free Response/Multiple Choice)
Test Form H- Mixed (Free Response/Multiple Choice)

Chapter 9
Test Form A- Free Response
Test Form B- Free Response
Test Form C- Multiple Choice
Test Form D- Multiple Choice
Test Form E- Mixed (Free Response/Multiple Choice)
Test Form F- Mixed (Free Response/Multiple Choice)
Test Form G- Mixed (Free Response/Multiple Choice)
Test Form H- Mixed (Free Response/Multiple Choice)

Chapter 10
Test Form A- Free Response
Test Form B- Free Response
Test Form C- Multiple Choice
Test Form D- Multiple Choice
Test Form E- Mixed (Free Response/Multiple Choice)
Test Form F- Mixed (Free Response/Multiple Choice)
Test Form G- Mixed (Free Response/Multiple Choice)
Test Form H- Mixed (Free Response/Multiple Choice)

Chapter 11
Test Form A- Free Response
Test Form B- Free Response
Test Form C- Multiple Choice
Test Form D- Multiple Choice
Test Form E- Mixed (Free Response/Multiple Choice)
Test Form F- Mixed (Free Response/Multiple Choice)
Test Form G- Mixed (Free Response/Multiple Choice)
Test Form H- Mixed (Free Response/Multiple Choice)

Chapter 12
Test Form A- Free Response
Test Form B- Free Response
Test Form C- Multiple Choice
Test Form D- Multiple Choice
Test Form E- Mixed (Free Response/Multiple Choice)
Test Form F- Mixed (Free Response/Multiple Choice)
Test Form G- Mixed (Free Response/Multiple Choice)
Test Form H- Mixed (Free Response/Multiple Choice)

Chapter 13
Test Form A- Free Response
Test Form B- Free Response
Test Form C- Multiple Choice
Test Form D- Multiple Choice
Test Form E- Mixed (Free Response/Multiple Choice)
Test Form F- Mixed (Free Response/Multiple Choice)
Test Form G- Mixed (Free Response/Multiple Choice)
Test Form H- Mixed (Free Response/Multiple Choice)

Chapter 14
Test Form A- Free Response
Test Form B- Free Response
Test Form C- Multiple Choice
Test Form D- Multiple Choice
Test Form E- Mixed (Free Response/Multiple Choice)
Test Form F- Mixed (Free Response/Multiple Choice)
Test Form G- Mixed (Free Response/Multiple Choice)
Test Form H- Mixed (Free Response/Multiple Choice)

Chapter 15
Test Form A- Free Response
Test Form B- Free Response
Test Form C- Multiple Choice
Test Form D- Multiple Choice
Test Form E- Mixed (Free Response/Multiple Choice)
Test Form F- Mixed (Free Response/Multiple Choice)
Test Form G- Mixed (Free Response/Multiple Choice)
Test Form H- Mixed (Free Response/Multiple Choice)

Chapter 16
Test Form A- Free Response
Test Form B- Free Response
Test Form C- Multiple Choice
Test Form D- Multiple Choice
Test Form E- Mixed (Free Response/Multiple Choice)
Test Form F- Mixed (Free Response/Multiple Choice)
Test Form G- Mixed (Free Response/Multiple Choice)
Test Form H- Mixed (Free Response/Multiple Choice)

Chapter 17
Test Form A- Free Response
Test Form B- Free Response
Test Form C- Multiple Choice
Test Form D- Multiple Choice
Test Form E- Mixed (Free Response/Multiple Choice)
Test Form F- Mixed (Free Response/Multiple Choice)
Test Form G- Mixed (Free Response/Multiple Choice)
Test Form H- Mixed (Free Response/Multiple Choice)

Final Exam
Test Form A- Free Response
Test Form B- Multiple Choice
Test Form C- Mixed (Free Response/Multiple Choice)

1. A spherical balloon with radius r inches has volume $\frac{4}{3}\pi r^3$.

    Find a function that represents the amount of air required to inflate the balloon from a radius of r inches to a radius of $r + 1$ inches.

2. Find the domain of the function.

    $g(u) = \sqrt{u} - \sqrt{2 - u}$

3. Find the range of the function.

    $h(x) = \sqrt{16 - x^2}$

4. Find an expression for the function $y = f(x)$ whose graph is the bottom half of the parabola $x + (8 - y)^2 = 0$.

5. A rectangle has perimeter 28 m.

    Express the area of the rectangle as a function $A(l)$ of the length l of one of its sides.

6. An open rectangular box with volume 3 m^3 has a square base.

    Express the surface area of the box as a function $S(x)$ of the length x of a side of the base.

7. If the point $(7, 3)$ is on the graph of an even function, what other point must also be on the graph?

8. In the function $f(x) = 3x + d$, what must be the coefficient d, if $f(6) = 1$?

9. Compare the functions $f(x) = x^8$ and $g(x) = e^x$ by graphing both f and g in several viewing rectangles.

    When does the graph of g finally surpass the graph of f?

10. Use the table to evaluate the expression $(f \circ g)(3)$.

x	1	2	3	4	5	6
$f(x)$	3	2	1	0	1	2
$g(x)$	6	5	2	3	4	6

11. Find the domain of the function.

$$f(x) = \frac{5}{1 - e^{-x}}$$

12. Suppose that the graph of $y = \log_2 x$ is drawn on a coordinate grid where the unit of measurement is an inch. How many miles to the right of the origin do we have to move before the height of the curve reaches 2 ft?

13. Use a graph to estimate the values of x such that $e^x > 10,000,000,000$. Round your answer to one decimal place.

14. Jason leaves Detroit at 3:00 P.M. and drives at a constant speed west along I-90. He passes Ann Arbor, 40 mi from Detroit, at 3:30 P.M.

    The graph of the function of the distance traveled (in miles) in terms of the time elapsed (in hours) is given below.

    Find the slope of the function.

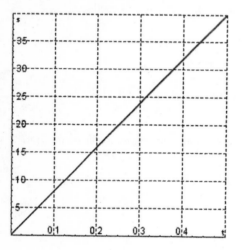

15. The monthly cost of driving a car depends on the number of miles driven. Samantha found that in October it cost her $312.5 to drive 500 mi and in February it cost her $375 to drive 1,000 mi.

    Express the monthly cost C as a function of the distance driven d assuming that a linear relationship gives a suitable model.

16. Find a formula for the inverse of the function.

    $$y = \ln(x + 5)$$

17. Use a graph to decide whether f is one-to-one.

$f(x) = x^9 - x$

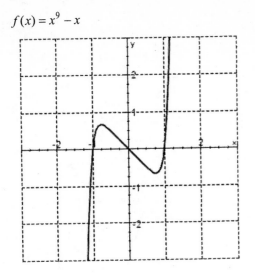

18. Find the exponential function $f(x) = Ca^x$ whose graph is given.

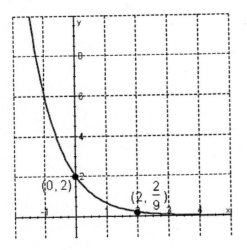

19. Fill in the blanks.

Find the exact value of each expression.

$\log_{10} 25 + \log_{10} 40 =$ _____

$\log_5 20 + \log_5 10 - 3\log_5 2 =$ _____

20. If $f(x) = x + 3$ and $h(x) = 4x - 4$, find a function g such that $g \circ f = h$.

1. $\dfrac{4}{3}\pi(3r^2 + 3r + 1)$

2. $0 \le u \le 2$

3. $0 \le h(x) \le 4$

4. $y = 8 - \sqrt{-x}$

5. $A(l) = (14 - l)l$

6. $S(x) = x^2 + \dfrac{12}{x}$

7. $(-7, 3)$

8. -17

9. $x \approx 26.1$

10. 2

11. $(-\infty, 0) \cup (0, \infty)$

12. 265

13. $x > 23.0$

14. 80

15. $C = 0.125d + 250$

16. $y = e^x - 5$

17. no

18. $f(x) = 2\left(\dfrac{1}{3}\right)^x$

19. $3, 2$

20. $4x - 16$

1. An open rectangular box with volume 6 m^3 has a square base.

   Express the surface area of the box as a function $S(x)$ of the length x of a side of the base.

2. A box with an open top is to be constructed from a rectangular piece of cardboard with dimensions $b = 13$ in. by $a = 20$ in. by cutting out equal squares of side x at each corner and then folding up the sides as in the figure.

   Express the volume V of the box as a function of x.

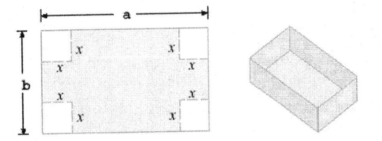

3. If the point (2, 9) is on the graph of an even function, what other point must also be on the graph?

4. In the function $f(x) = 6x + b$, what must be the coefficient b, if $f(5) = 1$?

5. Decide what type of function you might choose as a model for the data.

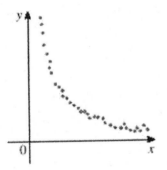

6. Use a graph to estimate the values of x such that $e^x > 10,000,000,000$. Round your answer to one decimal place.

7. Simplify the expression.

   $\sin(2\cos^{-1} 4x)$

8. The monthly cost of driving a car depends on the number of miles driven. Ann found that in October it cost her $285 to drive 100 mi and in May it cost her $335 to drive 300 mi.

   Express the monthly cost C as a function of the distance driven d assuming that a linear relationship gives a suitable model.

9. A study by the U. S. Office of Science and Technology in 1972 estimated the cost (in 1972 dollars) to reduce automobile emissions by certain percentages, and the graph gives the linear model of this table.

Reduction in emissions (%)	Cost per car (in $)
50	20
55	25.05
60	29.95
65	34.95
70	39.95

Find the cost, if the reduction in emissions is 80%, using this model.

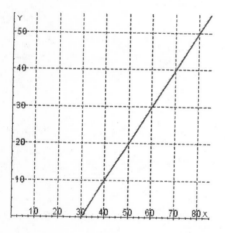

10. Suppose that the graph of $y = \log_2 x$ is drawn on a coordinate grid where the unit of measurement is an inch. How many miles to the right of the origin do we have to move before the height of the curve reaches 3 ft?

11. Find $f + g$.

   $$f(x) = x^3 + 4x^2$$
   $$g(x) = 5x^2 - 3$$

12. Use the table to evaluate the expression $(f \circ g)(3)$.

x	1	2	3	4	5	6
$f(x)$	0	1	2	3	4	5
$g(x)$	4	5	2	4	1	5

13. If $f(x) = x + 3$ and $h(x) = 3x - 5$, find a function g such that $g \circ f = h$.

14. How many solutions does the equation have?

$$\cos \frac{1}{5} x = 14.5$$

15. For what values of x is the inequality true $8 \,|\sin x - (x - 4\pi)| \, < \, 0.8$?

Write your answer correct to two decimal places.

16. Find the exponential function $f(x) = Ca^x$ whose graph is given.

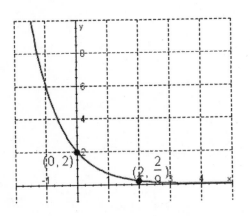

17. Decide what type of function you might choose as a model for the data.

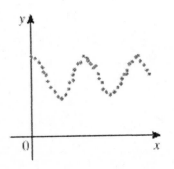

18. Jason leaves Detroit at 6:00 P.M. and drives at a constant speed west along I-90. He passes Ann Arbor, 60 mi from Detroit, at 6:50 P.M. The graph of the function of the distance traveled (in miles) in terms of the time elapsed (in hours) is given below.

    Find the slope of this function.

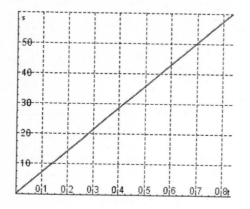

19. Find a formula for the inverse of the function.

    $y = \ln(x + 8)$

20. Compare the functions $f(x) = x^{10}$ and $g(x) = e^x$ by graphing both f and g in several viewing rectangles.

    When does the graph of g finally surpass the graph of f?

1. $S(x) = x^2 + \dfrac{24}{x}$

2. $V(x) = x(20 - 2x)(13 - 2x)$

3. $(-2, 9)$

4. -29

5. exponential

6. $x > 16.1$

7. $8x\sqrt{1 - 16x^2}$

8. $C = 0.25d + 260$

9. 50

10. 1084588

11. $x^3 + 9x^2 - 3$

12. 1

13. $3x - 14$

14. 1

15. $(11.72, 13.42)$

16. $f(x) = 2\left(\dfrac{1}{3}\right)^x$

17. trigonometric

18. 72

19. $y = e^x - 8$

20. $x \approx 35.8$

1. Find the domain of the function.

   $g(u) = \sqrt{u} - \sqrt{9-u}$

   Select the correct answer.

   a. $u \in [0, \ +\infty)$

   b. $u \in (-\infty, \ 0]$

   c. $u \in (0, \ 9)$

   d. $u \in [0, \ 9]$

   e. $u \in (-\infty, \ 9]$

2. Find the domain and range of the function.

   $g(x) = \sin^{-1}(5x + 1)$

   Select the correct answer.

   a.   Domain $\left[-\dfrac{2}{5}, \ 0 \right]$

   Range $\left[-\dfrac{\pi}{2}, \ \dfrac{\pi}{2} \right]$

   b.   Domain $\left[-\dfrac{2}{5}, \ 0 \right]$

   Range $\left[0, \ \pi \right]$

   c.   Domain $\left[-\dfrac{1}{5}, \ 0 \right]$

   Range $\left[-\dfrac{\pi}{2}, \ \dfrac{\pi}{2} \right]$

   d.   Domain $\left[-\dfrac{1}{5}, \ 0 \right]$

   Range $\left[0, \ \pi \right]$

   e.   Domain $\left[-\dfrac{1}{5}, \ 0 \right]$

   Range $\left[0, \ 2\pi \right]$

3. Suppose that the graph of $y = \log_2 x$ is drawn on a coordinate grid where the unit of measurement is an inch. How many miles to the right of the origin do we have to move before the height of the curve reaches 2 ft? Select the correct answer.

    a.   265 mi
    b.   269 mi
    c.   259 mi
    d.   261 mi
    e.   271 mi

4. Which function is represented by the following graph?

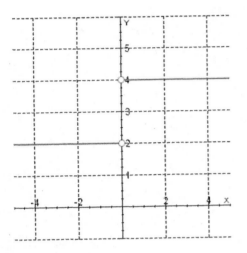

    Select the correct answer.

    a. $G(x) = \dfrac{3x - |-x|}{x}$

    b. $G(x) = \dfrac{3x + |x|}{x}$

    c. $G(x) = \dfrac{3x - |x|}{x}$

    d. $G(x) = \dfrac{3x + |-x|}{x}$

    e. $G(x) = \dfrac{3 + |x|}{x}$

5. Which of the following graphs is neither even nor odd.

    Select the correct answer.

    a. $f(x) = 6x^3 + 8x^2 + 7$
    b. $f(x) = x^4 - 4x^2$
    c. $f(x) = x^3 - 5x$

6. What is the equation of this graph?

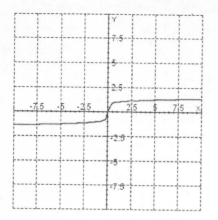

Select the correct answer.

a. $y = \sqrt[7]{x}$

b. $y = \sqrt[5]{x}$

c. $y = x^7$

d. $y = x^5$

e. $y = -x^7$

7 Jason leaves Detroit at 6:00 P.M. and drives at a constant speed west along I-90. He passes Ann Arbor, 40 mi from Detroit, at 6:50 P.M.

Find the slope of the function.

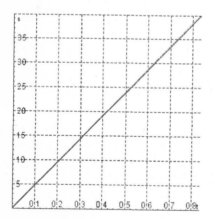

Select the correct answer.

a. 48

b. 36

c. 64

d. 24

e. 14

8. Find the exact value of each expression.

    $\sin(\sin^{-1} 0.6)$

    Select the correct answer.

    a.   1
    b.   0.6
    c.   - 0.6
    d.   - 1
    e.   0

9. The manager of a furniture factory finds that it costs $2200to manufacture 100 chairs in one day and $4800 to produce300 chairs in one day.

    Find the cost, if the factory produced 200 chairs.

    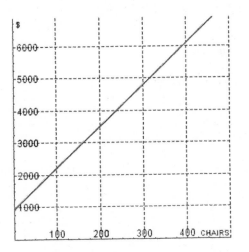

    Select the correct answer.

    a.   3,500
    b.   2,100
    c.   500
    d.   700
    e.   1,500

10. Find the domain of f^{-1}.

$$f(x) = \sqrt{6 - e^{6x}}$$

Select the correct answer.

a. $[0, \sqrt{6})$

b. $[0, \sqrt{6}]$

c. $(0, \sqrt{6})$

d. $(0, \infty)$

e. $(-\infty, \sqrt{6})$

11. The table shows (lifetime) peptic ulcer rates (per 100 population) for various family incomes as reported by the 1989National Health Interview Survey.

Find a slope of linear model using the first and last data points.

Number of data point	Ulcer rate (per 100 population)	Income
First	14.1	4,000
Second	13.6	5,000
Third	13.9	8,000
Forth	13.3	14,000
Fifth	12.1	20,000

Select the correct answer.

a. -0.00008
b. -0.0005
c. -0.000125
d. -0.00125
e. -0.01

12. What is $\sqrt[6]{x}$, given that $H = f \circ g \circ h$ and $H(x) = \sqrt[6]{\sqrt{x} - 4}$?

Select the correct answer.

a. $g(x)$
b. $h(x)$
c. $f(x)$

13. Use a graphing calculator or computer to determine which viewing rectangle produces the most appropriate graph of the function.

$$f(x) = \sqrt{4x - x^2}$$

Select the correct answer.

a.　　[-5, 5] by [0, 100]
b.　　[-2, 2] by [-2, 2]
c.　　[-4, 4] by [-4, 4]
d.　　[- 1, 5] by [-1, 4]
e.　　[1, 5] by [1, 4]

14. Use graphs to determine which of the functions $f(x) = 5x^2$ or $g(x) = \dfrac{x^3}{5}$ is eventually larger (that is, larger when x is very large).

Select the correct answer.

a.　　$g(x) = \dfrac{x^3}{5}$

b.　　$f(x) = 5x^2$

15. Starting with the graph of $y = e^x$, find the equation of the graph that results from reflecting about the line $y = 5$.

Select the correct answer.

a.　　$y = -e^x$

b.　　$y = -e^{x+10}$

c.　　$y = -e^x + 10$

d.　　$y = e^{-x} + 10$

e.　　$y = -e^{-5x} + 10$

16. Suppose you are offered a job that lasts two months. Which of the following methods of payment is more profitable?

Select the correct answer.

a.　　One cent on the first day, two cents on the second day, four cents on the third day, and, in general, 2^{n-1} cents on the n-th day.

b.　　One million dollars at the end of each month.

17. Suppose the graphs of $f(x) = x^2$ and $f(x) = 2^x$ are drawn on a coordinate grid where the unit of measurement is 1 inch. At a distance 1 ft to the right of the origin, the height of the graph of f is 12 ft. Find the height of the graph of g.

    Select the correct answer.

    a.   331 ft
    b.   341 ft
    c.   171 ft
    d.   3,410 ft
    e.   3,110 ft

18. Compare the functions $f(x) = x^{12}$ and $g(x) = e^x$ by graphing both f and g in several viewing rectangles. When does the graph of g finally surpass the graph of f ?

    Select the correct answer.

    a.   35.9
    b.   47.9
    c.   32.0
    d.   45.9
    e.   40.2

19. Under ideal conditions a certain bacteria population is known to double every three hours. Suppose that there are initially 25 bacteria. What is the size of the population after 15 hours?

    Select the correct answer.

    a.   820 bacteria
    b.   800 bacteria
    c.   6,100 bacteria
    d.   400 bacteria
    e.   2,100 bacteria

20. Find a formula for the inverse of the function.

    $y = \ln(x + 5)$

    Select the correct answer.

    a. $y = 5e^x$
    b. $y = e^{x+5}$
    c. $y = e^x + 5$
    d. $y = e^x - 5$
    e. $y = -e^{5x} - 5$

ANSWER KEY

Stewart - Calculus ET 5e Chapter 1 Form C

1. d

2. a

3. a

4. b

5. a

6. a

7. a

8. b

9. a

10. a

11. c

12. c

13. d

14. a

15. c

16. a

17. b

18. d

19. b

20. d

1. A rectangle has perimeter 18 m.

   Express the area of the rectangle as a function $A(l)$ of the length l of one of its sides.

   Select the correct answer.

   a. $A(l) = 9l + l^2$

   b. $A(l) = 9l - l^2$

   c. $A(l) = 18l + l^2$

   d. $A(l) = 18l - l^2$

   e. $A(l) = l - 9l^2$

2. Consider the functions.

   $f(x) = \sin x$

   $g(x) = 5 - \sqrt{x}$

   Find $f \circ g$.

   Select the correct answer.

   a. $(f \circ g)(x) = 5 - \sqrt{\sin x}$

   b. $(f \circ g)(x) = \sin(\sin x)$

   c. $(f \circ g)(x) = \sin(5 - \sqrt{x})$

   d. $(f \circ g)(x) = 5 - \sqrt{5 - \sqrt{x}}$

   e. $(f \circ g)(x) = \sin x - \sqrt{\sin \sqrt{x} - 5}$

3. Determine an appropriate viewing rectangle for the given function.

   $f(x) = 6^{\cos(x^2)}$

   Select the correct answer.

   a. $[-8, 8]$ by $[0, 7]$
   b. $[0, 7]$ by $[0, 8]$
   c. $[-8, 0]$ by $[0, 7]$
   d. $[-8, 8]$ by $[-7, 7]$
   e. $[8, 10]$ by $[-100, 7]$

4. We consider the family of functions $f(x) = \sqrt[n]{x}$, where n is a positive integer. Graph the root functions $y = \sqrt{x}$, $y = \sqrt[3]{x}$, $y = \sqrt[5]{x}$ on the same screen using the viewing rectangle $[-1, 4]$, $[-1, 3]$.

Select the correct answer.

a.

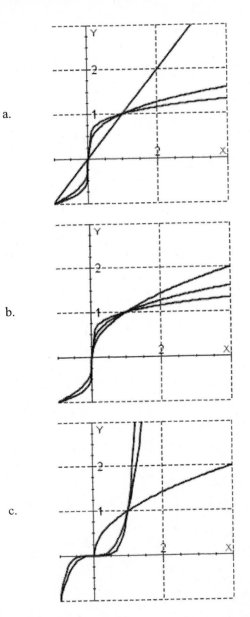

b.

c.

5. The function $f(x) = \sqrt{1 + cx^2}$ is graphed below.

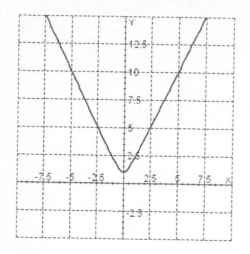

Choose the correct statement.

a. $c = 0$
b. $c > 0$
c. $c < 0$

6. Simplify the expression.

$\sin(2\cos^{-1} 6x)$

Select the correct answer.

a. $12x\sqrt{1 - 72x^2}$
b. $6x\sqrt{2 - 36x^2}$
c. $24x\sqrt{1 - 36x^2}$
d. $12x\sqrt{1 - 36x^2}$
e. $6x\sqrt{1 - x^2}$

7. Sketch the general shape of the graph of the exponential function for the case $0 < a < 1$.

 Select the correct answer.

 a.

 b.

 c.

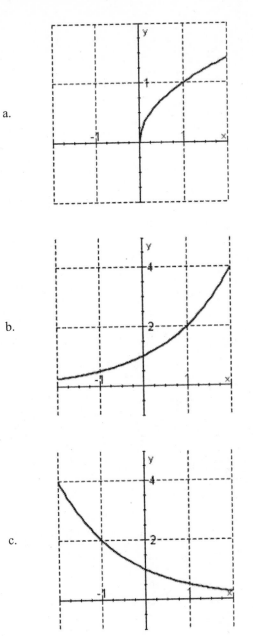

8. Graph the given function.

$y = e^x$

Select the correct answer.

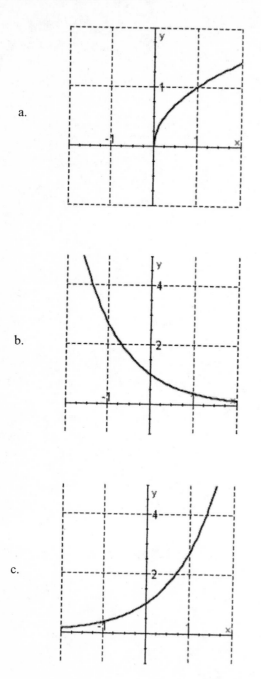

a.

b.

c.

9. Graph the given function.

$$y = \left(\frac{1}{5}\right)^x$$

Select the correct answer.

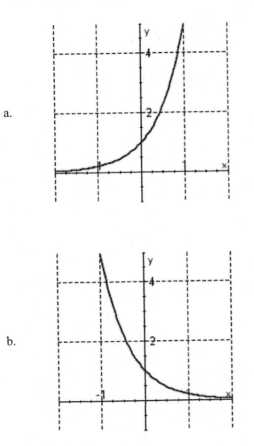

a.

b.

10. What is the natural exponential function?

Select the correct answer.

    a. $f(x) = ex$

    b. $f(x) = \dfrac{e}{x}$

    c. $f(x) = e^x$

    d. $f(x) = x^e$

    e. $f(x) = x^{\sqrt{e}}$

11. Make a rough sketch of the graph of the function. Do not use a calculator.

$$y = -3^x$$

Select the correct answer.

a.

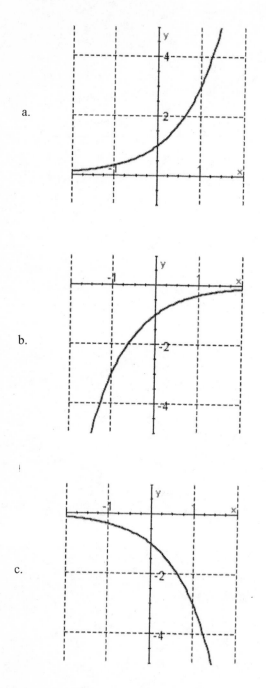

b.

c.

12. Make a rough sketch of the graph of the function. Do not use a calculator.

$$y = 2 + 3(1 - e^{-x})$$

Select the correct answer.

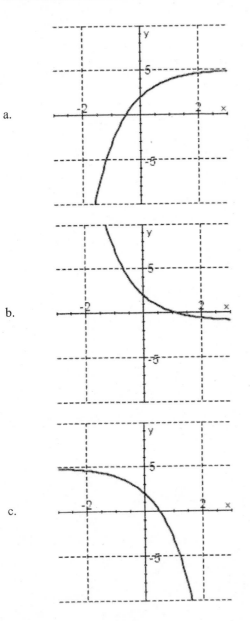

a.

b.

c.

13. Starting with the graph of $y = e^x$, write the equation of the graph that results from shifting 2 units right.

   Select the correct answer.

   a. $y = e^x - 2$

   b. $y = e^{x+2}$

   c. $y = e^x + 2$

   d. $y = e^{x-2}$

   e. $y = 2e^{x-2}$

14. Find the exponential function $f(x) = Ca^x$ whose graph is given.

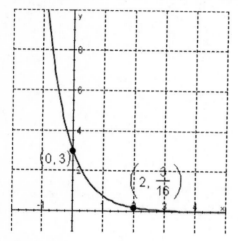

   Select the correct answer.

   a. $f(x) = \dfrac{1}{3^x}$

   b. $f(x) = 4\left(\dfrac{1}{3}\right)^x$

   c. $f(x) = \left(\dfrac{3}{4}\right)^x$

   d. $f(x) = 3\left(\dfrac{1}{4}\right)^x$

   e. $f(x) = \left(\dfrac{2}{3}\right)^x$

15. Use a graph to estimate the values of x such that $e^x > 100,000,000$.

    Select the correct answer.

    a. $x > 28.4$
    b. $x > 18.4$
    c. $x > 29.0$
    d. $x > 20.4$
    e. $x > 40.4$

16. The table gives the population of the United States, in millions, for the years 1900 - 2000. Use a graphing calculator with exponential regression capability to model the U.S. population since 1900. Use the model to estimate the population in 1955 and to predict the population in the year 2015.

Year	1900	1910	1920	1930	1940	1950	1960	1970	1980	1990	2000
Population (millions)	76	92	106	123	131	150	179	203	227	250	281

    Select the correct answer.

    a.   113 millions, 288 millions
    b.   163 millions, 412 millions
    c.   163 millions, 352 millions
    d.   113 millions, 352 millions
    e.   163 millions, 163 millions

17. Find a formula for the inverse of the function.

    $y = \ln(x + 8)$

    Select the correct answer.

    a. $y = e^{x+8}$

    b. $y = e^x - 8$

    c. $y = e^x + 8$

    d. $y = 8e^x$

    e. $y = -8e^x$

18. Suppose that the graph of $y = \log_2 x$ is drawn on a coordinate grid where the unit of measurement is an inch. How many miles to the right of the origin do we have to move before the height of the curve reaches 3 ft? Select the correct answer.

    a.   1,084,592 mi
    b.   1,084,588 mi
    c.   1,084,582 mi
    d.   1,084,584 mi
    e.   1,084,425 mi

19. Find the exact value of the expression.

$$\log_5 10 + \log_5 40 - 4\log_5 2$$

Select the correct answer.

a.   2
b.   5
c.   3
d.   4
e.   1

20. Express the given quantity as a single logarithm.

$$y = \ln p + w\ln q - v\ln t$$

Select the correct answer.

a. $\ln(p + q^w - t^v)$

b. $\ln\left(\dfrac{pqw}{tv}\right)$

c. $\ln\left(\dfrac{pq^w}{t^v}\right)$

d. $\ln\left(\dfrac{pt^v}{q^w}\right)$

e. $v\ln pqt$

ANSWER KEY

Stewart - Calculus ET 5e Chapter 1 Form D

1. b

2. c

3. d

4. b

5. b

6. d

7. c

8. c

9. b

10. c

11. c

12. a

13. d

14. d

15. b

16. c

17. b

18. b

19. a

20. c

ANSWER KEY

1. The graphs of $f(x)$ and $g(x)$ are given. For what values of x is $f(x) = g(x)$?

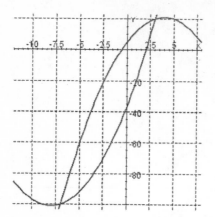

   Select the correct answer.

   a.   -7, 4
   b.   -2, 2
   c.   -7, 3
   d.   -5, 2
   e.   -9, 4

2. Find the range of the function.

   $$h(x) = \sqrt{64 - x^2}$$

3. If the point (5, 3) is on the graph of an even function, what other point must also be on the graph?

4. In the function $f(x) = 5x + d$, what must be the coefficient d, if $f(4) = 1$?

5. Simplify the expression.

   $$\sin(2\cos^{-1} 4x)$$

6. Find the domain of the function.

   $$f(x) = \frac{1}{1 - e^x}$$

7. Jason leaves Detroit at 3:00 P.M. and drives at a constant speed west along I-90. He passes Ann Arbor, 60 mi from Detroit, at 3:50 P.M.

Find the slope of this function.

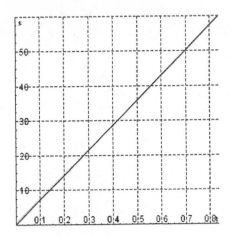

Select the correct answer.

a.   91
b.   73
c.   72
d.   88
e.   82

8. The table shows (lifetime) peptic ulcer rates (per 100 population) for various family incomes as reported by the 1989 National Health Interview Survey.

Find the slope of the linear model using the first and last data points.

Number of data point	Ulcer rate (per 100 population)	Income
First	14.3	3,000
Second	13.8	4,000
Third	14.2	8,000
Forth	13.5	13,000
Fifth	12.3	19,000

Select the correct answer.

a.   -0.0005
b.   -0.00008
c.   -0.000125
d.   -0.125
e.   -1.5

9. A study by the U. S. Office of Science and Technology in 1972 estimated the cost (in dollars) to reduce automobile emissions by certain percentages and the graph gives the linear model of this table.

Reduction in emissions (%)	Cost per car (in $)
50	24
55	29.05
60	33.95
65	38.95
70	43.95

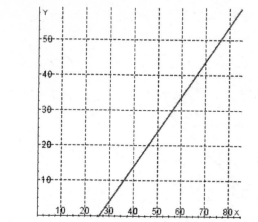

Find the cost, if the reduction in emissions is 80%, using this model.

Select the correct answer.

a. $63
b. $259
c. $44
d. $54
e. $70

10. Which of the following graphs is the graph of the function $f(x) = \sin |3x|$?

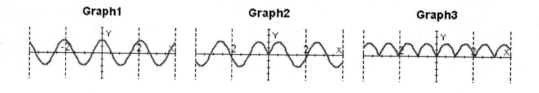

Graph1   Graph2   Graph3

11. Find $f - g$.

$$f(x) = \sqrt{1+x}$$
$$g(x) = \sqrt{1-x}$$

12. What is $\sqrt[10]{x}$, given that $H = f \circ g \circ h$ and $H(x) = \sqrt[10]{\sqrt{x} - 3}$?

Select the correct answer.

    a. $f(x)$

    b. $g(x)$

    c. $h(x)$

    d.   none

13. If $f(x) = x + 3$ and $h(x) = 6x - 2$, find a function g such that $g \circ f = h$.

Select the correct answer.

    a. $g(x) = 6x + 20$

    b. $g(x) = 6x - 20$

    c. $g(x) = 6x - 16$

    d. $g(x) = x + 20$

    e. $g(x) = 20x - 16$

14. How many solutions does the equation have?

$$\cos \frac{1}{10} x = 3.5x$$

Select the correct answer.

    a.   one solution

    b.   no solutions

    c.   two solutions

    d.   three solutions

15. For what values of x is the inequality true?

$$15 \left| \sin - (x - 30\pi) \right| < 1.5$$

Select the answer that is correct to two decimal places.

    a.   (23.58, 25.28)

    b.   (24.28, 25.98)

    c.   (23.78, 25.48)

    d.   (25.58, 26.98)

    e.   (26.58, 27.28)

16. Use a graphing calculator or computer to determine which viewing rectangle produces the most appropriate graph of the function.

$$f(x) = 48 + 28x - x^3$$

Select the correct answer.

a.   [-4, 4] by [-4, 4]
b.   [-10, 10] by [-10, 10]
c.   [-100, 100] by [-200, 200]
d.   [-0.5, 0.5] by [0, 5]
e.   [-10, 0] by [-10, 0]

17. We consider the family of functions $f(x) = \sqrt[n]{x}$, where n is a positive integer. Graph the root functions $y = x$, $y = \sqrt[4]{x}$, $y = \sqrt[5]{x}$ on the same screen using the viewing rectangle [-1, 4], [-1, 3].

Select the correct answer.

a.

b.

c.

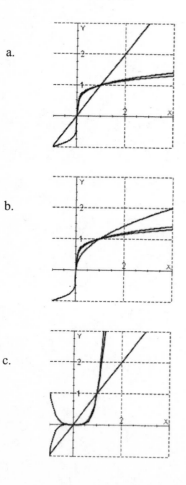

18. Express the given quantity as a single logarithm.

$\ln x + a \ln y - b \ln z$

19. Suppose that the graph of $y = \log_2 x$ is drawn on a coordinate grid where the unit of measurement is an inch. How many miles to the right of the origin do we have to move before the height of the curve reaches 3 ft?

20. Find a formula for the inverse of the function.

$y = \ln(x + 8)$

1. c

2. $0 \le h(x) \le 8$

3. (-5, 3)

4. -19

5. $8x\sqrt{1-16x^2}$

6. $(-\infty, 0) \cup (0, \infty)$

7. c

8. c

9. d

10. 2

11. $\sqrt{1+x} - \sqrt{1-x}$

12. a

13. b

14. a

15. b

16. c

17. a

18. $\ln\left(\dfrac{xy^a}{z^b}\right)$

19. 1084588

20. $y = e^x - 8$

1. Find the domain of the function.

    $g(u) = \sqrt{u} - \sqrt{8-u}$

    Select the correct answer.

    a. $u \in (0, \ 8]$
    b. $u \in [0, \ 8)$
    c. $u \in (0, \ 8)$
    d. $u \in [0, \ 8]$
    e. $u \in (-\infty, \ 0]$

2. Find the range of the function.

    $h(x) = \sqrt{9-x^2}$

3. Find an expression for the function $y = f(x)$ whose graph is the bottom half of the parabola
    $x + (3-y)^2 = 0$.

4. A rectangle has perimeter 18 m.

    Express the area of the rectangle as a function $A(l)$ of the length l of one of its sides.

5. An open rectangular box with volume 5 m^3 has a square base.

    Express the surface area of the box as a function $S(x)$ of the length x of a side of the base.

    Select the correct answer.

    a. $S(x) = x^2 + \dfrac{20}{x^2}$

    b. $S(x) = 2x + \dfrac{5}{x}$

    c. $S(x) = 2x^2 + \dfrac{5}{x^2}$

    d. $S(x) = x^2 + \dfrac{10}{x}$

    e. $S(x) = x^2 + \dfrac{20}{x}$

6. A box with an open top is to be constructed from a rectangular piece of cardboard with dimensions $b = 17$ in. by $a = 23$ in. by cutting out equal squares of side x at each corner and then folding up the sides as in the figure.

Express the volume V of the box as a function of x.

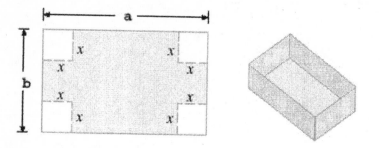

7. What is the equation of this graph?

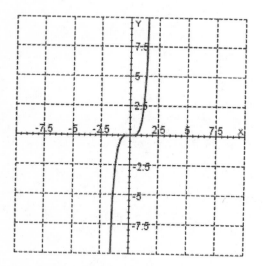

Select the correct answer.

a. $y = x^6$

b. $y = x^2$

c. $y = x^5$

d. $y = x^4$

e. $y = \sqrt[3]{x}$

8. If the point (9, 8) is on the graph of an even function, what other point must also be on the graph?

9. Find the domain of the function.

$$f(x) = \frac{2}{1 + e^x}$$

10. Under ideal conditions a certain bacteria population is known to double every three hours. Suppose that there are initially 25 bacteria. What is the size of the population after 15 hours?

    Select the correct answer.

    a.   810 bacteria
    b.   1,600 bacteria
    c.   3,000 bacteria
    d.   800 bacteria
    e.   950 bacteria

11. Jason leaves Detroit at 5:00 P.M. and drives at a constant speed west along I-90. He passes Ann Arbor, 40 mi from Detroit, at 5:50 P.M.

    Find the slope this function.

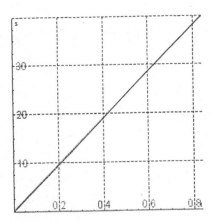

    Select the correct answer.

    a.   58
    b.   48
    c.   38
    d.   28
    e.   68

12. The monthly cost of driving a car depends on the number of miles driven. Mary found that in December it cost her $267.5 to drive 300 mi and in May it cost her $317.5 to drive 700 mi.

Express the monthly cost C as a function of the distance driven d assuming that a linear relationship gives a suitable model.

Select the correct answer.

    a. $C = 0.125d + 230$
    b. $C = 230d + 0.125$
    c. $C = 0.125d - 230$
    d. $C = 230d - 0.125$
    e. $C = 0.125d + 200$

13. A stone is dropped into a lake, creating a circular ripple that travels outward at a speed of 58 cm/s.

Express the radius r of this circle as a function of the time t (in seconds) and find $A \circ r$, if A is the area of this circle as a function of the radius.

14. Find a formula for the inverse of the function.

$y = \ln(x + 2)$

15. When a camera flash goes off, the batteries immediately begin to recharge the flash's capacitor, which stores electric charge given by

$$Q(t) = Q_0 \left(1 - e^{-t/a} \right)$$

(The maximum charge capacity is Q_0 and t is measured in seconds.) How long does it take to recharge the capacitor to 90% of capacity if $a = 4$?

Select the correct answer.

    a. $-4 \ln(1)$ seconds

    b. $-4 \ln\left(\dfrac{9}{10} \right)$ seconds

    c. $-4 \ln(10)$ seconds

    d. $-4 \ln\left(\dfrac{1}{10} \right)$ seconds

    e. $-\ln\left(\dfrac{4}{9} \right)$ seconds

16. A study by the U. S. Office of Science and Technology in 1972 estimated the cost (in 1972 dollars) to reduce automobile emissions by certain percentages given by the table, and the graph gives the linear model of this table.

Reduction in emissions (%)	Cost per car (in $)
50	73
55	83.05
60	92.95
65	102.95
70	112.95

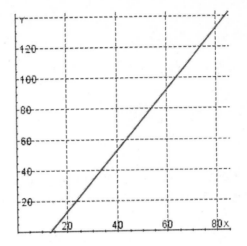

Find the cost, if the reduction in emissions is 80%, using this model.

Select the correct answer.

a. $115
b. $154
c. $133
d. $268
e. $130

17. Find $f - g$.

$$f(x) = \sqrt{5 + x}$$
$$g(x) = \sqrt{5 - x}$$

18. How does the graph of the function $f(x) = 8x^4 + cx^2 + x$ change when c changes?

Select the correct statement.

a.   at $c = 0$ one of the humps disappears

b.   the humps get flatter as c decreases

c.   if $c < 0$ the graph has three humps

19. Find the exact value of the expression.

$\sin(\sin^{-1} 0.5)$

Select the correct answer.

a.   1
b.   - 0.5
c.   - 1
d.   0.5
e.   0

20. Compare the functions $f(x) = x^6$ and $g(x) = e^x$ by graphing both f and g in several viewing rectangles. When does the graph of g finally surpass the graph of f ?

1. d

2. $0 \le h(x) \le 3$

3. $y = 3 - \sqrt{-x}$

4. $A(l) = (9 - l)l$

5. e

6. $v(x) = x(23 - 2x)(17 - 2x)$

7. c

8. $(-9, 8)$

9. $(-\infty, \infty)$

10. d

11. b

12. a

13. $r(t) = 58t, \ 3364\pi t^2$

14. $y = e^x - 2$

15. d

16. c

17. $\sqrt{5 + x} - \sqrt{5 - x}$

18. c

19. d

20. $x \approx 17$

1. Starting with the graph of $y = e^x$, write the equation of the graph that results from shifting 2 units left.

   Select the correct answer.

   a. $y = e^{x-2}$

   b. $y = e^{x+2}$

   c. $y = e^x - 2$

   d. $y = e^x + 2$

   e. $y = -2e^x + 2$

2. Find the range of the function.

   $$h(x) = \sqrt{16 - x^2}$$

3. Find the domain of the function.

   $$g(u) = \sqrt{u} - \sqrt{3-u}$$

   Select the correct answer.

   a. $u \in [0, \ \infty)$

   b. $u \in (0, \ 3)$

   c. $u \in (0, \ 3]$

   d. $u \in (-\infty, \ 0]$

   e. $u \in [0, \ 3]$

4. Which function is represented by the following graph?

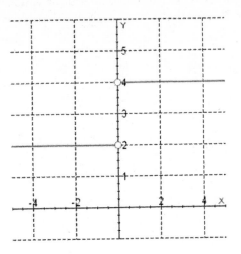

Select the correct answer.

a. $G(x) = \dfrac{3x - |x|}{x}$

b. $G(x) = \dfrac{3x + |x|}{x}$

c. $G(x) = \dfrac{3x + |-x|}{x}$

d. $G(x) = \dfrac{|x|}{x}$

e. $G(x) = |3x|$

5. Use a graph to estimate the values of x such that $e^x > 10,000,000$. Round your answer to one decimal place.

6. A rectangle has perimeter 20 m.

   Express the area of the rectangle as a function $A(l)$ of the length l of one of its sides.

7. A box with an open top is to be constructed from a rectangular piece of cardboard with dimensions $b = 15$ in. by $a = 24$ in. by cutting out equal squares of side x at each corner and then folding up the sides as in the figure.

    Express the volume V of the box as a function of x.

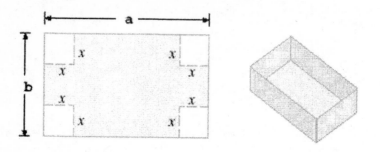

8. If the point $(8, 2)$ is on the graph of an even function, what other point must also be on the graph?

9. Which of the following functions is a trigonometric function?

    Select the correct answer.

    a. $f(q) = q^5 + q^3$

    b. $f(q) = \tan 2q$

    c. $f(q) = \dfrac{q^2 + 7}{q^3 - 5}$

    d. $f(q) = \sqrt{q}$

    e. $f(q) = \log_3 q$

10. Fill in the blanks.

    Let $f(x) = 3 + x^2 + \tan(\pi x / 2)$, where $-1 < x < 1$.

    $f^{-1}(3) = $ _____

    $f(f^{-1}(5)) = $ _____

11. The relationship between the Fahrenheit and Celsius temperature scales is given by the linear function

$$F = \frac{9}{5}C + 32.$$

Complete the table and find the slope.

C	F
15	
-25	
slope	

12. Fill in the blanks. Find the exact value of each expression.

$\log_{10} 2.5 + \log_{10} 40 =$ _____

$\log_5 75 + \log_5 15 - 2\log_5 3 =$ _____

13. The monthly cost of driving a car depends on the number of miles driven. Mary found that in January it cost her $395 to drive 700 mi and in July it cost her $420 to drive 800 mi.

Express the monthly cost C as a function of the distance driven d assuming that a linear relationship gives a suitable model.

Select the correct answer.

    a. $C = 0.25d + 220$
    b. $C = 220d + 0.25$
    c. $C = 220d - 0.25$
    d. $C = 0.25d - 220$
    e. $C = 0.125d + 230$

14. Suppose that the graph of $y = \log_2 x$ is drawn on a coordinate grid where the unit of measurement is an inch. How many miles to the right of the origin do we have to move before the height of the curve reaches 2 ft?

Select the correct answer.

    a.   259 mi
    b.   257 mi
    c.   265 mi
    d.   273 mi
    e.   298 mi

15. A stone is dropped into a lake, creating a circular ripple that travels outward at a speed of 51 cm/s.

    Express the radius r of this circle as a function of the time t (in seconds) and find $A \circ r$, if A is the area of this circle as a function of the radius.

16. If $f(x) = x + 2$ and $h(x) = 3x - 4$, find a function g such that $g \circ f = h$.

    Select the correct answer.

    a. $g(x) = 3x + 10$
    b. $g(x) = 3x - 2$
    c. $g(x) = 3x - 10$

17. How many solutions does the equation have?
    $$\cos \frac{1}{7} x = 19.5x$$

18. For what values of x is the inequality true?

    $$12 \,|\, \sin x - (x - 24)\pi \,| < 1.2$$

    Select the correct answer to two decimal places.

    a. $(29.37, 31.07)$
    b. $(33.07, 34.77)$
    c. $(30.57, 32.27)$
    d. $(29.37, 34.07)$
    e. $(29.01, 32.07)$

19. We consider the family of functions $f(x) = \sqrt[n]{x}$, where n is a positive integer. Graph the root functions $y = \sqrt{x}$, $y = \sqrt[4]{x}$, $y = \sqrt[6]{x}$ on the same screen using the viewing rectangle $[-1, 4]$, $[-1, 3]$.

Select the correct answer.

a.

b.

c.

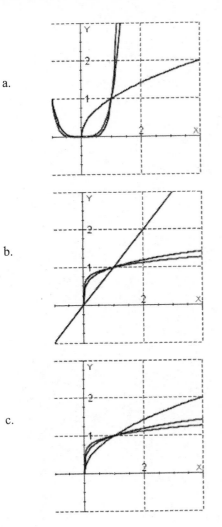

20. Simplify the expression.

$$\sin(2\cos^{-1} 6x)$$

1. b

2. $0 \le h(x) \le 4$

3. e

4. b

5. $x > 16.1$

6. $A(l) = (10 - l)l$

7. $V(x) = x(24 - 2x)(15 - 2x)$

8. (-8,2)

9. b

10. 0, 5

11. 15, 59, -25, -13, slope, 1.8

12. 2, 3

13. a

14. c

15. $r(t) = 51t$, $2601\pi t^2$

16. c

17. 1

18. c

19. c

20. $12x\sqrt{1 - 36x^2}$

1. The graph of function f is given. State the value of $f(-1)$.

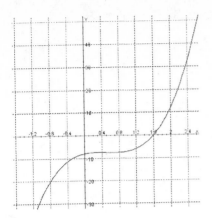

   Select the correct answer.

   a. -22
   b. -24
   c. -29
   d. -27
   e. -30

2. Find the domain of the function.

   $$f(x) = \frac{1}{1-e^x}$$

3. Find the domain of the function.

   $$g(u) = \sqrt{u} - \sqrt{8-u}$$

4. Find an expression for the function $y = f(x)$ whose graph is the bottom half of the parabola
   $x + (3-y)^2 = 0$.

   Select the correct answer.

   a. $y = 3 + \sqrt{-x}$
   b. $y = 3 - \sqrt{x}$
   c. $y = 3 + \sqrt{x}$
   d. $y = 3 - \sqrt{-x}$
   e. $y = 3 - x^2$

5. A rectangle has perimeter 24 m.

    Express the area of the rectangle as a function $A(l)$ of the length l of one of its sides.

    Select the correct answer.

    a. $A(l) = 12l + l^2$

    b. $A(l) = 24l - l^2$

    c. $A(l) = 24l + l^2$

    d. $A(l) = 12 - l$

    e. $A(l) = 12l - l^2$

    f. $A(l) = 24 + l$

6. An open rectangular box with volume 8 m^3 has a square base.

    Express the surface area of the box as a function $S(x)$ of the length x of a side of the base.

    Select the correct answer.

    a. $S(x) = 2x + \dfrac{8}{x}$

    b. $S(x) = x^2 + \dfrac{16}{x}$

    c. $S(x) = x^2 + \dfrac{32}{x}$

    d. $S(x) = x^2 + \dfrac{16}{x^2}$

    e. $S(x) = x^2 + \dfrac{32}{x^2}$

7. A box with an open top is to be constructed from a rectangular piece of cardboard with dimensions $b = 7$ in. by $a = 28$ in. by cutting out equal squares of side x at each corner and then folding up the sides as in the figure.

Express the volume V of the box as a function of x.

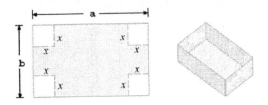

Select the correct answer.

a. $V(x) = x^3 - 35x^2 + 196x$

b. $V(x) = 4x^3 - 70x^2 + 196x$

c. $V(x) = x^3 - 70x^2 + 196x$

d. $V(x) = 4x^3 + 35x^2 + 196x$

e. $V(x) = 4x^3 + 70x^2 + 196x$

8. If the point $(8, 3)$ is on the graph of an even function, what other point must also be on the graph?

9. For what values of x is the inequality true?

$$6 |\sin x - (x - 12\pi)| < 0.6$$

Select the correct answer to two decimal places.

a. $(18.8, 20.5)$
b. $(17.5, 19.2)$
c. $(18, 19.7)$
d. $(16.8, 21.5)$
e. $(17.5, 18.5)$

10. In the function $f(x) = 7x + d$, what must be the coefficient d, if $f(1) = 1$?

Select the correct answer.

a. $d = -6$
b. $d = 8$
c. $d = 6$
d. $d = -8$
e. $d = 1$

11. Biologists have noticéd that the chirping rate of crickets of certain species is related to temperature, and the relationship appears to be very nearly linear. A cricket produces 113 chirps per minute at 70°F and 173 chirps at 80°F per minute.

Find the rate of chirping, if the temperature is 100°F.

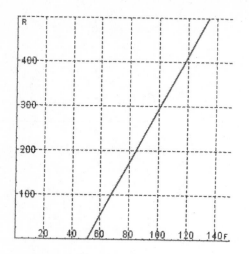

Select the correct answer.

   a.   907
   b.   −7
   c.   293
   d.   173
   e.   55

12. Find the exponential function $f(x) = Ca^x$ whose graph is given.

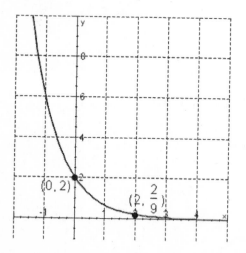

13. An isotope of sodium, ^{24}Na, has a half-life of 15 hours. A sample of this isotope has mass 1 g. Find the amount remaining after 60 hours.

   Select the correct answer.

   a.   0.015625 g
   b.   0.0625 g
   c.   0.0385 g
   d.   0.0001 g
   e.   0.0051 g

14. At the surface of the ocean, the water pressure is the same as the air pressure above the water is 15 lb/in ^{2}. Below the surface, the water pressure increases by 4.34 lb/in ^{2} for every 10 ft of descent.

   Find the depth, if the pressure 80 lb/in ^{2}.

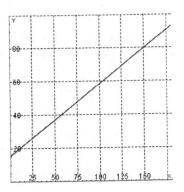

   Select the correct answer.

   a.   169 ft
   b.   150 ft
   c.   129 ft
   d.   20 ft
   e.   179 ft

15. Find $f + g$.

$$f(x) = x^3 + 6x^2$$
$$g(x) = 4x^2 - 2$$

   Select the correct answer.

   a. $(f + g)(x) = x^3 + 10x - 2$
   b. $(f + g)(x) = x^3 + 10x^2 - 2$
   c. $(f + g)(x) = x^3 + 2x + 2$
   d. $(f + g)(x) = x^3 + 10x$
   e. $(f + g)(x) = x^3 + x^2 - 1$

16. Find $f - g$.

$$f(x) = \sqrt{11 + x}$$
$$g(x) = \sqrt{11 - x}$$

17. What is $\sqrt[4]{x}$, given that $H = f \circ g \circ h$ and $H(x) = \sqrt[4]{\sqrt{x} - 4}$.

Select the correct answer.

    a. $g(x)$

    b. $h(x)$

    c. $f(x)$

18. A stone is dropped into a lake, creating a circular ripple that travels outward at a speed of 40 cm/s. Express the radius r of this circle as a function of the time t (in seconds) and find $A \circ r$, if A is the area of this circle as a function of the radius.

19. If $f(x) = x + 6$ and $h(x) = 6x - 2$, find a function g such that $g \circ f = h$.

20. When a camera flash goes off, the batteries immediately begin to recharge the flash's capacitor, which stores electric charge given by $Q(t) = Q_0 \left(1 - e^{-t/a} \right)$ (The maximum charge capacity is Q_0 and t is measured in seconds.) How long does it take to recharge the capacitor to 70% of capacity if $a = 3$?

Select the correct answer.

    a. $-3 \ln 3$ seconds

    b. $-3 \ln \left(\dfrac{7}{10} \right)$ seconds

    c. $-3 \ln \left(\dfrac{3}{10} \right)$ seconds

    d. $-3 \ln 10$ seconds

    e. $-7 \ln 10$ seconds

Stewart - Calculus ET 5e Chapter 1 Form H

1. d

2. $(-\infty, 0) \cup (0, \infty)$

3. $0 \le u \le 8$

4. d

5. e

6. c

7. b

8. $(-8,3)$

9. c

10. a

11. c

12. $f(x) = 2\left(\dfrac{1}{3}\right)^x$

13. b

14. b

15. b

16. $\sqrt{11+x} - \sqrt{11-x}$

17. c

18. $r(t) = 40t, \ 1600\pi t^2$

19. $6x - 38$

20. c

1. The point $P(4,2)$ lies on the curve $y = \sqrt{x}$. If Q is the point $\left(x, \sqrt{x}\right)$, use your calculator to find the slope of the secant line PQ (correct to six decimal places) for the value $x = 3.99$.

2. If a ball is thrown into the air with a velocity of 45 ft/s, its height in feet after t seconds is given by $y = 45t - 13t^2$.

   Find the instantaneous velocity when $t = 2$.

3. The position of a car is given by the values in the following table.

t (seconds)	0	1	2	3	4	5
s (feet)	0	19	33	74	114	178

   Estimate the instantaneous velocity when $t = 2$ by averaging the average velocities for the periods $[1, 2]$ and $[2, 3]$.

4. Determine the infinite limit.

   $$\lim_{x \to 0} \frac{x-1}{x^2(x+5)}$$

5. The slope of the tangent line to the graph of the exponential function $y = 5^x$ at the point $(0, 1)$ is

   $$\lim_{x \to 0} \frac{5^x - 1}{x}$$

   Estimate the slope to three decimal places.

6. Evaluate the limit.

   $$\lim_{x \to 5} \left(9x^2 + 7x + 3\right)$$

7. Evaluate the limit.

   $$\lim_{x \to 0} \frac{(2+x)^{-1} - 2^{-1}}{x}$$

8. If $1 \le f(x) \le x^2 + 2x + 2$, for all x find the limit.

$$\lim_{x \to -1} f(x)$$

9. Evaluate the limit and justify each step by indicating the appropriate properties of limits.

$$\lim_{x \to \infty} \frac{7x^2 - 2x + 9}{3x^2 + 5x - 9}$$

10. Use a graph to find a number N such that $\left| \dfrac{6x^2 + 5x - 3}{2x^2 - 1} - 3 \right| < 0.3$ whenever $x > N$.

11. Find an equation of the tangent line to the curve $y = 5x^3$ at the point $(-3, -135)$.

12. Use the given graph of $f(x) = \sqrt{x}$ to find a number δ such that $\left| \sqrt{x} - 2 \right| < 0.4$ whenever $\left| x - 4 \right| < \delta$.

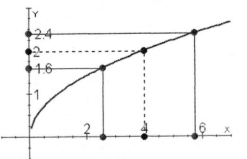

13. Use a graph to find a number δ such that $\left| \sqrt{4x + 1} - 3 \right| < 0.6$ whenever $\left| x - 2 \right| < \delta$.

14. For the limit, illustrate the definition by finding values of δ that correspond to $\varepsilon = 0.25$.

$$\lim_{x \to 1} \left(4 + x - 3x^3 \right) = 2$$

15. A machinist is required to manufacture a circular metal disk with area 1000 cm^2. If the machinist is allowed an error tolerance of ± 7 cm^2 in the area of the disk, how close to the ideal radius must the machinist control the radius?

16. For $x = 5$, determine whether f is continuous from the right, from the left, or neither.

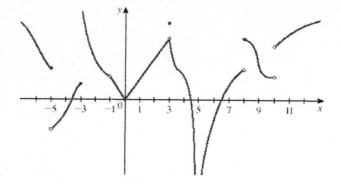

17. The limit represents the derivative of some function f at some number a. State f and a.

$$\lim_{t \to -0} \frac{\sin\left(\dfrac{\pi}{2} + t\right) - 1}{t}$$

18. Find the derivative of the function using the definition of derivative.

$$f(x) = 14 - 3x + 5x^2$$

19. If $f(t) = \dfrac{13}{3 + t^2}$ find $f'(t)$.

20. At what point is the function $f(x) = |6 - x|$ not differentiable.

ANSWER KEY

Stewart - Calculus ET 5e Chapter 2 Form A

1. 0.250156

2. -7

3. 27.5

4. $-\infty$

5. 1.609

6. 263

7. -1/4

8. 1

9. $\dfrac{7}{3}$

10. $N \geq 9$

11. $y = 135x + 270$

12. $\delta \leq 1.44$

13. $\delta \leq 0.81$

14. $\delta \leq 0.030$

15. 0.06234

16. neither

17. $f = \sin(x), \quad a = \dfrac{\pi}{2}$

18. $10x - 3$

19. $\dfrac{-26t}{(3+t)^2}$

20. 6

1. The point $P(4, 2)$ lies on the curve $y = \sqrt{x}$. If Q is the point $\left(x, \sqrt{x}\right)$, use your calculator to find the slope of the secant line PQ (correct to six decimal places) for the value of $x = 4.01$.

2. The displacement (in feet) of a certain particle moving in a straight line is given by $s = \dfrac{t^3}{6}$ where t is measured in seconds. Find the instantaneous velocity when $t = 4$.

3. The position of a car is given by the values in the following table.

t (seconds)	0	1	2	3	4	5
s (feet)	0	13	37	72	113	176

    Estimate the instantaneous velocity when $t = 2$ by averaging the average velocities for the periods $[1, 2]$ and $[2, 3]$.

4. If $G(x) = x/(1 + 6x)$, find $G'(a)$ and use it to find an equation of the tangent line to the curve $y = x/(1 + 6x)$ at the point $\left(-\dfrac{1}{4}, \dfrac{1}{2}\right)$.

5. Find $f'(a)$.

    $f(x) = 2 + x - 5x^2$

6. Evaluate the function $f(x) = 2\dfrac{\sqrt{x} - \sqrt{2}}{x - 2}$ at the given numbers (correct to six decimal places). Use the results to guess the value of the limit $\lim\limits_{x \to 2} f(x)$.

x	$f(x)$
1.6	
1.8	
1.9	
1.99	
1.999	
2.4	
2.2	
2.1	
2.01	
2.001	
Limit	

7. The graph of f is given. State the numbers at which f is not differentiable.

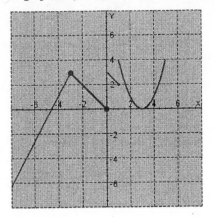

8. Evaluate the limit.

$$\lim_{x \to 0} x^9 \cos\left(\frac{3}{x}\right)$$

9. If $1 \le f(x) \le x^2 + 6x + 6$ for all x find the limit.

$$\lim_{x \to -1} f(x)$$

10. Evaluate the limit.

$$\lim_{x \to 5}\left(7x^2 + 6x + 8\right)$$

11. Find the derivative of the function using the definition of the derivative.

$$f(x) = 16 - 9x + 4x^2$$

12. If an arrow is shot upward on the moon, with a velocity of 70 m/s its height (in meters) after t seconds is given by $H(t) = 70t - 0.99t^2$. With what velocity will the arrow hit the moon?

13. The cost (in dollars) of producing x units of a certain commodity is $C(x) = 4{,}336 + 13x + 0.08x^2$.

Find the average rate of change with respect to x when the production level is changed from $x = 101$ to $x = 103$.

14. Prove the statement using the δ, ε definition of a limit.

$$\lim_{x \to 5} x^3 = 125$$

(use a separate sheet to answer if necessary)

15. If f and g are continuous functions with $f(3) = 3$ and $\lim_{x \to 3}[3f(x) - g(x)] = 3$, find $g(3)$.

16. Evaluate the limit.

$$\lim_{x \to -9} |x + 9|$$

17. Find the derivative of the function using the definition of the derivative.

$$f(x) = 14x + 18\sqrt{x}$$

18. If a cylindrical tank holds 100,000 gallons of water, which can be drained from the bottom of the tank in an hour, then Torricelli's Law gives the volume of water remaining in the tank after t minutes as

$$V(t) = 100,000\left(1 - \frac{t}{65}\right)^2, \quad 0 \le t \le 60$$

Find the rate at which the water is flowing out of the tank (the instantaneous rate of change of V with respect to t) as a function of t.

19. Evaluate the limit.

$$\lim_{x \to 0} \frac{(9 + x)^{-1} - 9^{-1}}{x}$$

20. For the function f whose graph is shown, state the following.

$$\lim_{x \to -4} f(x)$$

ANSWER KEY

Stewart - Calculus ET 5e Chapter 2 Form B

1. 0.249844

2. 8

3. 29.5

4. $\dfrac{1}{(1+6x)^2}$, $\quad y = 4x + \dfrac{3}{2}$

5. $1 - 10a$

6. $1.6, 0.746512, 1.8, 0.725728, 1.9, 0.716174, 1.99, 0.707993, 1.999, 0.707195,$

   $2.4, 0.674899, 2.2, 0.690261, 2.1, 0.698482, 2.01, 0.706225, 2.001, 0.707018,$

   $\text{Limit}, 0.707107$

7. $-3, 0, 1$

8. 0

9. 1

10. 213

11. $8x - 9$

12. -70

13. 29.32

14. Given $\varepsilon > 0$, we need $\delta > 0$ such that if $|x - 5| < \delta$, then $|x^3 - 125| < \varepsilon$. Now $|x^3 - 125| = |(x - 5)$ $(x^2 + 5x + 25)|$. If $|x - 5| < 1$, that is, $4 < x < 6$, then $x^2 + 5x + 25 < 6^2 + 5(6) + 25 = 91$ and so $|x^3 - 125| = |x - 5|(x^2 + 5x + 25)| < 91|x - 5|$.

    So if we take $\delta = \min\{1, \dfrac{\varepsilon}{91}\}$, then $|x - 5| < \delta \implies |x^3 - 125| = |x - 5|(x^2 + 5x + 25)| < 91$.

    $\dfrac{\varepsilon}{91} = \varepsilon.$

    So by the definition of a limit, $\lim\limits_{x \to 5} x^3 = 125$

15. 6

16. 0

17. $14 + \dfrac{9}{\sqrt{x}}$

18. $y = \dfrac{-200000}{65}\left(1 - \dfrac{t}{65}\right)$

19. $-\dfrac{1}{81}$

20. $-\infty$

1. A cardiac monitor is used to measure the heart rate of a patient after surgery. It compiles the number of heartbeats after t minutes. When the data in the table are graphed, the slope of the tangent line represents the heart rate in beats per minute. The monitor estimates this value by calculating the slope of a secant line. Use the data to estimate the patient's heart rate after 42 minutes using the secant line between the points with $t = 38$ and $t = 42$.

t (min)	36	38	40	42	44
Heartbeats	2,570	2,640	2,840	3,000	3,070

Select the correct answer.

    a.   -89
    b.   180
    c.   90
    d.   100
    e.   89
    f.   95

2. If an arrow is shot upward on the moon with a velocity of 55 m/s, its height in meters after t seconds is given by $h = 55t - 0.04t^2$. Find the average velocity over the interval $[1, 1.04]$.

Select the correct answer.

    a.   54.9194
    b.   55.0284
    c.   54.8174
    d.   54.9184
    e.   54.9084

3. The displacement (in feet) of a certain particle moving in a straight line is given by $s = \dfrac{t^3}{8}$ where t is measured in seconds. Find the average velocity over the interval $[1, 1.8]$.

Select the correct answer.

    a.   0.865
    b.   0.654
    c.   0.765
    d.   0.756
    e.   0.745
    f.   0.755

4. For the function f whose graph is shown, find the following.

$$\lim_{x \to -4} f(x)$$

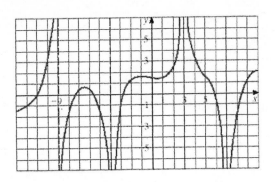

Select the correct answer.

a. ∞
b. $-\infty$
c. 1
d. -3
e. 0

5. Guess the value of the limit.

$$\lim_{x \to 0} 3 \frac{\tan 5x - 5x}{x^3}$$

Select the correct answer.

a. 116
b. 118
c. 129
d. 127
e. 125

6. For the function f whose graph is shown, find the equations of the vertical asymptotes.

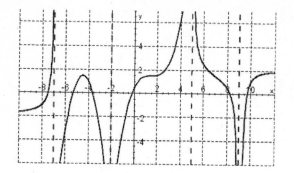

Select the correct answer.

a. $x = -7$
b. $x = 9$
c. $x = 5$
d. $x = -3$
e. $x = 10$
f. $x = -2$

7. Evaluate the limit.

$$\lim_{x \to 1} (x + 2)^3 (x^2 - 6)$$

Select the correct answer.

a.   27
b.   -45
c.   -135
d.   29
e.   -125

8. If $1 \le f(x) \le x^2 + 8x + 8$ for all x, find $\lim_{x \to -1} f(x)$.

Select the correct answer.

a.   1
b.   8
c.   -1/8
d.   -1/16
e.   The limit does not exist

9. Evaluate the limit.

$$\lim_{x \to 0} x^9 \cos\left(\frac{5}{x}\right)$$

Select the correct answer.

a. -5
b. 1
c. 0
d. 5
e. The limit does not exist

10. Use a graph to find a number δ such that $\left| \sin x - \frac{1}{2} \right| < 0.2$ whenever $\left| x - \frac{\pi}{6} \right| < \delta$.

Round down the answer to the nearest thousandth.

Select the correct answer.

a. $\delta \leq 0.218$
b. $\delta \leq 0.368$
c. $\delta \leq 0.401$
d. $\delta \leq 0.251$
e. $\delta \leq 0.425$

11. A machinist is required to manufacture a circular metal disk with area 1000 cm^2. If the machinist is allowed an error tolerance of $\pm 10 \text{ cm}^2$ in the area of the disk, how close to the ideal radius must the machinist control the radius? Round down the answer to the nearest hundred thousandth.

Select the correct answer.

a. $\delta \leq 0.08898 \ cm$
b. $\delta \leq 0.08908 \ cm$
c. $\delta \leq 0.08999 \ cm$
d. $\delta \leq 0.08913 \ cm$
e. $\delta \leq 0.09913 \ cm$

12. Consider the function $f(x) = \dfrac{1}{2 + e^{1/x}}$. Find the value of $\lim_{x \to 0^-} f(x)$.

Select the correct answer.

a. 1.5
b. -0.1
c. 0.1
d. 0.9
e. 0.5

13. Choose an equation from the following that expresses the fact that a function f is continuous at the number 6.

Select the correct answer.

a. $\lim\limits_{x \to \infty} f(x) = 6$

b. $\lim\limits_{x \to 6} f(x) = f(6)$

c. $\lim\limits_{x \to \infty} f(x) = f(6)$

d. $\lim\limits_{x \to 6} f(x) = 0$

e. $\lim\limits_{x \to 6} f(x) = \infty$

14. Find the horizontal and vertical asymptotes of each curve. Check your work by graphing the curve and estimating the asymptotes.

$$y = \frac{x}{x-2}$$

Select the correct answer.

a.

b.

c.

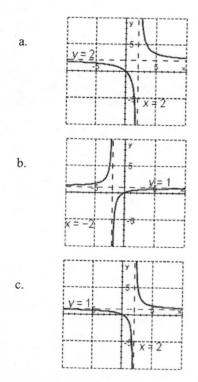

15. Find a, such that the function $f(x) = 4x + \sqrt{a - x^2}$ has the domain $\left(-5, 5 \right)$.

Select the correct answer.

a. $a = 5$
b. $a = 25$
c. $a = -25$
d. $a = \sqrt{5}$
e. $a = -\sqrt{5}$

16. Use continuity to evaluate the limit.

$$\lim_{x \to 25} \frac{39 + \sqrt{x}}{\sqrt{39 + x}}$$

Select the correct answer.

a. 17/4
b. ∞
c. 11/2
d. 11/4
e. $-\infty$

17. For the function $g(x)$ whose graph is given, which of the following numbers is greater?

$g'(0)$ or 0.

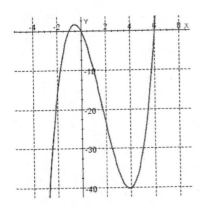

Select the correct answer.

a. $g'(0)$
b. $g'(0) = 0$
c. 0

18. Find an equation of the tangent line to the curve $y = x^3 - 5x + 3$ at the point (2, 1).

Select the correct answer.

    a. $y = 8x + 13$
    b. $y = -9x - 13$
    c. $y = 7x - 13$
    d. $y = -7x + 13$
    e. $y = 7x - 15$

19. The cost (in dollars) of producing x units of a certain commodity is $C(x) = 4{,}571 + 19x + 0.01x^2$. Find the instantaneous rate of change with respect to x when $x = 103$. (This is called the *marginal cost*.)

Select the correct answer.

    a.   26.06
    b.   20.06
    c.   21.06
    d.   18.06
    e.   31.06

20. If the tangent line to $y = f(x)$ at (8, 4) passes through the point (5, -32), find $f'(8)$.

Select the correct answer.

    a. $f'(8) = 24$
    b. $f'(8) = 20$
    c. $f'(8) = -12$
    d. $f'(8) = 12$
    e. $f'(8) = 32$

Stewart - Calculus ET 5e Chapter 2 Form C

1. c

2. d

3. f

4. b

5. e

6. a, b, c, f

7. c

8. a

9. c

10. a

11. a

12. e

13. b

14. c

15. b

16. c

17. c

18. c

19. c

20. d

1. The position of a car is given by the values in the following table.

t (seconds)	0	1	2	3	4	5
s (feet)	0	18	35	74	110	175

Find the average velocity for the time period beginning when $t = 2$ and lasting 2 seconds.

Select the correct answer.

a. 35.5
b. 47.5
c. 39
d. 37.5
e. 33.5

2. For the function f whose graph is shown, find the equations of the vertical asymptotes.

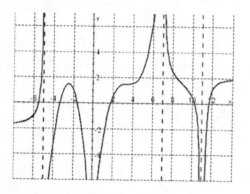

Select the correct answer.

a. $x = 0$
b. $x = 11$
c. $x = 1$
d. $x = 9$
e. $x = -5$
f. $x = -6$
g. $x = 7$

3. Determine the infinite limit.

$$\lim_{x \to 0} \frac{x+1}{x^2(x+7)}$$

Select the correct answer.

a. 0
b. $\dfrac{1}{7}$
c. $-\dfrac{1}{7}$
d. $-\infty$
e. ∞

4. Find the limit.

$$\lim_{x \to \infty} \frac{1}{2x + 7}$$

Select the correct answer.

a. $-\infty$

b. $\dfrac{1}{7}$

c. ∞

d. 0

e. $\dfrac{1}{2}$

5. The slope of the tangent line to the graph of the exponential function $y = 8^x$ at the point (0, 1) is

$$\lim_{x \to 0} \frac{8^x - 1}{x}.$$

Estimate the slope to three decimal places.

Select the correct answer.

a. 1.293
b. 2
c. 2.026
d. 1.568
e. 2.079
f. 2.556

6. Guess the value of $\displaystyle\lim_{x \to 0} \left(x^4 - \frac{2^x}{8,000} \right)$.

Select the correct answer.

a. 0.0005
b. 0.00075
c. 0.000125
d. -0.00125
e. -0.000375
f. -0.000125

7. Guess the value of $\lim\limits_{x \to 0} 3\dfrac{\tan(3x) - 3x}{x^3}$.

Select the correct answer.

    a.   32
    b.   22
    c.   27
    d.   20
    e.   33
    f.   17

8. Let $F(x) = \dfrac{x^2 - 1}{|x - 1|}$.

Find the following limits.

$$\lim_{x \to 1^+} F(x), \quad \lim_{x \to 1^-} F(x)$$

Select the correct answer.

    a.   both 2
    b.   2 and 1
    c.   2 and - 2
    d.   2 and – 1
    e.   both 1

9. Use continuity to evaluate the limit.

$$\lim_{x \to 13\pi} \sin(x + 4\sin x)$$

Select the correct answer.

    a. 13π
    b.   - 1
    c.   0
    d. ∞
    e.   1

10. Find the points at which f is discontinuous. At which of these points is f continuous from the right, from the left, or neither?

$$f(x) = \begin{cases} (x - 2)^3 & \text{if} \quad x \le 0 \\ (x + 4)^3 & \text{if} \quad x > 0 \end{cases}$$

Select the correct answer.

    a. $x = 0$, continuous from the left
    b. $x = 2$, continuous from the left
    c. $x = - 4$, continuous from the right
    d. $x = 0$, continuous from the right
    e. $x = 1$, continuous from the left

11. For what value of the constant c is the function f continuous on $(-\infty, \infty)$?

$$f(x) = \begin{cases} cx + 7 & for & x \le 2 \\ cx^2 - 5 & for & x > 2 \end{cases}$$

Select the correct answer.

a. $c = 1$
b. $c = 2$
c. $c = 6$
d. $c = -2$
e. $c = 7$

12. Find a function g that agrees with f for $x \ne 25$ and is continuous on $\Re$.

$$f(x) = \frac{5 - \sqrt{x}}{25 - x}$$

Select the correct answer.

a. $g(x) = \dfrac{1}{5 - x}$

b. $g(x) = \dfrac{1}{25 + x}$

c. $g(x) = \dfrac{1}{5 + \sqrt{x}}$

d. $g(x) = \dfrac{1}{5 - \sqrt{x}}$

e. $g(x) = \dfrac{\sqrt{5}}{5 - x}$

13. For what values of x is f continuous?

$$f(x) = \begin{cases} 7 & x \ is \ rational \\ 0 & x \ is \ irrational \end{cases}$$

Select the correct answer.

a.   all rational x
b.   all negative real numbers
c.   all real x
d.   all irrational x
e.   none

14. Find the limit.

$$\lim_{t \to \infty} \frac{t^2 + 3}{t^3 + t^2 - 1}$$

Select the correct answer.

a. ∞
b. 0
c. -3
d. 3
e. 2

15. Find the derivative of the function using the definition of derivative. State the domain of the function and the domain of its derivative.

$$G(x) = \frac{2 - 5x}{3 + x}$$

Select the correct answer.

a. $G'(x) = -\dfrac{13}{(3+x)^2}$; domain of $G' = \{x \mid x \neq -3\}$

b. $G'(x) = -\dfrac{17}{(3+x)^2}$; domain of $G' = \{x \mid x \neq -2\}$

c. $G'(x) = -\dfrac{17}{(3+x)^2}$; domain of $G' = \{x \mid x \neq -3\}$

16. The cost (in dollars) of producing x units of a certain commodity is $C(x) = 4{,}280 + 13x + 0.03x^2$.

Find the average rate of change with respect to x when the production level is changed from $x = 102$ to $x = 118$.

Select the correct answer.

a. 29.6
b. 19.6
c. 18.6
d. 26.6
e. 24.6
f. 16.6

17. Evaluate the limit.

$$\lim_{x \to -2} |x + 2|$$

Select the correct answer.

a.   2
b.   4
c.   - 2
d.   0
e.   The limit does not exist

18. If a ball is thrown into the air with a velocity of 58 ft/s, its height (in feet) after t seconds is given by

$H = 58t - 11t^2$. Find the velocity when $t = 4$.

Select the correct answer.

a.   27ft/s
b.   30ft/s
c.   31ft/s
d.   25ft/s
e.   37ft/s

19. Is there a number a such that $\displaystyle\lim_{x \to -3} \frac{6x^2 + ax + a + 2}{x^2 + x - 6}$ exists? If so, find the value of a and the value of

the limit.

Select the correct answer.

a. $a=14$, limit equals 1.4
b. $a=17$, limit equals 1.6
c. $a=28$, limit equals 1.4
d. $a=28$, limit equals 1.6
e. $a=14$, limit equals 1.6

20. Evaluate the limit.

$$\lim_{x \to 0} x^8 \cos\left(\frac{2}{x}\right)$$

Select the correct answer.

a.   1
b.   3
c.   0
d.   2
b.   The limit does not exist

1. d

2. a, b, e, g

3. e

4. d

5. e

6. f

7. c

8. c

9. c

10. a

11. c

12. c

13. e

14. b

15. c

16. b

17. d

18. b

19. d

20. c

1. A tank holds 1000 gallons of water, which drains from the bottom of the tank in half an hour. The values in the table show the volume V of water remaining in the tank (in gallons) after t minutes.

   If P is the point (15, 263) on the graph of V, fill the table with the slopes of the secant lines PQ where Q is the point on the graph with the corresponding t.

t (min)	5	10	15	20	25	30
V (gal)	686	481	263	171	22	0

   Enter your answer to two decimal places.

t	
5	
10	
20	
25	
30	

2. If an arrow is shot upward on the moon with a velocity of 57 m/s, its height in meters after t seconds is given by $h = 57t - 0.82t^2$. Find the instantaneous velocity after one second.

   Select the correct answer.

   a. 55.46
   b. 55.35
   c. 55.25
   d. 55.36
   e. 55.37

3. The displacement (in feet) of a certain particle moving in a straight line is given by $s = \dfrac{t^3}{4}$ where t is measured in seconds.

   Find the instantaneous velocity when $t = 2$.

4. Given that, $\lim\limits_{x \to 7} f(x) = -3$ and $\lim\limits_{x \to 7} g(x) = 9$.

Evaluate the limit.

$$\lim_{x \to 7} \frac{2f(x)}{g(x) - f(x)}$$

5. The position of a car is given by the values in the following table.

t (seconds)	0	1	2	3	4	5
s (feet)	0	19	38	76	128	173

Estimate the instantaneous velocity when $t = 2$ by averaging the average velocities for the periods [1, 2] and [2, 3].

Select the correct answer.

    a.   27.5
    b.   28.5
    c.   28
    d.   30
    e.   28.51
    f.   30.5

6. For the function f whose graph is shown, find the following.

$$\lim_{x \to 7} f(x)$$

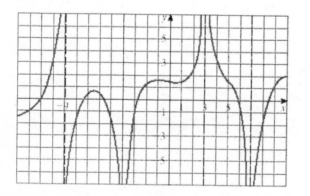

7. Consider the following function.

$$f(x) = \begin{cases} 3-x & x < -1 \\ x & -1 \le x < 3 \\ (x-3)^2 & x \ge 3 \end{cases}$$

Determine the values of a for which $\lim\limits_{x \to a} f(x)$ exists.

8. Evaluate the function $f(x) = 2\dfrac{\sqrt{x}-1}{x-1}$ at the given numbers (correct to six decimal places). Use the results to guess the value of the limit.

$$\lim_{x \to 1} f(x)$$

x	0.6	0.8	0.9	0.99	0.999	1.4	1.2	1.1	1.01	1.001
$f(x)$	1.127017	1.055728	1.026334	1.002513	1.00025	0.91608	0.954451	0.976177	0.997512	0.99975

Select the correct answer.

a. 1
b. 0.946535
c. 0.656983
d. 1.62569
e. 0.00713
f. 0.450455

9. Evaluate the limit.

$$\lim_{x \to 0} \frac{(7+x)^{-1} - 7^{-1}}{x}$$

10. Let $F(x) = \dfrac{x^2 - 1}{|x-1|}$

Find the following limits.

$$\lim_{x \to 1^+} F(x), \qquad \lim_{x \to 1^-} F(x)$$

11. Use a graph to find a number δ such that $|\sqrt{4x+1} - 3| < 0.6$ whenever $|x-2| < \delta$.

Round down the answer to the nearest hundredth.

12. Is there a number a such that $\lim\limits_{x \to -3} \dfrac{10x^2 + ax + a + 8}{x^2 + x - 6}$ exists? If so, find the value of a and the value of the limit.

Select the correct answer.

a. $a = 49$, limit equals 1.6
b. $a = 13$, limit equals 2.2
c. $a = 49$, limit equals 2.2
d. $a = 19$, limit equals 1.6
e. $a = 49$, limit equals 2.7

13. How close to 2 do we have to take x so that $5x + 3$ is within a distance of 0.025 from 13?

14. Find a function g that agrees with f for $x \neq 25$ and is continuous on $\Re$.

$$f(x) = \frac{5 - \sqrt{x}}{25 - x}$$

15. Use the given graph of $f(x) = \sqrt{x}$ to find a number δ such that $|\sqrt{x} - 2| < 0.4$ whenever $|x - 4| < \delta$.

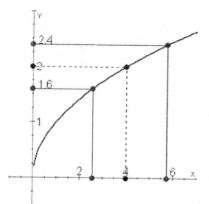

16. Use the given graph of $f(x) = x^2$ to find a number δ such that $|x^2 - 1| < \dfrac{1}{2}$ whenever

$|x - 1| < \delta$.

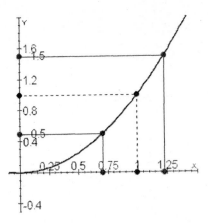

17. Use a graph to find a number δ such that $|\sin x - \dfrac{1}{2}| < 0.05$ whenever $|x - \dfrac{\pi}{6}| < \delta$.

Round down the answer to the nearest thousandth.

18. At what point is the function $f(x) = |6 - x|$ not differentiable.

19. How close to - 9 do we have to take x so that $\dfrac{1}{(x+9)^4} > 10000$?

20. Find the limit.

$\lim\limits_{x \to \infty} \dfrac{1}{2x + 3}$

1. 5, -42.3, 10, -43.6, 20, -18.4, 25, -24.1, 30, -17.53

2. d

3. 3

4. -1/2

5. b

6. $\lim\limits_{x \to 4^-} F(x)$

7. $y = 8x + 13$

8. a

9. -1/49

10. 2, -2

11. $\delta \le 0.81$

12. c

13. $|x - 2| < 0.005$

14. $g = \dfrac{1}{\left(5 + \sqrt{x}\right)}$

15. $\delta \le 1.44$

16. $\delta \le 0.22$

17. $\delta \le 0.056$

18. 6

19. $|x + 9| < 0.1$

20. 0

1. A tank holds 1000 gallons of water, which drains from the bottom of the tank in half an hour. The values in the table show the volume V of water remaining in the tank (in gallons) after t minutes.

   If P is the point (15, 220) on the graph of V, estimate the slope of the tangent line at P by averaging the slopes of two secant lines, passing through P and the points on the graph with $t = 10$ and $t = 20$.

t (min)	5	10	15	20	25	30
V (gal)	689	440	220	186	23	0

   Select the correct answer.

   a.   -24.4
   b.   -25.4
   c.   -37.4
   d.   -14.4
   e.   -35.4

2. If a ball is thrown into the air with a velocity of 45 ft/s, its height in feet after t seconds is given by $y = 45t - 15t^2$.

   Find the instantaneous velocity when $t = 4$.

3. If $\lim_{x \to 3^-} f(x) = 4.5$, then if $\lim_{x \to 3} f(x)$ exists, to what value does it converge?

   Select the correct answer.

   a.   6.5
   b.   4.5
   c.   1
   d.   2
   e.   6

4. For the function f whose graph is shown, find the limit.

   $$\lim_{x \to -9^+} f(x)$$

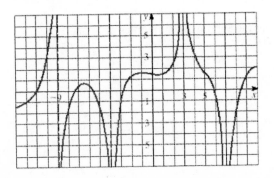

5. Evaluate the function at the given numbers (correct to six decimal places). Use the results to guess the value of the limit.

$$f(x) = 2\frac{\sqrt{x}-1}{x-1}$$

$$\lim_{x\to 1} f(x) = \underline{\hspace{2cm}}$$

x	0.6	0.8	0.9	0.99	0.999	1.4	1.2	1.1	1.01	1.001
$f(x)$	1.127017	1.055728	1.026334	1.002513	1.00025	0.91608	0.954451	0.976177	0.997512	0.99975

Select the correct answer.

a. 1.255039
b. 1.911314
c. 1.969944
d. 1.473889
e. 1

6. Evaluate the limit.

$$\lim_{x\to 1} (x+4)^5 (x^2 - 10)$$

7. Evaluate the limit.

$$\lim_{x\to 0} \frac{(2+x)^{-1} - 2^{-1}}{x}$$

8. Evaluate the limit.

$$\lim_{x\to 0} x^4 \cos\left(\frac{2}{x}\right)$$

9. Evaluate the limit and justify each step by indicating the appropriate properties of limits.

$$\lim_{x\to\infty} \frac{8x^2 - 9x + 1}{3x^2 + 9x - 3}$$

10. Find an equation of the tangent line to the curve $y = 4x^3$ at the point $(-4, -256)$.

11. A curve has equation $y = h(x)$.

Write an expression for the slope of the secant line through the points P(8, $h(8)$) and Q(x, $h(x)$).

12. Use a graph to find a number δ such that $\left| \sin x - \dfrac{1}{2} \right| < 0.1$ whenever $\left| x - \dfrac{\pi}{6} \right| < \delta$.

Round down the answer to the nearest thousandth.

13. Use the definition of the limit to find values of δ that correspond to $\varepsilon = 0.75$.

Round down the answer to the nearest thousandth.

$$\lim_{x \to 1} \left(4 + x - 3x^3 \right) = 2$$

14. Find the limit of the function $h(x)$.

$$h(x) = \begin{cases} 0 & \text{if } x \text{ is rational} \\ 1 & \text{if } x \text{ is irrational} \end{cases}$$

Select the correct answer.

    a.   1
    b.   20
    c.   10
    d.   0
    e.   does not exist

15. If f and g are continuous functions with $f(2) = 2$ and $\lim_{x \to 2} [2f(x) - g(x)] = 2$, find $g(2)$.

16. Find the limit.

$$\lim_{x \to \infty} \left(\sqrt{x^2 + ax} - \sqrt{x^2 + bx} \right)$$

17. State the domain.

$$F(x) = \sqrt{x - 6} \, \sin x$$

18. Find the derivative of the function using the definition of derivative.

$$f(x) = 19 - 9x + 2x^2$$

19. Find a function g that agrees with f for $x \neq 4$ and is continuous on $\Re$.

$$f(x) = \frac{2 - \sqrt{x}}{4 - x}$$

20. Find the derivative of the function using the definition of derivative.

$$f(x) = 13x + 4\sqrt{x}$$

ANSWER KEY

Stewart - Calculus ET 5e Chapter 2 Form F

1. b

2. -75

3. b

4. $-\infty$

5. e

6. -28125

7. -1/4

8. 0

9. $\dfrac{8}{3}$

10. $y = 192x + 512$

11. $\dfrac{h(x) - h(8)}{x - 8}$

12. $\delta \le 0.112$

13. $\delta \le 0.085$

14. e

15. 2

16. $\dfrac{a - b}{2}$

17. $[6,\ \infty)$

18. $4x - 9$

19. $g = \dfrac{1}{2 + \sqrt{x}}$

20. $13 + \dfrac{2}{\sqrt{x}}$

1. If $\lim\limits_{x \to 2^-} f(x) = 4.5$, then if $\lim\limits_{x \to 2} f(x)$ exists, to what value does it converge?

   Select the correct answer.

   a. 2
   b. 1
   c. 5
   d. 4.5
   e. 1.5

2. Consider the following function.

   $$f(x) = \begin{cases} 1-x & x < -1 \\ x & -1 \le x < 1 \\ (x-1)^2 & x \ge 1 \end{cases}$$

   Determine the values of a for which $\lim\limits_{x \to a} f(x)$ exists.

3. Evaluate the limit and justify each step by indicating the appropriate properties of limits.

   $$\lim_{x \to \infty} \frac{8x^2 - 9x + 3}{3x^2 + 4x - 4}$$

4. Find $f'(a)$.

   $$f(x) = 3 + x - 3x^2$$

5. Guess the value of the limit.

   $$\lim_{x \to 0} 3 \frac{\tan 5x - 5x}{x^3}$$

   Select the correct answer.

   a. 121
   b. 135
   c. 134
   d. 130
   e. 125

6. Given that $\lim\limits_{x \to 7} f(x) = -8$ and $\lim\limits_{x \to 7} g(x) = 10$.

Evaluate the limit.

$$\lim\limits_{x \to 7} \left(f(x) + g(x) \right)$$

7. Evaluate the limit.

$$\lim\limits_{x \to 1} (x+1)^3 \left(x^2 - 10 \right)$$

8. Evaluate the limit.

$$\lim\limits_{x \to 3} \left(\frac{x^3 - 5}{x^2 - 4} \right)$$

9. Find the derivative of the function using the definition of the derivative.

$$f(x) = 10 - x + 6x^2$$

10. Let

$$F(x) = \frac{x^2 - 81}{|x - 9|}$$

Find the following limits.

$$\lim\limits_{x \to 9^+} F(x), \quad \lim\limits_{x \to 9^-} F(x)$$

Select the correct answer.

a. 18 and 9
b. 18 and - 18
c. both 18
d. 18 and $-$ 9
e. 81 and 9

11. Use the given graph of $f(x) = \sqrt{x}$ to find a number δ such that $|\sqrt{x} - 2| < 0.4$ whenever $|x - 4| < \delta$.

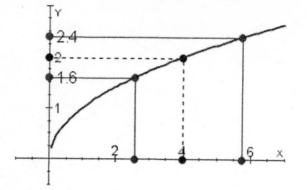

12. Use a graph to find a number δ such that $|\sqrt{4x+1} - 3| < 0.5$ whenever $|x - 2| < \delta$.

    Round down the answer to the nearest hundredth.

13. For the limit, illustrate the definition by finding values of δ that correspond to $\varepsilon = 0.5$.

    Round down the answer to the nearest thousandth.

    $$\lim_{x \to 1} \left(4 + x - 3x^3 \right) = 2$$

14. Find the slope of the tangent line to the curve $y = 5x^3$ at the point (-4, -320).

15. At what point is the function $f(x) = |8 - x|$ not differentiable.

16. Which of the given functions is discontinuous?

    a. $f(x) = \begin{cases} \dfrac{1}{x-2}, & x \geq 5 \\ \dfrac{1}{3}, & x < 5 \end{cases}$

    b. $f(x) = \begin{cases} \dfrac{1}{x-5}, & x \neq 5 \\ 3, & x = 5 \end{cases}$

17. Select the right number for the following limit and prove the statement using the δ, ε definition of the limit.

$$\lim_{x \to 3} \frac{x^2 + 3x - 18}{x - 3}$$

Select the correct answer.

a. 6
b. 8
c. 5
d. 9
e. 18

18. Prove the statement using the δ, ε definition of the limit.

$$\lim_{x \to 2} |x - 2| = 0$$

(use a separate sheet to answer if necessary)

19. Prove the statement using the δ, ε definition of the limit.

$$\lim_{x \to -5} \left(x^2 - 1\right) = 24$$

(use a separate sheet to answer if necessary)

20. Use continuity to evaluate the limit.

$$\lim_{x \to -17\pi} \sin(x + 3 \sin x)$$

Select the correct answer.

a. -17π

b. ∞

c. -1

d. 0

e. 1

1. d

2. $\left(-\infty,\ -1\right)\ \cup\ \left(-1,\ 1\right)\ \cup\ \left(1,\ \infty\right)$

3. $\dfrac{8}{3}$

4. $1 - 6a$

5. e

6. 2

7. -72

8. 22/5

9. $12x - 1$

10. b

11. $\delta \leq 1.44$

12. $\delta \leq 0.6875$

13. $\delta \leq 0.056$

14. 240

15. 8

16. b

17. d

18. Given $\varepsilon > 0$, we need $\delta > 0$ such that if $|x - 2| < \delta$ then $||x - 2| - 0| < \varepsilon$. But $||x - 2|| = |x - 2|$. So this is true if we pick $\delta = \varepsilon$.

19. Given $\varepsilon > 0$, we need $\delta > 0$ such that if $|x - (-5)| < \delta$ then $|(x^2 - 1) - 24| < \varepsilon$ or upon simplifying we need $|x^2 - 25| < \varepsilon$ whenever $|x + 5| < \delta$. Notice that if $|x + 5| < 1$, then $-1 < x + 5 < 1 \Rightarrow -11 < x - 5 < -9 \Rightarrow |x - 5| < 11$. So take $\delta = \min\{\varepsilon / 11, 1\}$. Then $|x - 5| < 11$ and $|x + 5| < \varepsilon / 11$, so $|(x^2 - 1) - 24| = |(x + 5)(x - 5)| = |x + 5||x - 5| < (\varepsilon / 11) \cdot (11) = \varepsilon$. Therefore, by the definition of a limit, $\lim_{x \to -5} (x^2 - 1) = 24$.

20. d

1. The point $P(4, 2)$ lies on the curve $y = \sqrt{x}$. If Q is the point $\left(x, \sqrt{x}\right)$, use your calculator to find the slope of the secant line PQ (correct to six decimal places) for the value of $x = 3.99$.

   Select the correct answer.

   a. $m_{PQ} = 0.250157$
   b. $m_{PQ} = 0.250156$
   c. $m_{PQ} = -0.250154$
   d. $m_{PQ} = -0.250156$
   e. $m_{PQ} = 0.250154$

2. If an arrow is shot upward on the moon with a velocity of 58 m/s, its height in meters after t seconds is given by $h = 58t - 0.47t^2$. Find the instantaneous velocity after one second.

   Select the correct answer.

   a.   56.95
   b.   57.16
   c.   57.06
   d.   57.05
   e.   57.07

3. The displacement (in feet) of a certain particle moving in a straight line is given by $s = \dfrac{t^3}{8}$ where t is measured in seconds. Find the instantaneous velocity when $t = 3$.

4. If $\lim\limits_{x \to 2^+} f(x) = 7.5$, then if $\lim\limits_{x \to 2} f(x)$ exists, to what value does it converge?

   Select the correct answer.

   a.   5
   b.   8.5
   c.   8
   d.   11.5
   e.   7.5

5. If f and g are continuous functions with $f(2) = 3$ and $\lim\limits_{x \to 2}[3f(x) - g(x)] = 5$, find $g(2)$.

6. The slope of the tangent line to the graph of the exponential function $y = 4^x$ at the point $(0, 1)$ is

$$\lim_{x \to 0} \frac{4^x - 1}{x}.$$

Estimate the slope to three decimal places.

Select the correct answer.

   a.   1.045
   b.   1.136
   c.   0.786
   d.   1.126
   e.   1.386

7. Given that $\lim_{x \to 7} f(x) = -2$ and $\lim_{x \to 7} g(x) = 3$.

Evaluate the limit.

$$\lim_{x \to 7} \frac{f(x)}{g(x)}$$

8. Evaluate the limit.

$$\lim_{x \to 0} \frac{(5 + x)^{-1} - 5^{-1}}{x}$$

9. How close to 2 do we have to take x so that $5x + 3$ is within a distance of 0.075 from 13?

10. Evaluate the limit and justify each step by indicating the appropriate properties of limits.

$$\lim_{x \to \infty} \frac{8x^2 - 5x + 9}{3x^2 + 9x - 6}$$

11. Use the given graph of $f(x) = \sqrt{x}$ to find a number δ such that $\left| \sqrt{x} - 2 \right| < 0.5$ whenever $\left| x - 4 \right| < \delta$.

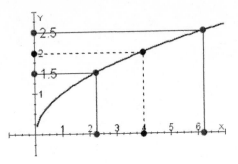

12. Use the given graph of $f(x) = x^2$ to find a number δ such that $\left| x^2 - 1 \right| < \dfrac{1}{2}$ whenever $\left| x - 1 \right| < \delta$.

Round down the answer to the nearest hundredth.

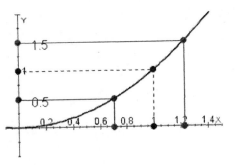

13. Use a graph to find a number δ such that $\left| \sqrt{4x + 1} - 3 \right| < 0.4$ whenever $\left| x - 2 \right| < \delta$.

Round down the answer to the nearest hundredth.

14. Use a graph to find a number δ such that $\left| \sin x - \dfrac{1}{2} \right| < 0.1$ whenever $\left| x - \dfrac{\pi}{6} \right| < \delta$.

Round down the answer to the nearest thousandth.

15. Write an equation that expresses the fact that a function f is continuous at the number 3.

16. Which of the given functions is discontinuous?

a. $f(x) = \begin{cases} \dfrac{1}{x-2}, & x \geq 5 \\ \dfrac{1}{3}, & x < 5 \end{cases}$

b. $f(x) = \begin{cases} \dfrac{1}{x-5}, & x \neq 5 \\ 3, & x = 5 \end{cases}$

17. If a ball is thrown into the air with a velocity of 62 ft/s, its height (in feet) after t seconds is given by

$H = 62t - 16t^2$.

Find the velocity when $t = 5$.

18. Use continuity to evaluate the limit.

$\lim\limits_{x \to 8\pi} \sin(x + 6 \sin x)$

Select the correct answer.

a. ∞
b. -1
c. 1
d. 0
e. 8π

19. Find a function g that agrees with f for $x \neq 16$ and is continuous on $\mathfrak{R}$.

$f(x) = \dfrac{4 - \sqrt{x}}{16 - x}$

20. Consider the function $f(x) = \dfrac{1}{1 + e^{1/x}}$.

Find the value of $\lim\limits_{x \to 0^+} f(x)$.

Select the correct answer.

a.   -0.8
b.   -0.5
c.   0.3
d.   0
e.   0.8

1. b

2. c

3. 3.375

4. e

5. 4

6. e

7. -2/3

8. -1/25

9. $|x-2| < 0.015$

10. $\dfrac{8}{3}$

11. $\delta \le 1.75$

12. $\delta \le 0.22$

13. $\delta \le 0.56$

14. $\delta \le 0.112$

15. $\lim\limits_{x \to 3} f(x) = f(3)$

16. b

17. -98

18. d

19. $g = \dfrac{1}{4 + \sqrt{x}}$

20. d

1. If $f(3) = 4$, $g(3) = 2$, $f'(3) = -5$, $g'(3) = 6$, find the following numbers.

   $(f + g)'(3) =$ _____

   $(fg)'(3) =$ _____

   $(f / g)'(3) =$ _____

   $\left(\dfrac{f}{f - g}\right)'(3) =$ _____

2. Find the points on the curve $y = 2x^3 + 3x^2 - 12x + 1$ where the tangent is horizontal.

3. Find an equation of the tangent line to the curve $y = x^7 \cos x$ at the point $\left(\pi, \, -\pi^7\right)$.

4. Differentiate.

   $g(x) = x^7 \cos x$

5. Find y' by implicit differentiation.

   $xy + 7x + 6x^2 = 5$

6. If a ball is thrown vertically upward with a velocity of 200 ft/s, then its height after t seconds is $s = 200t - 10t^2$.

   What is the maximum height reached by the ball?

7. Find the limit.

   $\displaystyle \lim_{x \to \pi/4} \frac{\sin x - \cos x}{\cos 2x}$

8. Find the derivative of the following function.

   $y(x) = c^3 + 6\cos^3 x$

9. A spherical balloon is being inflated. Find the rate of increase of the surface area $S = 4\pi r^2$ with respect to the radius r when $r = 1$ ft.

10. Differentiate the function.

$$f(x) = \frac{\sqrt{7}}{x^5}$$

11. Find an equation of the tangent line to the curve.

$$y = \frac{\sqrt{x}}{x+6} \text{ at } (4, \ 0.2)$$

12. A plane flying horizontally at an altitude of 4 mi and a speed of 465 mi/h passes directly over a radar station. Find the rate at which the distance from the plane to the station is increasing when it is 10 mi away from the station. Round the result to the nearest integer.

13. Find y' by implicit differentiation.

$$17 \cos x \sin y = 12$$

14. A company makes computer chips from square wafers of silicon. It wants to keep the side length of a wafer very close to 16 mm. The area is $A(x)$. Find $A'(16)$.

15. Find y' by implicit differentiation.

$$7x^2 + 7y^2 = 4$$

16. Find the first and the second derivatives of the function.

$$y = \frac{x}{3-x}$$

17. Find the first and the second derivatives of the function.

$$g(v) = v \csc v$$

18. If $y = 2x^3 + 5x$ and $\dfrac{dx}{dt} = 3$, find $\dfrac{dy}{dt}$ when $x = 5$.

19. The turkey is removed from the oven when its temperature reaches 185 F and is placed on a table in a room where the temperature is 60 F. After 10 minutes the temperature of the turkey is 162 F and after 20 minutes it is 152 F.

Use a linear approximation to predict the temperature of the turkey after half an hour.

20. If $f(t) = \dfrac{18}{3+t^2}$ find $f'(t)$.

1. 1, 14, -8.5, 8.5

2. (1, -6), (-2, 21)

3. $y = -7\pi^6(x - \pi) - \pi^7$

4. $\dfrac{dg(x)}{dx} = 7x^6 \cos(x) - x^7 \sin(x)$

5. $\dfrac{(-7 - y - 12x)}{x}$

6. 1000

7. $-\dfrac{\sqrt{2}}{2}$

8. $-18\cos^2 x \sin x$

9. 8π

10. $\dfrac{df}{dx} = -\dfrac{5\sqrt{7}}{x^6}$

11. $y = \dfrac{1}{200}(x - 4) + 0.2$

12. 456

13. $\tan(x)\tan(y)$

14. 32

15. $-\dfrac{x}{y}$

16. $3(3 - x)^{-2}, \ 6(3 - x)^{-3}$

17. $-v\csc(v)\cot(v) + \csc(v), \ \csc(v)\big(v\csc(v)\csc(v) + v\cot(v)\cot(v) - 2\cot(v)\big)$

18. 465

19. 142

20. $\dfrac{-36t}{\left(3 + t^2\right)^2}$

1. If $f(3) = -4$, $f'(3) = 4$, $g(3) = 2$ and $g'(3) = 0$, find $(f + g)'(3)$.

2. Evaluate.

$$\lim_{x \to 1} \frac{x^{7.000} - 1}{x - 1}$$

3. Differentiate.

$$f(x) = x^4 e^x$$

4. The position function of a particle is given by

$$s = t^3 - 10.5t^2 - 2t, \quad t \geq 0$$

When does the particle reach a velocity of 52 m/s?

5. Differentiate the function.

$$f(x) = \cos(\ln(5x))$$

6. Use the table to estimate the value of $h'(10.5)$, where $h(x) = f(g(x))$.

x	10	10.1	10.2	10.3	10.4	10.5	10.6
$f(x)$	4.5	3.5	5.6	4.3	2.5	9.9	7.8
$g(x)$	6.5	5.9	4.7	4.2	5.4	10.1	6.3

7. A spherical balloon is being inflated. Find the rate of increase of the surface area $S = 4\pi r^2$ with respect to the radius r when $r = 1$ ft.

8. If $h(2) = 7$ and $h'(2) = -2$, find $\dfrac{d}{dx}\left(\dfrac{h(x)}{x} \right)\Bigg|_{x=2}$

9. Differentiate.

$$y = \frac{\sin x}{7 + \cos x}$$

10. Differentiate.

$$y = \frac{\tan x - 2}{\sec x}$$

11. Find an equation of the tangent line to the curve $y = 3 \tan x$ at the point $\left(\frac{\pi}{4}, 3\right)$.

12. Find the derivative of the following function and calculate it for $x = 36$ to the nearest tenth.

$$y(x) = \sqrt{x + \sqrt{x + \sqrt{x}}}$$

13. Find the differential of the function.

$$y = x^4 + 5x$$

14. Find all points at which the tangent line is horizontal on the graph of the function.

$$y(x) = 6 \sin x + \sin^2 x$$

15. Regard y as the independent variable and x as the dependent variable and use implicit differentiation to find dx/dy.

$$y^4 + x^2 y^2 + yx^4 = y + 6$$

16. If $f(x) = 10 \cos x + \sin^2 x$, find $f'(x)$ and $f''(x)$.

17. Use implicit differentiation to find an equation of the tangent line to the curve $4x^2 + 3y^2 = 7$ at the point $(1, 1)$.

18. Find y''', if $y = \sqrt{2x + 1}$.

19. Find a formula for $f^{(n)}(x)$

$$f(x) = (5 + x)^{-1}$$

20. A baseball diamond is a square with side 90 ft. A batter hits the ball and runs toward first base with a speed of 28 ft/s. At what rate is his distance from second base decreasing when he is halfway to first base? Round the result to the nearest hundredth if necessary.

ANSWER KEY

Stewart - Calculus ET 5e Chapter 3 Form B

1. 4

2. 7000

3. $f'(x+4)x^3 e^x$

4. 9

5. $\dfrac{-\sin(\ln(5x))}{x}$

6. 24.75

7. 8π

8. -2.75

9. $\dfrac{dy}{dx} = \dfrac{7\cos x + 1}{(7 + \cos x)^2}$

10. $\dfrac{dy}{dx} = \cos(x) + 2\sin(x)$

11. $y = 6x + 3\left(1 - \dfrac{\pi}{2}\right)$

12. 0.1

13. $dy = \left(4x^3 + 5\right) dx$

14. $\left(\left(\dfrac{\pi}{2}\right) + 2\pi n, \ 7\right), \ \left(\dfrac{3\pi}{2} + 2\pi n, \ -5\right)$

15. $y = \dfrac{\left(1 - 4y^3 - 2x^2 y - x^4\right)}{\left(2xy^2 + 4yx^3\right)}$

16. $-10\sin(x) + \sin(2x), -10\cos(x) + 2\cos(2x)$

17. $y = -\dfrac{4}{3}x + \dfrac{7}{3}$

18. $3(2x + 1)^{-5/2}$

19. $(-1)^n \, n! \cdot (5 + x)^{-(n+1)}$

20. 12.52

1. Differentiate the function.

$$v = t^8 - \frac{1}{\sqrt[9]{t^8}}$$

Select the correct answer.

a. $\quad v' = 8t^7 + \dfrac{8}{9t\sqrt[9]{t^8}}$

b. $\quad v' = 8t^9 + \dfrac{9}{8\sqrt[9]{t^8}}$

c. $\quad v' = 9t^9 - \dfrac{9}{8t\sqrt[8]{t^9}}$

d. $\quad v' = 8t^7 - \dfrac{8\sqrt[9]{t^8}}{9}$

e. $\quad v' = t^7 + \dfrac{1}{9t\sqrt[9]{t^8}}$

2. Find an equation of the tangent line to the curve at the given point.

$$y = x^3 + 4e^x, \quad (0, \ 4)$$

Select the correct answer.

a. $\quad y = 4x + 4$
b. $\quad y = 2x + 4$
c. $\quad y = 3x + 5$
d. $\quad y = 5x + 4$
e. $\quad y = 4x + 5$

3. Compute Δy and dy for the given values of x and $dx = \Delta x$.

$$y = x^2, \quad x = 1, \quad \Delta x = 0.5$$

Select the correct answer.

a. $\quad \Delta y = 1.25, \quad dy = 1$
b. $\quad \Delta y = 0.25, \quad dy = 1$
c. $\quad \Delta y = 0.25, \quad dy = 0$
d. $\quad \Delta y = 1.25, \quad dy = 0$
e. $\quad \Delta y = 1.25, \quad dy = 0.25$

4.   Find the equation of the tangent line to the given curve at the specified point.

$$y = \frac{\sqrt{x}}{2x+2}, \quad (4, \ 0.2)$$

Select the correct answer.

a. $y = -\dfrac{19}{50}x + \dfrac{9}{50}$

b. $y = \dfrac{37}{70}x + \dfrac{129}{130}$

c. $y = -\dfrac{3}{200}x + \dfrac{13}{50}$

d. $y = \dfrac{109}{120}x + \dfrac{7}{90}$

e. $y = \dfrac{107}{120}x + \dfrac{13}{90}$

5.   Find equations of the tangent lines to the curve $y = \dfrac{x-8}{x+8}$ that are parallel to the line $x - y = 8$.

Select the correct answer(s).

a. $x - y = -17$
b. $x - y = -12$
c. $x - y = -15$
d. $x - y = -1$
e. $x - y = -4$

6.   The position function of a particle is given by $s = t^3 - 1.5t^2 - 2t, \ t \geq 0$.

When does the particle reach a velocity of 166 m/s?

Select the correct answer.

a. $t = 7$ sec
b. $t = 8$ sec
c. $t = 5$ sec
d. $t = 3$ sec
e. $t = 12$ sec

7. The mass of the part of a metal rod that lies between its left end and a point x meters to the right is $S = 4x^2$.

   Find the linear density when x is 1 m.

   Select the correct answer.

   a.   4
   b.   16
   c.   8
   d.   12
   e.   18

8. If f is the focal length of a convex lens and an object is placed at a distance v from the lens, then its image will be at a distance u from the lens, where f, v, and u are related by the *lens equation*

   $$\frac{1}{f} = \frac{1}{v} + \frac{1}{u}.$$

   Find the rate of change of v with respect to u.

   Select the correct answer.

   a. $\dfrac{dv}{du} = -\dfrac{f}{(u-f)^2}$

   b. $\dfrac{dv}{du} = -\dfrac{f^2}{(u-f)^2}$

   c. $\dfrac{dv}{du} = -\dfrac{f^2}{u-f}$

   d. $\dfrac{dv}{du} = \dfrac{f^2}{(u-f)^2}$

   e. $\dfrac{dv}{du} = \dfrac{2f^2}{(u-f)^2}$

9. The gas law for an ideal gas at absolute temperature T (in elvins), pressure P (in atmospheres), and volume V (in liters) is $PV = nRT$, where n is the number of moles of the gas and $R = 0.0821$ is the gas constant. Suppose that, at a certain instant, $P = 7$ atm and is increasing at a rate of 0.10 atm/min and $V = 10$L and is decreasing at a rate of 0.15 L/min. Find the rate of change of T with respect to time at that instant if $n = 10$ moles.

   Select the correct answer.

   a.   2.497
   b.   -0.041
   c.   -0.061
   d.   0.061
   e.   0.161

10. Find the limit.

$$\lim_{\theta \to 0} \frac{\cos(\cos\theta)}{\sec\theta}$$

Select the correct answer.

a.   1
b.   sin 1
c.   cos 1
d.   0
e.   2

11. Find the derivative of the following function and calculate it for $x = 25$ to the nearest tenth.

$$y(x) = \sqrt{x + \sqrt{x + \sqrt{x}}}$$

Select the correct answer.

a.   1.1
b.   -0.9
c.   0.1
d.   0.2
e.   0.3

12. Suppose that $F(x) = f(g(x))$ and $g(14) = 2$, $g'(14) = 5$, $f'(14) = 15$, and $f'(2) = 12$.

Find $F'(14)$.

Select the correct answer.

a.   60
b.   140
c.   24
d.   17
e.   20

13. Find the tangent to the ellipse $\dfrac{x^2}{4} + \dfrac{y^2}{4} = 1$ at the point $\left(1, \ \sqrt{3} \ \right)$.

Select the correct answer.

a. $y = -0.58x + 3.31$
b. $y = -0.58x + 2.31$
c. $y = 0.42x + 2.31$
d. $y = -1.58x + 1.31$
e.   none of these

14. Find the numerical value of the expression.

cosh(4)

Select the correct answer.

   a.   -6.8154
   b.   297.4354
   c.   27.3082
   d.   -92.8150
   e.   92.8150

15. Evaluate.

$$\lim_{x \to \infty} \frac{\sinh x}{e^x}$$

Select the correct answer.

   a. $-\infty$
   b. $1/2$
   c. ∞
   d.   0
   e. $-1/2$

16. Use differentials to estimate the amount of paint needed to apply a coat of paint 0.18 cm thick to a hemispherical dome with diameter 60 m.

Select the correct answer.

   a. 2.52π
   b. 3.24π
   c. 3.82π
   d. 2.28π
   e. 4.11π

17. Gravel is being dumped from a conveyor belt at a rate of 35 ft^3/min and its coarseness is such that it forms a pile in the shape of a cone whose base diameter and height are always equal. How fast is the height of the pile increasing when the pile is 15 ft high? Round the result to the nearest hundredth.

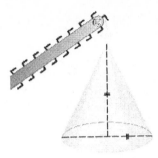

Select the correct answer.

a.   0.27 ft/min
b.   1.24 ft/min
c.   0.14 ft/min
d.   0.2 ft/min
e.   0.6 ft/min

18. Two carts, A and B, are connected by a rope 33 ft long that passes over a pulley (see the figure below). The point Q is on the floor 16 ft directly beneath and between the carts. Cart A is being pulled away from Q at a speed of 5 ft/s. How fast is cart B moving toward Q at the instant when cart A is 4 ft from Q? Round the result to the nearest hundredth.

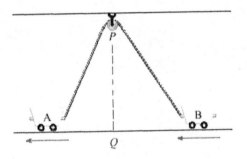

Select the correct answer.

a.   4.94 ft/s
b.   4.93 ft/s
c.   5.43 ft/s
d.   4.73 ft/s
e.   2.73 ft/s

19. The table lists the amount of U.S. cash per capita in circulation as of June 30 in the given year. Use a linear approximation to estimate the amount of cash per capita in circulation in the year 2000.

t	1960	1970	1980	1990
$C(t)$	$176	$270	$574	$1,068

Choose the correct answer from the following.

   a. $1,491
   b. $1,524
   c. $1,587
   d. $1,562
   e. $1,572

20. Two sides of a triangle are 6 m and 7 m in length and the angle between them is increasing at a rate of 0.07 rad/s. Find the rate at which the area of the triangle is increasing when the angle between the sides of fixed length is $\dfrac{\pi}{3}$.

Select the correct answer.

   a. $1.035 \text{ m}^2/\text{s}$
   b. $1.835 \text{ m}^2/\text{s}$
   c. $-1.265 \text{ m}^2/\text{s}$
   d. $0.735 \text{ m}^2/\text{s}$
   e. $5.735 \text{ m}^2/\text{s}$

ANSWER KEY

Stewart - Calculus ET 5e Chapter 3 Form C

1. a

2. a

3. a

4. c

5. a, d

6. b

7. c

8. b

9. c

10. c

11. c

12. a

13. b

14. c

15. b

16. b

17. d

18. b

19. d

20. d

1. Atmospheric pressure V decreases as altitude h increases. At a temperature of 10 C the pressure is 100.8 kilopascals (kPa) at sea level, 87.2 kPa at $h = 1$ km, and 73.6 kPa at $h = 2$ km. Use a linear approximation to estimate the atmospheric pressure at an altitude of 3 km.

   Select the correct answer.

   a.   59.2
   b.   55.7
   c.   60
   d.   61.6
   e.   62

2. If $f(x) = 4\cos x + \sin^2 x$, find $f'(x)$ and $f''(x)$.

   Select the correct answers.

   a. $f''(x) = -4\cos(x) + 2\cos(2x)$
   b. $f''(x) = -2\cos(2x) + 4\cos(x)$
   c. $f'(x) = -4\sin(2x) + \sin(x)$
   d. $f'(x) = -4\sin(x) + \sin(2x)$
   e. $f''(x) = -4\cos(2x) + 2\cos(x)$

3. The equation of motion is given for a particle, where s is in meters and t is in seconds. Find the acceleration after 4.5 seconds.

   $s = \sin 2\pi t$

   Select the correct answer.

   a. $9\pi \text{ m}/s^2$
   b. $-9\pi \text{ m}/s^2$
   c. $0 \text{ m}/s^2$
   d. $81\pi^2 \text{ m}/s^2$
   e. $-81\pi^2 \text{ m}/s^2$

4. Differentiate the function.

$$G(u) = \ln \sqrt{\frac{5u+6}{5u-6}}$$

Select the correct answer.

a. $\quad G'(u) = -\dfrac{30}{25u^2 - 36}$

b. $\quad G'(u) = -\dfrac{11}{25u^2 - 36}$

c. $\quad G'(u) = \sqrt{\dfrac{5u-6}{5u+6}}$

d. $\quad G'(u) = -\dfrac{5u-6}{2(5u+6)}$

e. $\quad G'(u) = \dfrac{5u}{2(5u+6)}$

5. Use logarithmic differentiation to find the derivative of the function.

$$y = (3x+1)^3 (x^4 - 6)^5$$

Select the correct answer.

a. $\quad y' = (20x+9)(3x+1)^3(x^4-6)^5$

b. $\quad y' = 9(3x+1)^2(x^4-6)^5 + 20x^3(3x+1)^3(x^4-6)^4$

c. $\quad y' = 9(3x+1)^2(x^4-6)^5 + 20x(3x+1)^3(x^4-6)^5$

d. $\quad y' = 9(3x+1)^2(x^4-6)^5 + (3x+1)^3(x^4-6)^5$

e. $\quad y' = (x+1)^2(x^4-6)^5 + 20x(3x+1)^3(x^3-6)^4$

6. Use logarithmic differentiation to find the derivative of the function.

$$y = \sqrt[5]{\frac{x^2+1}{x^2-1}}$$

Select the correct answer.

a. $y' = -\dfrac{4x}{5(x^4-1)}\sqrt[5]{\dfrac{x^2+1}{x^2-1}}$

b. $y' = -\dfrac{5x}{(x^4-1)}\sqrt[5]{\dfrac{x^2+1}{x^2-1}}$

c. $y' = -\dfrac{20x}{x^4-1}$

d. $y' = -\dfrac{20x}{x^4-1}\sqrt[5]{\dfrac{x^2+1}{x^2-1}}$

e. $y' = \dfrac{5x}{4x^4-1}\sqrt[5]{\dfrac{x^2+1}{x^2-1}}$

7. Use logarithmic differentiation to find the derivative of the function.

$$y = x^{6x}$$

Select the correct answer.

a. $y' = 6x^{6x}(6\ln x+1)$
b. $y' = 6(\ln x+1)$
c. $y' = 6x^{6x}(\ln x+1)$
d. $y' = -6x^{6x}(\ln x+6)$
e. $y' = x^x(\ln 6x+1)$

8. Use the linear approximation of the function $f(x) = \sqrt{9-x}$ at $a = 0$ to approximate the number $\sqrt{9.09}$.

Select the correct answer.

a. 3.02
b. 0.15
c. 7.44
d. 7.4
e. 2.25

9. Determine the values of x for which the given linear approximation is accurate to within 0.07 at $a = 0$.

   $\tan x \approx x$

   Select the correct answer.

   a. $-0.71 < x < 0.48$
   b. $0.06 < x < 0.68$
   c. $-1.04 < x < 1.55$
   d. $-0.57 < x < 0.57$
   e. $-0.19 < x < 0.28$

10. The turkey is removed from the oven when its temperature reaches 175 F and is placed on a table in a room where the temperature is 70 F. After 10 minutes the temperature of the turkey is 160 F and after 20 minutes it is 150 F. Use a linear approximation to predict the temperature of the turkey after half an hour.

    Select the correct answer.

    a.   136
    b.   130
    c.   134
    d.   140
    e.   160

11. Two cars start moving from the same point. One travels south at 28 mi/h and the other travels west at 70 mi/h. At hat rate is the distance between the cars increasing 5 hours later? Round the result to the nearest hundredth.

    Select the correct answer.

    a.   75.42 mi/h
    b.   75.49 mi/h
    c.   76.4 mi/h
    d.   75.39 mi/h
    e.   75.38 mi/h

12. A baseball diamond is a square with side 90 ft. A batter hits the ball and runs toward first base with a speed of 26 ft/s. At what rate is his distance from second base decreasing when he is halfway to first base?

Select the correct answer.

a. $\dfrac{12}{\sqrt{5}}$ ft/s

b. $\dfrac{90}{\sqrt{5}}$ ft/s

c. $\dfrac{26}{\sqrt{5}}$ ft/s

d. $\dfrac{\sqrt{5}}{26}$ ft/s

e. $\dfrac{\sqrt{5}}{5}$ ft/s

13. A water trough is 10 m long and a cross-section has the shape of an isosceles trapezoid that is 40 cm wide at the bottom, 75 cm wide at the top, and has height 55 cm. If the trough is being filled with water at the rate of 0.7 m^3/min, how fast is the water level rising when the water is 45 cm deep?

Round the result to the nearest hundredth.

Select the correct answer.

a.   10.3 cm/min
b.   10 cm/min
c.   10.2 cm/min
d.   10.25 cm/min
e.   11.25 cm/min

14. A plane flying horizontally at an altitude of 2 mi and a speed of 490 mi/h passes directly over a radar station. Find the rate at which the distance from the plane to the station is increasing when it is 10 mi away from the station.

Select the correct answer.

   a.   ≈ 495 mi/h
   b.   ≈ 485 mi/h
   c.   ≈ 455 mi/h
   d.   ≈ 970 mi/h
   e.   ≈ 870 mi/h

15. Two sides of a triangle are 2 m and 3 m in length and the angle between them is increasing at a rate of 0.03 rad/s. Find the rate at which the area of the triangle is increasing when the angle between the sides of fixed length is $\dfrac{\pi}{3}$.

Select the correct answer.

   a.   5.045 m^2/s
   b.   -0.955 m^2/s
   c.   0.045 m^2/s
   d.   -1.955 m^2/s
   e.   1.145 m^2/s

16. If two resistors with resistances R_1 and R_2 are connected in parallel, as in the figure, then the total resistance R measured in ohms (Ω), is given by $\dfrac{1}{R} = \dfrac{1}{R_1} + \dfrac{1}{R_2}$. If R_1 and R_2 are increasing at rates of 0.1 Ω/s and 0.4 Ω/s respectively, how fast is R changing when $R_1 = 75$ and $R_2 = 100$? Round the result to the nearest thousandth.

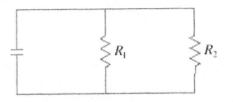

Select the correct answer.

   a.   0.159 Ω/s
   b.   0.145 Ω/s
   c.   1.196 Ω/s
   d.   0.106 Ω/s
   e.   0.168 Ω/s

17. Use logarithmic differentiation to find the derivative of the function.

$$y = x^{2/x}$$

Select the correct answer.

a. $y' = \dfrac{2x^{2/x}(1 - \ln x)}{x}$

b. $y' = \dfrac{2x^{2/x}(1 - \ln x)}{x^2}$

c. $y' = \dfrac{2x^{2/x}(1 + \ln x)}{x^2}$

d. $y' = \dfrac{x^{2/x}(1 - \ln x)}{x^2}$

e. $y' = \dfrac{x^{1/x}(1 + \ln x)}{2x}$

18. Determine the values of x for which the linear approximation $\dfrac{1}{(1 + 2x)^3} \approx 1 - 6x$ is accurate to within 0.17.

Select the correct answer.

a. $-0.23 < x < 0.93$
b. $-0.32 < x < 0.92$
c. $-0.07 < x < 0.09$
d. $-0.34 < x < 0.82$
e. $-0.34 < x < 0.19$

19. Find $\dfrac{d^4}{dx^4}(x^3 \ln x)$.

Select the correct answer.

a. $\dfrac{d^4}{dx^4}(x^3 \ln x) = \dfrac{6}{x^4}$

b. $\dfrac{d^4}{dx^4}(x^3 \ln x) = \dfrac{3}{x^4}$

c. $\dfrac{d^4}{dx^4}(x^3 \ln x) = \dfrac{3}{x}$

d. $\dfrac{d^4}{dx^4}(x^3 \ln x) = \dfrac{6}{x}$

e. $\dfrac{d^4}{dx^4}(x^3 \ln x) = \dfrac{6}{x^2}$

20. Gravel is being dumped from a conveyor belt at a rate of 30 ft^3/min and its coarseness is such that it forms a pile in the shape of a cone whose base diameter and height are always equal. How fast is the height of the pile increasing when the pile is 12 ft high? Round the result to the nearest hundredth.

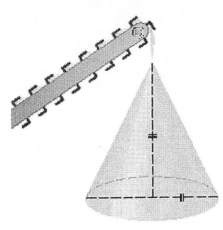

Select the correct answer.

a.   0.21 ft/min
b.   1.31 ft/min
c.   0.27 ft/min
d.   0.44 ft/min
e.   0.34 ft/min

1. c

2. a, d

3. c

4. a

5. b

6. a

7. c

8. a

9. d

10. d

11. d

12. c

13. c

14. b

15. c

16. d

17. b

18. c

19. d

20 c

1. Differentiate the function.

   $f(x) = \sqrt{70}$

2. Differentiate the function.

   $f(t) = \dfrac{1}{3}t^6 - 2t^4 + t$

3. Differentiate the function.

   $G(x) = \sqrt{x} - 5e^x$

4. Find y' by implicit differentiation.

   $8 \cos x \sin y = 7$

5. Find an equation of the tangent line to the curve $15(x^2 + y^2)^2 = 289(x^2 - y^2)$ at the point $(4, 1)$.

   Select the correct answer.

   a. $y = -1.11x + 17$
   b. $y = -1.11x + 3.43$
   c. $y = -1.11x + 5.43$
   d. $y = 1.11x + 5.43$
   e. none of these

6. Given a diagram with two tangent lines to the parabola $y = x^2$ that pass through the point $(0, -4)$. Find the coordinates of the points where these tangent lines intersect the parabola.

   Select the correct answer.

   a. $(\pm 2.5,\ 6.25)$
   b. $(\pm 2,\ 4)$
   c. $(\pm 1.5,\ 2.25)$
   d. $(\pm 3,\ 9)$
   e. $(\pm 3,\ 6.25)$

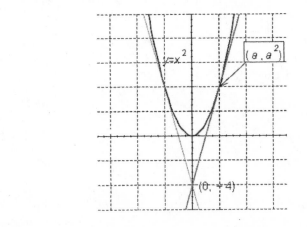

7. Evaluate.

    $$\lim_{x \to 1} \frac{x^{4.000} - 1}{x - 1}$$

8. Differentiate.

    $$f(x) = x^3 e^x$$

9. Find the average rate of change of the area of a circle with respect to its radius r as r changes from 4 to 5.

10. Find an equation of the tangent line to the curve $4x^2 + 3y^2 = 7$ at the point (1, 1).

11. If a tank holds 5000 gallons of water, and that water can drain from the tank in 40 minutes, then Torricelli's Law gives the volume V of water remaining in the tank after t minutes as

    $$V = 5000 \left(1 - \frac{t}{40} \right)^2.$$

    Find the rate at which water is draining from the tank after 6 minutes.

12. The quantity Q of charge in coulombs C that has passed through a point in a wire up to time t (measured in seconds), is given by $Q(t) = t^3 - 4t^2 + 4t + 10$.

    Find the current when $t = 2s$.

13. The gas law for an ideal gas at absolute temperature T (in kelvins), pressure P (in atmospheres), and volume V (in liters) is $PV = nRT$, where n is the number of moles of the gas and $R = 0.0821$ is the gas constant. Suppose that, at a certain instant, $P = 9$ atm and is increasing at a rate of 0.10 atm/min and $V = 11$L and is decreasing at a rate of 0.15 L/min. Find the rate of change of T with respect to time at that instant if $n = 10$ moles.

14. Find the derivative of $f(x)$.

    $$f(x) = x \cosh x$$

15. Evaluate

    $$\lim_{x \to \infty} \frac{\sinh x}{e^x}$$

16. Differentiate.

$g(x) = 5 \sec x + \tan x$

17. Find the derivative of the function.

$G(x) = (7x+10)^{12}(8x^2+3x-6)^{15}$

18. The displacement of a particle on a vibrating string is given by the equation $s(t) = 8 + \dfrac{1}{7}\sin(4\pi t)$

where s is measured in centimeter and t in seconds.

Find the velocity of the particle after t seconds.

19. Find $\dfrac{d}{dx}(\sin^{38} x \cos 38x)$.

20. A baseball diamond is a square with side 90 ft. A batter hits the ball and runs toward first base with a speed of 30 ft/s. At what rate is his distance from second base decreasing when he is halfway to first base? Round the result to the nearest hundredth.

1. 0

2. $f'(t) = 2t^5 - 8t^3 + 1$

3. $G'(x) = \dfrac{1}{2\sqrt{x}} - 5e^x$

4. $\tan(x)\tan(y)$

5. c

6. b

7. 4000

8. $f'(x) = (x+3)x^2 e^x$

9. 9π

10. $y = -1.33x + 2.33$

11. -212.5

12. 0

13. -0.305

14. $\cosh(x) + x\sinh(x)$

15. $\dfrac{1}{2}$

16. $\dfrac{dg(x)}{dx} = 5\sec(x)\tan(x) + \sec^2 x$

17. $84(7x+10)^{11}(8x^2+3x-6)^{15} + 15(7x+10)^{12}(8x^2+3x-6)^{14}(16x+3)$

18. $\dfrac{4\pi}{7}\cos(4\pi t)$

19. $38\sin^{37}(x)\cos(39x)$

20. 13.42

1. Differentiate the function.

   $$f(x) = \sqrt{30}$$

   Select the correct answer.

   a. $\quad f'(x) = 0$
   b. $\quad f'(x) = 1$
   c. $\quad f'(x) = 2\sqrt{30}$
   d. $\quad f'(x) = \dfrac{1}{2\sqrt{30}}$
   e. $\quad f'(x) = 2\sqrt{30}$

2. Differentiate the function.

   $$V(r) = \frac{4}{3}\pi r^3$$

3. Differentiate the function.

   $$f(t) = 9\sqrt{t} - \frac{5}{\sqrt{t}}$$

4. Find an equation of the tangent line to the curve at the given point.

   $$y = x^3 + 7e^x, \quad (0, \ 7)$$

5. Evaluate.

   $$\lim_{x \to 1} \frac{x^{4.000} - 1}{x - 1}$$

6. A television camera is positioned 4,600 ft from the base of a rocket launching pad. The angle of elevation of the camera has to change at the correct rate in order to keep the rocket in sight. Also, the mechanism for focusing the camera has to take into account the increasing distance from the camera to the rising rocket. Let's assume the rocket rises vertically and its speed is 680 ft/s when it has risen 2,600 ft. If the television camera is always kept aimed at the rocket, how fast is the camera's angle of elevation changing at this moment? Round the result to the nearest thousandth.

7. Determine the values of x for which the linear approximation $\sqrt{1+x} \approx 1 + \dfrac{x}{2}$ is accurate to within 0.03.

8. Differentiate.

$$y = \frac{1}{x^6 + x^3 + 1}$$

9. The table lists the amount of U.S. cash per capita in circulation as of June 30 in the given year. Use a linear approximation to estimate the amount of cash per capita in circulation in the year 2000.

t	1960	1970	1980	1990
$C(t)$	$172	$254	$571	$1,068

10. Use the linear approximation of the function $f(x) = \sqrt{7-x}$ at $a = 0$ to approximate the number $\sqrt{7.1}$.

11. Find the equation of the tangent line to the given curve at the specified point.

$$y = 2xe^x, \quad (0,\ 0)$$

12. The position function of a particle is given by $s = t^3 - 3t^2 - 5t, \quad t \ge 0$.

When does the particle reach a velocity of 4 m/s?

13. A company makes computer chips from square wafers of silicon. It wants to keep the side length of a wafer very close to 19 mm. The area is $A(x)$. Find $A'(19)$.

14. Determine the values of x for which the given linear approximation is accurate to within 0.07 at $a = 0$.

$$\tan x \approx x$$

15. If a tank holds 5000 gallons of water, and that water can drain from the tank in 40 minutes, then Torricelli's Law gives the volume V of water remaining in the tank after t minutes as

$$V = 5000\left(1 - \frac{t}{40}\right)^2 .$$

Find the rate at which water is draining from the tank after 15 minutes.

16. The quantity Q of charge in coulombs C that has passed through a point in a wire up to time t (measured in seconds) is given by $Q(t) = t^3 - 3t^2 + 4t + 3$. Find the current when $t = 2$ s.

    Select the correct answer.

    a.   13
    b.   4
    c.   2
    d.   3
    e.   1

17. Newton's Law of Gravitation says that the magnitude F of the force exerted by a body of mass m on a body of mass M is $F = \dfrac{GmM}{r^2}$.

    Find $\dfrac{dF}{dr}(6)$.

18. Suppose that the cost, in dollars, for a company to produce x pairs of jeans is

    $C(x) = 290 + 5x + 0.03x^2 + 0.0005x^3$.

    Find $C'(130)$.

    Select the correct answer.

    a. $328.15
    b. $21.25
    c. $38.15
    d. $34.25
    e. $344.25

19. Use the linear approximation of the function $f(x) = \sqrt{4+x}$ at $a = 0$ to approximate the number $\sqrt{4.04}$.

20. Two carts, A and B, are connected by a rope 40 ft long that passes over a pulley (see the figure below). The point Q is on the floor 10 ft directly beneath and between the carts. Cart A is being pulled away from Q at a speed of 5 ft/s. How fast is cart B moving toward Q at the instant when cart A is 8 ft from

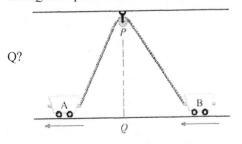

1. a

2. $V'(r) = 4\pi r^2$

3. $f'(t) = \dfrac{9}{2\sqrt{t}} + \dfrac{5}{2t\sqrt{t}}$

4. $y = 7x + 7$

5. 4000

6. 0.112

7. (-0.43, 0.55)

8. $y' = \dfrac{-(6x^5 + 3x^2)}{(x^6 + x^3 + 1)^2}$

9. 1565

10. 2.66

11. $y = 2x$

12. 3

13. 38

14. $-0.57 < x < 0.57$

15. -156.25

16. b

17. $\dfrac{-2GmM}{216}$

18. c

19. 2.01

20. 3.36

1. Differentiate the function.

$$S(r) = 4\pi r^2$$

2. Differentiate the function.

$$z = \frac{A}{y^{50}} + Be^y$$

3. Find the points on the curve $y = 2x^3 + 3x^2 - 36x + 7$ where the tangent is horizontal.

Select the correct answer.

a. $(-4, \ 71), \ (4, \ 39)$

b. $(-3, \ 88), \ (4, \ 39)$

c. $(-4, \ 71), \ (2, \ -37)$

d. $(-3, \ 88), \ (2, \ -37)$

e. $(-3, \ 37), \ (2, \ -37)$

4. Evaluate.

$$\lim_{x \to 1} \frac{x^{1.000} - 1}{x - 1}$$

5. Differentiate.

$$Y(u) = (u^{-2} + u^{-3})(2u^5 - u^3)$$

6. Differentiate.

$$y = \frac{1}{x^6 + x^4 + 5}$$

7. The position function of a particle is given by $s = t^3 - 3t^2 - 5t, \ t \ge 0$.

When does the particle reach a velocity of 139 m/s?

8. If a ball is thrown vertically upward with a velocity of 72 ft/s, then its height after t seconds is $s = 72t - 6t^2$.

   What is the maximum height reached by the ball?

   Select the correct answer.

   a.   6 ft
   b.   216 ft
   c.   36 ft
   d.   225 ft
   e.   81 ft

9. The mass of the part of a metal rod that lies between its left end and a point x meters to the right is $5x^2$ kg.

   Find the linear density when x is 4 m.

10. A telephone line hangs between two poles at 12 m apart in the shape of the catenary $y = 30\cosh(x/30) - 25$, where x and y are measured in meters.

    Find the slope of this curve where it meets the right pole.

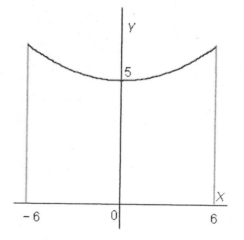

   Select the correct answer.

   a.   0.1630
   b.   0.2072
   c.   0.6162
   d.   0.2013
   e.   0.4013

11. Evaluate.

$$\lim_{x \to \infty} \frac{\cosh x}{e^x}$$

12. If a snowball melts so that its surface area decreases at a rate of $4 \text{ cm}^2 /\text{min}$, find the rate at which the diameter decreases when the diameter is 39 cm.

13. Two cars start moving from the same point. One travels south at 27 mi/h and the other travels west at 50 mi/h. At what rate is the distance between the cars increasing 3 hours later? Round the result to the nearest hundredth.

14. A baseball diamond is a square with side 90 ft. A batter hits the ball and runs toward first base with a speed of 28 ft/s. At what rate is his distance from second base decreasing when he is halfway to first base? Round the result to the nearest hundredth if necessary.

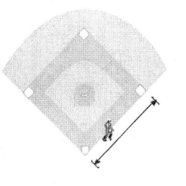

15. The altitude of a triangle is increasing at a rate of 3 cm/min while the area of the triangle is increasing at a rate of $4 \text{ cm}^2 /\text{min}$. At what rate is the base of the triangle changing when the altitude is 10 cm and the area is 90 cm^2.

16. A water trough is 20 m long and a cross-section has the shape of an isosceles trapezoid that is 20 cm wide at the bottom, 60 cm wide at the top, and has height 50 cm. If the trough is being filled with water at the rate of $0.7 \text{ m}^3 /\text{min}$, how fast is the water level rising when the water is 45 cm deep? Round the result to the nearest hundredth.

17. A boat is pulled into a dock by a rope attached to the bow of the boat and passing through a pulley on the dock that is 1 m higher than the bow of the boat. If the rope is pulled in at a rate of 2 m/s how fast is the boat approaching the dock when it is 3 m from the dock? Round the result to the nearest hundredth if necessary.

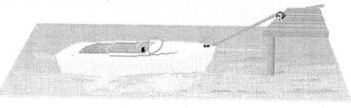

18. Two sides of a triangle are 3 m and 6 m in length and the angle between them is increasing at a rate of 0.04 rad/s. Find the rate at which the area of the triangle is increasing when the angle between the sides of fixed length is $\dfrac{\pi}{3}$.

19. Two carts, A and B, are connected by a rope 36 ft long that passes over a pulley (see the figure below). The point Q is on the floor 14 ft directly beneath and between the carts. Cart A is being pulled away from Q at a speed of 4 ft/s. How fast is cart B moving toward Q at the instant when cart A is 8 ft from Q? Round the result to the nearest hundredth.

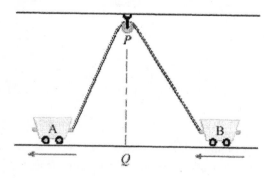

20. The circumference of a sphere was measured to be 90 cm with a possible error of 0.5 cm. Use differentials to estimate the maximum error in the calculated volume.

1. $S'(r) = 8\pi r$

2. $z'(y) = -\dfrac{50A}{y^{51}} + Be^{y}$

3. d

4. 1000

5. $Y'(u) = 6u^2 + 4u - 1$

6. $y'(x) = -\dfrac{(6x^5 + 4x^3)}{(x^6 + x^4 + 5)^2}$

7. 8

8. b

9. 40

10. d

11. $\dfrac{1}{2}$

12. $\dfrac{2}{39\pi}$

13. 56.82

14. 12.52

15. -4.6

16. 6.25

17. 2.11

18. 0.18

19. 2.8

20. 205

1. Differentiate the function.

    $f(x) = \sqrt{10}$

2. Evaluate.

    $$\lim_{x \to 1} \frac{x^{1.000} - 1}{x - 1}$$

3. The curve $y = \dfrac{1}{1 + x^2}$ is called a **witch of Maria Agnesi**.

    Find an equation of the tangent line to this curve at the point $(-2, \ 1/5)$.

    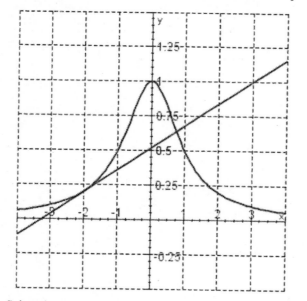

    Select the correct answer.

    a. $y = 0.06x + 0.45$
    b. $y = 0.16x + 0.52$
    c. $y = 0.4x + 0.39$
    d. $y = 0.19x + 0.29$
    e. $y = 0.16x + 0.29$

4. In this exercise we estimate the rate at which the total personal income is rising in the Richmond-Petersburg, Virginia, metropolitan area. In 1999, the population of this area was 961,600, and the population was increasing at roughly 9,400 people per year. The average annual income was $30,591 per capita, and this average was increasing at about $1,300 per year (a little above the national average of about $1,225 yearly). Use the Product Rule and these figures to estimate the rate at which total personal income was rising in the Richmond-Petersburg area in 1999.

5. The mass of the part of a metal rod that lies between its left end and a point x meters to the right is
$S = 3x^2$.

Find the linear density when x is 1 m.

Select the correct answer.

a. 9
b. 3
c. 6
d. 2
e. 1

6. If a tank holds 5000 gallons of water, and that water can drain from the tank in 40 minutes, then Torricelli's Law gives the volume V of water remaining in the tank after t minutes as

$$V = 5000\left(1 - \frac{t}{40}\right)^2.$$

Find the rate at which water is draining from the tank after 14 minutes.

7. Refer to the law of laminar flow. Consider a blood vessel with radius 0.01 cm, length 3 cm, pressure difference 3,500 dynes/ cm^2 and viscosity $\eta = 0.028$.

Find the velocity of the blood at radius $r = 0.004$.

8. Differentiate.

$g(x) = 8 \sec x + \tan x$

9. Find an equation of the tangent line to the curve $y = \sec x - 9 \cos x$ at the point $(\pi/3, -2.5)$.

10. Find the limit.

$$\lim_{\theta \to 0} \frac{\sin(\sin \theta)}{\sec \theta}$$

11. Use logarithmic differentiation to find the derivative of the function.

$$\sqrt[3]{\frac{x^2+1}{x^2-1}}$$

12. Differentiate the function.

$$y = \frac{\ln x}{4 + x}$$

13. Find, correct to three decimal places, the area of the region above the hyperbola $y = 5/(x-2)$, below the x-axis, and between the lines $x = -6$ and $x = -2$.

14. The curve with equation $y^2 = 26x^4 - x^2$ is called a **kampyle of Eudoxus**.

    Find an equation of the tangent line to this curve at the point (1, 4).

15. Find the tangent to the ellipse $\dfrac{x^2}{9} + \dfrac{y^2}{4} = 1$ at the point $(1.5, \ \sqrt{3})$.

16. Find the first and the second derivatives of the function.

    $$G(r) = \sqrt{r} + \sqrt[5]{r}$$

17. Find the equation of the tangent line to the given curve at the specified point.

    $$y = 4xe^x, \quad (0, \ 0)$$

18. Find a third-degree polynomial Q such that $Q(1) = 2$, $Q'(1) = 7$, $Q''(1) = 14$, and $Q'''(1) = 18$.

19. Differentiate the function.

    $$G(u) = \ln \sqrt{\frac{3u + 6}{3u - 6}}$$

20. If $f(x) = \dfrac{x}{\ln x}$, find $f'(e^3)$.

Stewart - Calculus ET 5e Chapter 3 Form H

1. 0

2. 1000

3. b

4. $1,537,635,400

5. c

6. -162.5

7. 0.88

8. $\dfrac{dg(x)}{dx} = 8\sec(x)\tan(x) + \sec^2 x$

9. $y = 6.5\sqrt{3}(x - \pi/3) - 2.5$

10. 0

11. $\dfrac{-4x}{3(x^4 - 1)}\sqrt[3]{\dfrac{x^2 + 1}{x^2 - 1}}$

12. $\dfrac{4 + x - x\ln x}{x(x+4)^2}$

13. 3.466

14. $y = 12.75x - 8.75$

15. $y = -0.38x + 2.31$

16. $\dfrac{1}{2}r^{-1/2} + \dfrac{1}{5}r^{-4/5}, \dfrac{-1}{4}r^{-3/2} - \dfrac{4}{25}r^{-9/5}$

17. $y = 4x$

18. $Q = 3x^3 - 2x^2 + 2x - 1$

19. $\dfrac{-18}{9u^2 - 36}$

20. 0.222222

1. Find the absolute maximum value of $y = 8\sin\left(\dfrac{\pi x}{8}\right)$.

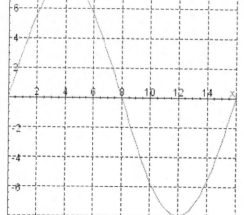

2. Find the absolute maximum of the function.

$$f(x) = \sin(6x) + \cos(6x) \text{ on the interval } \left[0, \ \frac{\pi}{18}\right]$$

3. Find the critical numbers of the function.

$$y = \frac{x}{x^2 + 25}$$

4. Verify that the function satisfies the three hypotheses of Rolle's Theorem on the given interval. Then find all numbers c that satisfy the conclusion of Rolle's Theorem.

$$f(x) = x^3 - 21x^2 + 80x + 2, \ [\,0, 16\,]$$

5. Find the inflection points for the function.

$$f(x) = 8x + 3 - 2\sin x, \ \ 0 < x < 3\pi$$

6. The graph of the derivative $f'(x)$ of a continuous function f is shown. On what intervals is f decreasing?

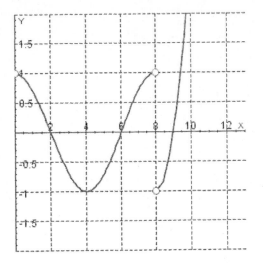

7. Find the value of the limit.

$$\lim_{x \to \infty} \frac{x^7}{7^x}$$

8. Find a cubic function $f(x) = ax^3 - bx^2 + cx - d$ that has a local maximum value of 40 at 1 and a local minimum value of -68 at 4.

9. Find the limit.

$$\lim_{x \to 1} \frac{x^4 - 1}{x^5 - 1}$$

10. A rectangular storage container with an open top is to have a volume of 10 m^3. The length of its base is twice the width. Material for the base costs \$13 per square meter. Material for the sides costs \$10 per square meter. Find the cost of the materials for the cheapest such container. Round the result to the nearest cent.

11. Find the dimensions of the rectangle of largest area that can be inscribed in an equilateral triangle of side $L = 6$ cm if one side of the rectangle lies on the base of the triangle. Round each dimension to the nearest tenth.

12. Estimate the extreme values of the function.

$$y(x) = \frac{1}{3}x^3 - 7x^2 + 40x + 7$$

Round the answers to the nearest hundredth.

13. The average cost of producing x units of a commodity is given by the equation $c(x) = 20.4 - 0.0007x$.

Find the marginal cost at a production level of 1,255 units.

14. Find the most general antiderivative of the function.

$$f(x) = 24x^2 - 16x + 6$$

15. Find the limit.

$$\lim_{x \to 0} \frac{e^x - 1 - x}{5x^2}$$

16. Use the graph of f to estimate the values of c that satisfy the conclusion of the Mean Value Theorem for the interval $[0, 7]$.

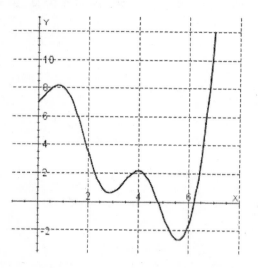

17. Verify that the function satisfies the hypotheses of The Mean Value Theorem on the given interval. Then find all numbers c that satisfy the conclusion of The Mean Value Theorem.

$$f(x) = 8x^2 + 8x + 3, \ [-8, 8]$$

18. Find the most general antiderivative of the function.

$$f(x) = 3\cos x - 6\sin x$$

19. Use Newton's method with the specified initial approximation x_1 to find x_3, the third approximation to the root of the given equation. (Give your answer to four decimal places.)

$$x^4 - 12 = 0, \quad x_1 = 8$$

20. Ornithologists have determined that some species of birds tend to avoid flights over large bodies of water during daylight hours. It is believed that more energy is required to fly over water than land because air generally rises over land and falls over water during the day. A bird with these tendencies is released from an island that is 6 km from the nearest point B on a straight shoreline, flies to a point C on the shoreline, and then flies along the shoreline to its nesting area D. Assume that the bird instinctively chooses a path that will minimize its energy expenditure. Points B and D are 12 km apart. In general, if it takes 1.4 times as much energy to fly over water as land, to what point C should the bird fly in order to minimize the total energy expended in returning to its nesting area? Your answer will be the distance between B and C (correct to one decimal place).

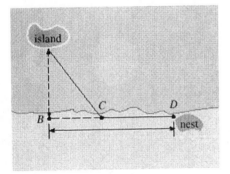

1. 8

2. $f\left(\dfrac{\pi}{24}\right) = \sqrt{2}$

3. 5, -5

4. $7 + \dfrac{\sqrt{201}}{3}, \ 7 - \dfrac{\sqrt{201}}{3}$

5. $\left(\pi, \ 8\pi + 3\right), \ \left(2\pi, \ 16\pi + 3\right)$

6. $(2,6) \ \cup \ (8,9)$

7. 0

8. $8x^3 - 60x^2 + 96x - 4$

9. $\dfrac{4}{5}$

10. 250.9

11. 3, 2.6

12. 40.33, 76.33

13. 18.64

14. $8x^3 - 8x^2 + 6x + C$

15. $\dfrac{1}{10}$

16. 0.7, 3, 3.9, 5.7

17. 0

18. $3\sin(x) + 6\cos(x) + C$

19. 4.5182

20. 6.1

1. Find the critical numbers of the function.

   $g(x) = 7x + \sin(7x)$

2. Find the absolute minimum value of $y = 3x^2 + \dfrac{6}{x}$ on the interval $[0, 6]$.

3. Estimate the absolute maximum value of the function $y = x\sqrt{3x - x^2}$ to two decimal places on the interval $[0, 3]$.

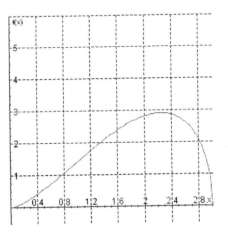

4. Verify that the function satisfies the three hypotheses of Rolle's Theorem on the given interval. Then find all numbers c that satisfy the conclusion of Rolle's Theorem.

   $f(x) = \sin 3\pi x, \quad \left[-\dfrac{2}{3}, \dfrac{2}{3}\right]$

5. Find an equation of the line through the point $(8, 16)$ that cuts off the least area from the first quadrant.

6. At 4:00 P.M. a car's speedometer reads 29 mi/h. At 4:15 it reads 71 mi/h. At some time between 4:00 and 4:15 the acceleration is exactly x mi/h^2. Find x.

7. Find the intervals of increasing or decreasing of the following function and complete the table.

$$y(x) = x^3 - 9x^2 + 24x$$

To complete the table, enter " i ", if the function is increasing on the interval, and " d ", if the function is decreasing on the interval.

$x < 2$	
$2 < x < 4$	
$x > 4$	

8. Find a cubic function $f(x) = ax^3 - bx^2 + cx - d$ that has a local maximum value of 112 at 1 and a local minimum value of -1,184 at 7.

9. Verify that the function satisfies the three hypotheses of Rolle's Theorem on the given interval. Then find all numbers c that satisfy the conclusion of Rolle's Theorem.

$$f(x) = x^3 - 15x^2 + 56x + 2, \ [\, 0, 8\,]$$

10. Find the limit.

$$\lim_{x \to 0} \frac{e^x - 2}{\sin 7x}$$

11. Find the limit.

$$\lim_{x \to \infty} \frac{x^7 - 3}{x^6 + 6}$$

12. A company estimates that the marginal cost (in dollars per item) of producing items is 2.75 - 0.002x. If the cost of producing one item is $589 find the cost of producing 100 items.

13. Find the limit.

$$\lim_{x \to 0} (1 - 10x)^{1/x}$$

14. Consider the following problem: A farmer with 800 ft of fencing wants to enclose a rectangular area and then divide it into four pens with fencing parallel to one side of the rectangle. What is the largest possible total area of the four pens?

15. Find the most general antiderivative of the function.

$$f(x) = 8x^{\frac{1}{7}} - 10x^{\frac{1}{9}}$$

16. A fence 9 ft tall runs parallel to a tall building at a distance of 7 ft from the building. What is the length of the shortest ladder that will reach from the ground over the fence to the wall of the building? Round the result to the nearest hundredth.

17. For the cost function (given in dollars), find the average cost of 1,105 units.

$$C(x) = 46,410 + 180x + x^2$$

18. A conical drinking cup is made from a circular piece of paper of radius $R = 7$ cm by cutting out a sector and joining the edges CA and CB. Find the maximum capacity of such a cup.

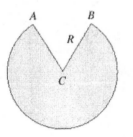

19. A painting in an art gallery has height $h = 60$ cm and is hung so that its lower edge is a distance $d = 17$ cm above the eye of an observer (as seen in the figure below). How far from the wall should the observer stand to get the best view? (In other words, where should the observer stand so as to maximize the angle θ subtended at his eye by the painting?)

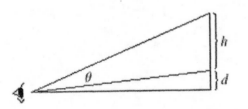

20. A steel pipe is being carried down a hallway 15 ft wide. At the end of the hall there is a right-angled turn into a narrower hallway 9 ft wide. What is the length of the longest pipe that can be carried horizontally around the corner?

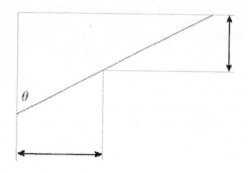

1. $\dfrac{\pi(2n+1)}{7}$

2. 9

3. 2.92

4. $\dfrac{1}{6}, \dfrac{-1}{6}, \dfrac{1}{2}, \dfrac{-1}{2}$

5. $y = -2x + 32$

6. $x = 168$

7. increase, decrease, increase

8. $12x^3 - 144x^2 + 252x - 8$

9. $5 + \dfrac{\sqrt{57}}{3}, \; 5 - \dfrac{\sqrt{57}}{3}$

10. $\dfrac{1}{7}$

11. ∞

12. $851.25

13. e^{-10}

14. 16000

15. $7x^{8/7} - 9x^{10/9} + C$

16. 22.57

17. 1327

18. 138.25

19. 36.18

20. 33.58

1. Find the absolute maximum value of $y = 7\sin\left(\dfrac{\pi}{10}\right)$.

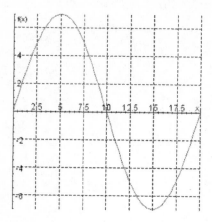

Select the correct answer.

   a.   7
   b.   15
   c.   0
   d.   5
   e.   -6

2. Find the critical numbers of the function.

$$y = \frac{x}{x^2 + 64}$$

Select the correct answer.

   a.   8, 0
   b.   8, -8
   c.   64, -64
   d.   0, -8
   e.   8, 0

3. Find the value of the limit.

$$\lim_{x \to \infty} \frac{x^3}{3^x}$$

Select the correct answer.

   a. ∞
   b.   0
   c.   3
   d.   2
   e.   1

4. Verify that the function satisfies the three hypotheses of Rolle's Theorem on the given interval. Then find all numbers c that satisfy the conclusion of Rolle's Theorem.

$$f(x) = x^3 - 21x^2 + 80x^2 + 7, \ [0, 16]$$

Select the correct answer.

   a. $c_1 = 201 + \dfrac{\sqrt{7}}{3}, c_2 = 201 - \dfrac{\sqrt{7}}{3}$

   b. $c = 7 - \dfrac{\sqrt{201}}{3}$

   c. $c_1 = 7 + \dfrac{\sqrt{201}}{3}, c_2 = 7 - \dfrac{\sqrt{201}}{3}$

   d. $c = 7 + \dfrac{\sqrt{201}}{3}$

   e. $c = \dfrac{\sqrt{201}}{3}$

5. Use the graph of f to estimate the values of c that satisfy the conclusion of the Mean Value Theorem for the interval $[0, 7]$.

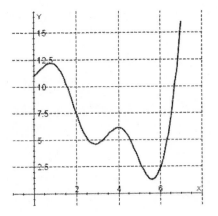

Select all that apply.

   a. $c = 3$
   b. $c = 3.7$
   c. $c = 0.3$
   d. $c = 5.7$
   e. $c = 1.3$
   f. $c = 3.5$
   g. $c = 3.9$
   h. $c = 0.7$

6. Find the exact values of the numbers c that satisfy the conclusion of The Mean Value Theorem for the function $f(x) = x^3 - 5x$ for the interval $[-5, 5]$.

Select the correct answer.

   a. $c = \dfrac{5\sqrt{3}}{3}$

   b. $c = -\dfrac{5\sqrt{3}}{3}$

   c. $c = \pm\dfrac{5\sqrt{3}}{3}$

   d. $c = \pm 5\sqrt{3}$

   e.   none of these

7. Find the inflection points for the function given.

   $f(x) = 8x + 2 - \sin x, \quad 0 < x < 3\pi$

   Select the correct answer.

   a. $\left(\pi,\ 8\pi\right),\ \left(2\pi,\ 16\pi + 2\right)$

   b. $\left(\pi,\ 2\right),\ \left(2\pi,\ 16\pi + 2\right)$

   c. $\left(\pi,\ 8\pi\right),\ \left(2\pi,\ 16\pi\right)$

   d. $\left(\pi,\ 8\pi + 2\right),\ \left(2\pi,\ 16\pi + 2\right)$

   e. $\left(\pi,\ 8\pi + 2\right),\ \left(2\pi\ ,16\pi\right)$

8. How many points of inflection are on the graph of the function?

   $f(x) = 18x^3 + 5x^2 - 12x - 17$

   Select the correct answer.

   a.   1
   b.   2
   c.   4
   d.   3
   e.   5

9. Sketch the curve.

$y = 3x^3 + 3x$

Select the correct answer.

a.

b.

c.

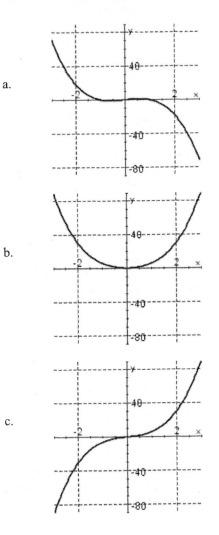

10. Sketch the curve.

$$y = \sqrt{\dfrac{x}{x-1}}$$

Select the correct answer.

a.

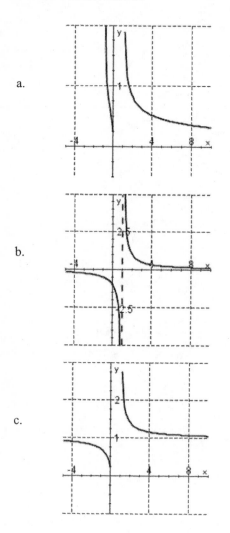

b.

c.

11. Sketch the curve.

$$y = x \tan 2x, \quad -\frac{\pi}{2} < x < \frac{\pi}{2}$$

Select the correct answer.

a.

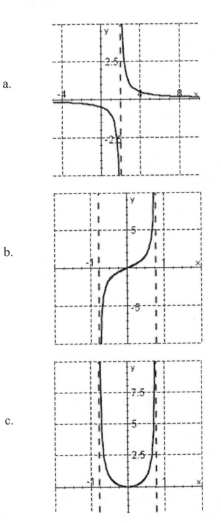

b.

c.

12. Estimate the extreme values of the function.

$$y(x) = \frac{1}{3}x^3 - 9x^2 + 72x + 2$$

Select the correct answer.

a.   146, 182
b.   1,226, -223
c.   383.18, 200.95
d.   150, -223
e.   1,226, 182

13.   Find the limit.

$$\lim_{x \to -\infty} x^7 e^x$$

Select the correct answer.

a. $-\infty$

b. $\dfrac{1}{7}$

c.   0
d. ∞
e.   7

14.   Find two positive numbers whose product is 144 and whose sum is a minimum.

Select the correct answer.

a.   4, 36
b.   2, 72
c.   12, 12

15. A rectangular storage container with an open top is to have a volume of 10 m^3. The length of its base is twice the width. Material for the base costs $12 per square meter. Material for the sides costs $5 per square meter. Find the cost of materials for the cheapest such container.

Select the correct answer.

a. $153.92
b. $158.1
c. $152.9
d. $151.6
e. $153.9
f. $152.4

16. Find the dimensions of the rectangle of largest area that can be inscribed in an equilateral triangle of side $L = 9$ cm if one side of the rectangle lies on the base of the triangle. Round the result to the nearest tenth.

    Select the correct answer.

    a. 9.5 cm , 3.9 cm
    b. 7.5 cm , 2.9 cm
    c. 4.5 cm , 4 cm
    d. 4.5 cm , 3.9 cm
    e. 4 cm , 3.91 cm
    f. 5.5 cm , 4.4 cm

17. What is the function of the graph?

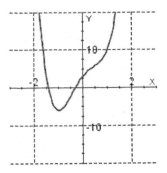

    Select the correct answer.

    a. $y = 5x^4 - 6x^2 + 8x + 3$

    b. $y = 6x^3 - 8x^2 + 5$

    c. $y = 6x^4 - 8x^3 + 5x$

    d. $y = x^7 - 8x^3 + 5x$

    e. $y = x^6 - 8x^2 + 5x$

18. A woman at a point A on the shore of a circular lake with radius 2 mi wants to arrive at the point C diametrically opposite on the other side of the lake in the shortest possible time. She can walk at the rate of 6 mi/h and row a boat at 2 mi/h. How should she proceed? (Find θ). Round the result, if necessary, to the nearest hundredth.

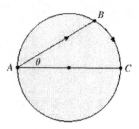

Select the correct answer.

a.   0.55 radians
b.   She should walk around the lake from point A to point C.
c.   She should row from point A to point C radians
d.   0.34 radians
e.   0.98 radians

19. Find the most general antiderivative of the function.

$$f(x) = 18x^2 - 14x + 9$$

Select the correct answer.

a. $F(x) = 30x^5 - 28x^4 + 9x + C$

b. $F(x) = 6x^3 - 7x^2 + 9x + C$

c. $F(x) = 18x^3 - 14x^2 + 9x + C$

d. $F(x) = 36x - 14 + C$

e. $F(x) = 6x^2 - 14x + C$

20. Given that the graph of f passes through the point (4, 69) and that the slope of its tangent line at $(x, f(x))$ is 10x - 4, find $f(1)$.

Select the correct answer.

a.   1
b.   12
c.   11
d.   6
e.   0

1. a

2. b

3. b

4. c

5. a, d, g, h

6. c

7. d

8. a

9. c

10. c

11. c

12. a

13. c

14. c

15. e

16. d

17. a

18. b

19. b

20. d

1. Find the critical numbers of the function.

   $y = 5x^2 + 20x$

   Select the correct answer.

   a. 5
   b. -2
   c. 20
   d. 0
   e. -1

2. Find the absolute maximum value of $y = \sqrt{36 - x^2}$ on the interval [- 6, 6].

   Select the correct answer.

   a. 5
   b. 6
   c. 7
   d. 0
   e. 1

3. Evaluate $f(x) = \sin(x^2)$, and tell whether its antiderivative F is increasing or decreasing at the point $x = -4$ radians.

   Select the correct answer (to the nearest thousandth).

   a. 0.757, decreasing
   b. 0.757, increasing
   c. -0.288, increasing
   d. -0.288, decreasing
   a. 0.277, decreasing

4. Find any absolute or local maximum and minimum values of $f(x) = 8 - 2x$ if $x \geq 6$.

   Select the correct answer.

   a. -4 is an absolute maximum
   b. 6 is an absolute minimum
   c. 6 is an absolute maximum
   d. 6 is a local minimum
   e. -4 is a local maximum
   f. -4 is an absolute minimum

5. Estimate the absolute maximum value of the function $y = x\sqrt{2x - x^2}$ to two decimal places on the interval $[0, 2]$.

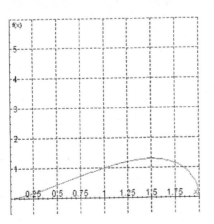

Select the correct answer.

a. 0.87
b. 1.3
c. 1.95
d. 1.5
e. -0.87

6. How many real roots does the equation $x^5 - 7x + c = 0$ have in the interval $[-1, 1]$?

Select the correct answer.

a. at most two real roots
b. no real roots
c. at most three real roots
d. at most one real root
e. at most five real roots

7. Find the critical numbers of $f(x) = x^4(x-3)^3$.

Select the correct answer.

a. $0, 2, \dfrac{12}{7}$ b. $0, 3, \dfrac{12}{11}$ c. $0, 3, \dfrac{12}{7}$ d. $0, 2, \dfrac{12}{11}$ e. $0, 2, \dfrac{7}{12}$

8. How many points of inflection are on the graph of the function?

$$f(x) = 12x^3 + 14x^2 - 7x - 9$$

Select the correct answer.

a.   3
b.   1
c.   4
d.   2
e.   5

9. Let $f(x) = \dfrac{x^3 + 2}{x}$, Show that $\lim\limits_{x \to \pm\infty} \left[f(x) - x^2 \right] = 0$.

This shows that the graph of f approaches the graph of $y = x^2$, and we say that the curve $y = f(x)$ is asymptotic to the parabola $y = x^2$. Use this fact to help sketch the graph of f.

Select the correct answer.

a.

b.

c.

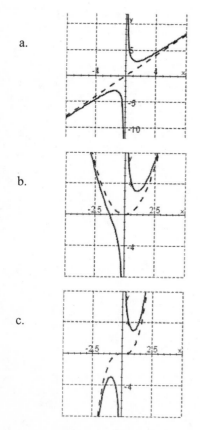

10. Sketch the curve.

$$y = x + 2x^{2/3}$$

Select the correct answer.

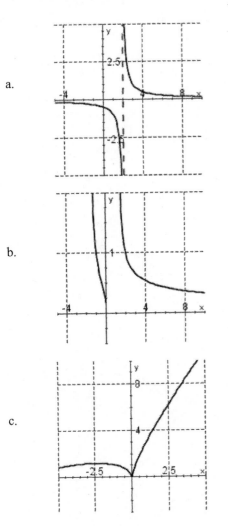

a.

b.

c.

11. Discuss the asymptotic behavior of $f(x) = \dfrac{x^2 + 7}{x}$. Find the asymptote of f.

Select the correct answer.

a. $y = x^3$
b. $y = x^2$
c. $y = 1$
d. $y = x$
e. $y = x^7$

12. Find the maximum or minimum point(s) of the function.

$$F(x) = \left(1 - x^2\right)^2 + 6x^2$$

Select the correct answer.

a. (0, 1)
b. (-8.6, 6)
c. (-8, 2)
d. (8, 0)
e. (16, 1)

13. For what values of c does the curve have maximum and minimum points?

$$F(x) = 5x^3 + cx^2 + 10x$$

Select the correct answer.

a. $|c| > 15$

b. $|c| > \sqrt{150}$

c. $|c| > 1{,}500$

d. $|c| > \sqrt{30}$

e. $|c| > \sqrt{750}$

14. Find the point on the line $y = 4x + 8$ that is closest to the origin.

Select the correct answer.

a. $\left(\dfrac{-32}{17}, \dfrac{10}{17}\right)$

b. $\left(\dfrac{-34}{17}, \dfrac{9}{17}\right)$

c. $\left(\dfrac{-32}{17}, \dfrac{8}{17}\right)$

d. $\left(-2, \dfrac{8}{17}\right)$

e. $\left(\dfrac{-31}{17}, \dfrac{8}{17}\right)$

15. A piece of wire 10 m long is cut into two pieces. One piece is bent into a square and the other is bent into an equilateral triangle. How should the wire be cut for the square so that the total area enclosed is a minimum? Round the result to the nearest hundredth.

    Select the correct answer.

    a. 5.35 m
    b. 4.4 m
    c. 4.35 m
    d. 0 m
    e. 3.25 m

16. Let $P(x)$ and $Q(x)$ be polynomials.

    Find $\lim\limits_{x \to \infty} \dfrac{P(x)}{Q(x)}$ if the degree of $P(x)$ is 5 and the degree of $Q(x)$ is 9.

    Select the correct answer.

    a. -4
    b. 9
    c. 4
    d. 0
    e. 5

17. A conical drinking cup is made from a circular piece of paper of radius $R = 4$ cm by cutting out a sector and joining the edges CA and CB. Find the maximum capacity of such a cup. Round the result to the nearest hundredth.

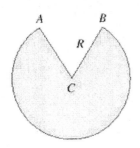

    Select the correct answer.

    a. 25.8 cm ^{3}
    b. 25.9 cm ^{3}
    c. 25.82 cm ^{3}
    d. 24.8 cm ^{3}
    e. 24.79 cm ^{3}
    f. 25.85 cm ^{3}

18. Find f.

$$f''(x) = 12x + 24x^2$$

Select the correct answer.

a. $f(x) = 6x^3 + 4x^4 + Cx + D$

b. $f(x) = 2x^3 + 2x^4 + Cx + D$

c. $f(x) = 4x^3 + 8x^4 + Cx + D$

d. $f(x) = 2x^3 + x^4 + Cx + D$

e. $f(x) = x^3 + 4x^4 + Cx + D$

19. A right circular cylinder is inscribed in a sphere of radius $r = 4$ cm. Find the largest possible surface area of such a cylinder. Round the result to the nearest hundredth.

Select the correct answer.

a. 162.66 cm^2

b. 163.16 cm^2

c. 162.68 cm^2

d. 161.55 cm^2

e. 168.55 cm^2

20. Use Newton's method with the specified initial approximation x_1 to find x_3, the third approximation to the root of the given equation. (Give your answer to four decimal places.)

$$x^4 - 23 = 0, \quad x_1 = 7$$

Select the correct answer.

a. $x_3 = 5.2794$

b. $x_3 = 7.8594$

c. $x_3 = 5.2668$

d. $x_3 = 3.9894$

e. $x_3 = 7.1122$

ANSWER KEY

Stewart - Calculus ET 5e Chapter 4 Form D

1. b

2. b

3. d

4. a

5. b

6. d

7. c

8. b

9. b

10. c

11. d

12. a

13. b

14. c

15. c

16. d

17. a

18. b

19. a

20. d

1. Find the critical numbers of the function.

   $g(x) = 6x + \sin(6x)$

2. Find the critical numbers of the function.

   $y = 3x^2 + 12x$

3. Find the absolute minimum value(s) of $y = 2x^2 - 20x + 9$ on the interval [0, 6].

4. The graph of the first derivative $f'(x)$ of a function f is shown below. At what values of x does f have a local maximum or minimum?

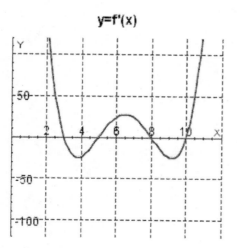

5. Find the critical numbers of $f(x) = x^4(x-2)^3$.

6. Find an equation of the line through the point (9, 36) that cuts off the least area from the first quadrant.

7. The graph of the derivative $f'(x)$ of a continuous function f is shown. At what values of x does f have a local maximum or minimum?

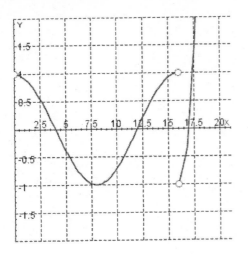

8. Find the limit.

$$\lim_{x \to 0^+} \frac{\ln 5x}{x}$$

Select the correct answer.

   a.   5
   b. π
   c. ∞
   d.   0
   e. $-\infty$

9. Find the minimum points of the function.

$$F(x) = x^4 - 500x$$

10. If 1,100 cm^2 of material is available to make a box with a square base and an open top, find the largest possible volume of the box.

11. Sketch the curve.

$$y = x + 3x^{2/3}$$

Select the correct answer.

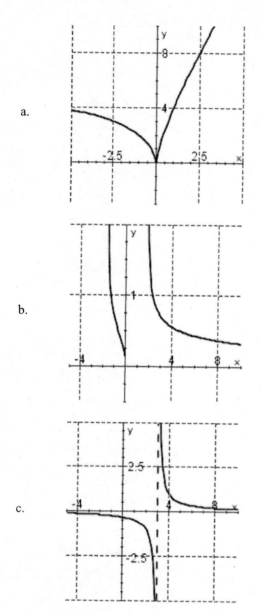

a.

b.

c.

12. Find all the maximum and minimum values of the function.

$$F(x) = \frac{x-5}{(x-4)^2}$$

13. Which of the following functions is graphed below?

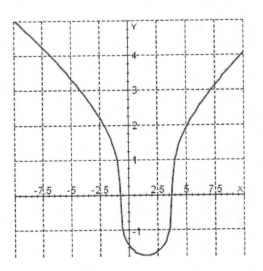

Select the correct answer.

a. $y = \sqrt[3]{x^2 - 3x - 3}$

b. $y = \sqrt[3]{x^3 + 3x + 3}$

c. $y = \sqrt{x^2 + 3x - 3}$

d. $y = x^2 + 3x - 3$

e. $y = \sqrt{x^2 - 6}$

14. Find the point on the line $y = 10x + 9$ that is closest to the origin.

Select the correct answer.

a. $\left(\dfrac{-90}{101}, \dfrac{9}{101}\right)$

b. $\left(\dfrac{-90}{100}, \dfrac{9}{101}\right)$

c. $\left(\dfrac{-90}{101}, \dfrac{11}{101}\right)$

d. $\left(\dfrac{-92}{101}, \dfrac{10}{101}\right)$

e. $\left(\dfrac{-89}{101}, \dfrac{9}{101}\right)$

15. A steel pipe is being carried down a hallway 10 ft wide. At the end of the hall there is a right-angled turn into a narrower hallway 6 ft wide. What is the length of the longest pipe that can be carried horizontally around the corner? Round the result to the nearest hundredth.

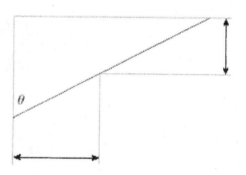

16. Find the maximum area of a rectangle that can be circumscribed about a given rectangle with length $L = 8$ and width $W = 3$.

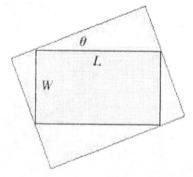

17. Find the limit.

$$\lim_{x \to -\infty} x^2 e^x$$

Select the correct answer.

a.   2

b.   0

c. $\dfrac{1}{2}$

d. ∞

e. $-\infty$

18. Use Newton's method to find all the roots of the equation, correct to six decimal places.

$$2x^5 - 6x^4 - 177x^3 - 11x^2 - 19x - 5 = 0$$

19. Find f .

$$f''(x) = 9\cos(3x)$$

Select the correct answer.

a. $f(x) = y = -\cos(3x) + Cx^2 + D$

b. $f(x) = y = 9\cos(x) + Cx + D$

c. $f(x) = y = -\cos(3x) + Cx + D$

d. $f(x) = y = \cos(9x) + Cx^2 + D$

e.   none of these

20. Find f.

$$f'(x) = 3\cos(x) + 10\sin(x)$$

$$f(0) = 9$$

1. $\dfrac{\pi(2n+1)}{6}$

2. -2

3. -41

4. 3, 5, 8, 10

5. $0, 2, \dfrac{8}{7}$

6. $y = -4x + 72$

7. 4, 12, 17

8. e

9. 5

10. 3511

11. a

12. $\dfrac{1}{4}$

13. a

14. a

15. 22.39

16. 60.5

17. b

18. 5, -1.707107, -0.292893

19. c

20. $f(x) = 3\sin(x) - 10\cos(x) + 19$

1. Find all the critical numbers of the function.

   $g(x) = 4x + \sin(4x)$

   Select the correct answer.

   a. $\dfrac{\pi}{4}$

   b. $\dfrac{\pi(2n+1)}{8}$

   c. $\dfrac{\pi n}{2}$

   d. $\dfrac{\pi(2n+1)}{4}$

   e. none

2. Find the critical numbers of the function.

   $y = 3x^2 + 30x$

   Select the correct answer.

   a. -5
   b. 30
   c. 3
   d. 0
   e. 5

3. Find the limit.

   $\lim\limits_{t \to 0} \dfrac{3^t - 2^t}{t}$

4. Verify that the function satisfies the three hypotheses of Rolle's Theorem on the given interval. Then find all numbers c that satisfy the conclusion of Rolle's Theorem.

$$f(x) = \sin 5\pi x, \quad \left[-\frac{2}{5}, \frac{2}{5}\right]$$

Select the correct answer.

a. $c_1 = \pm\dfrac{1}{10}, \quad c_2 = \dfrac{3}{10}$

b. $c_1 = -\dfrac{1}{10}, \quad c_2 = \pm\dfrac{1}{10}$

c. $c_1 = \dfrac{1}{10}, \quad c_2 = \pm\dfrac{3}{10}$

d. $c_1 = \pm\dfrac{1}{10}, \quad c_2 = \pm\dfrac{3}{10}$

e. none

5. Show that the equation $x^5 + 3x + 1 = 0$ has exactly one real root.
    (use a separate sheet to answer if necessary)

6. The graph of the second derivative $f''(x)$ of a function f is shown. State the x-coordinates of the inflection points of f.

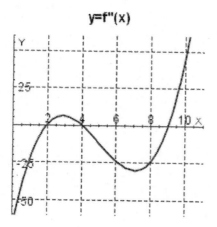

$y=f''(x)$

7. The graph of the derivative $f'(x)$ of a continuous function f is shown. On what intervals is f decreasing?

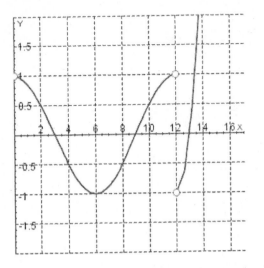

8. For what values of c does the curve have maximum and minimum points?

$$F(x) = 4x^3 + cx^2 + 4x$$

9. Suppose the line $y = 5x - 1$ is tangent to the curve $y = f(x)$ when $x = -8$. If Newton's method is used to locate a root of the equation $f(x) = 0$ and the initial approximation is $x_1 = -8$, find the second approximation x_2.

10. Find the limit.

$$\lim_{x \to 0} \frac{x}{\tan^{-1}(7x)}$$

11. Consider the following problem: A farmer with 890 ft of fencing wants to enclose a rectangular area and then divide it into four pens with fencing parallel to one side of the rectangle. What is the largest possible total area of the four pens?

Select the correct answer.

    a. $19,825.5 \text{ ft}^2$
    b. $19,802.5 \text{ ft}^2$
    c. $19,801.5 \text{ ft}^2$
    d. $19,902.5 \text{ ft}^2$
    e. $19,791.5 \text{ ft}^2$

12. Find the dimensions of the rectangle of largest area that can be inscribed in an equilateral triangle of side $L = 9$ cm if one side of the rectangle lies on the base of the triangle. Round the result to the nearest tenth.

    Select the correct answer.

    a. 5.5 cm, 4.4 cm
    b. 4 cm, 3.91 cm
    c. 7.5 cm, 2.9 cm
    d. 4.5 cm, 3.9 cm
    e. 4.5 cm, 4 cm

13. Find the most general antiderivative of the function.

    $$f(x) = 9x^2 - 10x + 3$$

14. Consider the figure below, where $a = 7$, $b = 1$ and $l = 6$. How far from the point A should the point P be chosen on the line segment AB so as to maximize the angle θ?

    Round the result to the nearest hundredth.

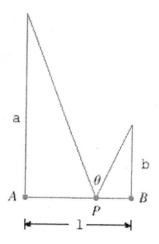

15. Sketch the curve.

$$y = 2x^3 + 3x$$

Select the correct answer.

a.

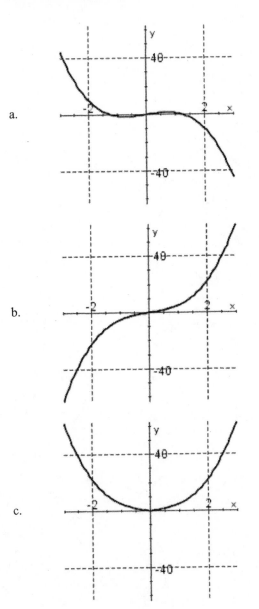

b.

c.

16. Sketch the curve.

$$y = \frac{x^2}{3x+6}$$

Select the correct answer.

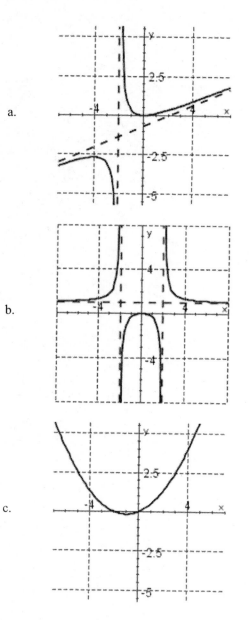

a.

b.

c.

17. Which of the following functions is graphed below?

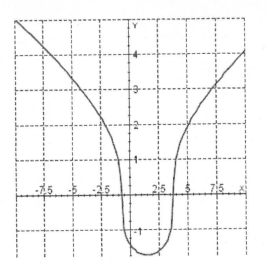

Select the correct answer.

a. $y = \sqrt[3]{x^2 - 3x - 3}$

b. $y = \sqrt[3]{x^3 + 3x + 3}$

c. $y = \sqrt{x^2 + 3x - 3}$

d. $y = x^2 + 3x - 3$

e. $y = \sqrt{x^2 - 6}$

18. Find two positive numbers whose product is 196 and whose sum is a minimum.

Select the correct answer.

a.   4, 49
b.   2, 98
c.   14, 14

19. Use Newton's method with the specified initial approximation x_1 to find x_3, the third approximation to the root of the given equation. (Give your answer to four decimal places.)

$x^4 - 13 = 0$, $x_1 = 2$

20. An aircraft manufacturer wants to determine the best selling price for a new airplane. The company estimates that the initial cost of designing the airplane and setting up the factories in which to build it will be 900 million dollars. The additional cost of manufacturing each plane can be modeled by the function $m(x) = 1{,}600x + 10x^{4/5} + 0.17x^2$ where x is the number of aircraft produced and m is the manufacturing cost, in millions of dollars. The company estimates that if it charges a price p (in millions of dollars) for each plane, it will be able to sell $x(p) = 390 - 5.8p$.

Find the cost function.

1. d

2. a

3. $\ln\left(\dfrac{3}{2}\right)$

4. d

5. $f(x) = x^5 + 3x + 1$. Since f is continuous and $f(-1) = -3$ and $f(0) = 1$, the equation $f(x) = 0$ has at least one root at $(-1, 0)$ by the Intermediate Value Theorem. Suppose that the equation has more than one root; say a and b are both roots with $a < b$. Then $f(a) = 0 = f(b)$ so by Rolle's Theorem $f'(x) = 5x^4 + 3 = 0$ has a root in (a, b). But this is impossible since clearly $f'(x) \geq 3 > 0$ for all real x.

6. 2, 4, 9

7. $(3, 9) \cup (12, 13)$

8. $|c| > \sqrt{48}$

9. 1/5

10. 1/7

11. b

12. d

13. $3x^3 - 5x^2 + 3x + C$

14. 3.26

15. b

16. a

17. a

18. c

19. 1.8989

20. $C(x) = 900 + 1600x + 10x^{4/5} + 0.17x^2$

1. Find the maximum value of $f(x) = 6 - 3x$ if $x \geq 2$. Is the maximum absolute or local?

2. Find the critical numbers of the function.

   $g(x) = 8x + \sin 8x$

3. Find the critical numbers of the function.

   $$y = \frac{x}{x^2 + 49}$$

4. Verify that the function satisfies the three hypotheses of Rolle's Theorem on the given interval. Then find all numbers c that satisfy the conclusion of Rolle's Theorem.

   $$f(x) = x^3 - 6x^2 + 8x + 4, \quad [0, \ 4]$$

   Select the correct answer.

   a. $c = 2 + \dfrac{2\sqrt{3}}{3}$

   b. $c = 2 - \dfrac{2\sqrt{3}}{3}$

   c. $c_1 = 12 + \dfrac{\sqrt{2}}{3}, \quad c_2 = 12 - \dfrac{\sqrt{2}}{3}$

   d. $c_1 = 2 + \dfrac{2\sqrt{3}}{3}, \quad c_2 = 2 - \dfrac{2\sqrt{3}}{3}$

   e. $c_1 = 2 + \dfrac{2\sqrt{3}}{3}, \quad c_2 = \dfrac{2\sqrt{3}}{3}$

5. A grain silo consists of a cylindrical main section, with a height of 33 ft, and a hemispherical roof. In order to achieve a total volume of 17,000 ft ^{3} (including the part inside the roof section), what would the radius of the silo have to be? Find the result and round to four decimal places.

6. Find the most general antiderivative of the function.

   $$f(x) = x^{1/5} - 4x^{1/3}$$

7. Find the point on the line $y = 5x + 9$ that is closest to the origin.

8.   Find any absolute, local maximum and minimum values of $f(x) = 2 - 5x$, $x \geq 1$.

     Select the correct answer.

     a.   1 is a local minimum
     b.   -3 is an absolute minimum
     c.   1 is an absolute minimum
     d.   1 is an absolute maximum
     e.   -3 is an absolute maximum

9.   Use the graph of f to estimate the values of c that satisfy the conclusion of the Mean Value Theorem for the interval $[0, 7]$.

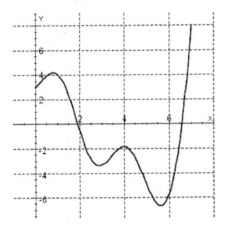

     Select the correct answer.

     a. $c = 0.6$
     b. $c = 3$
     c. $c = 5.7$
     d. $c = 0.7$
     e. $c = 1.3$
     f. $c = 5.6$
     g. $c = 3.9$
     h. $c = 5$

10. Consider the following problem.

     A farmer with 710 ft of fencing wants to enclose a rectangular area and then divide it into four pens with fencing parallel to one side of the rectangle. What is the largest possible total area of the four pens?

11. The graph of the first derivative $f'(x)$ of a function f is shown below. At what values of x does f have a local maximum or minimum?

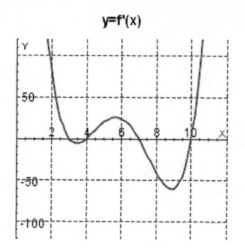

Select the correct answer.

    a.   8
    b.   9
    c.   4
    d.   7
    e.   10
    f.   3

12. Find the inflection points for the function.

$$f(x) = 6 - 5x - 2\sin x, \quad 0 < x < 3\pi$$

Select the correct answer.

    a. $\left(\pi,\ -5\pi + 6\right)$, $\left(2\pi,\ -10\pi\right)$

    b. $\left(\pi,\ -5\pi\right)$, $\left(2\pi,\ -10\pi + 6\right)$

    c. $\left(\pi,\ -5\pi + 6\right)$, $\left(2\pi,\ -10\pi + 6\right)$

    d. $\left(\pi,\ -5\pi\right)$, $\left(2\pi,\ -10\pi\right)$

    e. $\left(\pi,\ 6\right)$, $\left(2\pi,\ -10\pi + 6\right)$

13. How many points of inflection are on the graph of the function?

$$f(x) = -14x^3 + 7x^2 - 11x - 6$$

14. For the function f whose graph is given, find the limit.

$$\lim_{x \to -1^-} f(x)$$

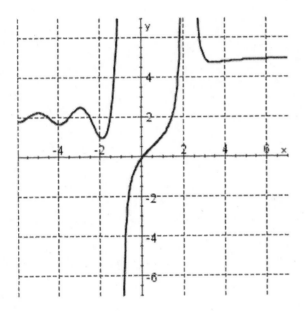

15. Use l'Hospital's Rule to calculate the exact value of the limit $\dfrac{f(x)}{g(x)}$ as $x \to 0$.

$$f(x) = e^x - 1 \text{ and } g(x) = x^5 + 4x$$

16. A Norman window has the shape of a rectangle surmounted by a semicircle. (Thus the diameter of the semicircle is equal to the width of the rectangle.) If the perimeter of the window is 22 ft, find the dimensions of the window so that the greatest possible amount of light is admitted.

17. Estimate the extreme values of the function.

$$y(x) = \frac{1}{3}x^3 - 9x^2 + 72x + 6$$

18. Find the maximum and minimum points of the function.

$$F(x) = \frac{6x}{1 + 36x^2}$$

19. Ornithologists have determined that some species of birds tend to avoid flights over large bodies of water during daylight hours. It is believed that more energy is required to fly over water than land because air generally rises over landand falls over water during the day. A bird with these tendencies is released from an island that is 8 km from the nearest point B on a straight shoreline, flies to a point C on the shoreline, and then flies along the shoreline to its nesting area D. Assume that the bird instinctively chooses apath that will minimize its energy expenditure. Points B and D are 13 km apart. In general, if it takes 1.9 times as much energy to fly over water as land, to what point C should the bird fly in order to minimize the total energy expended in returning to its nesting area? Your answer will be the distance between B and C.

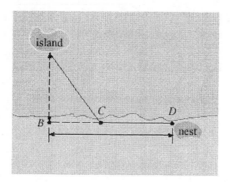

20. The upper left-hand corner of a piece of paper 14 in. wide by 18 in. long is folded over to the right-hand edge as in the figure. How would you fold it so as to minimize the length of the fold? In other words, how would you choose x to minimize y?

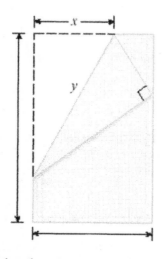

Select the correct answer.

a. $x = 3.5$ in
b. $x = 10.75$ in
c. $x = 10.5$ in
d. $x = 14$ in
e. $x = 10$ in

ANSWER KEY

Stewart - Calculus ET 5e Chapter 4 Form G

1. 0, absolute

2. $\dfrac{\pi(2n+1)}{8}$

3. 7, -7

4. d

5. 11.5323

6. $\dfrac{5}{6}x^{6/5} - 3x^{4/3} + C$

7. $\left(\dfrac{-45}{26}, \dfrac{9}{26}\right)$

8. e

9. b,c,d,g

10. 12602.5

11. c,d,e,f

12. c

13. 1

14. ∞

15. 1/4

16. 6.16, 3.08

17. 150, 186

18. $\dfrac{1}{6}, -\dfrac{1}{6}$

19. 5

20. c

1. Find the absolute maximum value of $y = \sqrt{81 - x^2}$ on the interval $[-9, 9]$.

   Select the correct answer.

   a. 10
   b. 0
   c. 9
   d. 8
   e. 1

2. Find the absolute maximum of the function $f(x) = \sin(2x) + \cos(2x)$ on the interval $\left[0, \dfrac{\pi}{6}\right]$.

3. Estimate the absolute minimum value of the function $y = x^3 - 6x + 3$ to two decimal places on the interval $[0, 10]$.

4. Verify that the function satisfies the three hypotheses of Rolle's Theorem on the given interval. Then find all numbers c that satisfy the conclusion of Rolle's Theorem.

   $f(x) = x^3 - 12x^2 + 35x + 7, \ [0, 7]$

5. Find a cubic function $f(x) = ax^3 - bx^2 + cx - d$ that has a local maximum value of 60 at 1 and a local minimum value of -4 at 3.

6. Find the maximum and minimum points of the function.

$$F(x) = \left(1 - x^2\right)^2 + 6x^2$$

7. For what values of c does the curve have maximum and minimum points?

$$F(x) = 2x^3 + cx^2 + 10x$$

Select the correct answer.

a. $\left| c \right| > 600$

b. $\left| c \right| > 6$

c. $\left| c \right| > \sqrt{120}$

d. $\left| c \right| > \sqrt{60}$

e. $\left| c \right| > \sqrt{30}$

8. Find the maximum area of a rectangle that can be circumscribed about a given rectangle with length $L = 7$ and width $W = 4$.

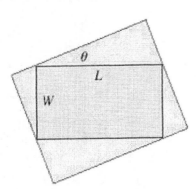

9. Let $P(x)$ and $Q(x)$ be polynomials.

Find $\lim\limits_{x \to \infty} \dfrac{P(x)}{Q(x)}$ if the degree of $P(x)$ is 2 and the degree of $Q(x)$ is 14.

10. A baseball team plays in a stadium that holds 56,000 spectators. With ticket prices at $9, the average attendance had been 32,000. When ticket prices were lowered to $8, the average attendance rose to 36,000.

How should ticket prices be set to maximize revenue?

11. A manufacturer has been selling 1,200 television sets a week at $400 each. A market survey indicates that for each $30 rebate offered to the buyer, the number of sets sold will increase by 60 per week. Find the demand function.

Select the correct answer.

    a. $p(x) = 0.5\,x + 1{,}000$
    b. $p(x) = -0.5\,x + 1{,}000$
    c. $p(x) = -0.5\,x + 400.5$
    d. $p(x) = -0.5\,x + 600$
    e. $p(x) = 0.5\,x$

12. The manager of a 138-unit apartment complex knows from experience that all units will be occupied if the rent is $860 per month. A market survey suggests that, on the average, one additional unit will remain vacant for each $10 increase in rent.

What rent should the manager charge to maximize revenue?

13. Use Newton's method to approximate the indicated root of $x^4 + x - 9 = 0$ in the interval $[1, 2]$, correct to six decimal places.

Use $x_1 = 1.5$ as the initial approximation.

14. Find f.

$$f'(x) = 3\cos(x) + 4\sin(x), \quad f(0) = 7$$

Select the correct answer.

    a. $f(x) = 3\sin(x) + 4\cos(x) + 11$
    b. $f(x) = -3\sin(x) - 4\cos(x) + 7$
    c. $f(x) = 3\sin(x) - 4\cos(x) + 11$
    d. $f(x) = 3\sin(3x) + 4\cos(4x) + 7$
    e. $f(x) = \sin(x) + \cos(x) + 7$

15. A car braked with a constant deceleration of $40\ ft/\sec^2$, producing skid marks measuring 55 ft before coming to a stop. How fast was the car traveling when the brakes were first applied?

16. Evaluate and determine whether the function's antiderivative is increasing or decreasing at the point $x = -2$ radians.

$$f(x) = \sin\left(x^2\right)$$

Select the correct answer (to the nearest thousandth).

a. -0.909, decreasing
b. -0.909, increasing
c. -0.757, decreasing
d. -0.757, increasing
e. none of these

17. A particle moves along a straight line with velocity function $v(t) = 2\sin(t) - 4\cos t$ and its initial displacement is $s(0) = 4$.

Find its position function.

18. A company estimates that the marginal cost (in dollars per item) of producing items is $2.07 - 0.002x$. If the cost of producing one item is $561 find the cost of producing 100 items.

19. What constant acceleration is required to increase the speed of a car from 20 ft/s to 45 ft/s in 5 s?

20. How many points of inflection are on the graph of the function?

$$f(x) = 4x^3 + 16x^2 - 6x - 7$$

Select the correct answer.

a. 2
b. 1
c. 4
d. 3
e. 5

1. c

2. $f\left(\dfrac{\pi}{8}\right) = \sqrt{2}$

3. -2.66

4. $4 \pm \dfrac{\sqrt{39}}{3}$

5. $16x^3 - 96x^2 + 144x - 4$

6   0

7   d

8   60.5

9. 0

10. p=8.5

11. b

12. 1120

13. 1.646722

14. c

15. 66.33

16. c

17. $s(t) = 6 - 2\cos(t) - 4\sin(t)$

18. $755.93

19. 5

20. b

1. Approximate the area under the curve $y = \sin x$ from 0 to $\pi/4$ using ten approximating rectangles of equal widths and right endpoints.

2. The speed of a runner increased steadily during the first three seconds of a race. Her speed at half-second intervals is given in the table. Find a lower estimate for the distance that she traveled during these three seconds.

t (s)	0	0.5	1.0	1.5	2.0	2.5	3.0
(ft/s)	0	3.7	8.3	13.2	15.1	15.7	16.2

3. The velocity graph of a braking car is shown. Use it to estimate to the nearest foot the distance traveled by the car while the brakes are applied.

   Use a left sum with $n = 7$.

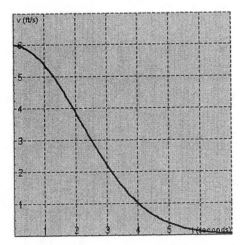

4. Evaluate the Riemann sum for $f(y) = 9 - y^2$, $0 \le y \le 2$ with four subintervals, taking the sample points to be right endpoints.

5. If $f(x) = \sqrt{x} - 2$, $1 \le x \le 6$, find the Riemann sum with $n = 5$ correct to 3 decimal places, taking the sample points to be midpoints.

6. Evaluate the definite integral.

$$\int_{-\pi/8}^{\pi/8} \frac{x^2 \sin x}{5 + x^6}\, dx$$

7. The velocity function (in meters per second) is given for a particle moving along a line. Find the distance traveled by the particle during the given time interval.

    $v(t) = 4t - 3, \ 0 \le t \le 6$

8. The table gives the values of a function obtained from an experiment. Use the values to estimate

    $\int_{0}^{6} f(t) \ dt$ using three equal subintervals with left endpoints.

t	$f(t)$
0	9.9
1	9.4
2	7.8
3	6.2
4	4.1
5	-6.8
6	-10.3

9. Find the area of the region that lies under the given curve.

    $y = \sqrt{5x + 2}, \quad 0 \le x \le 1$

    Round the result to the nearest thousandth.

10. Express the limit as a definite integral on the given interval.

    $\lim\limits_{n \to \infty} \sum\limits_{i=1}^{n} 7r_i \sin r_i \Delta r, \quad \left[\ 7, \ 10 \ \right]$

11. Evaluate the indefinite integral.

    $\int \dfrac{4 + 6x}{\sqrt{6 + 4x + 3x^2}} \, dx$

12. Evaluate the integral by interpreting it in terms of areas.

    $\int_{1}^{3} (1 + 4x) \ dx$

13. Express the sum as a single integral in the form

$$\int_a^b f(z)\ dz$$

$$\int_2^8 f(z)\ dz + \int_8^{11} f(z)\ dz$$

14. Use Part 1 of the Fundamental Theorem of Calculus to find the derivative of the function.

$$g(x) = \int_x^4 8\tan(t)\ dt$$

15. Evaluate the definite integral.

$$\int_0^1 x^2 \left(3 + 4x^3\right)^3 dx$$

16. Evaluate the integral.

$$\int_{\pi/6}^{\pi/4} \sin(t)\ dt$$

17. Evaluate the integral.

$$\int_0^{\pi/6} \frac{3 + \cos^2 \theta}{\cos^2 \theta}\ d\theta$$

18. The marginal cost of manufacturing x yards of a certain fabric is $C'(x) = 3 - 0.01x + 0.000006x^2$ (in dollars per yard). Find the increase in cost if the production level is raised from 500 yards to 3,000 yards.

19. Alabama Instruments Company has set up a production line to manufacture a new calculator. The rate of production of these calculators after t weeks is $\dfrac{dx}{dt} = 4{,}500\left(1 - \dfrac{130}{(t+9)^2}\right)$ calculators per week.

Production approaches 4,500 per week as time goes on, but the initial production is lower because of the workers' unfamiliarity with the new techniques. Find the number of calculators produced from the beginning of the third week to the end of the fourth week.

Round the answer to the nearest integer.

20. Evaluate the indefinite integral.

$$\int \cos^5 x \sin x \ dx$$

ANSWER KEY

Stewart – Calculus ET 5e Chapter 5 Form A

1. 0.32

2. 28

3. 19

4. 14.25

5. -0.857

6. 0

7. 54

8. 43.6

9. 2.092

10. $\displaystyle\int_{7}^{10} 7r\sin r\ dr$

11. $2\sqrt{6+4x+3x^2} + C$

12. 18

13. $\displaystyle\int_{2}^{11} f(z)\ dz$

14. $\dfrac{dg(x)}{dx} = -8\tan x$

15. 145/3

16. 0.158919

17. $1.732051 + \dfrac{\pi}{6}$

18. 17500

19. 818

20. $-\dfrac{1}{6}\cos^6 x + C$

1. Estimate the area from 0 to 5 under the graph of $f(x) = 81 - x^2$ using five approximating rectangles and right endpoints.

2. If $f(x) = \sin(\sin(x))$, $0 \le x \le \pi/5$, approximate the area under the curve using ten approximating rectangles of equal widths and left endpoints.

3. Evaluate the indefinite integral.

$$\int \frac{7+x}{9+x^2}\ dx$$

4. The velocity graph of a car accelerating from rest to a speed of 5 km/h over a period of 10 seconds is shown. Estimate to the nearest integer the distance traveled during this period. Use a right sum with $n = 10$.

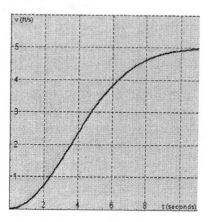

5. A table of values of an increasing function $f(x)$ is shown. Use the table to find an upper estimate of

$$\int_0^{25} f(x)\ dx$$

x	f(x)
0	-43
5	-32
10	-22
15	-7
20	6
25	35

6. Evaluate the integral by interpreting it in terms of areas.

$$\int_{-1}^{3} (5-x)\, dx$$

7. Given that $\int_{4}^{6} f(x)\, dx = \dfrac{6}{57}$, find $\int_{6}^{4} f(x)\, dx$.

8. Use Part 1 of the Fundamental Theorem of Calculus to find the derivative of the function.

$$g(x) = \int_{1}^{x} \sqrt{2+3t}\, dt$$

9. Use Part 1 of the Fundamental Theorem of Calculus to find the derivative of the function.

$$g(x) = \int_{4}^{x^2} 5\sqrt{1+t^2}\, dt$$

10. Find $g'(x)$ by evaluating the integral using Part 2 of the Fundamental Theorem and then differentiating.

$$g(x) = \int_{\pi}^{x} (5+\cos(t))\, dt$$

11. Evaluate the integral.

$$\int_{0}^{9} \left(10+6y-y^2\right) dy$$

12. If $F(x) = \int_{1}^{x} f(t)\, dt$, where $f(t) = \int_{1}^{t^2} \dfrac{\sqrt{10+u^4}}{u}\, du$, find $F''(2)$.

13. Evaluate the indefinite integral.

$$\int \cos^4 x \sin x\, dx$$

14. Find the indefinite integral.

$$\int x(5+10x^4)\ dx$$

15. Evaluate the integral.

$$\int_0^{\pi/6} \frac{2+\cos^2\theta}{\cos^2\theta}\ d\theta$$

16. Evaluate the integral by making the given substitution.

$$\int x^2\sqrt{x^3+1}\ dx,\ \ u=x^3+1$$

17. Evaluate the indefinite integral.

$$\int \frac{e^x}{e^x+9}\ dx$$

18. Evaluate the integral.

$$\int \left(x^2+2+\frac{1}{x^2+1}\right)\ dx$$

19. Evaluate the indefinite integral.

$$\int 6x(x^2+4)^4\ dx$$

20. Evaluate the indefinite integral.

$$\int t^2\cos(2-t^3)\ dt$$

1. 350

2. 0.17

3. $\frac{7}{3}\arctan\left(\frac{x}{3}\right) + \frac{1}{2}\ln\left(9 + x^2\right) + C$

4. 12

5. -100

6. 16

7. -0.105263

8. $\dfrac{dg(x)}{dx} = \sqrt{2 + 3x}$

9. $\dfrac{dg(x)}{dx} = 10x\sqrt{1 + x^4}$

10. $\dfrac{dg(x)}{dx} = 5 + \cos(x)$

11. 90

12. $\sqrt{266}$

13. $-\dfrac{1}{5}\cos^5 x + C$

14. $\dfrac{5x^2}{2} + \dfrac{10x^6}{6} + C$

15. $1.154701 + \dfrac{\pi}{6}$

16. $\dfrac{2}{9}(x^3 + 1)^{3/2} + C$

17. $\ln(e^x + 9) + C$

18. $\dfrac{x^3}{3} + 2x + (\tan x)^{-1} + C$

19. $\dfrac{3}{5}\left(x^2 + 4\right)^5 + C$

20. $-\dfrac{1}{3}\sin\left(2 - t^3\right) + C$

1. Estimate to the hundredth the area from 1 to 5 under the graph of $f(x) = \dfrac{4}{x}$ using four approximating rectangles and right endpoints.

    Select the correct answer.

    a. 5.13
    b. 6.65
    c. 5.83
    d. 3.65
    e. 4.23
    f. 4.55

2. Evaluate the Riemann sum for $f(r) = 2 - r^2$, $0 \le r \le 2$, with four subintervals, taking the sample points to be right endpoints.

    Select the correct answer.

    a. 0.25
    b. 1.5
    c. 2.5
    d. 0.36
    e. 0.2

3. The table gives the values of a function obtained from an experiment. Use the values to estimate $\displaystyle\int_0^6 f(z)\ dz$ using three equal subintervals with left endpoints.

z	$f(z)$
0	9.9
1	9.5
2	7.9
3	6.2
4	4.2
5	-7
6	-10.1

    Select the correct answer.

    a. 37.2
    b. 44
    c. 17
    d. 3.2
    e. 30.2

4. Use the Midpoint Rule with $n = 5$ to approximate the integral.

$$\int_0^{10} 6 \sin \sqrt{y} \; dy$$

Select the correct answer.

a.   14.344
b.   38.786
c.   26.995
d.   10.344
e.   12.374

5. Evaluate the integral.

$$\int_{\pi/3}^{\pi/2} \sin t \; dt$$

Select the correct answer.

a.   -1.000
b.   0.250
c.   1.000
d.   -0.500
e.   0.500

6. Find the area of the region that lies beneath the given curve.

$$y = \sin x, \; 0 \le x \le \frac{\pi}{3}$$

Select the correct answer.

a.   1.500
b.   - 1.500
c.   0.500
d.   - 0.500
e.   1.450

7. Find the general indefinite integral.

$$\int \frac{\sin 20t}{\sin 10t}\,dt$$

Select the correct answer.

a. $\dfrac{\sin 10t}{5} + C$

b. $\dfrac{\cos 10t}{5} + C$

c. $\dfrac{\sin 10t}{10} + C$

d. $-\dfrac{\cos 10t}{5} + C$

e. $-\dfrac{\sin 10t}{5} + C$

8. Evaluate the integral.

$$\int_{4}^{9} \frac{x^2 + 4}{\sqrt{x}}\,dx$$

Select the correct answer.

a. 215
b. 92.4
c. 430
d. 150
e. 25

9. An animal population is increasing at a rate of $13 + 51t$ per year (where t is measured in years). By how much does the animal population increase between the fourth and tenth years?

Select the correct answer.

a. 2,220
b. 4,362
c. 2,155
d. 2,064
e. 2,100

10. Evaluate the integral.

$$\int_0^3 \left(6 + 6y - y^2\right) dy$$

Select the correct answer.

    a.   -18
    b.   45
    c.   54
    d.   36
    e.   -12

11. The marginal cost of manufacturing x yards of a certain fabric is $C'(x) = 3 - 0.01x + 0.000006x^2$ (in dollars per yard). Find the increase in cost if the production level is raised from 1,000 yards to 4,500 yards.

Select the correct answer.

    a. $94,500.00
    b. $97,500.00
    c. $95,500.00
    d. $92,500.00
    e. $94,600.00

12. Evaluate the integral.

$$\int \left(x^3 + 2 + \frac{1}{x^2 + 1}\right) dx$$

Select the correct answer.

    a. $\dfrac{x^4}{4} + 2x + \tan^{-1} x + C$

    b. $x^4 + 2 + \tan^{-1} x + C$

    c. $\dfrac{x^4}{4} + 2x + \dfrac{3}{x^3 + 3} + C$

    d. $\dfrac{x^4}{4} + 2x + \tan^{-1} 2x^2 + C$

    e. $4 + 2x + \tan^{-1} x + C$

13. Alabama Instruments Company has set up a production line to manufacture a new calculator. The rate of production of these calculators after t weeks is $\dfrac{dx}{dt} = 5{,}700\left(1 - \dfrac{130}{(t+18)^2}\right)$ calculators per week.

Production approaches 5,700 per week as time goes on, but the initial production is lower because of the workers' unfamiliarity with the new techniques. Find the number of calculators produced from the beginning of the third week to the end of the fourth week.

Select the correct answer. The choices are rounded to the nearest integer.

    a.   8,031
    b.   8,027
    c.   8,034
    d.   8,042
    e.   8,142
    f.   8,032

14. Evaluate the indefinite integral.

$$\int \cos^7 x \sin x \; dx$$

Select the correct answer.

    a. $\dfrac{1}{8}\cos^8 x + C$

    b. $-\dfrac{1}{8}\sin^8 x + C$

    c. $-\dfrac{1}{8}\cos^7 x + C$

    d. $\dfrac{1}{8}\sin^8 x + C$

    e. $-\dfrac{1}{8}\cos^8 x + C$

15. Evaluate the definite integral.

$$\int_{25}^{81} \frac{dx}{x\sqrt{\ln x}}$$

Select the correct answer.

    a.   0.075
    b.   6.604
    c.   8.104
    d.   0.604
    e.   11.68
    f.   9

16. Evaluate the integral.

$$\int_{-2}^{5} \left| 4x - x^2 \right| dx$$

Select the correct answer. The choices are rounded to the nearest hundredth.

    a.   109.00
    b.   123.67
    c.   102.33
    d.   209.00
    e.   23.67

17. Evaluate the definite integral.

$$\int_{-\pi/2}^{\pi/2} \frac{x^2 \sin x}{4 + x^6} dx$$

Select the correct answer.

    a.   -2
    b.   1
    c.   3
    d.   0
    e.   -0.5

18. If h' is a child's rate of growth in pounds per year, which of the following expressions represent the increase in the child's weight (in pounds) between the years 2 and 5?

Select the correct answer.

a. $\displaystyle\int_2^5 h'(t)\ dt$

b. $h'(5) - h'(2)$

19. The acceleration function (in m / s ^{2}) and the initial velocity are given for a particle moving along a line. Find the velocity at time t and the distance traveled during the given time interval.

$a(t) = t + 4,\ \ v(0) = 3,\ \ 0 \le t \le 10$

Select the correct answer.

a. $v(t) = \dfrac{t^2}{2} + 4t + 3\ \ m/s,\ \ 396\dfrac{2}{3}\ m$

b. $v(t) = \dfrac{t^2}{2} + 4t + 3\ \ m/s,\ \ 391\dfrac{2}{3}\ m$

c. $v(t) = \dfrac{t^2}{2} + 3\ \ m/s,\ \ 411\dfrac{2}{3}\ m$

d. $v(t) = \dfrac{t^2}{2} + 4t\ \ m/s,\ \ 406\dfrac{2}{3}\ m$

e. $v(t) = \dfrac{t^2}{2} + 4t\ \ m/s,\ \ 415\dfrac{2}{3}\ m$

20. Evaluate the definite integral.

$$\int_0^1 x^2\left(3 + 4x^3\right)^3\ dx$$

Select the correct answer.

a. $\dfrac{145}{3}$

b. $\dfrac{775}{16}$

c. $\dfrac{2323}{48}$

d. $\dfrac{2320}{49}$

e. $\dfrac{707}{16}$

1. a

2. a

3. b

4. b

5. e

6. c

7. a

8. b

9. a

10. d

11. a

12. a

13. f

14. e

15. d

16. e

17. d

18. a

19. a

20. a

1. Estimate to the hundredth the area from 1 to 5 under the graph of $f(x) = \dfrac{4}{x}$ using four approximating rectangles and right endpoints.

   Select the correct answer. The choices are rounded to the nearest hundredth.

   a.   6.87
   b.   5.85
   c.   4.77
   d.   5.13
   e.   4.59

2. Approximate the area under the curve $y = \sin x$ from 0 to $\pi/2$ using ten approximating rectangles of equal widths and right endpoints.

   Select the correct answer. The choices are rounded to the nearest hundredth.

   a.   0.72
   b.   0.98
   c.   0.02
   d.   1.08
   e.   0.36

3. If $f(x) = \sqrt[5]{x}$, $1 \le x \le 4$, approximate the area under the curve using ten approximating rectangles of equal widths and left endpoints.

   Select the correct answer. The choices are rounded to the nearest hundredth.

   a.   3.52
   b.   2.94
   c.   1.66
   d.   4.76
   e.   2.50

4. The speed of a runner increased steadily during the first three seconds of a race. Her speed at half-second intervals is given in the table. Find a lower estimate for the distance that she traveled during these three seconds.

t (s)	0	0.5	1.0	1.5	2.0	2.5	3.0
v (ft/s)	0	4.6	8.5	13	14.5	15.5	15.7

   Select the correct answer.

   a.   28.15
   b.   27.05
   c.   28.75
   d.   28.05
   e.   29.55

5. Use Part 1 of the Fundamental Theorem of Calculus to find the derivative of the function.

$$g(x) = \int_5^x t^5 \sin t \ dt$$

Select the correct answer.

a. $\dfrac{dg(x)}{dx} = 4x^4 \sin x$

b. $\dfrac{dg(x)}{dx} = \dfrac{x^6}{6} \cos x$

c. $\dfrac{dg(x)}{dx} = x^5 \sin x$

d. $\dfrac{dg(x)}{dx} = x^2 \sin x$

e. $\dfrac{dg(x)}{dx} = 2x^3 \sin x$

6. If w' is a child's rate of growth in pounds per year, which of the following expressions represents the increase in the child's weight (in pounds) between the years 2 and 10?

Select the correct answer.

a. $w'(10) - w'(2)$

b. $\displaystyle\int_2^{10} w'(t) \ dt$

7. The area of the region that lies to the right of the y-axis and to the left of the parabola $x = 5y - y^2$ (the shaded region in the figure) is given by the integral $\displaystyle\int_0^5 (5y - y^2) \ dy$.

Find the area.

Select the correct answer.

a. 125

b. $\dfrac{25}{6}$

c. 6.25

d. $\dfrac{125}{6}$

e. 45.6

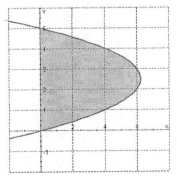

8.   Evaluate the integral.

$$\int_0^1 x^{3/7}\, dx$$

Select the correct answer.

a. $\dfrac{10}{7}$

b. $\dfrac{10}{3}$

c. $\dfrac{3}{10}$

d. $\dfrac{7}{10}$

e. $\dfrac{3}{7}$

9.   Evaluate the integral.

$$\int_{\pi/4}^{\pi/2} \sin t\, dt$$

Select the correct answer.

a.   1.414
b.   -0.707
c.   0.354
d.   0.707
e.   -1.414

10.   Evaluate the integral.

$$\int_1^4 \frac{x^2 + 6}{\sqrt{x}}\, dx$$

Select the correct answer.

a.   24.4
b.   37
c.   74
d.   49.2
e.   21.4

11. Evaluate the integral by making the given substitution.

$$\int x^2 \sqrt{x^3 + 2}\ dx, \quad u = x^3 + 2$$

Select the correct answer.

a. $\quad -\dfrac{2}{9}(x^3 + 2)^{3/2} + C$

b. $\quad \dfrac{1}{9}(x^3 + 2)^{1/2} + C$

c. $\quad \dfrac{2}{9}(x^3 + 2)^{1/2} + C$

d. $\quad \dfrac{2}{9}(x^3 + 3)^{3/2}$

e. $\quad \dfrac{2}{9}(x^3 + 2)^{3/2} + C$

12. The velocity function (in meters per second) is given for a particle moving along a line. Find the distance traveled by the particle during the given time interval.

$$v(t) = 6t - 6, \quad 0 \le t \le 5$$

Select the correct answer.

a. 105 m
b. -15 m
c. 45 m
d. 148.8 m
e. 115 m

13. An animal population is increasing at a rate of $29 + 37t$ per year (where t is measured in years). By how much does the animal population increase between the fourth and tenth years?

Select the correct answer.

a. 1,728
b. 1,583
c. 1,380
d. 3,282
e. 1,528

14. The velocity of a car was read from its speedometer at ten-second intervals and recorded in the table. Use the Midpoint Rule to estimate the distance traveled by the car.

$t(s)$	$v(mi/h)$		$t(s)$	$v(mi/h)$
0	0		60	63
10	39		70	60
20	57		80	70
30	54		90	49
40	69		100	43
50	65			

Select the correct answer.

    a.   1.7 miles
    b.   1.2 miles
    c.   1.5 miles
    d.   1.6 miles
    e.   1.9 miles

15. Evaluate the integral.

$$\int \left(x^3 + 4 + \frac{1}{x^2+1} \right) dx$$

Select the correct answer.

    a. $x^4 + 4 + \tan^{-1} x + C$

    b. $\dfrac{x^4}{4} + 4x + \dfrac{3}{x^3+3} + C$

    c. $\dfrac{x^4}{4} + 4x + \tan^{-1} x + C$

    d. $\dfrac{x^4}{4} + 4x + \tan^{-1} x + C$

    e. $\dfrac{3x^4}{4} + x + \tan^{-1} 4x + C$

16. Evaluate the definite integral.

$$\int_0^{\pi/8} \sin 8t \; dt$$

Select the correct answer.

    a.   0.25
    b.   3.25
    c.   0.35
    d.   1.25
    e.   -0.25

17. Find the area of the region that lies under the given curve.

$$y = \sqrt{2x+2}, \ \ 0 \le x \le 1$$

Select the correct answer.

a.   1.834
b.   1.727
c.   1.704
d.   1.724
e.   1.824

18. Evaluate the indefinite integral.

$$\int \frac{e^x}{e^x+1} \, dx$$

Select the correct answer.

a. $-\dfrac{1}{2}\ln\!\left(e^x+1\right)+C$

b. $\dfrac{1}{2}\ln\!\left(e^x+1\right)+C$

c. $\ln\!\left(e^x-1\right)+C$

d. $\ln\!\left(e^x+1\right)+C$

e. $-\ln\!\left(e^x+1\right)+C$

19. If $F(x) = \int_1^x f(t)\, dt$, where $f(t) = \int_1^{t^2} \dfrac{\sqrt{2+u^2}}{u}\, du$, find $F''(2)$.

Select the correct answer.

   a. $\dfrac{3\sqrt{2}}{2}$

   b. $3\sqrt{2}$

   c. $6\sqrt{2}$

   d. $6\sqrt{3}$

   e. $3\sqrt{3}$

20. Find the interval on which the curve $F(x) = \int_0^x \dfrac{1}{3+7t}\, dt$ is concave downward.

Select the correct answer.

   a. $\left(-\dfrac{3}{7},\ \infty\right)$

   b. $\left(-\infty,\ -\dfrac{3}{7}\right)$

   c. $\left(-\infty,\ \infty\right)$

   d. $\left(-\dfrac{5}{7},\ \infty\right)$

   e. $\left(-\dfrac{7}{3},\ \infty\right)$

Stewart - Calculus ET 5e Chapter 5 Form D

1. d

2. d

3. a

4. d

5. c

6. b

7. d

8. d

9. d

10. a

11. e

12. c

13. a

14. c

15. c

16. a

17. d

18. d

19. b

20. a

1.   The speed of a runner increased steadily during the first three seconds of a race. Her speed at half-second intervals is given in the table. Find a lower estimate for the distance that she traveled during these three seconds.

t (s)	0	0.5	1.0	1.5	2.0	2.5	3.0
v (ft/s)	0	4.5	8.4	12.1	13.2	13.3	13.8

2.   When we estimate distances from velocity data, it is sometimes necessary to use times t_0, t_1, t_2, ... that are not equally spaced. We can still estimate distances using the time periods $\Delta t = t_i - t_{i-1}$. For

example, on May 7, 1992, the space shuttle Endeavor was launched on mission STS-49, the purpose of which was to install a new perigee kick motor in an Intelsat communications satellite. The table, provided by NASA, gives the velocity data for the shuttle between liftoff and the jettisoning of the solid rocket boosters. Use this data to estimate an upper bound for the space shuttle Endeavor's height above Earth's surface 59 seconds after liftoff.

Event	Time (s)	Velocity (ft/s)
Launch	0	0
Begin roll maneuver	8	185
End roll maneuver	16	309
Throttle to 89%	20	427
Throttle to 67%	32	753
Throttle to 104%	58	1,350
Maximum dynamic pressure	59	1,407
Solid rocket booster separation	127	4,238

Select the correct answer.

a.   50,591
b.   50,452
c.   51,846
d.   50,436
e.   51,203

3. Evaluate the definite integral.

$$\int\limits_{e^9}^{e^{64}} \frac{dx}{x\sqrt{\ln x}}$$

4. The velocity graph of a braking car is shown. Use it to estimate to the nearest foot the distance traveled by the car while the brakes are applied.

   Use a left sum with $n = 7$.

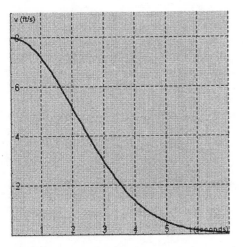

5. Evaluate the Riemann sum for $f(z) = 6 - z^2$, $0 \le z \le 2$ with four subintervals, taking the sample points to be right endpoints.

6. Evaluate the indefinite integral.

$$\int \sec^6 x \tan x \ dx$$

7. Use the Midpoint Rule with $n = 10$ to approximate the integral. Round each answer to 3 decimal places.

$$\int\limits_1^2 \sqrt{9 + w^2} \ dw$$

8. Express the integral as a limit of sums. Then evaluate the limit.

$$\int_0^\pi \sin 9x \, dx$$

9. Evaluate the integral by interpreting it in terms of areas.

$$\int_{-2}^2 \sqrt{4-x^2} \, dx$$

Select the correct answer.

    a. 4π
    b. 2π
    c. 8π
    d. 5π
    e. 3π

10. Evaluate the integral by interpreting it in terms of areas.

$$\int_{-4}^0 \left(1+\sqrt{16-x^2}\right) dx$$

11. If $\int_3^{15} f(x) \, dx = 4.4$ and $\int_8^{15} f(x) \, dx = 0.5$, find $\int_3^8 f(x) \, dx$.

12. Find the interval on which the curve $F(x) = \int_0^x \dfrac{1}{6+8t} \, dt$ is concave downward.

13. Find the general indefinite integral.

$$\int \frac{\sin 20t}{\sin 10t} \, dt$$

14. The area of the region that lies to the right of the y-axis and to the left of the parabola $x = 3y - y^2$ (the shaded region in the figure) is given by the integral $\int\limits_{0}^{3} \left(3y - y^2\right) dy$.

Find the area of the region.

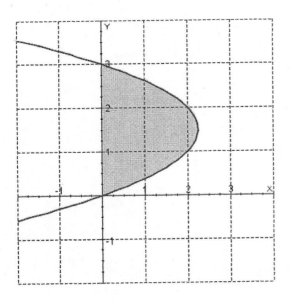

Select the correct answer.

a.   3/2
b.   9/2
c.   2.25
d.   27
e.   7/2

15. Evaluate the integral.

$$\int\limits_{3}^{6} \frac{x^2 + 6}{\sqrt{x}}\, dx$$

16. The acceleration function (in m / s ^{2}) and the initial velocity are given for a particle moving along a line.

   Find the velocity at time t and the distance traveled during the given time interval.

   $$a(t) = t + 4, \quad v(0) = 2, \quad 0 \le t \le 10$$

   Select the correct answer.

   a. $v(t) = \dfrac{t^2}{2} + 4t + 2 \;\; m/s, \;\; 391\dfrac{2}{3} \; m$

   b. $v(t) = \dfrac{t^2}{2} + 4t \;\; m/s, \;\; 392\dfrac{2}{3} \; m$

   c. $v(t) = \dfrac{t^2}{2} + 4t + 2 \;\; m/s, \;\; 386\dfrac{2}{3} \; m$

   d. $v(t) = \dfrac{5t^2}{2} + 2t + 2 \;\; m/s, \;\; 371\dfrac{2}{3} \; m$

   e. $v(t) = \dfrac{t^2}{4} + 4t + 2 \;\; m/s, \;\; 396\dfrac{2}{3} \; m$

17. An animal population is increasing at a rate of $29 + 36t$ per year (where t is measured in years). By how much does the animal population increase between the fourth and tenth years?

18. Evaluate the integral.

   $$\int \left(x^3 + 1 + \frac{1}{x^2 + 1} \right) dx$$

19. Evaluate the integral by making the given substitution.

   $$\int \cos 4x \; dx, \quad u = 4x$$

20. Evaluate the indefinite integral.

   $$\int \cos^8 x \sin x \; dx$$

1. 25.75

2. e

3. 10

4. 25

5. 8.25

6. $\dfrac{1}{6}\sec^6 x + C$

7. 3.36

8. 2/9

9. b

10. 16.566

11. 3.9

12. $\left(-0.75,\ \infty\right)$

13. $\dfrac{\sin 10t}{5} + C$

14. b

15. 37.646537

16. c

17. 1686

18. $\dfrac{x^4}{4} + x + \left(\tan x\right)^{-1} + C$

19. $\dfrac{1}{4}\sin 4x + C$

20. $-\dfrac{1}{9}\cos^9 x + C$

1. Use Part 1 of the Fundamental Theorem of Calculus to find the derivative of the function.

$$g(x) = \int_{3}^{\sqrt{x}} \frac{2\cos t}{t} \, dt$$

2. Evaluate the integral

$$\int_{0}^{1} x^{5/7} \, dx$$

3. Evaluate the integral.

$$\int_{2\pi}^{4\pi} \cos\theta \, d\theta$$

4. Find the area of the region that lies beneath the given curve.

$$y = \sin x, \ 0 \le x \le \frac{\pi}{2}$$

5. Use Part I of the Fundamental Theorem of Calculus to find the derivative of the function.

$$g(x) = \int_{9x}^{10x} \frac{t^2 + 3}{t^2 - 3} \, dt$$

6. Use Part I of the Fundamental Theorem of Calculus to find the derivative of the function.

$$g(x) = \int_{\cos x}^{7x} \cos\left(t^3\right) \, dt$$

7. Find the interval on which the curve $F(x) = \int_{0}^{x} \frac{dt}{8 + 8t}$ is concave downward.

8. Evaluate the indefinite integral.

$$\int \sec^2 x \tan x \ dx$$

9. Find a function $f(x)$ such that $5 + \int_a^x \frac{f(t)}{t^2} dt = 8\sqrt{x}$ for $x > 0$ and some number a.

10. Find the general indefinite integral.

$$\int x(10 + 8x^4) \ dx$$

Select the correct answer.

a. $5x^2 + \frac{4}{3}x^6 + C$

b. $5x^2 + \frac{8}{5}x^5 + C$

c. $10x + \frac{4}{3}x^6 + C$

d. $5x^2 + 8x^6 + C$

e. $5x^2 + \frac{8}{7}x^6 + C$

11. Evaluate the indefinite integral.

$$\int \cos^3 \sin x \ dx$$

12. Evaluate the integral.

$$\int_{-1}^3 \left| 2x - x^2 \right| dx$$

Select the correct answer. The choices are rounded to the nearest hundredth.

a. 19.33
b. 22.00
c. 14.67
d. 4.00
e. 32.67

13. The velocity of a car was read from its speedometer at ten-second intervals and recorded in the table. Use the Midpoint Rule to estimate the distance traveled by the car.

Round your answer to the nearest tenth.

$t(s)$	$v(mi/h)$		$t(s)$	$v(mi/h)$
0	0		60	65
10	37		70	57
20	55		80	60
30	67		90	47
40	69		100	44
50	53			

14. Evaluate the integral.

$$\int \left(x^2 + 2 + \frac{1}{x^2 + 1} \right) dx$$

15. Evaluate the definite integral.

$$\int_{e^{25}}^{e^{64}} \frac{dx}{x\sqrt{\ln x}}$$

16. Evaluate the integral by making the given substitution.

$$\int x^2 \sqrt{x^3 + 9} \; dx, \quad u = x^3 + 9$$

Select the correct answer.

a. $\dfrac{1}{9}\left(x^3 + 9\right)^{1/2} + C$

b. $\dfrac{2}{9}\left(x^3 + 9\right)^{3/2} + C$

c. $\dfrac{2}{9}\left(x^3 - 9\right)^{3/2} + C$

d. $-\dfrac{2}{9}\left(x^3 + 9\right)^{3/2} + C$

e. $\dfrac{2}{9}\left(x^3 + 9\right)^{1/2} + C$

17. Evaluate the indefinite integral.

$$\int 4x\left(x^2+3\right)^4 dx$$

18. Evaluate the indefinite integral.

$$\int \frac{4+10x}{\sqrt{7+4x+5x^2}}\,dx$$

Select the correct answer.

a. $2\sqrt{7+4x+5x^2}+C$

b. $\sqrt{7+4x+5x^2}+C$

c. $-2\sqrt{7+4x+5x^2}$

d. $-2\sqrt{7+4x+5x^2}+C$

e. $3\sqrt{7+4x+5x^2}+C$

19. Evaluate the definite integral.

$$\int_0^1 x^2\left(3+2x^3\right)^2 dx$$

20. Evaluate the indefinite integral.

$$\int t^2 \cos\left(1-t^3\right) dt$$

Select the correct answer.

a. $-\frac{1}{3}\cos\left(1-t^3\right)+C$

b. $-\sin\left(1-t^3\right)+C$

c. $-\frac{1}{3}\sin\left(1-t^3\right)+C$

d. $\frac{1}{3}\sin\left(1-t^3\right)+C$

e. $\frac{1}{3}\sin\left(1-t^2\right)+C$

1. $\dfrac{dg(x)}{dx} = \dfrac{\cos\left(\sqrt{x}\right)}{x}$

2. 0.583333

3. 0

4. 1

5. $\dfrac{dg(x)}{dx} = -9\left(\dfrac{81x^2+3}{81x^2-3}\right) + 10\left(\dfrac{100x^2+3}{100x^2-3}\right)$

6. $\dfrac{dg(x)}{dx} = 7\cos\left((7x)^3\right) + \sin x \cos\left(\cos^3 x\right)$

7. $\left(-1, \ \infty\right)$

8. $\dfrac{1}{2}\sec^2 x + C$

9. $f(x) = 4x^{3/2}$

10. a

11. $-\dfrac{1}{4}\cos^4 x + C$

12. d

13. 1.5

14. $\dfrac{x^3}{3} + 2x + \left(\tan x\right)^{-1} + C$

15. 6

16. c

17. $\dfrac{2}{5}\left(x^2+3\right)^5 + C$

18. a

19. $\dfrac{4}{9} + 5$

20. c

1. Estimate to the hundredth the area from 1 to 5 under the graph of $f(x) = \dfrac{4}{x}$ using four approximating rectangles and right endpoints.

2. Estimate the area from 0 to 5 under the graph of $f(x) = 81 - x^2$ using five approximating rectangles and right endpoints.

3. Approximate the area under the curve $y = \dfrac{2}{x^2}$ from 1 to 2 using ten approximating rectangles of equal widths and right endpoints. Round the answer to the nearest hundredth.

4. If $f(x) = \sin(\sin x)$, $0 \le x \le \pi/6$, approximate the area under the curve using ten approximating rectangles of equal widths and left endpoints.

   Round the answer to the nearest hundredth.

5. The speed of a runner increased steadily during the first three seconds of a race. Her speed at half-second intervals is given in the table. Find a lower estimate for the (distance that she traveled during these three seconds.

t (s)	0	0.5	1.0	1.5	2.0	2.5	3.0
v (ft/s)	0	3	7.6	11.7	13	13.7	14.6

6. Find $g'(x)$ by evaluating the integral using Part 2 of the Fundamental Theorem and then differentiating.

   $$g(x) = \int_{\pi}^{x} (3 + \cos t)\, dt$$

7. Use Part 1 of the Fundamental Theorem of Calculus to find the derivative of the function.

$$g(x) = \int_1^x \sqrt{2 + 7t} \ dt$$

8. When we estimate distances from velocity data, it is sometimes necessary to use times $t_0, t_1, t_2, \ldots$ that are not equally spaced. We can still estimate distances using the time periods $\Delta t = t_i - t_{i-1}$. For example, on May 7, 1992, the space shuttle Endeavor was launched on mission STS-49, the purpose of which was to install a new perigee kick motor in an Intelsat communications satellite. The table, provided by NASA, gives the velocity data for the shuttle between liftoff and the jettisoning of the solid rocket boosters. Use this data to estimate an upper bound for the space shuttle Endeavor's height above Earth's surface 60 seconds after liftoff.

Event	Time (s)	Velocity (ft/s)
Launch	0	0
Begin roll maneuver	8	178
End roll maneuver	15	338
Throttle to 89%	18	430
Throttle to 67%	30	754
Throttle to 104%	55	1,362
Maximum dynamic pressure	60	1,461
Solid rocket booster separation	129	4,231

Select the correct answer.

a.   54,786
b.   54,550
c.   56,381
d.   55,483
e.   55,996

9. The velocity graph of a car accelerating from rest to a speed of 7 km/h over a period of 10 seconds is shown. Estimate to the nearest integer the distance traveled during this period. Use a right sum with $n = 10$.

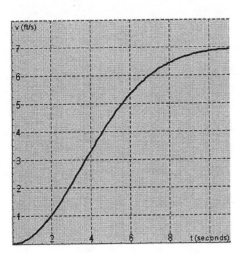

10. Determine a region whose area is equal to $\displaystyle\lim_{n\to\infty}\sum_{i=1}^{n}\frac{\pi}{3n}\tan\frac{i\pi}{3n}$.

Select the correct answer.

a. $y = \tan x, \ 0 \le x \le \dfrac{\pi}{13}$

b. $y = \tan x, \ 0 \le x \le \dfrac{\pi}{10}$

c. $y = \tan x, \ 0 \le x \le \dfrac{\pi}{3}$

d. $y = \tan x, \ 0 \le x \le \dfrac{\pi}{5}$

e. $y = \tan x, \ 0 \le x \le \dfrac{\pi}{8}$

f. $y = \tan x, \ 0 \le x \le \dfrac{\pi}{7}$

11. The table gives the values of a function obtained from an experiment. Use the values to estimate $\int_0^6 f(x)dx$ using three equal subintervals with left endpoints.

x	$f(x)$
0	9.9
1	8.8
2	7.4
3	6.3
4	4.1
5	-7.2
6	-10.3

12. Use the Midpoint Rule with $n = 10$ to approximate the integral.

$$\int_1^2 \sqrt{4+t^2}\,dt$$

Select the correct answer.

a. 2.510608
b. 1.731856
c. 10.042434
d. 2.810608
e. 3.510608

13. Use the Midpoint Rule with $n = 5$ to approximate the integral. Round the answer to 3 decimal places.

$$\int_0^{10} 2\sin\sqrt{t}\,dt$$

14. Express the limit as a definite integral on the given interval.

$$\lim_{n\to\infty}\sum_{i=1}^{n} 4r_i \sin r_i \Delta r, \quad \left[\,4,\,9\,\right]$$

15. Express the limit as a definite integral on the given interval.

$$\lim_{n\to\infty}\sum_{i=1}^{n}\left[2r_i^2 - 14r_i\right]\Delta r, \quad \left[\,4,\,8\,\right]$$

16. Evaluate the integral by interpreting it in terms of areas.

$$\int_{1}^{3} (4+7x)\, dx$$

17. Evaluate the integral by interpreting it in terms of areas.

$$\int_{-4}^{4} \sqrt{16-x^2}\, dx$$

18. Evaluate the integral by interpreting it in terms of areas.

$$\int_{-1}^{3} (3-x)\, dx$$

19. Given that $\int_{4}^{8} f(x)\, dx = \dfrac{2}{67}$, find $\int_{8}^{4} f(x)\, dx$.

20. Use Part 1 of the Fundamental Theorem of Calculus to find the derivative of the function.

$$g(x) = \int_{6}^{x} t^7 \sin(t)\, dt$$

1.   5.13

2.   350

3.   0.93

4.   0.12

5.   24.5

6. $\dfrac{dg(x)}{dx} = 3 + \cos x$

7. $\dfrac{dg(x)}{dx} = \sqrt{2 + 7x}$

8.   d

9.   17

10. c

11. 42.8

12. a

13. 12.929

14. $\displaystyle\int_{4}^{9} 4r \sin r \; dr$

15. $\displaystyle\int_{4}^{8} \left(2r^2 - 14r\right) dr$

16. 36

17. 25.133

18. 8

19. -0.029851

20. $\dfrac{dg(x)}{dx} = x^7 \sin x$

1. By reading values from the given graph of f, use five rectangles to find a lower estimate, to the nearest tenth, for the area from 0 to 10 under the given graph of f.

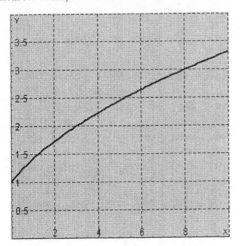

2. Approximate the area under the curve $y = \dfrac{4}{x^2}$ from 1 to 2 using ten approximating rectangles of equal widths and right endpoints. Round the answer to the nearest hundredth.

3. If $f(x) = \sin(\sin x)$, $0 \le x \le \pi/5$, approximate the area under the curve using ten approximating rectangles of equal widths and left endpoints.

    Select the correct answer. The choices are rounded to the nearest hundredth.

    a.   1.99
    b.   0.17
    c.   0.83
    d.   0.13
    e.   1.29

4. The speed of a runner increased steadily during the first three seconds of a race. Her speed at half-second intervals is given in the table. Find a lower estimate for the distance that she traveled during these three seconds.

t (s)	0	0.5	1.0	1.5	2.0	2.5	3.0
v (ft/s)	0	4.9	9.2	13.7	15.5	16.1	16.6

5. The velocity graph of a braking car is shown. Use it to estimate to the nearest foot the distance traveled by the car while the brakes are applied.

   Use a left sum with $n = 7$.

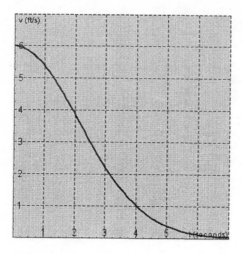

6. Evaluate the Riemann sum for $f(z) = 9 - z^2$, $0 \le z \le 2$, with four subintervals, taking the sample points to be right endpoints.

7. If $f(r) = \sqrt{r} - 2$, $1 \le r \le 6$, find the Riemann sum with $n = 5$ correct to 3 decimal places, taking the sample points to be midpoints.

8. The table gives the values of a function obtained from an experiment. Use the values to estimate $\int_0^6 f(w)\, dw$ using three equal subintervals with left endpoints.

w	$f(w)$
0	9.7
1	9.1
2	7.7
3	6.1
4	4.2
5	-6.6
6	-10.3

9. Use the Midpoint Rule with $n = 5$ to approximate the integral.

$$\int_0^{10} 2\sin\sqrt{q}\ dq$$

Select the correct answer. The choices are rounded to 3 decimal places.

a.   8.998
b.   4.781
c.   12.929
d.   9.998
e.   5.781

10. Use Part 1 of the Fundamental Theorem of Calculus to find the derivative of the function.

$$g(x) = \int_7^{x^2} 9\sqrt{1+t^8}\ dt$$

11. Evaluate the integral.

$$\int_0^9 \left(6 + 6y - y^2\right) dy$$

12. Evaluate the integral.

$$\int_0^1 x^{2/5} dx$$

13. Evaluate the integral.

$$\int_{6\pi}^{8\pi} \cos\theta\ d\theta$$

14. The marginal cost of manufacturing x yards of a certain fabric is $C'(x) = 3 - 0.01x + 0.000006x^2$ (in dollars per yard). Find the increase in cost if the production level is raised from 1,500 yards to 4,500 yards.

15. Find the general indefinite integral.

$$\int \frac{\sin 14t}{\sin 7t}\, dt$$

16. Evaluate the integral.

$$\int_{-4}^{3} \left| 2x - x^2 \right| dx$$

17. The area of the region that lies to the right of the y-axis and to the left of the parabola $x = 5y - y^2$ (the shaded region in the figure) is given by the integral $\int_{0}^{5} \left(5y - y^2\right) dy$.

Find the area of the region.

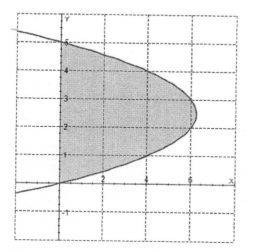

18. Evaluate the indefinite integral.

$$\int \frac{4+10x}{\sqrt{1+4x+5x^2}}\, dx$$

19. Evaluate the indefinite integral.

$$\int \frac{e^x}{e^x + 9} \, dx$$

20. Evaluate the definite integral

$$\int_{e^{16}}^{e^{64}} \frac{dx}{x\sqrt{\ln x}} \, dx$$

Select the correct answer.

a.   9
b.   8
c.   6
d.   11
e.   8.1

1. 21.2

2. 1.86

3. b

4. 29.7

5. 19

6. 14.25

7. -0.857

8. 43.2

9. c

10. $\dfrac{dg(x)}{dx} = 18x\sqrt{1+x^{16}}$

11. 54

12. 0.714286

13. 0

14. 94500

15. $\dfrac{2\sin 7t}{7} + C$

16. 40

17. 20.833

18. $2\sqrt{1+4x+5x^2} + C$

19. $\ln\!\left(e^x + 9\right) + C$

20. b

1. Sketch the region enclosed by $x = 4 - y^2$ and $x = y^2 - 2$. Decide whether to integrate with respect to x or y. Draw a typical approximating rectangle and label its height and width. Then find the area of the region.

2. Find the volume of the solid obtained by rotating about the x axis the region under the curve $y = \dfrac{1}{x}$ from $x = 1$ to $x = 6$.

3. Find the volume of the solid obtained by rotating the region bounded by $y = x^6$ and $x = y^6$ about the x axis.

4. Find the volume of the solid obtained by rotating the region bounded by $y = \sqrt[3]{x}$ and $y = x$ about the line $y = 1$.

5. True or False?

    The volume of the frustum of a right circular cone with height $h = 12$, lower base radius $R = 3$ and top radius $r = 3$ is 108π.

    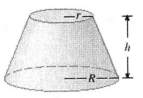

6. The linear density of a 15 m long rod is $22.5 / \sqrt{x+1}$ kg/m, where x is measured in meters from one end of the rod. Find the average density of the rod?

7. Find the volume of the frustum of a pyramid with square base of side $b = 19$, square top of side $a = 5$, and height $h = 15$.

    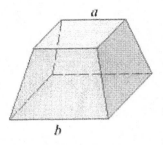

8. The base of S is an elliptical region with boundary curve $16x^2 + 16y^2 = 4$. Cross-sections perpendicular to the x axis are isosceles right triangles with hypotenuse in the base.

    Find the volume of S.

9. The base of S is the parabolic region $\left\{ (x, y) \mid x^2 \le y \le 10 \right\}$. Cross-sections perpendicular to the y axis are equilateral triangles.

    True or False?

    The volume of S is $100\sqrt{3}$.

10. *Cavalieri's Principle* states that if a family of parallel planes gives equal cross-sectional areas for two solids S_1 and S_2 then the volumes of S_1 and S_2 are equal.

    True or False?

    If $r = 2$ and $h = 5$, then the volume of the oblique cylinder shown in the figure is 20.

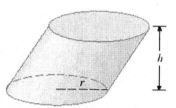

11. Find the volume common to two spheres, each with radius $r = 6$ if the center of each sphere lies on the surface of the other sphere.

12. Use the method of cylindrical shells to find the volume generated by rotating the region bounded by the given curves about the y axis.

    $$y = \frac{1}{x}, \ y = 0, \ x = 1, \ x = 2$$

13. Use the method of cylindrical shells to find the volume of solid obtained by rotating the region bounded by the given curves about the x axis.

    $$y^2 - 3y + x = 0, \ x = 0$$

14. Find the work done in pushing a car a distance of 12 m while exerting a constant force of 300 N.

15. True or False?

    If a force of 6 lbs is required to hold a spring stretched 5 inches beyond its natural length, then 60 lb-in. of work is done in stretching it from its natural length to 10 in. beyond its natural length.

16. An aquarium 3 m long, 6 m wide, and 1 m deep is full of water. Find the work (in J) needed to pump half of the water out of the aquarium. (Use the facts that the density of water is 1000 kg/m^3 and $g \approx 9.8$.)

17. In a steam engine the pressure and volume of steam satisfy the equation $PV^{1.4} = k$, where k is a constant. (This is true for adiabatic expansion, that is, expansion in which there is no heat transfer between the cylinder and its surroundings.) Calculate the work done by the engine (in ft-lb) during a cycle when the steam starts at a pressure of 100 lb/in^2 and a volume of 400 in^3 and expands to a volume of 1,100 in^3.

    Use the fact that the work done by the gas when the volume expands from volume V_1 to volume V_2 is

    $$W = \int_{V_1}^{V_2} P\,dV$$

18. Find the average value of the function $u(x) = 10x\sin(x^2)$ on the interval $\left[0, \sqrt{\pi} \right]$.

19. True or False?

    The Mean Value Theorem for Integrals says that if $u(x)$ is continuous on $[c, b]$, then there exists a number k in $[c, b]$ such that

    $$u(k) = u_{ave} = \frac{1}{c-b}\int_{c}^{b} u(x)\,dx$$

20. In a certain city the temperature x hours after 6 A.M. was modeled by the function

    $$U(x) = 28 + 10\sin\frac{\pi x}{11}$$

    Find the average temperature during the period from 6 A.M. to 6 P.M.

1. 13.86

2. $0.833333\,\pi$

3. $\dfrac{35}{52}\pi$

4. $\dfrac{4}{15}\pi$

5. T

6. 9

7. 2405

8. $\dfrac{1}{6}$

9. F

10. F

11. 90π

12. 2π

13. 13.5π

14. 3600

15. T

16. 22050

17. 2773

18. $\dfrac{10}{\sqrt{\pi}}$

19. F

20. 33.7

1. Find the volume of a cap of a sphere with radius $r = 50$ and height $h = 3$.

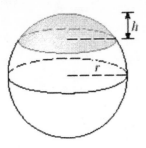

2. The base of S is an elliptical region with boundary curve $4x^2 + 9y^2 = 16$.
    Cross-sections perpendicular to the x axis are isosceles right triangles with hypotenuse in the base.

    Find the volume of S.

3. The base of S is the parabolic region $\left\{ (x, y) \mid x^2 \le y \le 2 \right\}$. Cross-sections perpendicular to the y axis are squares.

    Find the volume of S.

4. By interpreting the integral for the volume of a solid torus (the donut-shaped solid shown in the figure) with $r = 5$ and $R = 18$ as an area, find the volume of the torus.

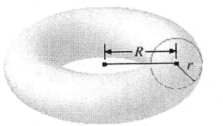

5. The linear density of an 8 m long rod is $12/\sqrt{x+1}$ kg/m, where x is measured in meters from one end of the rod.

    Find the average density of the rod?

6. The temperature of a metal rod, 6 m long, is $5x$ (C°) at a distance x meters from one end of the rod.

    What is the average temperature of the rod?

7. *Cavalieri's Principle* states that if a family of parallel planes gives equal cross-sectional areas for two solids S_1 and S_2 then the volumes of S_1 and S_2 are equal.

    True or False?

    If $r = 5$ and $h = 1$, then the volume of the oblique cylinder shown in the figure is 25.

    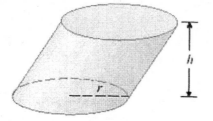

8. True or False?

    If the center of each of two spheres, each having radius $r = 2$, lies on the surface of the other sphere, then the volume common to both spheres is $\dfrac{10}{3}\pi$.

9. The region bounded by the given curves is rotated about the specified axis. Find the volume of the resulting solid by any method.

    $y = 5, \quad y = x^2 - 3x + 7; \quad \text{about } x = -1$

10. The region bounded by the given curves is rotated about the specified axis. Find the volume of the resulting solid by any method.

    $x^2 + (y-1)^2 = 1$ about the y axis

11. Use cylindrical shells to find the volume of the solid.

    A sphere of radius d.

12. A force of 10 lb is required to hold a spring stretched 4 in. beyond its natural length. How much work (in pound-inches) is done in stretching it from its natural length to 9 in. beyond its natural length?

13. If 432 J of work are needed to stretch a spring from 8 cm to 14 cm and another 580 J are needed to stretch it from 14 cm to 19 cm, what is the natural length of the spring?

14. A cable that weighs 2 lb/ft is used to lift 610 lb of coal up a mineshaft 470 ft deep.

True or False?

The work required is 507,600 ft-lb.

15. The tank shown is full of water. Given that water weighs 62.5 lb/ft and R = 5, find the work (in lb-ft) required to pump the water out of the tank.

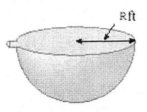

Rft

hemisphere

16. True or False?

The average value of the function $u(t) = \dfrac{8}{(3+t)^2}$ on the interval [0, 2] is less than 1.6.

17. True or False?

The average value of the function $z(v) = 7 - v^2$ on the interval [0, 6] is 2.61.

18. Find the average value of the function $u(x) = 10x \sin(x^2)$ on the interval $\left[\; 0, \;\; \sqrt{\pi} \;\right]$.

19. Find the number(s) a such that the average value of the function $f(t) = 25 - 20t + 3t^2$ on the interval $[0, a]$ is equal to 4.

20. The velocity v of blood that flows in a blood vessel with radius R and length l at a distance r from the central axis is $v(r) = \dfrac{P}{4ql}\left(R^2 - r^2\right)$. Where P is the pressure difference between the ends of the vessel and q is the viscosity of the blood.

Find the average velocity (with respect to r) over the interval $0 \le r \le R$

1. $\dfrac{1323}{3}\pi$

2. $\dfrac{128}{27}$

3. 8

4. $900\pi^2$

5. 6

6. 15

7. F

8. T

9. $\dfrac{5\pi}{6}$

10. $\dfrac{4\pi}{3}$

11. $\dfrac{4}{3}\pi\left(d^3\right)$

12. $\dfrac{405}{4}$

13. 2

14. T

15. 30680

16. T

17. F

18. $\dfrac{10}{\sqrt{\pi}}$

19. $a{=}3$ or $a{=}7$

20. $\dfrac{PR^2}{6ql}$

1. Sketch the region enclosed by the curves $y = x + 2$, $y = 16 - x^2$, $x = -2$, and $x = 2$. Decide whether to integrate with respect to x or y. Draw a typical approximating rectangle and label its height and width. Then find the area of the region.

   Select the correct answer.

   a.   50.67
   b.   51.67
   c.   8.44
   d.   16.89
   e.   101.33
   f.   152

2. Use calculus to find the area of the triangle with the given vertices.

   $(0, 0)$, $(10, 1)$, $(-1, 2)$

   Select the correct answer.

   a. $S = 11.5$
   b. $S = 12$
   c. $S = 11$
   d. $S = 10.5$
   e. $S = 15.5$

3. Use the Midpoint Rule with $n = 4$ to approximate the area of the region bounded by the given curves.

   $y = \sqrt{1 + x^3}$, $y = 1 - 7x$, $x = 2$

   Select the correct answer.

   a. $S = 18.22$
   b. $S = 15.22$
   c. $S = 14.22$
   d. $S = 13.22$
   e. $S = 17.22$

4. Find the volume of the solid obtained by rotating the region in the first quadrant bounded by $y = x^2$ and $y = 9$ about the y axis.

    Select the correct answer.

    a. $\dfrac{9}{2}\pi$

    b. $\dfrac{81}{2}$

    c. $\dfrac{81}{2}\pi$

    d. $\dfrac{81}{4}\pi$

    e. 9π

5. An aquarium 1 m long, 9 m wide, and 1 m deep is full of water. Find the work needed to pump half of the water out of the aquarium.

    (Use the facts that the density of water is 1000 kg/m^3 and $g \approx 9.8$.)

    Select the correct answer.

    a. 10,025 J
    b. 10,875 J
    c. 11,025 J
    d. 11,036 J
    e. 11,035 J

6. Find the volume of the solid obtained by rotating the region bounded by $y = x^3$ and $x = y^3$ about the x axis.

    Select the correct answer.

    a. $\dfrac{16}{35}\pi$

    b. $\dfrac{16}{7}\pi$

    c. $\dfrac{18}{35}$

    d. $\dfrac{7}{2}$

    e. 16π

7. Find the volume of the solid obtained by rotating the region bounded by $x = y^2$ and $x = 3y$ about the y axis.

Select the correct answer.

a. $\dfrac{-243}{3}\pi$

b. $\dfrac{1,458}{15}\pi$

c. $\dfrac{243}{15}\pi$

d. $\dfrac{256}{15}$

e. $\dfrac{-\pi}{15}$

8. Use the method of cylindrical shells to find the volume generated by rotating the region bounded by the given curves about the y-axis.

$$y = \frac{1}{x}, \quad y = 0, \quad x = 1, \quad x = 6$$

Select the correct answer.

a. $V = 10\pi$
b. $V = 5\pi$
c. $V = 11\pi$
d. $V = 4\pi$
e. $V = \pi$

9. Find the number(s) a such that the average value of the function $f(x) = 80 - 34x + 3x^2$ on the interval $[0, a]$ is equal to 10.

Select all that apply.

a. $a = 8$
b. $a = 10$
c. $a = 7$
d. $a = -7$
e. $a = -10$

10. Use the method of cylindrical shells to find the volume of solid obtained by rotating the region bounded by the given curves about the x axis $x = 6 + y^2$, $x = 0$, $y = 1$, $y = 3$.

Select the correct answer.

a. $V = 176\pi$
b. $V = 86\pi$
c. $V = 93\pi$
d. $V = 88\pi$
e. $V = 76\pi$

11. Use the method of cylindrical shells to find the volume generated by rotating the region bounded by the given curves about the specified axis.

$y = x^2$, $y = 0$, $x = 1$, $x = 8$; about $x = 1$

Select the correct answer.

a. $V = 20,482\pi$
b. $V = 10,246\pi$
c. $V = 10,239\pi$
d. $V = \dfrac{10,241}{6}\pi$
e. $V = 3413\pi$

12. The region bounded by the given curves is rotated about the specified axis. Find the volume of the resulting solid by any method.

$y = x^2 + 3x - 10$; about the x axis

Select the correct answer.

a. $V = 560.23\pi$
b. $V = 557.73\pi$
c. $V = 565.68\pi$
d. $V = 580.57\pi$
e. $V = 555.57\pi$

13. The region bounded by the given curves is rotated about the specified axis. Find the volume of the resulting solid by any method.

$y = 5, \ y = x^2 - 6x + 10$; about the line $x = -1$

Select the correct answer.

a. $V = 105.67\pi$
b. $V = 82.83\pi$
c. $V = 83.83\pi$
d. $V = 90.78\pi$
e. $V = 95.33\pi$

14. The region bounded by the given curves is rotated about the specified axis. Find the volume of the resulting solid by any method.

$x^2 + (y - 1)^2 = 1$; about the y axis

Select the correct answer.

a. $V = \dfrac{5}{3}\pi$

b. $V = \dfrac{2}{3}\pi$

c. $V = \dfrac{1}{3}\pi$

d. $V = \dfrac{4}{3}\pi$

e. $V = \dfrac{7}{3}\pi$

15. If 132 J of work are needed to stretch a spring from 9 cm to 12 cm and another 588 J are needed to stretch it from 12 cm to 19 cm, what is the natural length of the spring?

Select the correct answer.

a. 6 cm
b. 5 cm
c. 3 cm
d. 4 cm
e. 1 cm

16. A heavy rope, 40 ft long, weighs 0.8 lb/ft and hangs over the edge of a building 110 ft high. How much work is done in pulling the rope to the top of the building?

    Select the correct answer.

    a.   640 ft-lb
    b.   590 ft-lb
    c.   641 ft-lb
    d.   489 ft-lb
    e.   740 ft-lb

17. A tank is full of water. Find the work required to pump the water out of the outlet. Round the answer to the nearest thousand.

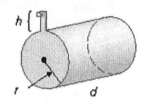

    $h = 2$ m , $r = 2$ m , $d = 5$ m

    Select the correct answer.

    a. $W = 2,013,000$ J
    b. $W = 2,184,000$ J
    c. $W = 2,462,000$ J
    d. $W = 2,585,000$ J

18. Find a number a in $[0, 2]$ at which the value of the function $f(x) = 7 - x^2$ is equal to the average value of the function on the interval $[0, 2]$.

    Select the correct answer.

    a. $a = -\dfrac{2\sqrt{3}}{3}$

    b. $a = \dfrac{2\sqrt{3}}{3}$

    c. $a = \dfrac{4\sqrt{3}}{3}$

    d. $a = \dfrac{2\sqrt{2}}{3}$

    e.   none of these

19. Find the average value of the function $z(t) = 4t \sin(t^2)$ on the interval $\left[0, \sqrt{\pi}\right]$.

Select the correct answer.

a. $\dfrac{8}{\pi}$

b. $\dfrac{8}{\sqrt{\pi}}$

c. $\dfrac{4}{\pi}$

d. $\dfrac{4}{\sqrt{\pi}}$

e.   none of these

20. The temperature of a metal rod, 4 m long, is $3x$ (in degrees Celsius) at a distance x meters from one end of the rod. What is the average temperature of the rod?

Select the correct answer.

a. $T_{ave} = 6°C$

b. $T_{ave} = 22°C$

c. $T_{ave} = 34°C$

d. $T_{ave} = 24°C$

e. $T_{ave} = 46°C$

1. a

2. d

3. b

4. c

5. c

6. a

7. b

8. a

9. b, c

10. d

11. d

12. a

13. c

14. d

15. b

16. a

17. c

18. b

19. d

20. a

1. The region bounded by the given curves is rotated about the specified axis. Find the volume of the resulting solid by any method.

   $x^2 + (y-1)^2 = 1$; about the y axis

   Select the correct answer.

   a. $V = \dfrac{1}{3}\pi$

   b. $V = \dfrac{4}{3}\pi$

   c. $V = \dfrac{5}{3}\pi$

   d. $V = \dfrac{2}{3}\pi$

   e. $V = \dfrac{7}{3}\pi$

2. Use cylindrical shells to find the volume of the solid.

   A sphere of radius r.

   Select the correct answer.

   a. $V = \dfrac{2}{3}\pi r^3$

   b. $V = \dfrac{4}{3}\pi r^3$

   c. $V = \dfrac{1}{3}\pi r^3$

   d. $V = \dfrac{5}{3}\pi r^3$

   e. $V = \dfrac{7}{3}\pi r^3$

3. Suppose you make napkin rings by drilling holes with different diameters through two wooden balls (which also have different diameters). You discover that both napkin rings have the same height h as shown in the figure. Use cylindrical shells to compute the volume of a napkin ring created by drilling a hole with radius d through the center of a sphere of radius D and express the answer in terms of h.

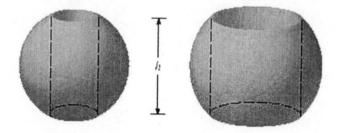

Select the correct answer.

a. $V = \dfrac{1}{6}\pi h^2$

b. $V = \dfrac{1}{6}\pi h^3$

c. $V = \dfrac{1}{4}\pi h^3$

d. $V = \dfrac{1}{3}\pi h^2$

e. $V = \dfrac{1}{3}\pi h^3$

4. Sketch a graph to estimate the x-coordinates of the points of intersection of the given curves. Then use this information to estimate the volume of the solid obtained by rotating about the y axis the region enclosed by these curves.

Rounded to the nearest hundredth.

$y = 0, \quad y = -x^4 + 6x^3 - x^2 + 6x$

Select the correct answer.

a. $V = 3{,}346.96\pi$
b. $V = 3{,}331.63\pi$
c. $V = 3{,}323.88\pi$
d. $V = 3{,}326.40\pi$
e. $V = 3{,}745.96\pi$

5. Find the number(s) a such that the average value of the function $z(v) = 51 - 26v + 3v^2$ on the interval $[0, a]$ is equal to 9.

    Select the correct answer(s).

    a.   6
    b.   -6
    c.   3
    d.   7
    e.   -7

6. A spring has a natural length of 22 cm. If a force of 15 N is required to keep it stretched to a length of 32 cm, how much work is required to stretch it from 22 cm to 40 cm?

    Select the correct answer.

    a.   3.43 J
    b.   1.93 J
    c.   2.93 J
    d.   3.93 J
    e.   2.43 J

7. If 90 J of work are needed to stretch a spring from 8 cm to 13 cm and another 294 J are needed to stretch it from 13 cm to 20 cm, what is the natural length of the spring?

    Select the correct answer.

    a.   5 cm
    b.   6 cm
    c.   7 cm
    d.   4 cm
    e.   2 cm

8. Use the Midpoint Rule with $n = 4$ to estimate the volume obtained by rotating about the region under the y-axis the region under the curve.

    $$y = \tan x, \quad 0 \le x \le \frac{\pi}{4}$$

    Select the correct answer. The choices are rounded to the nearest hundredth.

    a. $V = 1.142$
    b. $V = 1.851$
    c. $V = 0.825$
    d. $V = 0.491$
    e. $V = 0.156$

9. The region bounded by the given curves is rotated about the specified axis. Find the volume of the resulting solid by any method.

$y = 5$, $y = x^2 - 4x + 8$; about the line $x = -1$

Select the correct answer.

a. $V = 13.45\pi$
b. $V = 28.34\pi$
c. $V = 5.50\pi$
d. $V = 8\pi$
e. $V = 12.34\pi$

10. A bucket that weighs 5 lb and a rope of negligible weight are used to draw water from a well that is 70 ft deep. The bucket starts with 50 lb of water and is pulled up at a rate of 10 ft/s, but water leaks out of a hole in the bucket at a rate of 0.5 lb/s. Find the work done in pulling the bucket to the top of the well.

Select the correct answer.

a.   3,728.5 ft-lb
b.   3,837.5 ft-lb
c.   3,677.5 ft-lb
d.   3,727.5 ft-lb
e.   3,745.5 ft-lb

11. A tank is full of water. Find the work required to pump the water out of the outlet. Round the answer to the nearest thousand.

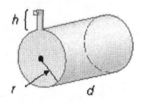

$h = 1$ m , $r = 1$ m , $d = 5$ m

Select the correct answer.

a. $W = 30,000$ J
b. $W = 308,000$ J
c. $W = 757,000$ J
d. $W = 431,000$ J
e. $W = 305,000$ J

12. Newton's Law of Gravitation states that two bodies with masses m_1 and m_2 attract each other with a force $F = G\dfrac{m_1 m_2}{r^2}$ where r is the distance between the bodies and G is the gravitation constant. If one of bodies is fixed, find the work needed to move the other from $r = a$ to $r = d$.

Select the correct answer.

a. $W = Gm_1 m_2 \left(\dfrac{1}{a^2} - \dfrac{1}{d^2} \right)$

b. $W = Gm_1 m_2 \left(\dfrac{1}{a} - \dfrac{1}{d} \right)$

c. $W = Gm_1 m_2 \left(\dfrac{1}{d} - \dfrac{1}{a} \right)$

d. $W = Gm_1 m_2 \left(\dfrac{1}{d^2} - \dfrac{1}{a^2} \right)$

e. $W = Gm_1 m_2 \left(\dfrac{1}{a^2} + \dfrac{1}{d^2} \right)$

13. Find the average value of the function $y(x) = 8\sqrt{x}$ on the interval $[1, 36]$.

Select the correct answer.

a. $\dfrac{688}{63}$

b. $\dfrac{688}{7}$

c. $\dfrac{688}{21}$

d. $\dfrac{2064}{7}$

e. $\dfrac{10{,}320}{10{,}321}$

14. The linear density of a 48 m long rod is $72 / \sqrt{x+1}$ kg/m, where x is measured in meters from one end of the rod.

Find the average density of the rod?

Select the correct answer.

a. $\rho_{ave} = 19$ kg/m

b. $\rho_{ave} = 8$ kg/m

c. $\rho_{ave} = 14$ kg/m

d. $\rho_{ave} = 18$ kg/m

e. $\rho_{ave} = 22$ kg/m

15. An aquarium 7 m long, 1 m wide, and 1 m deep is full of water. Find the work needed to pump half of the water out of the aquarium. (Use the facts that the density of water is 1000 kg/m^3 and $g \approx 9.8$.)

   Select the correct answer.

    a.   8,575 J
    b.   7,575 J
    c.   8,425 J
    d.   8,586 J
    e.   8,585 J

16. In a certain city the temperature x hours after 7 A.M. was modeled by the function

$$T(x) = 48 + 30\sin\frac{\pi x}{12}$$

   Find the average temperature during the period from 7 A.M. to 7 P.M.

   Select the correct answer.

    a.   67.099
    b.   14.956
    c.   43.203
    d.   1.402
    e.   69.029

17. The velocity v of blood that flows in a blood vessel with radius R and length l at a distance r from the central axis is $v(r) = \dfrac{P}{4ql}\left(R^2 - r^2\right)$ where P is the pressure difference between the ends of the vessel and q is the viscosity of the blood. Suppose that Vessel 1 has length 1.7 cm and outer radius 0.5 mm, and Vessel 2 has length 4.3 cm and outer radius 0.8 mm. Find the average velocities (with respect to r) over the interval $0 \leq r \leq R$ for each vessel. Which vessel has the higher average velocity?

   Select the correct answer.

    a.   Vessel 1
    b.   Vessel 2

18. The temperature of a metal rod, 7 m long, is $6x$ (in degrees Celsius) at a distance x meters from one end of the rod. What is the average temperature of the rod?

   Select the correct answer.

    a. $T_{ave} = 21°C$
    b. $T_{ave} = 38°C$
    c. $T_{ave} = 42°C$
    d. $T_{ave} = 23°C$
    e. $T_{ave} = 32°C$

19. The tank shown is full of water. Given that water weighs 62.5 lb/ft and $R = 7$, find the work required to pump the water out of the tank.

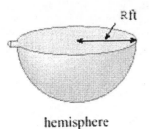

R ft

hemisphere

Select the correct answer.

a.   117,859 ft-lb
b.   116,858 ft-lb
c.   116,859 ft-lb
d.   117,879 ft-lb
e.   117,749 ft-lb

20. A heavy rope, 20 ft long, weighs 0.6 lb/ft and hangs over the edge of a building 100 ft high. How much work is done in pulling the rope to the top of the building?

Select the correct answer.

a.   220 ft-lb
b.   70 ft-lb
c.   -31 ft-lb
d.   120 ft-lb
e.   121 ft-lb

1. b

2. b

3. b

4. d

5. a, d

6. e

7. b

8. a

9. d

10. d

11. b

12. b

13. c

14. d

15. a

16. a

17. b

18. a

19. a

20. d

1. Sketch the region enclosed by $y = 2x + 1$ and $y = 6x^2$. Decide whether to integrate with respect to x or y. Draw a typical approximating rectangle and label its height and width. Then find the area of the region.

2. Sketch the region enclosed by $y = 2 + \sqrt{x}$ and $y = \dfrac{8+x}{8}$. Decide whether to integrate with respect to x or y. Draw a typical approximating rectangle and label its height and width. Then find the area of the region.

    Select the correct answer.

    a.   155.798646
    b.   31.159729
    c.   311.597293
    d.   778.993231
    e.   156.798646

3. Sketch the region enclosed by $y = 4x^2$ and $y = x^2 + 9$. Decide whether to integrate with respect to x or y. Draw a typical approximating rectangle and label its height and width. Then find the area of the region.

4. Find the average value of the function $z(t) = 6\cos(t)$ on the interval $\left[0, \dfrac{\pi}{2}\right]$.

5. Racing cars driven by Chris and Kelly are side by side at the start of a race. The table shows the velocities of each car (in miles per hour) during the first ten seconds of the race. Use the Midpoint Rule to estimate how much farther Kelly travels than Chris does during the ten seconds.

t	V_C	V_K		t	V_C	V_K
0	0	0		6	72	83
1	25	27		7	75	86
2	33	38		8	85	97
3	42	48		9	89	101
4	53	60		10	90	102
5	62	71				

6. Find the area of the region bounded by the parabola $y = x^2$, the tangent line to this parabola at (6, 36), and the x axis.

7. True or False?

   The volume of the frustum of a right circular cone with height $h = 6$, lower base radius $R = 6$ and top radius $r = 5$ is 182π.

8. Find the volume of a pyramid with height 4 and base an equilateral triangle with side $a = 13$.

   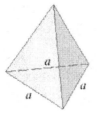

9. The base of S is an elliptical region with boundary curve $16x^2 + 4y^2 = 16$. Cross-sections perpendicular to the x axis are isosceles right triangles with hypotenuse in the base.

   Find the volume of S.

10. True or False?

    The volume of a solid torus (the donut-shaped solid shown in the figure) with $r = 3$ and $R = 19$ is $342\pi^2$.

    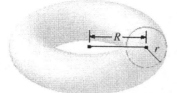

11. Use the method of cylindrical shells to find the volume generated by rotating the region bounded by the given curves about the specified axis.

    $y = \sqrt{x-1}$, $y = 0$, $y = 10$; about the line $y = 3$

12. Find the average value of the function $f(t) = 8 - t^2$ on the interval $[0, 9]$.

13. The region bounded by the given curves is rotated about the specified axis. Find the volume of the resulting solid by any method.

$y = x^2 - 2x - 3$; about the x axis

14. Use cylindrical shells to find the volume of the solid.

A sphere of radius a.

15. Suppose you make napkin rings by drilling holes with different diameters through two wooden balls (which also have different diameters). You discover that both napkin rings have the same height h as shown in the figure. Use cylindrical shells to compute the volume of a napkin ring created by drilling a hole with radius b through the center of a sphere of radius B and express the answer in terms of h.

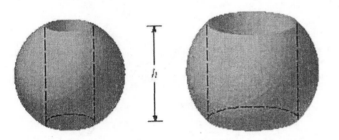

16. Find the work done in pushing a car a distance of 9 m while exerting a constant force of 200 N.

17. A force of 9 lb is required to hold a spring stretched 6 in. beyond its natural length. How much work (in pound-inches) is done in stretching it from its natural length to 8 in. beyond its natural length?

18. A tank is full of water. Find the work required to pump the water out of the outlet.

Round the answer to the nearest thousand.

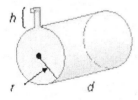

$h = 1$ m , $r = 2$ m , $d = 7$ m

19. The tank shown is full of water. Given that water weighs 62.5 lb/ft and R = 9, find the work required to pump the water out of the tank.

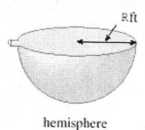

hemisphere

Select the correct answer.

a.   321,061 ft-lb
b.   322,062 ft-lb
c.   322,082 ft-lb
d.   321,952 ft-lb
e.   321,062 ft-lb

20. Newton's Law of Gravitation states that two bodies with masses m_1 and m_2 attract each other with a force $F = G\dfrac{m_1 m_2}{r^2}$ where r is the distance between the bodies and G is the gravitation constant. If one of bodies is fixed, find the work needed to move the other from $r = k$ to $r = c$.

1. 0.69

2. a

3. 20.78

4. $\dfrac{12}{\pi}$

5. $\dfrac{352}{3}$

6. $\dfrac{216}{3}$

7. T

8. $\dfrac{169\sqrt{3}}{3}$

9. $\dfrac{16}{3}$

10. T

11. 67.5π

12. -19

13. $\dfrac{512}{15}\pi$

14. $\dfrac{4}{3}\pi a^3$

15. $\dfrac{1}{6}\pi h^3$

16. 1800

17. 48

18. 2586000

19. b

20. $W = Gm_1 m_2 \left(\dfrac{1}{k} - \dfrac{1}{c} \right)$

1. Sketch the region enclosed by $y = 3x^2$ and $y = x^2 + 9$. Decide whether to integrate with respect to x or y. Draw a typical approximating rectangle and label its height and width. Then find the area of the region.

2. Use calculus to find the area of the triangle with the given vertices.

    $(0, 0), (10, 1), (-1, 4)$

3. Find the area of the region bounded by the parabola $y = x^2$, the tangent line to this parabola at $(5, 25)$, and the x-axis.

    Select the correct answer.

    a.   44.666667
    b.   42.666667
    c.   41.666667
    d.   47.666667
    e.   46.666667

4. Find the number b such that the line $y = b$ divides the region bounded by the curves $y = 5x^2$ and $y = 7$ into two regions with equal area.

5. Find the volume of the solid obtained by rotating about the x-axis the region under the curve $y = \dfrac{1}{x}$ from $x = 4$ to $x = 5$.

6. Find the volume of the solid obtained by rotating the region bounded by $y = x^4$ and $x = y^4$ about the x-axis.

7. True or False?

    The volume of the frustum of a right circular cone with height $h = 9$, lower base radius $R = 10$ and top radius $r = 2$ is 372π.

8. Find the volume of the frustum of a pyramid with square base of side $b = 12$, square top of side $a = 2$, and height $h = 3$.

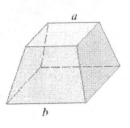

9. The base of S is an elliptical region with boundary curve $4x^2 + 4y^2 = 25$. Cross-sections perpendicular to the x-axis are isosceles right triangles with hypotenuse in the base.

True or false?

The volume of S is $\dfrac{125}{6}$.

10. The base of S is the parabolic region $\left\{ (x, y) \mid x^2 \leq y \leq 11 \right\}$. Cross-sections perpendicular to the y-axis are equilateral triangles. Find the volume of S .

11. True or False?

The volume of a solid torus (the donut-shaped solid shown in the figure) with $r = 4$ and $R = 14$ is $448\pi^2$.

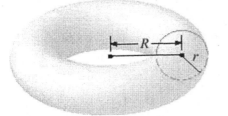

12. *Cavalieri's Principle* states that if a family of parallel planes gives equal cross-sectional areas for two solids S_1 and S_2 then the volumes of S_1 and S_2 are equal.

True or False?

If $r = 10$ and $h = 7$, then the volume of the oblique cylinder shown in the figure is 700.

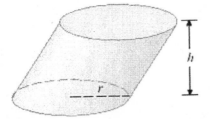

13. Find the volume common to two spheres, each with radius $r = 1$ if the center of each sphere lies on the surface of the other sphere.

14. Use the method of cylindrical shells to find the volume generated by rotating the region bounded by the given curves about the specified axis.

   $y = x^2$, $y = 0$, $x = 1$, $x = 6$; about $x = 1$

15. Set up, but do not evaluate, an integral for the volume of the solid obtained by rotating the region bounded by the given curves about the specified axis.

   $y = \sin x$, $y = 0$, $x = 2\pi$, $x = 8\pi$; about the y-axis

16. The region bounded by the given curves is rotated about the specified axis. Find the volume of the resulting solid by any method.

   $y = x^2 - 2x - 15$; about the x-axis

   Select the correct answer.

   a. $V = 1{,}112.61\pi$
   b. $V = 1{,}092.27\pi$
   c. $V = 1{,}092.72\pi$
   d. $V = 1{,}089.77\pi$
   e. $V = 2{,}089.77\pi$

17. The temperature of a metal rod, 8 m long, is $7x$ (in degrees C) at a distance x meters from one end of the rod. What is the average temperature of the rod?

18. Use cylindrical shells to find the volume of the solid.

   A sphere of radius r.

   Select the correct answer.

   a. $V = \dfrac{5}{3}\pi r^3$

   b. $V = \dfrac{4}{3}\pi r^3$

   c. $V = \dfrac{1}{3}\pi r^3$

   d. $V = \dfrac{2}{3}\pi r^3$

   e. $V = \dfrac{7}{3}\pi r^3$

19. Find the average value of the function $f(x) = 3x \sin(x^2)$ on the interval $[0, \sqrt{\pi}]$.

20. Find the number(s) b such that the average value of the function $z(v) = 23 - 18v + 3v^2$ on the interval $[0, b]$ is equal to 5.

    Select all that apply.

    a.   6
    b.   3
    c.   9
    d.   -6
    e.   -7

1. 25.46

2. 20.5

3. c

4. 4.41

5. 0.05π

6. $\dfrac{5}{9}\pi$

7. T

8. 172

9. T

10. $\dfrac{121\sqrt{3}}{2}$

11. T

12. F

13. $\dfrac{5}{12}\pi$

14. $\dfrac{3025\pi}{6}$

15. $\displaystyle\int\limits_{2\pi}^{8\pi} 2\pi x \sin x \ dx$

16. b

17. 28

18. b

19. $\dfrac{3}{\sqrt{\pi}}$

20. a, b

1. Use a graph to find approximate x-coordinates of the points of intersection of the given curves.

   $y = x^{14}, \quad y = 2\cos x$

   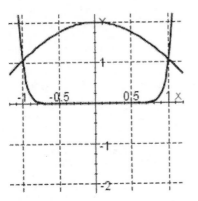

2. Find the area of the region bounded by the parabola $y = x^2$, the tangent line to this parabola at $(10, \; 100)$, and the x-axis.

3. Find the number b such that the line $y = b$ divides the region bounded by the curves $y = 3x^2$ and $y = 9$ into two regions with equal area.

4. True or False?

   If a force of 6 lbs is required to hold a spring stretched 5 inches beyond its natural length, then 38.4 lb-in. of work is done in stretching it from its natural length to 8 in. beyond its natural length.

5. Find (approximately) the area of the region bounded by the curves.

   $y = 6 + x^2, \quad y = 6 + e^{-x^2}$

   Select the correct answer.

   a. $S = 0.98$
   b. $S = 0.96$
   c. $S = 0.99$
   d. $S = 1.01$
   e. $S = 0.89$

6. Find the volume of the solid obtained by rotating about the x-axis the region under the curve $y = \dfrac{1}{x}$

   from $x = 6$ to $x = 7$.

7. Find the volume of the solid obtained by rotating the region bounded by $y = x^2$ and $x = y^2$ about the x-axis.

   Select the correct answer.

   a. $\dfrac{6\pi}{5}$

   b. $\dfrac{3\pi}{10}$

   c. $\dfrac{2}{5}$

   d. $\dfrac{\pi}{5}$

   e. $\dfrac{2\pi}{5}$

8. Find the volume of the solid obtained by rotating the region bounded by $y = x^3$ and $x = y^3$ about the line $x = -1$.

9. Use the method of cylindrical shells to find the volume of solid obtained by rotating the region bounded by the given curves about the x - axis.

   $$y^2 - 3y + x = 0, \quad x = 0$$

10. Find the volume of a cap of a sphere with radius $r = 20$ and height $h = 10$.

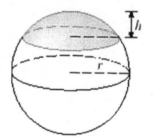

11. True or False?

   The volume of the frustum of a pyramid with square base of side $b = 17$, square top of side $a = 5$, and height $h = 8$ is 3,192.

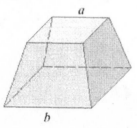

12. Find the volume of a pyramid with height $h = 9$ and rectangular base with dimensions 5 and 10.

13. Use cylindrical shells to find the volume of the solid.

    A right circular cone with height z and base radius d.

14. Use the method of cylindrical shells to find the volume generated by rotating the region bounded by the given curves about the specified axis.

    $y = x^2$, $y = 0$, $x = 1$, $x = 4$; *about* $x = 1$

15. True or False?

    The base of S is the parabolic region $\left\{ (x, \ y) \mid x^2 \leq y \leq 7 \right\}$. Cross-sections perpendicular to the y-axis are squares. The volume of S is 98.

16. True or False?

    The volume of a solid torus (the donut-shaped solid shown in the figure) with $r = 2$ and $R = 12$ is $96\pi^2$.

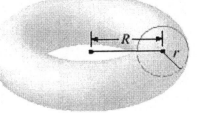

17. Find the volume common to two spheres, each with radius $r = 5$ if the center of each sphere lies on the surface of the other sphere.

18. Use the method of cylindrical shells to find the volume generated by rotating the region bounded by the given curves about the y-axis.

    $y = \dfrac{1}{x}$, $y = 0$, $x = 1$, $x = 9$

19. Set up, but do not evaluate, an integral for the volume of the solid obtained by rotating the region bounded by the given curves about the specified axis.

$$x = \sqrt{\sin y}, \ 0 \le y \le \pi, \ x = 0 \ ; \ about \ y = 3$$

Select the correct answer.

a. $$V = \int_0^\pi \pi(3 - y)\sqrt{\sin y} \ dy$$

b. $$V = \int_0^\pi 2\pi(3 - y)\sqrt{\sin y} \ dy$$

c. $$V = \int_0^\pi 2(3 - y)\sqrt{\sin y} \ dy$$

d. $$V = \int_0^\pi (3 - y)\sqrt{\sin y} \ dy$$

e. $$V = \int_0^\pi (\pi - y)\sqrt{\sin y} \ dy$$

20. The region bounded by the given curves is rotated about the specified axis. Find the volume of the resulting solid by any method.

$$x^2 + (y - 1)^2 = 1 \ ; \ about \ the \ x - axis$$

Select the correct answer.

a. $V = 2\pi^2$
b. $V = 2\pi^3$
c. $V = 3\pi^2$
d. $V = 4\pi^2$
e. $V = 4\pi^3$

1. -1, 1

2. $\dfrac{1000}{3}$

3. 5.67

4. T

5. a

6. 0.02381π

7. b

8. $\dfrac{51\pi}{35}$

9. 13.5π

10. $\dfrac{5000\pi}{3}$

11. F

12. 150

13. $\dfrac{\pi z d^2}{3}$

14. $\dfrac{513\pi}{6}$

15. T

16. T

17. $\dfrac{625\pi}{12}$

18. 16π

19. b

20. a

1. Use calculus to find the area of the triangle with the given vertices.

    $$\left(0,\ 0\right),\ \left(4,\ 1\right),\ \left(-1,\ 15\right)$$

2. Use a graph to find approximate x - coordinates of the points of intersection of the given curves.

    $$y = x^6, \quad y = 2\cos x$$

    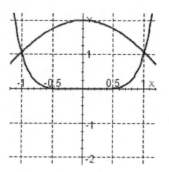

3. The linear density of a 24 m long rod is $36 / \sqrt{x+1}$ kg/m, where x is measured in meters from one end of the rod. Find the average density of the rod?

4. Find the area of the region bounded by the parabola $y = x^2$, the tangent line to this parabola at (2, 4), and the x-axis.

5. Find the number b such that the line $y = b$ divides the region bounded by the curves $y = 7x^2$ and $y = 9$ into two regions with equal area.

6. Find the positive value of c such that the area of the region bounded by the parabolas $y = x^2 - c^2$ and $y = c^2 - x^2$ is 576.

7. Find the volume of the solid obtained by rotating about the x-axis the region under the curve $y = \dfrac{1}{x}$ from $x = 2$ to $x = 6$.

8. Find the volume of the solid obtained by rotating the region bounded by $x = y^2$ and $x = 5y$ about the y-axis.

9.   True or False?

The Mean Value Theorem for Integrals says that if $f(t)$ is continuous on $[a, b]$, then there exists a

number m in $[a, b]$ such that $f(m) = f_{ave} = \dfrac{1}{a - b} \displaystyle\int_a^b f(t)\ dt$.

10.   Find the volume of the solid obtained by rotating the region bounded by $y = \sqrt[4]{x}$ and $y = x$ about the
line $y = 1$.

Select the correct answer.

a. $\dfrac{4\pi}{9}$

b. $\dfrac{\pi}{3}$

c. $\dfrac{1}{3}$

d. $\dfrac{4}{9}$

e. $\dfrac{\pi}{9}$

11.   Find the volume of the solid obtained by rotating the region bounded by $y = x^5$ and $x = y^5$ about the
line $x = -1$.

12.   Find the volume of a right circular cone with height $h = 48$ and base radius $r = 4$.

13.   The velocity v of blood that flows in a blood vessel with radius R and length l at a distance r from the
central axis is $v(r) = \dfrac{P}{4ql}\left(R^2 - r^2\right)$ where P is the pressure difference between the ends of the vessel
and q is the viscosity of the blood. Find the average velocity (with respect to r) over the
interval $0 \le r \le R$.

14.   The volume of the frustum of a pyramid with square base of side $b = 18$, square top of side $a = 5$, and
height $h = 5$ is 2.195.

True or false?

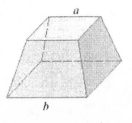

15. Find the volume of a pyramid with height $h = 27$ and rectangular base with dimensions 10 and 20.

16. Find the volume of a pyramid with height 5 and base an equilateral triangle with side $a = 4$.

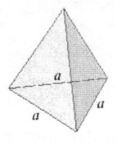

Select the correct answer.

   a.   2.89
   b.   23.09
   c.   11.55
   d.   46.19
   e.   12.89

17. True or False?

If the center of each of two spheres, each having radius $r = 7$, lies on the surface of the other sphere, then the volume common to both spheres is $\dfrac{1715\pi}{12}$.

18. Find the average value of the function $f(t) = 5t \sin\left(t^2 \right)$ on the interval $\left[0, \sqrt{\pi} \right]$.

Select the correct answer.

   a. $\dfrac{10}{\sqrt{\pi}}$

   b. $\dfrac{5}{\sqrt{\pi}}$

   c. $\dfrac{10}{\pi}$

   d. $\dfrac{5}{\pi}$

   e. $\dfrac{1}{\pi}$

19. In a certain city the temperature t hours after 4 A.M. was modeled by the function

$$T(t) = 11 + 30\sin\left(\frac{\pi t}{19}\right).$$

Find the average temperature during the period from 4 A.M. to 4 P.M.

20. The temperature of a metal rod, 3 m long, is $2x$ (in degrees C) at a distance x meters from one end of the rod. What is the average temperature of the rod?

Select the correct answer.

a. $T_{ave} = 41°\,C$

b. $T_{ave} = 3°\,C$

c. $T_{ave} = 30°\,C$

d. $T_{ave} = 43°\,C$

e. $T_{ave} = 0°\,C$

1. 30.5

2. -1, 1

3. 12

4. 8/3

5. 5.67

6. 6

7. $\dfrac{\pi}{3}$

8. $\dfrac{1250\pi}{3}$

9. F

10. b

11. $\dfrac{452\pi}{231}$

12. 256π

13. $\dfrac{PR^2}{6ql}$

14. F

15. 1800

16. c

17. T

18. b

19. 32.2

20. b

1. Evaluate the integral.

    $$\int_0^4 te^{-t}\ dt$$

2. Evaluate the integral.

    $$\int_0^{\pi/20} \cos^5 10x\ dx$$

3. Find the average value of the function $f(x)$ in the interval $\left[-\pi,\ \pi\right]$.

    $$f(x) = \sin^3 x \cos^3 x$$

4. Household electricity is supplied in the form of alternating current that varies from 170 V to -170 V with a frequency of 60 cycles per second (Hz). The voltage is thus given by the function $E(t)$, where t is the time in seconds. Voltmeters read the RMS (root-mean-square) voltage, which is the square root of the average value of $[E(t)]^2$ over one cycle. Calculate the RMS voltage of household current. Round your answer to the nearest integer.

    $$E(t) = 170\sin(120\pi t)$$

5. Evaluate the integral using the indicated trigonometric substitution.

    $$\int \frac{dx}{x^2\sqrt{x^2-16}};\ \ x = 4\sec\theta$$

6. Evaluate the integral.

    $$\int \frac{dx}{\left(x^2+2x+2\right)^2}$$

7. A torus is generated by rotating the circle $x^2 + (y-7)^2 = 1$ about the x axis. Find the volume enclosed by the torus. Round the answer to the nearest hundredth.

8. Use long division to evaluate the integral.

$$\int \frac{x^2}{x+5}\, dx$$

9. Find the volume of the resulting solid if the region under the curve $y = 1/\left(x^2 + 3x + 2\right)$ from $x = 0$ to $x = 1$ is rotated about the x-axis. Round your answer to four decimal places.

10. Evaluate the integral.

$$\int \frac{\cos x}{4 + \sin^2 x}\, dx$$

11. Evaluate the integral.

$$\int_{-1}^{\sqrt{3}} \frac{e^{\arctan y}}{1 + y^2}\, dy$$

12. Evaluate the integral.

$$\int \frac{1}{\sqrt{x+1} + \sqrt{x}}\, dx$$

13. Use Simpson's Rule to approximate the given integral with the specified value of n. Round your answer to six decimal places.

$$\int_0^{1/2} \sin\left(e^{t/4}\right) dt, \qquad n = 8$$

14. Estimate the area of the shaded region in the graph by using the Trapezoidal Rule with $n = 4$.

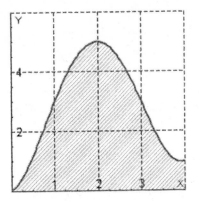

Round the answer to the nearest tenth.

15. For what values of K is the following integral improper?

$$\int_0^K \frac{x}{x^2 - 19x + 90} \, dx$$

Give your answer as an inequality.

16. Find the area under the curve from $x = 1$ to $x = t$.

$$y(x) = \frac{109}{x^5}$$

Evaluate it for $t = 10$, 100, and 1000 in order to find the total area under the curve for to $x \geq 1$.

17. Evaluate the following integral if it is convergent.

$$\int_0^\infty e^{-6x} \, dx$$

Give your answer as an expression in terms of e. If the integral is not convergent, enter "divergent."

18. Evaluate the following integral.

$$\int_0^1 \frac{3\ln 4x}{\sqrt{x}} \, dx$$

19. Evaluate the following integral.

$$\int_0^1 \frac{5}{x^{0.2}} \, dx$$

20. A manufacturer of lightbulbs wants to produce bulbs that last about 800 hours but, of course, some bulbs burn out faster than others. Let $F(t)$ be the fraction of the company's bulbs that burn out before t hours. $F(t)$ lies between 0 and 1.

Let $r(t) = F'(t)$. What is the value of $\int_0^\infty r(t) \, dt$?

ANSWER KEY

Stewart - Calculus ET 5e Chapter 7 Form A

1. $1 - 5e^{-4}$

2. $\dfrac{4}{75}$

3. 0

4. 120

5. $\dfrac{\frac{1}{16}\sqrt{x^2 - 16}}{x} + c$

6. $\dfrac{1}{2}\left((\tan x + 1)\right)^{-1} + \dfrac{1}{2}\left(\dfrac{x+1}{x^2 + 2x + 2}\right) + c$

7. 138.17

8. $\dfrac{x^2}{2} - 5x + 25\ln\left(\left|\,x + 5\,\right|\right) + C$

9. 0.286835

10. $\dfrac{1}{2}\left(\tan\left(\dfrac{\sin(x)}{2}\right)\right)^{-1} + c$

11. $e^{\pi/3} - e^{-\pi/4}$

12. $\dfrac{2}{3}\left((x+1)^{3/2} - x^{3/2}\right) + C$

13. 0.437117

14. 11.5

15. $K \geq 9$

16. 27.25

17. $\dfrac{1}{6}$

18. $6\ln(4) - 12$

19. 6.25

20. 1

1. Evaluate the integral.

$$\int 20xe^{5x} \, dx$$

2. Evaluate the integral.

$$\int x^2 \ln(19x) \, dx$$

3. Evaluate the integral.

$$\int t^3 e^{3t} \, dt$$

4. Evaluate the integral.

$$\int_0^1 (x^2 + 1)e^{-x} \, dx$$

Enter your answer in terms of e.

5. Evaluate the integral.

$$\int_0^{100} \sqrt{t} \ln t \, dt$$

6. Evaluate the integral.

$$\int_4^7 e^{\sqrt{t}} \, dt$$

7. Evaluate the integral.

$$\int_0^{\pi/20} \cos^5 10x \, dx$$

8. Evaluate the integral.

$$\int_{\pi/6}^{\pi/2} \cot^2 x \, dx$$

9. Evaluate the integral.

$$\int \frac{\tan^2 x - 1}{\sec^2 x} \, dx$$

10. Find the average value of the function $f(x)$ in the interval $[-\pi, \pi]$.

$$f(x) = \sin^4 x \cos^3 x$$

11. Find the volume obtained by rotating the region bounded by the given curves about $y = -1$.

$$y = \sin x, \quad x = 0, \quad x = \pi, \quad y = 0$$

12. Evaluate the integral.

$$\int \frac{x^2}{\left(36 - x^2\right)^{3/2}} \, dx$$

13. Evaluate the integral.

$$\int_{1/2}^{2/3} x^3 \sqrt{4 - 9x^2} \, dx$$

14. Evaluate the integral.

$$\int \frac{dx}{\left(x^2 + 8x + 17\right)^2}$$

15. Evaluate the integral.

$$\int e^t \sqrt{49 - e^{2t}} \, dt$$

16. Find the average value of $f(x) = \left(25 - x^2\right)^{3/2}$ on the interval $[\,0\,,5\,]$.

17. A water storage tank has the shape of a cylinder with diameter 10 ft. It is mounted so that the circular cross-sections are vertical. If the depth of the water is 8 ft, what percentage of the total capacity is being used? Round the answer to the nearest tenth.

18. Evaluate the integral.

$$\int \frac{x+12}{(x+5)(x-2)}\ dx$$

19. Evaluate the integral.

$$\int_{-1/\sqrt{3}}^{1/\sqrt{3}} \frac{e^{\arctan y}}{1+y^2}\ dy$$

20. Evaluate the integral.

$$\int_{-\sqrt{2}/2}^{\sqrt{2}/2} \frac{x^2}{\sqrt{1-x^2}}\ dx$$

1. $4xe^{5x} - \dfrac{4}{5}e^{5x} + C$

2. $\dfrac{1}{3}x^3 \ln(19x) - \dfrac{1}{9}x^3 + C$

3. $\dfrac{e^{3t}\left(27t^3 - 27t^2 + 18t - 6\right)}{81} + C$

4. $-6e^{-1} + 3$

5. $\dfrac{4000}{3}\ln 2 + \dfrac{4000}{3}\ln 5 - \dfrac{4000}{9}$

6. 31.61

7. $\dfrac{4}{75}$

8. $\sqrt{3} - \dfrac{\pi}{3}$

9. $-\dfrac{1}{2}\sin(2x) + C$

10. 0

11. $\dfrac{\pi^2}{2} + 4\pi$

12. $\dfrac{x}{\sqrt{36 - x^2}} - \left(\sin\left(\dfrac{x}{6}\right)\right)^{-1} + C$

13. $\dfrac{413}{38880}\sqrt{7}$

14. $\dfrac{1}{2}\left(\left(\tan(x+4)\right)^{-1} + \dfrac{x+4}{x^2 + 8x + 17}\right) + C$

15. $\dfrac{7^2}{2}\arcsin\left(\dfrac{e^t}{7}\right) + \dfrac{1}{2}e^t\sqrt{49 - e^{2t}} + C$

16. $\dfrac{125(3\pi)}{16}$

17. 85.8

18. $-\ln\left(|\,x+5\,|\right) + 2\ln\left(|\,x-2\,|\right) + C$

19. $e^{\pi/6} - e^{-\pi/6}$

20. $\left(\dfrac{\pi}{4} - \dfrac{1}{2}\right)$

1. Find the average value of the function $f(x)$ in the interval $[-\pi, \pi]$.

$$f(x) = \sin^2 x \cos^3 x$$

Select the correct answer.

a. π

b. 0

c. $\dfrac{\pi}{5}$

d. $\dfrac{\pi}{6}$

e. $\dfrac{\pi}{12}$

2. Find the reduction formula for the integral.

$$\int \left(\ln(15x + 7)\right)^n \, dx$$

Select the correct answer.

a. $\dfrac{(15x+7)\ln(15x+7)^n}{15} - n\int \left(\ln(15x+7)\right)^{n-2} \, dx$

b. $\dfrac{(15x+7)\ln(15x+7)^{n-1}}{15} - n\int \left(\ln(15x+7)\right)^{n-2} \, dx$

c. $\dfrac{(15x+7)\ln(15x+7)^n}{15} + n\int \left(\ln(15x+7)\right)^{n-1} \, dx$

d. $\dfrac{(15x+7)\ln(15x+7)^n}{15} - n\int \left(\ln(15x+7)\right)^{n-1} \, dx$

e. none of these

3. A particle moves on a straight line with velocity function $v(t) = \sin \omega t \cos^3 \omega t$. Find its position function $s = f(t)$ if $f(0) = 0$.

Select the correct answer.

a. $\dfrac{\sin^5 \omega t - 1}{5\omega}$

b. $\dfrac{\cos^3 \omega t + 1}{3\omega}$

c. $\dfrac{1 - \cos^4 \omega t + 1}{3\omega}$

d. $\dfrac{1 - \cos^4 \omega t}{4\omega}$

e. $\dfrac{\sin^4 \omega t + 1}{4\omega}$

4. Evaluate the integral using the indicated trigonometric substitution.

$$\int \frac{x^3}{\sqrt{x^2 + 25}}\, dx; \quad x = 5 \tan \theta$$

Select the correct answer.

a. $-\dfrac{2}{3}\left(x^2 + 25\right)^{3/2} + x^2 \sqrt{x^2 + 25} + C$

b. $\left(x^2 + 25\right)^{3/2} - 5\sqrt{x^2 + 25} + C$

c. $\dfrac{1}{3}\left(x^2 + 25\right)^{3/2} - \sqrt{x^2 + 25} + C$

d. $\left(x^2 + 25\right)^{3/2} - \sqrt{x^2 + 25} + C$

e. $\dfrac{3}{2}\left(x + 25\right)^{3/2} - 25\sqrt{x + 25} + C$

5. Evaluate the integral.

$$\int \frac{dx}{x\sqrt{x^2+6}}$$

Select the correct answer.

a. $\dfrac{1}{\sqrt{6}} \ln\left|\dfrac{\sqrt{x^2+6}-\sqrt{6}}{x^2}\right| + C$

b. $\dfrac{1}{\sqrt{6}} \ln\left|\dfrac{\sqrt{x^2+6}-\sqrt{6}}{x}\right| + C$

c. $\dfrac{1}{\sqrt{6}} \ln\left(\dfrac{\sqrt{x^2+6}-\sqrt{6}}{x^2}\right) + C$

d. $\dfrac{1}{\sqrt{6}} \ln\left(\dfrac{\sqrt{x^2+6}-\sqrt{6}}{x}\right) + C$

e. $\dfrac{1}{\sqrt{6}} \ln\left(\dfrac{\sqrt{6x^2+1}-\sqrt{6}}{x^2}\right) + C$

6. Use long division to evaluate the integral.

$$\int \frac{x^2}{x+2}\, dx$$

Select the correct answer.

a. $\dfrac{x^2}{2} - 2x + 4\ln(x+2) + C$

b. $\dfrac{x^2}{2} + 2x + 4\ln(x-2) + C$

c. $\dfrac{x^2}{2} + 2x + 4\ln|x+2| + C$

d. $\dfrac{x^2}{2} - 2x + 4\ln|x+2| + C$

e. $\dfrac{x^2}{2} - 2x + 2\ln|x+2| + C$

f. $x - 2x + 4\ln|x-2| + C$

7. Evaluate the integral.

$$\int \frac{8t^3 - 3t^2 + 13t - 3}{(t^2 + 1)(t^2 + 2)} \, dx$$

Select the correct answer.

a. $\frac{5}{2}\ln(t^2 + 1) + \frac{15}{2}\ln(t^2 + 2) - (3/\sqrt{2})\tan^{-1}(t/\sqrt{2}) + C$

b. $\frac{7}{2}\ln(t^2 + 1) + \frac{3}{2}\ln(t^2 + 2) - (3/\sqrt{2})\tan^{-1}(t/\sqrt{2}) + C$

c. $\frac{5}{2}\ln(t^2 + 1) + \frac{3}{2}\ln(t^2 + 2) - (3/\sqrt{2})\tan^{-1}(t/\sqrt{2}) + C$

d. $\frac{7}{2}\ln(t^2 + 1) + \frac{15}{2}\ln(t^2 + 2) - (3/\sqrt{2})\tan^{-1}(t/\sqrt{2}) + C$

e. $\frac{3}{2}\ln(t^2 + 1) + \frac{17}{2}\ln(t^2 + 2) - (3/\sqrt{2})\tan^{-1}(t/\sqrt{2}) + C$

8. Evaluate the integral.

$$\int \frac{1 + 5e^x}{1 - e^x} \, dx$$

Select the correct answer.

a. $6x - 5\ln(e^x - 1) + C$

b. $x + 8\ln(e^x - 1) + C$

c. $8x + 6\ln|e^x - 1| + C$

d. $x - 6\ln|e^x - 1| + C$

e. $6x - 5\ln(e^x + 1) + C$

9. Evaluate the integral.

$$\int_{\pi/6}^{\pi/3} \frac{\ln(\tan x)}{\sin x \cos x}\, dx$$

Select the correct answer.

a. 0

b. $-\dfrac{1}{8}(\ln 3)^2$

c. $\dfrac{1}{8}(\ln 3)^2$

d. $-\dfrac{1}{6}(\ln 3)^2$

e. $\dfrac{1}{6}(\ln 3)^2$

10. Use the Table of Integrals to evaluate the integral.

$$\int \frac{dx}{e^x(5+10e^x)}$$

Select the correct answer.

a. $\dfrac{-e^{-x} + 2\ln(5e^{-x} + 2)}{25} + C$

b. $-5e^{-x} + 2\ln(5e^{-x} + 2) + C$

c. $\dfrac{-5e^{-x} + 2\ln(5e^{-x} + 2)}{5} + C$

d. $-5e^{-x} + 2\ln(5e^{-x} + 2)$

e. $\dfrac{-e^{-x} + 2\ln(e^{-x} + 2)}{5} + C$

11. Find the volume of the resulting solid if the region under the curve $y = 1/(x^2 + 3x + 2)$ from $x = 0$ to $x = 5$ is rotated about the x-axis.

    Select the correct answer.

    a. $\pi\left(\dfrac{25}{21} + \ln\left(\dfrac{49}{144}\right)\right)$

    b. $\pi\left(\dfrac{17}{15} + \ln\left(\dfrac{9}{25}\right)\right)$

    c. $\pi\left(\dfrac{25}{21} + \ln\left(\dfrac{9}{25}\right)\right)$

    d. $\pi\left(\dfrac{17}{15} + \ln\left(\dfrac{49}{144}\right)\right)$

    e. $\pi\left(\dfrac{9}{25} + \ln\left(\dfrac{25}{144}\right)\right)$

12. Use the Table of Integrals to evaluate the integral.

$$\int \frac{x^5 dx}{\sqrt{x^{12} - 3}}$$

    Select the correct answer.

    a. $\dfrac{1}{6}\ln\left|x^6 + \sqrt{x^{12} - 3}\right| + C$

    b. $\dfrac{1}{6}\ln\left(x^6 + \sqrt{x^6 - 3}\right) + C$

    c. $\ln\left(x^6 + \sqrt{x^{12} - 3}\right) + C$

    d. $\ln\left|x^6 + \sqrt{x^{12} - 3}\right| + C$

    e. $\dfrac{1}{6}\ln\left|x^6 + \sqrt{x^6 - 3}\right| + C$

13. Evaluate the integral $\displaystyle\int_0^1 \frac{1}{x^p}\ dx$ for different values of p. Which of the following integrals is equal to 1.25?

Select the correct answer.

a. $\displaystyle\int_0^1 \frac{1}{x^{0.2}}\ dx$

b. $\displaystyle\int_0^1 \frac{1}{x^{0.5}}\ dx$

c. $\displaystyle\int_0^1 \frac{1}{x^{0.7}}\ dx$

d. $\displaystyle\int_0^1 \frac{1}{x^2}\ dx$

e. $\displaystyle\int_0^1 \frac{1}{x^{2.5}}\ dx$

14. Evaluate the integral.

$$\int t^3 e^{10t}\ dt$$

Select the correct answer.

a. $\dfrac{e^{10t}\left(1{,}000t^3 + 300t^2 - 60t + 6\right)}{10{,}000} + C$

b. $\dfrac{e^{10t}\left(1{,}000t^3 - 300t^2 - 60t - 6\right)}{10{,}000} + C$

c. $\dfrac{e^{10t}\left(1{,}000t^3 - 300t^2 + 60t + 6\right)}{10{,}000} + C$

d. $\dfrac{e^{10t}\left(1{,}000t^3 - 300t^2 + 60t - 6\right)}{10{,}000} + C$

e. none of these

15. Evaluate the integral.

$$\int\limits_0^4 \left(x^2 + 1\right) e^{-x} \, dx$$

Select the correct answer.

    a. $-27e^4 + 3$

    b. $-27e^{-4} - 1$

    c. $27e^{-4} + 3$

    d. $-27e^{-4} + 3$

    e.   none of these

16. Evaluate the indefinite integral.

$$\int x \cos 7x \, dx$$

Select the correct answer.

    a. $\dfrac{1}{49} \sin 7x + \dfrac{x}{7} \cos 7x + C$

    b. $\dfrac{1}{7} \cos 7x + \dfrac{x}{7} \sin 7x + C$

    c. $\dfrac{x}{49} \cos 7x + \dfrac{x}{7} \sin 7x + C$

    d. $\dfrac{1}{49} \cos 7x + \dfrac{x}{7} \sin 7x + C$

    e.   none of these

17. Evaluate the integral.

$$\int \frac{dx}{\left(x^2 + 2x + 2\right)^2}$$

Select the correct answer.

a. $\dfrac{1}{2}\left(\tan^{-1}(x+1) + \dfrac{x+1}{x^2 + 2x + 2} \right) + C$

b. $\dfrac{1}{2}\left(\tan(x+1) + \dfrac{1}{x^2 + 2x + 2} \right) + C$

c. $\dfrac{1}{2}\left(\tan(x+1) + \dfrac{x+1}{x^2 + 2x + 2} \right) + C$

d. $\dfrac{1}{2}\left(\tan^{-1}(x+1) + \dfrac{1}{x^2 + 2x + 2} \right) + C$

e. $\dfrac{1}{2}\left(\tan^{-1}(x+2) + \dfrac{1}{x^2 + 2} \right) + C$

18. Evaluate the integral.

$$\int e^t \sqrt{25 - e^{2t}}\ dt$$

Select the correct answer.

a. $\dfrac{25}{2}\arcsin\left(\dfrac{e^t}{5}\right) + \dfrac{1}{2}e^t\sqrt{25 - e^{2t}} + C$

b. $\arcsin\left(\dfrac{e^t}{5}\right) + \dfrac{1}{2}\sqrt{25 - e^{2t}} + C$

c. $\dfrac{25}{2}\arcsin\left(\dfrac{e^t}{5}\right) + \dfrac{1}{2}\sqrt{25 - e^{2t}} + C$

d. $\arcsin\left(\dfrac{e^t}{5}\right) + \dfrac{1}{2}e^t\sqrt{25 - e^{2t}} + C$

e. $\dfrac{25}{2}\arcsin\left(\dfrac{e^{2t}}{5}\right) + \dfrac{1}{2}\sqrt{5 - e^t} + C$

19. Find the area of the region bounded by the hyperbola $9x^2 - 4y^2 = 36$ and the line $x = 5$.

Select the correct answer.

a. $\dfrac{15}{2}\sqrt{21} - 6\ln\left|\dfrac{5+\sqrt{21}}{2}\right|$

b. $\dfrac{\pi}{2}\sqrt{21} + \ln\left|\dfrac{5+\sqrt{21}}{2}\right|$

c. $\dfrac{15}{2}\sqrt{21} + \ln\left|\dfrac{5+\sqrt{21}}{2}\right|$

d. $\dfrac{\pi}{2}\sqrt{21} - 6\ln\left|\dfrac{5+\sqrt{21}}{2}\right|$

e. $\dfrac{13}{2}\sqrt{21} - \ln\left|\dfrac{6+\sqrt{21}}{2}\right|$

20. Evaluate the integral using integration by parts with the indicated choices of u and dv.

$$\int 12\theta\cos\theta\ d\theta, \quad u = 12\theta, \quad dv = \cos\theta\ d\theta$$

Select the correct answer.

a. $12\theta\sin\theta + 12\cos\theta + C$

b. $12\theta\sin\theta - 12\cos\theta + C$

c. $12\theta\cos\theta + 12\sin\theta + C$

d. $12\theta\sin\theta + 12\cos 2\theta + C$

e.   none of these

1. b

2. d

3. d

4. a

5. b

6. d

7. c

8. d

9. a

10. e

11. a

12. a

13. a

14. d

15. d

16. d

17. a

18. a

19. a

20. a

1. Evaluate the integral.

$$\int \sin^2 x \cos^5 x \; dx$$

Select the correct answer.

a. $-\sin^3 x + \sin^5 x - \sin^7 x + C$

b. $\dfrac{1}{3}\sin^3 x - \dfrac{2}{5}\sin^5 x + \dfrac{1}{7}\sin^7 x + C$

c. $-\dfrac{1}{3}\sin^3 x + \dfrac{2}{5}\sin^5 x - \dfrac{1}{7}\sin^7 x + C$

d. $\sin^3 x - \sin^5 x + \sin^7 x + C$

e. $-\sin^3 x + \dfrac{2}{5}\sin^5 x - \sin^7 x + C$

2. Evaluate the integral.

$$\int x \ln(1+x) \; dx$$

Select the correct answer.

a. $\dfrac{1}{4}x - \dfrac{1}{8}x^2 + \dfrac{1}{12}x^3 - \dfrac{1}{16}x^4 + \dfrac{x^4}{4}\ln(1+x) - \dfrac{1}{4}\ln(1+x) + C$

b. $\dfrac{1}{2}x - \dfrac{1}{4}x^2 + \dfrac{x^2}{2}\ln(1+x) - \dfrac{1}{2}\ln(1+x) + C$

c. $-\dfrac{1}{3}x + \dfrac{1}{6}x^2 - \dfrac{1}{9}x^3 + \dfrac{x^3}{3}\ln(1+x) + \dfrac{1}{3}\ln(1+x) + C$

d. $\dfrac{1}{6}x^2 - \dfrac{1}{9}x^3 + \dfrac{x^3}{3}\ln(1+x) + \dfrac{1}{3}\ln(1+x) + C$

e. $-\dfrac{1}{3}x + \dfrac{1}{6}x^2 - \dfrac{1}{9}x^4 + \dfrac{1}{3}\ln(1+x) + C$

3. Evaluate the integral.

$$\int \frac{1}{e^{3x} - e^x} \, dx$$

Select the correct answer.

a. $e^{-x} + \dfrac{1}{2} \ln \left| \dfrac{e^x + 1}{e^x - 1} \right| + C$

b. $-e^{-x} - \dfrac{1}{2} \ln \left| \dfrac{e^x - 1}{e^x + 1} \right| + C$

c. $-e^{-x} - \dfrac{1}{2} \ln \left| \dfrac{e^x + 1}{e^x - 1} \right| + C$

d. $e^{-x} + \dfrac{1}{2} \ln \left| \dfrac{e^x - 1}{e^x + 1} \right| + C$

e. $e^{-2x} + \ln \left| \dfrac{e^x - 1}{e^x + 1} \right| + C$

4. Use the Table of Integrals to evaluate the integral.

$$\int_1^4 \frac{1}{x^2 \sqrt{4x^2 - 1}} \, dx$$

Select the correct answer. The choices are rounded to the nearest thousandth.

a. 0.252
b. 0.112
c. 0.762
d. 1.272
e. 0.225

5. Use the Table of Integrals to evaluate the integral.

$$\int \frac{\sqrt{25x^2 - 1}}{x^2} \, dx$$

Select the correct answer.

a. $\dfrac{\sqrt{25x^2 - 1}}{x} + \ln\left|5x + \sqrt{25x^2}\right| + C$

b. $5\ln\left|5x + \sqrt{25x^2 - 1}\right| + C$

c. $\dfrac{\sqrt{25x^2 - 1}}{x} + 5\ln\left|5x + \sqrt{25x^2 - 1}\right|$

d. $-\dfrac{\sqrt{25x^2 - 1}}{x} + 5\ln\left|5x + \sqrt{25x^2 - 1}\right| + C$

e. $\dfrac{\sqrt{5x^2 - 1}}{x} + \ln\left|x + \sqrt{5x^2 - 1}\right| + C$

6. Use the Comparison Theorem to determine which of the following integrals is convergent.

Select the correct answer.

a. $\displaystyle\int_1^\infty \frac{5\sqrt{1 + \sqrt{3x}}}{\sqrt{3x}} \, dx$

b. $\displaystyle\int_1^\infty \frac{6\sin^2 5x}{9 + x^2} \, dx$

7. The left, right, Trapezoidal, and Midpoint Rule approximations were used to estimate $\int_0^2 f(x)\ dx$, where f is the function whose graph is shown. The estimates were 0.5864, 0.8161, 0.2317, and 0.7618, and the same number of subintervals were used in each case.

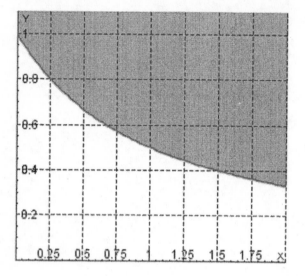

Choose the correct statement.

a. $L_n = 0.5864$, $T_n = 0.7618$, $M_n = 0.8161$ and $R_n = 0.2317$

b. $L_n = 0.8161$, $T_n = 0.2317$, $M_n = 0.5864$ and $R_n = 0.7618$

c. $L_n = 0.5864$, $T_n = 0.2317$, $M_n = 0.8161$ and $R_n = 0.7618$

d. $L_n = 0.8161$, $T_n = 0.7618$, $M_n = 0.5864$ and $R_n = 0.2317$

e.   none of these

8. Evaluate the integral.

$$\int_{\pi/6}^{\pi/3} \frac{\ln(\tan x)}{\sin x \cos x} dx$$

Select the correct answer.

a. $-\frac{1}{8}(\ln 3)^2$

b. 0

c. $\frac{1}{8}(\ln 3)^2$

d. 1.5

e. $-\frac{1}{3}(\ln 8)^2$

9. Use the Midpoint Rule to approximate the given integral with the specified value of n. Compare your result to the actual value and find the error in the approximation.

$$\int_{2}^{3} e^{-\sqrt{x}} dx, \quad n = 6$$

Choose the correct answer from below. The choices give the error only.

a. 0.00014
b. 0.00004
c. 0.10004
d. -0.00016
e. -0.00096
f. -0.00496

10. Use the Trapezoidal Rule to approximate $\int_{2}^{3} e^{3/x} dx$ for $n = 4$.

Select the correct answer. The choices are rounded to four decimal places.

a. 3.4215
b. 3.4437
c. 3.4227
d. 3.5227
e. 3.4232
f. 3.4177

11. Find the approximation T_{10} for the integral $\displaystyle\int_0^1 e^x \, dx$ and the corresponding error E_T .

Select the correct answer. Only the error is given.

    a.   -0.001432
    b.   -0.001232
    c.   -0.000432
    d.   -0.101432
    e.   -0.001833
    f.   -0.003568

12. Evaluate the following integral if it is convergent.

$$I = \int_0^\infty e^{-2x} \, dx$$

Select the correct answer.

    a. $I = \dfrac{1}{2}$

    b. $I = 2$

    c. $I = -2$

    d. $I = -\dfrac{1}{2}$

    e.   the integral is divergent

13. The region $\left\{ (x,\ y) \mid x \geq -5,\ 0 \leq y \leq e^{-x/3} \right\}$ is represented below.

Find the area of this region.

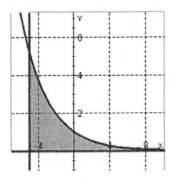

Select the correct answer. The choices are rounded to the nearest hundredth.

a.   Area = 15.89
b.   Area = 15.88
c.   Area = 16.08
d.   Area = 15.87
e.   Area = 17.89

14. A manufacturer of lightbulbs wants to produce bulbs that last about 600 hours but, of course, some bulbs burn out faster than others. Let $F(t)$ be the fraction of the company's bulbs that burn out before t hours. $F(t)$ lies between 0 and 1.

Let $r(t) = F'(t)$. What is the value of $\int_{0}^{\infty} r(t)dt$?

Select the correct answer.

a. $\int_{0}^{\infty} r(t)dt = 600$

b. $\int_{0}^{\infty} r(t)dt = 1$

c. $\int_{0}^{\infty} r(t)dt = 0$.

d. $\int_{0}^{\infty} r(t)dt = 2$

e.   The integral is divergent.

15. Let a and b be real numbers. What integral must appear in place of the question mark "?" to make the following statement true?

$$\int_{-\infty}^{a} \frac{8}{x^2+5}\,dx \;+\; \int_{a}^{\infty} \frac{8}{x^2+5}\,dx = ? \;+\; \int_{b}^{\infty} \frac{8}{x^2+5}\,dx$$

Select the correct answer.

a. $\displaystyle\int_{b}^{-\infty} \frac{8}{x^2+5}\,dx$

b. $\displaystyle\int_{-\infty}^{a} \frac{5}{x^2+8}\,dx$

c. $\displaystyle\int_{-\infty}^{b} \frac{8}{x^2+5}\,dx$

d. $\displaystyle\int_{b}^{-\infty} \frac{8}{x^2-5}\,dx$

e. none of these

16. Use a computer algebra system to evaluate the integral.

$$\int 5\sin^4 x\;dx$$

Select the correct answer.

a. $-\dfrac{5}{4}\sin^3 x\cos x - \dfrac{15}{8}\sin^2 x + \dfrac{15}{8}x + C$

b. $-\dfrac{5}{2}\sin^2 x\cos x - \dfrac{15}{8}\cos x\sin x + \dfrac{15}{6}x + C$

c. $-\dfrac{5}{2}\sin^3 x\cos x - \dfrac{5}{8}\cos x\sin x + \dfrac{5}{8}x + C$

d. $-\dfrac{5}{4}\sin^2 x\cos x + \dfrac{15}{8}\cos x\sin x + x + C$

e. $-\dfrac{5}{4}\sin^3 x\cos x - \dfrac{15}{8}\cos x\sin x + \dfrac{15}{8}x + C$

17. Evaluate the integral.

$$\int \frac{x \ln x}{\sqrt{x^2 - 1}} \, dx$$

Select the correct answer.

a. $\sqrt{x^2 - 1}(\ln x) - \sqrt{x^2 - 1} + \tan^{-1} \sqrt{x^2 - 1} + C$

b. $2\sqrt{x} \tan^{-1} \sqrt{x} - \ln(1 + x) + C$

c. $\frac{2}{3}(x + 1)^{3/2} - \frac{2}{3} x^{3/2} + C$

d. $\frac{2}{3}(x + 1)^{3/2} - \frac{3}{2} x^{4/3} + C$

c. $\frac{2}{3}\sqrt{x^2 - 1} - x \ln\left(\sqrt{x^2 - 1}\right) + C$

18. Use the Table of Integrals to evaluate the integral.

$$\int \frac{x}{\sqrt{x^2 - 8x}} \, dx$$

Select the correct answer.

a. $\sqrt{x^2 - 8x} + 4 \ln\left|x - 4 + \sqrt{x^2 - 8x}\right| + C$

b. $\sqrt{x^2 - 4x} - 4 \ln\left|x - 4 + \sqrt{x^2 - 8x}\right| + C$

c. $\sqrt{x^2 - 8x} + 4 \ln\left(x - 4 + \sqrt{x^2 - 8x}\right) + C$

d. $\sqrt{x^2 - 8x} + \ln\left|x - 4 + \sqrt{x^2 - 8x}\right| + C$

e. $\sqrt{x^2 - 4x} + 2 \ln\left(x - 4 + \sqrt{x^2 - 8x}\right) + C$

19. Evaluate the integral.

$$\int \frac{1}{-e^{-x}+e^{x}}\,dx$$

Select the correct answer.

a. $\ln\left(\dfrac{|e^{x}-1|}{e^{x}+1}\right)+C$

b. $\dfrac{1}{2}\ln\left(\dfrac{|e^{x}-1|}{e^{x}+1}\right)+C$

c. $-\dfrac{1}{2}\ln\left(\dfrac{|e^{x}-1|}{e^{x}+1}\right)+C$

d. $-\ln\left(\dfrac{|e^{x}-1|}{e^{x}+1}\right)+C$

e. $-\ln\left(\dfrac{|e^{x}-1|}{e^{x}}\right)+C$

20. Use the Table of Integrals to evaluate the integral.

$$\int e^{4x}\sin 2x\,dx$$

Select the correct answer.

a. $-\dfrac{1}{5}e^{4x}\sin 2x-\dfrac{1}{10}e^{4x}\cos 2x$

b. $\dfrac{1}{5}e^{4x}\sin 2x-\dfrac{1}{10}e^{4x}\cos 2x+C$

c. $\dfrac{1}{5}e^{4x}\sin 2x-2e^{4x}\cos 2x+C$

d. $e^{4x}\sin 2x-\dfrac{1}{8}e^{4x}\cos 2x+C$

e. $\dfrac{1}{5}e^{x}\sin x-\dfrac{1}{10}e^{x}\cos x+C$

1. b

2. b

3. d

4. a

5. d

6. b

7. d

8. b

9. b

10. c

11. a

12. a

13. b

14. b

15. c

16. e

17. a

18. a

19. b

20. b

1. Evaluate the integral using integration by parts with the indicated choices of u and dv.

$$\int 9\theta \cos\theta \; d\theta, \quad u = 9\theta, \quad dv = \cos\theta \, d\theta$$

Select the correct answer.

a. $9\theta \sin\theta + 9\cos\theta + C$
b. $9\sin\theta + 9\cos\theta + C$
c. $9\theta \cos\theta + 9\sin\theta + C$
d. $9\theta \sin\theta - 9\cos\theta + C$
e. none of these

2. Evaluate the integral.

$$\int_0^1 \frac{x^3}{\sqrt{36 - x^2}} \, dx$$

3. Find the area of the region bounded by the hyperbola $9x^2 - 4y^2 = 36$ and the line $x = 4$.

4. A torus is generated by rotating the circle $x^2 + (y - 8)^2 = 25$ about the x-axis. Find the volume enclosed by the torus. Round the answer to the nearest hundredth.

5. Evaluate the integral using the indicated trigonometric substitution.

$$\int \frac{x^3}{\sqrt{x^2 + 36}} \, dx; \quad x = 6 \tan\theta$$

6. Evaluate the integral.

$$\int \sin^3 10x \; dx$$

7. Write the form of the partial fraction decomposition of the expression. Do not determine the numerical values of the coefficients.

$$\frac{13}{(8x + 9)(x - 9)}$$

8. Use long division to evaluate the integral.

$$\int \frac{x^2}{x+8} \, dx$$

Select the correct answer.

a. $x - 8x + 64 \ln |x - 8| + C$

b. $\frac{x^2}{2} - 8x + 64 \ln(x+8) + C$

c. $\frac{x^2}{2} - 8x + 8 \ln |x+8| + C$

d. $\frac{x^2}{2} + 8x + 64 \ln |x+8| + C$

e. $\frac{x^2}{2} + 8x + 64 \ln(x-8) + C$

f. $\frac{x^2}{2} - 8x + 64 \ln |x+8| + C$

9. Use long division to evaluate the integral.

$$\int \frac{y}{y+3} \, dy$$

10. Use long division to evaluate the integral.

$$\int_0^8 \frac{x^3 + 4x^2 - 12x + 1}{x^2 + 4x - 12} \, dx$$

Select the correct answer. The choices are rounded to 3 decimal places.

a. 31.757
b. 31.969
c. 8.0310
d. 32.031
e. 34.032

11. Use the Table of Integrals to evaluate the integral.

$$\int_3^5 \frac{1}{x^2\sqrt{4x^2 - 1}} \, dx$$

12. If f is a quadratic function such that $f(0) = 1$ and $\displaystyle\int \frac{f(x)}{x^2(x+1)^3}\,dx$ is a rational function, find the value of $f'(0)$.

Select the correct answer.

    a. $f'(0) = 1$
    b. $f'(0) = 2$
    c. $f'(0) = 3$
    d. $f'(0) = 0$
    e. $f'(0) = 5$

13. Evaluate the integral.

$$\int \frac{\cos x}{9 + \sin^2 x}\,dx$$

14. Evaluate the integral.

$$\int x^2 \ln(1 + x)\,dx$$

15. Evaluate the integral.

$$\int \frac{1}{\sqrt{x+1} + \sqrt{x}}\,dx$$

16. Use the Table of Integrals to evaluate the integral.

$$\int \frac{x^2}{\sqrt{x^6 - 4}}\,dx$$

17. Use Simpson's Rule to approximate the given integral with the specified value of n.

$$\int_0^{1/2} \sin\left(e^{t/2}\right) dt, \quad n = 8$$

Select the correct answer. The choices are rounded to six decimal places.

    a.   0.463076
    b.   0.707476
    c.   -0.548035
    d.   0.551976
    e.   0.481335
    f.   0.451976

18. Use the Midpoint Rule to approximate $\int_0^4 \sqrt{x} \sin x\,dx$ for $n = 8$. Round the result to four decimal places.

19. The intensity of light with wavelength λ traveling through a diffraction grating with N slits at an angle θ is given by $I(\theta) = N^2 \dfrac{\sin^2 k}{k^2}$, where $k = \dfrac{\pi N d \sin(\theta)}{\lambda}$ and d is the distance between adjacent slits. A helium-neon laser with wavelength $\lambda = 645.3 \times 10^{-9}$ m is emitting a narrow band of light, given by $-10^{-6} < \theta < 10^{-6}$, through a grating with 1,000 slits spaced 0.0001 m apart. Use the Midpoint Rule with $n = 10$ to estimate the total light intensity $\int_{-10^{-6}}^{10^{-6}} I(\theta)\,d\theta$ emerging from the grating. Round the result to the nearest thousandth.

20. A radar gun was used to record the speed of a runner during the first 5 seconds of a race (see the table). Use Simpson's Rule to estimate the distance the runner covered during those 5 seconds. Round the result to the nearest thousandth.

t (s)	v(m/s)
0	0
0.5	4.22
1.0	7.29
1.5	8.78
2.0	9.38
2.5	10.26
3.0	10.53
3.5	10.66
4.0	10.73
4.5	10.82
5.0	10.97

Select the correct answer.

a. 44.288m
b. 44.798m
c. 44.309m
d. 42.287m
e. 44.398m
f. 44.298m

Stewart - Calculus ET 5e Chapter 7 Form E

1. a

2. 0.042059

3. $6\left(2\sqrt{3} - \ln\left(2 + \sqrt{3}\right)\right)$

4. 3947.84

5. $216\left(\dfrac{\frac{1}{3}\left(x^2 + 36\right)^{1.5}}{6^3} - \dfrac{\sqrt{x^2 + 36}}{6}\right) + C$

6. $\dfrac{1}{30}\left(\cos(10x)\right)^3 - \dfrac{1}{10}\cos(10x) + C$

7. $\dfrac{A}{8x + 9} + \dfrac{B}{x - 9}$

8. f

9. $y - 3\ln\left(|\,y + 3\,|\right) + C$

10. d

11. 0.018

12. c

13. $\dfrac{1}{3}\left(\tan\left(\dfrac{\sin(x)}{3}\right)\right)^{-1} + C$

14. $c - 0.333333x + 0.166667x^2 - 0.111111x^3 + \ln(1 + x)\left(0.333333x^3 + 0.333333\right)$

15. $\left(\dfrac{2}{3}\right)\left((x + 1)^{3/2} - x^{3/2}\right) + C$

16. $\dfrac{1}{3}\ln|\,x^3 + \sqrt{x^6 - 4}\,| + C$

17. f

18. 1.7874

19. 1.949

20. f

1. Evaluate the integral.

$$\int_1^6 e^{\sqrt{t}} \, dt$$

Round your answer to the nearest hundredth.

2. Use integration by parts to find the integral.

$$\int 16xf' \, dx$$

3. Evaluate the integral.

$$\int \cos^4 8t \, dt$$

Select the correct answer.

a. $\dfrac{3}{4}t + \dfrac{1}{16}\sin 16t + \dfrac{1}{128}\sin 32t + C$

b. $\dfrac{3}{8}t + \dfrac{1}{32}\sin 16t + \dfrac{1}{256}\sin 32t + C$

c. $\dfrac{3}{8}t + \dfrac{1}{32}\cos 16t + \dfrac{1}{256}\cos 32t + C$

d. $\dfrac{3}{8}t + \dfrac{1}{4}\cos 16t + \dfrac{1}{32}\cos 32t + C$

e. $\dfrac{3}{8}t + \dfrac{1}{4}\sin 16t + \dfrac{1}{32}\sin 32t + C$

4. Find the average value of the function $f(x)$ in the interval $[-\pi, \pi]$.

$$f(x) = \sin^3 x \cos^3 x$$

5. Find the area of the region bounded by the given curves.

$$y = \cos x, \quad y = \cos^3 x, \quad x = 0, \quad x = \frac{\pi}{2}$$

6. Evaluate the integral.

$$\int_0^{0.5} \frac{x^3}{\sqrt{16-x^2}}\, dx$$

7. Evaluate the integral.

$$\int \frac{dx}{x\sqrt{x^2+5}}$$

8. Evaluate the integral.

$$\int \frac{x^2}{\left(36-x^2\right)^{3/2}}\, dx$$

9. If f is a quadratic function such that $f(0) = 1$ and $\int \dfrac{2f(x)}{x^2(x+1)^3}\, dx$ is a rational function, find the value of

$f'(0)$.

Select the correct answer.

a. $f'(0) = 3$
b. $f'(0) = 1$
c. $f'(0) = 2$
d. $f'(0) = 0$
e. $f'(0) = 5$

10. Evaluate the integral.

$$\int_{-\sqrt{3}}^{1/\sqrt{3}} \frac{e^{\arctan y}}{1+y^2}\, dy$$

11. Evaluate the integral.

$$\int_{\pi/6}^{\pi/3} \frac{\ln(\tan x)}{\sin x \cos x}\, dx$$

Select the correct answer.

a. $-\dfrac{1}{8}(\ln 3)^2$

b. 0

c. $\dfrac{1}{8}(\ln 3)^2$

d. $-\dfrac{1}{8}(\ln 3)$

e. $-\dfrac{1}{3}(\ln 8)^2$

12. Use the Table of Integrals to evaluate the integral.

$$\int_{3}^{6} \frac{1}{x^2\sqrt{4x^2-4}}\, dx$$

13. Use the Table of Integrals to evaluate the integral.

$$\int \frac{x}{\sqrt{x^2-6x}}\, dx$$

14. Find $\displaystyle\lim_{t\to\infty} \int_{-t}^{t} -3x\,dx$.

15. Evaluate the following integral.

$$\int_{0}^{1} 3\frac{\ln 8x}{\sqrt{x}}\, dx$$

16. Use the Trapezoidal Rule to approximate $\displaystyle\int_{2}^{3} e^{2/x}\, dx$ for $n = 4$. Round the result to four decimal places.

17. Use the Midpoint Rule to approximate $\int_{1}^{5} \sqrt{x} \sin x \, dx$ for $n = 8$. Round the result to four decimal places.

18. A radar gun was used to record the speed of a runner during the first 5 seconds of a race (see the table). Use Simpson's Rule to estimate the distance the runner covered during those 5 seconds. Round the result to the nearest thousandth.

t (s)	v(m/s)
0	0
0.5	4.25
1.0	7.47
1.5	8.71
2.0	9.59
2.5	10.3
3.0	10.3
3.5	10.67
4.0	10.76
4.5	10.81
5.0	10.95

Select the correct answer.

a. 44.348m
b. 42.347m
c. 44.858m
d. 44.458m
e. 44.358m
f. 44.369m

19. The intensity of light with wavelength λ traveling through a diffraction grating with N slits at an angle θ is given by $I(\theta) = N^2 \dfrac{\sin^2 k}{k^2}$, where $k = \dfrac{\pi N d \sin(\theta)}{\lambda}$ and d is the distance between adjacent slits. A helium-neon laser with wavelength $\lambda = 645.3 \times 10^{-9}$ m is emitting a narrow band of light, given by $-10^{-6} < \theta < 10^{-6}$, through a grating with 1,000 slits spaced 0.0001 m apart. Use the Midpoint Rule with $n = 10$ to estimate the total light intensity $\int_{-10^{-6}}^{10^{-6}} I(\theta) \, d\theta$ emerging from the grating. Round the result to the nearest thousandth.

20. Evaluate the following integral.

$$\int_{-\infty}^{0} \frac{6}{10x - 7} \, dx$$

1. 33.58

2. $16xf(x) - 16\int f(x)dx$

3. b

4. 0

5. 1/3

6. 0.003927

7. $\dfrac{1}{\sqrt{5}}\ln\left(\left|\dfrac{\sqrt{x^2+5}-\sqrt{5}}{x}\right|\right)+C$

8. $\dfrac{x}{\sqrt{36-x^2}}-\left(\sin\left(\dfrac{x}{6}\right)\right)^{-1}+C$

9. a

10. $e^{\pi/6}-e^{-\pi/3}$

11. b

12. 0.022

13. $\sqrt{x^2-6x}+3\ln\left(\left|x-3+\sqrt{x^2-6x}\right|\right)+C$

14. 0

15. $6\ln(8)-12$

16. 2.2651

17. -0.5811

18. e

19. 1.949

20. divergent

17. Use the Midpoint Rule to approximate $\int_1^5 \sqrt{x} \sin x \; dx$ for $n = 8$. Round the result to four decimal places.

18. A radar gun was used to record the speed of a runner during the first 5 seconds of a race (see the table). Use Simpson's Rule to estimate the distance the runner covered during those 5 seconds. Round the result to the nearest thousandth.

t (s)	v(m/s)
0	0
0.5	4.25
1.0	7.47
1.5	8.71
2.0	9.59
2.5	10.3
3.0	10.3
3.5	10.67
4.0	10.76
4.5	10.81
5.0	10.95

Select the correct answer.

a. 44.348m
b. 42.347m
c. 44.858m
d. 44.458m
e. 44.358m
f. 44.369m

19. The intensity of light with wavelength λ traveling through a diffraction grating with N slits at an angle θ is given by $I(\theta) = N^2 \dfrac{\sin^2 k}{k^2}$, where $k = \dfrac{\pi N d \sin(\theta)}{\lambda}$ and d is the distance between adjacent slits. A helium-neon laser with wavelength $\lambda = 645.3 \times 10^{-9}$ m is emitting a narrow band of light, given by $-10^{-6} < \theta < 10^{-6}$, through a grating with 1,000 slits spaced 0.0001 m apart. Use the Midpoint Rule with $n = 10$ to estimate the total light intensity $\int_{-10^{-6}}^{10^{-6}} I(\theta) \; d\theta$ emerging from the grating. Round the result to the nearest thousandth.

20. Evaluate the following integral.

$$\int_{-\infty}^{0} \frac{6}{10x - 7} \, dx$$

1. 33.58

2. $16xf(x) - 16\int f(x)dx$

3. b

4. 0

5. 1/3

6. 0.003927

7. $\dfrac{1}{\sqrt{5}}\ln\left(\left|\dfrac{\sqrt{x^2+5}-\sqrt{5}}{x}\right|\right) + C$

8. $\dfrac{x}{\sqrt{36-x^2}} - \left(\sin\left(\dfrac{x}{6}\right)\right)^{-1} + C$

9. a

10. $e^{\pi/6} - e^{-\pi/3}$

11. b

12. 0.022

13. $\sqrt{x^2-6x} + 3\ln\left(\left|x-3+\sqrt{x^2-6x}\right|\right) + C$

14. 0

15. $6\ln(8) - 12$

16. 2.2651

17. -0.5811

18. e

19. 1.949

20. divergent

17. Use the Midpoint Rule to approximate $\int_1^5 \sqrt{x} \sin x \, dx$ for $n = 8$. Round the result to four decimal places.

18. A radar gun was used to record the speed of a runner during the first 5 seconds of a race (see the table). Use Simpson's Rule to estimate the distance the runner covered during those 5 seconds. Round the result to the nearest thousandth.

t (s)	v(m/s)
0	0
0.5	4.25
1.0	7.47
1.5	8.71
2.0	9.59
2.5	10.3
3.0	10.3
3.5	10.67
4.0	10.76
4.5	10.81
5.0	10.95

Select the correct answer.

    a.   44.348m
    b.   42.347m
    c.   44.858m
    d.   44.458m
    e.   44.358m
    f.   44.369m

19. The intensity of light with wavelength λ traveling through a diffraction grating with N slits at an angle θ is given by $I(\theta) = N^2 \dfrac{\sin^2 k}{k^2}$, where $k = \dfrac{\pi N d \sin(\theta)}{\lambda}$ and d is the distance between adjacent slits. A helium-neon laser with wavelength $\lambda = 645.3 \times 10^{-9}$ m is emitting a narrow band of light, given by $-10^{-6} < \theta < 10^{-6}$, through a grating with 1,000 slits spaced 0.0001 m apart. Use the Midpoint Rule with $n = 10$ to estimate the total light intensity $\int_{-10^{-6}}^{10^{-6}} I(\theta) \, d\theta$ emerging from the grating. Round the result to the nearest thousandth.

20. Evaluate the following integral.

$$\int_{-\infty}^0 \frac{6}{10x - 7} \, dx$$

1. 33.58

2. $16xf(x) - 16\int f(x)dx$

3. b

4. 0

5. 1/3

6. 0.003927

7. $\dfrac{1}{\sqrt{5}}\ln\left(\left|\dfrac{\sqrt{x^2+5}-\sqrt{5}}{x}\right|\right) + C$

8. $\dfrac{x}{\sqrt{36-x^2}} - \left(\sin\left(\dfrac{x}{6}\right)\right)^{-1} + C$

9. a

10. $e^{\pi/6} - e^{-\pi/3}$

11. b

12. 0.022

13. $\sqrt{x^2-6x} + 3\ln\left(\left|x-3+\sqrt{x^2-6x}\right|\right) + C$

14. 0

15. $6\ln(8) - 12$

16. 2.2651

17. -0.5811

18. e

19. 1.949

20. divergent

1. Evaluate the integral.

$$\int e^{4x} \cos(9x)\ dx$$

Select the correct answer.

a. $\dfrac{e^{4x}\left(4\cos(9x)+9\sin(9x)\right)}{97}$

b. $\dfrac{e^{4x}\left(4\sin(9x)+9\cos(9x)\right)}{97}$

c. $\dfrac{e^{4x}\left(4\sin(9x)-9\cos(9x)\right)}{97}$

d. $\dfrac{e^{4x}\left(4\cos(9x)+9\sin(9x)\right)}{13}$

e. none of these

2. Evaluate the integral.

$$\int_{1}^{81} \sqrt{t}\ \ln t\ dx$$

3. Use integration by parts to find the integral.

$$\int 10xf'\ dx$$

4. Evaluate the integral.

$$\int \sin^3 2x \cos^2 2x\ dx$$

5. Household electricity is supplied in the form of alternating current that varies from 165 V to -165 V with a frequency of 60 cycles per second (Hz). The voltage is thus given by the function $E(t)$, where t is the time in seconds. Voltmeters read the RMS (root-mean-square) voltage, which is the square root of the average value of $[E(t)]^2$ over one cycle. Calculate the RMS voltage of household current. Round your answer to the nearest integer.

$$E(t) = 165\sin(120\pi t)$$

6. Evaluate the integral.

$$\int_0^1 \frac{x^3}{\sqrt{4-x^2}}\, dx$$

7. Find the area of the region bounded by the hyperbola $9x^2 - 4y^2 = 36$ and the line $x = 6$.

8. Find $\displaystyle\lim_{t\to\infty}\int_{-t}^{t} -8x\; dx$.

9. If f is a quadratic function such that $f(0) = 1$ and $\displaystyle\int \frac{5f(x)}{x^2(x+1)^3}\, dx$ is a rational function, find the value

    of $f'(0)$.

    Select the correct answer.

    a. $f'(0) = 0$
    b. $f'(0) = 1$
    c. $f'(0) = 2$
    d. $f'(0) = 3$
    e. $f'(0) = 5$

10. Evaluate the integral.

$$\int_{-1}^{\sqrt{3}} \frac{e^{\arctan y}}{1+y^2}\, dy$$

11. Evaluate the integral.

$$\int \frac{\sqrt{36-x^2}}{x}\, dx$$

12. Evaluate the integral.

$$\int \frac{\arctan \sqrt{x}}{\sqrt{x}}\, dx$$

13. Use the Midpoint Rule to approximate $\int_1^5 \sqrt{x} \sin x \, dx$ for $n = 8$.

Select the correct answer. The choices are rounded to four decimal places.

    a.   0.5861
    b.   0.576
    c.   0.5833
    d.   0.5701
    e.   0.5811
    f.   0.4811

14. Determine how large the number a has to be so that $\int_a^\infty \dfrac{2}{x^2 + 1} \, dx \leq 0.007$.

15. Estimate the area of the shaded region in the graph by using the Trapezoidal Rule with $n=4$.

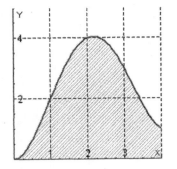

Select the correct answer.

    a.   1.5
    b.   7.5
    c.   6.4
    d.   5.9
    e.   9.5
    f.   11

16. Evaluate the following integral.

$$I = \int_{-\infty}^{0} \frac{3}{4x - 3} \, dx$$

Select the correct answer.

    a. $I = 5.3$
    b. $I = 3.1$
    c. $I = 2.2$
    d.   The integral is divergent

17. Evaluate the following integral.

$$\int_{-\infty}^{-7} \frac{1}{\sqrt{8-x}}\, dx$$

18. Determine whether the following integral is convergent or divergent.

$$\int_{1}^{\infty} \frac{6\ln 4x}{x}\, dx$$

Select the correct answer.

a. The integral is divergent
b. The integral is convergent

19. The region $\left\{ (x,y)\,|\, x \ge -3,\ 0 \le y \le e^{-x/3} \right\}$ is represented below.

Find the area of this region. Round to the nearest hundredth.

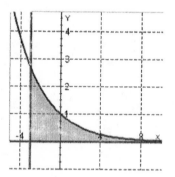

20. Evaluate the integral $\int_0^1 \frac{1}{x^p} \, dx$ for different values of p. Which of the following integrals is equal to 1.25?

Select the correct answer.

a. $\int_0^1 \frac{1}{x^{0.8}} \, dx$

b. $\int_0^1 \frac{1}{x^{0.3}} \, dx$

c. $\int_0^1 \frac{1}{x^{0.2}} \, dx$

d. $\int_0^1 \frac{1}{x^2} \, dx$

e. none of these

1. a

2. $1944 \ln 3 - \dfrac{2912}{9}$

3. $10xf(x) - 10\displaystyle\int f(x)dx$

4. $\dfrac{1}{10}(\cos(2x))^5 - \dfrac{1}{6}(\cos(2x))^3 + C$

5. 117

6. 0.137181

7. $6\left(6\sqrt{2} - \ln\left(3 + 2\sqrt{2}\right)\right)$

8. 0

9. d

10. $e^{\pi/3} - e^{-\pi/4}$

11. $\sqrt{36 - x^2} + 6\ln\left(\left|\dfrac{6 - \sqrt{36 - x^2}}{x}\right|\right) + C$

12. $2\sqrt{t}\arctan\left(\sqrt{t}\right) - \ln(1 + t) + C$

13. e

14. $a \geq 286$

15. e

16. d

17. divergent

18. a

19. 8.15

20. c

1. Make a substitution to express the integrand as a rational function and then evaluate the integral.

$$\int_{4}^{25} \frac{\sqrt{x}}{x-36} \, dx$$

Give your answer as a decimal, rounded to four decimal places.

2. Evaluate the integral.

$$\int_{\pi/3}^{\pi/2} \cot^2 x \, dx$$

3. Find the area of the region bounded by the given curves.

$$y = \cos x, \quad y = \cos^3 x, \quad x = 0, \quad x = \frac{\pi}{2}$$

4. Evaluate the integral.

$$\int_{0}^{0.5} \frac{x^3}{\sqrt{16-x^2}} \, dx$$

5. Write the form of the partial fraction decomposition of the expression. Do not determine the numerical values of the coefficients.

$$\frac{10}{(9x+4)(x-7)}$$

6. Evaluate the integral.

$$\int \frac{\sqrt{4-x^2}}{x}\,dx$$

Select the correct answer.

a. $\sqrt{4-x^2} + 2\ln\left|\dfrac{2-\sqrt{4-x^2}}{x}\right| + C$

b. $\sqrt{4-x^2} - 2\ln\left|\dfrac{4-\sqrt{4-x^2}}{x}\right| + C$

c. $-\sqrt{4-x^2} + 4\ln\left|\dfrac{2-\sqrt{4-x^2}}{x}\right| + C$

d. $\sqrt{4-x^2} + 4\ln\left|\dfrac{4-\sqrt{4-x^2}}{x}\right| + C$

e. $\sqrt{2-x^2} + \ln\left|\dfrac{\sqrt{4-x^2}}{x}\right| + C$

7. Evaluate the integral.

$$\int \frac{1+4e^x}{1-e^x}\,dx$$

8. Evaluate the integral.

$$\int \frac{1}{e^{3x}-e^x}\,dx$$

9. Evaluate the integral.

$$\int \frac{1}{\sqrt{x+1}+\sqrt{x}}\,dx$$

10. Evaluate the integral.

$$\int \frac{1}{-e^{-x} + e^x}\, dx$$

11. Use the Trapezoidal Rule to approximate $\int_1^2 e^{3/x}\, dx$ for $n = 4$. Round the result to four decimal places.

12. Use the Midpoint Rule to approximate $\int_3^7 \sqrt{x} \sin x\, dx$ for $n = 8$. Round the result to four decimal places.

13. Estimate the area of the shaded region in the graph by using the Trapezoidal Rule with $n = 4$.

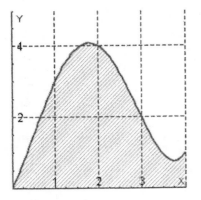

Round the answer to the nearest tenth.

14. Evaluate the integral.

$$\int_{-\frac{1}{\sqrt{3}}}^{\sqrt{3}} \frac{e^{\arctan y}}{1 + y^2}\, dy$$

15. If f is a quadratic function such that $f(0) = 1$ and $\int \dfrac{6f(x)}{x^2 (x+1)^3} \, dx$ is a rational function, find the value of $f'(0)$.

16. Evaluate the integral using integration by parts with the indicated choices of u and dv.

$$\int 4x \ln x \, dx, \quad u = 4 \ln x, \quad dv = x dx$$

Select the correct answer.

    a. $2x^2 \ln x + x^2 + C$

    b. $2x^2 \ln x - x^2 + C$

    c. $2x^2 \ln x - x + C$

    d. $2x \ln x - x^2 + C$

    e. $2x^2 \ln x - 4x^2 + C$

    f.   none of these

17. Make a substitution to express the integrand as a rational function and then evaluate the integral.

$$\int \dfrac{3e^{6x}}{e^{6x} + 3e^{3x} + 2} \, dx$$

Select the correct answer.

    a. $\ln\left[\left(e^x + 2\right)^2 / \left(e^x + 4\right) \right] + C$

    b. $\ln\left[\left(e^{3x} + 1\right) / \left(e^{3x} + 2\right) \right] + C$

    c. $\ln\left[\left(e^{3x} + 2\right)^2 / \left(e^{3x} + 1\right) \right] + C$

    d. $2\ln\left[\left(e + 2\right)^2 / \left(e^x + 1\right) \right] + C$

    e.   none of these

18. Evaluate the integral.

$$\int 20xe^{4x}\ dx$$

19. Evaluate the integral.

$$\int e^{7x}\cos 8x\ dx$$

Select the correct answer.

a. $\dfrac{e^{7x}\left(7\sin 8x + 8\cos 8x\right)}{113}$

b. $\dfrac{e^{7x}\left(7\cos 8x + 8\sin 8x\right)}{15}$

c. $\dfrac{e^{7x}\left(7\cos 8x + 8\sin 8x\right)}{113}$

d. $\dfrac{e^{7x}\left(7\sin 8x - 8\cos 8x\right)}{113}$

e. none of these

20. Evaluate the integral.

$$\int_{0}^{\pi/12}\cos^{5}6x\ dx$$

1. -4.2285

2. $\dfrac{1}{\sqrt{3}} - \dfrac{\pi}{6}$

3. 1/3

4. 0.003927

5. $\dfrac{A}{(9x+4)} + \dfrac{B}{(x-7)}$

6. a

7. $x - 5\ln\left(\left|e^x - 1\right|\right) + c$

8. $\left(e^{-x} + \dfrac{1}{2}\ln\left(\left|\dfrac{e^x - 1}{e^x + 1}\right|\right)\right) + C$

9. $\dfrac{2}{3}\left((x+1)^{3/2} - x^{3/2}\right) + C$

10. $\dfrac{1}{2}\ln\left(\left|e^x - 1\right|\right) - \dfrac{1}{2}\ln\left(e^x + 1\right) + C$

11. 9.0621

12. -3.7127

13. 9.5

14. $e^{\pi/3} - e^{-\pi/6}$

15. 3

16. b

17. c

18. $e^{4x}\left(5x - \dfrac{5}{4}\right) + C$

19. c

20. $\dfrac{4}{45}$

1. A steady wind blows a kite due west. The kite's height above ground from horizontal position $x = 0$ to $x = 50$ ft is given by $y = 140 - \frac{1}{40}(x - 20)^2$.

   True or False?

   The distance traveled by the kite is approximately 61.95 ft.

2. Find the length of the curve for the interval $1 \le x \le 16$.

   $$y = \int_1^x \sqrt{t^3 - 1}\, dt$$

3. Set up, but do not evaluate, an integral for the area of the surface obtained by rotating the curve about the given axis.

   $y = \ln x, \;\; 2 \le x \le 5; \;\; x - axis$

4. Set up, but do not evaluate, an integral for the area of the surface obtained by rotating the curve about the given axis.

   $y = e^x, \;\; 1 \le y \le 5; \;\; y - axis$

5. Find the area of the surface obtained by rotating the curve about the x-axis.

   $y = \frac{1}{3}(y^2 + 2)^{3/2}, \;\;\; 0 \le y \le 1$

6. Use either a CAS or a table of integrals to find the exact area of the surface obtained by rotating the given curve about the x-axis.

   $y = \sqrt{x^2 + 1}, \;\;\; 0 \le x \le 3$

7. Sketch the region bounded by the curves $y = x^2$, $x = 0$, and $y = 81$.

   True or False?

   The centroid of this region is $\left(\frac{27}{4}, \frac{243}{10} \right)$.

8. Find the centroid of the region bounded by the curves.

$$y = \ln 2x, \quad y = 0, \quad x = \frac{e}{2}$$

9. True or False?

   If the lamina shown in the figure below has density $\rho = 2$, then its center of mass is $\left(0, \dfrac{19}{3}\right)$.

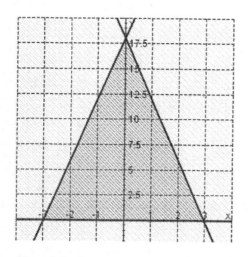

10. Set up, but do not evaluate, an integral for the length of the curve.

$$y = e^x \sin x, \quad 0 \le x \le \pi$$

11. If $f(x)$ is the probability density function for the blood cholesterol level of men over the age of 40, where x is measured in milligrams per deciliter, express as an integral the probability that the cholesterol level of such a man lies between 170 and 240.

12. The manager of a fast-food restaurant determines that the average time that her customers wait for service is 2 minutes.

    The manager wants to advertise that anybody who isn't served within a certain number of minutes gets a free hamburger. But she doesn't want to give away free hamburgers to more than 3% of her customers. What value of x must she use in the advertisement "if you aren't served within x minutes, you get a free hamburger"?

13. True or False?

The center of mass of a lamina with density $\rho = 3$ in the shape of a circle with radius 24 as shown below is $\left(\dfrac{32}{\pi}, \dfrac{32}{\pi} \right)$.

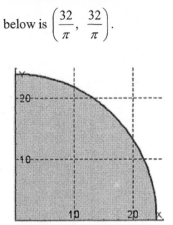

14. Find the centroid of the region shown, not by integration, but by locating the centroids of the rectangles and triangles and using additivity of moments.

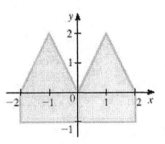

15. Let the function whose graph is shown be a probability density function. Calculate the mean.

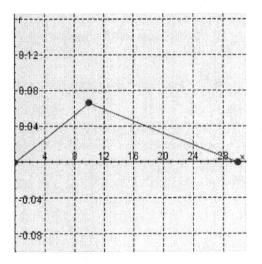

16. A type of lightbulb is labeled as having an average lifetime of 1,000 hours. It's reasonable to model the probability of failure of these bulbs by an exponential density function with mean $\mu = 1,000$.
    What is the median lifetime of these lightbulbs?

17. Set up, but do not evaluate, an integral that represents the length of the curve.

    $y = 5^x, \ 0 \le x \le 8$

18. Set up, but do not evaluate, an integral for the length of the curve.

    $y = 4x + \sin x, \ 0 \le x \le 2\pi$

19. The standard deviation for a random variable with probability density function f and mean μ is

    defined by $\sigma = \left[\displaystyle\int_{-\infty}^{\infty} (x - \mu)^2 f(x) dx \right]^{1/2}$.

    Find the standard deviation for an exponential density function with mean 9.

20. Use the arc length formula to find the length of the curve.

    $y = 3 - 5x, \ -3 \le x \le 2$

    Check your answer by noting that the curve is a line segment and calculating its length using the distance formula.

1. T

2. $\dfrac{2046}{5}$

3. $S = \displaystyle\int_{2}^{5} 2\pi \ln x \sqrt{1 + \left(\dfrac{1}{x}\right)^2} \, dx$

4. $S = \displaystyle\int_{0}^{\ln 5} 2\pi x \sqrt{1 + e^{2x}} \, dx$

5. $\dfrac{3\pi}{2}$

6. $3\sqrt{19}\,\pi + \dfrac{\pi}{\sqrt{2}} \ln\left(3\sqrt{2} + \sqrt{19}\right)$

7. T

8. $\left(\dfrac{e^2 + 1}{8}, \dfrac{2e - 3}{8}\right)$

9. T

10. $L = \displaystyle\int_{0}^{\pi} \sqrt{1 + e^{2x}\left(\cos x + \sin x\right)^2} \, dx$

11. $\displaystyle\int_{170}^{240} f(x)\, dx$

12. 7

13. T

14. $\left(0, \dfrac{1}{12}\right)$

15. 13.3333

16. 693.15

17. $\displaystyle\int_{0}^{8} \sqrt{1 + \left(\ln 5\right)^2 5^{2x}} \, dx$

18. $\displaystyle\int_{0}^{2\pi} \sqrt{\cos^2 x + 8\cos x + 17} \, dx$

19. 9

20. $5\sqrt{26}$

1. Set up, but do not evaluate, an integral for the length of the curve.

    $y = 3x + \sin x, \ 0 \le x \le 6\pi$

2. Find the arc length function for the curve $y = 10x^{3/2}$ with starting point $P_0 \ (\ 1, \ 10 \ )$.

3. A hawk flying at an altitude of 225 m accidentally drops its prey. The parabolic trajectory of the falling prey is described by the equation $y = 225 - \dfrac{x^2}{36}$ until it hits the ground, where y is its height above the ground and x is the horizontal distance traveled in meters.

    True or False?

    The distance traveled by the prey from the time it is dropped until the time it hits the ground is approximately 250.27 m.

4. A movie theater has been charging $9.00 per person and selling about 300 tickets on a typical weeknight. After surveying their customers, the theater estimates that for every $1.00 that they lower the price, the number of moviegoers will increase by 40 per night. Find the demand function and calculate the consumer surplus when the tickets are priced at $4.

5. A steady wind blows a kite due west. The kite's height above ground from horizontal position $x = 0$ to $x = 40$ ft is given by

    $$y = 180 - \frac{1}{40}(x - 40)^2$$

    Find the distance traveled by the kite.

6. Set up, but do not evaluate, an integral for the area of the surface obtained by rotating the curve about the given axis.

    $y = \ln x, \ 2 \le x \le 8; \ x \ axis$

7. Set up, but do not evaluate, an integral for the area of the surface obtained by rotating the curve about the given axis.

    $y = e^x, \ 1 \le y \le 3; \ y \ axis$

8. Find the area of the surface obtained by rotating the curve about the x-axis.

$$y = \frac{x^2}{4} - \frac{\ln x}{2}, \quad 1 \le x \le 7$$

9. Find the area of the surface obtained by rotating the curve about the x-axis.

$$x = \frac{1}{2\sqrt{2}} \left(y^2 - \ln y \right), \quad 1 \le y \le 5$$

10. Use Simpson's Rule with $n = 10$ to find the area of the surface obtained by rotating the curve about the x-axis. Please round the answer to the nearest hundred.

$$y = x^4, \quad 0 \le x \le \frac{1}{2}$$

11. The ellipse $\dfrac{x^2}{m^2} + \dfrac{y^2}{p^2} = 1, \quad m > p$ is rotated about the x-axis to form a surface called an *ellipsoid*. Find the surface area of this ellipsoid.

12. The masses $m_1 = 7$ and $m_2 = 33$ are located at the points $P_1(-8,-17)$ and $P_1(15,16)$.

   True or False?
   The center of mass of the system is $\left(\dfrac{439}{40}, \dfrac{409}{40} \right)$.

13. Sketch the region bounded by the curves $y = x^2$, $x = 0$, and $y = 81$.

   True or False?
   The centroid of this region is $\left(\dfrac{27}{4}, \dfrac{243}{10} \right)$.

14. Find the exact coordinates of the centroid.

$$y = e^{3x}, \quad y = 0, \quad x = 0, \quad x = \frac{1}{3}$$

15. True or False?

If the lamina shown in the figure below has density $\rho = 2$, then its center of mass is $\left(0, \dfrac{7}{3}\right)$.

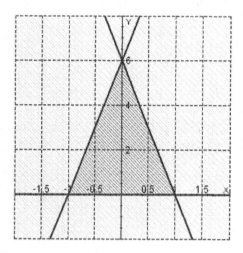

16. Calculate the center of mass of a lamina with density $\rho = 2$ in the shape of a quarter-circle with radius 27 as shown below.

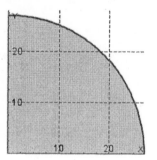

17. Find the centroid of the region shown, not by integration, but by locating the centroids of the rectangles and triangles and using additivity of moments.

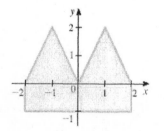

18. A demand curve is given by $\rho = \dfrac{300}{x+8}$.

   Find the consumer surplus when the selling price is $20.

19. For a given commodity and pure competition, the number of units produced and the price per unit are determined as the coordinates of the point of intersection of the supply and demand curves. Given the demand curve $\rho = 60 - \dfrac{x}{30}$ and the supply curve $\rho = 30 + \dfrac{x}{20}$, find the consumer surplus.

20. A company modeled the demand curve for its product (in dollars) by

$$\rho = \frac{1{,}000{,}000e^{-x/5}}{x+10{,}000}$$

   Use a graph to estimate the sales level when the selling price is $36.78. Then find (approximately, using Simpson's Rule with $n = 10$) the consumer surplus for this sales level.

1. $\displaystyle\int_0^{6\pi} \sqrt{\cos^2 x + 6\cos x + 10}\ dx$

2. $L = \dfrac{2}{675}\left(\left(1 + 225x\right)^{3/2} - 226\sqrt{226}\right)$

3. F

4. 3125

5. 59.16

6. $S = \displaystyle\int_2^8 2\pi\left(\ln x\right)\sqrt{1 + \left(\dfrac{1}{x}\right)^2}\ dx$

7. $S = \displaystyle\int_0^{\ln 3} 2\pi x\sqrt{1 + \left(e\right)^{2x}}\ dx$

8. $\dfrac{\pi}{4}\left(648 - 49\ln 7 - \left(\ln(7)\right)^2\right)$

9. $\dfrac{\pi}{8}\left(672 - 50\ln 5 - \left(\ln(5)\right)^2\right)$

10. 0.04

11. $2\pi\left(p^2 + \dfrac{m^2 p\left(\sin\left(\dfrac{\sqrt{m^2 - p^2}}{m}\right)\right)^{-1}}{\sqrt{m^2 - p^2}}\right)$

12. T

13. T

14. $\left(\dfrac{1}{3(e-1)},\ \dfrac{e+1}{4}\right)$

15. T

16. $\left(\dfrac{36}{\pi},\ \dfrac{36}{4}\right)$

17. $\left(0,\ \dfrac{1}{12}\right)$

18. 48.58

19. 2160

20. 90849

1. An integral for the length of the curve.

    $$y = 2x + \sin x, \ \ 0 \le x \le 2\pi$$

    Select the correct answer.

    a. $$\int_0^{2\pi} \sqrt{\cos^2 x + 2\cos x + 5} \ \ dx$$

    b. $$\int_0^{\pi} \sqrt{\cos^2 x + 4\cos x + 5} \ \ dx$$

    c. $$\int_0^{2\pi} \sqrt{\cos^2 x + 4\cos x + 4} \ \ dx$$

    d. $$\int_0^{2\pi} \sqrt{\cos^2 x + 4\cos x + 5} \ \ dx$$

    e. $$\int_0^{\pi} \sqrt{\cos^2 x + 5\cos x + 3} \ \ dx$$

2. A tank contains 1,100 L of brine with 10 kg of dissolved salt. Pure water enters the tank at a rate of 14 L/min. The solution is kept thoroughly mixed and drains from the tank at the same rate. How much salt is in the tank after 15 minutes?

    Select the correct answer.

    a. 8.47 kg
    b. 7.73 kg
    c. 7.92 kg
    d. 8.26 kg
    e. 8.8 kg
    f. 7.47 kg

3. Find the length of the curve for the interval $1 \le x \le 4$.

$$y = \int_1^x \sqrt{t^3 - 1} \; dt$$

Select the correct answer.

a. $L = \dfrac{1}{62}$

b. $L = \dfrac{62}{13}$

c. $L = \dfrac{5}{62}$

d. $L = \dfrac{62}{5}$

e. $L = \dfrac{61}{3}$

4. Set up, but do not evaluate, an integral for the area of the surface obtained by rotating the curve about the given axis.

$$y = \ln x, \;\; 1 \le x \le 4; \;\; x - axis$$

Select the correct answer.

a. $\displaystyle \int_4^1 2\pi x \sqrt{1 + (1/x)^2} \; dx$

b. $\displaystyle \int_1^4 2\pi x \sqrt{1 + (1/x)^2} \; dx$

c. $\displaystyle \int_1^4 2\pi x \ln(x)\sqrt{1 + (1/x)^2} \; dx$

d. $\displaystyle \int_4^1 2\pi x \ln(x)\sqrt{1 + (1/x)^2} \; dx$

e. $\displaystyle \int_4^1 2\pi \sqrt{x + (1/x)^2} \; dx$

5. The manager of a fast-food restaurant determines that the average time that her customers wait for service is 2 minutes. Find the probability that a customer is served within the first 4 minutes.

   Select the correct answer.

   a.   0.86
   b.   0.78
   c.   0.43
   d.   0.95
   e.   1.21
   f.   0.69

6. Set up, but do not evaluate, an integral for the area of the surface obtained by rotating the curve about the given axis.

   $y = e^x, \ 1 \le y \le 3; \ y - axis$

   Select the correct answer.

   a. $\displaystyle\int_1^3 2\pi e^x \sqrt{1 + e^{2x}} \ dx$

   b. $\displaystyle\int_0^{\ln 3} 2\pi \sqrt{1 + e^{2x}} \ dx$

   c. $\displaystyle\int_0^{\ln 3} 2\pi x \sqrt{1 + e^{2x}} \ dx$

   d. $\displaystyle\int_1^3 2\pi x \sqrt{1 + e^{2x}} \ dx$

   e. $\displaystyle\int_1^3 2\pi x e^x \sqrt{1 + e^x} \ dx$

7. Find the area of the surface obtained by rotating the curve about the x-axis.

$$x = \frac{1}{3}\left(y^2 + 2\right)^{3/2}, \quad 0 \le y \le 3$$

Select the correct answer.

a. $\dfrac{101\pi}{2}$

b. $\dfrac{93\pi}{2}$

c. $\dfrac{99\pi}{2}$

d. $\dfrac{95\pi}{2}$

e. $\dfrac{97\pi}{2}$

8. The demand function for a certain commodity is $\rho = 4 - \dfrac{x}{11}$. Find the consumer surplus when the sales level is 20.

Select the correct answer.

a. $21.82
b. $27.27
c. $23.64
d. $16.36
e. $20.00
f. $18.18

9. The ellipse $\dfrac{x^2}{a^2} + \dfrac{y^2}{p^2} = 1, \quad a > p$ is rotated about the x-axis to form a surface called an *ellipsoid*. Find the surface area of this ellipsoid.

Select the correct answer.

a. $2\pi\left[p^2 + a^2 p \sin^{-1}\left(\sqrt{a^2 - p^2}\,/a\right)/\sqrt{a^2 - p^2}\right]$

b. $2\pi\left[p^2 + a^2 p \sin^{-1}\left(\sqrt{a^2 - p^2}\,/a\right)\right]$

c. $2\pi\left[p^2 + a^2 p \sin^{-1}\left(\sqrt{a^2 - p^2}\right)/\sqrt{a^2 - p^2}\right]$

d. $2\pi\left[a^2 + p^2 \sin^{-1}\left(\sqrt{p^2 - a^2}\,/p\right)/\sqrt{p^2 - a^2}\right]$

e. $2\pi\left[p^2 + p\sin\left(\sqrt{a^2 - p^2}\,/a\right)/\sqrt{a^2 - p^2}\right]$

10. If the curve $y = f(x)$, $q \leq x \leq b$ is rotated about the horizontal line $y = c$, where $f(x) \leq c$.

Find a formula for the area of the resulting surface.

Select the correct answer.

a. $\displaystyle\int_{q}^{b} 2\pi(c - f(x))\sqrt{1 + \left(\frac{df(x)}{dx}\right)^2}\; dx$

b. $\displaystyle\int_{q}^{b} 2\pi(c + f(x))\sqrt{1 + \left(\frac{df(x)}{dx}\right)^2}\; dx$

c. $\displaystyle\int_{b}^{q} 2\pi(c - f(x))\sqrt{1 + \left(\frac{df(x)}{dx}\right)^2}\; dx$

d. $\displaystyle\int_{b}^{q} 2\pi(c + f(x))\sqrt{1 + \left(\frac{df(x)}{dx}\right)^2}\; dx$

e. $\displaystyle\int_{b}^{q} \pi(c + 2f(x))\sqrt{1 + \left(\frac{df(x)}{dx}\right)^2}\; dx$

11. Find the area of the surface obtained by rotating the circle $x^2 + y^2 = a^2$ about the line $y = a$.

Select the correct answer.

a. $2\pi^2 a^2$
b. $3\pi^2 a^2$
c. $7\pi^2 a^2$
d. $4\pi^2 a^2$
e. $\pi^2 a^2$

12. A large tank is designed with ends in the shape of the region between the curves $y = \dfrac{x^2}{2}$ and $y = 15$, measured in feet. Find the hydrostatic force on one end of the tank if it is filled to a depth of 5 ft with gasoline. (Assume the gasoline's density is 42.0 lb/ft^3 .)

Select the correct answer.

a. 1, 771 lb
b. 1, 683 lb
c. 1, 855 lb
d. 1, 850 lb
e. 1, 785 lb
f. 1, 918 lb

13. A trough is filled with a liquid of density 855 kg / m^3. The ends of the trough are equilateral triangles with sides 6 m long and vertex at the bottom. Find the hydrostatic force on one end of the trough.

Select the correct answer.

    a. 2.10×10^5 N

    b. 1.50×10^5 N

    c. 2.26×10^5 N

    d. 3×10^5 N

    e. 5.10×10^5 N

14. Find the exact coordinates of the centroid.

$$y = e^{5x}, \quad y = 0, \quad x = 0, \quad x = \frac{1}{5}$$

Select the correct answer.

    a. $\left(\dfrac{1}{5(e-1)}, \dfrac{e+5}{4} \right)$

    b. $\left(\dfrac{1}{(e-1)}, \dfrac{e+1}{4} \right)$

    c. $\left(\dfrac{1}{5(e-1)}, \dfrac{e+1}{4} \right)$

    d. $\left(\dfrac{1}{(e-1)}, \dfrac{e+5}{4} \right)$

    e. $\left(\dfrac{1}{5(e-1)}, \dfrac{5}{4} \right)$

15. Suppose the average waiting time for a customer's call to be answered by a company representative (modeled by exponentially decreasing probability density functions) is 10 minutes. Find the median waiting time.

Select the correct answer.

    a.   10.4 minutes
    b.   4.16 minutes
    c.   8.32 minutes
    d.   7.62 minutes
    e.   4.85 minutes
    f.   6.93 minutes

16. Find the centroid of the region bounded by the curves.

$y = \sin 5x, \quad y = 0, \quad x = 0, \quad x = \pi/5$

Select the correct answer.

a. $\left(\dfrac{\pi}{10}, \dfrac{\pi}{8}\right)$

b. $\left(\dfrac{\pi}{10}, \pi\right)$

c. $\left(\pi, \dfrac{\pi}{8}\right)$

d. $\left(-\dfrac{\pi}{10}, \dfrac{\pi}{8}\right)$

e. $\left(-\dfrac{1}{10}, \dfrac{1}{8}\right)$

17. For a given commodity and pure competition, the number of units produced and the price per unit are determined as the coordinates of the point of intersection of the supply and demand curves. Given the demand curve $p = 70 - \dfrac{x}{50}$ and the supply curve $p = 30 + \dfrac{x}{20}$, find the producer surplus.

Select the correct answer.

a. $3,275.31
b. $3,265.31
c. $3,320.31
d. $3,264.81
e. $3,267.35
f. $3,234.31

18. A movie theater has been charging $8.00 per person and selling about 500 tickets on a typical weeknight. After surveying their customers, the theater estimates that for every $1.50 that they lower the price, the number of moviegoers will increase by 35 per night. Find the demand function and calculate the consumer surplus when the tickets are priced at $3.

Select the correct answer.

a. $7,333.93
b. $10,593.45
c. $8,963.69
d. $5,704.17
e. $8,148.81

19. A hot, wet summer is causing a mosquito population explosion in a lake resort area. The number of mosquitoes is increasing at an estimated rate of $2,100 + 7e^{0.7t}$ per week (where t is measured in weeks). By how much does the mosquito population increase between the 4th and 8th weeks of summer?

Select the correct answer.

a. 14,222
b. 10,940
c. 15,316
d. 6,564
e. 7,658

20. *Poiseuille's Law* states that the rate of blood flow in a small human artery is given by $\dfrac{\pi PR^4}{8\eta l}$ where P is the pressure difference between the ends of the vessel, R and l are the radius and length of the vessel, and η is the viscosity of the blood.

Use Poiseuille's Law to calculate the rate of flow in an artery for which $\eta = 0.0029$, $R = 0.006$ *cm*, $l = 2$ *cm*, and $P = 7,000$ *dynes/cm^2*.

Select the correct answer.

a. $0.00314 \ cm^3 / s$
b. $0.000614 \ cm^3 / s$
c. $1.100614 \ cm^3 / s$
d. $0.0314 \ cm^3 / s$
e. $0.6144 \ cm^3 / s$

ANSWER KEY

Stewart - Calculus ET 5e Chapter 8 Form C

1. d

2. d

3. d

4. c

5. a

6. c

7. c

8. f

9. a

10. a

11. d

12. a

13. c

14. c

15. f

16. a

17. b

18. e

19. b

20. b

1. The marginal cost function $C'(x)$ is defined to be the derivative of the cost function. If the marginal cost of manufacturing x units of a product is $C'(x) = 0.009x^2 - 1.8x + 9$ (measured in dollars per unit) and the fixed start-up cost is $C(0) = \$1,800,000$, use the Total Change Theorem to find the cost of producing the first 5,000 units.

   Select the correct answer.

   a. $355,009,000
   b. $355,309,000
   c. $354,109,000
   d. $353,509,000
   e. $354,309,000
   f. $354,409,000

2. The marginal revenue from producing x units of a certain product is $100 + x - 0.001x^2 + 0.00003x^3$ (in dollars per unit). Find the increase in revenue if the production level is raised from 1,100 units to 1,400 units.

   Select the correct answer.

   a. $19,541,775
   b. $14,212,200
   c. $10,659,150
   d. $17,765,250
   e. $12,435,675
   f. $24,871,350

3. The demand function for a certain commodity is $p = 5 - \dfrac{x}{14}$. Find the consumer surplus when the sales level is 40.

   Select the correct answer.

   a. $40.00
   b. $62.86
   c. $85.71
   d. $57.14
   e. $80.00
   f. $74.29

4. A demand curve is given by $p = \dfrac{500}{x+8}$. Find the consumer surplus when the selling price is $20.

Select the correct answer.

    a. $254.73
    b. $228.61
    c. $229.72
    d. $239.82
    e. $235.22
    f. $227.67

5. A supply curve is given by $p = 4 + \dfrac{\sqrt{x}}{10}$.

Find the producer surplus when the selling price is $20.

Select the correct answer.

    a. $150,186.67
    b. $109,226.67
    c. $191,146.67
    d. $204,800.00
    e. $136,533.33
    f. $177,493.33

6. For a given commodity and pure competition, the number of units produced and the price per unit are determined as the coordinates of the point of intersection of the supply and demand curves. Given the demand curve $p = 40 - \dfrac{x}{10}$ and the supply curve $p = 50 + \dfrac{x}{10}$, find the producer surplus.

Select the correct answer.

    a. $124.50
    b. $125.00
    c. $180.00
    d. $94.00
    e. $135.00
    f. $127.04

7. A movie theater has been charging $6.00 per person and selling about 300 tickets on a typical weeknight. After surveying their customers, the theater estimates that for every $0.50 that they lower the price, the number of moviegoers will increase by 35 per night. Find the demand function and calculate the consumer surplus when the tickets are priced at $3.

    Select the correct answer.

    a. $928.93
    b. $1,672.07
    c. $1,300.50
    d. $1,857.86
    e. $2,601.00
    f. $2,043.64

8. A hot, wet summer is causing a mosquito population explosion in a lake resort area. The number of mosquitoes is increasing at an estimated rate of $2,200 + 8e^{0.8t}$ per week (where t is measured in weeks). By how much does the mosquito population increase between the 4th and 9th weeks of summer?

    Select the correct answer.

    a.   16,904
    b.   26,564
    c.   21,734
    d.   24,149
    e.   14,489
    f.   31,394

9. *Poiseuille's Law* states that the rate of blood flow in a small human artery is given by $\dfrac{\pi P R^4}{8\eta l}$ where P is the pressure difference between the ends of the vessel, R and l are the radius and length of the vessel, and η is the viscosity of the blood.

    If the radius of an artery is suddenly reduced to $\dfrac{1}{2}$ of its former value, use Poiseuille's Law to find the factor by which the blood pressure difference increases.

    Select the correct answer.

    a.   16
    b.   14
    c.   8
    d.   12
    e.   19
    f.   13

10. *Dye dilution* is a method of measuring cardiac output. If A mg of dye is used and $c(t)$ is the concentration of the dye at time t, then the cardiac output over the time interval $[0, T]$ is given by

$$F = \frac{A}{\displaystyle\int_0^T c(t)\ dt}$$

Find the cardiac output over the time interval $[0, 15]$ if the dye dilution method is used with 10 mg of dye and the dye concentration, in mg/L, is modeled by $c(t) = \frac{1}{2}t(15 - t)$, $0 \le t \le 15$, where t is measured in seconds.

Select the correct answer.

    a.   0.049778
    b.   0.053333
    c.   0.039111
    d.   0.042667
    e.   0.028444
    f.   0.035556

11. If $f(x)$ is the probability density function for the blood cholesterol level of men over the age of 40, where x is measured in milligrams per deciliter, express as an integral the probability that the cholesterol level of such a man lies between 195 and 230.

Select the correct answer.

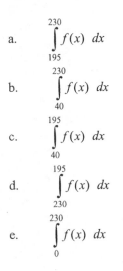

    a. $\displaystyle\int_{195}^{230} f(x)\ dx$

    b. $\displaystyle\int_{40}^{230} f(x)\ dx$

    c. $\displaystyle\int_{40}^{195} f(x)\ dx$

    d. $\displaystyle\int_{230}^{195} f(x)\ dx$

    e. $\displaystyle\int_{0}^{230} f(x)\ dx$

12. A spinner from a board game randomly indicates a real number between 0 and 50. The spinner is fair in the sense that it indicates a number in a given interval with the same probability as it indicates a number in any other interval of the same length. Find the mean.

Select the correct answer.

    a.   7.07
    b.   49
    c.   50
    d.   25
    e.   12.5
    f.   2,500

13. Let the function whose graph is shown be a probability density function. Use the graph to find $P(14 \le X \le 41)$.

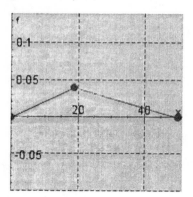

Select the correct answer.

    a.   0.74
    b.   0.59
    c.   0.52
    d.   1.11
    e.   0.89
    f.   1.04

14. Let the function whose graph is shown be a probability density function. Calculate the mean.

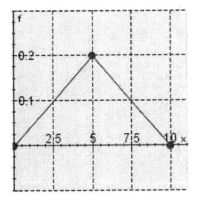

Select the correct answer.

a.   3.5
b.   7.5
c.   4
d.   6.5
e.   3
f.   5

15. Suppose the average waiting time for a customer's call to be answered by a company representative (modeled by exponentially decreasing probability density functions) is 25 minutes. Find the median waiting time.

Select the correct answer.

a.   10.4 minutes
b.   24.26 minutes
c.   13.86 minutes
d.   25.99 minutes
e.   12.13 minutes
f.   17.33 minutes

16. A type of lightbulb is labeled as having an average lifetime of 1,500 hours. It's reasonable to model the probability of failure of these bulbs by an exponential density function with mean $\mu = 1,500$.

What is the median lifetime of these lightbulbs?

Select the correct answer.

a.   831.78 hours
b.   623.83 hours
c.   1,455.61 hours
d.   935.75 hours
e.   1,143.69 hours
f.   1,039.72 hours

17. The manager of a fast-food restaurant determines that the average time that her customers wait for service is 3 minutes. Find the probability that a customer is served within the first 7 minutes.

Select the correct answer.

    a.   0.99
    b.   1.35
    c.   1.26
    d.   0.45
    e.   1.17
    f.   0.9

18. The manager of a fast-food restaurant determines that the average time that her customers wait for service is 5 minutes.

The manager wants to advertise that anybody who isn't served within a certain number of minutes gets a free hamburger. But she doesn't want to give away free hamburgers to more than 4% of her customers. What value of x must she use in the advertisement "If you aren't served within x minutes, you get a free hamburger"?

Select the correct answer.

    a.   23
    b.   16
    c.   29
    d.   12
    e.   26
    f.   31

19. According to the National Health Survey, the heights of adult males in the United States are (normally distributed with mean) 73 inches, and standard deviation of 2.8 inches. What is the probability that an adult male chosen at random is between 65 inches and 75 inches tall?

Select the correct answer.

    a.   0.46
    b.   0.38
    c.   0.61
    d.   0.76
    e.   0.91
    f.   0.68

20. The standard deviation for a random variable with probability density function f and mean μ is

defined by $\sigma = \left[\displaystyle\int_{-\infty}^{\infty} (x - \mu)^2 f(x) \; dx \right]^{1/2}$.

Find the standard deviation for an exponential density function with mean 7.

Select the correct answer.

a.   3.5
b.   8.4
c.   9.1
d.   7
e.   19.5

1. e

2. d

3. d

4. c

5. e

6. b

7. d

8. d

9. a

10. f

11. a

12. d

13. a

14. f

15. f

16. f

17. f

18. b

19. d

20. d

1. True or False?

   An integral for the length of the curve $y = x\sqrt[3]{3-x}$, $0 \le x \le 3$ is $\displaystyle\int_0^3 \sqrt{1 + \left[\frac{4x}{3(3-x)^{2/3}}\right]^2}\ dx$.

2. Find the length of the curve for the interval $1 \le x \le 16$.

   $$y = \int_1^x \sqrt{t^3 - 1}\ dt$$

3. Set up, but do not evaluate, an integral for the area of the surface obtained by rotating the curve about the given axis.

   $y = e^x$, $1 \le y \le 6$; $y - axis$

4. Find the area of the surface obtained by rotating the curve about the x-axis.

   $y = x^3$, $0 \le x \le 3$

   Select the correct answer.

   a. $\dfrac{\pi}{27}\left(731\sqrt{731} - 1\right)$

   b. $\dfrac{\pi}{27}\left(730\sqrt{730} - 1\right)$

   c. $\dfrac{\pi}{27}\left(733\sqrt{733} - 1\right)$

   d. $\dfrac{\pi}{27}\left(728\sqrt{728} - 1\right)$

   e. $\dfrac{\pi}{27}\left(707\sqrt{707} - 1\right)$

5. Let L be the length of the curve $y = f(x)$, $a \le x \le u$, where f is positive and has a continuous derivative. Let S_f be the surface area generated by rotating the curve about the x-axis. If c is a positive constant, define $g(x) = f(x) + c$ and let S_g be the corresponding surface area generated by the curve $y = g(x)$, $a \le x \le u$. Express S_g in terms of S_f and L.

   Select the correct answer.

   a. $S_g = S_f - 2\pi u L$

   b. $S_g = S_f + 2\pi a L$

   c. $S_g = S_f + 2\pi c L$

   d. $S_g = S_f - 2\pi c L$

   e. $S_g = S_f - 2\pi a L$

   f. $S_g = S_f + 2\pi u L$

6. A swimming pool is 10 ft wide and 36 ft long and its bottom is an inclined plane, the shallow end having a depth of 2 ft and the deep end, 12 ft. If the pool is full of water, find the hydrostatic force on the shallow end. (Use the fact that water weighs 62.5 lb / ft^3.)

7. Sketch the region bounded by the curves $y = x^2$, $x = 0$, and $y = 49$.

   True or False?

   The centroid of this region is $\left(\dfrac{21}{4}, \dfrac{147}{10} \right)$.

8. If the curve $y = f(x)$, $w \le x \le u$, is rotated about the horizontal line $y = r$, where $f(x) \le r$, find a formula for the area of the resulting surface.

9. Find the centroid of the region bounded by the curves.

    $y = \sin 5x, \ \ y = 0, \ \ x = 0, \ \ x = \pi/5$

    Select the correct answer.

    a. $\left(-\dfrac{\pi}{10}, \dfrac{\pi}{8}\right)$

    b. $\left(\dfrac{\pi}{10}, \dfrac{\pi}{8}\right)$

    c. $\left(\dfrac{\pi}{10}, \pi\right)$

    d. $\left(\pi, \dfrac{\pi}{8}\right)$

    e. $\left(\dfrac{\pi}{10}, -\dfrac{\pi}{8}\right)$

10. *Poiseuille's Law* states that the rate of blood flow in a small human artery is given by $\dfrac{\pi P R^4}{8\eta l}$

    where P is the pressure difference between the ends of the vessel, R and l are the radius and length of the vessel, and η is the viscosity of the blood.

    Use Poiseuille's Law to calculate the rate of flow in an artery for which

    $\eta = 0.0025$, $R = 0.008$ *cm*, $l = 4$ *cm*, and $P = 5{,}000$ *dynes*$/cm^2$.

11. If $f(x)$ is the probability density function for the blood cholesterol level of men over the age of 40, where x is measured in milligrams per deciliter, express as an integral the probability that the cholesterol level of such a man lies between 190 and 235.

12. A type of lightbulb is labeled as having an average lifetime of 2,000 hours. It's reasonable to model the probability of failure of these bulbs by an exponential density function with mean $\mu = 2{,}000$.

    What is the median lifetime of these lightbulbs?

13. Find the length of the curve for the interval $c \le v \le d$.

$$y = \ln\left(\frac{e^v + 1}{e^v - 1}\right)$$

Select the correct answer.

a. $L = \ln\left(\dfrac{e^d + e^{-d}}{e^c + e^{-c}}\right)$

b. $L = \ln\left(\dfrac{e^c - e^{-c}}{e^d - e^{-d}}\right)$

c. $L = \ln\left(\dfrac{e^d - e^{-d}}{e^c - e^{-c}}\right)$

d. $L = \ln\left(\dfrac{e^c + e^{-d}}{e^c + e^{-d}}\right)$

e. $L = \ln\left(\dfrac{e^d e^{-d}}{e^c + e^{-c}}\right)$

14. Use the arc length formula to find the length of the curve.

$$y = 5 - 3x, \ -5 \le x \le -2$$

15. Set up, but do not evaluate, an integral for the length of the curve.

$$y = e^x \cos x, \ 0 \le x \le 3\pi/2$$

16. Find the area of the surface obtained by rotating the curve about the x-axis.

$$y = \frac{x^2}{4} - \frac{\ln x}{2}, \ 1 \le x \le 3$$

17. Find the area of the surface obtained by rotating the curve about the x-axis.

$$x = \frac{1}{2\sqrt{2}}\left(y^2 - \ln y\right), \ 1 \le y \le 2$$

18. If the infinite curve $y = e^{-x}$, $x \geq 0$, is rotated about the x-axis, find the area of the resulting surface.

Select the correct answer.

a. $\dfrac{\pi}{6}\left[\sqrt{2} + \ln\left(1 + \sqrt{2}\right)\right]$

b. $\dfrac{\pi}{4}\left[\sqrt{2} + \ln\left(1 + \sqrt{2}\right)\right]$

c. $\pi\left[\sqrt{2} + \ln\left(1 + \sqrt{2}\right)\right]$

d. $\dfrac{\pi}{3}\left[\sqrt{2} + \ln\left(1 + \sqrt{2}\right)\right]$

e. $\dfrac{\pi}{6}\left[\sqrt{3} + \ln\left(1 + \sqrt{3}\right)\right]$

19. The manager of a fast-food restaurant determines that the average time that her customers wait for service is 2.5 minutes.

The manager wants to advertise that anybody who isn't served within a certain number of minutes gets a free hamburger. But she doesn't want to give away free hamburgers to more than 5% of her customers. What value of x must she use in the advertisement "If you aren't served within x minutes, you get a free hamburger"?

20. Boxes are labeled as containing 500 g of cereal. The machine filling the boxes produces weights that are normally distributed with standard deviation 12 g. If the target weight is 500 g, what is the probability that the machine produces a box with less than 480 g of cereal? Round your answer to four decimal places.

1. F

2. 2046/5

3. $S = \int\limits_{0}^{\ln 6} 2\pi x \sqrt{1 + e^{2x}} \ dx$

4. b

5. c

6. 1250

7. T

8. $\int\limits_{w}^{u} 2\pi \bigl(r - f(x)\bigr)\sqrt{1 + \left(\dfrac{df(x)}{dx}\right)^2} \ dx$

9. b

10. 0.000804

11. $\int\limits_{190}^{235} f(x) \ dx$

12. 1386.29

13. c

14. $3\sqrt{10}$

15. $L = \int\limits_{0}^{3\pi/2} \sqrt{1 + e^{2x}\bigl(\cos x - \sin x\bigr)^2} \ dx$

16. $\dfrac{\pi}{4}\left(28 - 9\ln 3 - \bigl(\ln 3\bigr)^2\right)$

17. $\dfrac{\pi}{8}\left(21 - 8\ln 2 - \bigl(\ln 2\bigr)^2\right)$

18. c

19. 7

20. 0.0478

1.   Find the length of the curve for the interval $1 \le x \le 3$.

$$y = \frac{x^4}{4} + \frac{1}{8x^2}$$

Select the correct answer.

a. $L = \dfrac{181}{2}$

b. $L = 9$

c. $L = \dfrac{9}{181}$

d. $L = \dfrac{181}{9}$

e. $L = \dfrac{8}{9}$

2.   Find the length of the curve for the interval $a \le t \le b$.

$$y = \ln\left(\frac{e^t + 1}{e^t - 1}\right)$$

3.   Set up, but do not evaluate, an integral that represents the length of the curve.

$$y = 6^x, \quad 4 \le x \le 10$$

4.   Set up, but do not evaluate, an integral for the length of the curve.

$$y = e^x \sin x, \quad 0 \le x \le 3\pi/2$$

Select the correct answer.

a. $L = \displaystyle\int_{0}^{3\pi/2} \sqrt{1 - e^{2x}(1 + \sin 2x)} \; dx$

b. $L = \displaystyle\int_{0}^{3\pi/2} \sqrt{1 + e^{2x}(1 + \sin 2x)} \; dx$

c. $L = \displaystyle\int_{0}^{3\pi/2} \sqrt{1 - e^{2x}(1 - \sin 2x)} \; dx$

d. $L = \displaystyle\int_{0}^{3\pi/2} \sqrt{1 + e^{2x}(1 - \sin 2x)} \; dx$

e. $L = \displaystyle\int_{0}^{3\pi/2} \sqrt{1 + e^{x}(1 - \sin x)} \; dx$

5. Set up, but do not evaluate, an integral for the length of the curve.

$$y = x\sqrt[3]{5-x}, \ 0 \le x \le 6$$

6. True or False?

An integral for the length of the curve $y = x\sqrt[3]{6-x}, \ 0 \le x \le 5$ is $\displaystyle\int_0^5 \sqrt{1 + \left[\frac{18-4x}{3(6-x)^{2/3}}\right]^2} \ dx$.

7. A hawk flying at an altitude of 169 m accidentally drops its prey. The parabolic trajectory of the falling prey is described by the equation $y = 169 - \dfrac{x^2}{36}$ until it hits the ground, where y is its height above the ground and x is the horizontal distance traveled in meters.

True or False?

The distance traveled by the prey from the time it is dropped until the time it hits the ground is approximately 192.99 m.

8. A steady wind blows a kite due west. The kite's height above ground from horizontal position $x = 0$ to $x = 50$ ft is given by $y = 190 - \dfrac{1}{80}(x - 40)^2$.

True or False?

The distance traveled by the kite is approximately 56.01 ft.

9. Find the length of the curve for the interval $1 \le x \le 9$.

$$y = \int_1^x \sqrt{t^3 - 1} \ dt$$

Select the correct answer.

a. $L = \dfrac{5}{484}$

b. $L = \dfrac{484}{5}$

c. $L = \dfrac{484}{13}$

d. $L = \dfrac{1}{484}$

e. $L = \dfrac{1}{256}$

10. Set up, but do not evaluate, an integral for the area of the surface obtained by rotating the curve about the given axis.

$y = \ln x, \ 3 \le x \le 7 \ ; \ x-axis$

11. Set up, but do not evaluate, an integral for the area of the surface obtained by rotating the curve about the given axis.

$y = e^x, \ 1 \le x \le 3 \ ; \ y-axis$

12. Find the area of the surface obtained by rotating the curve about the x-axis.

$y = \dfrac{x^2}{4} - \dfrac{\ln x}{2}, \ 1 \le x \le 7$

Select the correct answer.

a. $\dfrac{\pi}{4} \left[1{,}720 - 81\ln(7) - (\ln(7))^2 \right]$

b. $\dfrac{\pi}{4} \left[648 - 49\ln(7) - (\ln(7))^2 \right]$

c. $\dfrac{\pi}{4} \left[79 - 16\ln(7) - (\ln(7))^2 \right]$

d. $\dfrac{\pi}{4} \left[359 - 36\ln(7) - (\ln(7))^2 \right]$

e. $\dfrac{\pi}{4} \left[49 - \ln(7) - (\ln(7))^2 \right]$

13. Find the area of the surface obtained by rotating the curve about the x-axis.

$x = \dfrac{1}{2\sqrt{2}}\left(y^2 - \ln y\right), \ 1 \le y \le 2$

14. If the infinite curve $y = e^x$, $x \le 0$, is rotated about the x-axis , find the area of the resulting surface.

15. A large tank is designed with ends in the shape of the region between the curves $y = \dfrac{x^2}{4}$ and $y = 16$, measured in feet. Find the hydrostatic force on one end of the tank if it is filled to a depth of 7 ft with gasoline. (Assume the gasoline's density is $42.0 \ lb/ft^3$.)

Select the correct answer.

   a.   5,808 lb
   b.   5,720 lb
   c.   5,955 lb
   d.   5,892 lb
   e.   5,887 lb

16. A trough is filled with a liquid of density 880 kg/m^3. The ends of the trough are equilateral triangles with sides 4 m long and vertex at the bottom. Find the hydrostatic force on one end of the trough.

17. For any normal distribution, find $P(\mu - 1.6\sigma \le X \le \mu + 1.6\sigma)$.

18. Sketch the region bounded by the curves $y = x^2$, $x = 0$, and $y = 81$.

True or False?

The centroid of this region is $\left(\dfrac{27}{4}, \dfrac{243}{10} \right)$.

19. According to the National Health Survey, the heights of adult males in the United States are (normally distributed with mean) 71 inches, and standard deviation of 2.8 inches. What is the probability that an adult male chosen at random is between 55 inches and 75 inches tall?

Select the correct answer.

   a.   0.55
   b.   1.2
   c.   0.83
   d.   0.46
   e.   0.92

20. Boxes are labeled as containing 500 g of cereal. The machine filling the boxes produces weights that are normally distributed with standard deviation 12 g. If the target weight is 500 g, what is the probability that the machine produces a box with less than 485 g of cereal? Round your answer to four decimal places.

1. d

2. $\ln\left(\dfrac{e^b - e^{-b}}{e^a - e^{-a}}\right)$

3. $\displaystyle\int_4^{10} \sqrt{1 + \left(\ln(6)\right)^2 6^{2x}}\ dx$

4. b

5. $\displaystyle\int_0^6 \sqrt{1 + \left(\dfrac{15 - 4x}{3(5 - x)^{2/3}}\right)^2}\ dx$

6. T

7. F

8. T

9. b

10. $S = \displaystyle\int_3^7 2\pi(\ln x)\sqrt{1 + \left(\dfrac{1}{x}\right)^2}\ dx$

11. $S = \displaystyle\int_0^{\ln 3} 2\pi x \sqrt{1 + e^{2x}}\ dx$

12. b

13. $\dfrac{\pi}{8}\left(21 - 8\ln 2 - (\ln 2)^2\right)$

14. $\pi\left(\sqrt{2} + \ln\left(1 + \sqrt{2}\right)\right)$

15. a

16. 0.69×10^5

17. 0.89

18. T

19. e

20. 0.1056

1. Use the arc length formula to find the length of the curve.

    $y = 5 - 2x, \quad -5 \le x \le -3$

2. Find the length of the curve for the interval $5 \le x \le 7$.

    $$y = \frac{x^4}{4} + \frac{1}{8x^2}$$

    Select the correct answer.

    a. $L = \dfrac{543,903}{2}$

    b. $L = 1,225$

    c. $L = \dfrac{1,225}{543,903}$

    d. $L = \dfrac{543,903}{1,225}$

    e. $L = \dfrac{1}{1,225}$

3. Find the length of the curve for the interval $a \le v \le b$.

    $$y = \ln\left(\frac{e^v + 1}{e^v - 1}\right)$$

    Select the correct answer.

    a. $L = \ln\left|\dfrac{e^b + e^{-b}}{e^a + e^{-a}}\right|$

    b. $L = \ln\left|\dfrac{e^b + e^{-b}}{e^a - e^{-a}}\right|$

    c. $L = \ln\left|\dfrac{e^a - e^{-a}}{e^b - e^{-b}}\right|$

    d. $L = \ln\left|\dfrac{e^b - e^{-b}}{e^a - e^{-a}}\right|$

    e. $L = \ln\left|\dfrac{e^{2b} - e^{-2b}}{e^{2a} - e^{-2a}}\right|$

4. Set up, but do not evaluate, an integral that represents the length of the curve.

$y = 3^x, \ 0 \le x \le 7$

5. Set up, but do not evaluate, an integral for the length of the curve.

$y = x\sqrt[3]{4-x}, \ 0 \le x \le 5$

6. Set up, but do not evaluate, an integral for the length of the curve.

$y = 3x + \sin x, \ 0 \le x \le 3\pi$

7. Find the arc length function for the curve $y = 2x^{3/2}$ with starting point $P_0\ (\,1, 2\,)$.

Select the correct answer.

a. $\quad L = \dfrac{2}{27}\left((1+9x)^{1/2} - 10\sqrt{10}\right)$

b. $\quad L = \dfrac{2}{27}\left((1+9x)^{3/2} - 10\sqrt{10}\right)$

c. $\quad L = \dfrac{2}{27}\left((1+9x)^{5/2} + 10\sqrt{10}\right)$

d. $\quad L = \dfrac{2}{27}\left((1+9x)^{3/2} + 10\right)$

e. $\quad L = \dfrac{1}{27}\left((9x)^{3/2} + 10\right)$

8. A swimming pool is 14 ft wide and 36 ft long and its bottom is an inclined plane, the shallow end having a depth of 6 ft and the deep end 14 ft.

True or False?

If the pool is full of water, the hydrostatic force on the shallow end is 15,645 lb.

Use the fact that water weighs $62.5 \ lb/ft^3$.

9. A hawk flying at an altitude of 144 m accidentally drops its prey. The parabolic trajectory of the falling prey is described by the equation $y = 144 - \dfrac{x^2}{36}$ until it hits the ground, where y is its height above the ground and x is the horizontal distance traveled in meters.

True or False?

The distance traveled by the prey from the time it is dropped until the time it hits the ground is approximately 167.28 m.

10. A steady wind blows a kite due west. The kite's height above ground from horizontal position $x = 0$ to $x = 60$ ft is given by $y = 150 - \dfrac{1}{100}(x - 40)^2$.

True or False?

The distance traveled by the kite is approximately 64.45 ft.

11. Set up, but do not evaluate, an integral for the area of the surface obtained by rotating the curve about the given axis.

$y = \ln x, \; 1 \le x \le 5; \; x - axis$

12. Find the area of the surface obtained by rotating the curve about the x-axis.

$y = x^3, \; 0 \le x \le 5$

13. Find the area of the surface obtained by rotating the curve about the x-axis.

$y = \dfrac{x^2}{4} - \dfrac{\ln x}{2}, \; 1 \le x \le 7$

14. Find the area of the surface obtained by rotating the curve about the x-axis.

$x = \dfrac{1}{2\sqrt{2}}\left(y^2 - \ln y\right), \; 1 \le y \le 2$

15. The ellipse $\dfrac{x^2}{m^2} + \dfrac{y^2}{p^2} = 1$, $m > p$ is rotated about the x-axis to form a surface called an *ellipsoid*. Find the surface area of this ellipsoid.

16. Find the area of the surface obtained by rotating the circle $x^2 + y^2 = b$ about the line $y = b$.

17. Let L be the length of the curve $y = f(x)$, $q \le x \le p$, where f is positive and has a continuous derivative. Let S_f be the surface area generated by rotating the curve about the x-axis and L be the length of the curve. If c is a positive constant, define $g(x) = f(x) + c$ and let S_g be the corresponding surface area generated by the curve $y = g(x)$, $q \le x \le p$. Express S_g in terms of S_f and L.

18. A trough is filled with a liquid of density 835 kg / m^3. The ends of the trough are equilateral triangles with sides 8 m long and vertex at the bottom. Find the hydrostatic force on one end of the trough.

Select the correct answer.

    a. $1.50 \times 10^5 \ N$
    b. $5.24 \times 10^5 \ N$
    c. $2.40 \times 10^5 \ N$
    d. $0.80 \times 10^5 \ N$
    e. $1.80 \times 10^5 \ N$

19. Sketch the region bounded by the curves $y = x^2$, $x = 0$, and $y = 16$, and visually estimate the location of the centroid. Then find the exact coordinates of the centroid.

20. The standard deviation for a random variable with probability density function f and mean μ is

    defined by $\sigma = \left[\displaystyle\int_{-\infty}^{\infty} (x - \mu)^2 f(x) \ dx \right]^{1/2}$.

    Find the standard deviation for an exponential density function with mean 3.

1. $2\sqrt{5}$

2. d

3. d

4. $\displaystyle\int_0^7 \sqrt{1+\left(\ln(3)\right)^2 3^{2x}}\,dx$

5. $\displaystyle\int_0^5 \sqrt{1+\left(\dfrac{12-4x}{3\left(4-x\right)^{2/3}}\right)^2}\,dx$

6. $\displaystyle\int_0^{3\pi} \sqrt{\cos^2 x + 6\cos x + 10}\,\,dx$

7. b

8. F

9. F

10. T

11. $S = \displaystyle\int_1^5 2\pi \ln x \sqrt{1+\left(\dfrac{1}{x}\right)^2}\,dx$

12. $\dfrac{\pi}{27}\left(5626\sqrt{5626}-1\right)$

13. $\dfrac{\pi}{4}\left(648 - 49\ln 7 - \left(\ln 7\right)^2\right)$

14. $\dfrac{\pi}{8}\left(21 - 8\ln 2 - \left(\ln 2\right)^2\right)$

15. $2\pi\left(p^2 + \dfrac{m^2 p\left(\sin\left(\dfrac{\sqrt{m^2-p^2}}{m}\right)\right)^{-1}}{\sqrt{m^2-p^2}}\right)$

16. $4\pi^2 b^2$

17. $S_g = S_f + 2\pi c L$

18. b

19. $\left(3,\ 4.8\right)$

20. 3

1. Find the length of the curve for the interval $a \le v \le b$.

$$y = \ln\left(\frac{e^v + 1}{e^v - 1}\right)$$

2. Set up, but do not evaluate, an integral for the length of the curve.

$$y = e^x \sin x, \quad 0 \le x \le \pi/2$$

Select the correct answer.

a. $L = \displaystyle\int_0^{\pi/2} \sqrt{1 + e^{2x}(1 - \sin 2x)} \; dx$

b. $L = \displaystyle\int_0^{\pi/2} \sqrt{1 - e^{2x}(1 - \sin 2x)} \; dx$

c. $L = \displaystyle\int_0^{\pi/2} \sqrt{1 + e^{2x}(1 + \sin 2x)} \; dx$

d. $L = \displaystyle\int_0^{\pi/2} \sqrt{1 - e^{2x}(1 + \sin 2x)} \; dx$

e. $L = \displaystyle\int_0^{\pi} \sqrt{1 - e^{2x}(1 + \sin x)} \; dx$

3. True or False?

An integral for the length of the curve $y = x\sqrt[3]{4 - x}$, $0 \le x \le 2$ is $\displaystyle\int_0^2 \sqrt{1 + \left[\frac{12 - x}{3(4 - x)^{2/3}}\right]^2} \; dx$.

4. Sketch the region bounded by the curves $y = x^2$, $x = 0$, and $y = 9$.

True or False?

The centroid of this region is $\left(\dfrac{9}{4}, \dfrac{27}{10}\right)$.

5. Let L be the length of the curve $y = f(x)$, $a \le x \le u$, where f is positive and has a continuous derivative. Let S_f be the surface area generated by rotating the curve about the x-axis. If c is a positive constant, define $g(x) = f(x) + c$ and let S_g be the corresponding surface area generated by the curve $y = g(x)$, $a \le x \le u$. Express S_g in terms of S_f and L.

Select the correct answer.

a. $S_g = S_f - 2\pi u L$

b. $S_g = S_f + 2\pi a L$

c. $S_g = S_f + 2\pi c L$

d. $S_g = S_f - 2\pi c L$

e. $S_g = S_f - 2\pi a L$

f. $S_g = S_f + 2\pi u L$

6. Find the arc length function for the curve $y = 10x^{3/2}$ with starting point $P_o (1, 10)$.

Select the correct answer.

a. $L = \dfrac{2}{675}\left((1 + 225x)^{1/2} - 226\sqrt{226}\right)$

b. $L = \dfrac{2}{675}\left((1 + 225x)^{5/2} + 226\sqrt{226}\right)$

c. $L = \dfrac{2}{675}\left((1 + 225x)^{3/2} + 226\right)$

d. $L = \dfrac{2}{675}\left((1 + 225x)^{3/2} - 226\sqrt{226}\right)$

e. $L = \dfrac{2}{225}\left((1 + 220x)^{3/2} - 226\sqrt{226}\right)$

7. Set up, but do not evaluate, an integral for the area of the surface obtained by rotating the curve about the given axis.

$y = e^x, \ 1 \le y \le 8 \ ; \ y - axis$

Select the correct answer.

a. $\displaystyle\int_1^8 2\pi x \sqrt{1 + e^{2x}} \, dx$

b. $\displaystyle\int_0^{\ln 8} 2\pi \sqrt{1 + e^{2x}} \, dx$

c. $\displaystyle\int_0^{\ln 8} 2\pi x \sqrt{1 + e^{2x}} \, dx$

d. $\displaystyle\int_1^8 2\pi e^x \sqrt{1 + e^{2x}} \, dx$

e. $\displaystyle\int_1^{\ln 8} 2\pi e^x \sqrt{1 + e^x} \, dx$

8. Find the area of the surface obtained by rotating the curve about the x-axis.

$y = x^3, \ 0 \le x \le 2$

Select the correct answer.

a. $\dfrac{\pi}{27}\left(145\sqrt{145} - 1 \right)$

b. $\dfrac{\pi}{27}\left(143\sqrt{143} - 1 \right)$

c. $\dfrac{\pi}{27}\left(142\sqrt{142} - 1 \right)$

d. $\dfrac{\pi}{27}\left(146\sqrt{146} - 1 \right)$

e. $\dfrac{\pi}{27}\left(147\sqrt{147} - 1 \right)$

9. Find the area of the surface obtained by rotating the curve about the x-axis.

$y = \dfrac{x^2}{4} - \dfrac{\ln x}{2}, \ 1 \le x \le 7$

10. Find the area of the surface obtained by rotating the curve about the *x*-axis.

$$x = \frac{1}{3}(y^2 + 2)^{3/2}, \quad 0 \le y \le 5$$

Select the correct answer.

a. $\dfrac{679\pi}{2}$

b. $\dfrac{675\pi}{2}$

c. $\dfrac{669\pi}{2}$

d. $\dfrac{677\pi}{2}$

e. $\dfrac{641\pi}{2}$

11. A large tank is designed with ends in the shape of the region between the curves $y = \dfrac{x^2}{2}$ and $y = 18$, measured in feet. Find the hydrostatic force on one end of the tank if it is filled to a depth of 9 ft with gasoline. (Assume the gasoline's density is $42.0 \; lb / ft^3$.)

12. The ellipse $\dfrac{x^2}{a^2} + \dfrac{y^2}{n^2} = 1, \quad a > n$ is rotated about the *x*-axis to form a surface called an *ellipsoid*. Find the surface area of this ellipsoid.

Select the correct answer.

a. $2\pi\left[n^2 + a^2 n \sin^{-1}\left(\sqrt{a^2 - n^2} \right) / \sqrt{a^2 - n^2} \right]$

b. $2\pi\left[a^2 + n^2 a \sin^{-1}\left(\sqrt{n^2 - a^2} / n \right) / \sqrt{n^2 - a^2} \right]$

c. $2\pi\left[n^2 + a^2 n \sin^{-1}\left(\sqrt{a^2 - n^2} / a \right) \right]$

d. $2\pi\left[n^2 + a^2 n \sin^{-1}\left(\sqrt{a^2 - n^2} / a \right) / \sqrt{a^2 - n^2} \right]$

e. $2\pi\left[n^2 + a^2 n \sin^{-1}\left(\sqrt{a^2 - n^2} / a \right) / n \right]$

13. The end of a tank containing water is vertical and is in the shape of a semicircle with radius 10 m. Find the hydrostatic force against the end of the tank. (Use $g = 9.8$).

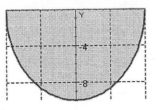

14. The end of a tank containing water is vertical and has the indicated shape, where $a = 13$, $b = 21$ and $h = 6$. Find the hydrostatic force against the end of the tank. Use the fact that water weighs 62.5 lb/ft^3 .

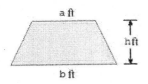

Select the correct answer.

a.   20,743.6 lb
b.   20,482.9 lb
c.   19,641.7 lb
d.   20,729.2 lb
e.   20,625.0 lb

15. Calculate the center of mass of the lamina with density $\rho = 10$ shown in the figure below.

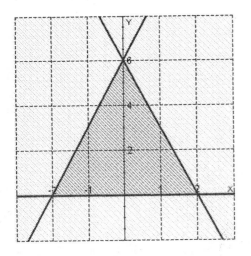

16. A hawk flying at an altitude of 225 m accidentally drops its prey. The parabolic trajectory of the falling prey is described by the equation $y = 225 - \dfrac{x^2}{36}$ until it hits the ground, where y is its height above the ground and x is the horizontal distance traveled in meters. Calculate the distance traveled by the prey from the time it is dropped until the time it hits the ground. Express your answer correct to the nearest centimeter.

17. True or False?

    The center of mass of a lamina with density $\rho = 4$ in the shape of a circle with radius 15 as shown below is $\left(\dfrac{20}{\pi}, \dfrac{20}{\pi} \right)$.

    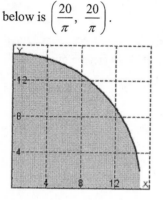

18. Find the centroid of the region shown, not by integration, but by locating the centroids of the rectangles and triangles and using additivity of moments.

    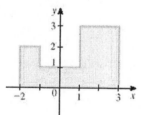

19. A steady wind blows a kite due west. The kite's height above ground from horizontal position $x = 0$ to $x = 80$ ft is given by $y = 130 - \dfrac{1}{100}(x - 20)^2$.

    True or False?

    The distance traveled by the kite is approximately 92.78 ft.

20. Find the length of the curve for the interval $1 \le x \le 4$.

    $$y = \int_1^x \sqrt{t^3 - 1} \; dt$$

1. $\ln\left(\dfrac{e^b - e^{-b}}{e^a - e^{-a}}\right)$

2. c

3. F

4. T

5. c

6. d

7. c

8. a

9. $\dfrac{\pi}{4}\left(648 - 49\ln 7 - (\ln 7)^2\right)$

10. b

11. 7698

12. d

13. 6533333

14. e

15. $(0, 2)$

16. 250.27

17. T

18. $\left(\dfrac{9}{10}, \dfrac{6}{5}\right)$

19. T

20. 62/5

1. For what values of r does the function $y = e^{rt}$ satisfy the differential equation?

   $$y'' - y' - 42y = 0$$

2. $y = Ce^{2x^2}$ is the solution of the differential equation $y' = 4xy$. Find the solution that satisfies the initial condition $y(1) = 1$.

3. A population is modeled by the differential equation $\dfrac{dP}{dt} = 1.8P\left(1 - \dfrac{P}{5,100}\right)$.

   For what values of P is the population decreasing?

4. A function $y(t)$ satisfies the differential equation $\dfrac{dy}{dt} = y^4 - 13y^3 + 40y^2$.

   What are the constant solutions of the equation?

5. The solution of the differential equation $y' = y^3 - 4y$ satisfies the initial condition $y(0) = 0.8$.

   Find the limit.

   $$\lim_{t \to \infty} y(t)$$

6. Use Euler's method with $h = 0.9$ to estimate the value of $y(1.8)$, where y is the solution of the initial-value problem.

   $$y' = y, \quad y(0) = 1$$

7. Kirchhoff's Law gives us the derivative equation $Q' = 12 - 4Q$.

   If $Q(0) = 0$, use Euler's method with step size 0.1 to estimate Q after 0.3 second.

8. Solve the differential equation.

   $$\frac{dy}{dx} = \frac{e^{7x}}{8y^7}$$

9. Solve the differential equation.

$$y' = \frac{8x^7 y}{\ln y}$$

10. Find the solution of the differential equation $\dfrac{du}{dt} = \dfrac{2t + \sec^2 t}{2u}$ that satisfies the initial condition $u(0) = 4$.

11. Find the solution of the differential equation $\dfrac{dy}{dx} = 7x^6 y$ that satisfies the initial condition $y(0) = 8$.

12. Find the orthogonal trajectories of the family of curves.

$$y = kx^5$$

13. **Newton's Law of Cooling** states that the rate of cooling of an object is proportional to the temperature difference between the object and its surroundings. Suppose that a roast turkey is taken from an oven when its temperature has reached $200°$ F and is placed on a table in a room where the temperature is $85°$ F. If $u(t)$ is the temperature of the turkey after t minutes, then Newton's Law of Cooling implies that $\dfrac{du}{dt} = k(u - 85)$.

This could be solved as a separable differential equation. Another method is to make the change of variable $y = u - 85$. If the temperature of the turkey is $170°$ F after half an hour, what is the temperature after 10 min?

14. Suppose that a population develops according to the logistic equation $\dfrac{dP}{dt} = 0.07P - 0.0007P^2$ where t is measured in weeks. What is the carrying capacity?

15. The Pacific halibut fishery has been modeled by the differential equation $\dfrac{dy}{dt} = ky\left(1 - \dfrac{y}{K}\right)$ where $y(t)$ is the biomass (the total mass of the members of the population) in kilograms at time t (measured in years), the carrying capacity is estimated to be $K = 30 \times 10^9$ kg and $k = 0.07$ per year. If $y(0) = 10 \times 10^9$ kg, find the biomass a year later.

16. The population of the world was about 5.3 billion in 1990. Birth rates in the 1990s range from 35 to 40 million per year and death rates range from 15 to 20 million per year. Let's assume that the carrying capacity for world population is 100 billion. Use the logistic model to predict the world population in the 2,000 year. Calculate your answer in billions to one decimal place. (Because the initial population is small compared to the carrying capacity, you can take k to be an estimate of the initial relative growth rate.)

17. Let

$$\frac{dP(t)}{dt} = 0.1P\left(1 - \frac{P}{890}\right) - \frac{1,870}{89}$$

What are the equilibrium solutions?

18. Consider the differential equation

$$\frac{dP(t)}{dt} = 0.6P\left(1 - \frac{P}{900}\right) - c$$

as a model for a fish population, where t is measured in weeks and c is a constant. For what values of c does the fish population always die out?

19. Determine whether the differential equation is linear.

$$y' + y \ln x = x^3 y^3$$

20. An object with mass m is dropped from rest and we assume that the air resistance is proportional to the speed of the object. If $s(t)$ is the distance dropped after t seconds, then the speed is $v = s'(t)$ and the acceleration is $a = v'(t)$. If g is the acceleration due to gravity, then the downward force on the object is $mg - cv$, where c is a positive constant, and Newton's Second Law gives $m\dfrac{dv}{dt} = mg - cv$.

Find the limiting velocity.

1. 7, -6

2. $\dfrac{1}{e^2}\left(e^{2x^2}\right)$

3. $(5100, \infty)$

4. 8, 5, 0

5. 0

6. 3.61

7. 2.352

8. $y = \pm\sqrt[8]{\dfrac{e^{7x}}{7} + C}$

9. $y = e^{\pm\sqrt{2x^8 + C}}$

10. $u = \sqrt{t^2 + \tan t + 16}$

11. $y = 8e^{x^7}$

12. $x^2 + 5y^2 = C$

13. 189

14. 100

15. 10.47×10^9

16. 5.5

17. $P(t) = 340, \quad P(t) = 550$

18. $c > 135$

19. no

20. $v = \dfrac{mg}{c}$

1. For what nonzero values of k does the function $y = \sin kt$ satisfy the differential equation?

    $$y'' + 4y = 0$$

2. Select a direction field for the differential equation $y' = y^2 - x^2$ from a set of direction fields labeled I-IV.

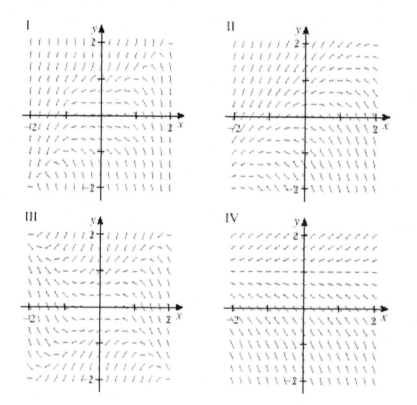

3. Use Euler's method with step size 0.5 to compute the approximate y-values y_1, y_2, y_3, and y_4 of the solution of the initial-value problem.

    $$y' = 1 + 7x - 4y, \quad y(1) = 2$$

4. Use Euler's method with step size 0.25 to estimate $y(1)$, where $y(x)$ is the solution of the initial-value problem. Round your answer to four decimal places.

    $$y' = 4x + y^2, \quad y(0) = 0$$

5. Solve the differential equation.

    $$5yy' = 3x$$

6. Solve the differential equation.

    $$y' = \frac{7x^6 y}{\ln y}$$

7. Solve the differential equation.

    $$\frac{du}{dt} = 15 + 5u + 3t + ut$$

8. Find the solution of the differential equation

    $$\frac{dy}{dx} = 6x^5 y$$

    that satisfies the initial condition $y(0) = 3$.

9. A bacteria culture starts with 440 bacteria and grows at a rate proportional to its size. After 6 hours there are 5,700 bacteria. When will the population reach 24,000?

10. Experiments show that if the chemical reaction $N_2O_5 \rightarrow 2NO_2 + \frac{1}{2}O_2$ takes place at $45°$ C, the rate of reaction of dinitrogen pentoxide is proportional to its concentration as follows :

    $$-\frac{d[N_2O_5]}{dt} = 0.0008[N_2O_5]$$

    How long will the reaction take to reduce the concentration of N_2O_5 to 50% of its original value?

11. After 3 days a sample of radon-222 decayed to 58% of its original amount. How long would it take the sample to decay to 43% of its original amount?

12. A thermometer is taken from a room where the temperature is $23°$ C to the outdoors, where the temperature is $0°$ C. After one minute the thermometer reads $11°$ C. Use Newton's Law of Cooling to answer the following question. When will the thermometer read $10°$ C?

13. The rate of change of atmospheric pressure P with respect to altitude h is proportional to P provided that the temperature is constant. At $15°$ C the pressure is 100.9 kPa at sea level and 85.18 kPa at $h = 1,080$. What is the pressure at an altitude of 2,000 m?

14. Suppose that a population grows according to a logistic model with carrying capacity 3,000 and $k = 0.08$ per year. If the initial population is 500, write a formula, P (t, for the population after t years).

15. Biologists stocked a lake with 500 fish and estimated the carrying capacity (the maximal population for the fish of that species in that lake) to be 6,000. The number of fish tripled in the first year.

    Assuming that the size of the fish population satisfies the logistic equation, how long will it take for the population to increase to 1,300?

16. Let $\dfrac{dP(t)}{dt} = 0.1P\left(1 - \dfrac{P}{730}\right) - \dfrac{129,000}{7,300}$.

    What are the equilibrium solutions?

17. Determine whether the differential equation is linear.

    $$xy' + e^x - x^7 y = 0$$

18. Solve the differential equation.

    $$(5 + t)\frac{du}{dt} + u = 5 + t, \quad t > 0$$

19. Solve the initial-value problem.

    $$x^2 \frac{dy}{dx} + 2xy = -\sin x, \quad y(\pi) = 0$$

20. A function $y(t)$ satisfies the differential equation $\dfrac{dy}{dt} = y^4 - 15y^3 + 54y^2$.

    For what values of y is y decreasing?

1. 2, -2

2. III

3. 2, 3.75, 3.75, 5.5

4. 1.6622

5. $y = \pm\sqrt{\dfrac{3}{5}x^2 + C}$

6. $y = e^{\pm\sqrt{2x^7 + C}}$

7. $u = -3 + Ce^{\frac{t^2}{2} + 5t}$

8. $y = 3e^{x^6}$

9. 9.04

10. 866

11. 4.65

12. 1.1

13. 73.7

14. $P(t) = \dfrac{3000}{1 + 5e^{-0.08t}}$

15. $t = 0.86$

16. $P(t) = 300, \quad P(t) = 430$

17. yes

18. $u = \dfrac{5t + 0.5t^2 + c}{5 + t}$

19. $y = x^{-2}(\cos x + 1)$

20. (6, 9)

1. Which equation does the function $y = e^{-3t}$ satisfy?

   Select the correct answer.

   a. $y'' + y' + 12y = 0$

   b. $y'' + y' - 12y = 0$

   c. $y'' - y' - 12y = 0$

   d. $y'' - y' + 12y = 0$

   e. $y'' - 3y' + 12y = 0$

2. Which of the following functions is a solution of the differential equation?

   $$y'' + 12y' + 36y = 0$$

   Select the correct answer.

   a. $y = t^2 e^{-6t}$

   b. $y = e^t$

   c. $y = e^{-6t}$

   d. $y = te^{-6t}$

   e. $y = 6e^{-6t}$

3. The equation $y = \dfrac{1}{\sqrt{C - 2x^2}}$ represents the family of solutions of the differential equation $y' = 2xy^3$, find the solution that satisfies the initial condition $y(0) = 10$.

   Select the correct answer.

   a. $y = \dfrac{10}{\sqrt{1 - 2x^2}}$

   b. $y = \dfrac{10}{\sqrt{1 - 200x^2}}$

   c. $y = \dfrac{10}{\sqrt{1 - 2x^2}} + 10$

   d. $y = \dfrac{10}{\sqrt{1 - 20x^2}}$

   e. $y = \dfrac{100}{\sqrt{1 - 20x^2}}$

4. A population is modeled by the differential equation.

$$\frac{dP}{dt} = 1.4P\left(1 - \frac{P}{4,700}\right)$$

For what values of P is the population increasing?

Select the correct answer.

   a. $0 < P < 4,700$
   b. $0 < P < 1.4$
   c. $P < 4,700$
   d. $P > 1.4$
   e. $P > 47$

5. Which of the following functions are the constant solutions of the equation

$$\frac{dy}{dt} = y^4 - 6y^3 + 8y^2$$

Select the correct answer.

   a. $y(t) = 2$
   b. $y(t) = 0$
   c. $y(t) = e^t$
   d. $y(t) = 4$
   e. $y(t) = 3$

6. Choose the differential equation corresponding to this direction field.

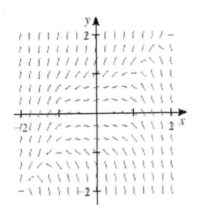

Select the correct answer.

   a. $y' = y^2 - x^2$
   b. $y' = y - x$
   c. $y' = y - 1$
   d. $y' = y^3 - x^3$
   e. $y' = 2y^3 + x^3$

7. Suppose that a population develops according to the logistic equation

$$\frac{dP}{dt} = 0.02P - 0.0002P^2$$

where t is measured in weeks. What is the carrying capacity?

Select the correct answer.

 a. $K = 0.02$
 b. $K = 0.0002$
 c. $K = 100$
 d. $K = 200$
 e. $K = 300$

8. Use Euler's method with step size 0.25 to estimate $y(1)$, where $y(x)$ is the solution of the initial-value problem. Round your answer to four decimal places.

$$y' = 5x + y^2, \quad y(0) = 0$$

Select the correct answer.

 a. $y(1) = 2.1307$
 b. $y(1) = 1.0429$
 c. $y(1) = 1.5219$
 d. $y(1) = 4.5157$
 e. $y(1) = 3.6127$

9. Solve the differential equation.

$$\frac{dy}{dx} = \frac{e^{2x}}{6y^5}$$

Select the correct answer.

 a. $y = \pm \sqrt[6]{\dfrac{e^{2x}}{2}}$

 b. $y = \pm \sqrt[6]{e^{2x}}$

 c. $y = \pm \sqrt[6]{e^{2x} + C}$

 d. $y = \pm \sqrt[6]{\dfrac{e^{6x}}{2} + C}$

 e. $y = \pm \sqrt[5]{\dfrac{e^{2x}}{2}}$

10. Solve the differential equation.

$7yy' = 5x$

Select the correct answer.

 a. $5x^2 - 7y^2 = C$

 b. $5x^2 + 7y^2 = C$

 c. $7x^2 - 5y^2 = C$

 d. $7x^2 + 5y^2 = C$

 e. $5x^2 + 7y^2 = 12$

11. Suppose that a population grows according to a logistic model with carrying capacity 3,000 and $k = 0.02$ per year. Choose the logistic differential equation for these data.

Select the correct answer.

 a. $\dfrac{dP(t)}{dt} = 0.02P\left(1 + \dfrac{P}{3,000}\right)$

 b. $\dfrac{dP(t)}{dt} = 3,000P\left(1 - \dfrac{P}{0.02}\right)$

 c. $\dfrac{dP(t)}{dt} = 0.02P\left(1 - \dfrac{P}{3,000}\right)$

 d. $\dfrac{dP(t)}{dt} = P\left(1 - \dfrac{P}{3,000}\right)$

 e. $\dfrac{dP(t)}{dt} = 0.002P\left(1 - \dfrac{P}{2}\right)$

12. Solve the differential equation.

$\dfrac{du}{dt} = 32 + 8u + 4t + ut$

Select the correct answer.

 a. $u = -4 + Ce^{t^2 - 8t}$

 b. $u = -4 + Ce^{\frac{t^2}{2} + 8t}$

 c. $u = -4 + Ce^{t^2 + 8t}$

 d. $u = -4 + Ce^{-8t}$

 e. $u = -4 + Ce^{8t^2}$

13. Find the solution of the differential equation $\dfrac{dy}{dx} = y^2 + 1$ that satisfies the initial condition $y(4) = 0$.

Select the correct answer.

   a. $y = \tan(x - 4)$
   b. $y = \tan(x - 9)$
   c. $y = \tan(x - 13)$
   d. $y = \tan(x - 12)$
   e. $y = \tan(x - 14)$

14. Find the solution of the differential equation $\dfrac{dy}{dx} = 5x^4 y$ that satisfies the initial condition $y(0) = 2$.

Select the correct answer.

   a. $y = 3e^{x^5}$

   b. $y = 2e^{x^4}$

   c. $y = 3e^{x^4} + C$

   d. $y = e^{x^5} + C$

   e. $y = 2e^{x^5}$

15. Solve the differential equation.

$$(6+t)\dfrac{du}{dt} + u = 6 + t, \quad t > 0$$

Select the correct answer.

   a. $u = \dfrac{6t + t^2}{t + 6} + C$

   b. $u = \dfrac{6t + t^3}{t + 6} + C$

   c. $u = \dfrac{6t + t^2 + C}{t + 6}$

   d. $u = \dfrac{6t + \dfrac{t^2}{2} + C}{t + 6}$

   e. $u = \dfrac{t - \dfrac{t^2}{2} + C}{t - 6}$

16. Each system of differential equations is a model for two species that either compete for the same resources or cooperate for mutual benefit (flowering plants and insect pollinators, for instance). Decide which of the following systems describes the competition model.

   Select the correct answer.

   a.
   $$\frac{dx}{dt} = 0.59x - 0.8212x^2 + 0.20093xy$$

   $$\frac{dy}{dt} = 0.09y + 0.17508xy$$

   b.
   $$\frac{dx}{dt} = 0.66x - 0.672x^2 + 0.4795xy$$

   $$\frac{dy}{dt} = 0.6y - 0.74321y^2 - 0.8992xy$$

   c.   none

17. A population of protozoa develops with a constant relative growth rate of 0.9264 per member per day. On day zero the population consists of 7 members. Find the population size after 4 days. Find the answer correct to the nearest whole number.

   Select the correct answer.

   a. $P=18$
   b. $P=285$
   c. $P=41$
   d. $P=275$
   e. $P=382$

18. Consider a population $P = P(t)$ with constant relative birth and death rates α and β, respectively, and a constant emigration rate m, where $\alpha = 0.9$, $\beta = 0.8$ and $m = 0.7$. Then the rate of change of the population at time t is modeled by the differential equation $\dfrac{dP}{dt} = kP - m$ where $k = \alpha - \beta$.

   Find the solution of this equation with the rate of change of the population at time $t = 3$ that satisfies the initial condition $P(0) = 3,400$.

   Select the correct answer.

   a.   655.3
   b.   4,602.1
   c.   7,987.1
   d.   4,587.1
   e.   1,187.1
   f.   none of these

19. The table gives estimates of the world population, in millions, from 1750 to 2000:

Year	Population	Year	Population
1750	900	1900	1,580
1800	1,080	1950	2,280
1850	1,240	2000	6,160

Use the exponential model and the population figures for 1750 and 1800 to predict the world population in 1950.

Select the correct answer.

   a. $P = 1,102,329$
   b. $P = 1,296$
   c. $P = 651,110,527$
   d. $P = 1,866$
   e. $P = 3,243$

20. Experiments show that if the chemical reaction $N_2O_5 \rightarrow 2NO_2 + \frac{1}{2}O_2$ takes place at $45°$ C, the rate of reaction of dinitrogen pentoxide is proportional to its concentration as follows :

$$-\frac{d[N_2O_5]}{dt} = 0.0004[N_2O_5]$$

How long will the reaction take to reduce the concentration of N_2O_5 to 90% of its original value? Select the correct answer.

   a. $t = 263$
   b. $t = 211$
   c. $t = 0$
   d. $t = 128$
   e. $t = 1,996$

1. c

2. c, d

3. b

4. a

5. a, b, d

6. d

7. c

8. a

9. d

10. a

11. c

12. b

13. a

14. e

15. d

16. b

17. b

18. d

19. d

20. a

1. A curve passes through the point $(4, 2)$ and has the property that the slope of the curve at every point P is 3 times the y-coordinate P. What is the equation of the curve?

    Select the correct answer.

    a. $y = \dfrac{1}{2}e^{3x-12}$

    b. $y = 2e^{3x+12}$

    c. $y = 2e^{x-12}$

    d. $y = 2e^{3x-4}$

    e. $y = 2e^{3x-12}$

2. A thermometer is taken from a room where the temperature is $17°\,C$ to the outdoors, where the temperature is $9°\,C$. After one minute the thermometer reads $13°\,C$. Use Newton's Law of Cooling to answer the following question. When will the thermometer read $10°\,C$?

    Select the correct answer.

    a. $t = 3.0$ min
    b. $t = 3.5$ min
    c. $t = 1.5$ min
    d. $t = 6.0$ min
    e. $t = 2.8$ min

3. A sum of $3,000 is invested at 25% interest. If $A(t)$ is the amount of the investment at time t for the case of continuous compounding, write a differential equation and an initial condition satisfied by $A(t)$.

    Select the correct answer.

    a. $\dfrac{dA}{dt} = 0.25A(0), \quad A(0) = 3{,}000$

    b. $\dfrac{dA}{dt} = 25A, \quad A(0) = 3{,}000$

    c. $\dfrac{dA}{dt} = 0.25A, \quad A(0) = 3{,}000$

    d. $\dfrac{dA}{dt} = 0.25A, \quad A(0) = 300$

    e. $\dfrac{dA}{dt} = 2{,}500A, \quad A(0) = 3{,}000$

4. Let c be a positive number. A differential equation of the form $\dfrac{dt}{dt} = ky^{1+c}$ where k is a positive constant, is called a *doomsday equation* because the exponent in the expression ky^{1+c} is larger than that for natural growth (that is, $k\,y$). An especially prolific breed of rabbits has the growth term $ky^{1.05}$. If 2 such rabbits breed initially and the warren has 27 rabbits after 5 months, then when is doomsday?

Select the correct answer.

   a.   40.98 months
   b.   38.98 months
   c.   1,106.35 months
   d.   35.98 months
   e.   81.95 months

5. Suppose that a population develops according to the logistic equation $\dfrac{dP}{dt} = 0.02P - 0.0002P^2$ where t is measured in weeks. What is the carrying capacity?

Select the correct answer.

   a. $K = 0.02$
   b. $K = 100$
   c. $K = 0.0002$
   d. $K = 200$
   e. $K = 2000$

6. Suppose that a population grows according to a logistic model with carrying capacity 2,000 and $k = 0.07$ per year. Choose the logistic differential equation for these data.

Select the correct answer.

   a. $\dfrac{dP(t)}{dt} = 0.07P\left(1 - \dfrac{P}{2{,}000}\right)$

   b. $\dfrac{dP(t)}{dt} = 2{,}000P\left(1 - \dfrac{P}{0.07}\right)$

   c. $\dfrac{dP(t)}{dt} = 0.07P\left(1 + \dfrac{P}{2{,}000}\right)$

   d. $\dfrac{dP(t)}{dt} = 0.07P\left(1 + \dfrac{P^2}{2{,}000}\right)$

   e. $\dfrac{dP(t)}{dt} = 0.02P\left(1 + \dfrac{P}{0.007}\right)$

7. The population of the world was about 5.3 billion in 1990. Birth rates in the 1990s range from 35 to 40 million per year and death rates range from 15 to 20 million per year. Let's assume that the carrying capacity for world population is 100 billion.

   Use the logistic model to predict the world population in the 2,450 year. Calculate your answer in billions to one decimal place.

   (Because the initial population is small compared to the carrying capacity, you can take k to be an estimate of the initial relative growth rate.)

   Select the correct answer.

   a.   32.9 billion
   b.   17.1 billion
   c.   24.1 billion
   d.   59.2 billion
   e.   78.3 billion

8. Determine whether the differential equation is linear.

   $$xy' + \sin x - x^5 y = 0$$

   Select the correct answer.

   a.   the equation is neither linear nor nonlinear
   b.   the equation is not linear
   c.   the equation is linear

9. Use the Bernoulli's method to solve the differential equation.

   $$y' + \frac{3y}{x} = \frac{y^3}{x^4}$$

   Select the correct answer.

   a. $y = \pm\left(Cx^6 + \dfrac{2}{9x^3}\right)^{1/2}$

   b. $y = \pm\left(Cx^6 + \dfrac{2}{9x^3}\right)^{-1/2}$

   c. $y = \left(Cx^6 \pm \dfrac{2}{9x^3}\right)^{1/2}$

   d. $y = \left(Cx^6 \pm \dfrac{2}{9x^3}\right)^{-1/2}$

   e. $y = \left(Cx^6 \pm \dfrac{2}{9x^3}\right)^{-3/2}$

10. In the circuit shown in Figure, a battery supplies a constant voltage of 40 V, the inductance is 2 H, the resistance is 10 Ω , and $I(0) = 0$. Find the current after 1 s. Round your answer to two decimal places.

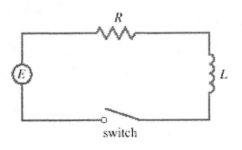

Select the correct answer.

   a.   4.11 A
   b.   3.63 A
   c.   3.97 A
   d.   3.76 A
   e.   7.0 A

11. The figure shows a circuit containing an electromotive force, a capacitor with a capacitance of C farads (F), and a resistor with a resistance of R ohms (Ω). The voltage drop across the capacitor is $\dfrac{Q}{C}$ where Q is the charge (in coulombs), so in this case Kirchhoff's Law gives $RI + \dfrac{Q}{C} = E(t)$.

But $I = \dfrac{dQ}{dt}$, so we have $R\dfrac{dQ}{dt} + \dfrac{1}{C}Q = E(t)$.

Suppose the resistance is 5 Ω , the capacitance is 0.05 F, a battery gives a constant voltage of 80 V, and the initial charge is $Q(0) = 0$ C. Find the charge and the current at time t.

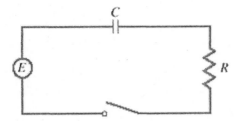

Select the correct answer.

   a. $Q = 16e^{-4t},\ I = 4\left(1 - e^{-4t}\right)$
   b. $I = 16e^{-4t},\ Q = 4\left(1 - e^{-4t}\right)$
   c. $Q = 16\left(1 - e^{-4t}\right),\ I = 4e^{-4t}$
   d. $Q = 4e^{-4t},\ I = 16\left(1 - e^{-4t}\right)$
   e. $Q = e^{-4t},\ I = \left(1 - e^{-t}\right)$

12. We modeled populations of aphids and ladybugs with a Lotka-Volterra system. Suppose we modify those equations as follows:

$$\frac{dA}{dt} = 3A(1 - 0.0001A) - 0.01AL \,,$$

$$\frac{dL}{dt} = -0.5L + 0.0001AL$$

Select the correct equilibrium solution.

    a. $A = 6{,}000, L = 350$
    b. $A = 5{,}000, L = 150$
    c. $A = 5{,}000, L = 50$
    d. $A = 1{,}000, L = 350$
    e. $A = 66{,}000, L = 35$

13. An object with mass m is dropped from rest and we assume that the air resistance is proportional to the speed of the object. If $s(t)$ is the distance dropped after t seconds, then the speed is $v = s'(t)$ and the acceleration is $a = v'(t)$. If g is the acceleration due to gravity, then the downward force on the object is $mg - cv$, where c is a positive constant, and Newton's Second Law gives $m\dfrac{dv}{dt} = mg - cv$.

Find the limiting velocity.

Select the correct answer.

    a. $v = \dfrac{g}{c}$

    b. $v = \dfrac{c}{g}$

    c. $v = \dfrac{mg}{c}$

    d. $v = \dfrac{mc}{g}$

    e. $v = mc$

14. A phase trajectory is shown for populations of rabbits (R) and foxes (F). Describe how each population changes as time goes by.

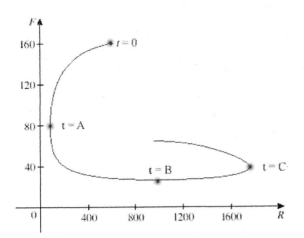

Select the correct statement.

    a.   At $t = B$ the population of foxes reaches a minimum of about 30.
    b.   At $t = B$ the number of rabbits rebounds to 500.
    c.   At $t = B$ the number of foxes reaches a maximum of about 2400.

15. A common inhabitant of human intestines is the bacterium *Escherichia coli*. A cell of this bacterium in a nutrient-broth medium divides into two cells every 20 minutes. The initial population of a culture is 25 cells. Find the number of cells after 5 hours.

Select the correct answer.

    a. $P = 1,000$
    b. $P = 6,553,600$
    c. $P = 32,768$
    d. $P = 1,476,225$
    e. $P = 819,200$

16. In the circuit shown in Figure, a generator supplies a voltage of $E(t) = 20 \sin 60t$ volts, the inductance is 2 H, the resistance is 40 Ω , and $I(0) = 2$ A. Find the current after 0.2 s. Round your answer to two decimal places.

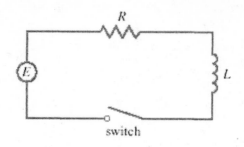

Select the correct answer.

   a.   -0.06 A
   b.   -0.11 A
   c.   -0.13 A
   d.   -0.75 A
   e.   -0.50 A

17. Solve the differential equation.

$$(2+t)\frac{du}{dt} + u = 2+t, \quad t > 0$$

Select the correct answer.

   a. $u = \dfrac{2t + t^2 + C}{t+2}$

   b. $u = \dfrac{t^2 + C}{t+2}$

   c. $u = \dfrac{2t + \frac{1}{2}t^2}{\frac{3}{2}t + 2} + C$

   d. $u = \dfrac{2t + \frac{t^2}{2} + C}{t+2}$

   e. $u = 2t + \dfrac{t^2}{2} + C$

18. The table gives the population of the United States, in millions, for the years 1900 - 2000.

Year	Population	Year	Population
1900	75	1960	166
1910	91	1970	200
1920	111	1980	228
1930	126	1990	253
1940	133	2000	276
1950	126		

Use the exponential model and the census figures for 1900 and 1910 to predict the population in 1,950.

Select the correct answer.

a. $P = 533$ million
b. $P = 1,004$ million
c. $P = 239$ million
d. $P = 394$ million
e. $P = 197$ million

19. Solve the initial-value problem.

$$x^2 \frac{dy}{dx} + 2xy = -\sin x, \quad y(\pi) = 0$$

Select the correct answer.

a. $y = \dfrac{\cos x + 1}{x^2}$

b. $y = \dfrac{\cos x - 1}{x^2}$

c. $y = \dfrac{-\sin x}{x^2}$

d. $y = \dfrac{\sin x}{x^2}$

e. $y = \dfrac{\sin^2 x}{x^3}$

20. Let $P(t)$ be the performance level of someone learning a skill as a function of the training time t. The graph of P is called a *learning curve*. We propose the differential equation $\dfrac{dP}{dt} = r(F - P(t))$ as a reasonable model for learning, where r is a positive constant. Solve it as a linear differential equation.

Select the correct answer.

a. $P(t) = F + Ce^{-rt}$

b. $P(t) = F + Ce^{rt}$

c. $P(t) = F - Ce^{-rt}$

d. $P(t) = F - Ce^{rt}$

e. $P(t) = FCe^{rt}$

ANSWER KEY

Stewart - Calculus ET 5e Chapter 9 Form D

1. e

2. a

3. c

4. a

5. b

6. a

7. c

8. c

9. b

10. c

11. b

12. b

13. c

14. a

15. e

16. b

17. d

18. e

19. a

20. a

1. For what nonzero values of k does the function $y = A \sin kt + B \cos kt$ satisfy the differential equation $y'' + 4y = 0$ for all values of A and B? Check all that apply.

   Select the correct answer.

   a. $k = 1$
   b. $k = -4$
   c. $k = 2$
   d. $k = -2$
   e. $k = 4$

2. $y = Ce^{4x^2}$ is the family of solutions to the differential equation $y' = 8xy$. Find the solution that satisfies the initial condition $y(0) = 8$.

3. $y = \dfrac{1}{10x + C}$ is the family of solutions of the differential equation $y' = -10y^2$, find the solution that satisfies the initial condition $y(0) = 6$.

4. A population is modeled by the differential equation $\dfrac{dP}{dt} = 1.6P\left(1 - \dfrac{P}{6,000}\right)$.

   What are the equilibrium solutions?

5. A function $y(t)$ satisfies the differential equation $\dfrac{dy}{dt} = y^4 - 10y^3 + 21y^2$.

   For what values of y is y increasing?

6. One model for the spread of a rumor is that the rate of spread is proportional to the product of the fraction of the population who have heard the rumor and the fraction who have not heard the rumor. Let's assume that the constant of proportionality is $k = 0.04$. Write a differential equation that is satisfied by y.

7. Biologists stocked a lake with 450 fish and estimated the carrying capacity (the maximal population for the fish of that species in that lake) to be 11,000. The number of fish tripled in the first year. Assuming that the size of the fish population satisfies the logistic equation, find an expression for the size of the population after t years.

8. Use the direction field of the differential equation to sketch a solution curve that passes through the given point.

$y' = y^2$, $(0, 1)$

Select the correct answer.

a.

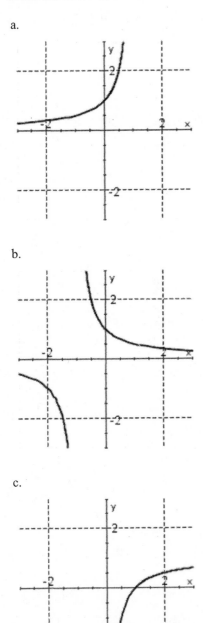

b.

c.

9. The solution of the differential equation $y' = y^3 - 4y$ satisfies the initial condition $y(0) = -0.1$.

    Find the limit $\lim\limits_{t \to \infty} y(t)$

10. Use Euler's method with step size 0.4 to estimate $y(2.0)$, where $y(x)$ is the solution of the initial-value problem. Round your answer to four decimal places.

    $$y' = x^2 + y^2, \quad y(0) = 1$$

11. Use Euler's method with step size 0.25 to estimate $y(0.5)$, where $y(x)$ is the solution of the initial-value problem. Round your answer to two decimal places.

    $$y' = 5xy^2, \quad y(0) = 1$$

12. Solve the differential equation.

    $$\frac{du}{dt} = 14 + 2u + 7t + ut$$

13. Find the solution of the differential equation $x + 4y^3 \sqrt{x^2 + 1} \; \dfrac{dy}{dx} = 0$ that satisfies the initial condition $y(0) = 3$.

    Select the correct answer.

    a. $y = \sqrt[4]{81 - \sqrt{x^2 + 1}}$

    b. $y = \sqrt[4]{81 - \sqrt{x^2 - 1}}$

    c. $y = \sqrt[4]{82 - \sqrt{x^2 - 1}}$

    d. $y = \sqrt[4]{81 + \sqrt{x^2 + 1}}$

    e. $y = \sqrt[4]{82 - \sqrt{x^2 + 1}}$

14. Find the solution of the differential equation $\dfrac{du}{dt} = \dfrac{2t + \sec^2 t}{2u}$ that satisfies the initial condition $u(0) = 7$.

15. Find the solution of the differential equation $\dfrac{dy}{dx} = 7x^6 y$ that satisfies the initial condition $y(0) = 7$.

16. Find the solution of the differential equation $\dfrac{dy}{dx} = \dfrac{y^2}{x^4}$ that satisfies the initial condition $y(1) = 1$.

17. Find the orthogonal trajectories of the family of curves.

$y = kx^7$

Select the correct answer.

a. $x^2 + 6y^2 = 0$

b. $x^2 - 6y^2 = 0$

c. $x^2 + 7y^2 = C$

d. $x^2 - 6y^2 = C$

e. $x^2 - 7y^2 = 0$

18. A tank contains 1,200 L of brine with 15 kg of dissolved salt. Pure water enters the tank at a rate of 14 L/min. The solution is kept thoroughly mixed and drains from the tank at the same rate. How much salt is in the tank after 15 minutes?

19. A common inhabitant of human intestines is the bacterium *Escherichia coli*. A cell of this bacterium in a nutrient-broth medium divides into two cells every 20 minutes. The initial population of a culture is 25 cells. Find the number of cells after 2 hours.

20. A bacteria culture starts with 150 bacteria and grows at a rate proportional to its size. After 2 hours there are 6,200 bacteria. When will the population reach 35,000?

1. c, d

2. $8e^{4x^2}$

3. $\dfrac{6}{60x+1}$

4. 0, 6000

5. $(-\infty,\ 0) \cup (0,\ 3) \cup (7,\ \infty)$

6. $\dfrac{dy}{dt} = 0.04y(1-y)$

7. $P(t) = \dfrac{11000}{1+23.44(0.3)^t}$

8. a

9. 0

10. 84.9998

11. 1.31

12. $u = -7 + Ce^{\frac{t^2}{2}+2t}$

13. e

14. $u = \sqrt{t^2 + \tan t + 49}$

15. $y = 7e^{x^7}$

16. $y = \dfrac{3x^3}{1+2x^3}$

17. c

18. 12.59

19. 1600

20. 2.93 hours

1. For what nonzero values of k does the function $y = \sin kt$ satisfy the differential equation?

    $$y'' + 9y = 0$$

    Select all that apply.

    a. $k = -9$
    b. $k = -3$
    c. $k = 1$
    d. $k = 9$
    e. $k = 3$

2. For what values of r does the function $y = e^{rt}$ satisfy the differential equation?

    $$y'' - y' - 30y = 0$$

3. Which of the following functions is a solution of the differential equation?

    $$y'' + 16y' + 64y = 0$$

    Select all that apply.

    a. $y = t^2 e^{-8t}$
    b. $y = te^{-8t}$
    c. $y = e^t$
    d. $y = e^{-8t}$
    e. $y = -8e^{-8t}$

4. $y = Ce^{2x^2}$ is the solution of the differential equation $y' = 4xy$.

    Find the solution that satisfies the initial condition $y(1) = 3$.

5. $y = \dfrac{1}{8x + C}$ is the family of solutions of the differential equation $y' = -8y^2$, find the solution that satisfies the initial condition $y(0) = 3$.

6. A population is modeled by the differential equation $\dfrac{dP}{dt} = 1.4\left(1 - \dfrac{P}{5{,}500}\right)$.

    For what values of P is the population decreasing?

7. Use Euler's method with step size 0.4 to estimate $y(2.0)$, where $y(x)$ is the solution of the initial-value problem. Round your answer to four decimal places.

    $$y' = x^2 + y^2, \quad y(0) = 1$$

8. A function $y(t)$ satisfies the differential equation $\dfrac{dy}{dt} = y^4 - 13y^3 + 30y^2$.

    For what values of y is y decreasing?

    Select the correct answer.

    a. $(-\infty, 3) \cup (10, \infty)$

    b. $(-\infty, 0) \cup (0, 3) \cup (10, \infty)$

    c. $(-\infty, 0) \cup (10, \infty)$

    d. $(0, 3) \cup (10, \infty)$

    e. $(3, 10)$

9. Choose the differential equation corresponding to this direction field.

    Select the correct answer.

    a. $y' = y - x$

    b. $y' = y^3 - x^3$

    c. $y' = y - 1$

    d. $y' = y^2 - x^2$

    e. $y' = 2y^2 - x^3$

10. The solution of the differential equation $y' = y^3 - 4y$ satisfies the initial condition $y(0) = 0.2$.

Find the limit.

$$\lim_{t \to \infty} y(t)$$

11. Solve the differential equation.

$$\frac{dy}{dx} = \frac{e^{2x}}{4y^3}$$

Select the correct answer.

a. $y = \pm\sqrt[3]{\dfrac{e^{2x}}{2} + C}$

b. $y = \pm\sqrt[3]{e^{2x}} + C$

c. $y = \pm\sqrt[4]{\dfrac{e^{3x}}{2}}$

d. $y = \pm\sqrt[4]{\dfrac{e^{2x}}{2} + C}$

e. $y = \pm\sqrt[4]{e^{2x}} + C$

12. Scientists can determine the age of ancient objects by a method called *radiocarbon dating*. The bombardment of the upper atmosphere by cosmic rays converts nitrogen to a radioactive isotope of carbon, ^{14}C, with a half-life of about 5730 years. Vegetation absorbs carbon dioxide through the atmosphere and animal life assimilates ^{14}C through food chains. When a plant or animal dies it stops replacing its carbon and the amount of ^{14}C begins to decrease through radioactive decay. Therefore, the level of radioactivity must also decay exponentially. A parchment fragment was discovered that had about 32% as much ^{14}C radioactivity as does plant material on Earth today. Estimate the age of the parchment.

Select the correct answer.

a. $t = 9{,}419$ years
b. $t = 9{,}231$ years
c. $t = 9{,}041$ years
d. $t = 10{,}926$ years
e. $t = 9{,}795$ years

13. A curve passes through the point $(9, 8)$ and has the property that the slope of the curve at every point P is 6 times the y-coordinate P. What is the equation of the curve?

14. Determine whether the differential equation is linear.

$$y' + y \cos x = x^7 y^7$$

15. Newton's Law of Cooling states that the rate of cooling of an object is proportional to the temperature difference between the object and its surroundings. Suppose that a roast turkey is taken from an oven when its temperature has reached $160°$ F and is placed on a table in a room where the temperature is $60°$ F. If $u(t)$ is the temperature of the turkey after t minutes, then Newton's Law of Cooling implies that $\dfrac{du}{dt} = k(u - 60)$.

This could be solved as a separable differential equation. Another method is to make the change of variable $y = u - 60$. If the temperature of the turkey is $150°$ F after half an hour, what is the temperature after 35 min?

Select the correct answer.

    a. $t = 298°$ F

    b. $t = 95°$ F

    c. $t = 143°$ F

    d. $t = 148°$ F

    e.   none of these

16. A sum of $2,150 is invested at 14% interest. If $A(t)$ is the amount of the investment at time t for the case of continuous compounding, write a differential equation and an initial condition satisfied by $A(t)$.

17. Consider a population $P = P(t)$ with constant relative birth and death rates α and β, respectively, and a constant emigration rate m, where $\alpha = 0.7$, $\beta = 0.4$ and $m = 0.8$. Then the rate of change of the population at time t is modeled by the differential equation $\dfrac{dP}{dt} = kP - m$ where $k = \alpha - \beta$.

Find the solution of this equation with the rate of change of the population at time $t = 5$ that satisfies the initial condition $P(0) = 3,500$.

18. Suppose that a population grows according to a logistic model with carrying capacity 7,500 and $k = 0.07$ per year.

Write the logistic differential equation for these data.

19. The Pacific halibut fishery has been modeled by the differential equation $\dfrac{dy}{dt} = k(1 - \dfrac{y}{K})$ where $y(t)$ is the biomass (the total mass of the members of the population) in kilograms at time t (measured in years), the carrying capacity is estimated to be $K = 20 \times 10^8$ kg and $k = 0.03$ per year. How long will it take for the biomass to reach 7×10^8 kg if $y(0) = 4 \times 10^8$?

20. One model for the spread of a rumor is that the rate of spread is proportional to the product of the fraction of the population who have heard the rumor and the fraction who have not heard the rumor. Let's assume that the constant of proportionality is $k = 0.02$. Write a differential equation that is satisfied by y.

1. b, e

2. 6, -5

3. b, d

4. $\dfrac{3}{e^2}e^{2x^2}$

5. $\dfrac{3}{24x+1}$

6. $(5500, \infty)$

7. 84.9998

8. e

9. b

10. 0

11. d

12. a

13. $y = 8e^{6x-54}$

14. no

15. d

16. $\dfrac{dA}{dt} = 0.14A, \ A(0) = 2150$

17. 15676.6

18. $\dfrac{dP(t)}{dt} = 0.07P\left(1 - \dfrac{P}{7500}\right)$

19. 25.58

20. $\dfrac{dy}{dt} = 0.02y(1-y)$

1. For what nonzero values of k does the function $y = A \sin kt + B \cos kt$ satisfy the differential equation $y'' + 25y = 0$ for all values of A and B?

2. Use Euler's method with step size 0.1 to estimate $y(0.2)$, where $y(x)$ is the solution of the initial-value problem. Round your answer to two decimal places.

$$y' = 4xy^2, \quad y(0) = 1$$

3. For the differential equation, find the equilibrium solutions.

$$\frac{dP(t)}{dt} = 0.5P\left(1 - \frac{P}{680}\right) - \frac{4{,}935}{68}$$

4. Solve the differential equation.

$$3yy' = 2x$$

Select the correct answer.

a. $3x^2 + 2y^2 = C$

b. $3x^2 + 2y^2 = 5$

c. $2x^2 + 3y^2 = 5$

d. $2x^2 + 3y^2 = C$

e. $2x^2 - 3y^2 = C$

5. Solve the differential equation.

$$y' = \frac{6x^5 y}{\ln y}$$

6. Solve the differential equation.

$$\frac{du}{dt} = 35 + 7u + 5t + ut$$

Select the correct answer.

a. $u = -5 + Ce^{t^2 - 7t}$

b. $u = -5 + Ce^{\frac{t}{2} + 7t^2}$

c. $u = -5 + Ce^{t^2 + 7t}$

d. $u = -5 + Ce^{\frac{t^2}{2} - 7t}$

e. $u = -5 + Ce^{\frac{t^2}{2} + 7t}$

7. Find the solution of the differential equation that satisfies the initial condition $y(0) = 6$.

$$\frac{dy}{dx} = 8x^7 y$$

8. Suppose that a population develops according to the logistic equation where t is measured in weeks.

   What is the carrying capacity?

$$\frac{dP}{dt} = 0.02P - 0.0002P^2$$

9. Solve the differential equation.

$$y' = \frac{5}{y}$$

   Select the correct answer.

   a. $y = \pm\sqrt{10x + C}$
   b. $y = \sqrt{5x}$
   c. $y = \pm\sqrt{5x + C}$
   d. $y = \sqrt{5x + 10} + C$
   e. $y = \pm\sqrt{5x}$

10. Find the orthogonal trajectories of the family of curves.

$$y = kx^6$$

11. Find the orthogonal trajectories of the family of curves.

$$y = (x + k)^{-8}$$

12. A common inhabitant of human intestines is the bacterium *Escherichia coli*. A cell of this bacterium in a nutrient-broth medium divides into two cells every 20 minutes. The initial population of a culture is 20 cells. Find the number of cells after 2 hours.

13. A bacteria culture starts with 120 bacteria and grows at a rate proportional to its size. After 5 hours there are 5,700 bacteria. When will the population reach 32,000?

    Select the correct answer.

    a. $t=7.2$
    b. $t=1.4$
    c. $t=27.9$
    d. $t=2.1$
    e.   none of those

14. The table gives estimates of the world population, in millions, from 1750 to 2000:

Year	Population	Year	Population
1750	620	1900	1,770
1800	930	1950	2,500
1850	1,350	2000	5,860

    Use the exponential model and the population figures for 1750 and 1800 to predict the world population in 1,900.

15. After 3 days a sample of radon-222 decayed to 58% of its original amount. How long would it take the sample to decay to 82% of its original amount?

16. Scientists can determine the age of ancient objects by a method called *radiocarbon dating*. The bombardment of the upper atmosphere by cosmic rays converts nitrogen to a radioactive isotope of carbon, ^{14}C, with a half-life of about 5730 years. Vegetation absorbs carbon dioxide through the atmosphere and animal life assimilates ^{14}C through food chains. When a plant or animal dies it stops replacing its carbon and the amount of ^{14}C begins to decrease through radioactive decay. Therefore, the level of radioactivity must also decay exponentially. A parchment fragment was discovered that had about 78% as much ^{14}C radioactivity as does plant material on Earth today. Estimate the age of the parchment.

17. A curve passes through the point (4, 4) and has the property that the slope of the curve at every point P is 4 times the y-coordinate P. What is the equation of the curve?

18. **Newton's Law of Cooling** states that the rate of cooling of an object is proportional to the temperature difference between the object and its surroundings. Suppose that a roast turkey is taken from an oven when its temperature has reached $170°$ F and is placed on a table in a room where the temperature is $70°$ F. If u (t) is the temperature of the turkey after t minutes, then Newton's Law of Cooling implies that $\dfrac{du}{dt} = k(u - 70)$.

    This could be solved as a separable differential equation. Another method is to make the change of variable $y = u - 70$. If the temperature of the turkey is $165°$ F after half an hour, what is the temperature after 45 min?

19. Let c be a positive number. A differential equation of the form $\dfrac{dy}{dt} = ky^{1+c}$ where k is a positive constant, is called a *doomsday equation* because the exponent in the expression ky^{1+c} is larger than that for natural growth (that is, ky). An especially prolific breed of rabbits has the growth term $ky^{1.01}$. If 5 such rabbits breed initially and the warren has 26 rabbits after 5 months, then when is doomsday?

20. The Pacific halibut fishery has been modeled by the differential equation $\dfrac{dy}{dt} = ky\left(1 - \dfrac{y}{K}\right)$ where $y(t)$ is the biomass (the total mass of the members of the population) in kilograms at time t(measured in years), the carrying capacity is estimated to be $K = 56 \times 10^8$ kg and $k = 0.07$ per year. How long will it take for the biomass to reach 9×10^8 kg if $y(0) = 7 \times 10^8$?

1. 5, -5

2. 1.04

3. $P(t) = 470, \quad P(t) = 210$

4. e

5. $y = e^{\pm\sqrt{2x^6 + C}}$

6. e

7. $y = 6e^{x^8}$

8. 100

9. a

10. $x^2 + 6y^2 = C$

11. $y = \left(\dfrac{64}{17x + C}\right)^{-8/17}$

12. 1280

13. a

14. 2093

15. 1.09

16. 2054

17. $y = 4e^{4x - 16}$

18. 163

19. 305.78

20. 4.19

1.   For what nonzero values of k does the function $y = A\sin kt + B\cos kt$ satisfy the differential equation $y'' + 36y = 0$ for all values of A and B?

Select all that apply.

a. $k = -36$
b. $k = -6$
c. $k = 36$
d. $k = 1$
e. $k = 6$

2.   For what values of r does the function $y = e^{rt}$ satisfy the differential equation?

$$y'' - y' - 30y = 0$$

3.   Use Euler's method with step size 0.1 to estimate $y(0.5)$, where $y(x)$ is the solution of the initial-value problem. Round your answer to four decimal places.

$$y' = x^2 + y^2, \quad y(0) = 1$$

4.   Solve the differential equation.

$$\frac{dy}{dx} = \frac{e^{2x}}{4y^3}$$

5.   Kirchhoff's Law gives us the derivative equation:

$$Q' = 12 - 4Q$$

If $Q(0) = 0$, use Euler's method with step size 0.4 to estimate Q after 1.2 second.

6.   Solve the differential equation.

$$5yy' = 4x$$

7.   Solve the differential equation.

$$y' = \frac{7x^6 y}{\ln y}$$

8. Find the orthogonal trajectories of the family of curves.

    $$y = (x + k)^{-7}$$

9. A certain small country has \$20 billion in paper currency in circulation, and each day \$70 million comes into the country's banks. The government decides to introduce new currency by having the banks replace old bills with new ones whenever old currency comes into the banks. Let $x = x(t)$ denote the amount of new currency in circulation at time t with $x(0) = 0$. Formulate and solve a mathematical model in the form of an initial-value problem that represents the "flow" of the new currency into circulation (in billions per day).

10. A population of protozoa develops with a constant relative growth rate of 0.7944 per member per day. On day zero the population consists of 2 members. Find the population size after 6 days.

11. Use the Bernoulli's method to solve the differential equation.

    $$y' + \frac{6y}{x} = \frac{y^3}{x^5}$$

    Select the correct answer.

    a. $y = \left(Cx^{12} \pm \dfrac{1}{8x^4} \right)^{-1/2}$

    b. $y = \pm \left(Cx^{12} + \dfrac{1}{8x^4} \right)^{1/2}$

    c. $y = \left(Cx^{12} \pm \dfrac{1}{8x^4} \right)^{1/2}$

    d. $y = \left(Cx^{12} + \dfrac{1}{8x^4} \right)^{-1/2}$

    e. $y = \left(Cx^{8} + \dfrac{1}{12x^4} \right)^{-1/2}$

12. Find the solution of the differential equation that satisfies the initial condition $y(1) = 1$.

$$\frac{dy}{dx} = \frac{y^2}{x^4}$$

Select the correct answer.

a. $y = \dfrac{3 + 2x^3}{4x^3}$

b. $y = \dfrac{1 - 2x^3}{4x^3}$

c. $y = \dfrac{4x^3}{1 - 2x^3}$

d. $y = \dfrac{1 - 3x^3}{1 + 2x^3}$

e. $y = \dfrac{3x^3}{1 + 2x^3}$

13. A common inhabitant of human intestines is the bacterium *Escherichia coli*. A cell of this bacterium in a nutrient-broth medium divides into two cells every 20 minutes. The initial population of a culture is 30 cells. Find the number of cells after 4 hours.

14. A bacteria culture starts with 110 bacteria and grows at a rate proportional to its size. After 3 hours there are 7,700 bacteria. When will the population reach 28,000?

15. Experiments show that if the chemical reaction $N_2O_5 \rightarrow 2NO_2 + \frac{1}{2}O_2$ takes place at $45°\,C$, the rate of reaction of dinitrogen pentoxide is proportional to its concentration as follows :

$$-\frac{d[N_2O_5]}{dt} = 0.0008[N_2O_5]$$

How long will the reaction take to reduce the concentration of N_2O_5 to 50% of its original value?

16. After 3 days a sample of radon-222 decayed to 58% of its original amount. How long would it take the sample to decay to 37% of its original amount?

17. A curve passes through the point $(7, 3)$ and has the property that the slope of the curve at every point P is 2 times the y-coordinate P. What is the equation of the curve?

18. A sum of $100 is invested at 27% interest. If $A(t)$ is the amount of the investment at time t for the case of continuous compounding, write a differential equation and an initial condition satisfied by $A(t)$.

19. Determine whether the differential equation is linear.

$$y' + y\cos x = x^9 y^9$$

20. Solve the initial-value problem.

$$t\frac{dy}{dt} + 2y = t^5, \quad t > 0, \quad y(1) = 0$$

ANSWER KEY

Stewart - Calculus ET 5e Chapter 9 Form H

1. b, e

2. 6, -5

3. 1.8371

4. $y = \pm\sqrt[4]{\dfrac{e^{2x}}{2} + C}$

5. 3.648

6. $y = \pm\sqrt{\dfrac{4}{5}x^2 + C}$

7. $y = e^{\pm\sqrt{2x^7 + C}}$

8. $y = \left(\dfrac{49}{15x + C}\right)^{-7/15}$

9. $x(t) = 20\left(1 - e^{-0.0035t}\right)$

10. 235

11. d

12. e

13. 122880

14. 3.9

15. 866

16. 5.48

17. $y = 3e^{2x-14}$

18. $\dfrac{dA}{dt} = 0.27A, \quad A(0) = 100$

19. no

20. $y = \dfrac{t^5}{7} - \dfrac{1}{7t^2}$

1. Eliminate the parameter to find a Cartesian equation of the curve.

   $$x = 100 \ t^2, \ \ y = -64 \ t^3$$

2. If a projectile is fired with an initial velocity of v_0 meters per second at an angle α above the horizontal and air resistance is assumed to be negligible, then its position after t seconds is given by the parametric equations $x = (v_0 \cos \alpha) \ t, \ \ y = (v_0 \sin \alpha) \ t - \dfrac{1}{2} g t^2$, where g is the acceleration of gravity $(9.8 \ m/s^2)$.

   If a gun is fired with $\alpha = 70°$ and $v_0 = 336 \ m/s$ when will the bullet hit the ground?

   Round the result to the nearest tenth.

3. Find an equation of the tangent to the curve at the point corresponding to the value of the parameter.

   $$x = e^{\sqrt{t}}, \ \ y = t - \ln t^9; \ \ t = 1$$

4. Find the points on the curve where the tangent is horizontal.

   $$x = 13\left(\cos \theta - \cos^2 \theta\right), \ \ y = 13\left(\sin \theta - \sin \theta \cos \theta\right)$$

5. Find the area bounded by the curve $x = t - \dfrac{1}{t}, \ \ y = t + \dfrac{3}{t}$ and the line $y = 6.5$.

6. Set up, but do not evaluate the integral that represents the length of the parametric curve.

   $$x = t - t^8, \ \ y = \dfrac{13}{12} t^{12/11}, \ \ 0 \le t \le 10$$

7. A cow is tied to a silo with radius 5 by a rope just long enough to reach the opposite side of the silo. Find the area available for grazing by the cow. Round the answer to the nearest hundredth.

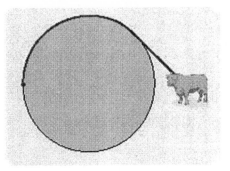

8. True or False?

    The exact length of the curve $x = e^t + e^{-t}$, $y = 1 - 2t$, $0 \le t \le 6$ is $\frac{1}{12}\left(e^{12} + 12 - e^{-12}\right)$.

9. True or False?

    The exact length of the parametric curve $x = e^t \cos t$, $y = e^t \sin t$, $0 \le t \le \frac{\pi}{5}$ is $\sqrt{2}e^{\pi/5}$.

10. Using the arc length formula, set up, but do not evaluate, an integral equal to the total arc length of the ellipse.

    $x = 5\sin\theta$, $y = 4\cos\theta$

11. Find the area of the surface obtained by rotating the curve about the x-axis.

    $x = a\cos^3\theta$, $y = a\sin^3\theta$, $0 \le \theta \le \pi$

12. Plot the point whose polar coordinates are given. Then find the Cartesian coordinates of the point.

    $\left(2, \frac{\pi}{2}\right)$

13. Find the area of the region that is bounded by the given curve and lies in the specified sector.

$r = \sqrt{\sin \theta}, \ 0 \le \theta \le 2\pi / 3$

14. Find an equation for the conic that satisfies the given conditions.

Hyperbola, vertices $\left(\pm 2, \ 0\right)$, asymptotes $y = \pm 3x$

15. Find the eccentricity of the conic.

$r = \dfrac{6}{1 - 9 \cos \theta}$

16. The graph of the following curve is given. Find the area that it encloses.

$r = \sin 3\theta$

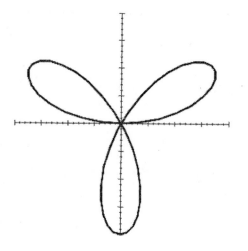

17. Find the area of the region that lies inside the first curve and outside the second curve.

$r = 3 \cos \theta, \ r = 1 + \cos \theta$

18. Find the area of the region that lies inside both curves.

$r = 8 + 2 \sin \theta, \ r = 7$

19. Write a polar equation in r and θ of a hyperbola with the focus at the origin, with the eccentricity 9 and the directrix $x = -2$.

20. Graph of the following curve is given. Find its length.

$r = \cos^2(\theta/2)$

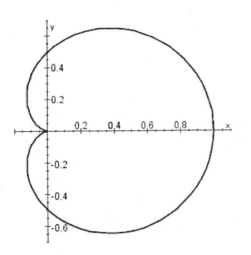

1. $x = 6.25y^{2/3}$

2. 64.4

3. $y = \dfrac{-16}{e}(x - e) + 1$

4. $\left(\dfrac{-39}{4}, -\dfrac{39\sqrt{3}}{4}\right), \left(\dfrac{-39}{4}, \dfrac{39\sqrt{3}}{4}\right)$

5. $\dfrac{143}{6} - 8\ln 2 - 4\ln 3$

6. $\displaystyle\int_{0}^{10} \sqrt{\left(1 - 8t^7\right)^2 + \left(\dfrac{13}{11}\right)^2 t^{2/11}}\ dt$

7. 645.96

8. F

9. F

10. $\displaystyle\int_{0}^{2\pi} \sqrt{25\cos^2(\theta) + 16\sin^2(\theta)}\ d\theta$

11. $S = \dfrac{12\pi a^2}{5}$

12. $(0, 2)$

13. $3/4$

14. $\dfrac{x^2}{4} - \dfrac{y^2}{36} = 1$

15. 9

16. $\dfrac{\pi}{4}$

17. π

18. $\dfrac{164\pi}{3} - \dfrac{31\sqrt{3}}{2}$

19. $r = \dfrac{18}{\left(1 - 9\cos\theta\right)}$

20. 4

1. Eliminate the parameter to find a Cartesian equation of the curve.

   $x = 25t^2, \quad y = -64t^3$

2. Eliminate the parameter to find a Cartesian equation of the curve.

   $x(t) = 10\ln(9t), \quad y(t) = \sqrt{t}$

3. Find parametric equations for the path of a particle that moves once clockwise along the circle $x^2 + (y-3)^2 = 4$, starting at (2, 3).

4. If a projectile is fired with an initial velocity of v_0 meters per second at an angle α above the horizontal and air resistance is assumed to be negligible, then its position after t seconds is given by the parametric equations $x = (v_0 \cos \alpha)\, t, \quad y = (v_0 \sin \alpha)\, t - \frac{1}{2}gt^2$, where g is the acceleration of gravity $\left(9.8 \; m/s^2\right)$.

   If a gun is fired with $\alpha = 55°$ and $v_0 = 497 \; m/s$ when will the bullet hit the ground?

   Round the result to the nearest tenth.

5. Find an equation of the tangent to the curve at the point corresponding to the value of the parameter.

   $x = t\sin t, \quad y = t\cos t \; ; \; t = 6\pi$

6. Find an equation of the tangent to the curve at the point by first eliminating the parameter.

   $x = e^t, \quad y = (t-7)^2; \quad (1, \; 49)$

7. Find the points on the curve where the tangent is horizontal.

   $x = 13\left(\cos\theta - \cos^2\theta\right), \quad y = 13\left(\sin\theta - \sin\theta\cos\theta\right)$

8. Try to estimate the coordinates of the highest point on the curve $x = 9te^t$, $y = 7te^{-t}$. Round the answer to the nearest hundredth.

9. Find the area of the region enclosed by each loop of the curve.

$$x = \sin t - 2\cos t \quad y = 3 + 3\sin t \cos t$$

10. True or False?

The length of the parametric curve $x = t - t^8$, $y = \dfrac{9}{8}t^{8/7}$, $5 \le t \le 7$ is given by the integral

$$\int_5^7 \sqrt{(1 - 8t)^7 + \left(\frac{9}{7}\right)^2 t^{2/7}} \ dt.$$

11. Find a Cartesian equation for the curve described by the given polar equation.

$$r = 5\sin\theta$$

12. Find the area of the region that is bounded by the given curve and lies in the specified sector.

$$r = \sqrt{\sin\theta}, \ 0 \le \theta \le \pi/2$$

13. The graph of the following curve is given. Find the area that it encloses.

$$r = \sin 3\theta$$

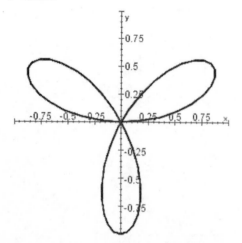

14. The graph of the following curve is given. Find the area that it encloses.

$r = 1 + 2\sin\theta$

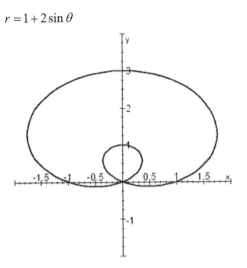

15. Find the area of the region that lies inside the first curve and outside the second curve.

$r = 8\sin\theta, \quad r = 4$

16. Find an equation for the conic that satisfies the given conditions.

Hyperbola, vertices $\left(\pm 3,\ 0\right)$, asymptotes $y = \pm 3x$

17. The point in a lunar orbit nearest the surface of the moon is called perilune and the point farthest from the surface is called apolune. The Apollo 11 spacecraft was placed in an elliptical lunar orbit with perilune altitude 108 km and apolune altitude 314 km (above the moon). Find an equation of this ellipse if the radius of the moon is 1728 km and the center of the moon is at one focus.

18. Write a polar equation in r and θ of a conic with the focus at the origin, and eccentricity $\dfrac{9}{2}$ and directrix $y = 7$.

19. Find the eccentricity of the conic.

$r = \dfrac{42}{7 + 6\sin\theta}$

20. The orbit of Hale-Bopp comet, discovered in 1995, is an ellipse with eccentricity 0.995 and one focus at the Sun. The length of its major axis is 356.3 AU. [An astronomical unit (AU) is the mean distance between Earth and the Sun, about 93 million miles.] Find the maximum distance from the comet to the Sun. (The perihelion distance from a planet to the Sun is $a(1 - e)$ and the aphelion distance is $a(1 + e)$.) Find the answer in AU and round to the nearest hundredth.

1. $x = 1.5625y^{2/3}$

2. $y = \dfrac{1}{3}\sqrt{e^{x/10}}$

3. $x = 2\cos t,\ \ y = 3 - 2\sin t,\ \ 0 \le t \le 2\pi$

4. 83.1

5. $y = \dfrac{x}{6\pi} + 6\pi$

6. $y = -14(x - 1) + 49$

7. $\left(\dfrac{-39}{4},\ -\dfrac{39\sqrt{3}}{4}\right),\ \left(\dfrac{-39}{4},\ \dfrac{39\sqrt{3}}{4}\right)$

8. $\left(24.46,\ 2.58\right)$

9. $\dfrac{6\sqrt{5}}{5}$

10. F

11. $x^2 + \left(y - \dfrac{5}{2}\right)^2 = \left(\dfrac{5}{2}\right)^2$

12. 1/2

13. $\dfrac{\pi}{4}$

14. $2\pi + \dfrac{3\sqrt{3}}{2}$

15. $\dfrac{16\pi}{3} + 8\sqrt{3}$

16. $\dfrac{x^2}{9} - \dfrac{y^2}{81} = 1$

17. $\dfrac{x^2}{3759721} + \dfrac{y^2}{3749112} = 1$

18. $r = \dfrac{63}{2 + 9\sin\theta}$

19. 6/7

20. 355.41

1. Eliminate the parameter to find a Cartesian equation of the following curve :

$$x(t) = \cos^2(4t), \quad y(t) = \sin^2(4t)$$

Select the correct answer.

   a. $\quad y(x) = 1 - 4x$

   b. $\quad y(x) = 1 + x$

   c. $\quad y(x) = 1 - x$

   d. $\quad y(x) = 4x$

   e. $\quad y(x) = 4 + x$

2. Eliminate the parameter to find a Cartesian equation of the following curve:

$$x(t) = 6 \ln(5t), \quad y(t) = \sqrt{t}$$

Select the correct answer.

   a. $\quad y = \sqrt{\dfrac{1}{5} e^{6/x}}$

   b. $\quad y = \sqrt{\dfrac{1}{5} e^{x/6}}$

   c. $\quad y = \sqrt{\dfrac{1}{6} e^{x/5}}$

   d. $\quad y = \sqrt{\dfrac{1}{6} e^{5/x}}$

   e. $\quad y = \sqrt{\dfrac{1}{6} x^{5e/6}}$

3. Describe the motion of a particle with position (x, y) as t varies in the given interval $0 \le t \le 2\pi$.

    $x = 6\sin t, \quad y = 3\cos t$

    Select the correct answer.

    a. Moves once clockwise along the circle $(6x)^2 + (3y)^2 = 1$ starting and ending at $(0, 3)$.

    b. Moves once clockwise along the ellipse $\dfrac{x^2}{36} + \dfrac{y^2}{9} = 1$ starting and ending at $(0, 3)$.

    c. Moves once counterclockwise along the ellipse $\dfrac{x^2}{36} + \dfrac{y^2}{9} = 1$ starting and ending at $(0, 3)$.

    d. Moves once counterclockwise along the circle $x^2 + (y)^2 = 1$ starting and ending at $(0, -3)$.

    e. Moves once counterclockwise along the ellipse $\dfrac{x^2}{6} + \dfrac{y^2}{3} = 1$ starting and ending at $(-3, 0)$.

4. Find a polar equation for the curve represented by the given Cartesian equation.

    $x^2 = 9y$

    Select the correct answer.

    a. $r = 9\tan\theta\sin\theta$
    b. $r = 9\cos\theta\sin\theta$
    c. $r = 9\tan\theta\sec\theta$
    d. $r = 9\tan\theta$
    e. $r = 9\tan\theta\csc\theta$

5. Find an equation of the tangent to the curve at the point $\left(\dfrac{9\sqrt{3}}{2}, \dfrac{5}{2}\right)$. Then graph the curve and the tangent.

$x = 9\sin 2t, \quad y = 5\sin t$

Select the correct answer.

a.

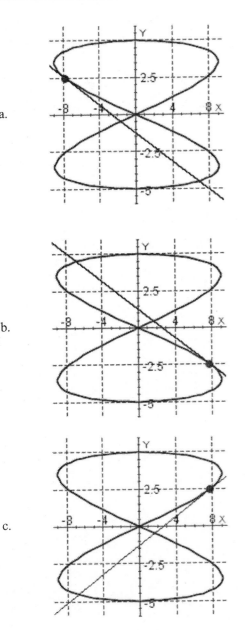

b.

c.

6. Find equations of the tangents to the curve $x = 3t^2 + 1$, $y = 2t^3 + 1$ that pass through the point (4, 3).

    Select the correct answer.

    a. $y = -8x + 11$, $y = x - 3$
    b. $y = x + 11$, $y = 2x - 1$
    c. $y = -2x + 12$, $y = x - 7$
    d. $y = -8x + 14$, $y = x - 7$
    e.   none of these

7. Plot the point whose polar coordinates are given. Then find the Cartesian coordinates of the point.

    $$\left(2, \frac{\pi}{2} \right)$$

    Select the correct answer.

    a.   (0 , 2)
    b.   (2 , 0)
    c.   (- 2 , 0)
    d.   (0 , - 2)
    e.   (2 , - 2)

8.   Sketch the region in the plane.

$$0 \leq \theta < \frac{\pi}{6}$$

Select the correct answer.

a.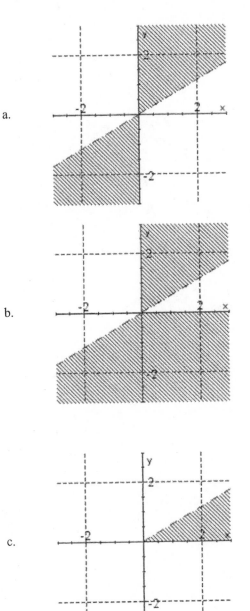

b.

c.

9. Sketch the curve with the given equation.

$r = \sin 6\theta$

Select the correct answer.

a.

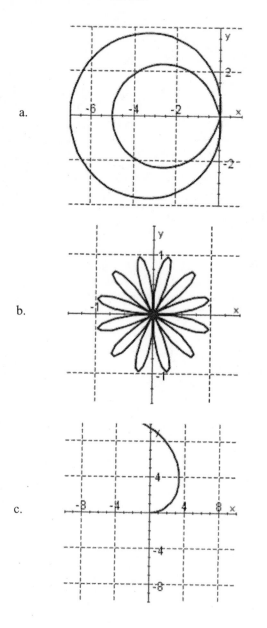

b.

c.

10. Find the slope of the tangent line to the given polar curve at the point specified by the value of θ.

$$r = \frac{1}{\theta}, \quad \theta = \pi$$

Select the correct answer.

a. $\dfrac{dy}{dx} = -2\pi$

b. $\dfrac{dy}{dx} = \dfrac{1}{4}$

c. $\dfrac{dy}{dx} = -\pi$

d. $\dfrac{dy}{dx} = 3$

e. $\dfrac{dy}{dx} = \dfrac{3}{\pi}$

11. Find the area of the region that is bounded by the given curve and lies in the specified sector.

$$r = \sqrt{\sin \theta}, \quad 0 \le \theta \le \pi/3$$

Select the correct answer.

a. $A = 1$

b. $A = \dfrac{1}{4}$

c. $A = \dfrac{1}{2}$

d. $A = \dfrac{3}{4}$

e. $A = \dfrac{\pi}{4}$

12. Find the length of the polar curve.

    $r = 7\cos\theta, \ 0 \le \theta \le 3\pi/4$

    Select the correct answer.

    a. $L = \dfrac{21}{4}$

    b. $L = \dfrac{21\pi}{4}$

    c. $L = \dfrac{\pi}{4}$

    d. $L = \dfrac{21\pi}{11}$

    e. $L = \dfrac{21}{4}$

13. Find the surface area generated by rotating the lemniscate $r^2 = 5\cos 2\theta$ about the line $\theta = \dfrac{\pi}{2}$.

    Select the correct answer.

    a. $L = \dfrac{\pi\sqrt{2}}{10}$

    b. $L = 10\sqrt{2}\pi$

    c. $L = \dfrac{\pi}{10}$

    d. $L = 5\sqrt{2}\pi$

    e. $L = \sqrt{2}\pi$

14. Sketch the hyperbola.

$$\frac{y^2}{36} - \frac{x^2}{81} = 1$$

Select the correct answer.

a.

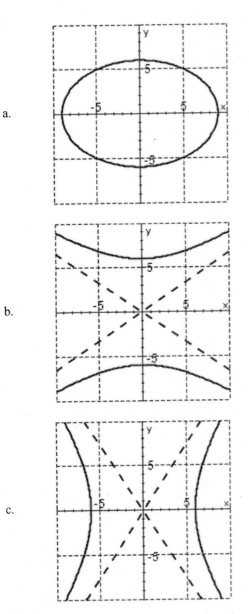

b.

c.

15. A family of curves is given by the equations $r = 1 + c \sin n\theta$, where c is a real number and n is a positive integer. Graph the curve with the given condition.

$c = 2, \quad n = 5$

Select the correct answer.

a.

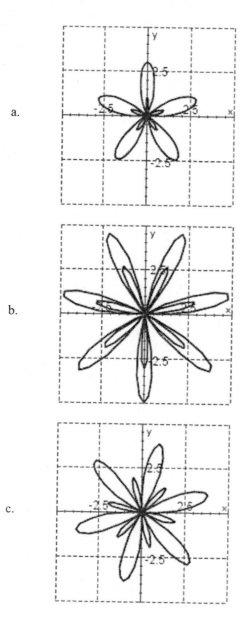

b.

c.

16. Find an equation for the conic that satisfies the given conditions.

Ellipse, foci $\left(\pm 1,\ 5\right)$, length of major axis 8

Select the correct answer.

a. $\dfrac{(x-3)^2}{16} - \dfrac{y^2}{15} = 1$

b. $\dfrac{x^2}{16} + \dfrac{y^2}{15} = 1$

c. $\dfrac{x^2}{16} + \dfrac{(y-5)^2}{15} = 1$

d. $4x^2 = y$

e. $x^2 = y$

17. A cross-section of a parabolic reflector is shown in the figure. The bulb is located at the focus and the opening at the focus is 18 cm. Find an equation of the parabola. Let V is the origin. Find the diameter of the opening $|CD|$, 19 cm from the vertex.

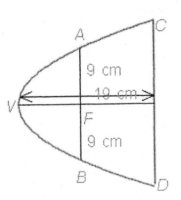

Select all that apply.

a. The equation is $y^2 - \dfrac{x^2}{18} = 1$

b. $|CD| = 4\sqrt{414}$

c. $|CD| = 2\sqrt{342}$

d. The equation is $y = 18x^2$

e. The equation is $y^2 = 18x$

f. $|CD| = 18$

18. In the LORAN (LOng RAnge Navigation) radio navigation system, two radio stations located at A and B transmit simultaneous signals to a ship or an aircraft located at P. The onboard computer converts the time difference in receiving these signals into a distance difference $|A| - |B|$, and this, according to the definition of a hyperbola, locates the ship or aircraft on one branch of a hyperbola (see the figure). Suppose that station is located L = 400 mi due east of station A on a coastline. A ship received the signal from B 1,200 microseconds (μs) before it received the signal from A. Assuming that radio signals travel at a speed of 980 $ft / \mu s$ and if the ship is due north of B, how far off the coastline is the ship? Round your answer to the nearest mile.

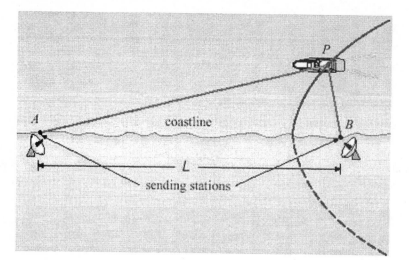

Select the correct answer.

a.   y = 246 miles
b.   y = 243 miles
c.   y = 248 miles
d.   y = 258 miles
e.   y = 278 miles

19. Write a polar equation in r and θ of an ellipse with the focus at the origin, with the eccentricity $\dfrac{6}{7}$ and directrix $x = -8$.

Select the correct answer.

a. $r = \dfrac{48}{7 - 6\cos\theta}$

b. $r = \dfrac{8}{3 - 2\sin\theta}$

c. $r = \dfrac{8}{7 - 6\sin\theta}$

d. $r = \dfrac{48}{6 + 7\sin\theta}$

e. $r = \dfrac{48}{1 + 7\sin\theta}$

20. The orbit of Hale-Bopp comet, discovered in 1995, is an ellipse with eccentricity 0.995 and one focus at the Sun. The length of its major axis is 356.3 AU. [An astronomical unit (AU) is the mean distance between Earth and the Sun, about 93 million miles.] Find the maximum distance from the comet to the Sun. (The perihelion distance from a planet to the Sun is $a(1-e)$ and the aphelion distance is $a(1+e)$.) Find the answer in AU and round to the nearest hundredth.

Select the correct answer.

a. 358.40 AU
b. 356.24 AU
c. 355.41 AU
d. 368.40 AU
e. 350.60 AU

1. c

2. b

3. b

4. c

5. c

6. e

7. a

8. c

9. b

10. c

11. b

12. b

13. b

14. b

15. a

16. c

17. c, e

18. c

19. a

20. c

1. Eliminate the parameter to find a Cartesian equation of the curve.

$$x(t) = \cos^2(10t), \quad y(t) = \sin^2(10t)$$

Select the correct answer.

a. $y(x) = 1 - 10x$
b. $y(x) = 1 + x$
c. $y(x) = 1 - x$
d. $y(x) = 10 - x$
e. $y(x) = 10 + x$

2. Eliminate the parameter to find a Cartesian equation of the curve.

$$x = 5e^t, \quad y = 21e^{-t}$$

Select the correct answer.

a. $y = \dfrac{5}{21x}$

b. $y = \dfrac{105}{x}$

c. $y = 105x$

d. $y = \dfrac{105}{e^x}$

e. $y = \dfrac{105x}{t}$

3. Find a polar equation for the curve represented by the given Cartesian equation.

$$x^2 = 2y$$

Select the correct answer.

a. $r = 2\tan\theta\sin\theta$
b. $r = 2\tan\theta$
c. $r = 2\tan\theta\sec\theta$
d. $r = 2\cot\theta$
e. $r = 2\sec\theta$

4. Find parametric equations to represent the line segment from (-1, 2) to (10, -6).

   Select the correct answer.

   a. $x = 10 - 8t, \ y = -1 + 11t, \ 0 \le t \le 1$

   b. $x = -1 + 11t, \ y = 2 - 8t, \ 0 \le t \le 1$

   c. $x = -1 + 11t, \ y = -6 - 8t, \ 0 \le t \le 1$

   d. $x = -1 - 11t, \ y = -8t, \ 0 \le t \le 1$

   e. $x = -1 + 11t, \ y = -6t, \ 0 \le t \le 1$

5. If a projectile is fired with an initial velocity of v_0 meters per second at an angle α above the horizontal and air resistance is assumed to be negligible, then its position after t seconds is given by the parametric equations $x = (v_0 \cos \alpha) \ t, \ y = (v_0 \sin \alpha) \ t - \frac{1}{2} gt^2$, where g is the acceleration of gravity $\left(9.8 \ m/s^2 \right)$.

   If a gun is fired with $\alpha = 50°$ and $v_0 = 486 \ m/s$ when will the bullet hit the ground?

   Select the correct answer.

   a. $t = 38$ s
   b. $t = 744.6$ s
   c. $t = 76$ s
   d. $t = 58$ s
   e. $t = 256.6$ s

6. Write a polar equation in r and θ of an ellipse with the focus at the origin, with the eccentricity 0.4 and vertex at (2, 0).

   Select the correct answer.

   a. $r = \dfrac{6}{5 + 2\cos\theta}$

   b. $r = \dfrac{6}{5 - 2\cos\theta}$

   c. $r = \dfrac{5}{5 - 2\cos\theta}$

   d. $r = \dfrac{5}{2 + 5\cos\theta}$

   e. $r = \dfrac{2}{5 - 6\cos\theta}$

7. Find an equation of the tangent to the curve at the point corresponding to the value of the parameter.

$x = t\sin t, \quad y = t\cos t ; \quad t = 11\pi$

Select the correct answer.

a. $y = \dfrac{x}{11\pi} + 12\pi$

b. $y = \dfrac{x}{11\pi} - 11\pi$

c. $y = \dfrac{x}{11\pi} + 11\pi$

d. $y = \dfrac{x}{11\pi} - 12\pi$

e. $y = \dfrac{x}{\pi} - 12\pi$

8. Find the area bounded by the curve $x = t - \dfrac{1}{t}, \quad y = t + \dfrac{2}{t}$ and the line $y = 4.5$

Select the correct answer.

a. $\dfrac{189}{25}$

b. $\dfrac{189}{16} - 9\ln 2$

c. $\dfrac{189}{16} - 3\ln 3$

d. $\dfrac{189}{25} - 9\ln 3$

e. $\dfrac{189}{16} - 2\ln 3$

9.   Sketch the region.

$$0 \le \theta < \frac{\pi}{8}$$

Select the correct answer.

a.

b.

c.

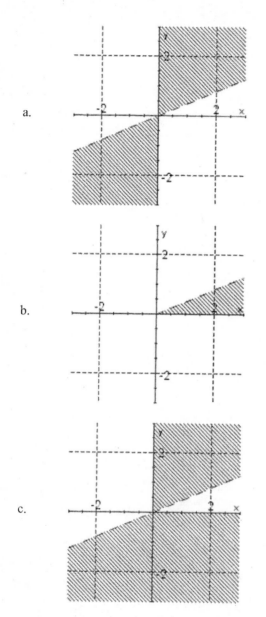

10. Sketch the curve with the given equation.

$r = 4\theta$

Select the correct answer.

a.

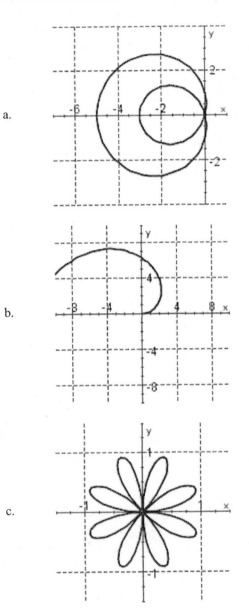

b.

c.

11. Sketch the curve with the given equation.

$$r = \sin(2\theta)$$

Select the correct answer.

a.

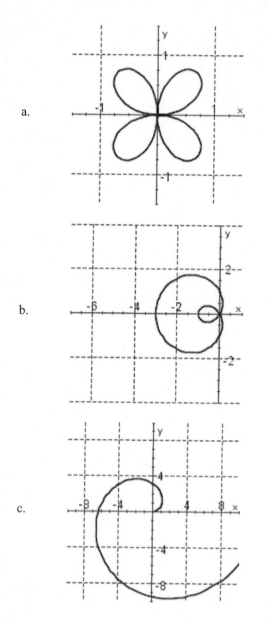

b.

c.

12. Find the area of the region enclosed by one loop of the curve.

$r = 7\cos 4\theta$

Select the correct answer.

a. $A = \dfrac{49\pi}{16}$

b. $A = 16\pi$

c. $A = \pi$

d. $A = \dfrac{49\pi}{11}$

e. $A = \dfrac{\pi}{11}$

13. The graph of the following curve is given. Find the area that it encloses.

$r = 3 + 6\sin\theta$

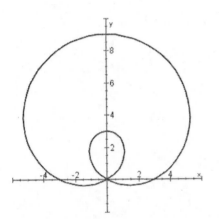

Select the correct answer.

a. $A = 18\pi + \dfrac{27\sqrt{5}}{2}$

b. $A = \dfrac{27\sqrt{5}}{2}$

c. $A = 18\pi$

d. $A = 18\pi + \dfrac{27\sqrt{3}}{2}$

e. $A = 18\pi + \dfrac{\sqrt{3}}{2}$

14. Find the area of the region that lies inside the first curve and outside the second curve.

$$r = 3\cos\theta, \quad r = 1 + \cos\theta$$

Select the correct answer.

a. $A = \dfrac{\pi}{4}$

b. $A = \pi$

c. $A = 2\pi$

d. $A = \dfrac{\pi}{2}$

e. $A = \dfrac{3\pi}{2}$

15. Use a graph to estimate the values of θ for which the curves $r = 9 + 3\sin 5\theta$ and $r = 18\sin\theta$ intersect.

Select all that apply. (rounded to two decimal places)

a. $\theta = 0.49$

b. $\theta = 2.57$

c. $\theta = 1.48$

d. $\theta = 0.58$

e. $\theta = 4.7$

16. Graph of the following curve is given. Find its length.

$$r = 4\cos^2\left(\frac{\theta}{2}\right)$$

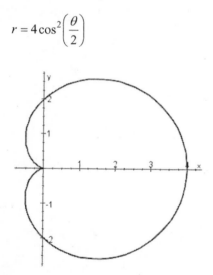

Select the correct answer.

a. $L = 17$

b. $L = 16$

c. $L = 19$

d. $L = 14$

e. $L = 22$

17. Sketch the hyperbola.

$$\frac{y^2}{9} - \frac{x^2}{81} = 1$$

Select the correct answer.

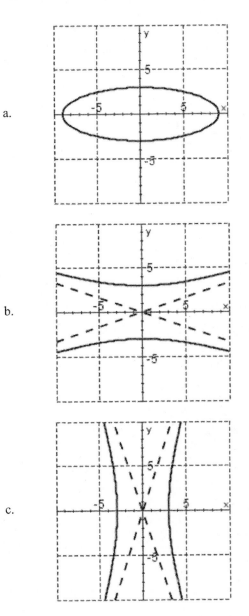

a.

b.

c.

18. Find an equation for the conic that satisfies the given conditions.

Parabola, Vertex $(0, 0)$, Focus $(0, -4)$

Select the correct answer.

a. $y^2 = -17x$

b. $x^2 + y^2 = 16y$

c. $x^2 = -16y$

d. $x^2 = 4y$

e. $x^2 = -y$

19. Find an equation for the conic that satisfies the given conditions.

Ellipse, foci $(\pm 2, 6)$, length of major axis 6

Select the correct answer.

a. $\dfrac{(x-5)^2}{9} - \dfrac{y^2}{5} = 1$

b. $\dfrac{x^2}{9} + \dfrac{(y-6)^2}{5} = 1$

c. $\dfrac{x^2}{9} + \dfrac{y^2}{5} = 1$

d. $3x^2 = y$

e. $\dfrac{1}{3}x^2 = y$

20. Find an equation for the conic that satisfies the given conditions.

Hyperbola, foci $(0, \pm 9)$, vertices $(0, \pm 1)$

Select the correct answer.

a. $y^2 - \dfrac{x^2}{80} = 1$

b. $9x^2 = y$

c. $\dfrac{(x-9)^2}{81} - \dfrac{y^2}{80} = 1$

d. $\dfrac{x^2}{81} + \dfrac{y^2}{80} = 1$

e. $\dfrac{9}{80}x^2 = y$

ANSWER KEY

Stewart - Calculus ET 5e Chapter 10 Form D

1. c

2. b

3. c

4. b

5. c

6. b

7. b

8. b

9. b

10. b

11. a

12. a

13. d

14. b

15. b, d

16. b

17. b

18. c

19. b

20. a

1.   Eliminate the parameter t to find a Cartesian equation of the curve.

$$y = 3t - 1, \quad x = t - 7$$

2.   Find an equation for the conic that satisfies the given conditions.

Hyperbola, foci $\left(0, \pm 9\right)$, vertices $\left(0, \pm 1\right)$

Select the correct answer.

a. $y^2 - \dfrac{1}{80}x^2 = 1$

b. $9x^2 = y$

c. $\dfrac{(x-9)^2}{81} - \dfrac{y^2}{80} = 1$

d. $\dfrac{x^2}{81} + \dfrac{y^2}{80} = 1$

e. $\dfrac{x^2}{81} + \dfrac{y^2}{9} = 1$

3.   Find parametric equations for the path of a particle that moves once clockwise along the circle $x^2 + (y-4)^2 = 81$, starting at $(9, 4)$.

4.   If a and b are fixed numbers, find parametric equations for the set of all points P determined as shown in the figure, using the angle ang as the parameter. Write the equations for $a = 8$ and $b = 3$.

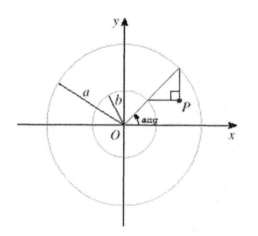

5. Find $\dfrac{dy}{dx}$.

$x = 6te^t, \quad y = 6t + e^t$

6. Find the points on the curve where the tangent is horizontal.

$x = 2\left(\cos\theta - \cos^2\theta \right), \quad y = 2\left(\sin\theta - \sin\theta\cos\theta \right)$

7. Try to estimate the coordinates of the highest point on the curve $x = 15te^t, \quad y = 3te^{-t}$. Round the answer to the nearest hundredth.

8. The curve $x = 2 - 4\cos^2 t, \quad y = \tan t(1 - 2\cos^2 t)$ cross itself at some point (x_0, y_0). Find the equations of both tangents at that point.

9. Find equations of the tangents to the curve $x = 3t^2 + 1, \quad y = 2t^3 + 1$ that pass through the point (4 , 3).

10. True or False?

The length of the parametric curve $x = t - t^{10}, \quad y = \dfrac{11}{10}t^{10/9}, \quad 2 \le t \le 9$ is given by the integral

$$\int_2^9 \sqrt{(1 - 10t)^9 + \left(\frac{11}{9}\right)^2 t^{2/9}} \; dt \, .$$

11. True or False?

The exact length of the curve $x = e^t + e^{-t}, \quad y = 5 - 12t, \quad 0 \le t \le 6$ is $\dfrac{1}{2}(e^{12} + 24 - e^{-12})$.

12. If the curve $x = t + t^3$, $y = t - \dfrac{3}{t^2}$, $1 \le t \le 2$ is rotated about the x-axis, estimate the area of the resulting surface to three decimal places. (If your calculator or CAS evaluates definite integrals numerically, use it. Otherwise, use Simpson's Rule.)

13. Graph of the following curve is given. Find its length.

$$r = 4\cos^2\left(\frac{\theta}{2}\right)$$

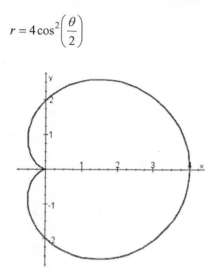

Select the correct answer.

a. $L = 17$
b. $L = 16$
c. $L = 19$
d. $L = 14$
e. $L = 22$

14. The graph of the following curve is given. Find the area that it encloses.

$$r = 2 + \cos 6\theta$$

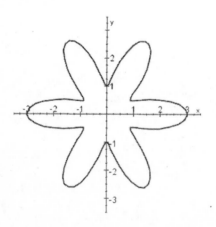

15. Find an equation for the conic that satisfies the given conditions.

    Hyperbola, foci (2, - 2) and (2, 8), vertices (2, 0) and (2, 6)

16. Find an equation for the conic that satisfies the given conditions.

    Hyperbola, vertices (3, 0), (-3, 0), asymptotes $y = \pm 2x$

17. Write a polar equation in r and θ of a hyperbola with the focus at the origin, with the eccentricity 6 and the directrix $x = - 2$.

18. Find the equation of the directrix of the conic.

    $$r = \frac{6}{3 + \sin \theta}$$

    Select the correct answer.

    a. $y = 6$
    b. $y = -3$
    c. $x = -6$
    d. $x = 3$
    e. $x = 2$

19. Find the eccentricity of the conic.

    $$r = \frac{9}{2 + 11\cos \theta}$$

20.   Find the area of the shaded region.

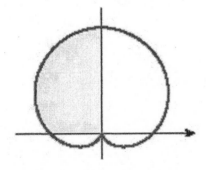

    $r = 1 + \sin \theta$

1. $y(x) = 3x + 20$

2. a

3. $x = 9\cos t, \quad y = 4 - 9\sin t, \quad 0 \le t \le 2\pi$

4. $x = 8\cos(ang), \quad y = 3\sin(ang), \quad 0 \le ang \le 2\pi$

5. $\dfrac{6 + e^t}{6e^t(1 + t)}$

6. $\left(-\dfrac{3}{2}, \ -\dfrac{3\sqrt{3}}{2} \right), \ \left(-\dfrac{3}{2}, \ \dfrac{3\sqrt{3}}{2} \right)$

7. (40.77, 1.10)

8. $y = \dfrac{x}{2}, \quad y = -\dfrac{x}{2}$

9. $y = -2(x - 13) - 15, \quad y = (x - 4) + 3$

10. F

11. F

12. $S = 8.923$

13. b

14. $\dfrac{9\pi}{2}$

15. $\dfrac{(y-3)^2}{9} - \dfrac{(x-2)^2}{16} = 1$

16. $\dfrac{x^2}{9} - \dfrac{y^2}{36} = 1$

17. $r = \dfrac{12}{(1 - 6\cos\theta)}$

18. a

19. 11/2

20. $\dfrac{3\pi}{8} + 1$

1. Eliminate the parameter to find a Cartesian equation of the curve.

    $x(t) = \cos^2 5t, \quad y = \sin^2 5t$

2. Find parametric equations to represent the line segment from (-9, 2) to (7, -8).

3. If a projectile is fired with an initial velocity of v_0 meters per second at an angle α above the horizontal and air resistance is assumed to be negligible, then its position after t seconds is given by the parametric equations $x = (v_0 \cos \alpha) \, t, \quad y = (v_0 \sin \alpha) \, t - \frac{1}{2} g t^2$, where g is the acceleration of gravity $(9.8 \ m/s^2)$.

    If a gun is fired with $\alpha = 20°$ and $v_0 = 470 \ m/s$ when will the bullet hit the ground?

    Round the result to the nearest tenth.

4. Find an equation of the tangent line to the curve at the point corresponding to the value of the parameter.

    $x = e^{\sqrt{t}}, \quad y = t - \ln t^3; \quad t = 1$

5. Find the points on the curve where the tangent line is horizontal.

    $x = 5(\cos \theta - \cos^2 \theta), \quad y = 5(\sin \theta - \sin \theta \cos \theta)$

6. Find equations of the tangent lines to the curve $x = 3t^2 + 1, \quad y = 2t^3 + 1$ that pass through the point (13, 17).

7. Find the area of the region enclosed by each loop of the curve.

    $$x = \sin t - 2\cos t, \quad y = 2 + 2\sin t \cos t$$

    Select the correct answer.

    a. $\dfrac{\sqrt{5}}{5}$

    b. $\dfrac{4}{5}\sqrt{\pi}$

    c. $\dfrac{2\pi}{5}\sqrt{5}$

    d. $\dfrac{4}{5}\sqrt{5}$

    e. $\dfrac{2}{5}\sqrt{5}$

8. Set up, but do not evaluate, an integral that represents the length of the parametric curve.

    $$x = t - t^9, \quad y = \frac{9}{8}t^{8/7}, \quad 3 \le t \le 12$$

9. True or False?

    The exact length of the curve $x = e^t + e^{-t}, \quad y = 10 - 2t, \quad 0 \le t \le 6$ is $\dfrac{1}{2}(e^{12} + 24 - e^{-12})$.

10. True or False?

    The exact length of the parametric curve $x = e^t \cos t, \quad y = e^t \sin t, \quad 0 \le t \le \dfrac{\pi}{3}$ is $\sqrt{2}e^{\pi/3}$.

11. True or False?

    If we use Simpson's Rule with $n = 10$ to estimate the arc length of the curve $x = \ln t, \quad y = e^{-t}, \quad 3 \le t \le 4$, we get $L \approx 0.084405$.

12. Using the arc length formula, set up, but do not evaluate, an integral equal to the total arc length of the ellipse.

    $$x = 4\sin\theta, \quad y = 2\cos\theta$$

13. If the curve $x = t + t^3$, $y = t - \dfrac{4}{t^2}$, $1 \le t \le 2$ is rotated about the x-axis, estimate the area of the resulting surface to three decimal places. (If your calculator or CAS evaluates definite integrals numerically, use it. Otherwise, use Simpson's Rule.)

14. If the arc of the curve $x = 2a \cot\theta$, $y = 2a \sin^2\theta$, $\dfrac{\pi}{4} \le \theta \le \dfrac{\pi}{2}$ is rotated about the x-axis, estimate the area of the resulting surface to two decimal places using Simpson's Rule with $n = 4$.

15. Find the surface area generated by rotating the lemniscate $r^2 = 5\cos 2\theta$ about the line $\theta = \dfrac{\pi}{2}$.

Select the correct answer.

a. $L = \dfrac{\pi\sqrt{2}}{10}$

b. $L = 10\sqrt{2}\pi$

c. $L = \dfrac{\pi}{10}$

d. $L = 5\sqrt{2}\pi$

e. $L = 10\sqrt{2}\pi$

16. The graph of the following curve is given. Find the area that it encloses.

$r = 11 \sin\theta$

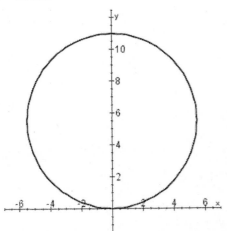

17. The graph of the following curve is given. Find the area that it encloses.

$r = \sin 4\theta$

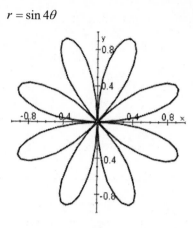

18. The graph of the following curve is given. Find the area that it encloses.

$r = 1 + \cos 6\theta$

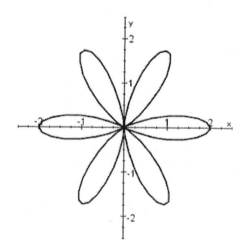

Select the correct answer.

a. $A = \dfrac{3\pi}{4}$

b. $A = \dfrac{3\pi}{2}$

c. $A = 3\pi$

d. $A = \dfrac{\pi}{2}$

e. $A = \dfrac{5\pi}{2}$

19. Find the area of the region that lies inside the first curve and outside the second curve.

$r = 3\cos\theta, \quad r = 1 + \cos\theta$

20. Graph of the following curve is given. Find its length.

$r = 2\cos^2(\theta/2)$

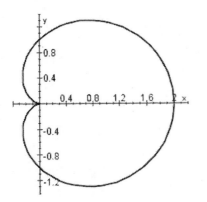

1. $x = 1 - y$

2. $x = -9 + 16t, \quad y = 2 - 10t, \quad 0 \le t \le 1$

3. 32.8

4. $y = \dfrac{-4}{e}(x - e) + 1$

5. $\left(-\dfrac{15}{4}, \ -\dfrac{15\sqrt{3}}{4} \right), \ \left(-\dfrac{15}{4}, \ \dfrac{15\sqrt{3}}{4} \right)$

6. $y + 127 = -4(x - 49), \quad y - 17 = 2(x - 13)$

7. d

8. $\displaystyle\int_{3}^{12} \sqrt{(1 - 9t^8)^2 + \left(\dfrac{9}{7}\right)^2 t^{2/7}} \ dt$

9. T

10. F

11. F

12. $\displaystyle\int_{0}^{2\pi} \sqrt{16\cos^2\theta + 4\sin^2\theta} \ d\theta$

13. $S = -21.601$

14. 22.15

15. b

16. $\dfrac{121\pi}{4}$

17. $\dfrac{\pi}{2}$

18. b

19. π

20. 8

1. If the curve $x = t + t^3$, $y = t - \dfrac{5}{t^2}$, $1 \le t \le 2$ is rotated about the x-axis, estimate the area of the resulting surface to three decimal places. (If your calculator or CAS evaluates definite integrals numerically, use it. Otherwise, use Simpson's Rule.)

2. Find the eccentricity of the conic.

    $$r = \frac{72}{9 + 8 \sin \theta}$$

3. Find the slope of the tangent line to the given polar curve at the point specified by the value of θ.

    $$r = \frac{1}{\theta}, \quad \theta = \pi$$

4. Sketch the curve with the given equation.

    $$r = \sin \frac{\theta}{2}$$

    Select the correct answer.

    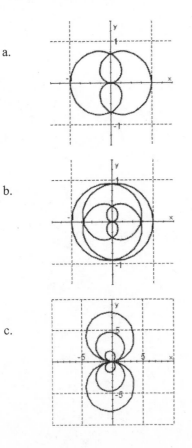

    a.

    b.

    c.

5. Use a graphing device to graph the polar curve. Choose the parameter interval to make sure that you produce the entire curve.

$$r = 1 + 4\cos\frac{\theta}{3}$$

6. The graph of the following curve is given. Find the area that it encloses.

$$r = \sin 2\theta$$

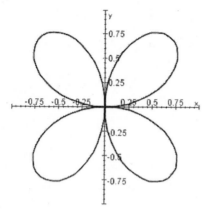

Select the correct answer.

a. $A = \dfrac{\pi}{6}$

b. $A = \dfrac{\pi}{5}$

c. $A = \dfrac{\pi}{2}$

d. $A = \dfrac{\pi}{3}$

e $A = \dfrac{5\pi}{3}$

7. Find a Cartesian equation for the curve described by the given polar equation.

$$r = 3\sin\theta$$

8. Find the equation of the directrix of the conic.

$$r = \frac{3}{6 - \sin\theta}$$

9. The graph of the following curve is given. Find the area that it encloses.

   $r = 2 + \cos 6\theta$

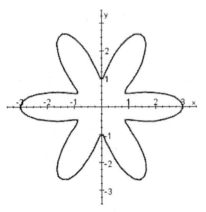

10. Find the eccentricity of the conic.

    $$r = \frac{2}{1 + 3\sin \theta}$$

11. Find the surface area generated by rotating the lemniscate $r^2 = 5\cos 2\theta$ about the line $\theta = \pi / 2$.

    Select the correct answer.

    a. $L = \dfrac{\pi}{10}$

    b. $L = \dfrac{\pi\sqrt{2}}{10}$

    c. $L = 5\sqrt{2}\pi$

    d. $L = 10\sqrt{2}\pi$

    e. $L = 2\sqrt{5}\pi$

12. Write a polar equation in r and θ of a conic with the focus at the origin, eccentricity $\dfrac{3}{2}$ and directrix $y = 9$.

Select the correct answer.

a. $r = 2\sin\theta$

b. $r = \dfrac{27}{2+3\sin\theta}$

c. $r = \dfrac{27}{2+3\cos\theta}$

d. $r = \dfrac{3}{3-2\sin\theta}$

e. $r = \dfrac{2}{27-2\sin\theta}$

13. Find the vertices, foci and asymptotes of the hyperbola.

$$16x^2 - 9y^2 + 64x - 72y = 224$$

Select all that apply.

a.   The foci are $(-7,\ -4)$, $(3,\ -4)$

b.   The vertices are $(-5,\ -4)$, $(1,\ -4)$

c.   The vertices are $(\pm 1,\ -4)$

d.   The asymptote is $y = \dfrac{5}{7}(x-2)$

e.   The foci are $(-7,\ -4)$, $(6,\ -5)$

f.   The asymptotes are $y = \pm\dfrac{3}{4}x$

14. Find an equation for the conic that satisfies the given conditions.

Ellipse, foci $(\pm 6,\ 0)$, vertices $(\pm 7,\ 0)$

Select the correct answer.

a. $7x^2 = y$

b. $\dfrac{x^2}{49} + \dfrac{y^2}{13} = 1$

c. $\dfrac{x^2}{6} + \dfrac{y^2}{8} = 1$

d. $\dfrac{x^2}{49} - \dfrac{y^2}{13} = 1$

e. $\dfrac{x^2}{49} + \dfrac{y^2}{8} = 1$

15. Find an equation for the conic that satisfies the given conditions.

Hyperbola, foci (4, - 1) and (4, 9), vertices (4, 1) and (4, 7)

16. Graph the conics $r = e/(1 - e\cos\theta)$ with e = 0.3, 0.6 and 1.0 on a common screen.

Select the correct answer.

a.

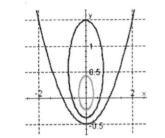

b.

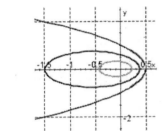

c.

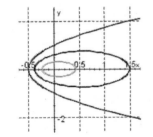

17. The planet Mercury travels in an elliptical orbit with eccentricity 0.203. Its minimum distance from the Sun is 4.6×10^7 km. If the perihelion distance from a planet to the Sun is $a(1-e)$ and the aphelion distance is $a(1+e)$, find the maximum distance (in km) from Mercury to the Sun.

Select the correct answer.

a. 6.9×10^7 km
b. 6.1×10^7 km
c. 7×10^7 km
d. 9.6×10^7 km
e. 7.5×10^7 km

18. Using the arc length formula, set up, but do not evaluate, an integral equal to the total arc length of the ellipse.

$$x = 5\sin\theta, \quad y = 4\cos\theta$$

19. Write a polar equation in r and θ of a hyperbola with the focus at the origin, with the eccentricity 5 and directrix $r = 9\csc\theta$.

    Select the correct answer

    a. $r = \dfrac{45}{1 - 45\cos\theta}$

    b. $r = \dfrac{45}{1 + 9\cos\theta}$

    c. $r = \dfrac{14}{5 + \sin\theta}$

    d. $r = \dfrac{45}{1 + 5\sin\theta}$

    e. $r = \dfrac{14}{4 + 5\sin\theta}$

20. Write a polar equation in r and θ of a hyperbola with the focus at the origin, with the eccentricity 6 and the directrix $y = -2$.

1. $S = -56.458$

2. $8/9$

3. $-\pi$

4. a

5. $[0,\ 6\pi]$

6. c

7. $x^2 + \left(y - \dfrac{3}{2}\right)^2 = \left(\dfrac{3}{2}\right)^2$

8. $y = -3$

9. $\dfrac{9\pi}{2}$

10. 3

11. d

12. b

13. a, b

14. b

15. $\dfrac{(y-4)^2}{9} - \dfrac{(x-4)^2}{16} = 1$

16. c

17. a

18. $\displaystyle\int_{0}^{2\pi} \sqrt{25\cos^2(\theta) + 16\sin^2(\theta)}\ d\theta$

19. d

20. $r = \dfrac{12}{1 - 6\sin\theta}$

1. If a and b are fixed numbers, find parametric equations for the set of all points P determined as shown in the figure, using the angle *ang* as the parameter. Write the equations for $a = 10$ and $b = 4$.

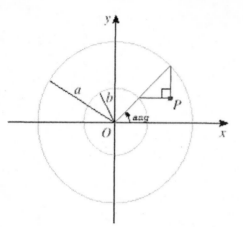

2. Find parametric equations to represent the line segment from (-5, 8) to (5, -4).

3. Find an equation for the conic that satisfies the given conditions.

   Ellipse, foci $(\pm 1, \ 5)$, length of major axis is 6

4. Find an equation for the conic that satisfies the given conditions.

   Hyperbola, foci (7, - 1) and (7, 9), vertices (7, 1) and (7, 7)

5. Try to estimate the coordinates of the highest point on the curve $x = 2te^{t}$, $y = 12te^{-t}$. Round the answer to the nearest hundredth.

6. If a projectile is fired with an initial velocity of v_0 meters per second at an angle α above the horizontal and air resistance is assumed to be negligible, then its position after t seconds is given by the parametric equations $x = (v_0 \cos \alpha) \ t$, $y = (v_0 \sin \alpha) \ t - \frac{1}{2} gt^2$, where g is the acceleration of gravity $(9.8 \ m/s^2)$.

   If a gun is fired with $\alpha = 62°$ and $v_0 = 264 \ m/s$ when will the bullet hit the ground?

   Round the result to the nearest tenth.

7. Find an equation of the tangent line to the curve at the point corresponding to the value of the parameter.

$$x = e^{\sqrt{t}}, \quad y = t - \ln t^7; \quad t = 1$$

8. Write a polar equation in r and θ of an ellipse with the focus at the origin, with the eccentricity $\dfrac{3}{4}$ and directrix $x = -5$.

9. Eliminate the parameter to find a Cartesian equation of the curve.

$$x(t) = \cos^2 6t, \quad y(t) = \sin^2 6t$$

10. Find the eccentricity of the conic.

$$r = \frac{5}{2 - 3\sin\theta}$$

Select the correct answer.

a. $e = \dfrac{5}{2}$

b. $e = \dfrac{2}{3}$

c. $e = \dfrac{3}{2}$

d. $e = 5$

e. $e = \dfrac{5}{3}$

11. Find an equation of the tangent line to the curve at the point corresponding to the value of the parameter.

$$x = t\sin t, \quad y = t\cos t \ ; \quad t = 3\pi$$

Select the correct answer.

a. $y = \dfrac{x}{3\pi} - 4\pi$

b. $y = \dfrac{x}{3\pi} + 3\pi$

c. $y = \dfrac{x}{3\pi} - 3\pi$

d. $y = \dfrac{x}{3\pi} + 4\pi$

e. $y = \dfrac{x}{4\pi} + 3\pi$

12. Find the points on the curve where the tangent line is horizontal.

$$x = 4(\cos\theta - \cos^2\theta), \quad y = 4(\sin\theta - \sin\theta\cos\theta)$$

13. The curve $x = 2 - 4\cos^2 t$, $y = \tan t(1 - 2\cos^2 t)$ cross itself at some point (x_0, y_0). Find the equations of both tangent lines at that point.

Select the correct answer.

a. $y = \dfrac{x}{2}, \quad y = -\dfrac{x}{2}$

b. $y = x + 6, \quad y = -x + 6$

c. $y = \dfrac{x}{8}, \quad y = -\dfrac{x}{8}$

d. $y = \dfrac{x}{2} + 8, \quad y = -\dfrac{x}{2} + 2$

e. $y = \dfrac{x}{2} - 8, \quad y = -\dfrac{x}{2} - 2$

14. Find the area of the region that lies inside the first curve and outside the second curve.

$$r = 10\sin\theta, \quad r = 5$$

Select the correct answer.

a. $A = \dfrac{25\pi}{3} + \dfrac{25\sqrt{3}}{2}$

b. $A = \dfrac{25\pi}{3}$

c. $A = \dfrac{25}{3} + \dfrac{25\sqrt{3}}{2}$

d. $A = \dfrac{25\sqrt{3}}{2}$

e. $A = \dfrac{3\sqrt{3}\pi}{2}$

15. The graph of the following curve is given. Find its length.

$$r = 4\cos^2(\theta/2)$$

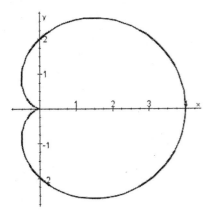

Select the correct answer.

a. $L = 19$
b. $L = 14$
c. $L = 16$
d. $L = 17$
e. $L = 27$

16. Find the vertex, focus, and directrix of the parabola.

$$x^2 + 10x - y + 30 = 0$$

Select all that apply.

a. The vertex is $(-5,\ 5)$

b. The vertex is $(0,\ 2)$

c. The directrix is $y = \dfrac{19}{4}$

d. The focus is $\left(-5,\ \dfrac{21}{4}\right)$

e. The focus is $\left(5,\ -\dfrac{21}{4}\right)$

17. Find the area of the region that lies inside both curves.

$$r = 4\sin\theta,\ \ r = 4\cos\theta$$

18. Find the area bounded by the curve $x = t - \dfrac{1}{t}$, $y = t + \dfrac{1}{t}$ and the line $y = 2.5$.

19. Find all points of intersection of the given curves.

$r^2 = 9\sin 2\theta, \ \ r^2 = 9\cos 2\theta$

20. Find the length of the polar curve.

$r = 7\cos\theta, \ \ 0 \le \theta \le \pi/4$

ANSWER KEY

Stewart - Calculus ET 5e Chapter 10 Form H

---

1. $x = 10\cos(ang), \ y = 4\sin(ang), \ 0 \le ang \le 2\pi$

2. $x = -5 + 10t, \ y = 8 - 12t, \ 0 \le t \le 1$

3. $\dfrac{x^2}{9} + \dfrac{(y-5)^2}{8} = 1$

4. $\dfrac{(y-4)^2}{9} - \dfrac{(x-7)^2}{16} = 1$

5. $(5.44, \ 4.41)$

6. 47.6

7. $y = -\dfrac{12}{e}(x-e) + 1$

8. $r = \dfrac{15}{4 - 3\cos\theta}$

9. $x = 1 - y$

10. c

11. c

12. $\left(-3, \ -3\sqrt{3}\right), \ \left(-3, \ 3\sqrt{3}\right)$

13. a

14. a

15. c

16. a, c, d

17. $2\pi - 4$

18. $\dfrac{15}{4} - 4\ln 2$

19. $(0, 0), \ \left(\dfrac{3}{\sqrt[4]{2}}, \ \dfrac{\pi}{8}\right), \ \left(\dfrac{3}{\sqrt[4]{2}}, \ \dfrac{9\pi}{8}\right)$

20. $\dfrac{7\pi}{4}$

---

1. Use the Integral Test to determine whether the series is convergent or divergent.

$$\sum_{n=1}^{\infty} \frac{1}{8n+1}$$

2. Find the partial sum s_{10} of the series.

$$\sum_{k=1}^{\infty} \frac{8}{k^2}$$

Approximate the answer to the nearest thousandth.

3. Use the sum of the first 9 terms to approximate the sum of the following series.

$$\sum_{n=1}^{\infty} \frac{8}{n^{10}+n^2}$$

Give your answer to six decimal places.

4. Given the series

$$\sum_{n=1}^{\infty} \frac{10n}{(10n+1)\, 4^n}$$

Estimate the error in using the partial sum s_8 by comparison with the series $\sum_{n=9}^{\infty} \frac{1}{4^n}$.

5. Test the series for convergence or divergence.

$$\frac{7}{\ln 2} - \frac{7}{\ln 3} + \frac{7}{\ln 4} - \frac{7}{\ln 5} + \frac{7}{\ln 6} - \cdots$$

6. Test the series for convergence or divergence.

$$\sum_{n=5}^{\infty} \frac{n^2-25}{n^2+5n}$$

7. Test the series for convergence or divergence.

$$\sum_{k=1}^{\infty} \frac{(-3)^{k+1}}{4^{2k}}$$

8. Test the series for convergence or divergence.

$$\sum_{k=1}^{\infty} (-1)^k \frac{\sqrt{k}}{k+7}$$

9. Test the series for convergence or divergence.

$$\sum_{k=2}^{\infty} \frac{1}{(\ln k)^{\ln k}}$$

10. Test the series for convergence or divergence.

$$\sum_{m=1}^{\infty} (\sqrt[m]{3}-1)^m$$

11. Find the interval of convergence of the series.

$$\sum_{n=1}^{\infty} \frac{6x^n}{\sqrt[5]{n}}$$

12. Find the radius of convergence of the series.

$$\sum_{n=1}^{\infty} \frac{8^n x^n}{(n+5)^2}$$

13. If the radius of convergence of the power series $\sum_{n=0}^{\infty} c_n z^n$ is 5, what is the radius of convergence of

the series $\sum_{n=1}^{\infty} n c_n z^{n-1}$?

14. Determine the interval of convergence for the function.

$$f(y) = \arctan\left(\frac{y}{9}\right)$$

15. Find the sum of the series.

$$\sum_{n=2}^{\infty} n(n-1)x^{n+1} \quad |x| < 1$$

16. Find the Maclaurin series for $f(x)$ using the definition of a Maclaurin series.

$$f(x) = (2+x)^{-3}$$

17. Evaluate the indefinite integral as an infinite series.

$$\int \sin(4x)^2 \, dx$$

18. Use series to evaluate the limit correct to four decimal places.

$$\lim_{x \to 0} \frac{\sin 6x - 6x + \dfrac{216}{6}x^3}{x^5}$$

19. Use the binomial series to expand the function as a power series. Find the radius of convergence.

$$\frac{1}{(2+x)^2}$$

20. Find the Taylor polynomial T_2 for the function f at the number $a = 1$.

$$f(x) = \sqrt{x}$$

1. divergent

2. 12.398

3. 4.007926

4. err ≤ 0.0000051

5. convergent

6. divergent

7. convergent

8. convergent

9. convergent

10. convergent

11. [-1, 1)

12. 1/8

13. 5

14. (-9, 9)

15. $\dfrac{2x^3}{(1-x)^3}$

16. $\displaystyle\sum_{n=0}^{\infty} \dfrac{(-1)^n (n+1)(n+2)\left(\dfrac{x}{2}\right)^n}{2 \cdot 2^3}$

17. $C + \displaystyle\sum_{n=0}^{\infty} \dfrac{(-1)^n 4^{4n+2} x^{4n+3}}{(4n+3)(2n+1)!}$

18. 64.8

19. $|x| < 2$

20. $T_2 = 1 + \dfrac{1}{2}(x-1) - \dfrac{1}{8}(x-1)^2$

1. Find a formula for the general term a_n of the sequence, assuming that the pattern of the first few terms continues.

$$\left\{ 1,\ -\frac{1}{3},\ \frac{1}{9},\ -\frac{1}{27},\ \dots \right\}$$

2. Find the value of the limit for the sequence.

$$\left\{ \arctan\left(\frac{3n}{3n+8} \right) \right\}$$

3. Find the exact value of the limit of the sequence defined by $a_1 = \sqrt{3}$, $a_{n+1} = \sqrt{3 + a_n}$.

4. Use the Integral Test to determine whether the series is convergent or divergent.

$$\sum_{n=1}^{\infty} \frac{1}{3n+1}$$

5. Find the partial sum s_{10} of the series $\displaystyle\sum_{n=1}^{\infty} \frac{9}{n^5}$.

Approximate the answer to the nearest thousandth.

6. Find the partial sum s_7 of the series $\displaystyle\sum_{m=1}^{\infty} \frac{3}{10 + 7^m}$.

Give your answer to five decimal places.

7. How many terms of the series $\displaystyle\sum_{m=2}^{\infty} \frac{18}{9m(\ln m)^2}$ would you need to add to find its sum to within 0.02?

8. Find all positive values of b for which the series $\displaystyle\sum_{n=1}^{\infty} 4b^{\ln 3n}$ converges.

9. Write the partial sum of the converging series which represent the decimal number 0.2523.

10. Test the series for convergence or divergence.

$$\sum_{n=2}^{\infty} (-1)^n \, \frac{n}{5 \ln n}$$

11. Approximate the sum to the indicated accuracy.

$$\sum_{n=1}^{\infty} \frac{(-1)^{n-1}}{n^7} \qquad \text{(five decimal places)}$$

12. Approximate the sum to the indicated accuracy.

$$\sum_{n=0}^{\infty} \frac{(-1)^n}{3^n \, n!} \qquad \text{(four decimal places)}$$

13. Test the series for convergence or divergence.

$$\sum_{k=5}^{\infty} \frac{5}{k(\ln k)^6}$$

14. Test the series for convergence or divergence.

$$\sum_{m=1}^{\infty} \frac{3^m m^5}{m!}$$

15. Test the series for convergence or divergence.

$$\sum_{k=1}^{\infty} \cos k$$

16. Test the series for convergence or divergence.

$$\sum_{m=1}^{\infty} (-1)^m \, \frac{\ln m}{\sqrt{m}}$$

17. Test the series for convergence or divergence.

$$\sum_{k=1}^{\infty} \frac{k \ln k}{(k+4)^3}$$

18. Use Taylor's Inequality to estimate the accuracy $|R_4|$ of the approximation $f(x)$ at the number $a = 1$, when $0 \le x \le 2$.

$f(x) = \cos(x)$

19. A car is moving with speed 23 m/s and acceleration 2m/s^2 at a given instant. Using a second-degree Taylor polynomial, estimate how far the car moves in the next second.

20. The resistivity of a conducting wire is the reciprocal of the conductivity and is measured in units of ohm-meters. The resistivity of a given metal depends on the temperature according to the equation $\rho(t) = \rho_{27}e^{\alpha(t-27)}$ where t is the temperature in C. There are tables that list the values of α (called the temperature coefficient) and ρ_{27} (the resistivity at $27°$ C) for various metals. Except at very low temperatures, the resistivity varies almost linearly with temperature and so it is common to approximate the expression for $\rho(t)$ by its first-degree Taylor polynomial at $t = 27$. Find the expression for this linear approximation.

1. $a_n = \left(-\dfrac{1}{3}\right)^{n-1}$

2. $\dfrac{\pi}{4}$

3. $\dfrac{1+\sqrt{13}}{2}$

4. divergent

5. 9.332

6. 0.23727

7. $m > e^{100}$

8. $b < \dfrac{1}{e}$

9. $\dfrac{1}{5} + \dfrac{5}{10^2} + \dfrac{2}{10^3} + \dfrac{3}{10^4}$

10. divergent

11. 0.99259

12. 0.7165

13. convergent

14. convergent

15. divergent

16. convergent

17. convergent

18. 0.0083

19. 24

20. $\rho_{27}(1 + \alpha(t - 27))$

1. Determine whether the sequence converges or diverges.

    $$a(n) = \frac{2^n}{5^{n+1}}$$

    Select the correct answer.

    a.   converges
    b.   diverges

2. Find the value of the limit for the sequence given.

    $$\left\{ \frac{1 \cdot 9 \cdot 17 \cdots (8n+1)}{(8n)^2} \right\}$$

    Select the correct answer.

    a. π
    b.   -1
    c.   3
    d.   0
    e.   1

3. A sequence $\{a_n\}$ is defined recursively by the equation $a_n = 0.5(a_{n-1} + a_{n-2})$ for $n \geq 3$ where $a_1 = 18$, $a_2 = 9$.

    Use your calculator to guess the limit of the sequence.

    Select the correct answer.

    a.   12
    b.   13
    c.   6
    d.   17
    e.   26

4. Find the partial sum s_7 of the series $\sum_{n=1}^{\infty} \frac{1}{2+5^n}$. Give your answer to five decimal places.

    Select the correct answer.

    a. $s_7 = 0.18976$

    b. $s_7 = 0.18985$

    c. $s_7 = 1.60976$

    d. $s_7 = 0.18975$

    e. $s_7 = 0.19176$

5. Given the series $\displaystyle\sum_{m=1}^{\infty} \frac{3m}{4^m(3m+5)}$ estimate the error in using the partial sum s_8 by comparison with

the series $\displaystyle\sum_{m=9}^{\infty} \frac{1}{4^m}$.

Select the correct answer.

a. $R_8 \geq 0.0000051$
b. $R_8 \leq 2.6130051$
c. $R_8 \leq 0.0000051$
d. $R_8 \leq 0.000005$
e. $R_8 \geq 0.0000052$

6. Find all positive values of u for which the series $\displaystyle\sum_{m=1}^{\infty} 4u^{\ln 7m}$ converges.

Select the correct answer.

a. $u < 4$

b. $4 < u < \dfrac{7}{e}$

c. $u > 7$

d. $0 < u < \dfrac{1}{e}$

e. $u > \ln 7$

7. Evaluate the function $f(x) = \cos x$ by a Taylor polynomial of degree 4 centered at $a = 0$, and $x = 2$.

Select the correct answer.

a.   0.67
b.   -0.33
c.   -1.33
d.   0.28
e.   -0.44

8. Given the series :

$$A = \sum_{k=1}^{\infty} \frac{1}{k^5+9} \quad \text{and} \quad B = \sum_{k=1}^{\infty} \frac{1}{k^4-k}$$

Select the correct answer.

a.   Both series are convergent.
b.   Both series are divergent.
c.   Series A diverges by the Integral Test.
d.   Series B and A converges by the Limit Comparison Test.
e.   Series B diverges by the Integral Test.

9. Test the series for convergence or divergence.

$$\frac{8}{\ln 2} - \frac{8}{\ln 3} + \frac{8}{\ln 4} - \frac{8}{\ln 5} + \frac{8}{\ln 6} - \cdots$$

Select the correct answer.

a.   the series is divergent
b.   the series is convergent

10. Use the power series for $f(x) = \sqrt[3]{5+x}$ to estimate $\sqrt[3]{5.08}$ correct to four decimal places.

Select the correct answer.

a.   1.7156
b.   1.7189
c.   1.7195
d.   1.7200
e.   1.7190

11. How many terms of the series do we need to add in order to find the sum to the indicated accuracy?

$$\sum_{n=1}^{\infty} \frac{(-1)^{n+1}}{n^2} \qquad (|\,error\,|) < 0.0399$$

Select the correct answer.

a. $n = 12$
b. $n = 5$
c. $n = 13$
d. $n = 6$
e. $n = 8$

12. Which of the given series are absolutely convergent?

Select the correct answer.

a. $$\sum_{n=1}^{\infty} \frac{\sin 3n}{n}$$

b. $$\sum_{n=1}^{\infty} \frac{\cos \frac{7\pi n}{8}}{n\sqrt{n}}$$

13. Determine whether the series is absolutely convergent, conditionally convergent, or divergent.

$$\sum_{n=1}^{\infty} \frac{(-1)^n \arctan n}{n^5}$$

Select the correct answer.

   a.   divergent
   b.   absolutely convergent
   c.   conditionally convergent

14. Test the series for convergence or divergence.

$$\sum_{m=1}^{\infty} \frac{(-6)^{m+1}}{4^{5m}}$$

Select the correct answer.

   a.   The series is convergent
   b.   The series is divergent

15. Test the series for convergence or divergence.

$$\sum_{m=1}^{\infty} (\sqrt[m]{5} - 1)^m$$

Select the correct answer.

   a.   The series is divergent
   b.   The series is convergent

16. Find the interval of convergence of the series.

$$\sum_{n=1}^{\infty} \frac{(-1)^n x^n}{n+4}$$

Select the correct answer.

   a.   [-1, 1)
   b.   [-1, 1]
   c.   (-1, 1]
   d.   (-1, 1)
   e.   diverges everywhere

17. Suppose that the radius of convergence of the power series $\displaystyle\sum_{n=0}^{\infty} c_n x^n$ is 16. What is the radius of convergence of the power series $\displaystyle\sum_{n=0}^{\infty} c_n x^{2n}$?

Select the correct answer.

a.   256
b.   4
c.   1
d.   16
e.   252

18. Evaluate the indefinite integral as a power series.

$$\int \tan^{-1}(t^2)\ dt$$

Select the correct answer.

a. $\displaystyle C + \sum_{n=0}^{\infty} \frac{(-1)^n t^{4n+3}}{(2n+1)(4n+3)}$

b. $\displaystyle C + \sum_{n=0}^{\infty} \frac{(-1)^n t^{4n+3}}{(4n+3)}$

c. $\displaystyle C + \sum_{n=0}^{\infty} \frac{(-1)^n t^{4n+2}}{(2n+1)(4n+3)}$

d. $\displaystyle C + \sum_{n=0}^{\infty} \frac{(-1)^n t^{2n+2}}{(2n+1)}$

e. $\displaystyle C + \sum_{n=0}^{\infty} \frac{(-1)^n t^{2n+3}}{(2n+3)}$

19. Use a power series to approximate the definite integral.

$$\int_{0}^{0.4} z^4 \tan^{-1}(z^4)\ dz$$

Select the correct answer.

a.   0.4
b.   0.000029
c.   1.400262
d.   1.399738
e.   1.004262

20. Find the Maclaurin series for $f(x)$ using the definition of the Maclaurin series.

$$f(x) = x\cos(4x)$$

Select the correct answer.

a. $\displaystyle\sum_{n=0}^{\infty} \frac{(-1)^n 4^{2n} x^{2n+1}}{n!}$

b. $\displaystyle\sum_{n=0}^{\infty} \frac{(-1)^n 4^{2n} x^{2n+1}}{(2n)!}$

c. $\displaystyle\sum_{n=0}^{\infty} \frac{(-1)^n 4^{2n} x^{2n}}{(2n)!}$

d. $\displaystyle\sum_{n=0}^{\infty} \frac{(-1)^{n+1} 4^{2n} x^{2n+1}}{(2n)!}$

e. $\displaystyle\sum_{n=0}^{\infty} \frac{(-1)^n 4^n x^{2n+1}}{(2n)!}$

1. a

2. d

3. a

4. a

5. c

6. d

7. b

8. a

9. b

10. e

11. b

12. b

13. b

14. a

15. b

16. c

17. b

18. a

19. b

20. b

1.   Find the value of the limit of the sequence defined by $a_1 = \sqrt{3}, \quad a_{n+1} = \sqrt{3 + a_n}$.

Select the correct answer.

   a. $\dfrac{1 - \sqrt{13}}{2}$

   b. $\dfrac{1 + \sqrt{13}}{2}$

   c. $\dfrac{3}{2}$

   d. $\dfrac{-1}{2}$

   e. $\dfrac{5}{2}$

2.   Determine whether the sequence is increasing, decreasing, or not monotonic. Is the sequence bounded?

   $$a_n = \dfrac{1}{2n + 1}$$

Select the correct answer.

   a.   decreasing
   b.   not monotonic
   c.   increasing
   d.   bounded

3.   Find the value of the limit of the sequence defined by $a_1 = 1, \quad a_{n+1} = 3 - \dfrac{1}{a_n}$.

Select the correct answer.

   a. $\dfrac{3 + \sqrt{5}}{2}$

   b. $\dfrac{3 - \sqrt{5}}{2}$

   c. $\dfrac{3 - \sqrt{10}}{2}$

   d. $\dfrac{3 + \sqrt{10}}{2}$

   e. $3 + \sqrt{10}$

4. Find the value of c.

$$\sum_{n=2}^{\infty} (1+c)^{-n} = 7$$

Select the correct answer.

a. $\quad 0$

b. $\quad \dfrac{\sqrt{77} - 7}{14}$

c. $\quad -\dfrac{\sqrt{77} + 7}{14}$

d. $\quad -\dfrac{\sqrt{7} + 7}{7}$

e. $\quad \dfrac{\sqrt{7} - 7}{2}$

5. Given the two series $A = 1 + \dfrac{1}{4} + \dfrac{1}{9} + \dfrac{1}{16} + \dfrac{1}{25} + \ldots$ and $B = \displaystyle\sum_{n=1}^{\infty} n^5 e^{-n^6}$ determine whether each series is convergent or divergent and choose the correct statement.

Select the correct answer.

a. Both series are divergent.
b. Series A is convergent, series B is divergent.
c. Both series are convergent.
d. Series A is divergent, series B is convergent.

6. Find the partial sum s_7 of the series $\displaystyle\sum_{k=1}^{\infty} \dfrac{3}{4 + 5^k}$. Give your answer to five decimal places.

Select the correct answer.

a. $s_7 = 0.46301$
b. $s_7 = 0.47999$
c. $s_7 = 2.276$
d. $s_7 = 0.466$
e. $s_7 = 0.566$

7. Given the series:

$$A = \sum_{m=1}^{\infty} \frac{\sin^2 5m}{m^{10}\sqrt{m}} \text{ and } B = \sum_{m=1}^{\infty} 8\cos\left(\frac{1}{7m}\right)$$

Determine whether each series is convergent or divergent.

a. A is convergent, B is divergent.
b. A is divergent, B is convergent.
c. The both series are convergent.
d. The both series are divergent.

8. Find the interval of convergence of the series.

$$\sum_{n=1}^{\infty} \frac{x^n}{n8^n}$$

Select the correct answer.

a. (-8, 8]
b. (-1,1)
c. [-1, 1]
d. [-8, 8]
e. [-8, 8)
f. diverges everywhere

9. Find the radius of convergence of the series.

$$\sum_{n=1}^{\infty} \frac{n^3 x^n}{3^n}$$

Select the correct answer.

a. $R = \infty$
b. $R = 0$
c. $R = \dfrac{1}{3}$
d. $R = 1$
e. $R = 3$

10. Find the interval of convergence of the series.

$$\sum_{n=1}^{\infty} (-1)^n \frac{(x+8)^n}{n6^n}$$

Select the correct answer.

a. (2, 14]
b. (-14, -2)
c. [-1,1]
d. (-8, 6]
e. [-14, -2)
f. diverges everywhere

11. Find a power series representation for

$$f(t) = \ln(10 - t)$$

Select the correct answer.

a. $\displaystyle\sum_{n=0}^{\infty} \frac{t^n}{n10^n}$

b. $\displaystyle\sum_{n=1}^{\infty} \frac{10t^n}{n^n}$

c. $\ln 10 - \displaystyle\sum_{n=1}^{\infty} \dfrac{t^n}{10^n}$

d. $\ln 10 - \displaystyle\sum_{n=1}^{\infty} \dfrac{t^n}{n10^n}$

e. $\ln 10 + \displaystyle\sum_{n=1}^{\infty} \dfrac{t^{2n}}{10^n}$

12. Find a power series representation for the function.

$$f(y) = \ln\left(\frac{7+y}{7-y}\right)$$

Select the correct answer.

a. $\displaystyle\sum_{n=0}^{\infty} 14 y^{2n+1}$

b. $\displaystyle\sum_{n=0}^{\infty} \dfrac{y^{2n+1}}{7}$

c. $\displaystyle\sum_{n=7}^{\infty} \dfrac{14 y^{2n+1}}{14}$

d. $\displaystyle\sum_{n=0}^{\infty} \dfrac{2 y^{2n+1}}{7^{n+1}(2n+1)}$

e. $\displaystyle\sum_{n=0}^{\infty} \dfrac{y^{2n+1}}{7^{n+1}(n+1)}$

13. Use series to approximate the definite integral to within the indicated accuracy.

$$\int_{0}^{0.9} x^2 e^{-x^2}\, dx \quad |error| < 0.001$$

Select the correct answer.

a.   0.1249
b.   0.0125
c.   0.1449
d.   0.0625
e.   0.0825

14. Use series to evaluate the limit correct to three decimal places.

$$\lim_{x \to 0} \frac{7x - \tan^{-1} 7x}{x^3}$$

Select the correct answer.

a.   114.133
b.   114.333
c.   34.3233
d.   115.933
e.   118.933

15. Use the binomial series to expand the function as a power series. Find the radius of convergence.

$$\frac{1}{(1+x)^4}$$

Select the correct answer.

a. $|x| < 8$
b. $|x| < 10$
c. $|x| < 1$
d. $|x| < 0.1$
e. $|x| < 1.8$

16. Use the binomial series to expand the function as a power series. Find the radius of convergence.

$$\frac{x}{\sqrt{16 + x^2}}$$

Select the correct answer.

a. $|x| < 8$
b. $|x| < 1$
c. $|x| < 4$
d. $|x| < 10$
e. $|x| < 1.8$

17. Find the Taylor polynomial T_3 for the function f at the number $a = 1$.

$f(x) = \ln x$

Select the correct answer.

a. $(x-1) - \dfrac{1}{2}(x-1)^2 + \dfrac{1}{3}(x-1)^3$

b. $(x-1) + \dfrac{1}{5}(x-1)^2 + \dfrac{1}{4}(x-1)^3$

c. $(x+1) - \dfrac{1}{4}(x+1)^2 + \dfrac{1}{3}(x+1)^3$

d. $(x+1) - \dfrac{1}{5}(x+1)^2 + \dfrac{1}{7}(x+1)^3$

e. $(x-1) - \dfrac{1}{5}(x-1)^2 - \dfrac{1}{7}(x-1)^3$

18. Find the Taylor polynomial T_3 for the function $f(x)$ at the number $a = 9$.

$f(x) = \cos x$

Select the correct answer.

a. $\cos(9) - \sin(9)(x+9) - \dfrac{\cos(9)}{2}(x+9)^2 + \dfrac{\sin(9)}{6}(x+9)^3$

b. $\cos(9) - \sin(9)(x-9) - \dfrac{\cos(9)}{2}(x-9)^2 + \dfrac{\sin(9)}{6}(x-9)^3$

c. $\cos(9) + \sin(9)(x-9) + \dfrac{\cos(9)}{2}(x-9)^2 + \dfrac{\sin(9)}{6}(x-9)^3$

d. $\cos(6) + \sin(6)(x-9) + \dfrac{\cos(6)}{6}(x-9)^2 + \dfrac{\sin(6)}{9}(x-9)^3$

e. $\cos(6) + \sin(6)(x-9) + \dfrac{\cos(2)}{2}(x-9)^2 + \dfrac{\sin(2)}{6}(x-9)^3$

19. Use Taylor's Inequality to estimate the accuracy $|R_2|$ of the approximation $f(x)$ at the number $a = 1$, when $0.71 \le x \le 1.29$.

$$f(x) = \frac{1}{x^2}$$

Select the correct answer.

    a.   1.0407
    b.   0.5407
    c.   1.5407
    d.   1.7407
    e.   1.8407

20. Estimate $\sin(35^\circ)$ correct to five decimal places.

Select the correct answer.

    a.   1.07358
    b.   1.57358
    c.   0.57358
    d.   1.77358
    e.   2.57358

1. b

2. a, d

3. a

4. b

5. c

6. d

7. a

8. e

9. e

10. b

11. d

12. d

13. a

14. b

15. c

16. c

17. a

18. b

19. b

20. c

1. Determine whether the sequence converges or diverges.

$$a_n = \frac{5+5n^2}{n+n^2}$$

Select the correct answer.

a. converges
b. diverges

2. If $1,600 is invested at 7% interest, compounded annually, then after n years the investment is worth $a_n = 1,600(1.07)^n$ dollars. Find the size of investment after 7 years.

3. Determine whether the series is convergent or divergent. If it is convergent, write its sum. Otherwise write *divergent*.

$$\sum_{n=1}^{\infty} 7\left(\frac{3}{4}\right)^{n-1}$$

4. Express the number $0.\overline{87}$ as a ratio of integers.

5. Use the binomial series to expand the function as a power series. Find the radius of convergence.

$$\sqrt[4]{1+x^6}$$

6. When money is spent on goods and services, those that receive the money also spend some of it. The people receiving some of the twice-spent money will spend some of that, and so on. Economists call this chain reaction the multiplier effect. In a hypothetical isolated community, the local government begins the process by spending D dollars. Suppose that each recipient of spent money spends $100c\%$ and saves $100s\%$ of the money that he or she receives. The values c and s are called the marginal propensity to consume and the marginal propensity to save and, of course, $c + s = 1$.

The number $k = 1/s$ is called the multiplier. What is the multiplier if the marginal propensity to consume is 80%?

Select the correct answer.

a. 6
b. 4
c. 5
d. 7
e. 3

7. Find the partial sum s_7 of the series $\displaystyle\sum_{m=1}^{\infty} \frac{5}{6+9^m}$.

   Write your answer to five decimal places.

8. Use the sum of the first 9 terms to approximate the sum of the following series:

   $$\sum_{n=1}^{\infty} \frac{6}{n^6 + n^2}$$

   Write your answer to six decimal places.

9. Determine whether the series converges or diverges.

   $$\sum_{n=1}^{\infty} \frac{4 + \cos n}{4^n}$$

   Select the correct answer.

   a. neither
   b. converges
   c. diverges

10. For what values of k does the series $\displaystyle\sum_{n=3}^{\infty} \frac{1}{n^k \ln n}$ converge?

11. Test the series for convergence or divergence.

   $$\sum_{n=2}^{\infty} \frac{(-1)^{n-1}}{\sqrt[3]{7 \ln n}}$$

12. Find the radius of convergence of the series.

   $$\sum_{n=1}^{\infty} \frac{5^n x^n}{(n+8)^3}$$

13. Find the Maclaurin series for $f(x)$ using the definition of a Maclaurin series.

   $$f(x) = (2+x)^{-3}$$

14. Find the Taylor series for $f(x)$ centered at $a = 1$.

$$f(x) = 2 + x + x^2$$

15. Use the binomial series to expand the function as a power series. Find the radius of convergence.

$$\frac{x^2}{\sqrt{2+x}}$$

16. Find the Maclaurin series for $f(x)$.

$$f(x) = x\cos(6x)$$

17. Use multiplication or division of power series to find the first three nonzero terms in the Maclaurin series for the function.

$$f(x) = e^{-x^2}\cos 4x$$

Select the correct answer.

a. $1 - 17x^2 + 19.17x^4$
b. $1 - 9x^2 + 11.17x^4$
c. $1 - 9x^2 + 19.17x^4$
d. $1 - 9x + 19.17x^2$
e. $1 - 17x^2 + 11.17x^4$

18. Use the binomial series to expand the function as a power series. Find the radius of convergence.

$$\frac{1}{(5+x)^6}$$

19. The following table contains the evaluation of the Taylor polynomial centered at $a = 1$ for $f(x) = 1/x$.

What is the degree of this polynomial?

x	$T(x)$
0.5	1.88
0.7	1.42
1.7	0.45
2.8	-3.39
3	-5.00

Select the correct answer.

a.   3
b.   2
c.   1
d.   5
e.   4

20. Use the Alternating Series Estimation Theorem or Taylor's Inequality to estimate the range of values of x for which the given approximation is accurate to within the stated error.

$$\cos x \approx 1 - \frac{x^2}{2} + \frac{x^4}{24} \quad |error| < 0.08$$

Write a such that $-a < x < a$.

1. a

2. 2569.25

3. 28

4. 29/33

5. $|x| < 1$

6. c

7. 0.39846

8. 3.098422

9. b

10. $k > 1$

11. convergent

12. 1/5

13. $\displaystyle\sum_{n=0}^{\infty} \frac{(-1)^n (n+1)(n+2)\left(\frac{x}{2}\right)^n}{2^4}$

14. $4 + 3(x-1) + (x+1)^2$

15. $|x| < 2$

16. $\displaystyle\sum_{n=0}^{\infty} \frac{(-1)^n 6^{2n} x^{2n+1}}{(2n)!}$

17. c

18. $|x| < 5$

19. a

20. $-1.965 < x < 1.965$

1. Find a formula for the general term a_n of the sequence, assuming that the pattern of the first few terms continues.

$$\left\{ 1,\ 7,\ 13,\ 19,\ \ldots \right\}$$

2. Find the value of the limit for the sequence.

$$\left\{ \frac{1 \cdot 8 \cdot 15 \cdots (7n+1)}{(7n)^2} \right\}$$

3. If $600 is invested at 4% interest, compounded annually, then after n years the investment is worth $a_n = 600(1.04)^n$ dollars. Find the size of investment after 7 years.

Select the correct answer.

   a. $789.56
   b. $430.21
   c. $1,321.06
   d. $1,230.81
   e. $1,860.81

4. Find the value of the limit of the sequence defined by $a_1 = 1$, $a_{n+1} = 3 - \dfrac{1}{a_n}$.

Select the correct answer.

   a. $\dfrac{3 + \sqrt{10}}{2}$

   b. $\dfrac{3 - \sqrt{10}}{2}$

   c. $\dfrac{3 - \sqrt{5}}{2}$

   d. $\dfrac{3 + \sqrt{5}}{2}$

   e. $\dfrac{2 + \sqrt{5}}{3}$

5. Use Taylor's Inequality to estimate the accuracy $|R_3|$ of the approximation $f(x)$ at the number $a = 0$, when $0 \le x \le 0.5$.

$$f(x) = \tan x$$

6. A right triangle ABC is given with $\theta = 1.1$ and $|AC| = b = 4$. CD is drawn perpendicular to AB, DE is drawn perpendicular to BC, EF $\perp$ AB and this process is continued indefinitely as shown in the figure. Find the total length of all the perpendiculars $|CD| + |DE| + |EF| + |FG| + ...$

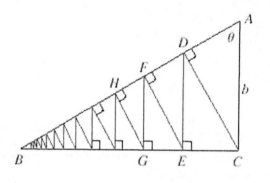

7. Let $A = \sum_{n=10}^{\infty} \frac{3}{n^{4.6}}$ and $B = \int_{9}^{\infty} \frac{3}{x^{4.6}} \, dx$. Compare A and B.

    Select the correct answer.

    a. $A \geq B$
    b. $A \leq B$
    c. $A < B$
    d. $A > B$
    e. $A = B$

8. Given the two series

    $$A = 1 + \frac{1}{16} + \frac{1}{81} + \frac{1}{256} + \frac{1}{625} + ... \text{ and } B = \sum_{n=1}^{\infty} n^8 e^{-n^9}$$ determine whether each series is convergent

    or divergent and choose the correct statement.

    Select the correct answer.

    a. Series A is divergent, series B is convergent.
    b. Both series are convergent.
    c. Series A is convergent, series B is divergent.
    d. Both series are divergent.

9. Find the values of s for which the series is convergent.

    $$\sum_{k=5}^{\infty} \frac{1}{m \ln m \left[\ln(\ln m)\right]^{s}}$$

10. Find the partial sum s_{10} of the series $\sum\limits_{n=1}^{\infty} \dfrac{7}{n^3}$.

Please approximate the answer to the nearest thousandth.

11. Find the partial sum s_7 of the series $\sum\limits_{m=1}^{\infty} \dfrac{8}{6+10^m}$.

Give your answer to five decimal places.

12. Use the sum of the first 9 terms to approximate the sum of the following series:

$$\sum_{n=1}^{\infty} \dfrac{4}{n^7 + n^5}$$

Give your answer to six decimal places.

13. Which of the given series is (are) convergent?

Select the correct answer.

a. $\quad \dfrac{7}{6} - \dfrac{7}{7} + \dfrac{7}{8} - \dfrac{7}{9} + \dfrac{7}{10} - \cdots$

b. $\quad -\dfrac{1}{6} + \dfrac{2}{7} - \dfrac{3}{8} + \dfrac{4}{9} - \dfrac{5}{10} + \cdots$

14. Test the series for convergence or divergence.

$$\dfrac{6}{\ln 2} - \dfrac{6}{\ln 3} + \dfrac{6}{\ln 4} - \dfrac{6}{\ln 5} + \dfrac{6}{\ln 6} - \cdots$$

Select the correct answer.

a.　　the series is divergent
b.　　the series is convergent

15. Approximate the sum to the indicated accuracy.

$$\sum_{n=0}^{\infty} \dfrac{(-1)^n}{3^n\, n!} \quad \text{(four decimal places)}$$

16. The terms of a series are defined recursively by the equations $a_1 = 5$, $a_{n+1} = \dfrac{7n+1}{6n+3} a_n$

   Determine whether $\sum a_n$ converges or diverges.

17. Estimate $\sin(33°)$ correct to five decimal places.

   Select the correct answer.

   a.   1.54464
   b.   1.04464
   c.   0.54464
   d.   2.04464
   e.   3.54464

18. Test the series for convergence or divergence.

   $$\sum_{k=1}^{\infty} \left(\sqrt[k]{3} - 1\right)^k$$

19. For which positive integers k is the series $\displaystyle\sum_{n=1}^{\infty} \dfrac{(n!)^6}{(kn)!}$ convergent?

   Select the correct answer.

   a. $k \geq 1$
   b. $k \leq 0$
   c. $k \geq 0$
   d. $k \geq 6$
   e. $k \leq -6$

20. Find the Taylor polynomial T_3 for the function $f(x)$ at the number $a = 1$.

   $f(x) = \sin x$

ANSWER KEY

Stewart - Calculus ET 5e Chapter 11 Form F

1. $a_n = 6n - 5$

2. 0

3. a

4. d

5. 0.0428

6. 32.77

7. c

8. b

9. $(1, \infty)$

10. 8.383

11. 0.58431

12. 2.026946

13. a

14. b

15. 0.7165

16. diverges

17. c

18. convergent

19. d

20. $T_3 = \sin(1) + \cos(1) \cdot (x-1) - \dfrac{\sin(1)}{2} \cdot (x-1)^2 - \dfrac{\cos(1)}{6} \cdot (x-1)^3$

1. Find the value of the limit for the sequence.

$$\left\{ \frac{n^8}{n!} \right\}$$

2. Find the exact value of the limit of the sequence defined by $a_1 = \sqrt{3}, \ a_{n+1} = \sqrt{3 + a_n}$.

3. Find the exact value of the limit of the sequence defined by $a_1 = 1, \ a_{n+1} = 6 - \dfrac{1}{a_n}$

4. A right triangle ABC is given with $\theta = 1.4$ and $|AC| = b = 10$. CD is drawn perpendicular to AB, DE is drawn perpendicular to BC, EF $\perp$ AB and this process is continued indefinitely as shown in the figure. Find the total length of all the perpendiculars $|CD| + |DE| + |EF| + |FG| + \ldots$

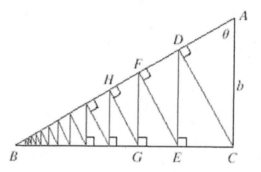

5. A sequence $\{a_n\}$ is defined recursively by the equation $a_n = 0.5(a_{n-1} + a_{n-2})$ for $n \geq 3$ where $a_1 = 21, \ a_2 = 21$. Use your calculator to guess the limit of the sequence.

6. Use the Integral Test to determine whether the series is convergent or divergent.

$$\sum_{n=1}^{\infty} \frac{1}{9n+1}$$

Select the correct answer.

a.   the series is divergent
b.   the series is convergent

7. Which of the following series is convergent?

    Select the correct answer.

    a. $$\sum_{m=1}^{\infty} \frac{10}{m^8 + 3}$$

    b. $$\sum_{m=1}^{\infty} 10\frac{\ln 6m}{m^2}$$

    c. $$\sum_{m=1}^{\infty} \frac{5}{m \ln 3m}$$

8. Find the partial sum s_{10} of the series $\sum_{m=1}^{\infty} \dfrac{5}{m^3}$.

    Please approximate the answer to the nearest thousandth.

9. Find all positive values of u for which the series $\sum_{n=1}^{\infty} 8u^{\ln 5n}$ converges.

10. A car is moving with speed 16 m/s and acceleration 6m/s² at a given instant. Using a second-degree Taylor polynomial, estimate how far the car moves in the next second.

    Select the correct answer.

    a. 19.5 m
    b. 19 m
    c. 20 m
    d. 25.5 m
    e. 30 m

11. Find the Taylor polynomial T_3 for the function f at the number $a = 1$.

$$f(x) = \ln x$$

Select the correct answer.

a. $(x+1) - \dfrac{1}{3}(x+1)^2 + \dfrac{1}{2}(x+1)^3$

b. $(x-1) - \dfrac{1}{2}(x-1)^2 + \dfrac{1}{3}(x-1)^3$

c. $(x-1) + \dfrac{1}{4}(x-1)^2 + \dfrac{1}{2}(x-1)^3$

d. $(x-1) + \dfrac{1}{4}(x-1)^2 + \dfrac{1}{2}(x-1)^3$

e. $(x-1) + \dfrac{1}{3}(x-1)^2 + \dfrac{1}{4}(x-1)^3$

12. Use Taylor's Inequality to estimate the accuracy $|R_4|$ of the approximation $f(x)$ at the number $a = 1.5$, when $0 \le x \le 3$.

$$f(x) = \cos x$$

13. How many terms of the series do we need to add in order to find the sum to the indicated accuracy?

$$\sum_{n=1}^{\infty} \frac{(-1)^n n}{2^n} \quad (\, |error| < 0.1562 \,)$$

14. Approximate the sum to the indicated accuracy.

$$\sum_{n=1}^{\infty} \frac{(-1)^{n-1}}{n^7} \quad \text{(five decimal places)}$$

Select the correct answer.

a.   0.99219
b.   0.99249
c.   0.97269
d.   0.99259
e.   0.98259

15. Which of the partial sums of the alternating series $\displaystyle\sum_{n=1}^{\infty} \frac{(-1)^{n-1}}{n}$ are overestimates of the total sum.

Select the correct answer.

   a. s_{100}
   b. s_{67}
   c. s_{82}
   d. s_{91}
   e. s_{55}

16. Determine whether the series is absolutely convergent, conditionally convergent, or divergent.

$$\sum_{n=1}^{\infty} \frac{(-1)^{n-1}}{n^4 \sqrt{n}}$$

Select the correct answer.

   a.   divergent
   b.   absolutely convergent
   c.   conditionally convergent

17. Determine whether the series is absolutely convergent, conditionally convergent, or divergent.

$$\sum_{n=1}^{\infty} \frac{(-1)^n \arctan n}{n^2}$$

Select the correct answer.

   a.   absolutely convergent
   b.   divergent
   c.   conditionally convergent

18. Find the Maclaurin series for the function $f(x)$.

$f(x) = x \cos 7x$

19. Use multiplication or division of power series to find the first three nonzero terms in the Maclaurin series for the function.

$f(x) = e^{-x^2} \cos 4x$

20. Use the binomial series to expand the function as a power series. Find the radius of convergence.

$\sqrt[4]{1 + x^5}$

1. 0

2. $\dfrac{1+\sqrt{13}}{2}$

3. $\dfrac{6+4\sqrt{2}}{2}$

4. 677.27

5. 21

6. a

7. a, b

8. 5.988

9. $u < \dfrac{1}{e}$

10. b

11. b

12. 0.0633

13. 5

14. d

15. b, d

16. b

17. a

18. $\displaystyle\sum_{n=0}^{\infty} \dfrac{(-1)^n \cdot 7^{2n} \cdot x^{2n+1}}{(2n)!}$

19. $1 - 9x^2 + 19.17x^4$

20. $|x| < 1$

1. Determine whether the series is convergent or divergent. If it is convergent, write its sum. Otherwise write *divergent*.

$$\sum_{n=1}^{\infty} 7 \left(\frac{3}{4} \right)^{n-1}$$

2. Use the sum of the first 9 terms to approximate the sum of the following series:

$$\sum_{n=1}^{\infty} \frac{6}{n^6 + n^2}$$

    Write your answer to six decimal places.

3. Determine whether the series converges or diverges.

$$\sum_{n=1}^{\infty} \frac{4 + \cos n}{4^n}$$

    Select the correct answer.

    a. neither
    b. converges
    c. diverges

4. Use multiplication or division of power series to find the first three nonzero terms in the Maclaurin series for the function.

$$f(x) = e^{-x^2} \cos 4x$$

    Select the correct answer.

    a. $1 - 17x^2 + 19.17x^4$
    b. $1 - 9x^2 + 11.17x^4$
    c. $1 - 9x^2 + 19.17x^4$
    d. $1 - 9x + 19.17x^2$
    e. $1 - 17x^2 + 11.17x^4$

5. Use the binomial series to expand the function as a power series. Find the radius of convergence.

$$\frac{1}{(5 + x)^6}$$

6. Find a formula for the general term a_n of the sequence, assuming that the pattern of the first few terms continues.

$$\left\{ 1,\ 7,\ 13,\ 19,\ \ldots \right\}$$

7. Find the value of the limit for the sequence.

$$\left\{ \frac{1 \cdot 8 \cdot 15 \cdots (7n+1)}{(7n)^2} \right\}$$

8. Find the value of the limit of the sequence defined by $a_1 = 1,\ a_{n+1} = 3 - \dfrac{1}{a_n}$.

Select the correct answer.

a. $\dfrac{3 + \sqrt{10}}{2}$

b. $\dfrac{3 - \sqrt{10}}{2}$

c. $\dfrac{3 - \sqrt{5}}{2}$

d. $\dfrac{3 + \sqrt{5}}{2}$

e. $\dfrac{2 + \sqrt{5}}{3}$

9. A right triangle ABC is given with $\theta = 1.1$ and $|AC| = b = 4$. CD is drawn perpendicular to AB, DE is drawn perpendicular to BC, EF ⊥ AB and this process is continued indefinitely as shown in the figure. Find the total length of all the perpendiculars $|CD| + |DE| + |EF| + |FG| + \ldots$

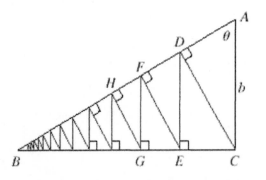

10. Find the partial sum s_{10} of the series $\displaystyle\sum_{n=1}^{\infty} \frac{7}{n^3}$.

    Please approximate the answer to the nearest thousandth.

11. The terms of a series are defined recursively by the equations $a_1 = 5$, $a_{n+1} = \dfrac{7n+1}{6n+3} a_n$.

    Determine whether $\displaystyle\sum a_n$ converges or diverges.

12. Find the Taylor polynomial T_3 for the function $f(x)$ at the number $a = 1$.

    $f(x) = \sin x$

13. Approximate the sum to the indicated accuracy.

    $$\sum_{n=1}^{\infty} \frac{(-1)^{n-1}}{n^7} \quad \text{(five decimal places)}$$

    Select the correct answer.

    a.   0.99219
    b.   0.99249
    c.   0.97269
    d.   0.99259
    e.   0.98259

14. Which of the partial sums of the alternating series $\displaystyle\sum_{n=1}^{\infty} \frac{(-1)^{n-1}}{n}$ are overestimates of the total sum.

    Select the correct answer.

    a. s_{100}
    b. s_{67}
    c. s_{82}
    d. s_{91}
    e. s_{55}

15. Determine whether the series is absolutely convergent, conditionally convergent, or divergent.

$$\sum_{n=1}^{\infty} \frac{(-1)^n \arctan n}{n^2}$$

Select the correct answer.

    a.   absolutely convergent
    b.   divergent
    c.   conditionally convergent

16. Find the Maclaurin series for the function $f(x)$.

$$f(x) = x \cos 7x$$

17. How many terms of the series do we need to add in order to find the sum to the indicated accuracy?

$$\sum_{n=1}^{\infty} \frac{(-1)^n n}{2^n} \quad (\, |error| < 0.1562 \,)$$

18. Test the series for convergence or divergence.

$$\sum_{m=1}^{\infty} (-1)^m \frac{\ln m}{\sqrt{m}}$$

19. The resistivity of a conducting wire is the reciprocal of the conductivity and is measured in units of ohm-meters. The resistivity of a given metal depends on the temperature according to the equation $\rho(t) = \rho_{27} e^{\alpha(t-27)}$ where t is the temperature in C. There are tables that list the values of α (called the temperature coefficient) and ρ_{27} (the resistivity at $27\degree$ C) for various metals. Except at very low temperatures, the resistivity varies almost linearly with temperature and so it is common to approximate the expression for $\rho(t)$ by its first-degree Taylor polynomial at $t = 27$. Find the expression for this linear approximation.

20. Suppose that the radius of convergence of the power series $\sum\limits_{n=0}^{\infty} c_n x^n$ is 16. What is the radius of convergence of the power series $\sum\limits_{n=0}^{\infty} c_n x^{2n}$?

Select the correct answer.

    a.   256
    b.   4
    c.   1
    d.   16
    e.   252

Stewart - Calculus ET 5e Chapter 11 Form H

1. 28

2. 3.098422

3. b

4. c

5. $|x| < 5$

6. $a_n = 6n - 5$

7. 0

8. d

9. 32.77

10. 8.383

11. diverges

12. $T_3 = \sin(1) + \cos(1) \cdot (x-1) - \dfrac{\sin(1)}{2} \cdot (x-1)^2 - \dfrac{\cos(1)}{6} \cdot (x-1)^3$

13. d

14. b, d

15. a

16. $\displaystyle\sum_{n=0}^{\infty} \dfrac{(-1)^n \cdot 7^{2n} \cdot x^{2n+1}}{(2n)!}$

17. 5

18. convergent

19. $\rho_{27}(1 + \alpha(t - 27))$

20. b

1. Draw a rectangular box with the origin and $(6, 6, 3)$ as opposite vertices and with its faces parallel to the coordinate planes. Find the length of the diagonal of the box.

2. Find an equation of the sphere with center $(1, -3, 5)$ that touches the xz - plane.

3. Write an inequality to describe the half-space consisting of all points to the left of a plane parallel to the xz - plane and 9 units to the right of it.

4. Write inequalities to describe the solid rectangular box in the first octant bounded by the planes $x = 1, y = 6$, and $z = 4$.

5. Write an inequality to describe the region consisting of all points between (but not on) the spheres of radius 5 and 7 centered at the origin.

6. Find $3\mathbf{a} + 9\mathbf{b}$.

   $\mathbf{a} = 6\mathbf{i} - 5\mathbf{j} + 8\mathbf{k}$, $\mathbf{b} = 5\mathbf{i} + 3\mathbf{j} + 6\mathbf{k}$

7. Find $6\mathbf{a} + 8\mathbf{b}$.

   $\mathbf{a} = 4\mathbf{i} - 8\mathbf{k}$, $\mathbf{b} = 8\mathbf{i} - 10\mathbf{j} + 9\mathbf{k}$

8. Velocities have both direction and magnitude and thus are vectors. The magnitude of a velocity vector is called *speed*. Suppose that a wind is blowing from the direction N 67° W at a speed of 23 km/h. (This means that the direction from which the wind blows is 67° west of the northerly direction.) A pilot is steering a plane in the direction N 24° E at an airspeed (speed in still air) of 230 km/h. The *true course*, or *track*, of the plane is the direction of the resultant of the velocity vectors of the plane and the wind. The *ground speed* of the plane is the magnitude of the resultant. Find the *ground speed* of the plane. Round the result to the nearest hundredth.

9. A woman walks due west on the deck of a ship at 4 mi/h. The ship is moving north at a speed of 20 mi/h. Find the speed of the woman relative to the surface of the water. Round the result to the nearest tenth.

10. The tension **T** at each end of the chain has magnitude 30 N and makes an angle $\angle a = 35°$ with the horizontal. What is the weight of the chain? Round the result to the nearest hundredth.

11. Find **a** • **b**, if **a** $= \langle 2,\ 9,\ -5 \rangle$ and **b** $= \langle 10,\ 7,\ 2 \rangle$.

12. Find **a** • **b**, if **a** $= 4\mathbf{i} + 24\mathbf{j} - 7\mathbf{k}$ and **b** $= 10\mathbf{i} + 8\mathbf{k}$.

13. Find the angle between the vectors, if **a** $= \langle 6,\ 0 \rangle$ and **b** $= \langle 6,\ 6 \rangle$.

14. Find the cosine of the angle between the following vectors.

    a $= 7\mathbf{j} + 5\mathbf{k}$
    b $= 2\mathbf{i} + 3\mathbf{j} + 6\mathbf{k}$

15. For what values of a are the vectors $\langle -7,\ a,\ -2 \rangle$ and $\langle a,\ a^2,\ a \rangle$ orthogonal?

16. Let P be a point not on the line L that passes through the points Q and R.

    Use the formula $\mathbf{d} = \dfrac{|\mathbf{a} \times \mathbf{b}|}{|\mathbf{a}|}$ where $\mathbf{a} = \vec{QR}$, $\mathbf{b} = \vec{QP}$, to find the distance from the point $P\ (-1, 2, -4)$ to the line through $Q\ (-4, 4, -2)$ and $R\ (-1, 3, -4)$.

17. Find an equation of the plane through the points $(0,\ -2,\ -2)$, $(-2,\ 0,\ -2)$ and $(-2,\ -2,\ 0)$.

18. Plot the point whose cylindrical coordinates are $(7,\ \pi/2,\ 6)$.

    Then find the rectangular coordinates of the point.

19. Change from spherical to cylindrical coordinates.

$(4, 0, 0)$

20. Write the equation in spherical coordinates.

$5x^2 + 5y^2 - 9z^2 = 4$

1. 9

2. $(x-1)^2 + (y+3)^2 + (z-5)^2 = 9$

3. $y < 9$

4. $0 \le x \le 1,\ 0 \le y \le 6,\ 0 \le z \le 4$

5. $25 < x^2 + y^2 + z^2 < 49$

6. $63i + 12j + 78k$

7. $88i - 80j + 24k$

8. 230.75

9. 20.4

10. 34.41

11. 73

12. -16

13. $\dfrac{\pi}{4}$

14. 0.85

15. 3, -3, 0

16. 1

17. $x + y + z = -4$

18. (0, 7, 6)

19. (0, 0, 4)

20. $\rho^2 (5(\sin(\phi))^2 - 9(\cos(\phi))^2) = 4$

1. Find an equation of the sphere that passes through the point $(-4,\ 9,\ 3)$ and has center $(10,\ -6,\ -1)$.

2. Write an equation or inequality that represents a plane containing all points with equal x and y coordinates.

3. Write an equation or inequality that represents all points on or inside a circular cylinder of radius 9 with the y-axis as its axis.

4. Write an inequality to describe the half-space consisting of all points to the left of a plane parallel to the xz - plane and 2 units to the right of it.

5. Write inequalities to describe the solid rectangular box in the first octant bounded by the planes $x = 4$, $y = 7$, and $z = 8$.

6. Write inequalities to describe the solid upper hemisphere of the sphere of radius 7 centered at the origin.

7. Find an equation of the set of all points equidistant from the points $A(0,\ 7,\ 1)$ and $B(3,\ 3,\ 5)$.

8. Find a vector a with representation given by the directed line segment $\overrightarrow{AB}$.

    $A(-4, 7, 6)$, $B(-9, -1, -9)$

9. Find the sum of the given vectors.

    $\langle 8,\ -2,\ -1 \rangle$, $\langle -8,\ 9,\ 1 \rangle$

10. Find $6\mathbf{a} + 2\mathbf{b}$.

    $\mathbf{a} = \langle 8,\ -2, \rangle$, $\mathbf{b} = \langle 7,\ -10, \rangle$

11. Find $3\mathbf{a} + 6\mathbf{b}$.

$\mathbf{a} = 10\mathbf{i} - 2\mathbf{j} + 4\mathbf{k}$, $\mathbf{b} = 2\mathbf{i} + 8\mathbf{j} + 10\mathbf{k}$

12. Two forces F_1 and F_2 with magnitudes 10 lb and 18 lb act on an object at a point P as shown in the figure. Find the magnitude of the resultant force F acting at P. Round the result to the nearest tenth.

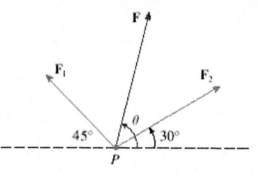

13. Change from rectangular to cylindrical coordinates.

$(3, -3, 6)$

14. Change from spherical to cylindrical coordinates.

$(2, 0, 0)$

15. Write the equation in cylindrical coordinates.

$2x^2 + 2y^2 + z^2 = 10$

16. Write the equation in spherical coordinates.

$7x^2 + 7y^2 - 2z^2 = 17$

17. For what values of d are the vectors $\langle -33, d, -3 \rangle$ and $\langle d, d^2, d \rangle$ orthogonal?

18. The tension T at each end of the chain has magnitude 22 N and makes an angle $\angle a = 42°$ with the horizontal. What is the weight of the chain? Round the result to the nearest hundredth.

19. Find $\mathbf{a} \cdot \mathbf{b}$, if $\mathbf{a} = \langle 5, -1, -4 \rangle$ and $\mathbf{b} = \langle 3, 4, -3 \rangle$.

20. Find the scalar projection of $\mathbf{b}$ onto $\mathbf{a}$.

$\mathbf{a} = \langle 4, 2 \rangle$
$\mathbf{b} = \langle 9, 10 \rangle$

Round your answer to the nearest hundredth.

1. $(x-10)^2 + (y+6)^2 + (z+1)^2 = 437$

2. $x = y$

3. $x^2 + z^2 \leq 81$

4. $y < 2$

5. $0 \leq x \leq 4,\ 0 \leq y \leq 7,\ 0 \leq z \leq 8$

6. $0 \leq x^2 + y^2 + z^2 \leq 49,\ z \geq 0$

7. $-3x + 4y - 4z = 3.5$

8. $\langle -5,\ -8,\ -15 \rangle$

9. $\langle 0,\ 7,\ 0 \rangle$

10. $\langle 62,\ -32 \rangle$

11. $42i + 42j + 72k$

12. 18.2 lb

13. $\left(3\sqrt{2},\ \dfrac{7\pi}{4},\ 6 \right)$

14. $(0, 0, 2)$

15. $2r^2 + z^2 = 10$

16. $\rho^2 \left(7(\sin\phi)^2 - 2(\cos\phi)^2 \right) = 17$

17. 6, -6, 0

18. 29.44

19. 23

20. 12.52

1. Suppose you start at the origin, move along the x-axis a distance of 8 units in the positive direction, and then move downward a distance of 1 units. What are the coordinates of your position?

   Select the correct answer.

   a.   (8, 0, 1)
   b.   (0, 8, 1)
   c.   (8, −1, 0)
   d.   (8, 0, −1)
   e.   (8, 1, 0)

2. Find that the midpoint of the line segment from $P1(-10, 10, 5)$ to $P2(2, 8, 3)$.

   Select the correct answer.

   a.   (−4, 9, 4)
   b.   (6, 0, −1)
   c.   (−6, 0, 1)
   d.   (4, −9, −4)
   e.   (1, 9, −4)

3. Find an equation of the set of all points equidistant from the points $A(7, -8, -9)$ and $B(-4, 2, -10)$.

   Select the correct answer.

   a. $11x - 10y + z = -37$
   b. $11x - 10y + z = 37$
   c. $-11x - 10y + z = 37$
   d. $11x - 10y - z = 37$
   e. $11x - 10y + z = 37$

4. Find the sum of the given vectors.

   $$\left\langle -6, 1, 5 \right\rangle, \ \left\langle 1, 4, 9 \right\rangle$$

   Select the correct answer.

   a. $\left\langle -5, 5, 14 \right\rangle$
   b. $\left\langle 5, -5, -14 \right\rangle$
   c. $\left\langle 5, -14, -5 \right\rangle$
   d. $\left\langle 5, -5, 14 \right\rangle$
   e. $\left\langle -14, -14, -5 \right\rangle$

5. Find $5\mathbf{a} + 3\mathbf{b}$.

$$\mathbf{a} = \langle -7,\ -6 \rangle,\quad \mathbf{b} = \langle -4,\ 7 \rangle$$

Select the correct answer.

a. $\langle 9,\ 47 \rangle$

b. $\langle -9,\ -47 \rangle$

c. $\langle -47,\ -9 \rangle$

d. $\langle 47,\ 9 \rangle$

e. $\langle 9,\ 9 \rangle$

6. Two forces F_1 and F_2 with magnitudes 8 lb and 12 lb act on an object at a point P as shown in the figure. Find the magnitude of the resultant force F acting at P. Round the result to the nearest tenth.

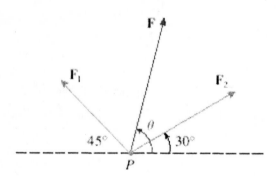

Select the correct answer.

a. 13.6 lb
b. 12.6 lb
c. 11.5 lb
d. 10.6 lb
e. 14.6 lb

7. Find $\mathbf{a} \bullet \mathbf{b}$, if $|\mathbf{a}| = 26$, $|\mathbf{b}| = 17$, and the angle between $\mathbf{a}$ and $\mathbf{b}$ is $\dfrac{\pi}{3}$.

Select the correct answer.

a. $\dfrac{442}{\sqrt{2}}$

b. $221\sqrt{3}$

c. 221

d. 884

e. $442\sqrt{3}$

8. Find the angle between the vectors, if $\mathbf{a} = \langle 6, 0 \rangle$ and $\mathbf{b} = \langle 6, 6 \rangle$.

    Select the correct answer.

    a. $\dfrac{\pi}{6}$

    b. $\dfrac{\pi}{3}$

    c. $\dfrac{\pi}{2}$

    d. $\dfrac{\pi}{4}$

    e. $\dfrac{5\pi}{6}$

9. Find a unit vector that is orthogonal to both $9\mathbf{i} + 9\mathbf{j}$ and $9\mathbf{i} + 9\mathbf{k}$.

    Select the correct answer.

    a. $\dfrac{\mathbf{i}}{3} - \dfrac{\mathbf{j}}{3} - \dfrac{\mathbf{k}}{3}$

    b. $\dfrac{\mathbf{i}}{\sqrt{3}} - \dfrac{\mathbf{j}}{\sqrt{3}} - \dfrac{\mathbf{k}}{\sqrt{3}}$

    c. $\dfrac{\mathbf{i}}{3} + \dfrac{\mathbf{j}}{3} + \dfrac{\mathbf{k}}{3}$

    d. $\dfrac{\mathbf{i}}{9} + \dfrac{\mathbf{j}}{9} + \dfrac{\mathbf{k}}{9}$

    e. $\dfrac{\mathbf{i}}{9} - \dfrac{\mathbf{j}}{9} - \dfrac{\mathbf{k}}{9}$

10. Find the cross product $\mathbf{a} \times \mathbf{b}$.

    $$\mathbf{a} = \langle 3, 5, 1 \rangle, \ \mathbf{b} = \langle -5, 2, -2 \rangle$$

    Select the correct answer.

    a. $\mathbf{a} \times \mathbf{b} = \langle -10, -5, 6 \rangle$

    b. $\mathbf{a} \times \mathbf{b} = \langle -12, 1, 31 \rangle$

    c. $\mathbf{a} \times \mathbf{b} = \langle 2, -6, -25 \rangle$

    d. $\mathbf{a} \times \mathbf{b} = \langle -8, -11, -19 \rangle$

    e. $\mathbf{a} \times \mathbf{b} = \langle -16, -23, 25 \rangle$

11. Let $\mathbf{v} = 7\,\mathbf{j}$ and let $\mathbf{u}$ be a vector with length 5 that starts at the origin and rotates in the xy - plane. Find the maximum value of the length of the vector $|\mathbf{u} \times \mathbf{v}|$.

Select the correct answer.

    a. $|\mathbf{u} \times \mathbf{v}| = 12$

    b. $|\mathbf{u} \times \mathbf{v}| = 140$

    c. $|\mathbf{u} \times \mathbf{v}| = 30$

    d. $|\mathbf{u} \times \mathbf{v}| = 1$

    e. $|\mathbf{u} \times \mathbf{v}| = 35$

12. Let P be a point not on the line L that passes through the points Q and R.

Use the formula $\mathbf{d} = \dfrac{|\mathbf{u} \times \mathbf{v}|}{|\mathbf{a}|}$ where $\mathbf{a} = \overrightarrow{QR}$, $\mathbf{b} = \overrightarrow{QP}$ to find the distance from the point P (4, -2, -2) to the line through Q (1, 3, 5) and R (-2, 4, 0).

Select the correct answer.

    a. $\mathbf{d} = 8.2$
    b. $\mathbf{d} = 9.0$
    c. $\mathbf{d} = 8.4$
    d. $\mathbf{d} = 10.1$
    e. $\mathbf{d} = 6.7$

13. Identify the planes that are perpendicular.

Select the correct answer.

    a. $x + 10y - z = 6,\ -9x - y - 19z = 2$

    b. $x = 5x + 3y,\ -10x - 6y + 2z = -1$

    c. $8x + 5y = -3,\ 9y + 6z = -1$

    d. $8x + 5y = -3,\ y + 6z = -1$

    e. $8x + 5y = -3,\ y + 6z = -1$

14. Identify the surface.

$$25x^2 + z^2 = 100 + 100y^2$$

Select the correct answer.

a. The surface is a hyperboloid of one sheet with axis the y-axis.
b. The surface is a hyperboloid of two sheets with axis the x-axis.

15. Find the equation of a hyperbolic paraboloid.

Select the correct answer.

a. $\dfrac{x^2}{3} - \dfrac{y^2}{10} = \dfrac{z}{8}$

b. $\dfrac{x^2}{8} + \dfrac{y^2}{10} = 1 - \dfrac{z^2}{4}$

c. $\dfrac{x^2}{7} + \dfrac{y^2}{5} = \dfrac{z^2}{4}$

d. $\dfrac{x^2}{4} + \dfrac{y^2}{7} = \dfrac{z}{5}$

e. $\dfrac{x}{4} + \dfrac{y}{10} = \dfrac{z}{5}$

16. Find $|\mathbf{u} \times \mathbf{v}|$ correct to three decimal places where $|\mathbf{u}| = 9$, $|\mathbf{v}| = 3$, $\angle\theta = 85°$.

Select the correct answer.

a. 26.897
b. 31.897
c. 2.989
d. 2.353
e. 8.966

17. Classify the surface.

$$25x^2 + y^2 - z^2 - 6y + 6z = 0$$

Select the correct answer.

a. A cone with axis parallel to the z-axis and vertex (0, 3, 3).
b. A circular paraboloid with vertex (0, 3, 1) and axis the z-axis.
c. A hyperboloid of one sheet with center (-5, 3, -1) and axis parallel to the z-axis.

18. Change from rectangular to cylindrical coordinates.

$(9, -9, 2)$

Select the correct answer.

a. $\left(9\sqrt{2}, \dfrac{7\pi}{4}, 2\right)$

b. $\left(9\sqrt{2}, \dfrac{\pi}{4}, 2\right)$

c. $\left(9\sqrt{2}, 0, 2\right)$

d. $\left(9, \dfrac{7\pi}{4}, 2\right)$

e. $\left(-9\sqrt{2}, \dfrac{\pi}{4}, 2\right)$

19. Change from spherical to cylindrical coordinates.

$(8, 0, 0)$

Select the correct answer.

a. $(0, 0, -8)$
b. $(8, 0, 8)$
c. $(-8, 0, -8)$
d. $(0, 0, 8)$
e. $(8, 0, 0)$

20. Write the equation in cylindrical coordinates:

$2x^2 + 2y^2 + z^2 = 15$

Select the correct answer.

a. $2r + z = 15$
b. $2r^2 - z^2 = 15$
c. $2r^2 + z^2 = 15$
d. $4r^2 + z^2 = 15$
e. $2r^2 + z^2 = 225$

1. d

2. a

3. e

4. a

5. c

6. b

7. c

8. d

9. b

10. b

11. e

12. c

13. a

14. a

15. a

16. a

17. a

18. a

19. d

20. c

1. Find the distance from $(-10,\ 2,\ -8)$ to the xy - plane.

    Select the correct answer.

    a.   10
    b.   8
    c.   2
    d.   16
    e.   4

2. Find an equation of the sphere with center $(8,\ -4,\ 8)$ that touches the xy - plane.

    Select the correct answer.

    a. $(x-8)^2 + (y+4)^2 + (z-8)^2 = 4096$

    b. $(x-8)^2 + (y+4)^2 + (z-8)^2 = 64$

    c. $(x-8)^2 + (y-4)^2 + (z-8)^2 = 8$

    d. $(x+8)^2 + (y-4)^2 + (z+8)^2 = 64$

    e. $(x+8)^2 - (y-4)^2 - (z+8)^2 = 64$

3. Write an equation that represents all points on and inside a circular cylinder of radius 6 with the y-axis as its axis.

    Select the correct answer.

    a. $y^2 + z^2 < 36$

    b. $x^2 + z^2 \le 36$

    c. $x^2 + z^2 \ge 36$

    d. $x^2 + y^2 \le 36$

    e. $x^2 + y^2 \le 6$

4. Find the sum of the given vectors.

    $$\langle -5,\ -6 \rangle,\ \langle -7,\ -1 \rangle$$

    Select the correct answer.

    a. $\langle 7,\ 12 \rangle$

    b. $\langle -12,\ -7 \rangle$

    c. $\langle -7,\ -12 \rangle$

    d. $\langle 12,\ 7 \rangle$

    e. $\langle -12,\ -5 \rangle$

5. Find the sum of the given vectors.

    $$\langle 6,\ -8,\ -4\rangle,\ \langle -7,\ 5,\ -4\rangle$$

    Select the correct answer.

    a. $\langle 1,\ 8,\ 3\rangle$
    b. $\langle -1,\ -3,\ -8\rangle$
    c. $\langle 1,\ 3,\ 8\rangle$
    d. $\langle -3,\ -1,\ -8\rangle$
    e. $\langle 3,\ 1,\ 8\rangle$

6. Find $7\mathbf{a} + 8\mathbf{b}$.

    $\mathbf{a} = 8\mathbf{i} - 7\mathbf{k}$, $\mathbf{b} = 7\mathbf{i} - 10\mathbf{j} + 5\mathbf{k}$

    Select the correct answer.

    a. $114\mathbf{i} + 80\mathbf{j} - 7\mathbf{k}$
    b. $113\mathbf{i} - 80\mathbf{j} - 7\mathbf{k}$
    c. $113\mathbf{i} - 79\mathbf{j} - 8\mathbf{k}$
    d. $112\mathbf{i} + 80\mathbf{j} - 9\mathbf{k}$
    e. $112\mathbf{i} - 80\mathbf{j} - 9\mathbf{k}$

7. Two forces F_1 and F_2 with magnitudes 10 lb and 6 lb act on an object at a point P as shown in the figure. Find the magnitude of the resultant force F acting at P. Round the result to the nearest tenth.

    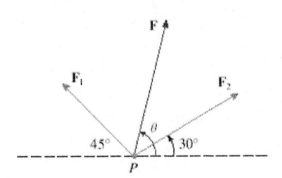

    Select the correct answer.

    a. 9.1 lb
    b. 11.3 lb
    c. 10.2 lb
    d. 12.4 lb
    e. 8.2 lb

8. Identify the coordinate system that best describes symmetry about the origin.

   Select the correct answer.

   a. cylindrical coordinate system
   b. spherical coordinate system
   c. rectangular coordinate system

9. Find the point at which the line given by the parametric equations below intersects the plane.

   $2x + 4y - 3y = -48$

   $x = 10 + 7t, \quad y = -10, \quad z = 7t$

   Select the correct answer.

   a. $(-38, -10, 28)$
   b. $(43, -10, -18)$
   c. $(38, -10, 28)$
   d. $(-43, -10, 18)$
   e. $(38, -10, -28)$

10. Find the traces of the surface in the planes $x = k$, $y = k$, $z = k$.

    $x^2 - y^2 + z^2 = 1$

    Select the correct answer.

    a.
    $$x = k, \quad z^2 - y^2 = 1 + k^2, \quad hyperbola$$
    $$y = k, \quad z^2 - x^2 = 1 + k^2, \quad hyperbola$$
    $$z = k, \quad x^2 + y^2 = k^2 - 1, \quad circle$$

    b.
    $$x = k, \quad z^2 - y^2 = 1 - k^2, \quad hyperbola$$
    $$y = k, \quad x^2 + z^2 = 1 + k^2, \quad circle$$
    $$z = k, \quad x^2 - y^2 = 1 - k^2, \quad hyperbola$$

    c.
    $$x = k, \quad z^2 - y^2 = k^2, \quad hyperbola$$
    $$y = k, \quad x^2 + z^2 = 1 + k^2, \quad hyperbola$$
    $$z = k, \quad x^2 - y^2 = 1 - k^2, \quad hyperbola$$

11. Find the distance between the given parallel planes.

$6x + 7y - 2z = 10$ and $12x + 14y - 4z = 60$

Select the correct answer.

a.   3.42
b.   2.13
c.   2.12
d.   3.14
e.   5.12

12. Reduce the equation to one of the standard forms.

$z^2 = 6x^2 + 2y^2 - 12$

Select the correct answer.

a. $x^2 + y^2 - \dfrac{z^2}{3} = 1$

b. $(x-1)^2 + \dfrac{y^2}{(1/3)^2} + z^2 = 1$

c. $\dfrac{x^2}{2} + \dfrac{y^2}{6} - \dfrac{z^2}{12} = 1$

d. $x^2 + \dfrac{y^2}{6} - \dfrac{z^2}{12} = 1$

e. $\dfrac{x^2}{2} + \dfrac{y^2}{6} - z^2 = 1$

13. Find an equation for the surface obtained by rotating the parabola $z = x^2$ about the z-axis.

Select the correct answer.

a. $z^2 + x^2 = y$
b. $y^2 + x^2 = z$
c. $x^2 + y^2 + z^2 = 1$
d. $y^2 - x^2 = z$
e. $y^2 - x^2 = z^2$

14. Find an equation for the surface consisting of all points that are equidistant from the point $(0, -3, 0)$ and the plane $y = 3$.

    Select the correct answer.

    a. $x^2 + 12y^2 + z^2 = 1$

    b. $x^2 + y^2 = z$

    c. $z^2 - y^2 = x$

    d. $z^2 + x^2 = -12y$

    e. $z^2 - x^2 = -12y$

15. Find an equation for the surface consisting of all points P for which the distance from P to the x-axis is three times the distance from P to the yz-plane.

    Select the correct answer.

    a. $x^2 - y^2 - z^2 = 3$

    b. $x^2 + y^2 + z^2 = 9$

    c. $9x^2 = y^2 + z^2$

    d. $3x^2 = y^2 - 3z^2$

    e. $3x^2 = y^2 + 3z$

16. Plot the point whose cylindrical coordinates are $(9, \pi/2, 7)$. Then find the rectangular coordinates of the point.

    Select the correct answer.

    a. $(0, 7, 9)$
    b. $(7, 0, 7)$
    c. $(9, 9, 7)$
    d. $(0, 9, 7)$
    e. $(0, 0, 7)$

17. Change from spherical to cylindrical coordinates.

    $(7, 0, 0)$

    Select the correct answer.

    a. $(0, 0, 7)$
    b. $(0, 0, -7)$
    c. $(-7, 0, -7)$
    d. $(7, 0, 7)$
    e. $(7, 0, 0)$

18. The sketch of the solid is given below. Given $a = 8$, write the inequalities that describe it.

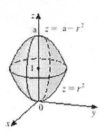

Select the correct answer.

a. $r^2 \le z \le 8 - r^2$

b. $r^2 \le z \le 8 + r^2$

c. $r^2 \le z \le 8$

d. $r^2 - 8 \le z \le r^2$

e.   none of these

19. A solid lies above the cone $z = 9\sqrt{x^2 + y^2}$ and below the sphere $x^2 + y^2 + z^2 = 6z$.

Describe the solid in terms of inequalities involving spherical coordinates.

Select the correct answer.

a. $0 \le \rho \le 6\cos\phi,\ 0 \le \theta \le 2\pi,\ 0 \le \phi \le \arctan\left(\dfrac{1}{9}\right)$

b. $0 \le \rho \le 9\cos\phi,\ 0 \le \theta \le 2\pi,\ 0 \le \phi \le \arctan(6)$

c. $0 \le \rho \le 12\cos\phi,\ 0 \le \theta \le 2\pi,\ 0 \le \phi \le \arctan(9)$

d. $0 \le \rho \le 6\cos\phi,\ 0 \le \theta \le \pi,\ 0 \le \phi \le \arctan(9)$

e. $0 \le \rho \le 2\cos\phi,\ 0 \le \theta \le \pi,\ 0 \le \phi \le \arctan(9)$

20. Find the graph of a silo consisting of a cylinder with radius a and height b surmounted by a hemisphere. Let $a = 9$, and $b = 10$.

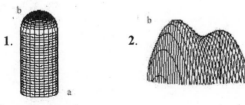

Select the correct answer.

a.   1

b.   2

c.   both 1 and 2

d.   none of these

1. b

2. b

3. b

4. b

5. b

6. e

7. c

8. b

9. c

10. b

11. c

12. c

13. b

14. d

15. c

16. d

17. a

18. a

19. a

20. a

1. Find the length of the median of side AB of the triangle with vertices $A(-2,\ 8,\ -7)$, $B(-6,\ -8,\ -3)$ and $C(2,\ -4,\ 9)$.

2. Find an equation of the sphere with center $(-9,\ 7,\ 8)$ that touches the xz - plane.

3. Write an equation or inequality that represents a plane containing all points with equal x and z coordinates.

4. Write an equation or inequality that represents all points on or inside a circular cylinder of radius 1 with the y-axis as its axis.

5. Write inequalities to describe the solid rectangular box in the first octant bounded by the planes $x = 9$, $y = 6$, and $z = 7$.

6. Find the sum of the given vectors.

    $$\left\langle -3,\ 8,\ -5 \right\rangle,\ \left\langle 2,\ 9,\ 3 \right\rangle$$

7. Find $5\mathbf{a} + 9\mathbf{b}$.

    $\mathbf{a} = 6\mathbf{i} - 5\mathbf{k}$, $\mathbf{b} = 9\mathbf{i} - 2\mathbf{j} + 10\mathbf{k}$

8. A bicycle pedal is pushed by a foot with a force of aN as shown. The shaft of the pedal is 15 cm long.

    Find the magnitude of the torque about P correct to two decimal places.

    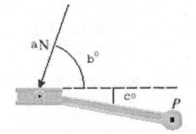

    $a = 70,\ b = 58°,\ c = 7°$

9. Write the equation in cylindrical coordinates.

    $z = 3x^2 - 3y^2$

10. Find the magnitude of the torque about P correct to two decimal places if a d-lb force is applied as shown

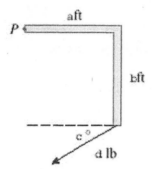

    $a = 1$ ft, $b = 1$ ft, $c = 30°$, $d = 44$ lb.

11. Find parametric equations for the line through the points $(5, 1, 10)$ and $(-6, -9, 6)$.

12. Find an equation of the plane that passes through the point $(4, 0, -2)$ and contains the line
    $x = 10 - 3t,\ y = 10 + 8t,\ z = 6 + 7t$.

13. Find an equation of the plane that passes through the line of intersection of the planes $x - z = 2$ and
    $y + 3z = 7$, and is perpendicular to the plane $5x + 3y - 2z = 8$.

14. Find an equation of the plane with x-intercept = 1, y-intercept = 10, and z-intercept = -10.

15. Find parametric equations for the line through the point $(4, 5, 2)$ that is parallel to the plane
    $x + y + z = -15$ and perpendicular to the line $x = 15 + t,\ y = 12 - t,\ z = 3t$.

    Select the correct answer.

    a. $x = 4t + 4,\ y = -2t + 5,\ z = -2t + 2$

    b. $x = 2t + 4,\ y = -4t + 5,\ z = 2t + 2$

    c. $x = 4t - 4,\ y = -2t - 5,\ z = -2t + 2$

    d. $x = 4t,\ y = 2t - 5,\ z = -2t$

    e. $x = 4t - 4,\ y = -2t,\ z = -2t + 5$

16. Find the distance between the given parallel planes.

    $5x + 8y - 10z = 3$ and $10x + 16y - 20z = 40$

    Select the correct answer.

    a. 2.54
    b. 1.24
    c. 1.3
    d. 2.24
    e. 5.3

17. Find an equation for the surface obtained by rotating the parabola $y = x^2$ about the y - axis.

    Select the correct answer.

    a. $y^2 + x^2 = z$
    b. $z^2 + x^2 = y$
    c. $z^2 - x^2 = y$
    d. $z^2 + x^2 + y^2 = 1$
    e. $z^2 - x^2 - y^2 = 1$

18. Find an equation for the surface consisting of all points P for which the distance from P to the x-axis is three times the distance from P to the yz-plane.

19. Change from rectangular to cylindrical coordinates.

    $(4, - 4, 2)$

    Select the correct answer.

    a. $\left(4\sqrt{2},\ \dfrac{\pi}{4},\ 2 \right)$

    b. $\left(4,\ \dfrac{7\pi}{4},\ 2 \right)$

    c. $\left(4\sqrt{2},\ 0,\ 2 \right)$

    d. $\left(4\sqrt{2},\ \dfrac{7\pi}{4},\ 2 \right)$

    e. $\left(-4\sqrt{2},\ \dfrac{\pi}{4},\ 2 \right)$

20. Write the equation in spherical coordinates.

$$x^2 + y^2 = 2y$$

Select the correct answer.

a. $\rho \sin \phi = 2 \sin \theta$

b. $\rho \cos \phi = 2 \sin \theta$

c. $\rho \sin \phi = 2 \cos \theta$

d. $\rho \sin \phi = 4 \sin \theta$

e. $4 \rho \sin \phi = \sin \theta$

Stewart - Calculus ET 5e Chapter 12 Form E

1. $\sqrt{248}$

2. $(x+9)^2 + (y-7)^2 + (z-8)^2 = 49$

3. $x = z$

4. $x^2 + z^2 \leq 1$

5. $0 \leq x \leq 9,\ 0 \leq y \leq 6,\ 0 \leq z \leq 7$

6. $\langle -1,\ 17,\ -2 \rangle$

7. $111\mathbf{i} - 18\mathbf{j} + 65\mathbf{k}$

8. 9.52

9. $z = 3r^2 \cos(2\theta)$

10. 60.11

11. $x = 5 + 11t,\ y = 1 + 10t,\ z = 10 + 4t$

12. $6x - 66y + 78z = -132$

13. $3x + 7y + 18z = 55$

14. $-100x - 10y + 10z = -100$

15. a

16. b

17. b

18. $y^2 + z^2 = 9x^2$

19. d

20. a

1. Suppose you start at the origin, move along the x-axis a distance of 4 units in the positive direction, and then move downward a distance of 8 units. What are the coordinates of your position?

   Select the correct answer.

   a. $(4,\ 0,\ -8)$
   b. $(0,\ 4,\ 8)$
   c. $(4,\ 8,\ 0)$
   d. $(4,\ 0,\ 8)$
   e. $(4,\ -8,\ 0)$

2. Find the length of the side AB of the triangle with vertices $A(5,\ 5,\ -10)$, $B(-3,\ -6,\ 1)$ and $C(-9,\ -2,\ -1)$.

3. Find an equation of the sphere that passes through the point $(7,\ -4,\ 9)$ and has center $(-4,\ 5,\ -5)$.

4. Given the following equation, find the radius of the sphere.

   $$x^2 + y^2 + z^2 = 6x + 2y + 4z$$

5. Find that the midpoint of the line segment from $P1(8,\ 10,\ -3)$ to $P2(-2,\ 10,\ 7)$.

   Select the correct answer.

   a. $(-5,\ 0,\ 5)$
   b. $(-3,\ -10,\ -2)$
   c. $(5,\ 0,\ -5)$
   d. $(3,\ 10,\ 2)$
   e. $(-3,\ 10,\ 2)$

6. Write an equation or inequality that represents a plane containing all points with equal x and y coordinates.

    Select the correct answer.

    a. $y \neq z$
    b. $x \leq y$
    c. $x = y$
    d. $x \geq y$
    e. $y = \dot{z}$

7. Write inequalities to describe the solid rectangular box in the first octant bounded by the planes $x = 4$, $y = 8$, and $z = 5$.

8. Find $9\mathbf{a} + 4\mathbf{b}$.

    $\mathbf{a} = 2\mathbf{i} - 9\mathbf{j} + 9\mathbf{k}$, $\mathbf{b} = 5\mathbf{i} + 2\mathbf{j} + 10\mathbf{k}$

9. Find $\mathbf{a} \cdot \mathbf{b}$, if $\mathbf{a} = 5\mathbf{i} + 13\mathbf{j} - 8\mathbf{k}$ and $\mathbf{b} = 14\mathbf{i} + 3\mathbf{k}$.

10. Find the angle between the vectors, if $\mathbf{a} = \langle 12, \ 0 \rangle$ and $\mathbf{b} = \langle 12, \ 12 \rangle$.

11. Find the cosine of the angle between the following vectors.

    $\mathbf{a} = 2\mathbf{j} + 6\mathbf{k}$
    $\mathbf{b} = 6\mathbf{i} + 4\mathbf{j} + 3\mathbf{k}$

12. Find the volume of the parallelepiped with adjacent edges PQ, PR, and PS.

    $P(1, 2, 3)$, $Q(3, 5, 4)$, $R(3, 2, 5)$, $S(4, 2, 3)$

13. Find a parametric equations for the line through the point $(-6, 9, 3)$ and parallel to the vector $\langle 7, \ 3, \ -7 \rangle$.

14. Find the point of intersection.

$$L_1 \; : \; \frac{x-17}{3} = \frac{y-58}{8} = \frac{z-23}{2}$$

$$L_2 \; : \; \frac{x-49}{7} = \frac{y-26}{4} = z-15$$

15. Find an equation of the plane that passes through the line of intersection of the planes $x - z = 10$ and $y + 5z = 9$, and is perpendicular to the plane $3x + 2y - 2z = 7$.

16. Find an equation of the plane with x-intercept = 9, y-intercept = 1, and z-intercept = -3.

17. Find an equation for the surface obtained by rotating the line $x = 6y$ about the x-axis.

18. Change from rectangular to cylindrical coordinates.

$(9, - 9, 1)$

Select the correct answer.

a. $\left(9\sqrt{2}, \; \frac{7\pi}{4}, \; 1 \right)$

b. $\left(9\sqrt{2}, \; \frac{\pi}{4}, \; 1 \right)$

c. $\left(9, \; \frac{7\pi}{4}, \; 1 \right)$

d. $\left(-9, \; \frac{7\pi}{4}, \; -1 \right)$

e. $\left(\sqrt{2}, \; \frac{7\pi}{4}, \; 1 \right)$

19. Identify the correct statement(s) below.

Select the correct answer.

    a. $r = 3$ is a circular cylinder, radius 3, axis the z-axis

    b. $\rho = 7$ is a circular cylinder, radius 7, axis the z-axis

    c. $\phi = \dfrac{\pi}{9}$ is a half-cone

    d. $\theta = \dfrac{\pi}{5}$ is a half-cone

    e.   none of these

20. The sketch of the solid is given below. Given $a = 2$, write the inequalities that describe it.

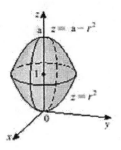

Select the correct answer.

    a. $r^2 \le z \le 2 + r^2$

    b. $r^2 \le z \le 2 - r^2$

    c. $r^2 \le z \le 2$

    d. $r \le z \le 2 - r$

    e. $r^2 - 2 \le z \le r^2$

1. a

2. $\sqrt{306}$

3. $(x+4)^2 + (y-5)^2 + (z+5)^2 = 398$

4. $\sqrt{14}$

5. d

6. c

7. $0 \le x \le 4,\ 0 \le y \le 8,\ 0 \le z \le 5$

8. $38i - 73j + 121k$

9. 46

10. $\dfrac{\pi}{4}$

11. 0.53

12. 18

13. $x = -6 + 7t,\ y = 9 + 3t,\ z = 3 - 7t$

14. $(-7,\ -6,\ 7)$

15. $8x + 5y + 17z = 125$

16. $-3x - 27y + 9z = -27$

17. $z^2 + y^2 = \dfrac{x^2}{36}$

18. a

19. a, c

20. b

1. Draw a rectangular box with the origin and $(6, 6, 3)$ as opposite vertices and with its faces parallel to the coordinate planes. Find the length of the diagonal of the box.

2. Find an equation of the sphere that passes through the point $(-6, -2, 5)$ and has center $(9, -9, 2)$.

3. Given the following equation, find the center of the sphere.

$$x^2 + y^2 + z^2 = 4x + 10y - 10z$$

Select the correct answer.

   a. $(-2, -5, 5)$
   b. $(2, 5, -5)$
   c. $(4, 10, -10)$
   d. $(2, 5, 5)$
   e. $(2, 4, 10)$

4. Find the point at which the line given by the parametric equations below intersects the plane.

$$10x + 4y - 4z = -32$$

$$x = -4 + 4t, \quad y = 2, \quad z = -7t$$

5. Write the equation in spherical coordinates.

$$x^2 + y^2 = 3y$$

6. A bicycle pedal is pushed by a foot with a force of a-N as shown. The shaft of the pedal is 15 cm long.

   Find the magnitude of the torque about P correct to two decimal places.

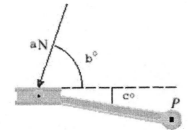

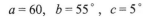

$a = 60, \quad b = 55°, \quad c = 5°$

7. Let P be a point not on the line L that passes through the points Q and R.

    Use the formula $\mathbf{d} = \dfrac{|\mathbf{a} \times \mathbf{b}|}{|\mathbf{a}|}$ where $a = \overrightarrow{QR}$, $b = \overrightarrow{QP}$ to find the distance from the point P (2, -1, 2) to the line through Q (-3, 3, 3) and R (4, 1, -2).

8. Find an equation of the plane through the points (0, 3, 3), (3, 0, 3) and (3, 3, 0).

    Select the correct answer.

    a. $x + y + z = 6$
    b. $9x - 6y - 9z = 1$
    c. $x + y + z = 3$
    d. $x + 3y + z = 1$
    e. $x - y + z = 1$

9. Find an equation of the plane with x-intercept = 7, y-intercept = 6 and z-intercept = 3.

    Select the correct answer.

    a. $\dfrac{x}{7} + \dfrac{y}{6} + \dfrac{z}{3} = 1$
    b. $7x + 6y + 3z = 1$
    c. $\dfrac{x}{7} + \dfrac{y}{6} + \dfrac{z}{3} = 0$
    d. $7x + 6y + 3z = 0$
    e. $\dfrac{7x}{3} + 6y + z = 0$

10. Witch of the given lines is parallel to the line $x = 8 + t$, $y = t$, $z = -7 - 10t$?

    Select the correct answer.

    a. $r = \left\langle -6, -10, 0 \right\rangle + t\left\langle 2, 2, -20 \right\rangle$
    b. $x + 8 = y - 2 = -9 - z$
    c. $x = -5 + t$, $y = 10 + t$, $z = -1 - t$
    d. $x = -5t$, $y = 10t$, $z = -1 - t$
    e. $x = -5 + 3t$, $y = 10 + t$, $z = -2 - t$

11. Find the distance between the point $(9, 9, 5)$ and the plane $10x - 3y - 8z = 10$.

    Select the correct answer.

    a.   0.99
    b.   2.51
    c.   0.08
    d.   1.51
    e.   0.8

12. Find the distance between the given parallel planes.

    $3x + 3y - 6z = 3$ and $6x + 6y - 12z = 30$

13. Find an equation for the surface obtained by rotating the parabola $x = z^2$ about the x - axis.

    Select the correct answer.

    a. $y^2 + z^2 = x$
    b. $x^2 + z^2 = y$
    c. $x^2 + y^2 + z^2 = 1$
    d. $y^2 - z^2 = x$
    e. $y^2 - 2z^2 = 3x$

14. Find an equation for the surface consisting of all points that are equidistant from the point $(0, -5, 0)$ and the plane $y = 5$.

15. Find an equation for the surface consisting of all points P for which the distance from P to the x-axis is three times the distance from P to the yz-plane.

    Select the correct answer.

    a. $3x^2 = y^2 - 3z^2$
    b. $9x^2 = y^2 + z^2$
    c. $x^2 - y^2 - z^2 = 3$
    d. $x^2 + y^2 + z^2 = 9$
    e. $x^2 + 2y^2 - z^2 = 0$

16. Write the equation in cylindrical coordinates.

$$5x^2 + 5y^2 + z^2 = 11$$

17. Identify the correct statement(s) below.

    Select all that apply.

    a. $\phi = \dfrac{\pi}{3}$ is a half-cone

    b. $\rho = 4$ is a circular cylinder, radius 4, axis the z-axis

    c. $\theta = \dfrac{\pi}{6}$ is a half-cone

    d. $r = 1$ is a circular cylinder, radius 1, axis the z-axis

    e.   none of these

18. Change from spherical to cylindrical coordinates.

    $(4, 0, 0)$

    Select the correct answer.

    a. $(-4, 0, -4)$
    b. $(0, 0, -4)$
    c. $(4, 0, 0)$
    d. $(4, 0, 4)$
    e. $(0, 0, 4)$

19. Write the equation in spherical coordinates.

    $$7x^2 + 7y^2 - 4z^2 = 12$$

    Select the correct answer.

    a. $\rho^2 (7 \sin \phi - 4 \cos \phi) = 12$
    b. $\rho^2 (7 \sin^2 \phi + \cos^2 \phi) = 12$
    c. $\rho(7 \sin^2 \phi - 4 \cos^2 \phi) = 12$
    d. $\rho^2 (7 \sin^2 \phi - 4 \cos^2 \phi) = 12$
    e. $\rho^2 (7 \sin^2 \phi + \cos^2 \phi) = 144$

20. Change from rectangular to cylindrical coordinates.

    $(3, -3, 1)$

1. 9

2. $(x-9)^2 + (y+9)^2 + (z-2)^2 = 283$

3. b

4. $(-4, 2, 0)$

5. $\rho \sin \phi = 3 \sin \theta$

6. 7.79

7. 3.5

8. a

9. a

10. a

11. a

12. 1.63

13. a

14. $x^2 + z^2 = -20y$

15. b

16. $5r^2 + z^2 = 11$

17. a, d

18. e

19. d

20. $\left(3\sqrt{2}, \ \dfrac{7\pi}{4}, \ 1 \right)$

1. Suppose you start at the origin, move along the x-axis a distance of 7 units in the positive direction, and then move downward a distance of 1 units. What are the coordinates of your position?

2. Write an equation or inequality that represents all points on or inside a circular cylinder of radius 3 with the y-axis as its axis.

3. Write inequalities to describe the solid rectangular box in the first octant bounded by the planes $x = 8$, $y = 3$, and $z = 5$.

4. Write inequalities to describe the solid upper hemisphere of the sphere of radius 2 centered at the origin.

5. Find a vector a with representation given by the directed line segment $\overrightarrow{AB}$.

   $A(-9, -8, 2)$, $B(7, 7, 7)$

6. Find the sum of the given vectors.

   $\langle -6, -5, 8 \rangle, \langle 8, 3, 6 \rangle$

7. Find $4\mathbf{a} + 8\mathbf{b}$.

   $\mathbf{a} = 4\mathbf{i} - 10\mathbf{j}$, $\mathbf{b} = 10\mathbf{i} + 4\mathbf{j}$

8. Find $5\mathbf{a} + 3\mathbf{b}$.

   $\mathbf{a} = 6\mathbf{i} - 6\mathbf{j} + 10\mathbf{k}$, $\mathbf{b} = 7\mathbf{i} + 3\mathbf{j} + 8\mathbf{k}$

   Select the correct answer.

   a. $52\mathbf{i} - 21\mathbf{j} + 76\mathbf{k}$
   b. $51\mathbf{i} + 21\mathbf{j} + 74\mathbf{k}$
   c. $53\mathbf{i} + 21\mathbf{j} + 76\mathbf{k}$
   d. $51\mathbf{i} - 21\mathbf{j} + 74\mathbf{k}$
   e. $52\mathbf{i} - 20\mathbf{j} + 75\mathbf{k}$

9. Find an equation for the surface obtained by rotating the line $x = 4z$ about the x-axis.

10. Find parametric equations for the line through the point (6, 0, 10) and perpendicular to the plane $-3x + 2y - 4z = 2$.

11. Find parametric equations for the line through the points (-6, 2, 1) and (-9, -4, 3).

12. Find an equation of the plane through the origin and parallel to the plane $-9x + 6y - 9z = -1$.

13. Find an equation of the plane that passes through the point (1, 0, -3) and contains the line
$x = 6 - 7t, \ y = 6 + 5t, \ z = 4 + 8t$.

14. Find an equation of the plane that passes through the line of intersection of the planes $x - z = 3$ and $y + 7z = 10$, and is perpendicular to the plane $3x + 5y - 4z = 4$.

15. Identify the planes that are perpendicular.

    Select the correct answer(s).

    a. $4x + 8y = 3, \ 10y + 8z = 5$
    b. $x + 5y - z = 2, \ -2x - y - 7z = 2$
    c. $x = 5x + 5y, \ -20x - 20y + 4z = 5$

16. Find an equation of the plane with x-intercept = -6, y-intercept = 1, and z-intercept = 9.

17. Let P be a point not on the line L that passes through the points Q and R. The distance d from the point
P to the line L is $d = \dfrac{|\mathbf{a} \times \mathbf{b}|}{|\mathbf{a}|}$ where $\mathbf{a} = \overrightarrow{QR}$ and $\mathbf{b} = \overrightarrow{QP}$. Use this formula to find the distance from
the point (-4, 1, -3) to the line $x = -3 + t, \ y = 4 - 4t, \ z = 2t$.

    Select the correct answer.

    a.   19.34
    b.   4.22
    c.   17.81
    d.   4.58
    e.   5.58

18. Find an equation for the surface consisting of all points P for which the distance from P to the x-axis is five times the distance from P to the yz-plane.

19. Write the equation in spherical coordinates.

    $$x^2 + y^2 = 9y$$

    Select the correct answer.

    a. $\rho \cos \phi = 9 \sin \theta$
    b. $\rho \sin \phi = 9 \sin \phi$
    c. $\rho \sin \phi = 9 \sin \theta$
    d. $\rho \sin \phi = 9 \cos \phi$
    e. $\rho^2 \sin \theta = 9 \cos \phi$

20. A solid lies above the cone $z = 7\sqrt{x^2 + y^2}$ and below the sphere $x^2 + y^2 + z^2 = 9z$.

    Describe the solid in terms of inequalities involving spherical coordinates.

1. $(7, 0, -1)$

2. $x^2 + z^2 \le 9$

3. $0 \le x \le 8,\ 0 \le y \le 3,\ 0 \le z \le 5$

4. $0 \le x^2 + y^2 + z^2 \le 4,\ z \ge 0$

5. $\langle 16,\ 15,\ 5 \rangle$

6. $\langle 2,\ -2,\ 14 \rangle$

7. $96i - 8j$

8. d

9. $y^2 + z^2 = \dfrac{x^2}{16}$

10. $x = 6 - 3t,\ y = 2t,\ z = 10 - 4t$

11. $x = -6 + 3t,\ y = 2 + 6t,\ z = 1 - 2t$

12. $-9x + 6y - 9z = 0$

13. $13x - 89y + 67z = -188$

14. $23x + 7y + 26z = 139$

15. b

16. $9x - 54y - 6z = -54$

17. b

18. $y^2 + z^2 = 25x^2$

19. c

20. $0 \le \rho \le 9\cos\phi,\ 0 \le \phi \le \arctan\left(\dfrac{1}{7}\right)$

1. Find the following limit.

    $$\lim_{t \to \infty} \left\langle \arctan t, \ e^{-7t}, \ \frac{\ln t}{t} \right\rangle$$

2. Find a vector function that represents the curve of intersection of the two surfaces:
    The cylinder $x^2 + y^2 = 16$ and the surface $z = xy$.

3. Find a vector function that represents the curve of intersection of the two surfaces:
    The cone $z = \sqrt{x^2 + y^2}$ and the plane $z = 2 + y$.

4. Find a vector function that represents the curve of intersection of the two surfaces:
    The paraboloid $z = 4x^2 + y^2$ and the parabolic cylinder $y = x^2$.

5. Find the derivative of the vector function.

    $$\mathbf{r}(t) = \mathbf{a} + t\mathbf{b} + t^3\mathbf{c}$$

6. Find the point of intersection of the tangent lines to the curve $r(t) = \left\langle \sin \pi t, \ 6 \sin \pi t, \ \cos \pi t \right\rangle$, at the points where $t = 0$ and $t = 0.5$.

7. The curves $r_1(t) = \left\langle t, \ t^6, \ t^7 \right\rangle$ and $r_2(t) = \left\langle \sin t, \ \sin 5t, \ t \right\rangle$ intersect at the origin. Find their angle of intersection correct to the nearest degree.

8. Evaluate the integral.

    $$\int \left(e^{6t}\mathbf{i} + 8t\mathbf{j} + \ln t\mathbf{k} \right) dt$$

9. If $\mathbf{u}(t) = \mathbf{i} - 9t^2\mathbf{j} + 3t^3\mathbf{k}$ and $\mathbf{v}(t) = t\mathbf{i} - \cos t\mathbf{j} + \sin t\mathbf{k}$, find $\dfrac{\partial}{\partial t}[\mathbf{u}(t) \cdot \mathbf{v}(t)]$.

10. Use *Simpson's Rule* with $n = 10$ to estimate the length of the arc of the twisted cubic
$x = t$, $y = t^2$, $z = t^3$ from the origin to the point $(2, 4, 8)$.

Give the answer to four decimal places.

11. Find the unit tangent vector $T(t)$.

$$r(t) = \left\langle \frac{25}{3}t^3,\ 25t^2,\ 50t \right\rangle$$

12. *Theorem*

The curvature of the curve given by the vector function **r** is:

$$k(t) = \frac{|r'(t) \times r''(t)|}{|r'(t)|^3}$$

Use Theorem to find the curvature of $r(t) = t^2 i + 10t k$.

13. Find the acceleration of a particle with the given position function.

$$r(t) = -2 \sin t i + 6t j - 4 \cos t k$$

14. A particle moves with position function $r(t) = 2 \cos t i + 2 \sin t j + 2t k$.

Find the normal component of the acceleration vector.

15. Find an expression for $\dfrac{d}{dt}\ [x(t) \cdot (y(t) \times z(t))]$.

16. At what point on the curve $x = t^3$, $y = 3y$, $z = t^4$ is the normal plane parallel to the plane
$9x + 9y - 12z = 7$?

17. Find the velocity of a particle with the given position function.

$$r(t) = 13e^{15t} i + 10e^{-18t} j$$

18. Find the domain of the following vector function.

$$r(t) = \left\langle t^8, \ \sqrt{t-1}, \ \sqrt{9-t} \right\rangle$$

19. Find equations of the normal plane to $x = t$, $y = t^2$, $z = t^3$ at the point $(3, 9, 27)$.

20. A particle moves with position function $\mathbf{r}(t) = (9t - 3t^3 - 2)\mathbf{i} + 9t^2\mathbf{j}$.

Find the tangential component of the acceleration vector.

1. $\mathbf{r}(t) = \dfrac{\pi}{2}\mathbf{i}$

2. $\mathbf{r}(t) = 4\cos(t)\mathbf{i} + 4\sin(t)\mathbf{j} + 16\sin(t)\cos(t)\mathbf{k}$

3. $\mathbf{r}(t) = t\mathbf{i} + \dfrac{(t^2 - 4)}{4}\mathbf{j} + \dfrac{(t^2 + 4)}{4}\mathbf{k}$

4. $\mathbf{r}(t) = t\mathbf{i} + t^2\mathbf{j} + (4t^2 + t^4)\mathbf{k}$

5. $\mathbf{b} + 3t^2\mathbf{c}$

6. $\left(1,\ 6,\ 1\right)$

7. $79\,°$

8. $\dfrac{e^{6t}}{6}\mathbf{i} + 4t^2\mathbf{j} + t(\ln t - 1)\mathbf{k} + C$

9. $1 - 18t\cos t + 18t^2\sin t + 3t^3\cos t$

10. 9.507

11. $\left\langle \dfrac{t^2}{t^2 + 2},\ \dfrac{2t}{t^2 + 2},\ \dfrac{2}{t^2 + 2} \right\rangle$

12. $\dfrac{20}{(4t^2 + 100)^{3/2}}$

13. $a = 2\sin t\mathbf{i} + 4\cos t\mathbf{k}$

14. 2

15. $\dfrac{\mathbf{d}x(t)}{\mathbf{d}t} \cdot (y(t) \times z(t)) - \dfrac{\mathbf{d}y(t)}{\mathbf{d}t}(x(t) \times z(t)) + \dfrac{\mathbf{d}z(t)}{\mathbf{d}t}(x(t) \times y(t))$

16. $(-1, -3, 1)$

17. $v = 195e^{15t}\mathbf{i} - 180e^{-18t}\mathbf{j}$

18. $1 \le t \le 9$

19. $x + 6y + 27z - 786 = 0$

20. $18t$

1. Find the following limit.

$$\lim_{t \to \infty}\left\langle \arctan t, \ e^{-7t}, \ \frac{\ln t}{t} \right\rangle$$

2. Find a vector function that represents the curve of intersection of the two surfaces:

   The cylinder $x^2 + y^2 = 16$ and the surface $z = xy$.

3. Find a vector function that represents the curve of intersection of the two surfaces:

   The cone $z = \sqrt{x^2 + y^2}$ and the plane $z = 2 + y$.

4. Find a vector function that represents the curve of intersection of the two surfaces:

   The paraboloid $z = 4x^2 + y^2$ and the parabolic cylinder $y = x^2$.

5. Find the unit tangent vector $T(t)$.

   $$\mathbf{r}(t) = \left\langle \frac{4}{3}t^3, \ 4t^2, \ 8t \right\rangle$$

6. What force is required so that a particle of mass m has the following position function?

   $$\mathbf{r}(t) = 5t^3\mathbf{i} + 2t^2\mathbf{j} + 7t^3\mathbf{k}$$

7. Find the derivative of the vector function $\mathbf{r}(t) = \mathbf{a} + t\mathbf{b} + t^3\mathbf{c}$.

8. Find the point of intersection of the tangent lines to the curve $\mathbf{r}(t) = \left\langle \sin \pi t, \ 6\sin \pi t, \ \cos \pi t \right\rangle$, at the points where $t = 0$ and $t = 0.5$.

9. *Formula*

    For a plane curve with equation $y = f(x)$ we have

    $$k(t) = \frac{|f''(x)|}{\left[1 + (f'(x))^2\right]^{3/2}}$$

    Use Formula to find the curvature of $y = x^5$.

10. Find the velocity of a particle with the given position function.

    $$\mathbf{r}(t) = 4e^{12t}\mathbf{i} + 14e^{-8t}\mathbf{j}$$

11. The curves $\mathbf{r}_1(t) = \left\langle t, \ t^6, \ t^7 \right\rangle$ and $\mathbf{r}_2(t) = \left\langle \sin t, \ \sin 5t, \ t \right\rangle$ intersect at the origin. Find their angle of intersection correct to the nearest degree.

12. Evaluate the integral.

    $$\int \left(e^{6t}\mathbf{i} + 8t\mathbf{j} + \ln t\mathbf{k}\right) \ dt$$

13. If $\mathbf{u}(t) = \mathbf{i} - 9t^2\mathbf{j} + 3t^3\mathbf{k}$ and $\mathbf{v}(t) = t\mathbf{i} - \cos t\mathbf{j} + \sin t\mathbf{k}$, find $\dfrac{\partial}{\partial t}[\mathbf{u}(t) \cdot \mathbf{v}(t)]$.

14. Use *Simpson's Rule* with $n = 10$ to estimate the length of the arc of the twisted cubic
    $x = t, \ y = t^2, \ z = t^3$ from the origin to the point $(2, 4, 8)$.

    Please give the answer to four decimal places.

15. Find the velocity of a particle with the given position function.

    $$\mathbf{r}(t) = 13e^{15t}\mathbf{i} + 10e^{-18t}\mathbf{j}$$

16. Find the domain of the following vector function.

    $$r(t) = \left\langle t^8, \ \sqrt{t-1}, \ \sqrt{9-t} \right\rangle$$

17. A force with magnitude 40 N acts directly upward from the xy-plane on an object with mass 5 kg. The object starts at the origin with initial velocity $v\,(0) = 5\mathbf{i} - 4\mathbf{j}$. Find its position function.

18. A ball is thrown at an angle of $15°$ to the ground. If the ball lands 67 m away, what was the initial speed of the ball? Let $g = 9.8 \ m/s^2$.

19. A particle moves with position function $\mathbf{r}(t) = (12t - 4t^3 - 2)\mathbf{i} + 12t^2\mathbf{j}$.

Find the tangential component of the acceleration vector.

20. A particle moves with position function $\mathbf{r}(t) = 8\cos t\mathbf{i} + \sin t\mathbf{j} + 8t\mathbf{k}$.

Find the normal component of the acceleration vector.

Stewart - Calculus ET 5e Chapter 13 Form B

1. $\mathbf{r}(t) = \dfrac{\pi}{2}\mathbf{i}$

2. $\mathbf{r}(t) = 4\cos t\mathbf{i} + 4\sin t\mathbf{j} + 16\sin t\cos t\mathbf{k}$

3. $\mathbf{r}(t) = t\mathbf{i} + \dfrac{t^2 - 4}{4}\mathbf{j} + \dfrac{t^2 + 4}{4}\mathbf{k}$

4. $\mathbf{r}(t) = t\mathbf{i} + t^2\mathbf{j} + (4t^2 + t^4)\mathbf{k}$

5. $\left\langle \dfrac{t^2}{t^2 + 2}, \dfrac{2t}{t^2 + 2}, \dfrac{2}{t^2 + 2} \right\rangle$

6. $\mathbf{F} = m(30t\mathbf{i} + 4\mathbf{j} + 42t\mathbf{k})$

7. $\mathbf{b} + 3t^2\mathbf{c}$

8. $\left(1,\ 6,\ 1\right)$

9. $\dfrac{20\,|x|^3}{(1 + 25x^8)^{3/2}}$

10. $v = 48e^{12t}\mathbf{i} - 112e^{-8t}\mathbf{j}$

11. $79°$

12. $\dfrac{e^{6t}}{6}\mathbf{i} + 4t^2\mathbf{j} + t(\ln t - 1)\mathbf{k} + C$

13. $1 - 18t\cos t + 18t^2\sin t + 3t^3\cos t$

14. 9.5706

15. $v = 195e^{15t}\mathbf{i} - 180e^{-18t}\mathbf{j}$

16. $1 \le t \le 9$

17. $\mathbf{r}(t) = 5t\mathbf{i} - 4t\mathbf{j} + 4t^2\mathbf{k}$

18. 36.2

19. $24t$

20. 8

1. Find the following limit.

    $$\lim_{t \to 0^+} \left\langle 2\cos t, \; 6\sin t, \; 3t \ln t \right\rangle$$

    Select the correct answer.

    a. $\mathbf{r}(t) = 2\mathbf{i}$
    b. $\mathbf{r}(t) = 2\mathbf{i} + 6\mathbf{j} + 3\mathbf{k}$
    c. $\mathbf{r}(t) = 2\mathbf{i} - 3\mathbf{k}$
    d. $\mathbf{r}(t) = 2\mathbf{j}$
    e. $\mathbf{r}(t) = 2\mathbf{k}$

2. Choose the parametric equations that correspond to the given graph.

    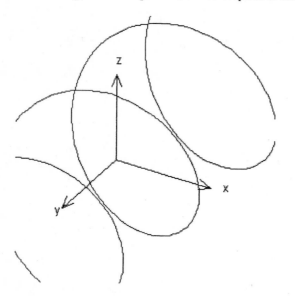

    Select the correct answer.

    a. $x = t, \; y = t^6, \; z = e^{-4t}$

    b. $x = \cos 4t, \; y = t, \; z = \sin 4t$

    c. $x = t, \; y = \dfrac{3t^6}{3+t^2}, \; z = t^4$

    d. $x = \cos 4t, \; y = \sin t, \; z = 4t$

    e. $x = t, \; y = t^2, \; z = \sin 4t$

3. A particle moves with position function $\mathbf{r}(t) = (21t - 7t^3 - 2)\mathbf{i} + 21t^2\mathbf{j}$.

    Find the tangential component of the acceleration vector.

    Select the correct answer.

    a. $a_T = 42\,t + 2$
    b. $a_T = 21\,t$
    c. $a_T = -42\,t$
    d. $a_T = 42\,t$
    e. $a_T = 242\,t$

4. Find a vector function that represents the curve of intersection of the two surfaces:

    The circular cylinder $x^2 + y^2 = 4$ and the parabolic cylinder $z = x^2$.

    Select the correct answer.

    a. $\mathbf{r}(t) = 4\cos t\mathbf{i} + 4\sin t\mathbf{j} + 16\cos^2 t\mathbf{k}$

    b. $\mathbf{r}(t) = 4\cos t\mathbf{i} + 4\sin t\mathbf{j} + 4\cos^2 t\mathbf{k}$

    c. $\mathbf{r}(t) = \cos t\mathbf{i} + \sin t\mathbf{j} - 4\cos^2 t\mathbf{k}$

    d. $\mathbf{r}(t) = 4\cos t\mathbf{i} - 4\sin t\mathbf{j} - 16\cos^2 t\mathbf{k}$

    e. $\mathbf{r}(t) = 16\cos t\mathbf{i} - \sin t\mathbf{j} + 16\cos^2 t\mathbf{k}$

5. A force with magnitude 12 N acts directly upward from the xy-plane on an object with mass 3 kg. The object starts at the origin with initial velocity $v(0) = 3\mathbf{i} - 4\mathbf{j}$. Find its position function.

    Select the correct answer.

    a. $\mathbf{r}(t) = 3t\mathbf{i} - 4t\mathbf{j} + 2t^2\mathbf{k}$

    b. $\mathbf{r}(t) = 3t^2\mathbf{i} - 4t^2\mathbf{j} + 2t^3\mathbf{k}$

    c. $\mathbf{r}(t) = 3t\mathbf{i} - 4t\mathbf{j} + 4t^2\mathbf{k}$

    d. $\mathbf{r}(t) = 3\mathbf{i} - 4\mathbf{j} + 2t^2\mathbf{k}$

    e. $\mathbf{r}(t) = 3t^3\mathbf{i} - 4\mathbf{j} + 2t^2\mathbf{k}$

6. The figure shows a curve C given by a vector function $\mathbf{r}(t)$. Choose the correct expression for $\mathbf{r}'(4)$.

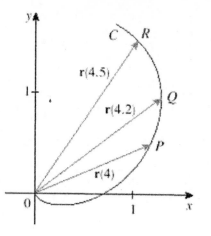

Select the correct answer.

a. $\displaystyle\lim_{h \to 0} \frac{\mathbf{r}(4+h)+\mathbf{r}(4)}{h}$

b. $\displaystyle\lim_{h \to 0} \frac{\mathbf{r}(4-h)-\mathbf{r}(4)}{h}$

c. $\displaystyle\lim_{h \to 0} \frac{\mathbf{r}(4-h)+\mathbf{r}(4)}{h}$

d. $\displaystyle\lim_{h \to 0} \frac{\mathbf{r}(4+h)-\mathbf{r}(4)}{h}$

e. $\displaystyle\lim_{h \to 0} \frac{\mathbf{r}(4+h)-\mathbf{r}(h)}{h}$

7. If $\mathbf{r}(t) = \left\langle t,\ t^7,\ t^9 \right\rangle$, find $\mathbf{r}''(t)$.

Select the correct answer.

a. $\left\langle 0,\ 42t^5,\ 72t^7 \right\rangle$

b. $\left\langle 0,\ 42t^6,\ 72t^8 \right\rangle$

c. $\left\langle 1,\ 42t^5,\ 72t^7 \right\rangle$

d. $\left\langle 0,\ 7t^5,\ 9t^7 \right\rangle$

e. $\left\langle 1,\ 7t^6,\ 9t^8 \right\rangle$

8. Which of the following curves is smooth?

Select the correct answer.

    a. $r(t) = \left\langle t^7,\ t^8,\ t^2 \right\rangle$

    b. $r(t) = \left\langle t^7 + t,\ t^4,\ t^8 \right\rangle$

9. Evaluate the integral.

$$\int (e^{7t} + 4t\mathbf{j} + \ln t\,\mathbf{k})\ dt$$

Select the correct answer.

    a. $\dfrac{e^{7t}}{7}\mathbf{i} + 2t^2\mathbf{j} + (\ln t - 1)\mathbf{k} + \mathbf{C}$

    b. $\dfrac{e^{7t}}{7}\mathbf{i} + 4t^2\mathbf{j} + (\ln t - 1)\mathbf{k} + \mathbf{C}$

    c. $e^{7t}\mathbf{i} + 2t^2\mathbf{j} + (\ln t - 1)\mathbf{k} + \mathbf{C}$

    d. $\dfrac{e^{7t}}{7}\mathbf{i} + 2t^2\mathbf{j} + t(\ln t - 1)\mathbf{k} + \mathbf{C}$

    e. $e^{7t}\mathbf{i} + 4t^2\mathbf{j} + (\ln t - 1)\mathbf{k} + \mathbf{C}$

10. Find $\mathbf{r}(t)$ if $\mathbf{r}'(t) = \sin t\,\mathbf{i} - \cos t\,\mathbf{j} + 6t\mathbf{k}$ and $r(0) = \mathbf{i} + \mathbf{j} + 5\mathbf{k}$.

Select the correct answer.

    a. $(-\cos t + 2)\mathbf{i} - (\sin t - 1)\mathbf{j} + (3t^2 + 5)\mathbf{k}$

    b. $(-\cos t + 2)\mathbf{i} + (\sin t + 1)\mathbf{j} + (3t^2 + 5)\mathbf{k}$

    c. $(\cos t)\mathbf{i} - (\sin t - 1)\mathbf{j} + (3t^2 + 5)\mathbf{k}$

    d. $(\cos t)\mathbf{i} + (\sin t + 1)\mathbf{j} + (3t^2 + 5)\mathbf{k}$

    e. $(-\cos t + 1)\mathbf{i} - (\sin t - 1)\mathbf{j} + (3t^2 + 5)\mathbf{k}$

11. Reparametrize the curve with respect to arc length measured from the point where $t = 0$ in the direction of increasing t.

$$\mathbf{r}(t) = (7 + 3t)\mathbf{i} + (8 + 9t)\mathbf{j} - (6t)\mathbf{k}$$

Select the correct answer.

a. $\mathbf{r}(t(s)) = (7 + \dfrac{3}{\sqrt{116}}s)\mathbf{i} + (8 + \dfrac{9}{\sqrt{116}}s)\mathbf{j} - (6s)\mathbf{k}$

b. $\mathbf{r}(t(s)) = (7 + \dfrac{3}{\sqrt{136}}s)\mathbf{i} + (8 + \dfrac{9}{\sqrt{136}}s)\mathbf{j} - (6s)\mathbf{k}$

c. $\mathbf{r}(t(s)) = (7 + \dfrac{3}{\sqrt{126}}s)\mathbf{i} + (8 + \dfrac{9}{\sqrt{126}}s)\mathbf{j} - (\dfrac{6s}{\sqrt{126}})\mathbf{k}$

d. $\mathbf{r}(t(s)) = (7 - \dfrac{3}{\sqrt{126}}s)\mathbf{i} - (8 + \dfrac{9}{\sqrt{126}}s)\mathbf{j} + (\dfrac{6s}{\sqrt{126}})\mathbf{k}$

e. $\mathbf{r}(t(s)) = (7 - \dfrac{3}{\sqrt{116}}s)\mathbf{i} - (8 + \dfrac{s}{\sqrt{116}})\mathbf{j} + (\dfrac{6s}{\sqrt{126}})\mathbf{k}$

12. Find the unit tangent vector $T(t)$.

$$\mathbf{r}(t) = \left\langle 3\sin t, \ 6t, \ 3\cos t \right\rangle$$

Select the correct answer.

a. $\left\langle \dfrac{3}{\sqrt{50}}\cos t, \ \dfrac{6}{\sqrt{44}}, \ -\dfrac{3}{\sqrt{47}}\sin t \right\rangle$

b. $\left\langle \dfrac{3}{\sqrt{46}}\cos t, \ \dfrac{6}{\sqrt{45}}, \ \dfrac{3}{\sqrt{45}}\sin t \right\rangle$

c. $\left\langle \dfrac{3}{\sqrt{46}}\cos t, \ \dfrac{6}{\sqrt{45}}, \ -\dfrac{3}{\sqrt{45}}\sin t \right\rangle$

d. $\left\langle \dfrac{3}{\sqrt{42}}\cos t, \ \dfrac{6}{\sqrt{42}}, \ -\dfrac{3}{\sqrt{42}}\sin t \right\rangle$

e. $\left\langle \dfrac{3}{\sqrt{42}}\cos t, \ \dfrac{3}{\sqrt{42}}, \ -\dfrac{3}{\sqrt{42}}\sin t \right\rangle$

13. *Formula*

For a plane curve with equation $y = f(x)$ we have

$$k(t) = \frac{|f''(x)|}{\left[1 + (f'(x))^2\right]^{3/2}}$$

Use Formula to find the curvature of $y = x^7$.

Select the correct answer.

a. $\dfrac{7x^6}{(1 + 49x^{12})^{3/2}}$

b. $\dfrac{42|x|^5}{(1 + 7x^6)^{3/2}}$

c. $\dfrac{42|x|^5}{(1 + 49x^{12})^{3/2}}$

d. $\dfrac{49|x|^5}{(1 + 7x^{12})^{3/2}}$

e. $\dfrac{|x|^5}{(1 + x^6)^{3/2}}$

14. Find the acceleration of a particle with the following position function.

$$r(t) = \left\langle 4t^2 - 2,\ 8t \right\rangle$$

Select the correct answer.

a. $\mathbf{a}(t) = (4 + 2t)\mathbf{i} - 8\mathbf{j}$
b. $\mathbf{a}(t) = 4\mathbf{i} - \mathbf{j}$
c. $\mathbf{a}(t) = 8\mathbf{i}$
d. $\mathbf{a}(t) = 8t\mathbf{i} + 8\mathbf{j}$
e. $\mathbf{a}(t) = 4t\mathbf{i} + 8\mathbf{j}$

15. Find the velocity of a particle with the given position function.

$$r(t) = 10e^{7t}\mathbf{i} + 7e^{-12t}\mathbf{j}$$

Select the correct answer.

    a. $\mathbf{v}(t) = 70e^t\mathbf{i} - 84e^{-t}\mathbf{j}$

    b. $\mathbf{v}(t) = 10e^{7t}\mathbf{i} - 7e^{-12t}\mathbf{j}$

    c. $\mathbf{v}(t) = 70e^{7t}\mathbf{i} - 84e^{-12t}\mathbf{j}$

    d. $\mathbf{v}(t) = 17e^{7t}\mathbf{i} + 19e^{-12t}\mathbf{j}$

    e. $\mathbf{v}(t) = 17e^{7t}\mathbf{i} + e^{-12t}\mathbf{j}$

16. Find the acceleration of a particle with the given position function.

$$r(t) = 6\sin t\mathbf{i} + 10t\mathbf{j} - 8\cos t\mathbf{k}$$

Select the correct answer.

    a. $\mathbf{a}(t) = -6\cos t\,\mathbf{i} + 8\sin t\,\mathbf{k}$

    b. $\mathbf{a}(t) = -6\sin t\,\mathbf{i} + 8\cos t\,\mathbf{k}$

    c. $\mathbf{a}(t) = -6\sin t\,\mathbf{i} + 8\cos t\,\mathbf{j}$

    d. $\mathbf{a}(t) = 6\sin t\,\mathbf{i} - 8\cos t\,\mathbf{k}$

    e. $\mathbf{a}(t) = 6\sin t\,\mathbf{i} - 8t\,\mathbf{k}$

17. Find the speed of a particle with the given position function.

$$r(t) = 5\sqrt{2}t\mathbf{i} + e^{5t}\mathbf{j} - e^{-5t}\mathbf{k}$$

Select the correct answer.

    a. $|\mathbf{v}(t)| = (e^{5t} + e^{-5t})$

    b. $|\mathbf{v}(t)| = \sqrt{10 + 5e^t + 5e^{-t}}$

    c. $|\mathbf{v}(t)| = \sqrt{10 + e^{10t} + e^{-10t}}$

    d. $|\mathbf{v}(t)| = 5(e^{5t} + e^{-5t})$

    e. $|\mathbf{v}(t)| = 5(e^t + e^{-t})$

18. Find the velocity of a particle that has the given acceleration and the given initial velocity.

$\mathbf{a}(t) = 2\mathbf{k}, \quad \mathbf{v}(0) = 10\mathbf{i} - 9\mathbf{j}$

Select the correct answer.

a. $\mathbf{v}(t) = (10t - 9)\mathbf{i} + 2t\mathbf{k}$
b. $\mathbf{v}(t) = 10\mathbf{i} - 9\mathbf{j} + 2\mathbf{k}$
c. $\mathbf{v}(t) = 9\mathbf{i} - 10\mathbf{j} + 2t\mathbf{k}$
d. $\mathbf{v}(t) = 10\mathbf{i} - 9\mathbf{j} + 2t\mathbf{k}$
e. $\mathbf{v}(t) = 10\mathbf{i} - \mathbf{j} + 2t\mathbf{k}$

19. Choose the parametric equations that correspond to the given graph.

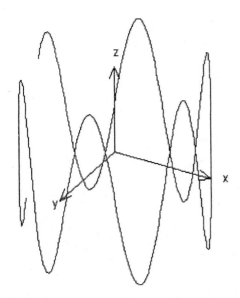

Select the correct answer.

a. $x = e^{-t}\cos 10t, \quad y = e^{-t}\sin 10t, \quad z = e^{-t}$
b. $x = \cos 8t, \quad y = \sin 8t, \quad z = \ln t$
c. $x = \cos t, \quad y = \sin t, \quad z = \sin 6t$
d. $x = t, \quad y = \sin t, \quad z = \cos t$
e. $x = \ln t, \quad y = t, \quad z = t^2$

20. The position function of a particle is given by

$$\mathbf{r}(t) = \left\langle 7t^2, \ 7t, \ 7t^2 - 140t \right\rangle$$

When is the speed a minimum?

Select the correct answer.

    a. $t = 5$
    b. $t = 0$
    c. $t = 20$
    d. $t = 10$
    e. $t = 30$

1. a

2. b

3. d

4. a

5. a

6. d

7. a

8. b

9. d

10. a

11. c

12. c

13. c

14. c

15. c

16. b

17. d

18. d

19. c

20. a

1. Find the following limit.

$$\lim_{t \to \infty} \left\langle \arctan t, \ e^{-7t}, \ \frac{\ln t}{t} \right\rangle$$

Select the correct answer.

a. $\mathbf{r}(t) = \dfrac{\pi}{2}\mathbf{i}$

b. $\mathbf{r}(t) = \dfrac{\pi}{2}\mathbf{i} + 8\mathbf{j}$

c. $\mathbf{r}(t) = \pi\mathbf{j}$

d. $\mathbf{r}(t) = 8\mathbf{j}$

e. $\mathbf{r}(t) = 8\mathbf{i}$

2. Choose the parametric equations that correspond to the given graph.

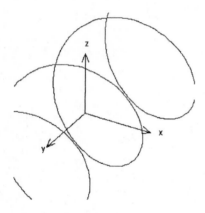

Select the correct answer.

a. $x = t, \ y = t^6, \ z = e^{-4t}$

b. $x = \cos 4t, \ y = t, \ z = \sin 4t$

c. $x = t, \ y = t^2, \ z = \sin 4t$

d. $x = \cos 4t, \ y = \sin t, \ z = 4t$

e. $x = t, \ y = \dfrac{3t^6}{3 + t^2}, \ z = t^4$

3. What force is required so that a particle of mass m has the following position function?

$r(t) = 3t^3 i + 7t^2 j + 9t^3 k$

Select the correct answer.

a. $F(t) = 9mt^2 i + 14mt j + 27mt^2 k$
b. $F(t) = mt^2 i + 4mt j + 27mt^2 k$
c. $F(t) = 18mt i + 14m j + 54t k$
d. $F(t) = 18mt i + 14m j + 54mt k$
e. $F(t) = 27mt i + 14m j + 18mt k$

4. A projectile is fired with an initial speed of 287 m/s and angle of elevation 16°. Find the range of the projectile.

Select the correct answer.

a. $d \approx 10 \ km$
b. $d \approx 28 \ km$
c. $d \approx 40 \ km$
d. $d \approx 2 \ km$
e. $d \approx 16 \ km$

5. Choose the parametric equations that correspond to the given graph.

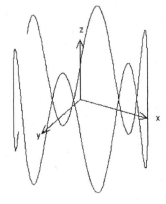

Select the correct answer.

a. $x = e^{-t} \cos 10t, \ y = e^{-t} \sin 10t, \ z = e^{-t}$
b. $x = \cos 8t, \ y = \sin 8t, \ z = \ln t$
c. $x = \cos t, \ y = \sin t, \ z = \sin 6t$
d. $x = t, \ y = \sin t, \ z = \cos t$
e. $x = \ln t, \ y = t, \ z = t^2$

6. Find a vector function that represents the curve of intersection of the two surfaces: the top half of the

    ellipsoid $x^2 + 6y^2 + 6z^2 = 36$ and the parabolic cylinder $y = x^2$.

    Select the correct answer.

    a. $\mathbf{r}(t) = t\mathbf{i} + t^2\mathbf{j} + \sqrt{\dfrac{6 - t^2 - 6t^4}{6}}\mathbf{k}$

    b. $\mathbf{r}(t) = t\mathbf{i} + t^4\mathbf{j} + \sqrt{\dfrac{36 - t^2 - 6t}{6}}\mathbf{k}$

    c. $\mathbf{r}(t) = t\mathbf{i} + t^2\mathbf{j} + \sqrt{\dfrac{36 - t^2 - 6t^4}{6}}\mathbf{k}$

    d. $\mathbf{r}(t) = t\mathbf{i} + t^2\mathbf{j} + \sqrt{\dfrac{36 - t^2 - 6t}{6}}\mathbf{k}$

    e. $\mathbf{r}(t) = t\mathbf{i} - t^2\mathbf{j} - \sqrt{\dfrac{36 - t^2 - 6t}{6}}\mathbf{k}$

7. Find the derivative of the vector function

    $\mathbf{r}(t) = \mathbf{a} + t\mathbf{b} + t^3\mathbf{c}$

    Select the correct answer.

    a. $\mathbf{b} + 3t^2\mathbf{c}$
    b. $\mathbf{b} + t^2\mathbf{c}$
    c. $\mathbf{b} - t^2\mathbf{c}$
    d. $\mathbf{b} - 3t^2\mathbf{c}$
    e. $\mathbf{b} - 2t^2\mathbf{c}$

8. Find the domain of the following vector function.

    $\mathbf{r}(t) = \left\langle t^7,\ \sqrt{t - 6},\ \sqrt{8 - t} \right\rangle$

    Select the correct answer.

    a. $6 \le t < 8$
    b. $t \ge 6$
    c. $6 \le t \le 8$
    d. $-6 \le t \le 8$
    e. $t \le 8$

9. Find parametric equations for the tangent line to the curve with the given parametric equations at the specified point.

$x = \cos t, \quad y = 4e^{6t}, \quad z = 4e^{-6t}; \quad (1, \ 4, \ 4)$

Select the correct answer.

a. $\quad x = t, \quad y = 4 + 24t, \quad z = 4 - 24t$

b. $\quad x = 1, \quad y = 4 - 24t, \quad z = 4 + 24t$

c. $\quad x = t, \quad y = 4 + 24t, \quad z = 4 + 24t$

d. $\quad x = 1, \quad y = 4 + 24t, \quad z = 4 - 24t$

e. $\quad x = 0, \quad y = 4 + 6t, \quad z = 4 - 6t$

10. Evaluate the integral.

$$\int (e^{7t} + 4t\mathbf{j} + \ln t\mathbf{k}) \ dt$$

Select the correct answer.

a. $\quad \dfrac{e^{7t}}{7}\mathbf{i} + 2t^2\mathbf{j} + (\ln t - 1)\mathbf{k} + \mathbf{C}$

b. $\quad \dfrac{e^{7t}}{7}\mathbf{i} + 4t^2\mathbf{j} + (\ln t - 1)\mathbf{k} + \mathbf{C}$

c. $\quad e^{7t}\mathbf{i} + 2t^2\mathbf{j} + (\ln t - 1)\mathbf{k} + \mathbf{C}$

d. $\quad \dfrac{e^{7t}}{7}\mathbf{i} + 2t^2\mathbf{j} + t(\ln t - 1)\mathbf{k} + \mathbf{C}$

e. $\quad e^{7t}\mathbf{i} + 4t^2\mathbf{j} + (\ln t - 1)\mathbf{k} + \mathbf{C}$

11. Reparametrize the curve with respect to arc length measured from the point where $t = 0$ in the direction of increasing t.

$\mathbf{r}(t) = (7 + 3t)\mathbf{i} + (8 + 9t)\mathbf{j} - (6t)\mathbf{k}$

Select the correct answer.

a. $\quad \mathbf{r}(t(s)) = (7 + \dfrac{3}{\sqrt{116}}s)\mathbf{i} + (8 + \dfrac{9}{\sqrt{116}}s)\mathbf{j} - (6s)\mathbf{k}$

b. $\quad \mathbf{r}(t(s)) = (7 + \dfrac{3}{\sqrt{136}}s)\mathbf{i} + (8 + \dfrac{9}{\sqrt{136}}s)\mathbf{j} - (6s)\mathbf{k}$

c. $\quad \mathbf{r}(t(s)) = (7 + \dfrac{3}{\sqrt{126}}s)\mathbf{i} + (8 + \dfrac{9}{\sqrt{126}}s)\mathbf{j} - (\dfrac{6s}{\sqrt{126}})\mathbf{k}$

d. $\quad \mathbf{r}(t(s)) = (7 - \dfrac{3}{\sqrt{126}}s)\mathbf{i} - (8 + \dfrac{9}{\sqrt{126}}s)\mathbf{j} + (\dfrac{6s}{\sqrt{126}})\mathbf{k}$

e. $\quad \mathbf{r}(t(s)) = (7 - \dfrac{3}{\sqrt{116}}s)\mathbf{i} - (8 + \dfrac{s}{\sqrt{116}})\mathbf{j} + (\dfrac{6s}{\sqrt{126}})\mathbf{k}$

12. Use Simpson's Rule with $n = 10$ to estimate the length of the arc of the twisted cubic $x = t, \ y = t^2, \ z = t^3$, from the origin to the point (2, 4, 8).

Select the correct answer.

    a.   9.5706
    b.   19.5706
    c.   7.5706
    d.   8.5706
    e.   10.5706

13. Find the following limit.

$$\lim_{t \to 0^+} \left\langle 2\cos t, \ 6\sin t, \ 3t \ln t \right\rangle$$

Select the correct answer.

    a. $\mathbf{r}(t) = 2\mathbf{i}$
    b. $\mathbf{r}(t) = 2\mathbf{i} + 6\mathbf{j} + 3\mathbf{k}$
    c. $\mathbf{r}(t) = 2\mathbf{i} - 3\mathbf{k}$
    d. $\mathbf{r}(t) = 2\mathbf{j}$
    e. $\mathbf{r}(t) = 2\mathbf{k}$

14. A particle moves with position function $\mathbf{r}(t) = (18t - 6t^3 + 2)\mathbf{i} + 18t^2\mathbf{j}$.

Find the tangential component of the acceleration vector.

Select the correct answer.

    a. $a_T = 36\,t + 2$
    b. $a_T = 36\,t$
    c. $a_T = 18\,t$
    d. $a_T = -\,36\,t$
    e. $a_T = -\,48\,t$

15. If $\mathbf{r}(t) = \left\langle t, \ t^9, \ t^4 \right\rangle$, find $\mathbf{r}''(t)$.

Select the correct answer.

    a. $\left\langle 0, \ 72t^7, \ 12t^2 \right\rangle$
    b. $\left\langle 1, \ 72t^7, \ 12t^2 \right\rangle$
    c. $\left\langle 1, \ 9t^8, \ 4t^3 \right\rangle$
    d. $\left\langle 0, \ 9t^6, \ 12t^2 \right\rangle$
    e. $\left\langle 0, \ 72t^8, \ 12t^3 \right\rangle$

16. **Theorem**

   The curvature of the curve given by the vector function **r** is

   $$k(t) = \frac{|\mathbf{r}'(t) \times \mathbf{r}''(t)|}{|\mathbf{r}'(t)|^3}$$

   Use Theorem to find the curvature of $\mathbf{r}(t) = \left\langle \sqrt{15}t,\ e^t,\ e^{-t} \right\rangle$ at the point $(0, 1, 1)$.

   Select the correct answer.

   a. $\dfrac{\sqrt{2}}{19}$

   b. $17\sqrt{2}$

   c. $\dfrac{\sqrt{2}}{17}$

   d. $\dfrac{1}{17}$

   e. $\dfrac{\sqrt{15}}{17}$

17. Find the velocity of a particle that has the given acceleration and the given initial velocity.

   $$\mathbf{a}(t) = 2\mathbf{k},\quad \mathbf{v}(0) = 10\mathbf{i} - 9\mathbf{j}$$

   Select the correct answer.

   a. $\mathbf{v}(t) = (10t - 9)\mathbf{i} + 2t\mathbf{k}$

   b. $\mathbf{v}(t) = 10\mathbf{i} - 9\mathbf{j} + 2\mathbf{k}$

   c. $\mathbf{v}(t) = 9\mathbf{i} - 10\mathbf{j} + 2t\mathbf{k}$

   d. $\mathbf{v}(t) = 10\mathbf{i} - 9\mathbf{j} + 2t\mathbf{k}$

   e. $\mathbf{v}(t) = 10\mathbf{i} - \mathbf{j} + 2t\mathbf{k}$

18. Which of the following curves is smooth?

   Select the correct answer.

   a. $\mathbf{r}(t) = \left\langle t^7,\ t^8,\ t^2 \right\rangle$

   b. $\mathbf{r}(t) = \left\langle t^7 + t,\ t^4,\ t^8 \right\rangle$

19. *Formula*

For a plane curve with equation $y = f(x)$ we have $k(t) = \dfrac{|f''(x)|}{\left[1 + (f'(x))^2\right]^{3/2}}$.

Use Formula to find the curvature of $y = x^8$.

Select the correct answer.

a. $\dfrac{56|x|^6}{(1 + 8x^7)^{3/2}}$

b. $\dfrac{56|x|^6}{(1 + 64x^{14})^{3/2}}$

c. $\dfrac{8x^7}{(1 + 64x^{14})^{3/2}}$

d. $\dfrac{x^7}{(1 + 64x^{14})^{3/2}}$

e. $\dfrac{8x^7}{(1 + 64x^{14})^{1/2}}$

20. The figure shows a curve C given by a vector function $\mathbf{r}(t)$. Choose the correct expression for $\mathbf{r}'(4)$.

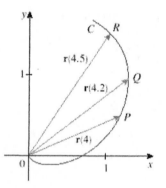

Select the correct answer.

a. $\displaystyle\lim_{h \to 0} \dfrac{\mathbf{r}(4 - h) - \mathbf{r}(4)}{h}$

b. $\displaystyle\lim_{h \to 0} \dfrac{\mathbf{r}(4 + h) - \mathbf{r}(4)}{h}$

c. $\displaystyle\lim_{h \to 0} \dfrac{\mathbf{r}(4 + h) + \mathbf{r}(4)}{h}$

d. $\displaystyle\lim_{h \to 0} \dfrac{\mathbf{r}(4 - h) + \mathbf{r}(4)}{h}$

e. $\displaystyle\lim_{h \to 0} \dfrac{\mathbf{r}(4 - h) + \mathbf{r}(h)}{h}$

1. a

2. b

3. d

4. d

5. c

6. c

7. a

8. c

9. d

10. d

11. c

12. a

13. a

14. b

15. a

16. c

17. d

18. b

19. b

20. b

1. Find the domain of the following vector function.

$$r(t) = \left\langle t^8, \ \sqrt{t-3}, \ \sqrt{10-t} \right\rangle$$

Select the correct answer.

a. $3 \le t \le 10$
b. $3 \le t < 10$
c. $t \ge 3$
d. $t \ge 10$
e. $t \ge -3$

2. Find a vector function that represents the curve of intersection of the two surfaces.
The circular cylinder $x^2 + y^2 = 4$ and the parabolic cylinder $z = x^2$.

3. Find the derivative of the vector function.

$$\mathbf{r}(t) = \mathbf{a} + t\mathbf{b} + t^2\mathbf{c}$$

4. Find parametric equations for the tangent line to the curve with the given parametric equations at the specified point.

$$x = t^8, \ y = t^3, \ z = t^7; \ (1, \ 1, \ 1)$$

Select the correct answer.

a. $x = 1 - 7t, \ y = 1 - 2t, \ z = 1 - 6t$
b. $x = 1 + 7t, \ y = 1 + 2t, \ z = 1 + 6t$
c. $x = 1 + 8t, \ y = 1 + 3t, \ z = 1 + 7t$
d. $x = 1 - 8t, \ y = 1 - 3t, \ z = 1 - 7t$
e. $x = 8t, \ y = 3t, \ z = 7t$

5. The curves $\mathbf{r}_1(t) = \left\langle t, \ t^5, \ t^3 \right\rangle$ and $\mathbf{r}_2(t) = \left\langle \sin t, \ \sin 4t, \ t \right\rangle$ intersect at the origin.

Find their angle of intersection correct to the nearest degree.

6. Find $\mathbf{r}(t)$ if $\mathbf{r}'(t) = t^9\mathbf{i} + 4t^3\mathbf{j} - t^5\mathbf{k}$ and $r(0) = \mathbf{j}$.

7. If $\mathbf{u}(t) = \mathbf{i} - 3t^2\mathbf{j} + 6t^3\mathbf{k}$ and $\mathbf{v}(t) = t\mathbf{i} - \cos t\mathbf{j} + \sin t\mathbf{k}$, find $\dfrac{\partial}{\partial t}[\mathbf{u}(t) \cdot \mathbf{v}(t)]$.

8. Use Simpson's Rule with $n = 10$ to estimate the length of the arc of the twisted cubic
    $x = t,\ y = t^2,\ z = t^3$, from the origin to the point $(2, 4, 8)$.

    Select the correct answer.

    a.   9.5706
    b.   19.5706
    c.   7.5706
    d.   8.5706
    e.   10.5706

9. Reparametrize the curve with respect to arc length measured from the point where $t = 0$ in the
    direction of increasing t.

    $r(t) = 8\sin t\mathbf{i} + t\mathbf{j} + 8\cos t\mathbf{k}$

10. Find the unit tangent vector $T(t)$.

    $r(t) = \langle 4\sin t,\ 9t,\ 4\cos t\rangle$

11. A force with magnitude 40 N acts directly upward from the xy-plane on an object with mass 5 kg. The
    object starts at the origin with initial velocity $\mathbf{v}(0) = 5\mathbf{i} - 4\mathbf{j}$. Find its position function.

12. *Formula*
    For a plane curve with equation $y = f(x)$ we have $\mathbf{k}(t) = \dfrac{|f''(x)|}{\left[1 + (f'(x))^2\right]^{3/2}}$.

    Use Formula to find the curvature of $y = x^8$.

    Select the correct answer.

    a. $\dfrac{56|x|^6}{(1+8x^7)^{3/2}}$

    b. $\dfrac{56|x|^6}{(1+64x^{14})^{3/2}}$

    c. $\dfrac{8x^7}{(1+64x^{14})^{3/2}}$

    d. $\dfrac{x^7}{(1+64x^{14})^{3/2}}$

    e. $\dfrac{8x^7}{(1+64x^{14})^{1/2}}$

13. At what point on the curve $x = t^3$, $y = 3t$, $z = t^4$ is the normal plane parallel to the plane $9x + 9y - 12z = 7$?

14. Find the velocity of a particle with the given position function.

$$\mathbf{r}(t) = 13e^{15t}\mathbf{i} + 10e^{-18t}\mathbf{j}$$

15. What force is required so that a particle of mass m has the following position function?

$$\mathbf{r}(t) = 5t^3\mathbf{i} + 2t^2\mathbf{j} + 7t^3\mathbf{k}$$

16. Find the speed of a particle with the given position function.

$$\mathbf{r}(t) = t\mathbf{i} + 6t^2\mathbf{j} + 2t^6\mathbf{k}$$

Select the correct answer.

a. $|v(t)| = \sqrt{1 + 12t + 12t^5}$

b. $|v(t)| = 1 + 144t^2 + 144t^{10}$

c. $|v(t)| = 1 + 12t + 12t^5$

d. $|v(t)| = \sqrt{1 + 144t^2 + 144t^{10}}$

e. $|v(t)| = \sqrt{1 + 144t + 144t^5}$

17. The position function of a particle is given by $\mathbf{r}(t) = \left\langle 8t^2,\ 2t,\ 8t^2 - 96t \right\rangle$.

When is the speed a minimum?

18. A ball is thrown at an angle of $15°$ to the ground. If the ball lands 67 m away, what was the initial speed of the ball? Let $g = 9.8\ m/s^2$.

19. A particle moves with position function $\mathbf{r}(t) = (12t - 4t^3 - 2)\mathbf{i} + 12t^2\mathbf{j}$.

Find the tangential component of the acceleration vector.

20. A particle moves with position function $\mathbf{r}(t) = 8\cos t\mathbf{i} + 8\sin t\mathbf{j} + 8t\mathbf{k}$.

Find the normal component of the acceleration vector.

ANSWER KEY

Stewart - Calculus ET 5e Chapter 13 Form E

1. a

2. $\mathbf{r}(t) = 4\cos(t)\mathbf{i} + 4\sin t\mathbf{j} + 16\cos^2 t\mathbf{k}$

3. $b + 2tc$

4. c

5. $76°$

6. $\dfrac{t^{10}}{10}\mathbf{i} + (t^4 + 1)\mathbf{j} - \dfrac{t^6}{6}\mathbf{k}$

7. $1 - 6t\cos t + 21t^2\sin t + 6t^3\cos t$

8. a

9. $\mathbf{r}(t(s)) = 4\sin\left(\dfrac{s}{\sqrt{65}}\right)\mathbf{i} + \left(\dfrac{s}{\sqrt{65}}\right)\mathbf{j} + 8\cos\left(\dfrac{s}{\sqrt{65}}\right)\mathbf{k}$

10. $\left\langle \dfrac{4}{\sqrt{97}}\cos t, \ \dfrac{9}{\sqrt{97}}, \ \dfrac{-4}{\sqrt{97}}\sin t \right\rangle$

11. $\mathbf{r}(t) = 5t\mathbf{i} - 4t\mathbf{j} + 4t^2\mathbf{k}$

12. b

13. $(-1, \ -3, \ 1)$

14. $\mathbf{v} = 195e^{15t}\mathbf{i} - 180e^{-18t}\mathbf{j}$

15. $\mathbf{F} = m(30t\mathbf{i} + 4\mathbf{j} + 42t\mathbf{k})$

16. d

17. $t = 3$

18. 36.2

19. $24t$

20. 8

1. Find the domain of the following vector function.

$$r(t) = \left\langle t^8, \ \sqrt{t-1}, \ \sqrt{9-t} \right\rangle$$

2. Find the following limit:

$$\lim_{t \to \infty} \left\langle \arctan t, \ e^{-4t}, \ \frac{\ln t}{t} \right\rangle$$

3. A particle moves with position function $r(t) = 2\cos t\, i + 2\sin t\, j + 2t k$.

   Find the normal component of the acceleration vector.

4. Find the unit tangent vector $T(t)$.

$$r(t) = \left\langle \frac{4}{3}t^3, \ 4t^2, \ 8t \right\rangle$$

5. What force is required so that a particle of mass m has the following position function?

$$\mathbf{r}(t) = 3t^3\mathbf{i} + 7t^2\mathbf{j} + 9t^3\mathbf{k}$$

   Select the correct answer.

   a. $\mathbf{F}(t) = 9mt^2\mathbf{i} + 14mt\mathbf{j} + 27mt^2\mathbf{k}$

   b. $\mathbf{F}(t) = mt^2\mathbf{i} + 4mt\mathbf{j} + 27mt^2\mathbf{k}$

   c. $\mathbf{F}(t) = 18mt\mathbf{i} + 14m\mathbf{j} + 54t\mathbf{k}$

   d. $\mathbf{F}(t) = 18mt\mathbf{i} + 14m\mathbf{j} + 54mt\mathbf{k}$

   e. $\mathbf{F}(t) = 27mt\mathbf{i} + 14m\mathbf{j} + 18mt\mathbf{k}$

6. Find a vector function that represents the curve of intersection of the two surfaces:

   The cylinder $x^2 + y^2 = 9$ and the surface $z = xy$.

7. Find a vector function that represents the curve of intersection of the two surfaces:

    The top half of the ellipsoid $x^2 + 6y^2 + 6z^2 = 36$ and the parabolic cylinder $y = x^2$.

    Select the correct answer.

    a. $r(t) = t\mathbf{i} + t^2\mathbf{j} + \sqrt{\dfrac{6 - t^2 - 6t^4}{6}}\mathbf{k}$

    b. $r(t) = t\mathbf{i} + t^4\mathbf{j} + \sqrt{\dfrac{36 - t^2 - 6t}{6}}\mathbf{k}$

    c. $r(t) = t\mathbf{i} + t^2\mathbf{j} + \sqrt{\dfrac{36 - t^2 - 6t^4}{6}}\mathbf{k}$

    d. $r(t) = t\mathbf{i} + t^2\mathbf{j} + \sqrt{\dfrac{36 - t^2 - 6t}{6}}\mathbf{k}$

    e. $r(t) = t\mathbf{i} - t^2\mathbf{j} - \sqrt{\dfrac{36 - t^2 - 6t}{6}}\mathbf{k}$

8. Find a vector function that represents the curve of intersection of the two surfaces:

    The circular cylinder $x^2 + y^2 = 4$ and the parabolic cylinder $z = x^2$.

9. Find the derivative of the vector function.

    $r(t) = \mathbf{a} + t\mathbf{b} + t^2\mathbf{c}$

10. Find the point of intersection of the tangent lines to the curve $r(t) = \langle \sin \pi t, \ 5\sin \pi t, \ \cos \pi t \rangle$, at the points where $t = 0$ and $t = 0.5$.

11. The curves $r_1(t) = \langle t, \ t^6, \ t^7 \rangle$ and $r_2(t) = \langle \sin t, \ \sin 5t, \ t \rangle$ intersect at the origin. Find their angle of intersection correct to the nearest degree.

12. Evaluate the integral.

    $\displaystyle\int (e^{6t}\mathbf{i} + 8t\mathbf{j} + \ln t\,\mathbf{k}) \ dt$

13. Reparametrize the curve with respect to arc length measured from the point where $t = 0$ in the direction of increasing t.

    $r(t) = 8\sin t\,\mathbf{i} + t\mathbf{j} + 8\cos t\,\mathbf{k}$

14. **Theorem**

The curvature of the curve given by the vector function **r** is

$$k(t) = \frac{|\mathbf{r}'(t) \times \mathbf{r}''(t)|}{|\mathbf{r}'(t)|^3}$$

Use Theorem to find the curvature of $\mathbf{r}(t) = \left\langle \sqrt{15}t, \ e^t, \ e^{-t} \right\rangle$ at the point (0, 1, 1).

15. Find the velocity of a particle with the given position function.

$$\mathbf{r}(t) = 10e^{7t}\mathbf{i} + 7e^{-12t}\mathbf{j}$$

Select the correct answer.

    a. $\mathbf{v}(t) = 70e^t\mathbf{i} - 84e^{-t}\mathbf{j}$

    b. $\mathbf{v}(t) = 10e^{7t}\mathbf{i} - 7e^{-12t}\mathbf{j}$

    c. $\mathbf{v}(t) = 70e^{7t}\mathbf{i} - 84e^{-12t}\mathbf{j}$

    d. $\mathbf{v}(t) = 17e^{7t}\mathbf{i} + 19e^{-12t}\mathbf{j}$

    e. $\mathbf{v}(t) = 17e^{7t}\mathbf{i} + e^{-12t}\mathbf{j}$

16. Find equations of the normal plane to $x = t, \ y = t^2, \ z = t^3$ at the point (3, 9, 27).

17. Find the acceleration of a particle with the given position function.

$$\mathbf{r}(t) = -2\sin t\mathbf{i} + 6t\mathbf{j} - 4\cos t\mathbf{k}$$

18. A projectile is fired with an initial speed of 834 m/s and angle of elevation 38°. Find the range of the projectile.

Select the correct answer.

    a. $d \approx 42 \ km$

    b. $d \approx 34 \ km$

    c. $d \approx 11 \ km$

    d. $d \approx 68 \ km$

    e. $d \approx 58 \ km$

19. A ball is thrown at an angle of $15°$ to the ground. If the ball lands 126 m away, what was the initial speed of the ball? Let $g = 9.8 \, m/s^2$.

Select the correct answer.

   a. $v_0 \approx 49.7$ m/s
   b. $v_0 \approx 16.6$ m/s
   c. $v_0 \approx 99.4$ m/s
   d. $v_0 \approx 24.8$ m/s

20. A particle moves with position function $r(t) = (9t - 3t^3 - 2)\mathbf{i} + 9t^2\mathbf{j}$.

Find the tangential component of the acceleration vector.

1. $1 \le t \le 9$

2. $r(t) = \dfrac{\pi}{2} i$

3. 2

4. $\left\langle \dfrac{t^2}{t^2+2}, \; \dfrac{2t}{t^2+2}, \; \dfrac{2}{t^2+2} \right\rangle$

5. d

6. $r(t) = 3\cos t i + 3\sin t j + 9\sin t \cos t k$

7. c

8. $r(t) = 4\cos t i + 4\sin t j + 16\cos^2 t k$

9. $b + 2tc$

10. $\left(1, \; 5, \; 1 \right)$

11. $79°$

12. $\dfrac{e^{6t}}{6} i + 4t^2 j + t(\ln t - 1)k + C$

13. $r(t(s)) = 4\sin\left(\dfrac{s}{\sqrt{65}}\right) i + \left(\dfrac{s}{\sqrt{65}}\right) j + 8\cos\left(\dfrac{s}{\sqrt{65}}\right) k$

14. $\dfrac{\sqrt{2}}{17}$

15. c

16. $x + 6y + 27z - 786 = 0$

17. $a(t) = 2\sin t i + 4\cos t k$

18. b

19. a

20. $18t$

1. Find the following limit.

    $$\lim_{t \to 0^+} \left\langle 2\cos t, \ 6\sin t, \ 3t \ln t \right\rangle$$

    Select the correct answer.

    a. $\mathbf{r}(t) = 2\mathbf{i}$
    b. $\mathbf{r}(t) = 2\mathbf{i} + 6\mathbf{j} + 3\mathbf{k}$
    c. $\mathbf{r}(t) = 2\mathbf{i} - 3\mathbf{k}$
    d. $\mathbf{r}(t) = 2\mathbf{j}$
    e. $\mathbf{r}(t) = 2\mathbf{k}$

2. Find a vector function that represents the curve of intersection of the two surfaces.

    The circular cylinder $x^2 + y^2 = 4$ and the parabolic cylinder $z = x^2$.

3. Find the derivative of the vector function.

    $$\mathbf{r}(t) = \mathbf{a} + t\mathbf{b} + t^3\mathbf{c}$$

4. The curves $\mathbf{r}_1(t) = \left\langle t, \ t^6, \ t^7 \right\rangle$ and $\mathbf{r}_2(t) = \left\langle \sin t, \ \sin 5t, \ t \right\rangle$ intersect at the origin. Find their angle of intersection correct to the nearest degree.

5. A force with magnitude 24 N acts directly upward from the xy-plane on an object with mass 4 kg. The object starts at the origin with initial velocity $\mathbf{v}(0) = 8\mathbf{i} - 2\mathbf{j}$. Find its position function.

6. Find a vector function that represents the curve of intersection of the two surfaces:

    The circular cylinder $x^2 + y^2 = 4$ and the parabolic cylinder $z = x^2$.

    Select the correct answer.

    a. $\mathbf{r}(t) = 4\cos t\mathbf{i} + 4\sin t\mathbf{j} + 16\cos^2 t\mathbf{k}$
    b. $\mathbf{r}(t) = 4\cos t\mathbf{i} + 4\sin t\mathbf{j} + 4\cos^2 t\mathbf{k}$
    c. $\mathbf{r}(t) = \cos t\mathbf{i} + \sin t\mathbf{j} - 4\cos^2 t\mathbf{k}$
    d. $\mathbf{r}(t) = 4\cos t\mathbf{i} - 4\sin t\mathbf{j} - 16\cos^2 t\mathbf{k}$
    e. $\mathbf{r}(t) = 16\cos t\mathbf{i} - \sin t\mathbf{j} + 16\cos^2 t\mathbf{k}$

7. Use *Simpson's Rule* with $n = 10$ to estimate the length of the arc of the twisted cubic $x = t$, $y = t^2$, $z = t^3$ from the origin to the point $(2, 4, 8)$.

    Give the answer to four decimal places.

8. Find the point of intersection of the tangent lines to the curve $r(t) = \left\langle \sin \pi t, \ 8 \sin \pi t, \ \cos \pi t \right\rangle$, at the points where $t = 0$ and $t = 0.5$.

9. *Theorem*

    The curvature of the curve given by the vector function **r** is

    $$k(t) = \frac{|\mathbf{r}'(t) \times \mathbf{r}''(t)|}{|\mathbf{r}'(t)|^3}$$

    Use Theorem to find the curvature of $\mathbf{r}(t) = \left\langle \sqrt{15}t, \ e^t, \ e^{-t} \right\rangle$ at the point $(0, 1, 1)$.

10. *Formula*

    For a plane curve with equation $y = f(x)$ we have $k(t) = \dfrac{|f''(x)|}{\left[1 + (f'(x))^2\right]^{3/2}}$.

    Use Formula to find the curvature of $y = x^8$.

    Select the correct answer.

    a. $\dfrac{56|x|^6}{(1 + 8x^7)^{3/2}}$

    b. $\dfrac{56|x|^6}{(1 + 64x^{14})^{3/2}}$

    c. $\dfrac{8x^7}{(1 + 64x^{14})^{3/2}}$

    d. $\dfrac{x^7}{(1 + 64x^{14})^{3/2}}$

    e. $\dfrac{8x^7}{(1 + 64x^{14})^{1/2}}$

11. At what point on the curve $x = t^3$, $y = 3t$, $z = t^4$ is the normal plane parallel to the plane $3x + 3y - 4z = 9$?

   Select the correct answer.

   a.   (-1, -3, 9)
   b.   (-1, -3, 1)
   c.   (-9, 3, 1)
   d.   (9, 3, -2)
   e.   (-1, 3, 9)

12. Find the unit tangent vector $T(t)$.

   $$r(t) = \left\langle \frac{25}{3}t^3, \ 25t^3, \ 50t \right\rangle$$

13. Find the speed of a particle with the given position function.

   $$\mathbf{r}(t) = 5\sqrt{2}t\mathbf{i} + e^{5t}\mathbf{j} - e^{-5t}\mathbf{k}$$

   Select the correct answer.

   a. $|\mathbf{v}(t)| = (e^{5t} + e^{-5t})$

   b. $|\mathbf{v}(t)| = \sqrt{10 + 5e^t + 5e^{-t}}$

   c. $|\mathbf{v}(t)| = \sqrt{10 + e^{10t} + e^{-10t}}$

   d. $|\mathbf{v}(t)| = 5(e^{5t} + e^{-5t})$

   e. $|\mathbf{v}(t)| = 5(e^t + e^{-t})$

14. A force with magnitude 40 N acts directly upward from the xy-plane on an object with mass 5 kg. The object starts at the origin with initial velocity $\mathbf{v}(0) = 5\mathbf{i} - 4\mathbf{j}$. Find its position function

15. Find the position vector of a particle that has the given acceleration and the given initial velocity and position.

   $\mathbf{a}(t) = -4\mathbf{k}$, $\mathbf{v}(0) = \mathbf{i} + \mathbf{j} - 10\mathbf{k}$, $\mathbf{r}(0) = 2\mathbf{i} + 9\mathbf{j}$

16. The position function of a particle is given by $r(t) = \left\langle 5t^2, \ 10t, \ 5t^2 - 40t \right\rangle$.

   When is the speed a minimum?

17. What force is required so that a particle of mass m has the following position function?

$$\mathbf{r}(t) = 3t^3\mathbf{i} + 7t^2\mathbf{j} + 9t^3\mathbf{k}$$

Select the correct answer.

a. $\mathbf{F}(t) = 9mt^2\mathbf{i} + 14mt\mathbf{j} + 27mt^2\mathbf{k}$

b. $\mathbf{F}(t) = mt^2\mathbf{i} + 4mt\mathbf{j} + 27mt^2\mathbf{k}$

c. $\mathbf{F}(t) = 18mt\mathbf{i} + 14m\mathbf{j} + 54t\mathbf{k}$

d. $\mathbf{F}(t) = 18mt\mathbf{i} + 14m\mathbf{j} + 54mt\mathbf{k}$

e. $\mathbf{F}(t) = 27mt\mathbf{i} + 14m\mathbf{j} + 18mt\mathbf{k}$

18. A projectile is fired with an initial speed of 748 m/s and angle of elevation $28°$. Find the range of the projectile in kilometers. Please enter your answer as a number, rounded to the nearest integer, without units.

19. A particle moves with position function $r(t) = (9t - 3t^3 - 2)\mathbf{i} + 9t^2\mathbf{j}$.

Find the tangential component of the acceleration vector.

20. A particle moves with position function $\mathbf{r}(t) = 8\cos t\mathbf{i} + 8\sin t\mathbf{j} + 8t\mathbf{k}$.

Find the normal component of the acceleration vector.

Stewart - Calculus ET 5e Chapter 13 Form G

1. a

2. $r(t) = 4\cos(t)\mathbf{i} + 4\sin(t)\mathbf{j} + 16\cos^2(t)\mathbf{k}$

3. $\mathbf{b} + 3t^2\mathbf{c}$

4. $79°$

5. $r(t) = 8t\mathbf{i} - 2t\mathbf{j} + 3t^2\mathbf{k}$

6. a

7. 9.5706

8. (1, 8, 1)

9. $\dfrac{\sqrt{2}}{17}$

10. b

11. b

12. $\left\langle \dfrac{t^2}{t^2 + 2}, \ \dfrac{2t}{t^2 + 2}, \ \dfrac{2}{t^2 + 2} \right\rangle$

13. d

14. $r(t) = 5t\mathbf{i} - 4t\mathbf{j} + 4t^2\mathbf{k}$

15. $r(t) = (t + 2)\mathbf{i} + (t + 9)\mathbf{j} - (2t^2 + 10t)\mathbf{k}$

16. $t = 2$

17. d

18. 24

19. $18t$

20. 8

1.   Find a vector function that represents the curve of intersection of the two surfaces.
      The circular cylinder $x^2 + y^2 = 4$ and the parabolic cylinder $z = x^2$.

2.   Choose the point that is not on the given curve.

      $r(t) = (8 + t)\mathbf{i} + 2t\mathbf{j} + t\mathbf{k}$

      Select the correct answer.

      a.   (12, 8, -4)
      b.   (11, 6, -1)
      c.   (8, 0, 0)
      d.   (1, 6, -1)
      e.   (8, 0, -4)

3.   Choose the parametric equations that correspond to the given graph.

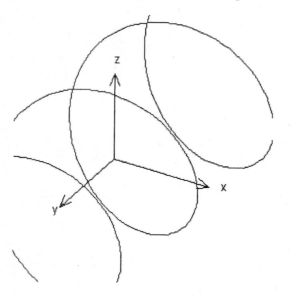

      Select the correct answer.

      a. $x = t, \ y = t^6, \ z = e^{-4t}$

      b. $x = \cos 4t, \ y = t, \ z = \sin 4t$

      c. $x = t, \ y = \dfrac{3t^6}{3 + t^2}, \ z = t^4$

      d. $x = \cos 4t, \ y = \sin t, \ z = 4t$

      e. $x = t, \ y = t^2, \ z = \sin 4t$

4. Find the point of intersection of the tangent lines to the curve $r(t) = \langle \sin \pi t, \ 4 \sin \pi t, \ \cos \pi t \rangle$, at the points where $t = 0$ and $t = 0.5$.

5. The curves $r_1(t) = \langle t, \ t^6, \ t^7 \rangle$ and $r_2(t) = \langle \sin t, \ \sin 5t, \ t \rangle$ intersect at the origin. Find their angle of intersection correct to the nearest degree.

6. If $\mathbf{u}(t) = \mathbf{i} - 3t^2 \mathbf{j} + 6t^3 \mathbf{k}$ and $\mathbf{v}(t) = t\mathbf{i} - \cos t\mathbf{j} + \sin t\mathbf{k}$, find $\dfrac{\partial}{\partial t}[\mathbf{u}(t) \cdot \mathbf{v}(t)]$.

7. Find the unit tangent vector $T(t)$.

$$r(t) = \langle 4 \sin t, \ 9t, \ 4 \cos t \rangle$$

8. Use *Simpson's Rule* with $n = 10$ to estimate the length of the arc of the twisted cubic $x = t, \ y = t^2, \ z = t^3$ from the origin to the point $(2, 4, 8)$.

   Give the answer to four decimal places.

9. **Theorem**

   The curvature of the curve given by the vector function $\mathbf{r}$ is

   $$k(t) = \frac{|\mathbf{r}'(t) \times \mathbf{r}''(t)|}{|\mathbf{r}'(t)|^3}$$

   Use Theorem to find the curvature of $\mathbf{r}(t) = \langle \sqrt{15}t, \ e^t, \ e^{-t} \rangle$ at the point $(0, 1, 1)$.

   Select the correct answer.

   a. $\dfrac{\sqrt{2}}{19}$

   b. $17\sqrt{2}$

   c. $\dfrac{\sqrt{2}}{17}$

   d. $\dfrac{1}{17}$

   e. $\dfrac{\sqrt{15}}{17}$

10. The position function of a particle is given by $r(t) = \langle 8t^2, \ 2t, \ 8t^2 - 96t \rangle$.

When is the speed a minimum?

11. **Formula**

For a plane curve with equation $y = f(x)$ we have

$$k(t) = \frac{|f''(x)|}{\left[1 + (f'(x))^2\right]^{3/2}}$$

Use Formula to find the curvature of $y = x^5$.

12. Find the speed of a particle with the given position function.

$$r(t) = 5\sqrt{2}t\mathbf{i} + e^{5t}\mathbf{j} - e^{-5t}\mathbf{k}$$

Select the correct answer.

   a. $|v(t)| = (e^{5t} + e^{-5t})$

   b. $|v(t)| = \sqrt{10 + 5e^t + 5e^{-t}}$

   c. $|v(t)| = \sqrt{10 + e^{10t} + e^{-10t}}$

   d. $|v(t)| = 5(e^{5t} + e^{-5t})$

   e. $|v(t)| = 5(e^t + e^{-t})$

13. Find the following limit.

$$\lim_{t \to \infty} \left\langle \arctan t, \ e^{-7t}, \ \frac{\ln t}{t} \right\rangle$$

14. Find the unit tangent vector $T(t)$.

$$r(t) = \langle 8t^2, \ 16t, \ 8\ln t \rangle$$

15. Find parametric equations for the tangent line to the curve with the given parametric equations at the specified point.

$$x = t^8, \ y = t^3, \ z = t^7; \ (1, \ 1, \ 1)$$

Select the correct answer.

a. $x = 1 - 7t, \ y = 1 - 2t, \ z = 1 - 6t$

b. $x = 1 + 7t, \ y = 1 + 2t, \ z = 1 + 6t$

c. $x = 1 + 8t, \ y = 1 + 3t, \ z = 1 + 7t$

d. $x = 1 - 8t, \ y = 1 - 3t, \ z = 1 - 7t$

e. $x = 8t, \ y = 3t, \ z = 7t$

16. Find the following limit.

$$\lim_{t \to 0^+} \left\langle 2\cos t, \ 6\sin t, \ 3t \ln t \right\rangle$$

Select the correct answer.

a. $\mathbf{r}(t) = 2\mathbf{i}$

b. $\mathbf{r}(t) = 2\mathbf{i} + 6\mathbf{j} + 3\mathbf{k}$

c. $\mathbf{r}(t) = 2\mathbf{i} - 3\mathbf{k}$

d. $\mathbf{r}(t) = 2\mathbf{j}$

e. $\mathbf{r}(t) = 2\mathbf{k}$

17. Find the domain of the following vector function.

$$r(t) = \left\langle t^8, \ \sqrt{t-1}, \ \sqrt{9-t} \right\rangle$$

18. Evaluate the integral.

$$\int \left(e^{6t}\mathbf{i} + 8t\mathbf{j} + \ln t\mathbf{k} \right) \ dt$$

19. A ball is thrown at an angle of $75°$ to the ground. If the ball lands 53 m away, what was the initial speed of the ball? Let $g = 9.8 \ m/s^2$.

20. The following table gives coordinates of a particle moving through space along a smooth curve.

t	x	Y	z
0.5	5.8	9.1	4.3
1	12.6	14.9	16.8
1.5	25.6	21.2	29.4
2	39.2	39.5	37.9
2.5	42.4	42.4	43

Find the average velocity over the time interval [0.5, 2.5].

Select the correct answer.

a. $\mathbf{v} = 18.3\,\mathbf{i} + 16.65\,\mathbf{j} + 19.35\,\mathbf{k}$
b. $\mathbf{v} = 26.6\,\mathbf{i} - 24.6\,\mathbf{j} - 21.1\,\mathbf{k}$
c. $\mathbf{v} = 13.6\,\mathbf{i} - 11.6\,\mathbf{j} + 25\,\mathbf{k}$
d. $\mathbf{v} = 19.8\,\mathbf{i} + 12.1\,\mathbf{j} - 25.1\,\mathbf{k}$
e. $\mathbf{v} = 21.1\,\mathbf{i} + 12.1\,\mathbf{j} - 11.6\,\mathbf{k}$

1. $r(t) = 4\cos(t)\mathbf{i} + 4\sin(t)\mathbf{j} + 16\cos^2 t\mathbf{k}$

2. b

3. b

4. $(1, 4, 1)$

5. $79°$

6. $1 - 14t\cos t + 13t^2\sin t + 2t^3\cos t$

7. $\left\langle -\dfrac{4}{\sqrt{97}}\cos t, \ \dfrac{9}{\sqrt{97}}, \ \dfrac{-4}{\sqrt{97}}\sin t \right\rangle$

8. 9.5706

9. c

10. $t = 3$

11. $\dfrac{20\,|x|^3}{(1 + 25x^8)^{3/2}}$

12. d

13. $r(t) = \dfrac{\pi}{2}\mathbf{i}$

14. $\left\langle \dfrac{2t^2}{2t^2 + 1}, \ \dfrac{2t}{2t^2 + 1}, \ \dfrac{1}{2t^2 + 1} \right\rangle$

15. c

16. a

17. $1 \le t \le 9$

18. $\dfrac{e^{6t}}{6}\mathbf{i} + 4t^2\mathbf{j} + t(\ln t - 1)\mathbf{k} + C$

19. 32.2

20. a

1. The *temperature-humidity index I* (or humidex, for short) is the perceived air temperature when the actual temperature is T and the relative humidity is h, so we can write $I = f(t, h)$. The following table of values of I is an excerpt from a table compiled by the National Oceanic and Atmospheric Administration. For what value of T is $f(T, 50) = 82$?

T ↓ \ h →	20	30	40	50	60	70
80	74	76	78	82	83	86
85	81	82	84	86	90	94
90	86	90	93	96	101	106
95	94	94	98	107	111	125
100	99	101	109	122	129	138

2. Find the limit.

$$\lim_{(x,y)\to(9,-5)} x^5 + 8x^3 y - 2xy^2$$

3. Find $h(x, y) = g(f(x, y))$, if $g(t) = t^2 + \sqrt{t}$ and $f(x, y) = 8x + 7y - 6$.

4. Find f_x for $f(x, y) = 3x^5 + 2x^3 y^2 + 9xy^4$.

5. Find the first partial derivatives of the function.

$$c = \ln\left(a + \sqrt{a^2 + b^2} \right)$$

6. Find the linearization $L(x, y)$ of the function at the given point.

$$f(x, y) = x\sqrt{y}, \quad (-5, 4)$$

Round the answers to the nearest hundredth.

7. Find the differential of the function.

$$u = e^{5t} \sin 3x$$

8. Find f_x for $f(x, y) = 7x^5 + 6x^3 y^2 + 7xy^4$.

9. Find $\dfrac{\partial^2 z}{\partial x^2}$ for $z = y \tan 8x$.

10. The length l, width w and height h of a box change with time. At a certain instant the dimensions are $l = 3$, and $w = h = 5$ and l and w are increasing at a rate of 10 m/s while h is decreasing at a rate of 1 m/s. At that instant find the rates at which the surface area is changing.

11. Find the directional derivative of f at the given point in the direction indicated by the angle θ .

$$f(x, y) = xe^{-4y}, \quad (2, \ 0), \quad \theta = \frac{\pi}{2}$$

12. Find the directional derivative of f at the given point in the direction indicated by the angle θ .

$$f(x, y) = \sqrt{6x - 5y}, \quad (5, \ 1), \quad \theta = -\frac{\pi}{6}$$

13. Find the maximum rate of change of f at the given point.

$$f(x, y) = \sin(xy), \quad (1, \ 0)$$

14. Find f_x for $f(x, y) = \displaystyle\int_{y}^{x} \cos(t^8) \ dt$.

15. Find equation of the tangent plane to the given surface at the specified point.

$$5x^2 + 3y^2 + 8z^2, \quad (3, \ 6, \ 5)$$

16. Find symmetric equations for the tangent line to the curve of intersection of the paraboloid $z = x^2 + y^2$ and the ellipsoid $2x^2 + y^2 + z^2 = 76$ at the point $(2, \ 2, \ 8)$.

17. Find the critical points of the function.

$$f(x, y) = 5 + 76xy + 38x^2 + 240y + \frac{y^4}{4}$$

18. Find the absolute maximum value of the function f on the set D.

$$D = \left\{ (x, y) \mid |x| \leq 1, \ |y| \leq 1 \right\}$$

$$f(x, y) = 4x^2 + 10y^2 + 9x^2y + 3$$

19. Find the dimensions of a rectangular box of maximum volume such that the sum of the lengths of its 12 edges is 24.

20. Use Lagrange multipliers to find the point whose coordinates are all positive at which the function $f(x, y, z) = 5xyz$ has its maximum value, subject to the constraint $5x^2 + 15y^2 + 25z^2 = 6$.

ANSWER KEY

Stewart - Calculus ET 5e Chapter 14 Form A

1. $T = 80$

2. 29439

3. $64x^2 + 49y^2 + 112xy + 36 - 96x - 84y + \sqrt{8x + 7y - 6}$

4. $15x^4 + 6x^2y^2 + 9y^4$

5. $\dfrac{1}{\sqrt{a^2 + b^2}}, \quad \dfrac{b}{a\sqrt{a^2 + b^2} + a^2 + b^2}$

6. $L = 2x - 1.25y + 5$

7. $du = 5e^{5t}\sin(3x)dt + 3e^{5t}\cos(3x)dx$

8. $35x^4 + 18x^2y^2 + 7y^4$

9. $128y\sec^2 8x \tan 8x$

10. 344

11. -8

12. 0.77

13. 1

14. $\cos(x^8)$

15. $15x + 18y + 40z = 353$

16. $\dfrac{x-2}{34} = \dfrac{y-2}{36}, \quad \dfrac{y-2}{36} = \dfrac{z-8}{-8}$

17. $(-6, 6), (-4, 4), (10, -10)$

18. 26

19. $2, 2, 2$

20. $\left(\sqrt{\dfrac{2}{5}}, \sqrt{\dfrac{2}{15}}, \sqrt{\dfrac{2}{25}}\right)$

1. Find the limit.

$$\lim_{(x,y)\to(9,-5)} x^5 + 8x^3y - 2xy^2$$

2. Find the directional derivative of f at the given point in the direction indicated by the angle θ.

$$f(x,y) = \sqrt{6x-5y}, \quad (5, \ 1), \quad \theta = -\frac{\pi}{6}$$

3. Find the maximum rate of change of f at the given point.

$$f(x,y) = \sin(xy), \quad (1, \ 0)$$

4. Find the direction in which the function $f(x,y) = x^4y - x^3y^2$ decreases fastest at the point (2, -1).

5. Find equation of the tangent plane to the given surface at the specified point.

$$5x^2 + 3y^2 + 8z^2 = 353, \quad (3, \ 6, \ 5)$$

6. Find symmetric equations for the tangent line to the curve of intersection of the paraboloid $z = x^2 + y^2$ and the ellipsoid $2x^2 + y^2 + z^2 = 76$ at the point (2, 2, 8).

7. Find the critical points of the function.

$$f(x,y) = 5 + 76xy + 38x^2 + 240y + \frac{y^4}{4}$$

8. Find f_x for $f(x,y) = 7x^5 + 6x^3y^2 + 7xy^4$.

9. Find the first partial derivatives of the function.

$$c = \ln(a + \sqrt{a^2 + b^2})$$

10. Find f_x for $f(x,y) = \int_y^x \cos(t^8) \ dt$.

11. Find $\dfrac{\partial^2 z}{\partial x^2}$ for $z = y \tan 8x$.

12. Find the directional derivative of f at the given point in the direction indicated by the angle θ.

$$f(x, y) = xe^{-4y}, \quad (2, \ 0), \quad \theta = \frac{\pi}{2}$$

13. Find an equation of the tangent plane to the given surface at the specified point.

$$z = \sqrt{18 - x^2 - 2y^2}, \quad (3, \ 2, \ -2)$$

14. Use the linearization $L(x, y)$ of the function $f(x, y, z) = \sqrt{x^2 + y^2 + z^2}$ at $(4, -1, 3)$ to approximate $f(3.97, -0.82, 2.87)$.

15. Find the differential of the function.

$$u = e^{5t} \sin 3x$$

16. The length l, width w and height h of a box change with time. At a certain instant the dimensions are $l = 3$, and $w = h = 5$ and l and w are increasing at a rate of 10 m/s while h is decreasing at a rate of 1 m/s. At that instant find the rates at which the surface area is changing.

17. Use differentials to estimate the amount of tin in a closed tin can with diameter 8 cm and height 11 cm if the tin is 0.04 cm thick.

18. A boundary stripe 1 in. wide is painted around a rectangle whose dimensions are 100 ft by 210 ft. Use differentials to approximate the number of square feet of paint in the stripe.

19. Find f_x for $f(x, y) = 3x^5 + 2x^3 y^2 + 9xy^4$.

20. Find $h(x, y) = g(f(x, y))$, if $g(t) = t^2 + \sqrt{t}$ and $f(x, y) = 8x + 7y - 6$.

1. 29439

2. 77

3. 1

4. $\begin{pmatrix} 44 \\ -32 \end{pmatrix}$

5. $15x + 18y + 40z = 353$

6. $\dfrac{x-2}{34} = \dfrac{y-2}{36}, \ \dfrac{y-2}{36} = \dfrac{z-8}{-8}$

7. (-6, 6), (-4, 4), (10, -10)

8. $35x^4 + 18x^2 y^2 + 7y^4$

9. $\dfrac{1}{\sqrt{a^2 + b^2}}, \ \dfrac{b}{a\sqrt{a^2 + b^2} + a^2 + b^2}$

10. $\cos(x^8)$

11. $128y\sec^2 8x \tan 8x$

12. -8

13. $z = -3x - 4y + 15$

14. 4.96

15. $du = 5e^{5t} \sin(3x)dt + 3e^{5t} \cos(3x)dx$

16. 344

17. 15.08

18. 51.67

19. $15x^4 + 6x^2 y^2 + 9y^4$

20. $64x^2 + 49y^2 + 112xy + 36 - 96x - 84y + \sqrt{8x + 7y - 6}$

1. A contour map for a function f is shown. Use it to estimate the value of $f(-3, 3)$.

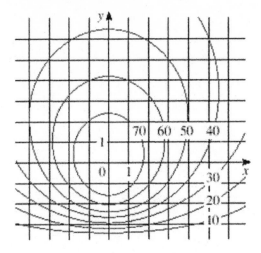

Select the correct answer.

   a. 56
   b. 48
   c. 28
   d. 65
   e. 78

2. Two contour maps are shown. One is for a function f whose graph is a cone. The other is for a function g whose graph is a paraboloid. Find the number of contour map of a cone.

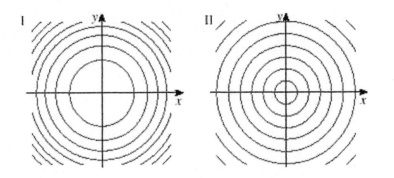

Select the correct answer.

   a. II
   b. I
   c. impossible to determine

3. Find the equation that describes the following surface.

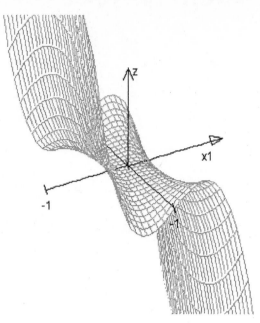

Select the correct answer.

   a. $f(x, y) = xy^2 - 3x^3$

   b. $f(x, y) = xy^2 - 3x^2$

   c. $f(x, y) = xy - 3x^3$

   d. $f(x, y) = xy^2 + 3x^3$

   e.   none of these

4. Use a table of numerical values of $f(x, y)$ for (x, y) near the origin to make a conjecture about the value of the limit of $f(x, y)$ as $(x, y) \to (0, 0)$.

$$f(x, y) = \frac{x^2 y^3 + x^3 y^2 - 3}{1 - xy}$$

Select the correct answer.

   a.   -1

   b.   3

   c.   -3

   d.   1

   e.   cannot determine the value from the given information

5. Find the limit, if it exists.

$$\lim_{(x,y)\to(0,0)} \frac{6xy^2}{x^2 + y^2}$$

Select the correct answer.

a. 0
b. 6
c. 2
d. 1
e. The limit does not exist

6. Determine the largest set on which the function is continuous.

$$F(x, y) = \arctan(10x + 8\sqrt{y-3})$$

Select the correct answer.

a. $\left\{ (x, y) \mid y \geq 3, \; \left| 10x + 8\sqrt{y} \right| \leq 1 \right\}$

b. $\left\{ (x, y) \mid y \geq 3 \right\}$

c. $\left\{ (x, y) \mid y \leq 0 \right\}$

d. $\left\{ (x, y) \mid x \geq 0 \right\}$

e. $\left\{ (x, y) \mid x \geq 1 \right\}$

7. Find $f_y(-36, \; 6)$ for $f(x, \; y) = \sin(2x + 12y)$.

Select the correct answer.

a. 2
b. 12
c. -2
d. 0
e. -12

8. Use the definition of partial derivatives as limits to find $f_x(x, \; y)$ if $f(x, y) = 4x^2 - 9xy + 2y^2$.

Select the correct answer.

a. $8x - 9xy$
b. $8x - 9y$
c. $8x - 9$
d. $4y - 9x$
e. $4x - 9y$

9. Find the indicated partial derivative.

$$f(x, y) = x^2 y^4 - 3x^4 y \; ; \quad f_{xxx}$$

Select the correct answer.

   a. $f_{xxx} = 3xy$

   b. $f_{xxx} = -3xy$

   c. $f_{xxx} = 72x^2 y$

   d. $f_{xxx} = -72xy$

   e. $f_{xxx} = -45xy$

10. Find the indicated partial derivative.

$$u = x^a y^b z^c; \quad \frac{\partial^6 u}{\partial x \partial y^2 \partial z^3}, \quad a > 1, \; b > 2, \; c > 3$$

Select the correct answer.

   a. $\dfrac{\partial^6 u}{\partial x \partial y^2 \partial z^3} = x^{a-1} y^{b-2} z^{c-3}$

   b. $\dfrac{\partial^6 u}{\partial x \partial y^2 \partial z^3} = x^{b-1} y^{c-2} z^{a-3}$

   c. $\dfrac{\partial^6 u}{\partial x \partial y^2 \partial z^3} = ab(b-1)c(c-1)(c-2)x^{a-1} y^{b-2} z^{c-3}$

   d. $\dfrac{\partial^6 u}{\partial x \partial y^2 \partial z^3} = cb(b-1)c(a-1)(a-2)x^{c-1} y^{b-2} z^{a-3}$

   e. $\dfrac{\partial^6 u}{\partial x \partial y^2 \partial z^3} = acb(a-1)(a-2)x^{a-1} y^{b-2} z^{c-3}$

11. Use the Chain Rule to find $\dfrac{\partial z}{\partial s}$.

$$z = e^r \cos(\theta), \quad r = 10st, \quad \theta = \sqrt{s^2 + t^2}$$

Select the correct answer.

a. $\quad \dfrac{\partial z}{\partial s} = e^r \left(10t \cos(\theta) - \dfrac{s \sin(\theta)}{\sqrt{s^2 + t^2}} \right)$

b. $\quad \dfrac{\partial z}{\partial s} = e^r \left(t \cos(\theta) - \dfrac{s \sin(\theta)}{\sqrt{s^2 + t}} \right)$

c. $\quad \dfrac{\partial z}{\partial s} = e^r \left(10t \cos(\theta) + \dfrac{s \sin(\theta)}{\sqrt{s^2 - t^2}} \right)$

d. $\quad \dfrac{\partial z}{\partial s} = e^t \left(\cos(\theta) + \dfrac{s \sin(\theta)}{\sqrt{s^2 - t^2}} \right)$

e. $\quad \dfrac{\partial z}{\partial s} = \left(10t \cos(\theta) + \dfrac{se^r \sin(\theta)}{\sqrt{s^2 + t^2}} \right)$

12. Use the Chain Rule to find $\dfrac{\partial u}{\partial p}$.

$$u = \dfrac{x + y}{y + z}$$

$$x = p + 6r + 5t, \quad y = p - 6r + 5t, \quad z = p + 6r - 5t$$

Select the correct answer.

a. $\quad \dfrac{\partial u}{\partial p} = \dfrac{5t}{p}$

b. $\quad \dfrac{\partial u}{\partial p} = -\dfrac{20t}{p^3}$

c. $\quad \dfrac{\partial u}{\partial p} = -\dfrac{5t}{p^2}$

d. $\quad \dfrac{\partial u}{\partial p} = -\dfrac{25t}{p^2}$

e. $\quad \dfrac{\partial u}{\partial p} = \dfrac{25t}{p^2} + t$

13. Find the directional derivative of $f(x, y) = \sqrt{xy}$ at $P(3, 5)$ in the direction of $Q(3.920, 0.795)$.

Select the correct answer. The choices are rounded to the nearest tenth.

    a.   0.7
    b.   3.5
    c.   -3.5
    d.   2.5
    e.   -1.6

14. Find the direction in which the maximum rate of change of f at the given point occurs.

$$f(x, y) = \sin(xy), \quad (1, 0)$$

Select the correct answer.

    a. $\left\langle \dfrac{1}{\sqrt{2}}, \dfrac{1}{\sqrt{2}} \right\rangle$

    b. $\langle 0, 1 \rangle$

    c. $\langle 1, 0 \rangle$

    d. $\langle \sqrt{2}, 0 \rangle$

    e. $\langle 1, -\sqrt{2} \rangle$

15. Find equation of the normal line to the given surface at the specified point.

$$2x^2 + 8y^2 + 3z^2 = 235, \quad (4, 4, 5)$$

Select the correct answer.

    a. $\dfrac{x-4}{55} = \dfrac{y-4}{55} = \dfrac{z-5}{55}$

    b. $\dfrac{x+4}{16} = \dfrac{y+4}{64} = \dfrac{z+5}{30}$

    c. $\dfrac{x-4}{16} = \dfrac{y-4}{64} = \dfrac{z-5}{30}$

    d. $16x + 64y + 30z = 235$

    e. $2x + 8y + 3z = 1$

16. Find equation of the tangent plane to the given surface at the specified point.

$z + 5 = xe^y \cos z, \quad (5, \ 0, \ 0)$

Select the correct answer.

a. $x + 5y + z = 5$
b. $x + y - 5z = 5$
c. $5x + y - z = 5$
d. $x + 5y - z = 5$
e. $x + y - z = 5$

17. At what point is the following function a local minimum?

$f(x, y) = 6x^2 + 3y^2$

Select the correct answer.

a. $(6, 3)$
b. $(3, 0)$
c. $(0, 0)$
d. $(6, 0)$
e. $(6, -3)$

18. Find the critical points of the function.

$f(x, y) = 8 + 76xy + 38x^2 + 240y + \dfrac{y^4}{4}$

Select the correct answer.

a. $(-4, 4), (-6, 6), (10, -10)$
b. $(-6,6), (-8,8), (8, -8)$
c. $(-4,6), (-6,-10), (10, 4)$
d. $(4, 4), (6, 6), (-10, 0)$
e. $(-4,6), (-8,6), (8, -6)$

19. Use *Lagrange multipliers* to find the maximum value of the function subject to the given constraint.

$$f(x, y) = 8x^2 - 4y^2, \quad 8x^2 + 4y^2 = 9$$

Select the correct answer.

    a. $f(x, y) = \dfrac{1}{9}$

    b. $f(x, y) = \dfrac{1}{4}$

    c. $f(x, y) = \dfrac{1}{8}$

    d. $f(x, y) = 8$

    e. $f(x, y) = 9$

20. Use *Lagrange multipliers* to find the maximum value of the function subject to the given constraint.

$$f(x, y, z) = 14x + 8y + 12z, \quad x^2 + y^2 + z^2 = 101$$

Select the correct answer.

    a. $f(20,\ 9,\ 18) = 568$
    b. $f(14,\ 8,\ 12) = 404$
    c. $f(8,\ 17,\ 5) = 308$
    d. $f(7,\ 4,\ 6) = 202$
    e. $f(8,\ 4,\ 12) = 212$

1. a

2. a

3. a

4. c

5. a

6. b

7. b

8. b

9. d

10. c

11. a

12. c

13. a

14. b

15. c

16. d

17. c

18. a

19. e

20. d

1. Find the indicated partial derivative.

   $$f(x, y) = x^2 y^4 - 3x^4 y \; ; \; f_{xxx}$$

   Select the correct answer.

   a. $f_{xxx} = 3xy$
   b. $f_{xxx} = -3xy$
   c. $f_{xxx} = 72x^2 y$
   d. $f_{xxx} = -72xy$
   e. $f_{xxx} = -45xy$

2. The ellipsoid $8x^2 + 3y^2 + z^2 = 14$ intersects the plane $y = 2$ in an ellipse. Find parametric equations for the tangent line to this ellipse at the point $(1, 2, 2)$.

   Select the correct answer.

   a. $x = 1 + t, \; y = 2, \; z = 4t - 2$
   b. $x = 1 + t, \; y = 1, \; z = 4t + 2$
   c. $x = 1 + t, \; y = 2, \; z = -4t + 2$
   d. $x = 1 + t, \; y = 2, z = -4t - 2$
   e. $x = t, \; y = 2, z = -4t + 2$

3. How many nth - order partial derivatives does a function of two variables have?

   Select the correct answer.

   a. $\dfrac{n}{2}$
   b. $2n$
   c. n^2
   d. 2^n
   e. $n2^n$

4. Find the maximum value of $f(x_1, \; x_2, ..., \; x_n) = \sqrt[n]{x_1 x_2 \cdot ... \cdot x_n}$ given that $x_1, x_2, ..., x_n$ are positive numbers and $x_1 + x_2 + ... + x_n = c$, where c is a constant.

   Find f for $n = 6$ and $c = 12$ and select the correct answer below.
   Select the correct answer.

   a. $f = 4.5$
   b. $f = 2$
   c. $f = 8.5$
   d. $f = 9.5$
   e. $f = 7.5$

5. If $z = x^2 - xy + 7y^2$ and (x, y) changes from $(1, 3)$ to $(0.95, 3.09)$, find dz.

Select the correct answer.

a. $dz = 2.87$
b. $dz = 3.74$
c. $dz = 4.87$
d. $dz = 3.42$
e. $dz = 3.6$

6. If is the total resistance of three resistors, connected in parallel, with resistances R_1, R_2, R_3, then
$\dfrac{1}{R} = \dfrac{1}{R_1} + \dfrac{1}{R_2} + \dfrac{1}{R_3}$. If the resistances are measured in ohms as $R_1 = 30 \ \Omega$, $R_2 = 35 \ \Omega$ and
$R_3 = 50 \ \Omega$, with a possible error of 0.8% in each case, estimate the maximum error in the calculated value of R.

Select the correct answer.

a. $0.291 \ \Omega$
b. $0.957 \ \Omega$
c. $0.347 \ \Omega$
d. $0.476 \ \Omega$
e. $0.098 \ \Omega$

7. Use the equation $\dfrac{dy}{dx} = -\dfrac{\dfrac{\partial F}{\partial x}}{\dfrac{\partial F}{\partial y}} = -\dfrac{F_x}{F_y}$ to find $\dfrac{dy}{dx}$.

$\cos(x - 9y) = xe^{3y}$

Select the correct answer.

a. $\dfrac{dy}{dx} = \dfrac{\sin(x-9y) + e^{3y}}{\sin(x-9y) - xe^{3y}}$

b. $\dfrac{dy}{dx} = \dfrac{\sin(x-y) + e^{3y}}{9\sin(x-9y) - xe^{3y}}$

c. $\dfrac{dy}{dx} = \dfrac{\sin(x-9y) + e^{3y}}{9\sin(x-9y) - 3xe^{3y}}$

d. $\dfrac{dy}{dx} = \dfrac{\sin(x-y) + e^{3y}}{\sin(x-y) - xe^{y}}$

e. $\dfrac{dy}{dx} = \dfrac{9\sin(x-y) + e^{3y}}{\sin(x-9y) - 9xe^{y}}$

8. Find the direction in which the maximum rate of change of f at the given point occurs.

$f(x, y) = \sin(xy), \quad (0, \; 1)$

Select the correct answer.

a. $\left\langle 0, \; 1 \right\rangle$

b. $\left\langle 1, \; 0 \right\rangle$

c. $\left\langle \dfrac{1}{\sqrt{2}}, \; \dfrac{1}{\sqrt{2}} \right\rangle$

d. $\left\langle 0, \; \dfrac{1}{\sqrt{2}} \right\rangle$

e. $\left\langle \dfrac{1}{\sqrt{2}}, \; 1 \right\rangle$

9. Suppose that over a certain region of space the electrical potential V is given by $V(x, y, z) = 8x^2 - 7xy + 7xyz$.

Find the rate of change of the potential at (-1, 1, -1) in the direction of the vector $v = 8i + 10j - 8k$.

Select the correct answer.

a.   -72
b.   20
c.   14.569856
d.   -44
e.   44

10. Which of the given equations are the parametric equations for the tangent line to the curve of intersection of the paraboloid $z = x^2 + y^2$ and the ellipsoid $6x^2 + y^2 + z^2 = 35$ at the point $(-1, \; 2, \; 5)$?

Select the correct answer.

a. $x = -1 - 22t, \;\; y = 2 + 16t, \;\; z = 5 - 20t$

b. $x = -1 + 2t, \;\; y = 2 - 4t, \;\; z = 5 + t$

c. $x = -1 + 6t, \;\; y = 2 - 2t, \;\; z = 5 - 5t$

d. $x = -t, \;\; y = 2 + 2t, \;\; z = 5t$

e. $x = -1 + 16t, \;\; y = 2 - 20t, \;\; z = -5t$

11. Suppose $(1, 1)$ is a critical point of a function f with continuous second derivatives. In the case of $f_{xx}(1, 1) = 7$, $f_{xy}(1, 1) = 8$, $f_{yy}(1, 1) = 10$ what can you say about f ?

Select the correct answer.

a. f has a local maximum at $(1,1)$
b. f has a saddle point at $(1,1)$
c. f has a local minimum at $(1,1)$

12. At what point is the following function a local maximum?

$$f(x, y) = 3 - 10x + 12y - 5x^2 - 6y^2$$

Select the correct answer.

a. $(1, -1)$
b. $(-1, 1)$
c. $(3, 1)$
d. $(0, 1)$
e. $(1, 1)$

13. At what point is the following function a local minimum?

$$f(x, y) = 2x^2 + 2y^2 + 2x^2 y + 6$$

Select the correct answer.

a. $(-1, 2)$
b. $(1, 6)$
c. $(0, 0)$
d. $(-1, 6)$
e. $(-1, -6)$

14. Find all the saddle points of the function.

$$f(x, y) = x \sin \frac{y}{3}$$

Select the correct answer.

a. $(0, \ 3\pi n)$

b. $\left(0, \ \dfrac{\pi}{3} n \right)$

c. $(3\pi n, \ 1)$

d. $\left(\dfrac{3n}{\pi}, \ 0 \right)$

e. $\left(3\pi n, \ 0 \right)$

15. Find the critical points of the function.

$$f(x, y) = \frac{x^4}{4} - 14x^2 + 4y^2 + 48x + 2$$

Select the correct answer.

   a. $(4, 0), (6, 0), (2, 0)$
   b. $(-4, 0), (-6, 0), (-2, 0)$
   c. $(4, 0), (-6, 0)$
   d. $(4, 0), (-6, 0), (2, 0)$
   e. $(0, 0), (6, 0), (2, 0)$

16. Find the absolute minimum value of the function f on the set D. D is the region bounded by the parabola $y = x^2$ and the line $y = 4$.

$$f(x, y) = 7 + 9xy - 4x - 8y$$

Select the correct answer.

   a.   -97
   b.   -89
   c.   0
   d.   -96
   e.   96

17. Find three positive numbers whose sum is 360 and whose product is a maximum.

Select the correct answer.

   a.   120, 120, 120
   b.   179.5, 179.5, 1
   c.   358, 1, 1

18. Use *Lagrange multipliers* to find three positive numbers whose sum is 297 and whose product is a maximum.

Select the correct answer.

   a. $x = y = z = 99$
   b. $x = 129, y = 79, z = 89$
   c. $x = 99, y = z = -99$
   d. $x = 109, y = 99, z = 89$

19. Use *Lagrange multipliers* to find the dimensions of the rectangular box with largest volume if the total surface area is given as $54 \, cm^2$.

Select the correct answer.

  a. $x = 9$ cm, $y = z = 3$ cm
  b. $x = y = z = 9$ cm
  c. $x = 6$ cm, $y = 6$ cm, $z = 2$ cm
  d. $x = y = z = 3$ cm

20. Use *Lagrange multipliers* to find the shortest distance from the point $(3, 9, 8)$ to the plane $3x + 9y + 4z = 16$.

Select the correct answer.

  a. $D = 106$
  b. $D = 90$
  c. $D = \sqrt{106}$
  d. $D = \sqrt{61}$
  e. $D = 61$

1. d

2. c

3. d

4. b

5. b

6. e

7. c

8. b

9. d

10. a

11. c

12. b

13. c

14. a

15. d

16. b

17. a

18. a

19. d

20. c

1. Use the contour map of f to estimate the value of $f(-3, 3)$.

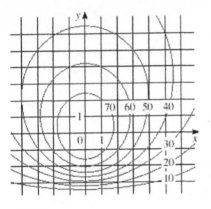

2. Find the limit.

$$\lim_{(x,y)\to(10,-3)} x^5 + 8x^3 y - 3xy^2$$

Select the correct answer.

a. 124,270
b. -24,270
c. 75,730
d. 100,000
e. 123,000

3. Determine the largest set on which the function is continuous.

$$f(x, y, z) = \frac{xyz}{7x^2 + 2y^2 - z}$$

4. A cardboard box without a lid is to have a volume of 6,912 cm^2. Find the dimensions that minimize the amount of cardboard used.

5. Use *Lagrange multipliers* to find the dimensions of the rectangular box with largest volume if the total surface area is given as 96 cm^2.

6. Find $f_y(-24, 8)$ for $f(x, y) = \sin(2x + 6y)$.

Select the correct answer.

a. 6
b. 2
c. 0
d. -6
e. -2

7. Use implicit differentiation to find $\partial z / \partial x$.

$$9x^2 + 8y^2 - 3z^2 = 2x(y + z)$$

8. Find $\dfrac{\partial^2 z}{\partial x^2}$ for $z = y \tan 8x$.

9. Find the indicated partial derivative.

$$f(x, y) = x^2 y^9 - 2x^4 y \; ; \; f_{xxx}$$

10. The ellipsoid $6x^2 + 3y^2 + z^2 = 14$ intersects the plane $y = 2$ in an ellipse. Find parametric equations for the tangent line to this ellipse at the point (1, 2, 2).

11. Use differentials to estimate the amount of metal in a closed cylindrical can that is 13 cm high and 6 cm in diameter if the metal in the top and bottom is 0.09 cm thick and the metal in the sides is 0.01 cm thick.

    Select the correct answer. (rounded to the nearest hundredth.)

    a.   8.34 cm^3
    b.   7.54 cm^3
    c.   6.99 cm^3
    d.   6.91 cm^3
    e.   6.7 cm^3

12. Use the Chain Rule to find $\dfrac{\partial w}{\partial s}$ where $s = 3, t = 0$.

$$w = x^2 + y^2 + z^2, \quad x = st, \quad y = s \cos t, \quad z = s \sin t$$

13. Find the directional derivative of the function at the given point in the direction of the vector v.

$$f(x, y) = -7 + 10x\sqrt{y}, \quad (5, 16), \quad v = \left\langle -4, \, 3 \right\rangle$$

14. Find the direction in which the maximum rate of change of f at the given point occurs.

$f(x,y,z) = x^3 y^4 z^2$, $(1, 1, 1)$

Select the correct answer.

a. $\langle 3, 4, 2 \rangle$

b. $\langle 3, 2, 4 \rangle$

c. $\langle 2, 4, 3 \rangle$

d. $\langle 4, 3, 2 \rangle$

e. $\langle 3, 3, 4 \rangle$

15. Find the dimensions of a rectangular box of maximum volume such that the sum of the lengths of its 12 edges is 96.

16. Find the equation of the tangent plane to the given surface at the specified point.

$2x^2 + 8y^2 + 8z^2 = 954$, $(-3, 6, 9)$

17. If $f(x, y) = x^2 + 9y^2$, use the gradient vector $\nabla f(-5, 10)$ to find the tangent line to the level curve $f(x, y) = 925$ at the point $(-5, 10)$.

18. Find all the saddle points of the function.

$f(x, y) = x \sin \dfrac{y}{5}$

19. Find the absolute minimum value of the function f on the set D. D is the region bounded by the parabola $y = x^2$ and the line $y = 4$.

$f(x, y) = 6 + 3xy - 2x - 4y$

Select the correct answer.

a. 0
b. -34
c. -36
d. -30
e. 30

20. Find the absolute maximum value of the function f on the set D.

$$D = \left\{ (x, y) \mid |x| \le 1, \ |y| \le 1 \right\}$$

$$f(x, y) = 8x^2 + 10y^2 + 5x^2y + 3$$

Select the correct answer

   a.   18
   b.   26
   c.   0
   d.   23
   e.   32

1. 56

2. c

3. $\left\{ (x,y),\ z \neq 7x^2 + 2y^2 \right\}$

4. 24, 24, 12

5. $x = 4,\ y = 4,\ z = 4$

6. a

7. $\dfrac{9x - y - z}{x + 3z}$

8. $\dfrac{128y\sin(8x)}{\cos^3(8x)}$

9. $-48xy$

10. $x = 1 + t,\ y = 2,\ z = -3t + 2$

11. b

12. 6

13. -28.25

14. a

15. 8, 8, 8

16. $-6x + 48y + 72z = 954$

17. $-5x + 90y = 925$

18. $(0,\ 5\pi n)$

19. d

20. b

1. The *temperature-humidity index I* (or humidex, for short) is the perceived air temperature when the actual temperature is T and the relative humidity is h, so we can write $I = f(t, h)$. The following table of values of I is an excerpt from a table compiled by the National Oceanic and Atmospheric Administration. For what value of h is $f(95, h) = 96$?

$T\downarrow$ $h\rightarrow$	20	30	40	50	60	70
80	70	75	80	81	83	86
85	80	84	85	86	89	94
90	88	93	96	100	102	104
95	93	96	99	103	114	123
100	99	102	112	121	128	144

2. A contour map for a function f is shown. Use it to estimate the value of $f(-3, 3)$.

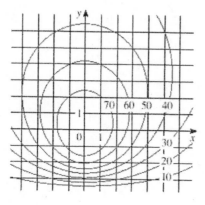

3. The radius of a right circular cone is increasing at a rate of 5 in/s while its height is decreasing at a rate of 3.6 in/s. At what rate is the volume of the cone changing when the radius is 115 in. and the height is 140 in.?

    Select the correct answer.

    a. 117,741.73 $\dfrac{in^3}{s}$

    b. 119,741.73 $\dfrac{in^3}{s}$

    c. 118,741.73 $\dfrac{in^3}{s}$

    d. 123,741.73 $\dfrac{in^3}{s}$

    e. 136,741.73 $\dfrac{in^3}{s}$

4. Find the gradient of f.

$$f(x, y) = 7xy^6 - 9x^7 y$$

5. Evaluate the gradient of f at the point P.

$$f(x, y, z) = xy^2 z^3, \quad P(-1, \ 3, \ -1)$$

6. Find the directional derivative of the function at the given point in the direction of the vector v.

$$f(x, y, z) = x \tan^{-1}\left(\frac{y}{z}\right), \quad (-8, \ -8, \ -8), \quad v = -10i + 7j + 7k$$

7. Suppose that over a certain region of space the electrical potential V is given by
$V(x, y, z) = 2x^2 - 2xy + 8xyz$.

Find the rate of change of the potential at $(-4, \ -6, \ -1)$ in the direction of the vector $v = 7i + 10j - 8k$.

Give your answer rounded to three decimal places.

8. Find equation of the normal line to the given surface at the specified point.

$$z + 2 = xe^y \cos z, \quad (2, \ 0, \ 0)$$

9. If $f(x, y) = x^2 + 9y^2$, use the gradient vector $\nabla f(10, \ 2)$ to find the tangent line to the level curve
$f(x, y) = 136$ at the point $(10, 2)$.

Select the correct answer.

a. $10x + 18y = 136$
b. $100x + 36y = 136$
c. $10x + 18y = 12$
d. $100x - 36y = 12$
e. $100x - 18y = 12$

10. Which of the given points are the points on the hyperboloid $x^2 - y^2 + 4z^2 = 4$ where the normal line is parallel to the line that joins the points (-1, 1, 3) and (0, 2, 5).

    Select all that apply.

    a.   (-2, 2, 1)
    b.   (2, -2, 1)
    c.   (-2, 2, -1)
    d.   (2, -2, -1)
    e.   (2, 2, 1)

11. At what point is the following function a local minimum?

    $$f(x, y) = 8x^2 + 8y^2 + 8x^2y + 6$$

12. At what point is the following function a local minimum?

    $$f(x, y) = 2x^2y + y^3 - 18x^2 - 18y^2 + 4$$

13. Find the points on the surface $z^2 = xy + 49$ that are closest to the origin.

    Select the correct answer.

    a.   (0, 0, 7)
    b.   (0, 0, 49) (0, 0, -49)
    c.   (0, 0, 7) (0, 0, -7)
    d.   (0, 0, -49)
    e.   (0, 0, 28)

14. Find three positive numbers whose sum is 500 and whose product is a maximum.

15. Use *Lagrange multipliers* to find the maximum value of the function subject to the given constraint.

    $$f(x, y, z) = 4x^4 + 4y^4 + 4z^4, \quad 4x^2 + 4y^2 + 4z^2 = 3$$

16. Use *Lagrange multipliers* to find the dimensions of the rectangular box with largest volume if the total surface area is given as 96 cm^2.

17. Use Lagrange multipliers to find the maximum and minimum values of the function
    $f(x, y, z) = 6x - y - 7z$ subject to the constraints $x + 5y - z = 0$ and $x^2 + 16y^2 = 1$.

18. Find all the saddle points of the function.

$$f(x, y) = x \sin \frac{y}{5}$$

19. Use *Lagrange multipliers* to find three positive numbers whose sum is 102 and whose product is a maximum.

    Select the correct answer.

    a. $x = 34, y = z = -34$
    b. $x = y = z = 34$
    c. $x = 44, y = 34, z = 24$
    d. $x = 64, y = 14, z = 24$
    e. $x = 34, y = 35, z = 33$

20. Use *Lagrange multipliers* to find the volume of the largest rectangular box with edges parallel to the axes that can be inscribed in the ellipsoid $9x^2 + 4y^2 + 9z^2 = 324$.

1. $h = 30$

2. 56

3. c

4. $\left(7y^6 - 63x^6y, \ 42y^5x - 9x^7\right)$

5. $\left\{-9, \ 6, \ -27\right\}$

6. -0.558

7. -56.734

8. $x - 2 = \dfrac{y}{2} = -z$

9. a

10. b, c

11. $(0, 0)$

12. $(0, 12)$

13. c

14. $\dfrac{500}{3}, \ \dfrac{500}{3}, \ \dfrac{500}{3}$

15. 3/4

16. $x = 4, \ y = 4, \ z = 4$

17. $f_{\min} = \dfrac{-\sqrt{1312}}{4}, \ f_{\max} = \dfrac{\sqrt{1312}}{4}$

18. $(0, \ 5\pi n)$

19. b

20. $V = \dfrac{108}{\sqrt{3}}$

1. Find the equation that describes the following surface.

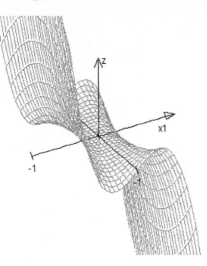

Select the correct answer.

a. $f(x, y) = xy^2 - 3x^3$

b. $f(x, y) = xy^2 - 3x^2$

c. $f(x, y) = xy^2 + 3x^3$

d. $f(x, y) = 2xy^2$

e.   none of these

2. Use a table of numerical values of $f(x, y)$ for (x, y) near the origin to make a conjecture about the value of the limit of $f(x, y)$ as $(x, y) \rightarrow (0, 0)$.

$$f(x, y) = \frac{x^2 y^3 + x^3 y^2 - 2}{1 - xy}$$

Select the correct answer.

a.   -2
b.   1
c.   -1
d.   2
e.   cannot determine the value from the given information

3. Find the limit.

$$\lim_{(x,y)\to(14,7)} xy \cos(x - 2y)$$

4.   Determine the largest set on which the function is continuous.

$$F(x, y) = \arctan\left(10x + 2\sqrt{y-3}\right)$$

5.   Use polar coordinates to find the limit.

$$\lim_{(x,y)\to(0,0)} \frac{x^4 + y^4}{x^3 + y^3}$$

6.   Use spherical coordinates to find the limit.

$$\lim_{(x,y)\to(0,0)} \frac{5xyz}{x^2 + y^2 + z^2}$$

7.   At what point is the following function a local minimum?

$$f(x, y) = 8x^2 + 9y^2$$

Select the correct answer.

   a. $(8, 9)$
   b. $(0, 0)$
   c. $(9, 0)$
   d. $(8, 0)$
   e. $(-8, 0)$

8.   Find the critical points of the function $f(x, y) = \sin 7x + \sin 7y + \sin(7x + 7y)$
for $0 < x < \dfrac{2\pi}{7},\ 0 < y < \dfrac{2\pi}{7}$.

9.   Find the critical points of the function.

$$f(x, y) = \frac{x^4}{4} - 14x^2 + 5y^2 + 48x + 10$$

Select the correct answer.

   a. $(-4, 0), (-6,0), (-2, 0)$
   b. $(4, 0), (-6,0)$
   c. $(4, 0), (6, 0), (2, 0)$
   d. $(4, 0), (-6, 0), (2, 0)$
   e. $(1, 0), (6, 0), (0, 0)$

10. Find the points on the surface $z^2 = xy + 4$ that are closest to the origin.

11. Find the dimensions of the rectangular box with largest volume if the total surface area is given as $294 \ cm^2$.

Select the correct answer.

   a.   28 cm, 1.75 cm, 1.75 cm
   b.   7 cm, 7 cm, 7 cm
   c.   294 cm, 7 cm, 7 cm
   d.   14 cm, 14 cm, 3.5 cm
   e.   714 cm, 14 cm, 1.75 cm

12. Find the dimensions of a rectangular box of maximum volume such that the sum of the lengths of its 12 edges is 96.

Select the correct answer

   a.   4, 8, 16
   b.   8, 8, 8
   c.   8, 96, 8
   d.   32, 32, 32
   e.   32, 8, 16

13. Use *Lagrange multipliers* to find the volume of the largest rectangular box with edges parallel to the axes that can be inscribed in the ellipsoid $16x^2 + 4y^2 + 9z^2 = 576$.

14. Use *Lagrange multipliers* to find the volume of the largest rectangular box in the first octant with three faces in the coordinate planes and one vertex in plane $x + 4y + 5z = 60$.

15. Use *Lagrange multipliers* to find the maximum value of the function subject to the given constraint.

$$f(x, y, z) = 13x^4 + 13y^4 + 13z^4, \ \ 13x^2 + 13y^2 + 13z^2 = 3$$

16. Use *Lagrange multipliers* to find the minimum value of the function subject to the given constraints.

$$f(x, y, z, t) = 7x + 7y + 7z + 7t, \ \ 7(x^2 + y^2 + z^2 + t^2) = 9$$

17. Use *Lagrange multipliers* to find the maximum value of the function subject to the given constraints.

$$f(x, y, z) = x + 3y \ ; \ \ x + y + z = 4, \ y^2 + z^2 = 4$$

18. Use *Lagrange multipliers* to find the shortest distance from the point $(8, 10, 8)$ to the plane $8x + 10y + 4z = 16$.

Select the correct answer

    a. $D = \sqrt{59}$
    b. $D = \sqrt{180}$
    c. $D = 19$
    d. $D = 180$
    e. $D = 18$

19. Use *Lagrange multipliers* to find three positive numbers whose sum is 279 and whose product is a maximum.

Select the correct answer.

    a. $x = 103, y = 93, z = 83$
    b. $x = 123, y = 73, z = 83$
    c. $x = 93, y = z = -93$
    d. $x = y = z = 93$
    e. $x = 92, y = 93, z = 94$

20. Use *Lagrange multipliers* to find the dimensions of the rectangular box with largest volume if the total surface area is given as $150 \ cm^2$.

1. a

2. a

3. 98

4. $\left\{ (x, y),\ y \ge 3 \right\}$

5. 0

6. 0

7. b

8. $\left(\dfrac{\pi}{21}, \dfrac{\pi}{21} \right), \left(\dfrac{\pi}{7}, \dfrac{\pi}{7} \right), \left(\dfrac{5\pi}{21}, \dfrac{5\pi}{21} \right)$

9. d

10. $(0, 0, 2), (0, 0, -2)$

11. b

12. b

13. $V = \dfrac{192}{\sqrt{3}}$

14. $V = 400$

15. 9/39

16. $6\sqrt{7}$

17. $4 + \dfrac{10\sqrt{5}}{5}$

18. b

19. d

20. $x = 5,\ y = 5,\ z = 5$

1. Find the limit.

$$\lim_{(x,y)\to(4,-8)} x^5 + 2x^3 y - 5xy^2$$

Select the correct answer.

   a.   -1,280
   b.   1,024
   c.   3,328
   d.   -2,304
   e.   -2,256

2. Use implicit differentiation to find $\partial z / \partial x$.

$$6x^2 + 3y^2 - 2z^2 = 2x(y+z)$$

3. Use implicit differentiation to find $\partial z / \partial x$ and $\partial z / \partial y$.

$$x\,y\,z = \sin(x+y+z)$$

4. Find all the second partial derivatives.

$$f(x,y) = x^4 - 8x^2 y^3$$

5. Find the indicated partial derivative.

$$u = x^a y^b z^c; \quad \frac{\partial^6 u}{\partial x \partial y^2 \partial z^3}, \quad a > 1, \ b > 2, \ c > 3$$

6. Find an equation of the tangent plane to the given surface at the specified point.

$$z = \sqrt{192 - x^2 - 8y^2}, \quad (12, \ 2, \ -3)$$

7. Use the linearization $L(x, y)$ of the function.

$$f(x,y) = \sqrt{9 - x^2 - 2y^2} \text{ at } (-1, 1) \text{ to approximate } f(-0.91, \ 0.82).$$

8. The wind-chill index I is the perceived temperature when the actual temperature is T and the wind speed is v so we can write $I = f(T, v)$. The following table of values is an excerpt from a table compiled by the National Atmospheric and Oceanic Administration. Use the table to find a linear approximation $L(T, v)$ to the wind chill index function when T is near $16°$ C and v is near 30 kmh.

T ↓	v → 10	20	30	40	50
20	18	17	14	13	12
16	15	12	10	7	8
12	8	6	2	2	-1
8	5	1	-2	-6	-7

9. If $z = x^2 - xy + 7y^2$ and (x, y) changes from $(2, 1)$ to $(1.95, 1.07)$, find dz.

10. A boundary stripe 2 in. wide is painted around a rectangle whose dimensions are 100 ft by 240 ft. Use differentials to approximate the number of square feet of paint in the stripe.

    Select the correct answer.

    a. $113.23 \ ft^2$
    b. $113.89 \ ft^2$
    c. $113 \ ft^2$
    d. $113.33 \ ft^2$
    e. $113.81 \ ft^2$

11. Find $\dfrac{\partial z}{\partial y}$.

    $xe^{4y} + 4yz + ze^{8x} = 0$

12. Find the direction in which the maximum rate of change of f at the given point occurs.

$f(x, y) = \sin(xy), \quad (1, \ 0)$

Select the correct answer.

a. $\left\langle 0, \ 1 \right\rangle$

b. $\left\langle \dfrac{\sqrt{2}}{2}, \ \dfrac{\sqrt{2}}{2} \right\rangle$

c. $\left\langle 1, \ 0 \right\rangle$

d. $\left\langle \dfrac{\sqrt{2}}{2}, \ \sqrt{2} \right\rangle$

e. $\left\langle 1, \ \sqrt{3} \right\rangle$

13. Find the maximum rate of change of f at the given point.

$f(x, y, z) - x^4 y^3 z^2, \quad (1, \ -1, \ 1)$

14. Find the absolute minimum value of the function f on the set D. D is the region bounded by the parabola $y = x^2$ and the line $y = 4$.

$f(x, y) = 5 + 8xy - 2x - 4y$

Select the correct answer.

a. -76
b. -75
c. -71
d. 0
e. 4

15. Find the absolute maximum value of the function f on the set D.

$D = \left\{ (x, y) \mid \ |x| \leq \ 1, \ |y| \leq \ 1 \right\}$

$f(x, y) = 3x^2 + 8y^2 + 10x^2 y + 9$

16. Use *Lagrange multipliers* to find the minimum value of the function subject to the given constraints.

$f(x, y, z, t) = 9x + 9y + 9z + 9t, \quad 9(x^2 + y^2 + z^2 + t^2) = 1$

17. Use Lagrange multipliers to find the maximum value of the function subject to the given constraints.

$$f(x, y, z) = x + 3y, \quad x + y + z = 2, \quad y^2 + z^2 = 25$$

Select the correct answer.

a. $f_{max} = 2 + \dfrac{25\sqrt{5}}{5}$

b. $f_{max} = 2 - 5\sqrt{5}$

c. $f_{max} = 2 + 6\sqrt{5}$

d. $f_{max} = 7 - 5\sqrt{19}$

e. $f_{max} = 2 + \sqrt{5}$

18. Use Lagrange multipliers to find the maximum and minimum values of the function
$f(x, y, z) = 5x - y - 5z$ subject to the constraints $x + 2y - z = 0$ and $x^2 + 4y^2 = 1$.

19. Use *Lagrange multipliers* to find the shortest distance from the point (1, 5, -5) to the plane
$2x + 9y - 3z = 6$.

20. Use *Lagrange multipliers* to find the dimensions of the rectangular box with largest volume if the total
surface area is given as 96 cm^2.

1. a

2. $\dfrac{6x - y - z}{x + 2z}$

3. $\dfrac{-(yz - \cos(x + y + z))}{(xy - \cos(x + y + z))}$, $\dfrac{-(xz - \cos(x + y + z))}{(xy - \cos(x + y + z))}$

4. $12x^2 - 16y^3$, $-48xy^2$, $-48xy^2$, $-48x^2 y$

5. $ab(b - 1)c(c - 1)(c - 2)x^{a-1}y^{b-2}z^{c-3}$

6. $z = -3x - 4y + 41$

7. 2.63

8. $L = -6.5 + 1.5T - 0.25v$

9. $dz = 0.69$

10. d

11. $\dfrac{\partial z}{\partial y} = -\dfrac{4xe^{4y} + 4z}{4y + e^{8x}}$

12. a

13. 5.385165

14. c

15. 30

16. $2\sqrt{9}$

17. a

18. $f_{\min} = \dfrac{-\sqrt{121}}{2}$, $f_{\max} = \dfrac{\sqrt{121}}{2}$

19. $\dfrac{28\sqrt{94}}{47}$

20. $x = 4$, $y = 4$, $z = 4$

1. Find an approximation for the integral.

$$\iint\limits_{R} (4x - 5y^2)\ dA$$

Use a double Riemann sum with $m = n = 2$ and the sample point in the upper right corner to approximate the double integral, where $R = \left\{\ (x, y)\ \mid\ 0 \le x \le 8,\ 0 \le y \le 4\ \right\}$.

2. Find $\displaystyle\int_0^5 f(x, y)\ dx$, if $f(x, y) = 8x + 3x^2 y$.

3. Calculate the iterated integral.

$$\int_1^4 \int_0^3 (1 + 2xy)\ dxdy$$

4. Calculate the iterated integral.

$$\int_0^6 \int_0^{10} \sqrt{x + y}\ dxdy$$

Round the answer to the nearest hundredth.

5. Find the average value of $f(x, y) = x^2 y$ over the rectangle with vertices $(-4,\ 0),\ (-4,\ 3),\ (4,\ 3),\ (4,\ 0)$.

Round the answer to the nearest hundredth.

6. Evaluate the iterated integral.

$$\int_1^4 \int_y^4 xy\ dxdy$$

7. Evaluate the double integral.

$$\iint\limits_{D} x \cos y\ dA$$

D is bounded by $y = 0$, $y = x^2$, and $x = 2$.

8. Evaluate the integral by changing to polar coordinates.

$$\iint\limits_D e^{-x^2-y^2}\, dA$$

D is the region bounded by the semicircle $x = \sqrt{16 - y^2}$ and the y-axis.

9. Find the region E for which the triple integral $\iiint\limits_E (1 - 9x^2 - 5y^2 - 5z^2)\, dV$ is a maximum.

10. A cylindrical drill with radius 1 is used to bore a hole through the center of a sphere of radius 5. Find the volume of the ring-shaped solid that remains. Please round the answer to the nearest hundredth.

11. An agricultural sprinkler distributes water in a circular pattern of radius 100 ft. It supplies water to a depth of e^{-r} feet per hour at a distance of r feet from the sprinkler. What is the total amount of water supplied per hour to the region inside the circle of radius 10 feet centered at the sprinkler?

Round the answer to the nearest thousandth.

12. Find the mass of the lamina that occupies the region D and has the given density function, if D is bounded by the parabola $x = y^2$ and the line $y = x - 2$.

$$\rho(x, y) = 7$$

13. Find the mass of the lamina that occupies the region D and has the given density function:

$$R = \left\{ (x, y) \mid 0 \le x \le \frac{\pi}{2},\ 0 \le y \le \cos x \right\} \quad \rho(x, y) = 10x$$

Round the answer to the nearest hundredth.

14. Find the area of the part of the plane $6x + 5y + z = 9$ that lies inside the cylinder $x^2 + y^2 = 49$.

15. Find the area of the surface.

$$z = \frac{2}{3}\left(x^{3/2} + y^{3/2} \right),\ 0 \le x \le 3,\ 0 \le y \le 3$$

Round the result to the nearest thousandth.

16. Find the area of the surface. The part of the sphere $x^2 + y^2 + z^2 = a^2$ that lies within the cylinder $x^2 + y^2 = ax$ and above xy - plane.

17. Use a triple integral to find the volume of the solid bounded by the cylinder $x = y^2$ and the planes $z = 0$ and $x + z = 4$.

    Round the answer to the nearest tenth.

18. Express the volume of the wedge in the first octant that is cut from the cylinder $y^2 + z^2 = 3$ by the planes $y = x$ and $x = 4$ as an iterated integral with respect to z, then to y, then to x.

19. Express the integral $\int_0^4 \int_y^4 \int_0^y f(x, y, z) \; dzdxdy$ in the form $\int_a^b \int_{u(x)}^{v(x)} \int_{c(x,y)}^{d(x,y)} f \; dxdzdy$.

20. The joint density function for random variables X, Y and Z is $f(x, y, z) = C xyz$ for $0 \le x \le 2$, $0 \le y \le 4$, $0 \le z \le 1$, and $f(x, y, z) = 0$ otherwise. Find the value of the constant C.

    Round the answer to the nearest thousandth.

1. -832

2. $100 + 125y$

3. 76.5

4. 165.22

5. 8

6. 225/8

7. $\dfrac{1 - \cos(4)}{2}$

8. $\dfrac{\left(1 - e^{-16}\right)\pi}{2}$

9. $9x^2 + 5y^2 + 5z^2 = 1$

10. 492.5

11. 6.28

12. 63/2

13. 5.71

14. $49\pi\sqrt{62}$

15. 17.771

16. $a^2(\pi - 2)$

17. 17.1

18. $\displaystyle\int_0^4 \int_0^x \int_0^{\sqrt{3-y^2}} dz\,dx\,dy$

19. $\displaystyle\int_0^4 \int_0^y \int_y^4 f\, dx\,dz\,dy$

20. 0.125

1. Find $\int\limits_{0}^{2} f(x, y)\ dx$ if $f(x, y) = 8x + 6x^2 y$.

2. Calculate the iterated integral.

$$\int\limits_{2}^{4}\int\limits_{0}^{3} (3 + 2xy)\ dxdy$$

3. Calculate the iterated integral.

$$\int\limits_{2}^{5}\int\limits_{4}^{5} \left(\frac{x}{y} + \frac{y}{x}\right) dxdy$$

Round the answer to the nearest hundredth.

4. Find the volume of the solid bounded by the surface $z = x\sqrt{3x^2 + 3y}$ and the planes $x = 1,\ x = 0$, $y = 1,\ y = 0$, and $z = 0$.

Round the answer to the nearest hundredth.

5. Find the volume of the solid bounded by the surface $z = 6 + (x - 5)^2 + 4y$ and the planes $x = 3,\ y = 1$ and coordinate planes.

6. Evaluate the double integral.

$$\iint\limits_{D} \frac{3y}{x^2 + 1}\ dA,\ \ D = \left\{\ 0 \le x \le 9,\ 0 \le y \le \sqrt{x}\ \right\}$$

7. Evaluate the double integral.

$$\iint\limits_{D} x\cos y\ dA,$$

D is bounded by $y = 0,\ y = x^2$, and $x = 2$.

8. Evaluate the double integral

$$\iint_D (5x - y) \ dA$$

D is bounded by the circle with center the origin and radius 9.

9. Evaluate the integral by reversing the order of integration.

$$\int_0^1 \int_{\arctan y}^{\pi/2} \cos x \sqrt{3 + \cos^2 x} \ dxdy$$

10. Compute $\iint_D \sqrt{25 - x^2 - y^2} \ dA$, where D is the disk $x^2 + y^2 \leq 25$, by first identifying the integral as the volume of a solid.

11. Use polar coordinates to find the volume of the solid under the paraboloid $z = x^2 + y^2$ and above the disk $x^2 + y^2 \leq 4$.

12. Find the exact area of the surface $z = x^2 + 2y$, $0 \leq x \leq 1$, $0 \leq y \leq 2$.

13. A cylindrical drill with radius 3 is used to bore a hole through the center of a sphere of radius 5. Find the volume of the ring-shaped solid that remains. Please round the answer to the nearest hundredth.

14. Evaluate the iterated integral by converting to polar coordinates.

$$\int_0^1 \int_0^{\sqrt{1-x^2}} e^{x^2+y^2} \ dydx$$

Round the answer to the nearest hundredth.

15. An agricultural sprinkler distributes water in a circular pattern of radius 100 ft. It supplies water to a depth of e^{-r} feet per hour at a distance of r feet from the sprinkler. What is the total amount of water supplied per hour to the region inside the circle of radius 85 feet centered at the sprinkler?

   Round the answer to the nearest thousandth.

16. Find the mass of the lamina that occupies the region D and has the given density function, if D is bounded by the parabola $x = y^2$ and the line $y = x - 2$.

   $\rho(x, y) = 7$

17. The joint density function for a pair of random variables X and Y is given.

   $$f(x, y) = \begin{cases} Cx(1 + y), & 0 \le x \le 2, \ 0 \le y \le 4 \\ 0, & \text{otherwise} \end{cases}$$

   Find the value of the constant C.

18. Find the area of the part of the plane $6x + 6y + z = 6$ that lies in the first octant.

19. Evaluate the triple integral.

   $$\iiint\limits_{E} 5x \ dV$$

   $$E = \left\{ (x, y, z) \ | \ 0 \le y \le 3, \ 0 \le x \le \sqrt{9 - y^2}, \ 0 \le z \le y \right\}$$

   Round to the nearest tenth.

20. Evaluate the triple integral.

   $$\iiint\limits_{E} 3xy \ dV$$

   E lies under the plane $z = 5 + x + y$ and above the region in the xy - plane bounded by the curves $y = \sqrt{x}$, $y = 0$, and $x = 4$.

   Round the answer to the nearest tenth.

1. $16 + 16y$

2. 72

3. 6.47

4. 0.84

5. 63

6. $0.75 \ln(82)$

7. $\dfrac{1 - \cos(4)}{2}$

8. 0

9. $\dfrac{-1}{3}(3^{1.5} - 4^{1.5})$

10. $\dfrac{250}{3}\pi$

11. $\dfrac{16\pi}{2}$

12. $3 + \dfrac{5}{4}\ln(5)$

13. 269.08

14. 1.35

15. 6.283

16. $63/2$

17. $C = \dfrac{1}{24}$

18. $\dfrac{36\sqrt{73}}{72}$

19. 50.625

20. 292.6

1. Estimate the volume of the solid that lies above the square $R = [0, \ 4] \times [0, \ 4]$ and below the elliptic paraboloid $f(x, y) = 68 - 2x^2 - 2y^2$.

   Divide R into four equal squares and use the Midpoint rule.

   Select the correct answer.

   a. 836
   b. 778
   c. 768
   d. 192
   e. 762

2. Evaluate the double integral by first identifying it as the volume of a solid.

   $$\iint\limits_{R} (15 - 2x) \ dA$$

   $$R = \left\{ (x, y) \mid 3 \le x \le 7, \ 3 \le y \le 8 \right\}$$

   Select the correct answer.

   a. 200
   b. -300
   c. 100
   d. -100
   e. -200

3. Calculate the double integral.

   $$\iint\limits_{R} (3x^2 y^3 - 4x^4) \ dA, \quad R = \left\{ (x, y) \mid 0 \le x \le 4, \ 0 \le y \le 4 \right\}$$

   Select the correct answer.

   a. 409.6
   b. 273.07
   c. 819.2
   d. 204.8
   e. 212.8

4. Find the volume of the solid bounded by the surface $z = 5 + (x-4)^2 + 2y$ and the planes $x = 3, y = 4$ and coordinate planes.

   Select the correct answer.

   a. $V = 384$
   b. $V = 768$
   c. $V = 192$
   d. $V = 576$
   e. $V = 256$

5. Evaluate the iterated integral.

   $$\int_1^3 \int_y^3 xy \; dx dy$$

   Select the correct answer.

   a.   18.1
   b.   8
   c.   5
   d.   10
   e.   10.3

6. Find the volume under $z = x^5 + y^5$ and above the region bounded by $y = x^2$ and $x = y^2$.

   Select the correct answer.

   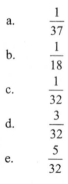

   a. $\dfrac{1}{37}$

   b. $\dfrac{1}{18}$

   c. $\dfrac{1}{32}$

   d. $\dfrac{3}{32}$

   e. $\dfrac{5}{32}$

7. For which of the following regions would you use rectangular coordinates?

    Select the correct answer.

    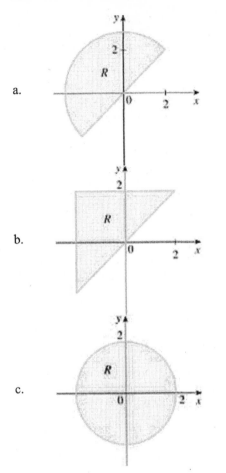

    a.

    b.

    c.

8. Use polar coordinates to find the volume of the solid under the paraboloid $z = x^2 + y^2$ and above the disk $x^2 + y^2 \leq 9$.

    Select the correct answer.

    a. 40.5π
    b. -7.5π
    c. 68.5π
    d. 140.5π
    e. -43.5π

9. Use polar coordinates to find the volume of the solid bounded by the paraboloid $z = 7 - 6x^2 - 6y^2$ and the plane $z = 1$.

   Select the correct answer.

   a. 13π
   b. 6π
   c. 4.5π
   d. 2π
   e. 3π

10. Evaluate the iterated integral by converting to polar coordinates.

$$\int_{-2}^{2} \int_{0}^{\sqrt{4-y^2}} (x^2 + y^2)^{3/2} \, dx \, dy$$

   Select the correct answer.

   a.   20.11
   b.   28.67
   c.   11.03
   d.   10.52
   e.   19.65

11. A swimming pool is circular with a 20-ft diameter. The depth is constant along east-west lines and increases linearly from 4 ft at the south end to 9 ft at the north end. Find the volume of water in the pool.

   Select the correct answer.

   a. $650\pi \ ft^3$
   b. $600\pi \ ft^3$
   c. $696.5\pi \ ft^3$
   d. $628\pi \ ft^3$
   e. $714.5\pi \ ft^3$

12. Find the center of mass of a lamina in the shape of an isosceles right triangle with equal sides of length $a = 5$ if the density at any point is proportional to the square of the distance from the vertex opposite the hypotenuse. Assume the vertex opposite the hypotenuse is located at (0, 0), and that the sides are along the positive axes.

   Select the correct answer.

   a.   (5, 3)
   b.   (2, 2)
   c.   (2, 4)
   d.   (3, 3)
   e.   none of these

13. Find the area of the surface. The part of the surface $z = x + y^2$ that lies above the triangle with vertices $(0, 0)$, $(2, 2)$, and $(0, 2)$.

Select the correct answer.

a. $A(S) = \dfrac{9}{\sqrt{2}} - \dfrac{1}{3\sqrt{2}}$

b. $A(S) = \dfrac{\sqrt{6}}{2} - \dfrac{1}{3\sqrt{2}}$

c. $A(S) = \dfrac{163\sqrt{163} - 1}{3\sqrt{2}}$

d. $A(S) = \dfrac{43\sqrt{129}}{\sqrt{2}} - \dfrac{1}{3\sqrt{2}}$

e. $A(S) = \dfrac{43\sqrt{129}}{\sqrt{2}}$

14. Find the area of the part of hyperbolic paraboloid $z = y^2 - x^2$ that lies between the cylinders $x^2 + y^2 = 1$ and $x^2 + y^2 = 16$.

Select the correct answer.

a. $\pi \dfrac{65\sqrt{65} - 5\sqrt{5}}{3}$

b. $\pi \dfrac{\sqrt{65} - \sqrt{5}}{6}$

c. $\pi \dfrac{65\sqrt{65} - 5\sqrt{5}}{6}$

d. $\pi \dfrac{\sqrt{65} - \sqrt{5}}{3}$

e. $\pi \dfrac{32\sqrt{65} - 4\sqrt{5}}{3}$

15. Find the area of the surface.

$$z = \dfrac{2}{3}\left(x^{\frac{3}{2}} + y^{\frac{3}{2}} \right), \quad 0 \le x \le 5, \ 0 \le y \le 3$$

Select the correct answer.

a. 36.238
b. 38.031
c. 31.017
d. 29.973
e. 33.018

16. Find the area of the surface. The part of the sphere $x^2 + y^2 + z^2 = 64$ that lies above the plane $z = 3$.

Select the correct answer.

    a. $A(S) = 80 - \pi$

    b. $A(S) = 80\pi$

    c. $A(S) = \pi$

    d. $A(S) = \dfrac{\pi}{80}$

    e. $A(S) = 80$

17. Find the area of the surface. The part of the sphere $x^2 + y^2 + z^2 = b^2$ that lies within the cylinder $x^2 + y^2 = bx$ and above xy - plane.

Select the correct answer.

    a. $A(S) = 2b^2$

    b. $A(S) = b^2\pi$

    c. $A(S) = b^2(\pi - 2)$

    d. $A(S) = 2\pi$

    e. $A(S) = 2\pi - b^2$

18. Evaluate the integral.

$$\int_0^2 \int_1^3 \int_0^{1-z^2} 5ze^{3y}\,dx\,dz\,dy$$

Select the correct answer.

    a.   -10,731.4

    b.   -9,658.3

    c.   -53,657.2

    d.   9,658.3

    e.   53,657.2

19. Use a triple integral to find the volume of the solid bounded by the cylinder $x = y^2$ and the planes $z = 0$ and $x + z = 3$.

Select the correct answer.

   a.   2.5
   b.   11.3
   c.   8.3
   d.   15.3
   e.   18.3

20. Find the Jacobian of the transformation.

$x = 5\alpha \sin \beta, \quad y = 4\alpha \cos \beta$

Select the correct answer.

   a. $\dfrac{\partial(x, y)}{\partial(\alpha, \beta)} = 9\alpha$

   b. $\dfrac{\partial(x, y)}{\partial(\alpha, \beta)} = -20\alpha \sin \beta \cos \beta$

   c. $\dfrac{\partial(x, y)}{\partial(\alpha, \beta)} = -20\alpha$

   d. $\dfrac{\partial(x, y)}{\partial(\alpha, \beta)} = -\alpha$

   e. $\dfrac{\partial(x, y)}{\partial(\alpha, \beta)} = 36\alpha$

1. c
2. c
3. c
4. c
5. b
6. b
7. b
8. a
9. e
10. a
11. a
12. b
13. a
14. c
15. e
16. b
17. c
18. a
19. c
20. c   .

1. Use the transformation $x = \sqrt{5}u - \sqrt{\frac{5}{3}}v$, $y = \sqrt{5}u + \sqrt{\frac{5}{3}}v$ to evaluate the integral

$\iint\limits_{R} \left(x^2 - xy + y^2\right) dA$, where R is the region bounded by the ellipse $x^2 - xy + y^2 = 5$.

Select the correct answer.

a. $\dfrac{100\pi}{3^{3/2}}$

b. $\dfrac{25}{\sqrt{3}}$

c. $\dfrac{25\pi}{\sqrt{3}}$

d. $\dfrac{5\pi^2}{\sqrt{3}}$

e. $\dfrac{5\pi}{\sqrt{3}}$

2. A swimming pool is circular with a 20-ft diameter. The depth is constant along east-west lines and increases linearly from 4 ft at the south end to 9 ft at the north end. Find the volume of water in the pool.

Select the correct answer.

a. $650\pi \ ft^3$

b. $600\pi \ ft^3$

c. $696.5\pi \ ft^3$

d. $628\pi \ ft^3$

e. $714.5\pi \ ft^3$

3. Use a triple integral to find the volume of the solid bounded by the cylinder $x = y^2$ and the planes $z = 0$ and $x + z = 3$.

Select the correct answer.

a. 2.5
b. 11.3
c. 8.3
d. 18.3
e. 15.3

4. Find the volume under $z = x^5 + y^5$ and above the region bounded by $y = x^2$ and $x = y^2$.

    Select the correct answer.

    a. $\dfrac{1}{36}$

    b. $\dfrac{1}{18}$

    c. $\dfrac{1}{32}$

    d. $\dfrac{3}{32}$

    e. $\dfrac{5}{36}$

5. Use polar coordinates to find the volume of the solid bounded by the paraboloid $z = 7 - 6x^2 - 6y^2$ and the plane $z = 1$.

    Select the correct answer.

    a. 13π
    b. 6π
    c. 4.5π
    d. 2π
    e. 3π

6. Use a computer algebra system to find the value of the integral.

    $$\iint\limits_{R} x^5 y^3 e^{xy} \, dA \ , \quad R = [0,\ 2] \times [0,\ 2]$$

    Select the correct answer.

    a. 815.97
    b. 13,045.96
    c. 791.97
    d. 12,067.96
    e. 706.97

7.   Find the volume of the solid bounded by the surface $z = 5 + (x-4)^2 + 2y$ and the planes $x = 3, y = 4$ and coordinate planes.

Choose your answer from below.

   a. $V = 384$
   b. $V = 768$
   c. $V = 192$
   d. $V = 576$
   e. $V = 525$

8.   Find the area of the surface. The part of the sphere $x^2 + y^2 + z^2 = 64$ that lies above the plane $z = 3$.

Select the correct answer.

   a. $A(S) = 80 - \pi$
   b. $A(S) = 80\pi$
   c. $A(S) = \pi$
   d. $A(S) = \dfrac{\pi}{80}$
   e. $A(S) = \dfrac{7\pi}{80}$

9.   Find the Jacobian of the transformation.

   $x = 5\alpha \sin \beta, \quad y = 4\alpha \cos \beta$

Select the correct answer.

   a. $\dfrac{\partial(x, y)}{\partial(\alpha, \beta)} = 9\alpha$

   b. $\dfrac{\partial(x, y)}{\partial(\alpha, \beta)} = -20\alpha \sin \beta$

   c. $\dfrac{\partial(x, y)}{\partial(\alpha, \beta)} = -20\alpha$

   d. $\dfrac{\partial(x, y)}{\partial(\alpha, \beta)} = -2\alpha$

   e. $\dfrac{\partial(x, y)}{\partial(\alpha, \beta)} = \alpha$

10. Find the area of the surface.

$$z = \frac{2}{3}\left(x^{3/2} + y^{3/2}\right), \ 0 \le x \le 5, \ 0 \le y \le 3$$

Select the correct answer.

   a.   36.238
   b.   38.031
   c.   31.017
   d.   29.973
   e.   33.018

11. Evaluate the integral.

$$\int_{0}^{2} \int_{1}^{3} \int_{0}^{1-z^2} 5ze^{3y} \, dx\,dz\,dy$$

Select the correct answer.

   a.   -10,731.4
   b.   -9,658.3
   c.   -53,657.2
   d.   9,658.3
   e.   53,657.2

12. Evaluate the double integral by first identifying it as the volume of a solid.

$$\iint_R (15 - 2x) \, dA \ \text{where} \ R = \left\{ (x, y) \ | \ 3 \le x \le 7, \ 3 \le y \le 8 \right\}$$

Select the correct answer.

   a.   200
   b.   -300
   c.   100
   d.   -100
   e.   -200

13. For which of the following regions would you use rectangular coordinates?

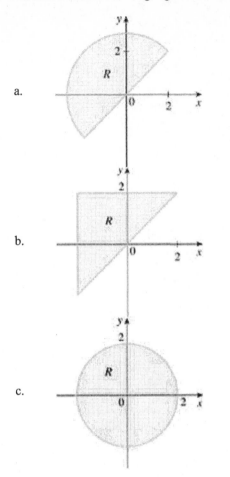

a.

b.

c.

14. Use cylindrical or spherical coordinates, whichever seems more appropriate, to evaluate the integral $\iiint\limits_{E} z \, dV$ where E lies above the paraboloid $z = x^2 + y^2$ and below the plane $z = 6y$.

Select the correct answer.

   a.   1,956.21
   b.   1,944.78
   c.   1,712.31
   d.   1,807.13
   e.   1,908.52

15. Calculate the double integral.

$$\iint_R (3x^2y^3 - 4x^4)\ dA, \quad R = \left\{ (x, y) \mid 0 \le x \le 4,\ 0 \le y \le 4 \right\}$$

Select the correct answer.

a.   409.6
b.   273.07
c.   819.2
d.   204.8
e.   215.8

16. Use polar coordinates to find the volume of the solid under the paraboloid $z = x^2 + y^2$ and above the disk $x^2 + y^2 \le 9$.

Select the correct answer.

a. 40.5π
b. -7.5π
c. 68.5π
d. 140.5π
e. -43.5π

17. Evaluate the iterated integral by converting to polar coordinates.

$$\int_{-2}^{2} \int_{0}^{\sqrt{4-y^2}} (x^2 + y^2)^{3/2}\ dx\,dy$$

Select the correct answer.

a.   20.11
b.   28.67
c.   11.03
d.   10.52
e.   19.65

18. Evaluate the iterated integral.

$$\int_1^3 \int_y^3 xy \ dxdy$$

Select the correct answer.

a.   18.1
b.   8
c.   5
d.   10
e.   10.3

19. Find the area of the surface. The part of the sphere $x^2 + y^2 + z^2 = b^2$ that lies within the cylinder $x^2 + y^2 = bx$ and above the xy - plane.

Select the correct answer.

a. $A(S) = 2b^2$

b. $A(S) = b^2 \pi$

c. $A(S) = b^2 (\pi - 2)$

d. $A(S) = 2\pi$

e. $A(S) = 2b\pi$

20. Use a computer algebra system to find the moment of inertia I_0 of the lamina that occupies the region D and has the density function $\rho(x, y) = 3xy$, if $D = \left\{ (x, y) \mid 0 \le x \le \pi, \ 0 \le y \le \sin(x) \right\}$.

Select the correct answer.

a.   14.1
b.   34.1
c.   24.1
d.   28.1
e.   none of these

1. c

2. a

3. c

4. b

5. e

6. a

7. c

8. b

9. c

10. e

11. a

12. c

13. b

14. e

15. c

16. a

17. a

18. b

19. c

20. a

1. Estimate the volume of the solid that lies above the square $R = [0, 8] \times [0, 8]$ and below the elliptic paraboloid $f(x, y) = 120 - 3x^2 - 4y^2$.

    Divide R into four equal squares and use the Midpoint Rule.

2. Compute $\iint\limits_{D} \sqrt{16 - x^2 - y^2}\, dA$, where D is the disk $x^2 + y^2 \le 16$, by first identifying the integral as the volume of a solid.

3. Use polar coordinates to find the volume of the solid under the paraboloid $z = x^2 + y^2$ and above the disk $x^2 + y^2 \le 49$.

    Select the correct answer.

    a. $1{,}277.5\pi$
    b. $1{,}205.5\pi$
    c. $1{,}200.5\pi$
    d. $1{,}163.5\pi$
    e. $1{,}267.5\pi$

4. Use polar coordinates to find the volume of the sphere of radius 6.

    Select the correct answer.

    b.   824.54
    b.   924.54
    c.   913.26
    d.   964.54
    e.   904.78

5. A cylindrical drill with radius 5 is used to bore a hole through the center of a sphere of radius 7. Find the volume of the ring-shaped solid that remains.

    Round the answer to the nearest hundredth.

6. Evaluate the iterated integral by converting to polar coordinates.

    $$\int_0^1 \int_0^{\sqrt{1-x^2}} e^{x^2+y^2}\, dy\, dx$$

    Round the answer to the nearest hundredth.

7. Find the center of mass of the lamina that occupies the region D and has the given density function, if D is bounded by the parabola $y = 64 - x^2$ and the x-axis.

$\rho(x, y) = y$

Select the correct answer.

a. (0, 36.57)
b. (16, 56.57)
c. (9, 40.57)
d. (8, 46.57)
e. none of these

8. Find the area of the surface.

The part of the sphere $x^2 + y^2 + z^2 = 9$ that lies above the plane $z = 2$.

9. Find the area of the part of the sphere $x^2 + y^2 + z^2 = 4z$ that lies inside the paraboloid $z = x^2 + y^2$.

10. Find, to four decimal places, the area of the part of the surface $z = 1 + x^2 y^2$ that lies above the disk $x^2 + y^2 \le 1$.

Select the correct answer.

a. $A(S) = 4.6447$
b. $A(S) = 3.3213$
c. $A(S) = 2.0979$
d. $A(S) = 3.4447$
e. $A(S) = 3.8747$

11. Evaluate the integral.

$$\int_1^3 \int_1^4 \int_1^{1-z^2} 5ze^{3y} \, dx\,dz\,dy$$

Round the answer to the nearest tenth.

12. Find the moment of inertia about the y - axis for a cube of constant density 3 and side length 5 if one vertex is located at the origin and three edges lie along the coordinate axes.

Round the answer to the nearest tenth.

13. Find the region E for which the triple integral $\iiint\limits_{E} (1 - 4x^2 - 5y^2 - 6z^2)\, dV$ is a maximum.

14. Use cylindrical coordinates to evaluate the triple integral $\iiint\limits_{E} y\, dV$ where E is the solid that lies

between the cylinders $x^2 + y^2 = 3$ and $x^2 + y^2 = 7$ above the xy-plane and below the plane $z = x + 4$.

Select the correct answer.

a. 3.4
b. 9.19
c. 0
d. 8.57
e. 0.54

15. Use spherical coordinates to evaluate the triple integral $\iiint\limits_{E} xe^{\left(x^2 + y^2 + z^2\right)^2}\, dV$ where E is the solid that

lies between the spheres $x^2 + y^2 + z^2 = 9$ and $x^2 + y^2 + z^2 = 16$ in the first octant.

16. Use spherical coordinates to find the volume of the solid that lies within the sphere $x^2 + y^2 + z^2 = 9$ above the xy-plane and below the cone $z = \sqrt{x^2 + y^2}$.

Round the answer to the nearest hundredth.

17. Use spherical coordinates to find the moment of inertia of the solid homogeneous hemisphere of radius 3 and density 1 about a diameter of its base.

Select the correct answer.

a. 203.58
b. 198.08
c. 205.13
d. 213.5
e. 195.22

18. Use cylindrical or spherical coordinates, whichever seems more appropriate, to evaluate
$\iiint\limits_{E} z \, dV$ where E lies above the paraboloid $z = x^2 + y^2$ and below the plane $z = 4y$.

Select the correct answer.

a.   160.28
b.   176.38
c.   167.55
d.   175.93
e.   175.37

19. Find the Jacobian of the transformation.

$$x = \frac{u}{2u + 7v}, \quad y = \frac{v}{4u - 8v}$$

20. Use cylindrical coordinates to evaluate $\iiint\limits_{E} \sqrt{x^2 + y^2} \, dV$ where E is the region that lies inside the cylinder $x^2 + y^2 = 4$ and between the planes $z = -4$ and $z = 7$.

Select the correct answer.

a.   252.61
b.   184.31
c.   195
d.   168.58
e.   126.99

ANSWER KEY

Stewart - Calculus ET 5e Chapter 15 Form E

1. -1280

2. $\dfrac{128}{3}\pi$

3. c

4. e

5. 492.5

6. 1.35

7. a

8. 6π

9. 4π

10. b

11. -858818.6

12. 6250

13. $4x^2 + 5y^2 + 6z^2 = 1$

14. c

15. $\dfrac{\pi}{16}\left(e^{256} - e^{81}\right)$

16. 39.99

17. a

18. c

19. 0

20. b

1. Let V be the volume of the solid that lies under the graph of $f(x, y) = \sqrt{73 - x^2 - y^2}$ and above the rectangle given by $R = \left\{ (x, y) \mid 2 \le x \le 4, \ 2 \le y \le 6 \right\}$.

    Use the lines $x = 3$ and $y = 5$ to divide R into subrectangles. Find the Riemann sum using lower left corners.

    Select the correct answer.

    a. 60.3
    b. 6.63
    c. 23.24
    d. 84.49
    e. 29.24

2. Find the volume of the "bumpy sphere" - the family of surfaces $\rho = 1 + \dfrac{1}{5} \sin \theta \sin n\phi$ with $m = 5$ and $n = 3$.

    Round the answer to the nearest hundredth.

3. Evaluate the integral by making an appropriate change of variables.

    $\displaystyle\iint\limits_{R} e^{x+y} \, dA$, where R is given by the inequality $|x| + |y| \le 3$.

    Round the answer to the nearest hundredth.

4. Calculate the double integral.

    $\displaystyle\iint\limits_{R} \frac{4 + x^2}{1 + y^2} \, dA, \quad R = \left\{ (x, y) \mid 0 \le x \le 9, \ 0 \le y \le 1 \right\}$

    Round the answer to the nearest hundredth.

5. Calculate the double integral.

    $\displaystyle\iint\limits_{R} x \sin(x + y) \, dA, \quad R = \left[0, \ \frac{\pi}{4} \right] \times \left[0, \ \frac{\pi}{6} \right]$

    Round the answer to the nearest hundredth.

6. Calculate the double integral.

$$\iint\limits_{R} xye^{y} \ dA, \quad R = \left\{ (x, y) \mid 0 \le x \le 1, \ 0 \le y \le 1 \right\}$$

Please round the answer to the nearest hundredth.

7. Find the volume of the solid in the first octant bounded by the cylinder $z = 9 - y^2$ and the plane $x = 1$.

8. Use the given transformation to evaluate the integral.

$$\iint\limits_{R} (x + y) \ dA, \text{ where } R \text{ is the square with vertices } (0, 0), (2, 3), (3, -2), (5, 1) \text{ and}$$

$$x = 2u + 3v, \quad y = 3u - 2v$$

9. A lamina occupies the part of the disk $x^2 + y^2 \le 25$ in the first quadrant. Find its center of mass if the density at any point is proportional to its distance from the x-axis.

10. Evaluate the iterated integral.

$$\int\limits_{1}^{5} \int\limits_{y}^{5} xy \ dxdy$$

11. Evaluate the double integral.

$$\iint\limits_{R} x \cos y \ dA, \text{ where } D \text{ is bounded by } y = 0, \ y = x^2, \text{ and } x = 2.$$

12. Evaluate the double integral.

$$\iint\limits_{D} y^3 \ dA, \text{ where } D \text{ is the triangular region with vertices } (0, 1), (7, 0) \text{ and } (1, 1).$$

13. Find the volume bounded by the cylinders $x^2 + y^2 = 25$ and $y^2 + z^2 = 25$.

14. Evaluate the integral by reversing the order of integration.

$$\int_0^1 \int_{4y}^4 e^{x^2} \, dx \, dy$$

15. Compute $\displaystyle\iint_D \sqrt{4 - x^2 - y^2} \, dA$, where D is the disk $x^2 + y^2 \le 4$, by first identifying the integral as the volume of a solid.

16. Evaluate the integral by changing to polar coordinates.

$\displaystyle\iint_D e^{-x^2 - y^2} \, dA$, where D is the region bounded by the semicircle $x = \sqrt{4 - y^2}$ and the y-axis.

17. Use polar coordinates to find the volume of the solid inside the cylinder $x^2 + y^2 = 9$ and the ellipsoid $2x^2 + 2y^2 + z^2 = 36$.

   Select the correct answer.

   a.   260.31
   b.   301.74
   c.   261.29
   d.   292.45
   e.   284.22

18. Find the Jacobian of the transformation.

   $x = 6uv, \quad y = 4vw, \quad z = 5uw$

19. Find the mass of the lamina that occupies the region D and has the given density function, if D is bounded by the parabola $x = y^2$ and the line $y = x - 2$.

$\rho(x, y) = 3$

Select the correct answer.

a. $\dfrac{27}{2}$

b. $\dfrac{9}{2}$

c. $\dfrac{3}{2}$

d. $\dfrac{7}{2}$

e. none of those

20. Find the area of the surface. The part of the surface $z = 9 - x^2 - y^2$ that lies above the xy - plane.

Select the correct answer.

a. $A(S) = \dfrac{1}{6}(37\sqrt{37} - 1)$

b. $A(S) = \dfrac{\pi}{6}(37\sqrt{37} - 1)$

c. $A(S) = \dfrac{\pi}{3}(37\sqrt{37} - 1)$

d. $A(S) = \dfrac{\pi}{3}(9\sqrt{7} - 1)$

e. $A(S) = \dfrac{\pi}{6}(3\sqrt{37} - 1)$

1. a

2. 4.32

3. 60.11

4. 219.13

5. 0.11

6. 0.5

7. 18

8. 39

9. $\left(\dfrac{15}{8}, \dfrac{15\pi}{16} \right)$

10. 72

11. $\dfrac{1 - \cos(4)}{2}$

12. $\dfrac{1}{5}$

13. 666.67

14. $\dfrac{e^{16} - 1}{8}$

15. $\dfrac{16}{3}\pi$

16. $\dfrac{\left(1 - e^{-4}\right)\pi}{2}$

17. d

18. $240uvw$

19. a

20. b

1. Evaluate the double integral by first identifying it as the volume of a solid.

$$\iint\limits_{R} (2-4x)\ dA, \qquad R = \left\{ (x,y) \mid 2 \le x \le 7,\ 3 \le y \le 7 \right\}$$

Select the correct answer.

   a.   -640
   b.   -320
   c.   320
   d.   640
   e.   960

2. Find $\displaystyle\int_{0}^{2} f(x,y)\ dx$, if $f(x,y) = 2x + 6x^2 y$.

3. Calculate the iterated integral.

$$\int_{0}^{6} \int_{0}^{3} \sqrt{x+y}\ dxdy$$

Select the correct answer.

   a.   18.56
   b.   111.38
   c.   37.13
   d.   74.26
   e.   79.26

4. Calculate the iterated integral.

$$\int_{0}^{\ln 4} \int_{0}^{\ln 5} e^{5x-y}\ dxdy$$

5. Calculate the double integral.

$$\iint\limits_{R} (3x^2 y^3 - 5x^4)\ dA, \qquad R = \left\{ (x,y) \mid 0 \le x \le 1,\ 0 \le y \le 4 \right\}$$

Select the correct answer.

   a.   30
   b.   60
   c.   15
   d.   20
   e.   25

6. Calculate the double integral.

$$\iint_R \frac{xy^2}{x^2+4}\, dA, \qquad R = \left\{ (x,y) \mid 0 \le x \le 2,\ -1 \le y \le 1 \right\}$$

Round the answer to the nearest hundredth.

7. Calculate the double integral.

$$\iint_R xye^y\, dA, \qquad R = \left\{ (x,y) \mid 0 \le x \le 2,\ 0 \le y \le 1 \right\}$$

Select the correct answer.

    a.   4.19
    b.   -2
    c.   12.87
    d.   2
    e.   2.57

8. Find the area of the surface.

The part of the surface $z = 1 - x^2 - y^2$ that lies above the xy - plane.

Select the correct answer.

    a. $A(S) = \dfrac{\pi}{6}(5\sqrt{5} - 1)$

    b. $A(S) = \dfrac{\pi}{3}(5\sqrt{5} - 1)$

    c. $A(S) = \dfrac{1}{6}(5\sqrt{5} - 1)$

    d. $A(S) = \dfrac{\pi}{6}(\sqrt{5} - 1)$

    e. $A(S) = \dfrac{\pi}{5}(6\sqrt{5} - 1)$

9. Find the area of the surface. The part of the sphere $x^2 + y^2 + z^2 = 9$ that lies above the plane $z = 1$.

Select the correct answer.

    a. $A(S) = \dfrac{\pi}{12}$

    b. $A(S) = 12\pi$

    c. $A(S) = 12 - \pi$

    d. $A(S) = \pi$

    e. $A(S) = \dfrac{1}{12}$

10. Find the region E for which the triple integral $\iiint\limits_{E} (1 - 2x^2 - 7y^2 - 2z^2)\ dV$ is a maximum.

11. Find the Jacobian of the transformation.

$$x = \frac{u}{10u + 3v}, \quad y = \frac{v}{10u - 3v}$$

12. Find the mass of the solid S bounded by the paraboloid $z = 6x^2 + 6y^2$ and the plane $z = 5$ if S has constant density 3.

   Select the correct answer.

   a.   24.91
   b.   16.25
   c.   19.63
   d.   13.92
   e.   15.07

13. Use spherical coordinates to evaluate the triple integral $\iiint\limits_{E} xe^{(x^2+y^2+z^2)^2}\ dV$ where E is the solid that lies between the spheres $x^2 + y^2 + z^2 = 4$ and $x^2 + y^2 + z^2 = 25$ in the first octant.

14. Use spherical coordinates to find the volume of the solid that lies within the sphere $x^2 + y^2 + z^2 = 16$ above the xy-plane and below the cone $z = \sqrt{x^2 + y^2}$.

   Round the answer to the nearest hundredth.

15. Use cylindrical or spherical coordinates, whichever seems more appropriate, to find the volume of the solid E that lies above the cone $z = \sqrt{x^2 + y^2}$ and below the sphere $x^2 + y^2 + z^2 = 9$.

   Select the correct answer.

   a.   10.57
   b.   16.56
   c.   7.57
   d.   18.56
   e.   17.57

16. Find the Jacobian of the transformation.

$$x = 2\alpha \sin \beta, \quad y = 2\alpha \cos \beta$$

17. Find the Jacobian of the transformation.

$$x = 7u + 7v, \quad y = 4u - 6v$$

Select the correct answer.

a. $\dfrac{\partial(x, y)}{\partial(u, v)} = 73$

b. $\dfrac{\partial(x, y)}{\partial(u, v)} = 70$

c. $\dfrac{\partial(x, y)}{\partial(u, v)} = 14$

d. $\dfrac{\partial(x, y)}{\partial(u, v)} = -14$

e. $\dfrac{\partial(x, y)}{\partial(u, v)} = -70$

18. Use the given transformation to evaluate the integral.

$$\iint\limits_{R} xy \, dA$$, where R is the region in the first quadrant bounded by the lines $y = x, \quad y = 3x$ and the hyperbolas $y = 2, \quad xy = 4$; $x = \dfrac{u}{v}, \quad y = v$.

Select the correct answer.

a. 4.447
b. 5.088
c. 3.296
d. 8.841
e. 9.447

19. Use the given transformation to evaluate the integral.

$$\iint\limits_{R} (x + y) \, dA$$, where R is the square with vertices $(0, 0)$, $(4, 6)$, $(6, -4)$, $(10, 2)$, and

$$x = 4u + 6v, \quad y = 6u - 4v$$

Select the correct answer.

a. 208
b. 52
c. 312
d. 42
e. 343

20. Evaluate the integral by making an appropriate change of variables.

$$\iint\limits_{R} xy \ dA \text{, where } R \text{ is the parallelogram bounded by the lines } 2x - 3y = -5, \ 2x - 3y = -2,$$

$$5x + 2y = -5, \ 5x + 2y = -3.$$

Round the answer to the nearest hundredth.

1. b

2. $4 + 16y$

3. c

4. 486.6

5. b

6. 0.23

7. d

8. a

9. b

10. $2x^2 + 7y^2 + 2z^2 = 1$

11. 0

12. c

13. $\dfrac{\pi}{16}\left(e^{625} - e^{16}\right)$

14. 94.78

15. b

16. -4α

17. e

18. c

19. c

20. -0.16

1. Estimate the volume of the solid that lies above the square $R = [0, 8] \times [0, 8]$ and below the elliptic paraboloid $f(x, y) = 129 - 4x^2 - 5y^2$.

   Divide R into four equal squares and use the Midpoint Rule.

2. Use the Midpoint Rule with four squares of equal size to estimate the triple integral.

   $$\iint\limits_{R} \cos(x^4 + y^4)\ dA, \quad R = \left\{ (x, y) \mid 0 \le x \le 0.75, \ 0 \le y \le 0.75 \right\}$$

   Select the correct answer.

   a.   0.562498
   b.   0
   c.   1.488658
   d.   1.984878
   e.   10.586016

3. Calculate the double integral.

   $$\iint\limits_{R} x \sin(x + y)\ dA, \quad R = \left[0, \ \frac{\pi}{6}\right] \times \left[0, \ \frac{\pi}{2}\right]$$

   Round the answer to the nearest hundredth.

4. Find the area of the part of the plane $36x + 9y + z = 27$ that lies in the first octant.

5. Find the area of the surface. The part of the surface $z = 9 - x^2 - y^2$ that lies above the xy - plane.

6. Find the area of the surface. The part of the surface $z = xy$ that lies within the cylinder $x^2 + y^2 = 64$.

7. Find the area of the part of the sphere $x^2 + y^2 + z^2 = 9z$ that lies inside the paraboloid $z = x^2 + y^2$.

   Select the correct answer.

   a. 81π
   b. 40.5π
   c. 4.5π
   d. 9π
   e. 7π

8. Use the Midpoint Rule for double integrals with m = n = 2 to estimate the area of the surface.

   $z = xy + x^2 + y^2, \ 0 \le x \le 5, \ 0 \le y \le 5$

   Round your answer to four decimal places.

9. Find the area of the finite part of the paraboloid $y = x^2 + z^2$ cut off by the plane $y = 4$.

   [*Hint* : *Project the surface onto the xz - plane.*]

   Select the correct answer.

   a. $A(S) = \dfrac{\pi}{6}\left(17\sqrt{17} - 1\right)$

   b. $A(S) = \dfrac{17\pi}{7}\left(\sqrt{17} - 1\right)$

   c. $A(S) = \dfrac{\pi}{6}\left(17 - \sqrt{17}\right)$

   d. $A(S) = \dfrac{\pi}{3}\left(17\sqrt{17} - 1\right)$

   e. $A(S) = \dfrac{\pi}{3}\left(\sqrt{17} - 1\right)$

10. Evaluate the triple integral.

    $\displaystyle\iiint\limits_{E} 5x \ dV \ , \ E = \left\{ \ (x, y, z) \ | \ 0 \le y \le 3, \ 0 \le x \le \sqrt{9 - y^2}, \ 0 \le z \le y \ \right\}$

    Round to the nearest tenth.

11. Express the integral as an iterated integral of the form $\displaystyle\int_{a}^{b}\int_{u(x)}^{v(x)}\int_{c(x,y)}^{d(x,y)} f \ dzdydx$ where E is the solid bounded by the surfaces $x^2 = 1 - y$, $z = 0$, and $z = y$.

    $\displaystyle\iiint\limits_{E} f(x, y, z) \ dV$

12. Express the integral $\displaystyle\int_{0}^{2}\int_{y}^{2}\int_{0}^{y} f(x, y, z) \ dzdxdy$ in the form $\displaystyle\int_{a}^{b}\int_{u(x)}^{v(x)}\int_{c(x,y)}^{d(x,y)} f \ dxdzdy$.

13. Find the mass of the solid E, if E is the cube given by $0 \le x \le 4$, $0 \le y \le 4$, $0 \le z \le 4$ and the density function ρ is $\rho(x, y, z) = x^2 + y^2 + z^2$.

14. Find the region E for which the triple integral $\iiint\limits_E (1 - 4x^2 - 6y^2 - 7z^2) \, dV$ is a maximum.

15. Use cylindrical coordinates to evaluate $\iiint\limits_E \sqrt{x^2 + y^2} \, dV$, where E is the region that lies inside the

    cylinder $x^2 + y^2 = 25$ and between the planes $z = -6$ and $z = 5$.

    Select the correct answer.

    a. 2,879.79
    b. 2,931.9
    c. 2,818.41
    d. 2,431.9
    e. 2,218.41

16. Use cylindrical coordinates to find the volume of the solid that the cylinder $r = 3\cos\theta$ cuts out of the sphere of radius 3 centered at the origin. Please round the answer to the nearest hundredth.

17. Find the mass of the solid S bounded by the paraboloid $z = 7x^2 + 7y^2$ and the plane $z = 3$ if S has constant density 5.

    Round the answer to the nearest hundredth.

18. Use spherical coordinates to evaluate $\iiint\limits_E xe^{(x^2 + y^2 + z^2)^2} \, dV$, where E is the solid that lies between the

    spheres $x^2 + y^2 + z^2 = 4$ and $x^2 + y^2 + z^2 = 25$ in the first octant.

19. Use the given transformation to evaluate the integral.

$$\iint\limits_{R} xy \ dA$$

R is the region in the first quadrant bounded by the lines $y = x$, $y = 3x$, and the hyperbolas $xy = 2$, $xy = 5$;

$$x = \frac{u}{v}, \ y = v$$

Select the correct answer.

a.   15.827
b.   7.559
c.   5.768
d.   8.96
e.   4.26

20. Find an approximation to $\iint\limits_{R} (4x - 3y^2) \ dA$.

Use a double Riemann sum with $m = n = 2$ and the sample point in the lower right corner to approximate the double integral, where $R = \left\{ (x, y) \mid 0 \le x \le 6, \ 0 \le y \le 4 \right\}$.

1. -3264

2. c

3. 0.17

4. $\dfrac{9\sqrt{1378}}{8}$

5. $\dfrac{\pi}{6}\left(37\sqrt{37}-1\right)$

6. $\dfrac{2\pi}{3}\left(65\sqrt{65}-1\right)$

7. d

8. 268.3542

9. a

10. 50.625

11. $\displaystyle\int_{-1}^{1}\int_{0}^{\sqrt{1-x^2}}\int_{0}^{y} f \; dzdydx$

12. $\displaystyle\int_{0}^{2}\int_{0}^{y}\int_{y}^{2} f \; dxdzdy$

13. 1024

14. $4x^2 + 6y^2 + 7z^2 = 1$

15. a

16. 32.55

17. 10.1

18. $\dfrac{\pi}{16}\left(e^{625}-e^{16}\right)$

19. c

20. 288

1. Find the gradient vector field of $f(x, y) = \ln(x + 8y)$.

2. Evaluate $\displaystyle\int_C xy^4 ds$, where C is the right half of the circle $x^2 + y^2 = 9$.

3. Evaluate $\displaystyle\int_C yz\ dy + xy\ dz$, where C is given by $x = 4\sqrt{t}$, $y = 5t$, $z = 2t^2$, $0 \le t \le 1$.

4. Find the work done by the force field $\mathbf{F}(x, y) = 6x\mathbf{i} + (6y + 3)\mathbf{j}$ in moving an object along an arch of the cycloid $\mathbf{r}(t) = (t - \sin(t))\mathbf{i} + (1 - \cos(t))\mathbf{j}$, $0 \le t \le 2\pi$.

5. Find the work done by the force field $\mathbf{F}(x, y) = xz\mathbf{i} + yx\mathbf{j} + zy\mathbf{k}$ on a particle that moves along the curve $\mathbf{r}(t) = t^2\mathbf{i} - t^3\mathbf{j} + t^4\mathbf{k}$, $0 \le t \le 1$.

6. Determine whether or not $\mathbf{F}$ is a conservative vector field. If it is, find a function f such that $\mathbf{F} = \nabla f$.

   $\mathbf{F} = (14x + 8y)\mathbf{i} + (8x + 18y)\mathbf{j}$

7. Determine whether or not F is a conservative vector field. If it is, find a function f such that $\mathbf{F} = \nabla f$.

   $\mathbf{F} = (8x\cos y - y\cos x)\mathbf{i} + (-4x^2 \sin y - \sin x)\mathbf{j}$

8. Find a function f such that $\mathbf{F} = \nabla f$, and use it to evaluate $\displaystyle\int_C \mathbf{F} \cdot dz$ along the given curve C.

   $\mathbf{F}(x, y) = x^5 y^6 \mathbf{i} + y^5 x^6 \mathbf{j}$

   $C : \mathbf{r}(t) = \sqrt{t}\mathbf{i} + (1 + t^3)\mathbf{j}$, $0 \le t \le 1$

9. Find a parametric representation for the part of the plane $z = 8$ that lies inside the cylinder $x^2 + y^2 = 9$.

10. Suppose that $\mathbf{F}$ is an inverse square force field, that is, $\mathbf{F} = \dfrac{5\mathbf{r}}{|\mathbf{r}|^3}$ where $\mathbf{r} = x\,\mathbf{i} + y\,\mathbf{j} + z\,\mathbf{k}$. Find the work done by $\mathbf{F}$ in moving an object from a point P_1 along a path to a point P_2 in terms of the distances d_1 and d_2 from these points to the origin.

11. Use Green's Theorem to evaluate the line integral along the given positively oriented curve.

$$\int_C (xy)\ dx + (6x^2)\ dy$$

C consists of the line segment from (-4, 0) to (4, 0) and the top half of the circle $y^2 + x^2 = 16$.

12. Find the curl of the vector field.

$\mathbf{F}(x, y, z) = 10e^x \sin(y)\mathbf{i} + 5e^x \cos(y)\mathbf{j} + 4z\mathbf{k}$

13. Let $\mathbf{r} = x\mathbf{i} + y\mathbf{j} + z\mathbf{k}$ and $r = |\mathbf{r}|$.

Find $\nabla \cdot (2r\ \mathbf{r})$.

14. Let $\mathbf{r} = x\mathbf{i} + y\mathbf{j} + z\mathbf{k}$ and $r = |\mathbf{r}|$.

Find $\nabla \times (4\mathbf{r})$.

15. Find a parametric representation for the part of the elliptic paraboloid $x + y^2 + 4z^2 = 16$ that lies in front of the plane $x = 0$.

16. Set up, but do not evaluate, a double integral for the area of the surface with parametric equations
$x = 3u \cos v$, $y = 5u \sin v$, $z = u^2$, $0 \le u \le 6$, $0 \le v \le 2\pi$.

17. Evaluate the surface integral.

$$\iint_S 48yz \; dS$$

S is the part of the plane $x + y + z = 2$ that lies in the first octant.

18. Evaluate the surface integral $\iint_S \mathbf{F} \; dS$ for the given vector field $\mathbf{F}$ and the oriented surface S. In other words, find the flux of F across S.

$\mathbf{F}(x, y, z) = 4\,x\mathbf{i} + 4\,y\mathbf{j} + 4\,z\mathbf{k}$, S is the sphere $x^2 + y^2 + 4z^2 = 3$.

19. Evaluate the surface integral $\iint_S \mathbf{F} \; dS$ for the given vector field $\mathbf{F}$ and the oriented surface S. In other words, find the flux of $\mathbf{F}$ across S.

$\mathbf{F}(x, y, z) = 43y\mathbf{j} - 11z\mathbf{k}$, S consists of the paraboloid $y = x^2 + z^2$, $0 \le y \le 3$, and the disk $x^2 + z^2 \le 3$, $y = 3$, with positive (outward) orientation.

20. Calculate the work done by the force field $\mathbf{F}(x, y, z) = (x^x + 10z^2)\,\mathbf{i} + (y^y + 14x^2)\,\mathbf{j} + (z^z + 12y^2)\,\mathbf{k}$ when a particle moves under its influence around the edge of the part of the sphere $x^2 + y^2 + z^2 = 16$ that lies in the first octant, in a counterclockwise direction as viewed from above.

ANSWER KEY

Stewart - Calculus ET 5e Chapter 16 Form A

1. $\dfrac{1}{x+8y}\mathbf{i} + \dfrac{8}{x+8y}\mathbf{j}$

2. 291.6

3. 35.36

4. $12\pi^2$

5. $\dfrac{23}{88}$

6. $7x^2 + 8yx + 9y^2 + K$

7. $4x^2\cos(y) - y\sin(x) + K$

8. $\dfrac{32}{3}$

9. $x = r\cos(\phi), \quad y = r\sin(\phi), \quad z = 8, \quad 0 \le r \le 3, \quad 0 \le \phi \le 2\pi$

10. $5\left(\dfrac{1}{d_2} - \dfrac{1}{d_1}\right)$

11. 0

12. $-5e^2\cos(y)k$

13. $8r$

14. 0

15. $x = 16 - y^2 - 4z^2, \quad z = z, \quad y = y, \quad y^2 + 4z^2 \le 16$

16. $\displaystyle\int_0^6 \int_0^{2\pi} \sqrt{100u^4\cos^2(v) + 36u^4\sin^2(v) + 225u^2}\;\; dvdu$

17. $32\sqrt{3}$

18. $48\sqrt{3}\pi$

19. 0

20. 1536

1. Find the gradient vector field of $f(x, y, z) = \sqrt{x^3 + y^5 + z^8}$.

2. Find the gradient vector field of $f(x, y, z) = x \cos \dfrac{2y}{9z}$.

3. The **flow lines** (or **streamlines**) of a vector field are the paths followed by a particle whose velocity field is the given vector field. Thus, the vectors in a vector field are tangent to the flow lines. The flow lines of the vector field $\mathbf{F}(x, y) = 8x\mathbf{i} - 24y\mathbf{j}$ satisfy the differential equations $\dfrac{dx}{dt} = 8x$ and $\dfrac{dy}{dt} - 24y$.

   Solve these differential equations to find the equations of the family of flow lines.

4. Find the mass of a thin wire in the shape of a quarter-circle $x^2 + y^2 = 9$, $x > 0$, $y > 0$ if the density function is $\rho(x, y) = x + y$.

5. Find the curl of the vector field.

   $\mathbf{F}(x, y, z) = (x - 9z)\mathbf{i} + (x + y + 6z)\mathbf{j} + (x - 9y)\mathbf{k}$

6. Find the curl of the vector field.

   $\mathbf{F}(x, y, z) = 2e^x \sin(y)\mathbf{i} + 4e^x \cos(y)\mathbf{j} + 9z\mathbf{k}$

7. Find the divergence of the vector field.

   $\mathbf{F}(x, y, z) = \dfrac{x}{2x^2 + 9y^2 + 7z^2}\mathbf{i} + \dfrac{y}{2x^2 + 9y^2 + 7z^2}\mathbf{j} + \dfrac{z}{2x^2 + 9y^2 + 7z^2}\mathbf{k}$

8. Determine whether or not the vector field is conservative. If it is conservative, find a function f such that $\mathbf{F} = \nabla f$.

   $\mathbf{F}(x, y, z) = 10x\mathbf{i} + 4y\mathbf{j} + 6z\mathbf{k}$

9. Determine whether or not the vector field is conservative. If it is conservative, find a function f such that $\mathbf{F} = \nabla f$.

   $\mathbf{F}(x, y, z) = 14xy\mathbf{i} + (7x^2 + 18yz)\mathbf{j} + 9y^2\mathbf{k}$

10. Determine whether or not the vector field is conservative. If it is conservative, find a function f such that $\mathbf{F} = \nabla f$.

$$\mathbf{F}(x, y, z) = 35yze^{7xz}\mathbf{i} + 5e^{7xz}\mathbf{j} + 35xye^{7xz}\mathbf{k}$$

11. Let $\mathbf{r} = x\mathbf{i} + y\mathbf{j} + z\mathbf{k}$ and $r = |\mathbf{r}|$.

   Find $\nabla \times (10\mathbf{r})$.

12. Evaluate the surface integral.

$$\iint\limits_{S} (y^2 + z^2) \ dS$$

   S is the part of the paraboloid $x = 1 - y^2 - z^2$ that lies in front of the plane $x = 0$.

   Round the answer to the nearest hundredth.

13. Evaluate the surface integral.

$$\iint\limits_{S} 4yz \ dS$$

   S is the part of the plane $z = y + 9$ that lies inside the cylinder $x^2 + y^2 = 8$.

14. Evaluate the surface integral $\iint\limits_{S} \mathbf{F} \ dS$ for the given vector field $\mathbf{F}$ and the oriented surface S.
   In other words, find the flux of $\mathbf{F}$ across S.

   $\mathbf{F}(x, y, z) = 6\,x\,y\,\mathbf{i} + 2\,y\,z\,\mathbf{j} + 7\,x\,z\,\mathbf{k}$, S is the part of the paraboloid $z = 4 - x^2 - y^2$, that lies above the square $0 \le x \le 1, \ 0 \le y \le 1$, and has upward orientation.

   Round the answer to four decimal places.

15. A fluid with density 1,330 flows with velocity $\mathbf{v} = y\mathbf{i} + \mathbf{j} + z\mathbf{k}$. Find the rate of flow upward through the paraboloid $z = 9 - \frac{1}{3}(x^2 + y^2), \ x^2 + y^2 \le 36$.

16. Use Stokes' Theorem to evaluate $\iint_C \mathbf{F} \cdot d\mathbf{r}$.

$\mathbf{F}(x, y, z) = 0.81x\mathbf{i} + 9y\mathbf{j} + 3(y^2 + x^2)\mathbf{k}$

C is the boundary of the part of the paraboloid $z = 0.81 - x^2 - y^2$ in the first octant. C is oriented counterclockwise as viewed from above.

17. Let $\mathbf{F}(x, y, z) = \left\langle 5ax^3 - xz^2, \ x^2y + by^3, \ 2cz^3 \right\rangle$ and consider all surfaces S whose boundary is a fixed closed curve C.

Find the values of a, b, and c for which $\iint_C \mathbf{F} \cdot d\mathbf{S}$ is independent of the choice of S.

18. Use the Divergence Theorem to calculate the surface integral $\iint_S \mathbf{F} \ d\mathbf{S}$.

$\mathbf{F}(x, y, z) = xy\mathbf{i} + yz\mathbf{j} + zx\mathbf{k}$

S is the surface of the solid cylinder $x^2 + y^2 \le 9, \ 0 \le z \le 2$.

19. Use the Divergence Theorem to calculate the surface integral $\iint_S \mathbf{F} \ d\mathbf{S}$, that is, calculate the flux of $\mathbf{F}$ across S.

$\mathbf{F}(x, y, z) = (x^3 + y \sin z)\mathbf{i} + (y^3 + z \cos x)\mathbf{j} + 3z\mathbf{k}$

S is the surface of the solid bounded by the hemispheres $z = \sqrt{25 - x^2 - y^2}$, $z = \sqrt{1 - x^2 - y^2}$, and the plane $z = 0$.

20. Use a computer algebra system to compute the flux of $\mathbf{F}$ across S.

$\mathbf{F}(x, y, z) = \sin x \cos^2 y\mathbf{i} + \sin^3 z \cos^4 z\mathbf{j} + \sin^5 z \cos^6 x\mathbf{k}$

S is the surface of the cube cut from the first octant by the planes $x = \dfrac{\pi}{2}, \ y = \dfrac{\pi}{2}, \ z = \dfrac{\pi}{2}$.

Round the answer to the nearest hundredth.

1. $\dfrac{3x^2}{2\sqrt{x^3+y^5+z^8}}\mathbf{i} - \dfrac{5y^4}{2\sqrt{x^3+y^5+z^8}}\mathbf{j} + \dfrac{8z^7}{2\sqrt{x^3+y^5+z^8}}\mathbf{k}$

2. $\cos\left(\dfrac{2y}{9z}\right)\mathbf{i} - \dfrac{2x}{9z}\sin\left(\dfrac{2y}{9z}\right)\mathbf{j} + \dfrac{2xy}{9z^2}\sin\left(\dfrac{2y}{9z}\right)\mathbf{k}$

3. $y = \dfrac{C}{x^3}$

4. 18

5. $-15\mathbf{i} - 10\mathbf{j} + \mathbf{k}$

6. $2e^x \cos(y)\mathbf{k}$

7. $\dfrac{1}{2x^2 + 9y^2 + 7z^2}$

8. $5x^2 + 2y^2 + 3z^2 + K$

9. $7x^2 y + 9y^2 z + K$

10. $5ye^{7xz} + K$

11. 0

12. 2.98

13. $64\sqrt{2}\pi$

14. 17.1722

15. 215460π

16. 0

17. $a = \dfrac{-1}{15}, \quad b = 0, \quad c = \dfrac{1}{6}$

18. 18π

19. 0

20. 2747.2π

1. Which plot illustrates the vector field $\mathbf{F}(x, y, z) = \mathbf{j}$?

   Select the correct answer.

   I.
   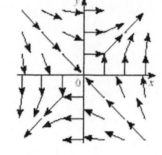

   II.
   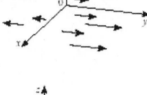

   III.
   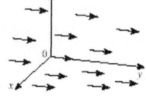

   IV.
   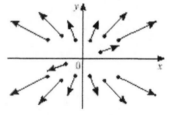

2. Which plot illustrates the vector field $\mathbf{F}(x, y, z) = y\mathbf{j}$?

Select the correct answer.

I.

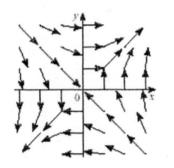

II.

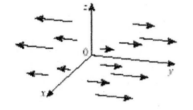

III.

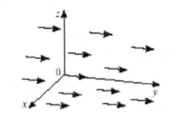

IV.

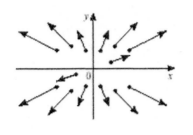

3. Evaluate the line integral $\displaystyle\int_C \mathbf{F}\cdot d\mathbf{r}$, where $\mathbf{F}(x,y) = (x-y)\mathbf{i} + (xy)\mathbf{j}$ and C is the arc of the circle

    $x^2 + y^2 = 9$ traversed counterclockwise from $(3, 0)$ to $(0, -3)$.

    Select the correct answer.

    a.   257.06
    b.   28.85
    c.   25.71
    d.   5.14
    e.   51.41

4. Find the exact mass of a thin wire in the shape of the helix $x = 2\sin(t)$, $y = 2\cos(t)$, $z = 3t$, $0 \le t \le 2\pi$
    if the density is 4.

    Select the correct answer.

    a. $8\sqrt{13}\pi$
    b. $4\sqrt{13}\pi$
    c. $8\sqrt{13}\pi^2$
    d. $8\sqrt{13}$
    e. $4\sqrt{13}$

5. Find the work done by the force field $\mathbf{F}(x,y) = x\sin(y)\mathbf{i} + y\mathbf{j}$ on a particle that moves along the
    parabola $y = x^2$ from $(1, 1)$ to $(2, 4)$.

    Select the correct answer.

    a. $\dfrac{1}{2}(17 - \cos(1) + \cos(4))$

    b. $\dfrac{1}{2}(17 + \cos(1) - \cos(4))$

    c. $\dfrac{1}{2}(15 + \sin(1) - \sin(4))$

    d. $\dfrac{1}{2}(15 + \cos(1) - \cos(4))$

    e. $\dfrac{1}{2}(15 + \sin(1) - \cos(4))$

6. Use Green's Theorem and/or a computer algebra system to evaluate $\int_C P\,dx + Q\,dy$, where

$P(x, y) = x^4 y^5$, $Q(x, y) = -x^7 y^6$, and C is the circle $x^2 + y^2 = 16$.

Select the correct answer.

a. $-2,703,361\pi$
b. $2,670,592$
c. $-1,335,296\pi$
d. $1,400,832\pi$
e. $8,011,776\pi^2$

7. Use Green's Theorem to evaluate the line integral along the given positively oriented curve.

$$\int_C (10xy)\,dx + (10x^2)\,dy$$

C consists of the line segment from (-3, 0) to (3, 0) and the top half of the circle $x^2 + y^2 = 9$.

Select the correct answer.

a. 0
b. 33.333333
c. 20
d. 100
e. 136

8. Find the correct identity, if f is a scalar field, $\mathbf{F}$ and $\mathbf{G}$ are vector fields.

Select the correct answer.

a. $\operatorname{div}(f\mathbf{F}) = f\operatorname{curl}(\mathbf{F}) + (\nabla f) \times \mathbf{F}$
b. $\operatorname{div}(f\mathbf{F}) = f\operatorname{div}(\mathbf{F}) + \mathbf{F} \cdot \nabla f$
c. $\operatorname{curl}(f\mathbf{F}) = f\operatorname{div}(\mathbf{F}) + \mathbf{F} \cdot \nabla f$
d. None of these

9. Which of the equations below is an equation of a cone?

Select the correct answer.

a. $r(x, \theta) = \langle x,\ \cos 7\theta,\ \sin 7\theta \rangle$

b. $r(x, \theta) = \langle x,\ x\cos 10\theta,\ x\sin 10\theta \rangle$

10. Suppose that $f(x, y, z) = g\left(\sqrt{x^2 + y^2 + z^2}\right)$ where g is a function of one variable such that $g(5) = 6$.

Evaluate $\displaystyle\iint_S f(x, y, z) \, dS$ where S is the sphere $x^2 + y^2 + z^2 = 25$.

Select the correct answer.

a. 150π
b. 300π
c. 600π
d. 250π
e.   None of these

11. Let $\mathbf{r} = x\mathbf{i} + y\mathbf{j} + z\mathbf{k}$ and $r = |\mathbf{r}|$.

Find $\nabla \cdot (6\mathbf{r})$.

Select the correct answer.

a.   24
b.   18
c.   30
d.   35
e.   None of these

12. Evaluate the surface integral.

$$\iint_S 6yz \, dS$$

S is the part of the plane $x + y + z = 6$ that lies in the first octant.

Select the correct answer.

a. $I = 648\sqrt{5}$
b. $I = 54\sqrt{7}$
c. $I = 324$
d. $I = 1{,}296$
e. $I = 324\sqrt{3}$

13. Evaluate the surface integral.

$$\iint\limits_{S} 6x \ dS$$

S is the surface $y = x^2 + 6z, \ 0 \le x \le 5, \ 0 \le z \le 4$.

Select the correct answer.

a. $I = 2{,}756.9733$
b. $I = 2{,}756.9633$
c. $I = 918.9878$
d. $I = 1{,}378.4817$
e. $I = 1{,}978.4817$

14. The temperature at the point (x, y, z) in a substance with conductivity $K = 2.5$ is $u(x, y, z) = 5x^2 + 5y^2$.

Find the rate of heat flow inward across the cylindrical surface $y^2 + z^2 = 2, \ 0 \le x \le 7$.

Select the correct answer.

a. 700π
b. 100π
c. 175π
d. 700
e. 720π

15. Let D be a region bounded by a simple closed path C in the xy. Then the coordinates of the centroid $(\bar{x}, \ \bar{y})$ of D are $\bar{x} = \dfrac{1}{2A}\int_{C} x^2 \ dy, \ \bar{y} = -\dfrac{1}{2A}\int_{C} y^2 \ dx$ where A is the area of D.

Find the centroid of the triangle with vertices $(0, 0)$, $(8, 0)$ and $(0, 8)$.

Select the correct answer.

a. $\left(\dfrac{8}{3}, \ -\dfrac{8}{3}\right)$

b. $\left(\dfrac{1}{24}, \ \dfrac{1}{8}\right)$

c. $\left(\dfrac{1}{8}, \ \dfrac{1}{64}\right)$

d. $\left(\dfrac{8}{3}, \ \dfrac{8}{3}\right)$

e. $\left(\dfrac{1}{8}, \ \dfrac{1}{8}\right)$

16. Let $\mathbf{F}(x, y, z) = \left\langle 5ax^3 - xz^2, \; x^2y + by^3, \; 2cz^3 \right\rangle$ and consider all surfaces S whose boundary is a fixed closed curve C. Find the values of a, b, and c for which $\iint_S \mathbf{F} \cdot d\mathbf{S}$ is independent of the choice of S.

Select the correct answer.

a. $a = 0, \; b = 0, \; c = 0$

b. $a = -\dfrac{1}{15}, \; b = 7, \; c = -\dfrac{1}{6}$

c. $a = -\dfrac{1}{15}, \; b = 0, \; c = \dfrac{1}{6}$

d. $a = \dfrac{1}{15}, \; b = 0, \; c = -\dfrac{1}{6}$

e. $a = \dfrac{1}{6}, \; b = 0, \; c = -\dfrac{1}{6}$

17. If S and C satisfy the hypotheses of Stokes' Theorem and f, g have continuous second-order partial derivatives, find $\int_C (10f\nabla3g) \cdot d\mathbf{r}$.

Select the correct answer.

a. 0

b. $\iint_S (10\nabla f \times 3\nabla g) \cdot d\mathbf{S}$

c. 1

d. 2

e. none of these

18. Use the Divergence Theorem to calculate the surface integral $\iint_S \mathbf{F} \; d\mathbf{S}$.

$\mathbf{F}(x, y, z) = xy\mathbf{i} + yz\mathbf{j} + zx\mathbf{k}$

S is the surface of the solid cylinder $x^2 + y^2 \le 25, \; 0 \le z \le 5$.

Select the correct answer.

a. 625π
b. 312.5π
c. 125π
d. 62.5π
e. 125

19. Use the Divergence Theorem to calculate the surface integral $\iint\limits_S \mathbf{F}\ d\mathbf{S}$.

$\mathbf{F}(x, y, z) = x\mathbf{i} + y\mathbf{j} + z\mathbf{k}$

S is the surface of the unit ball $x^2 + y^2 + z^2 \le 9$.

Select the correct answer.

a.   108
b. 9π
c. 3π
d.   3
e. 108π

20. Use the Divergence Theorem to calculate the surface integral $\iint\limits_S \mathbf{F}\ d\mathbf{S}$; that is, calculate the flux of $\mathbf{F}$ across S.

$\mathbf{F}(x, y, z) = 3xy^2\mathbf{i} + 2xe^z\mathbf{j} + z^3\mathbf{k}$

S is the surface of the solid bounded by the cylinder $y^2 + z^2 = 16$ and the planes $x = -1$ and $x = 4$.

Select the correct answer.

a. 640π
b. $1{,}152\pi$
c. $1{,}920\pi$
d. $1{,}280\pi$
e. $1{,}640\pi$

1. III

2. III

3. c

4. a

5. d

6. c

7. a

8. b

9. b

10. c

11. b

12. e

13. b

14. a

15. d

16. c

17. b

18. b

19. e

20. c

1. Use Green's Theorem and/or a computer algebra system to evaluate $\int_C P\ dx + Q\ dy$,

    where $P(x, y) = x^4 y^5$, $Q(x, y) = -x^7 y^6$, and C is the circle $x^2 + y^2 = 4$.

    Select the correct answer.

    a. $624\pi^2$
    b. $65{,}640\pi$
    c. $-32{,}977\pi$
    d. -104π
    e. 208

2. Use Green's Theorem to evaluate the line integral along the given positively oriented curve.

    $$\int_C (4xy)\ dx + (4x^2)\ dy$$

    C consists of the line segment from (-3, 0) to (3, 0) and the top half of the circle $y^2 + x^2 = 9$.

    Select the correct answer.

    a.   0
    b.   8
    c.   16
    d.   5.333333
    e.   18

3. Use Green's Theorem to evaluate the line integral along the given positively oriented curve.

    $$\int_C \mathbf{F}\ d\mathbf{r},\ \mathbf{F}(x, y) = (y^2 - x^2 y)\mathbf{i} + xy^2 \mathbf{j}$$

    C consists of the circle $x^2 + y^2 = 16$ from (4, 0) to (2, 2) and the line segments from (2, 2) to (0, 0) and from (0, 0) to (4, 0).

    Select the correct answer.

    a. $I \approx 37.77$
    b. $I \approx 42.71$
    c. $I \approx 41.39$
    d. $I \approx 35.43$
    e. $I \approx 32.43$

4. Use Green's Theorem to find the work done by the force $\mathbf{F}(x, y) = x(x + 5y)\mathbf{i} + 4xy^2\mathbf{j}$ in moving a particle from the origin along the x - axis to (4, 0) then along the line segment to (0, 4) and then back to the origin along the y-axis.

   Select the correct answer.

   a. -6
   b. 32
   c. -32
   d. 192
   e. -192

5. A particle starts at the point (-3, 0), moves along the x-axis to (3, 0) and then along the semicircle $y = \sqrt{9 - x^2}$ to the starting point. Use Green's Theorem to find the work done on this particle by the force field $\mathbf{F}(x, y) = \left\langle 24x,\ 8x^3 + 24xy^2 \right\rangle$.

   Select the correct answer.

   a. 486π
   b. 972π
   c. 486
   d. 0
   e. 48π

6. A plane lamina with constant density $\rho(x, y) = 12$ occupies a region in the xy - plane bounded by a simple closed path C. Its moments of inertia about the axes are $I_x = -\dfrac{\rho}{3}\int_C y^3\,dx$ and $I_y = \dfrac{\rho}{3}\int_C x^3\,dy$.

   Find the moments of inertia about the axes, if C is a rectangle with vertices (0, 0), (4, 0), (4, 5) and (0, 5).

   Select the correct answer.

   a. (2,000, 1,280)
   b. (-1,280, 1,280)
   c. (2,000, -1,280)
   d. (-2,000, 1,280)
   e. (-2,880, 1,200)

7. Find the curl of the vector field.

   $\mathbf{F}(x, y, z) = 2xy\mathbf{i} + 10yz\mathbf{j} + 5xz\mathbf{k}$

   Select the correct answer.

   a. $-10y\mathbf{i} - 5z\mathbf{j} - 2x\mathbf{k}$
   b. $-5y\mathbf{i} - 10z\mathbf{j} - 2x\mathbf{k}$
   c. $-2y\mathbf{i} - 5z\mathbf{j} - 10x\mathbf{k}$
   d. $2y\mathbf{i} - 5z\mathbf{j} + 10x\mathbf{k}$
   e.   none of these

8. Find the correct identity, if f is a scalar field, $\mathbf{F}$ and $\mathbf{G}$ are vector fields.

   Select the correct answer.

   a. $\operatorname{div}(\mathbf{F} + \mathbf{G}) = \operatorname{div}\mathbf{F} + \operatorname{div}\mathbf{G}$

   b. $\operatorname{div}(\mathbf{F} + \mathbf{G}) = \operatorname{curl}\mathbf{F} + \operatorname{div}\mathbf{G}$

   c. $\operatorname{div}(\mathbf{F} + \mathbf{G}) = \operatorname{curl}\mathbf{F} + \operatorname{curl}\mathbf{G}$

   d. $\operatorname{curl}(\mathbf{F} + \mathbf{G}) = \operatorname{div}\mathbf{F} + \operatorname{curl}\mathbf{G}$

   e.   none of these

9. Find the correct identity, if f is a scalar field, $\mathbf{F}$ and $\mathbf{G}$ are vector fields.

   Select the correct answer.

   a. $\operatorname{div}(f\mathbf{F}) = f\operatorname{curl}(\mathbf{F}) + (\nabla f) \times \mathbf{F}$
   b. $\operatorname{div}(f\mathbf{F}) = f\operatorname{div}(\mathbf{F}) + \mathbf{F} \cdot \nabla f$
   c. $\operatorname{curl}(f\mathbf{F}) = f\operatorname{div}(\mathbf{F}) + \mathbf{F} \cdot \nabla f$
   d.   None of these

10. Find a parametric representation for the part of the elliptic paraboloid $x + y^2 + 6z^2 = 9$ that lies in front of the plane $x = 0$.

    Select the correct answer.

    a. $x = x, \quad y = \pm\sqrt{9 - x + 6z^2}, \quad z = z$

    b. $x = x, \quad y = \sqrt{9 - x + 6z^2}, \quad z = z$

    c. $x = 9 - y^2 - 6z^2, \quad y = y, \quad z = y, \quad 0 \le y^2 + 6z^2 \le 3$

    d. $x = 9 - y^2 - 6z^2, \quad y = y, \quad z = y, \quad y^2 + 6z^2 \ge 9$

    e. $x = 9 - y^2 - 6z^2, \quad y = y, \quad z = y, \quad y^2 + 6z^2 \le 9$

11. Use Stokes' Theorem to evaluate.

$$\int_C \mathbf{F} \cdot d\mathbf{r}$$

$\mathbf{F}(x, y, z) = e^{-7x}\mathbf{i} + e^{4y}\mathbf{j} + e^{5z}\mathbf{k}$

C is the boundary of the part of the plane $8x + y + 8z = 8$ in the first octant.

Select the correct answer.

a.   0
b.   23
c.   49
d.   16
e.   69

12. Let S be the cube with vertices $(\pm 1, \pm 1, \pm 1)$. Approximate $\iint_S \sqrt{x^2 + 2y^2 + 7z^2}$ by using a Riemann sum as in Definition 1, taking the patches S_{ij} to be the squares that are the faces of the cube and the points P_{ij} to be the centers of the squares.

Select the correct answer.

a. $4(1 + \sqrt{2} + \sqrt{7})$

b. $8(1 + \sqrt{2} + \sqrt{7})$

c. $8(3 + \sqrt{7})$

d. $8(3 + \sqrt{2})$

e.   none of these

13. Suppose that $f(x, y, z) = g\left(\sqrt{x^2 + y^2 + z^2}\right)$ where g is a function of one variable such that $g(2) = 3$.

Evaluate $\iint_S f(x, y, z) \; dS$ where S is the sphere $x^2 + y^2 + z^2 = 4$.

Select the correct answer.

a. 24π
b. 48π
c. 12π
d. 18π
e.   none of these

14. Evaluate the surface integral.

$$\iint\limits_{S} 10yz \ dS$$

S is the surface with parametric equations $x = 7\,uv$, $y = 6\,(u + v)$, $z = 6\,(u - v)$, $u^2 + v^2 = 3$.

Select the correct answer.

a. $I = 10\pi$
b. $I = 3$
c. $I = 0$
d. $I = 10 + 7\pi$
e. $I = 10 + 3\pi$

15. The temperature at the point (x, y, z) in a substance with conductivity $K = 9$ is $u(x, y, z) = 6x^2 + 6y^2$.

Find the rate of heat flow inward across the cylindrical surface $y^2 + z^2 = 3$, $0 \le x \le 10$.

Select the correct answer.

a.   6,480
b. $6,480\pi$
c. $6,48\pi$
d. $1,620\pi$
e. 324π

16. Use Stokes' Theorem to evaluate $\iint\limits_{S} \text{curl } \mathbf{F} \cdot d\mathbf{S}$.

$$\mathbf{F}(x, y, z) = 7xy\mathbf{i} + 7e^z\mathbf{j} + 7xy^2\mathbf{k}$$

S consists of the four sides of the pyramid with vertices $(0, 0, 0)$, $(3, 0, 0)$, $(0, 0, 3)$, $(3, 0, 3)$ and $(0, 3, 0)$ that lie to the right of the xz - plane, oriented in the direction of the positive y - axis.

Select the correct answer.

a.   12
b.   16
c.   49
d.   0
e.   1

17. Use the Divergence Theorem to calculate the surface integral $\iint\limits_{S} \mathbf{F} \ d\mathbf{S}$; that is, calculate the flux of $\mathbf{F}$ across S.

$\mathbf{F}(x, y, z) = x^3\mathbf{i} + y^3\mathbf{j} + y^3\mathbf{k}$, S is the sphere $x^2 + y^2 + z^2 = 25$

Select the correct answer.

a. 500π
b. $2,500\pi$
c. 500
d. $7,500$
e. $7,500\pi$

18. Use a computer algebra system to compute the flux of $\mathbf{F}$ across S.

$\mathbf{F}(x, y, z) = \sin x \cos^2 y\mathbf{i} + \sin^3 z \cos^4 z\mathbf{j} + \sin^5 z \cos^6 x\mathbf{k}$

S is the surface of the cube cut from the first octant by the planes $x = \dfrac{\pi}{2}$, $y = \dfrac{\pi}{2}$, $z = \dfrac{\pi}{2}$.

Select the correct answer.

a. 0.67
b. 2
c. 4.01
d. 1
e. 3

19. Which of the equations below is an equation of a cone?

a. $r(x, \ \theta) = \langle x, \ \cos 7\theta, \ \sin 7\theta \rangle$

b. $r(x, \ \theta) = \langle x, \ \cos 5\theta, \ \sin 5\theta \rangle$

20. Use the Divergence Theorem to calculate the surface integral.

$\iint\limits_{S} \mathbf{F} \ d\mathbf{S}$

$\mathbf{F}(x, y, z) = 4x\mathbf{i} + 5xy\mathbf{j} + 3xz\mathbf{k}$

S is the surface of the box bounded by the planes $x = 0, x = 5, y = 0, y = 3, z = 0, z = 4$.

Select the correct answer.

a. $2,640$
b. $1,440$
c. -960
d. 120
e. 140

1. d

2. a

3. a

4. b

5. a

6. a

7. a

8. a

9. b

10. e

11. a

12. b

13. b

14. c

15. b

16. d

17. e

18. b

19. b

20. b

1. The **flow lines** (or **streamlines**) of a vector field are the paths followed by a particle whose velocity field is the given vector field. Thus, the vectors in a vector field are tangent to the flow lines. If the parametric equations of a flow line for the vector field $\mathbf{F}(x, y) = x\mathbf{i} - y\mathbf{j}$ are

    $x = x(t)$ and $y = y(t)$, then they satisfy the differential equations $\dfrac{dx}{dt} = x$ and $\dfrac{dy}{dt} = -y$.

    Solve these differential equations to find an equation of the flow line that passes through the point $(1, 2)$.

    Select the correct answer.

    a. $y = \dfrac{4}{x}$

    b. $y = 2x$

    c. $y = \dfrac{2}{x}$

    d. $y = \dfrac{1}{x+1}$

    e. $y = \dfrac{1}{2x-1}$

2. Consider the vector field $\mathbf{F}(x, y) = \mathbf{i} + x\mathbf{j}$. If a particle starts at the point $(10, 4)$ in the velocity field given by $\mathbf{F}$, find an equation of the path it follows.

3. If a wire with linear density 10 lies along a space curve C, its **moment of inertia** about the z-axis is given by $I_z = \displaystyle\int_C 10(x^2 + y^2)\, ds$. Find the moment of inertia for the wire in the shape of the helix

    $x = 2\sin(t), \quad y = \cos(t), \quad z = 3t, \quad 0 \le t \le 2\pi$

4. Find a function f such that $\mathbf{F} = \nabla f$, and use it to evaluate $\displaystyle\int_C \mathbf{F} \cdot d\mathbf{r}$ along the given curve C.

    $\mathbf{F} = e^{2y}\mathbf{i} + (1 + 2xe^{2y})\mathbf{j}$

    $C: \mathbf{r}(t) = te^t\mathbf{i} + (1+t)\mathbf{j}, \ 0 \le t \le 1$

5. Suppose that $\mathbf{F}$ is an inverse square force field, that is, $\mathbf{F} = \dfrac{2\mathbf{r}}{|\mathbf{r}|^3}$ where $\mathbf{r} = x\mathbf{i} + y\mathbf{j} + z\mathbf{k}$. Find the work done by $\mathbf{F}$ in moving an object from a point P_1 along a path to a point P_2 in terms of the distances d_1 and d_2 from these points to the origin.

6. Use Green's Theorem to find the work done by the force $F(x, y) = x(x + 5y)i + (4xy^2)j$ in moving a particle from the origin along the x-axis to (3, 0) then along the line segment to (0, 3) and then back to the origin along the y-axis.

    Select the correct answer.

    a.   49.5
    b.   -1.5
    c.   4.5
    d.   -4.5
    e.   -49.5

7. Let $r = xi + yj + zk$ and $r = |r|$.

    Find $\nabla \cdot (9 \ r \ r)$.

8. Which of the equations below is an equation of a plane?

    Select the correct answer.

    a. $r(u, v) = (5 + 10u)i + (-u + 9v)j + (2 + 6u + 4v)k$

    b. $r(u, v) = u \cos vi + u \sin vj + u^2 k$

9. Find a parametric representation for the part of the sphere $x^2 + y^2 + z^2 = 4$ that lies above the cone $z = \sqrt{x^2 + y^2}$.

10. Find the area of the part of paraboloid $x = y^2 + z^2$ that lies inside the cylinder $z^2 + y^2 = 25$.

11. Find the area of the part of the surface $y = 4x + z^2$ that lies between the planes $x = 0, x = 7, z = 0$, and $z = 3$.

    Select the correct answer.

    a.   121.339
    b.   113.269
    c.   107.759
    d.   110.234
    e.   111.239

12. Evaluate the surface integral.

$$\iint_S 4(x^2 y + z^2) \, dS$$

S is the part of the cylinder $x^2 + y^2 = 9$ between the planes $z = 0$ and $z = 4$.

13. Evaluate the surface integral.

$$\iint_S 10 yz \, dS$$

S is the surface with parametric equations $x = 4\,uv$, $y = 2(u + v)$, $z = 2(u - v)$, $x^2 + v^2 = 4$.

14. Find parametric equations for C, if C is the curve of intersection of the hyperbolic paraboloid

$z = y^2 - x^2$ and the cylinder $x^2 + y^2 = 16$ oriented counterclockwise as viewed from above.

15. Find the moment of inertia about the z-axis of a thin funnel in the shape of a cone $z = 5\sqrt{4x^2 + 4y^2}$,
$1 \le z \le 4$, if its density function is $\rho(x, y, z) = 3 - z$.

Round the answer to four decimal places.

16. Use *Gauss's Law* to find the charge contained in the solid hemisphere $x^2 + y^2 + z^2 \le 81$, $z \ge 0$, if the
electric field is $\mathbf{E}(x, y, z) = x\mathbf{i} + y\mathbf{j} + 2z\mathbf{k}$.

17. Use Stokes' Theorem to evaluate $\iint_S \text{curl } \mathbf{F} \cdot d\mathbf{S}$.

$\mathbf{F}(x, y, z) = 2xyz\mathbf{i} + 2xy\mathbf{j} + 2x^2 yz\mathbf{k}$

S consists of the top and the four sides (but not the bottom) of the cube with vertices $(\pm 3, \pm 3, \pm 3)$
oriented outward.

18. Use Stokes' Theorem to evaluate $\iint\limits_S \text{curl } \mathbf{F} \cdot d\mathbf{S}$.

$\mathbf{F}(x, y, z) = 2xy\mathbf{i} + 2e^z\mathbf{j} + 2xy^2\mathbf{k}$

S consists of the four sides of the pyramid with vertices $(0, 0, 0)$, $(7, 0, 0)$, $(0, 0, 7)$, $(7, 0, 7)$ and $(0, 7, 0)$ that lie to the right of the xz-plane, oriented in the direction of the positive y-axis.

19. Use Stokes' Theorem to evaluate $\iint\limits_C \mathbf{F} \cdot d\mathbf{r}$.

$\mathbf{F}(x, y, z) = 0.16x\mathbf{i} + 5y\mathbf{j} + 6(y^2 + x^2)\mathbf{k}$

C the boundary of the part of the paraboloid $z = 0.16 - x^2 - y^2$ in the first octant. C is oriented counterclockwise as viewed from above.

20. Use a computer algebra system to compute the flux of $\mathbf{F}$ across S.

$\mathbf{F}(x, y, z) = \sin x \cos^2 y\mathbf{i} + \sin^3 z \cos^4 z\mathbf{j} + \sin^5 z \cos^6 x\mathbf{k}$

S is the surface of the cube cut from the first octant by the planes $x = \dfrac{\pi}{2}$, $y = \dfrac{\pi}{2}$, $z = \dfrac{\pi}{2}$.

Round the answer to the nearest hundredth.

1.   c

2. $y = \dfrac{x^2}{2} - 46$

3. $80\sqrt{13}\pi$

4. $e^5 + 1$

5. $2\left(\dfrac{1}{d_2} - \dfrac{1}{d_1} \right)$

6.   c

7. $36r$

8.   a

9. $x = x, \; z = \sqrt{4 - x^2 - y^2}, \; y = y, \; 2 \le y^2 + x^2 \le 4$

10. $\dfrac{101\pi\sqrt{101} - 1}{6}$

11.   e

12. 512π

13.   0

14. $x = 4\cos(t), \; y = 4\sin(t), \; z = -16\cos(2t)$

15. -0.0843

16. $1944\pi\varepsilon_0$

17.   0

18.   0

19.   0

20.   2

1. Find the gradient vector field of $f(x, y) = \ln(x + 2y)$.

2. Find the gradient vector field of $f(x, y, z) = x\cos\dfrac{2y}{5z}$.

3. Consider the vector field $\mathbf{F}(x, y) = \mathbf{i} + x\mathbf{j}$. If a particle starts at the point $(10, 4)$ in the velocity field given by $\mathbf{F}$, find an equation of the path it follows.

4. Evaluate $\displaystyle\int_C xy^4 \, ds$, where C is the right half of the circle $x^2 + y^2 = 25$.

5. Evaluate $\displaystyle\int_C xy \, dx + (x - y) \, dy$, where C consists of line segments from $(0, 0)$ to $(3, 0)$ and from $(3, 0)$ to $(2, 5)$.

6. Evaluate $\displaystyle\int_C yz \, dy + xy \, dz$, where C is given by $x = 10\sqrt{t}, \ y = 3t, \ z = 10t^2, \ 0 \le t \le 1$.

   Select the correct answer.

   a.   193.93
   b.   20.82
   c.   208.23
   d.   1,939.29
   e.   225.25

7. A thin wire is bent into the shape of a semicircle $x^2 + y^2 = 4, \ x > 0$. If the linear density is 7, find the exact mass of the wire.

8. Find the curl of the vector field.

   $\mathbf{F}(x, y, z) = 5e^x \sin(y)\mathbf{i} + 3e^x \cos(y)\mathbf{j} + 8z\mathbf{k}$

9. If a wire with linear density 6 lies along a space curve C, its **moment of inertia** about the z-axis is given by $I_z = \int_C 6(x^2 + y^2) \, ds$. Find the moment of inertia for the wire in the shape of the helix $x = 2\sin(t)$, $y = 2\cos(t)$, $z = 3t$, $0 \le t \le 2\pi$.

Select the correct answer.

   a. $48\sqrt{13}\pi$
   b. $48\sqrt{13}\pi^2$
   c. $12\sqrt{13}$
   d. $24\sqrt{11}\pi$
   e. $12\sqrt{11}\pi$

10. Find the work done by the force field $F(x, y) = 3x\mathbf{i} + (3y + 10)\mathbf{j}$ in moving an object along an arch of the cycloid $\mathbf{r}(t) = (t - \sin(t))\mathbf{i} + (1 - \cos(t))\mathbf{j}$, $0 \le t \le 2\pi$.

11. Find the work done by the force field $F(x, y) = x\sin(y)\mathbf{i} + y\mathbf{j}$ on a particle that moves along the parabola $y = x^2$ from $(-2, 4)$ to $(1, 1)$.

12. Find the work done by the force field $F(x, y, z) = xz\mathbf{i} + yx\mathbf{j} + zy\mathbf{k}$ on a particle that moves along the curve $\mathbf{r}(t) = t^2\mathbf{i} + t^3\mathbf{j} + t^4\mathbf{k}$, $-1 \le t \le 0$.

13. Determine whether or not $\mathbf{F}$ is a conservative vector field. If it is, find a function f such that $\mathbf{F} = \nabla f$.

   $\mathbf{F} = (4 + 2xy + \ln x)\mathbf{i} + x^2\mathbf{j}$

14. Determine whether or not F is a conservative vector field. If it is, find a function f such that $\mathbf{F} = \nabla f$.

   $\mathbf{F} = (9ye^{9x} + \sin y)\mathbf{i} + (e^{9x} + x\cos y)\mathbf{j}$

15. Find a function f such that $\mathbf{F} = \nabla f$ and use it to evaluate $\int_C \mathbf{F} \cdot d\mathbf{r}$ along the given curve C.

   $\mathbf{F} = y\mathbf{i} + (x + 2y)\mathbf{j}$

   C is the upper semicircle that starts at $(1, 2)$ and ends at $(5, 2)$.

16. Determine whether or not the vector field is conservative. If it is conservative, find a function f such that $\mathbf{F} = \nabla f$.

$\mathbf{F}(x, y, z) = 10x\mathbf{i} + 10y\mathbf{j} + 10z\mathbf{k}$

17. Find the work done by the force field $\mathbf{F}$ in moving an object from P to Q.

$\mathbf{F}(x, y) = x^3 y^4 \mathbf{i} + x^4 y^3 \mathbf{j}$; $P(0, 0), Q(3, 2)$

18. Let $\mathbf{F} = \nabla f$, where $f(x, y) = \sin(x - 8y)$.

Which of the following equations does the line segment from $(0, 0)$ to $(0, \pi)$ satisfy?

Select the correct answer.

a. $\displaystyle\int_C \mathbf{F} \cdot d\mathbf{r} = 0$

b. $\displaystyle\int_C \mathbf{F} \cdot d\mathbf{r} = 1$

c. none of these

19. Suppose that $\mathbf{F} = \dfrac{9\mathbf{r}}{|\mathbf{r}|^3}$ is an inverse square force field, where $\mathbf{r} = x\mathbf{i} + y\mathbf{j} + z\mathbf{k}$.

Find the work done by $\mathbf{F}$ in moving an object from a point P_1 along a path to a point P_2 in terms of the distances d_1 and d_2 from these points to the origin.

20. Use Green's Theorem to find the work done by the force $\mathbf{F}(x, y) = x(x + 4y)\mathbf{i} + 4xy^2\mathbf{j}$ in moving a particle from the origin along the x-axis to $(1, 0)$ then along the line segment to $(0, 1)$ and then back to the origin along the y-axis.

1. $\dfrac{1}{x+2y}\mathbf{i}+\dfrac{2}{x+2y}\mathbf{j}$

2. $\cos\left(\dfrac{2y}{5z}\right)\mathbf{i}-\dfrac{2x}{5z}\sin\left(\dfrac{2y}{5z}\right)\mathbf{j}+\dfrac{2xy}{5z^2}\sin\left(\dfrac{2y}{5z}\right)\mathbf{k}$

3. $y=\dfrac{x^2}{2}-46$

4. 6250

5. -5.83

6. a

7. $\dfrac{1029}{5}-\cos(64)-\sin(16)$

8. $-2e^x\cos(y)k$

9. a

10. $6\pi^2$

11. -8.1

12. $\dfrac{-87}{88}$

13. $4x+yx^2+x(\ln x-1)+K$

14. $ye^{9x}+x\sin(y)+K$

15. 8

16. $f=5x^2+5y^2+5z^2+K$

17. 324

18. a

19. $9\left(\dfrac{1}{d_2}-\dfrac{1}{d}\right)$

20. -0.333333

1. Evaluate $\int\limits_{C} xy\ dx + (x-y)\ dy$, where C consists of line segments from $(0, 0)$ to $(4, 0)$ and from $(4, 0)$ to $(3, 4)$.

2. Find the exact value of $\int\limits_{C} xe^{yz}\ ds$, where C is the line segment from $(0, 0, 0)$ to $(1, 4, 3)$.

3. Find the exact value of the line integral $\int\limits_{C} \mathbf{F} \cdot d\mathbf{r}$, where $\mathbf{F}(x, y, z) = \sin(x)\mathbf{i} + \cos(y)\mathbf{j} + xz\mathbf{k}$ and C is given by $\mathbf{r}(t) = t^3\mathbf{i} - t^2\mathbf{j} + t\mathbf{k}, \ 0 \le t \le 1$.

4. Evaluate the line integral $\int\limits_{C} \mathbf{F} \cdot d\mathbf{r}$, where $\mathbf{F}(x, y) = (x - y)\mathbf{i} + (xy)\mathbf{j}$ and C is the arc of the circle $x^2 + y^2 = 4$ traversed counterclockwise from $(2, 0)$ to $(0, -2)$.

5. Find the exact value of $\int\limits_{C} \mathbf{F} \cdot d\mathbf{r}$, where $\mathbf{F}(x, y) = e^{x-1}\mathbf{i} + (xy)\mathbf{j}$ and C is given by $\mathbf{r}(t) = t^2\mathbf{i} + t^3\mathbf{j}, \ 0 \le t \le 1$.

6. Find the area of the part of the surface $y = 4x + z^2$ that lies between the planes $x = 0, \ x = 4, \ z = 0$, and $z = 1$.

   Select the correct answer.

   a. 19.148
   b. 17.118
   c. 13.638
   d. 27.218
   e. 16.113

7. Evaluate the surface integral.

   $$\iint\limits_{S} 10yz\ dS$$

   S is the surface with parametric equations $x = 5\ uv, \ y = 6\ (u + v), \ z = 6\ (u - v), \ u^2 + v^2 = 3$.

8. Evaluate the surface integral $\iint\limits_{S} \mathbf{F} \, dS$ for the given vector field $\mathbf{F}$ and the oriented surface S. In other words, find the flux of $\mathbf{F}$ across S.

   $\mathbf{F}(x, y, z) = 4x\mathbf{i} + 4y\mathbf{j} + 4z\mathbf{k}$, S is the sphere $x^2 + y^2 + z^2 = 2$.

9. A fluid with density 1,230 flows with velocity $\mathbf{v} = y\mathbf{i} + \mathbf{j} + z\mathbf{k}$. Find the rate of flow upward through the paraboloid $z = 9 - \frac{1}{4}(x^2 + y^2)$, $x^2 + y^2 \leq 36$.

10. Use Stokes' Theorem to evaluate $\iint\limits_{S} \mathbf{curl} \, \mathbf{F} \cdot dS$

    $\mathbf{F}(x, y, z) = 9xyz\mathbf{i} + 9xy\mathbf{j} + 9x^2yz\mathbf{k}$

    S consists of the top and the four sides (but not the bottom) of the cube with vertices $(\pm 9, \ \pm 9, \ \pm 9)$ oriented outward.

11. Use Stokes' Theorem to evaluate $\iint\limits_{S} \mathbf{curl} \, \mathbf{F} \cdot dS$

    $\mathbf{F}(x, y, z) = 8xy\mathbf{i} + 8e^z\mathbf{j} + 8xy^2\mathbf{k}$

    S consists of the four sides of the pyramid with vertices $(0, 0, 0)$, $(5, 0, 0)$, $(0, 0, 5)$, $(5, 0, 5)$, and $(0, 5, 0)$ that lie to the right of the xz-plane, oriented in the direction of the positive y-axis.

12. Use Stokes' Theorem to evaluate $\int\limits_{C} \mathbf{F} \cdot d\mathbf{r}$.

    $\mathbf{F}(x, y, z) = 4z\mathbf{i} + 2x\mathbf{j} + 6y\mathbf{k}$

    C is the curve of intersection of the plane $z = x + 9$ and the cylinder $x^2 + y^2 = 9$

13. Calculate the work done by the force field $\mathbf{F}(x, y, z) = (x^x + 14z^2)\mathbf{i} + (y^y + 6x^2)\mathbf{j} + (z^z + 12y^2)\mathbf{k}$ when a particle moves under its influence around the edge of the part of the sphere $x^2 + y^2 + z^2 = 4$ that lies in the first octant, in a counterclockwise direction as viewed from above.

    Select the correct answer.

    a. 512π
    b. 85.33
    c. 170.67
    d. 170.67π
    e. 85π

14. Use the Divergence Theorem to calculate the surface integral $\iint\limits_S \mathbf{F} \; dS$.

$\mathbf{F}(x,y,z) = xz\mathbf{i} + yz\mathbf{j} + 5z^2\mathbf{k}$

S is the surface of the solid bounded by the paraboloid $z = x^2 + y^2$ and the plane $z = 6$.

15. The temperature at the point (x, y, z) in a substance with conductivity $K = 14$ is
$u(x, y, z) = 5x^2 + 5y^2$.

Find the rate of heat flow inward across the cylindrical surface $y^2 + z^2 = 4$, $0 \le x \le 5$.

16. Use the Divergence Theorem to calculate the surface integral $\iint\limits_S \mathbf{F} \; dS$, that is, calculate the flux of $\mathbf{F}$ across S.

$\mathbf{F}(x,y,z) = x^3\mathbf{i} + 2xz^4\mathbf{j} + 3y^2\mathbf{k}$

S is the surface of the solid bounded by the paraboloid $z = 1 - x^2 - y^2$ and the xy-plane.

17. Use the Divergence Theorem to calculate the surface integral $\iint\limits_S \mathbf{F} \; dS$, that is, calculate the flux of $\mathbf{F}$ across S.

$\mathbf{F}(x,y,z) = x^3\mathbf{i} + y^3\mathbf{j} + z^3\mathbf{k}$

S is the sphere $x^2 + y^2 + z^2 = 25$.

Select the correct answer.

a. $2{,}500\pi$
b. 500π
c. $7{,}500$
d. 500
e. $7{,}500\pi$

18. Use the Divergence Theorem to calculate the surface integral $\iint\limits_S \mathbf{F} \; dS$, that is, calculate the flux of $\mathbf{F}$ across S.

$$\mathbf{F}(x,y,z) = e^y \cos z\mathbf{i} + y\sqrt{1-x^2}\,\mathbf{j} + x\cos y\mathbf{k}$$

S is the surface of the solid that lies above the xy-plane and below the surface $z = 5 - x^4 - y^4, \; -1 \le x \le 1, \; -1 \le y \le 1$.

Round the result to the nearest hundredth.

19. Evaluate the surface integral $\iint\limits_S \mathbf{F} \; dS$ for the given vector field $\mathbf{F}$ and the oriented surface S. In other words, find the flux of $\mathbf{F}$ across S.

$$\mathbf{F}(x,y,z) = 9x\mathbf{i} + 2y\mathbf{j} + 6z\mathbf{k}$$

S is the cube with vertices $(\pm 1, \; \pm 1, \; \pm 1)$.

20. Assume that S and $\mathbf{F}$ satisfy the conditions of the Divergence Theorem and the scalar functions and components of the vector fields have continuous second-order partial derivatives. Which of the following expressions is equal to zero?

Select the correct answer.

a. $\iint\limits_S (f \, \nabla \, g) \cdot \mathbf{n} \; dS$

b. $\iint\limits_S \mathbf{a} \cdot \mathbf{n} \; dS$, $\mathbf{a}$ is a constant vector

c. $\iint\limits_S (f \, \nabla \, g - g \, \nabla \, f) \cdot \mathbf{n} \; dS$

ANSWER KEY

1. -0.67

2. $\dfrac{\sqrt{26}(e^{12}-1)}{24}$

3. $\dfrac{6}{5} - \cos(1) - \sin(1)$

4. 10.09

5. $1 + \dfrac{3}{8} - \dfrac{1}{e}$

6. b

7. 0

8. $32\sqrt{2}\pi$

9. 199260π

10. 0

11. 0

12. -36π

13. c

14. 864π

15. 5600π

16. 0.5π

17. e

18. 0

19. 136

20. b

1. Evaluate $\displaystyle\int_C y\ ds$, where C is given by $x = t^2$, $y = t$, $2 \le t \le 9$.

2. Evaluate $\displaystyle\int_C xy^4\ ds$, where C is the right half of the circle $x^2 + y^2 = 4$.

   Select the correct answer.

   a.　　0.8
   b.　　267.0
   c.　　25.6
   d.　　97.4
   e.　　90.4

3. Evaluate $\displaystyle\int_C xy\ dx + (x - y)\ dy$, where C consists of line segments from $(0, 0)$ to $(4, 0)$ and from $(4, 0)$ to $(4, 2)$.

4. Evaluate $\displaystyle\int_C xy^3\ ds$, where C is given by $x = 9\sin t$, $y = \cos t$, $z = 9t$, $0 \le t \le \dfrac{\pi}{2}$.

5. Let $\mathbf{r} = x\mathbf{i} + y\mathbf{j} + z\mathbf{k}$ and $r = |\mathbf{r}|$.

   Find $\nabla \cdot (4\mathbf{r})$.

6. Evaluate $\displaystyle\int_C \mathbf{F} \cdot d\mathbf{r}$, where $\mathbf{F}(x, y) = \dfrac{x}{\sqrt{x^2 + y^2}}\mathbf{i} + \dfrac{y}{\sqrt{x^2 + y^2}}\mathbf{j}$ and C is the parabola $y = 1 + x^2$ from (-3, 10) to (-2, 5).

7. Find the exact value of $\displaystyle\int_C \mathbf{F} \cdot d\mathbf{r}$, where $\mathbf{F}(x, y) = e^{x-1}\mathbf{i} + xy\mathbf{j}$ and C is given by

   $\mathbf{r}(t) = t^2\mathbf{i} + t^3\mathbf{j}$, $0 \le t \le 1$.

8. Determine whether or not the vector field is conservative. If it is conservative, find a function f such that $\mathbf{F} = \nabla f$.

   $\mathbf{F}(x, y, z) = 5zy\mathbf{i} + 5xz\mathbf{j} + 5xy\mathbf{k}$

9. A thin wire is bent into the shape of a semicircle $x^2 + y^2 = 4$, $x > 0$. If the linear density is 3, find the mass of the wire.

   Select the correct answer.

   a. 18π
   b. $6\pi^2$
   c. 3π
   d. 6π
   e. 2π

10. Find the exact mass of a thin wire in the shape of the helix $x = 2\sin t$, $y = 2\cos t$, $z = 3t$, $0 \le t \le 2\pi$ if the density is 5.

11. Find the work done by the force field $\mathbf{F}(x, y) = 2x\mathbf{i} + (2y + 5)\mathbf{j}$ in moving an object along an arch of the cycloid $\mathbf{r}(t) = (t - \sin(t))\mathbf{i} + (1 - \cos(t))\mathbf{j}$, $0 \le t \le 2\pi$.

12. Determine whether or not $\mathbf{F}$ is a conservative vector field. If it is, find a function f such that $\mathbf{F} = \nabla f$.

   $$\mathbf{F} = (6ye^{6x} + \sin y)\mathbf{i} + (e^{6x} + x\cos y)\mathbf{j}$$

13. Find a function f such that $\mathbf{F} = \nabla f$ and use it to evaluate $\displaystyle\int_C \mathbf{F} \cdot d\mathbf{r}$ along the given curve C.

   $\mathbf{F} = y\mathbf{i} + (x + 2y)\mathbf{j}$; C is the upper semicircle that starts at $(1, 4)$ and ends at $(5, 4)$.

14. Find the work done by the force field $\mathbf{F}$ in moving an object from P to Q.

   $\mathbf{F}(x, y) = x^2 y^3 \mathbf{i} + x^3 y^2 \mathbf{j}$; $P(0, 0)$, $Q(4, 1)$

15. Use Green's Theorem to evaluate the double integral.

   $P(x, y) = 2x^2 \sin y$, $Q(x, y) = 3y^2 \sin x$

   C is a triangle with the vertices $(0, 0)$, $(4, 0)$ and $(4, 4)$.

   Round the answer to the nearest hundredth.

16. Use Green's Theorem to evaluate the line integral along the given positively oriented curve.

$$\int_C \left(7.5y^2 - \tan^{-1} x\right) dx + \left(12x + \sin y\right) dy$$

C is the boundary of the region enclosed by the parabola $y = x^2$ and the line $y = 49$.

17. Find the area of the region bounded by the hypocycloid with vector equation.

$$\mathbf{r}(t) = 12\cos^3 t\mathbf{i} + 80\sin^3 t\mathbf{j}, \ 0 \le t \le 2\pi$$

Select the correct answer.

    a.   360
    b. $360\pi^2$
    c. 360π
    d. 2.25π
    e. $2.25\pi^2$

18. Determine whether or not the vector field is conservative. If it is conservative, find a function f such that $\mathbf{F} = \nabla f$.

$$\mathbf{F}(x,y,z) = 27yze^{9xz}\mathbf{i} + 3e^{9xz}\mathbf{j} + 27xye^{9xz}\mathbf{k}$$

19. Use Stokes' Theorem to evaluate $\int_C \mathbf{F} \cdot d\mathbf{r}$, where $\mathbf{F}(x,y,z) = 6yx^2\mathbf{i} + 2x^3\mathbf{j} + 6xy\mathbf{k}$.

C is the curve of intersection of the hyperbolic paraboloid $z = y^2 - x^2$ and the cylinder $x^2 + y^2 = 25$ oriented counterclockwise as viewed from above.

20. Use the Divergence Theorem to calculate the surface integral

$$\iint_S \mathbf{F} \ dS \ ;$$ that is, calculate the flux of $\mathbf{F}$ across S.

$$\mathbf{F}(x,y,z) = 3xy^2\mathbf{i} + 10xe^z\mathbf{j} + z^3\mathbf{k}$$

S is the surface of the solid bounded by the cylinder $y^2 + z^2 = 16$ and the planes $x = -5$ and $x = 3x$.

Select the correct answer.

    a. $1{,}024\pi$
    b. $2{,}048\pi$
    c. $3{,}072\pi$
    d. -768π
    e. $-1{,}024\pi$

ANSWER KEY

Stewart - Calculus ET 5e Chapter 16 Form H

1. 482.41

2. c

3. 6

4. 20876.97

5. 12

6. −5.0551

7. $1 + \dfrac{3}{8} - \dfrac{1}{e}$

8. 1

9. d

10. $10\sqrt{13}\pi$

11. $4\pi^2$

12. $ye^{6x} + x\sin(y) + K$

13. 16

14. $\dfrac{64}{3}$

15. 37.77

16. -196196

17. c

18. $f = 3ye^{9xz} + K$

19. -3750π

20. c

1. Solve the differential equation.

   $y'' - 9y' + 14y = 0$

2. Solve the differential equation.

   $y'' + 10y' + 41y = 0$

3. Solve the differential equation.

   $y'' - 6y' + 9y = 0$

4. Solve the differential equation.

   $13y'' = 5y'$

5. Solve the differential equation.

   $4y'' + y' = 0$

6. Solve the initial-value problem.

   $2y'' + 21y' + 54y = 0$, $y(0) = 0$, $y'(0) = 1$

7. Solve the initial-value problem.

   $y'' - 25y' = 0$, $y(0) = 6$, $y'(0) = 0$

8. Solve the initial-value problem.

   $y'' + 49y = 0$, $y\left(\dfrac{\pi}{7}\right) = 0$, $y'\left(\dfrac{\pi}{7}\right) = 1$

9. Solve the boundary-value problem, if possible.

$$y'' - y' - 2y = 0 \ , \quad y(-1) = 1 \ , \quad y(1) = 0$$

10. Solve the differential equation using the method of undetermined coefficients.

$$y'' + 6y' + 9y = 1 + x$$

11. Solve the differential equation using the method of undetermined coefficients.

$$y'' - 4y' + 5y = e^{-x}$$

12. Solve the initial-value problem using the method of undetermined coefficients.

$$y'' + y' - 2y = x + \sin x \ , \quad y(0) = \frac{19}{20} \ , \quad y'(0) = 0$$

13. Solve the differential equation using the method of variation of parameters.

$$y'' - 2y' = e^{2x}$$

14. Solve the differential equation using the method of variation of parameters.

$$y'' - 4y = \frac{1}{x}$$

15. A spring with a 7-kg mass is held stretched 1.4 m beyond its natural length by a force of 80 N. If the spring begins at its equilibrium position but a push gives it an initial velocity of 1.2 m/s, find the position x (t) of the mass after t seconds.

16. A spring with a mass of 2 kg has damping constant 14, and a force of 3.6 N is required to keep the spring stretched 0.3 m beyond its natural length. Find the mass that would produce critical damping.

17. A series circuit consists of a resistor $R = 20 \ \Omega$, an inductor with $L = 1$ H, a capacitor with $C = 0.002$ F, and a 12-V battery. If the initial charge and current are both 0, find the charge Q(t) at time t.

18. A series circuit consists of a resistor $R = 24 \ \Omega$, an inductor with $L = 2$ H, a capacitor with $C = 0.005$ F, and a generator producing a voltage of $E(t) = 12\cos 10t$. If the initial charge is $Q = 0.001$ C and the initial current is 0, find the charge Q(t) at time t.

19. Use power series to solve the differential equation.

    $y' = 7xy$

20. Use power series to solve the differential equation.

    $y'' = 64y$

Stewart - Calculus ET 5e Chapter 17 Form A

---

1. $c_1 e^{7x} + c_2 e^{2x}$

2. $e^{-5x}(c_1 \cos(4x) + c_2 \sin(4x))$

3. $e^{3x}(c_1 + c_2 x)$

4. $c_1 + c_2 e^{\frac{5x}{13}}$

5. $c_1 + c_2 e^{\frac{-x}{4}}$

6. $\dfrac{2}{3} e^{\frac{-9x}{2}} - \dfrac{2}{3} e^{-6x}$

7. $3(e^{5x} + e^{-5x})$

8. $-\dfrac{1}{7} \sin(7x)$

9. $\dfrac{1}{e^6 - 1}(e^{5-x} - e^{2(x+1)})$

10. $y(x) = c_1 e^{-3x} + c_2 x e^{-3x} + \dfrac{1}{9}x + \dfrac{1}{27}$

11. $y(x) = e^{2x}(c_1 \cos(x) + c_2 \sin(x)) + \dfrac{1}{10} e^{-x}$

12. $y(x) = \dfrac{17}{15} e^x + \dfrac{1}{6} e^{-2x} - \dfrac{1}{2}x - \dfrac{1}{4} - \dfrac{1}{10}\cos(x) - \dfrac{3}{10}\sin(x)$

13. $y(x) = c_1 + c_2 e^{2x} + \dfrac{1}{2} x e^{2x}$

14. $y(x) = \left(c_1 - \displaystyle\int \dfrac{e^{2x}}{4x}\ dx \right) e^{-2x} + \left(c_2 + \displaystyle\int \dfrac{e^{-2x}}{4x}\ dx \right) e^{2x}$

15. $x(t) = 0.42 \sin\left(\dfrac{20t}{7} \right)$

16. $49/12$

17. $Q(t) = \dfrac{-e^{-10t}}{250}(6\cos(20t) + 3\sin(20t)) + \dfrac{3}{125}$

18. $Q(t) = e^{-6t}(0.001\cos(8t) - 0.06175\sin(8t)) + \dfrac{1}{20}\sin(10t)$

19. $y(x) = ce^{\frac{7x^2}{2}}$

20. $y(x) = c_1 \cosh(8x) + c_2 \sinh(8x)$

---

1. Solve the differential equation.

   $$y'' - 18y' + 106y = 0$$

2. Solve the differential equation.

   $$y'' - 12y' + 36y = 0$$

3. Solve the differential equation.

   $$7y'' = 2y'$$

4. Solve the differential equation.

   $$3y'' + y' = 0$$

5. Solve the differential equation.

   $$\frac{d^2 y}{dt^2} + \frac{dy}{dt} + 2y = 0$$

6. Solve the initial-value problem.

   $$y'' + 36y = 0, \quad y\left(\frac{\pi}{6}\right) = 0, \quad y'\left(\frac{\pi}{6}\right) = 1$$

7. Solve the boundary-value problem, if possible.

   $$y'' + 2y' - 15y = 0, \quad y(0) = 0, \quad y(2) = 1$$

8. Solve the boundary-value problem, if possible.

   $$y'' - y' - 30y = 0, \quad y(-1) = 1, \quad y(1) = 0$$

9. Solve the boundary-value problem, if possible.

$$y'' + 2y' + 37y = 0 \ , \quad y(0) = 1 \ , \quad y(\pi) = 2$$

10. Solve the differential equation using the method of undetermined coefficients.

$$y'' + 9y = e^{2x}$$

11. Solve the differential equation using the method of undetermined coefficients.

$$y'' - 8y' + 17y = e^{-x}$$

12. Solve the initial - value problem using the method of undetermined coefficients.

$$y'' - y = xe^{2x} \ , \quad y(0) = 0 \ , \quad y'(0) = 1$$

13. Solve the differential equation using the method of variation of parameters.

$$y'' + 9y = x$$

14. Solve the differential equation using the method of variation of parameters.

$$y'' - 5y' + 4y = \sin x$$

15. Solve the differential equation using the method of variation of parameters.

$$y'' + 6y' + 9y = \frac{e^{-3x}}{x^3}$$

16. A series circuit consists of a resistor $R = 24 \ \Omega$, an inductor with $L = 2$ H, a capacitor with $C = 0.005$ F, and a generator producing a voltage of $E(t) = 12\cos 10t$. If the initial charge is $Q = 0.001$ C and the initial current is 0, find the charge Q(t) at time t.

17. Use power series to solve the differential equation.

$y' = 5xy$

18. Use power series to solve the differential equation.

$y' = 5x^2 y$

19. The figure shows a pendulum with length L and the angle θ from the vertical to the pendulum. It can be shown that θ, as a function of time, satisfies the nonlinear differential equation $\dfrac{d^2\theta}{dt^2} + \dfrac{g}{L}\sin\theta = 0$ where g = 9.8 m/s^2 is the acceleration due to gravity. For small values of θ we can use the linear approximation $\sin\theta = \theta$ and then the differential equation becomes linear. Find the equation of motion of a pendulum with length 1 m if θ is initially 0.1 rad and the initial angular velocity is $\dfrac{d\theta}{dt} = 1$ rad/s.

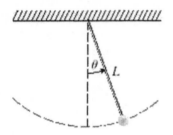

20. Use power series to solve the differential equation.

$y'' - xy' - y = 0$, $y(0) = 1$, $y'(0) = 0$

1. $e^{9x}(c_1 \cos(5x) + c_2 \sin(5x))$

2. $e^{6x}(c_1 + c_2 x)$

3. $c_1 + c_2 e^{\frac{2x}{7}}$

4. $c_1 + c_2 e^{\frac{-x}{3}}$

5. $e^{\frac{-t}{2}}\left(c_1 \cos\left(\frac{\sqrt{7}t}{2}\right) + c_2 \sin\left(\frac{\sqrt{7}t}{2}\right)\right)$

6. $-\dfrac{1}{6}\sin(6x)$

7. $\left(e^6 - e^{-10}\right)^{-1}\left(e^{3x} - e^{-5x}\right)$

8. $\dfrac{1}{e^{22} - 1}(e^{17-5x} - e^{6(x+1)})$

9. no solution

10. $y(x) = c_1 \cos(3x) + c_2 \sin(3x)) + \dfrac{1}{13}e^{2x}$

11. $y(x) = e^{4x}(c_1 \cos(x) + c_2 \sin(x)) + \dfrac{1}{26}e^{-x}$

12. $y(x) = e^x - \dfrac{5}{9}e^{-x} + e^{2x}\left(\dfrac{1}{3}x - \dfrac{4}{9}\right)$

13. $y(x) = c_1 \cos(3x) + c_2 \sin(3x)) + \dfrac{1}{9}x$

14. $y(x) = c_1 e^{4x} + c_2 e^x + \dfrac{5}{34}\cos(x) + \dfrac{3}{34}\sin(x)$

15. $y(x) = e^{-3x}\left(c_1 + c_2 x + \dfrac{1}{2x}\right)$

16. $Q(t) = e^{-6t}(0.001\cos(8t) - 0.06175\sin(8t)) + \dfrac{1}{20}\sin(10t)$

17. $y(x) = ce^{\frac{5x^2}{2}}$

18. $y(x) = ce^{\frac{5x^3}{3}}$

19. $\theta(t) = 0.1\cos(\sqrt{9.8}t) + \dfrac{1}{\sqrt{9.8}}\sin(\sqrt{9.8}t)$

20. $y(x) = e^{\frac{x^2}{2}}$

1. Solve the differential equation.

$$y'' + 10y' + 41y = 0$$

Select the correct answer.

    a. $y(x) = e^{-5x}(c_1 \cos(4x) + c_2 \sin(4x))$

    b. $y(x) = ce^{-5x} \cos(4x)$

    c. $y(x) = e^{-5x}(c_1 \cos(4x) + c_2 x \sin(4x))$

    d. $y(x) = e^{-4x}(c_1 \cos(5x) + c_2 \sin(5x))$

    e. $y(x) = e^{-x}(c_1 \cos(x) + c_2 \sin(x))$

2. Solve the initial-value problem.

$$y'' + 8y' + 41y = 0 \ , \ \ y(0) = 1, \ \ y'(0) = 2$$

Select the correct answer.

    a. $y(x) = e^{4x}\left(\cos(5x) - \dfrac{2}{5}\sin(5x) \right)$

    b. $y(x) = e^{-4x}\left(\cos(5x) + \dfrac{6}{5}\sin(5x) \right)$

    c. $y(x) = e^{5x}\left(\cos(5x) + \dfrac{6}{5}\sin(5x) \right)$

    d. $y(x) = e^{5x}\left(\cos(4x) + \dfrac{6}{5}\sin(4x) \right)$

    e. $y(x) = e^{-5x}\left(\cos(5x) + \dfrac{2}{5}\sin(5x) \right)$

3. Solve the initial-value problem.

$$y'' - 16y' + 64y = 0 \ , \ \ y(2) = 0, \ \ y'(2) = 1$$

Select the correct answer.

    a. $y(x) = (x - 2)e^{8(x-2)}$

    b. $y(x) = (x + 2)e^{8(x-2)}$

    c. $y(x) = (x + 2)e^{8(x+2)}$

    d. $y(x) = (x - 2)e^{8(x+2)}$

    e. $y(x) = (x - 8)e^{8(x+8)}$

4. Solve the boundary-value problem, if possible.

$$y'' + 5y' - 24y = 0, \quad y(0) = 0, \quad y(2) = 1$$

Select the correct answer.

a. $\quad y(x) = \left(e^6 - e^{-16} \right)\left(e^{6x} - e^{-8x} \right)$

b. $\quad y(x) = \left(e^6 - e^{-16} \right)^{-1}\left(e^{6x} - e^{-16x} \right)$

c. $\quad y(x) = \left(e^6 - e^{-16} \right)^{-1}\left(e^{3x} - e^{-8x} \right)$

d. $\quad y(x) = \left(e^8 - e^{-16} \right)^{-1}\left(e^{x} - e^{-8x} \right)$

e. $\quad$ No solution

5. Solve the differential equation using the method of undetermined coefficients.

$$y'' + 5y' + 6y = x^2$$

Select the correct answer.

a. $\quad y(x) = c_1 e^{-2x} + c_2 e^{-3x} + \dfrac{19}{108} c_3$

b. $\quad y(x) = \dfrac{1}{6}x^2 - \dfrac{5}{18}x + \dfrac{19}{108}$

c. $\quad y(x) = c_1 e^{-2x} + c_2 e^{-3x}$

d. $\quad y(x) = c_1 e^{-2x} + c_2 e^{-3x} + \dfrac{1}{6}x^2 - \dfrac{5}{18}x + \dfrac{19}{108}$

e. $\quad y(x) = c_1 e^{-2x} + c_2 e^{-3x} + \dfrac{1}{6}x^2$

6. Solve the differential equation using the method of undetermined coefficients.

$$y'' + 6y' + 9y = 1 + x$$

Select the correct answer.

a. $\quad y(x) = c_1 e^{-3x} + c_2 x e^{-3x}$

b. $\quad y(x) = c_1 e^{-3x} + c_2 x e^{-3x} + \dfrac{1}{9}x + \dfrac{1}{27}$

c. $\quad y(x) = c_1 e^{-3x} + \dfrac{1}{9}x + \dfrac{1}{27}$

d. $\quad y(x) = c_1 e^{-3x} + c_2 x e^{-3x} + \dfrac{2}{9}x$

e. $\quad y(x) = c_1 x e^{-3x} + c_2 x^2 e^{-3x} + \dfrac{1}{27}x$

7. Solve the differential equation using the method of variation of parameters.

$$y'' - 4y' + 3y = \sin x$$

Select the correct answer.

a. $y(x) = c_1 \sin 3x + \dfrac{c_2}{4} x + \cos 3x$

b. $y(x) = c_1 \sin x + \dfrac{c_2}{5} x + \dfrac{1}{10} \sin x$

c. $y(x) = c_1 e^{3x} + c_2 e^x + \dfrac{1}{5} \cos x + \dfrac{1}{10} \sin x$

d. $y(x) = c_1 e^{3x} + c_2 e^x + \dfrac{1}{10} \sin x$

e. $y(x) = c_1 e^{3x} + c_2 e^x + \dfrac{1}{5} \sin x$

8. Solve the differential equation using the method of variation of parameters.

$$y'' - y' = e^x$$

Select the correct answer.

a. $y(x) = c_1 + c_2 x e^x + e^x$

b. $y(x) = c_1 + c_2 e^x + x e^x$

c. $y(x) = c_1 + c_2 e^x$

d. $y(x) = c_1 + (1 + x) x e^x$

e. $y(x) = c_1 + x e^x$

9. Solve the differential equation using the method of variation of parameters.

$$y'' + y = \sec x \ , \quad \dfrac{\pi}{4} < x < \dfrac{\pi}{2}$$

Select the correct answer.

a. $y(x) = (c_1 + x) \sin x + c_2 + \ln(\cos x)$

b. $y(x) = \dfrac{\pi}{2} \sin x + \left[\dfrac{\pi}{2} + \ln(\cos x) \right] \cos x$

c. $y(x) = \left[\dfrac{\pi}{4} + \ln(\cos x) \right] \cos x$

d. $y(x) = (c_1 + x) \sin x + [c_2 + \ln(\cos x)] \cos x$

e. $y(x) = c_1 + [c_2 + \ln(\sin x)] \sin x$

10. A spring with a 3-kg mass is held stretched 0.9 m beyond its natural length by a force of 30 N. If the spring begins at its equilibrium position but a push gives it an initial velocity of 1.2 m/s, find the position x(t) of the mass after t seconds.

Select the correct answer.

a. $x(t) = 1.2\sin(7t)$

b. $x(t) = 0.36\sin\left(\dfrac{10}{3}t\right) + 0.48\cos\left(\dfrac{10}{3}t\right)$

c. $x(t) = 0.48\cos\left(\dfrac{10}{3}t\right)$

d. $x(t) = 0.36\sin\left(\dfrac{10}{3}t\right)$

e. $x(t) = \dfrac{10}{3}\sin(7t)$

11. A spring with a mass of 5 kg has damping constant 28 and spring constant 195. Find the damping constant that would produce critical damping.

Select the correct answer.

a. $c = 10\sqrt{77}$

b. $c = 10\sqrt{39}$

c. $c = 15\sqrt{39}$

d. $c = 15\sqrt{77}$

e. $c = 39\sqrt{10}$

12. A series circuit consists of a resistor $R = 16\ \Omega$, an inductor with $L = 2$ H, a capacitor with $C = 0.00625$ F, and a 12-V battery. If the initial charge is 0.0008 C and the initial current is 0, find the current I(t) at time t.

Select the correct answer.

a. $I(t) = 0.742e^{-4t}\sin(8t)$

b. $I(t) = 0.742e^{-8t}$

c. $I(t) = \dfrac{e^{-160t}}{160}(0.00625\cos(4t) + 8\sin(4t)) - \dfrac{1}{2}$

d. $I(t) = \dfrac{e^{-4t}}{160}\cos(8t)$

e. $I(t) = \dfrac{e^{-4t}}{160}\cos(8t) - \dfrac{1}{2}$

13. The figure shows a pendulum with length L and the angle θ from the vertical to the pendulum. It can be shown that θ, as a function of time, satisfies the nonlinear differential equation $\dfrac{d^2\theta}{dt^2} + \dfrac{g}{L}\sin\theta = 0$ where g = 9.8 m/s ^{2} is the acceleration due to gravity. For small values of θ we can use the linear approximation $\sin\theta = \theta$ and then the differential equation becomes linear. Find the equation of motion of a pendulum with length 1 m if θ is initially 0.1 rad and the initial angular velocity is $\dfrac{d\theta}{dt} = 1$ rad/s.

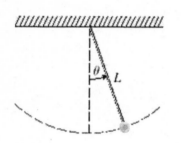

Select the correct answer.

a. $\theta(t) = 0.1\cos(\sqrt{9.8}t) + \dfrac{1}{\sqrt{9.8}}\sin(\sqrt{9.8}t)$

b. $\theta(t) = 0.1\sin(\sqrt{9.8}t) + \dfrac{1}{\sqrt{9.8}}\cos(\sqrt{9.8}t)$

c. $\theta(t) = 2\cos(9.8t) + \dfrac{1}{9.8}\sin(9.8t)$

d. $\theta(t) = 0.1\cos(\sqrt{9.8}t) + 2\sin(\sqrt{9.8}t)$

e. $\theta(t) = \dfrac{1}{9.8}\cos(\sqrt{9.8}t) + 0.1\sin(\sqrt{9.8}t)$

14. Use power series to solve the differential equation.

$y' = 4x^2 y$

Select the correct answer.

a. $y(x) = ce^{\frac{4x^3}{3}}$

b. $y(x) = ce^{4x}$

c. $y(x) = ce^{-\frac{4x^3}{3}}$

d. $y(x) = 4e^{\frac{x^3}{3}}$

e. $y(x) = e^{-\frac{x^3}{3}}$

15. Use power series to solve the differential equation.

$(x-6)y' + 2y = 0$

Select the correct answer.

a. $y(x) = c_0 \sum\limits_{n=0}^{\infty} \dfrac{n+1}{6^n} x^n$

b. $y(x) = c_0 \sum\limits_{n=0}^{\infty} \dfrac{x^n}{6^n}$

c. $y(x) = c_0 \sum\limits_{n=0}^{\infty} \dfrac{nx^n}{6^n}$

d. $y(x) = c_0 \sum\limits_{n=0}^{\infty} (n+1)x^n$

e. $y(x) = c_0 \sum\limits_{n=0}^{\infty} \dfrac{(n+1)}{x^n}$

16. Use power series to solve the differential equation.

$y'' - xy' - y = 0$, $y(0) = 5$, $y'(0) = 0$

Select the correct answer.

a. $y(x) = e^{5x}$

b. $y(x) = 5e^{\frac{x^2}{2}}$

c. $y(x) = 5e^x$

d. $y(x) = ce^{\frac{x^2}{2}}$

e. $y(x) = 5e^{-\frac{x^2}{2}}$

17. Use power series to solve the differential equation.

$$y'' + x^2 y = 0 \, , \quad y(0) = 6, \quad y'(0) = 0$$

Select the correct answer.

a. $y(x) = 6 - \sum\limits_{n=1}^{\infty} (-1)^n \dfrac{x^{4n}}{4n(4n-1)...4 \cdot 3}$

b. $y(x) = \sum\limits_{n=1}^{\infty} (-1)^n \dfrac{6x^{4n}}{4n(4n-1)...4 \cdot 3}$

c. $y(x) = 6 + \sum\limits_{n=1}^{\infty} (-1)^n \dfrac{6x^{4n}}{4n(4n-1)...4 \cdot 3}$

d. $y(x) = -6 + \sum\limits_{n=1}^{\infty} (-1)^n \dfrac{x^{4n}}{4n(4n-1)...4 \cdot 3}$

e. $y(x) = \sum\limits_{n=1}^{\infty} (-1)^n \dfrac{x^{4n}}{4n(4n-1)...4 \cdot 3}$

18. The solution of the initial-value problem $x^2 y'' + xy' + x^2 y = 0 \, , \quad y(0) = 1, \quad y'(0) = 0$ is called a Bessel function of order 0. Solve the initial - value problem to find a power series expansion for the Bessel function.

Select the correct answer.

a. $y(x) = x + \sum\limits_{n=0}^{\infty} (-1)^n \dfrac{x^{2n}}{2^{2n}(n!)^2}$

b. $y(x) = \sum\limits_{n=0}^{\infty} (-1)^{n+1} \dfrac{nx^{2n-1}}{2^{2n-1}(n!)^2}$

c. $y(x) = \sum\limits_{n=0}^{\infty} (-1)^n \dfrac{x^{2n}}{2^{2n}(n!)^2}$

d. $y(x) = \sum\limits_{n=0}^{\infty} (-1)^n \dfrac{x^n}{2^n(2n!)}$

e. $y(x) = 2^x + \sum\limits_{n=0}^{\infty} (-1)^n \dfrac{x^{2n}}{(n!)^2}$

19. Solve the differential equation.

$$y'' - 8y' + 25y = 0$$

Select the correct answer.

a. $y(x) = e^{4x}(c_1 \cos(3x) + c_2 \sin(3x))$

b. $y(x) = e^{4x}(c_1 \cos(3x) + c_2 x \sin(3x))$

c. $y(x) = ce^{4x} \cos(3x)$

d. $y(x) = c_1 \cos(3x) + c_2 x \sin(3x)$

e. $y(x) = e^{4x}(c_1 \cos(4x) + c_2 x \sin(4x))$

20. A series circuit consists of a resistor $R = 24 \ \Omega$, an inductor with $L = 2$ H, a capacitor with $C = 0.005$ F, and a generator producing a voltage of $E(t) = 12\cos 10t$. If the initial charge is $Q = 0.001$ C and the initial current is 0, find the charge Q(t) at time t.

Select the correct answer.

a. $Q(t) = e^{-2t}(0.051\cos(2t) - 0.06175\sin(2t)) + \dfrac{1}{20}\sin(10t)$

b. $Q(t) = e^{-6t}(0.001\cos(8t) - 0.06175\sin(8t)) + \dfrac{1}{20}\sin(10t)$

c. $Q(t) = e^{-3t}(\cos(5t) - 0.06175\sin(5t))$

d. $Q(t) = e^{-6t}(\cos(6t) - 0.06175\sin(6t))$

e. $Q(t) = e^{-6t}(0.001\cos(8t) - 0.06175\sin(8t))$

1.   a

2.   b

3.   a

4.   c

5.   d

6.   b

7.   c

8.   b

9.   d

10. d

11. b

12. a

13. a

14. a

15. a

16. b

17. c

18. c

19. a

20. b

1. Solve the differential equation.

   $$17y'' = 3y'$$

   Select the correct answer.

   a. $y(x) = c_1 x + c_2 e^{\frac{3x}{17}}$

   b. $y(x) = c_1 + c_2 e^{\frac{3x}{17}}$

   c. $y(x) = c_1 x + c_2 e^{-\frac{3x}{17}}$

   d. $y(x) = ce^{\frac{17x}{3}}$

   e. $y(x) = ce^{17x}$

2. A spring with a mass of 3 kg has damping constant 35 and spring constant 129. Find the damping constant that would produce critical damping.

   Select the correct answer.

   a. $c = 6\sqrt{43}$

   b. $c = 6\sqrt{7}$

   c. $c = 9\sqrt{7}$

   d. $c = 9\sqrt{43}$

   e. $c = 43\sqrt{7}$

3. Solve the differential equation.

   $$\frac{d^2 y}{dt^2} + \frac{dy}{dt} + 3y = 0$$

   Select the correct answer.

   a. $y(t) = ce^{-\frac{t}{2}} \cos\left(\sqrt{\frac{11t}{2}}\right)$

   b. $y(t) = e^{-\frac{t}{2}}\left[c_1 \cos\left(\frac{\sqrt{11}t}{2}\right) + c_2 \sin\left(\frac{\sqrt{11}t}{2}\right)\right]$

   c. $y(t) = t^2 e^{-\frac{t}{2}}\left[c_1 \cos\left(\sqrt{\frac{11t}{2}}\right) + c_2 \sin\left(\sqrt{\frac{11t}{2}}\right)\right]$

   d. $y(t) = te^{\frac{t}{2}}\left[c_1 \cos\left(\frac{\sqrt{11}t}{2}\right) + c_2 \sin\left(\frac{\sqrt{11}t}{2}\right)\right]$

   e. $y(t) = e^{\frac{\sqrt{t}}{2}}\left[c_1 \cos\left(\frac{\sqrt{t}}{2}\right) + c_2 \sin\left(\frac{\sqrt{t}}{2}\right)\right]$

4. Solve the differential equation.

$$36y'' + y = 0$$

Select the correct answer.

a. $y(x) = c_1 \cos\left(-\dfrac{x}{36}\right) + c_2 \sin\left(-\dfrac{x}{6}\right)$

b. $y(x) = c_1 \cos(6x) + c_2 \sin(6x)$

c. $y(x) = c_1 \cos(-6x) + c_2 \sin(-6x)$

d. $y(x) = c_1 \cos\left(\dfrac{x}{6}\right) + c_2 \sin\left(\dfrac{x}{6}\right)$

e. $y(x) = c_1 \cos(36x) - c_2 \sin(36x)$

5. Solve the initial-value problem.

$$y'' - 2y' - 24y = 0 , \quad y(1) = 4, \quad y'(1) = 1$$

Select the correct answer.

a. $y(x) = \dfrac{1}{10} e^{4(x-1)} + \dfrac{1}{23} e^{-6(x-1)}$

b. $y(x) = e^{6x} - e^{-4x}$

c. $y(x) = \dfrac{17}{10} e^{6(x-1)} + \dfrac{23}{10} e^{-4(x-1)}$

d. $y(x) = \dfrac{1}{10} e^{4x} - \dfrac{1}{23} e^{-6x}$

e. $y(x) = \dfrac{1}{10} e^{x} - \dfrac{1}{23} e^{-x}$

6. Use power series to solve the differential equation.

$$y'' - xy' - y = 0 , \quad y(0) = 6, \quad y'(0) = 0$$

Select the correct answer.

a. $y(x) = 6e^{x}$

b. $y(x) = 6e^{\frac{x^2}{2}}$

c. $y(x) = e^{6x}$

d. $y(x) = ce^{\frac{x^2}{2}}$

e. $y(x) = e^{-6x}$

7. Solve the boundary-value problem, if possible.

$$y'' + 2y' - 63y = 0 \ , \quad y(0) = 0, \quad y(2) = 1$$

Select the correct answer.

a. $\quad y(x) = \left(e^{14} - e^{-18} \right)^{-1} \left(e^{14x} - e^{-18x} \right)$

b. $\quad y(x) = \left(e^{14} - e^{-18} \right)^{-1} \left(e^{7x} - e^{-9x} \right)$

c. $\quad y(x) = \left(e^{14} - e^{-18} \right)^{-1} \left(e^{14x} - e^{-9x} \right)$

d. $\quad y(x) = \left(e^{14} - e^{-18} \right)^{-1} \left(e^{8x} - e^{-9x} \right)$

e. No solution

8. Solve the boundary-value problem, if possible.

$$y'' - y' - 6y = 0 \ , \quad y(-1) = 1, \quad y(1) = 0$$

Select the correct answer.

a. $\quad y(x) = \dfrac{1}{e^{10} + 1} \left(e^{8-2x} - e^{3(x+1)} \right)$

b. $\quad y(x) = \dfrac{1}{e^{10} - 1} \left(e^{8-2x} + e^{3(x+1)} \right)$

c. $\quad y(x) = \dfrac{1}{e^{10} - 1} \left(e^{8-2x} - e^{3(x+1)} \right)$

d. $\quad y(x) = \dfrac{1}{e^{10} + 1} \left(e^{8x} + e^{3(x+1)} \right)$

e. No solution

9. Graph the particular solution and several other solutions.

    $2y'' + 3y' + y = 2 + \cos 2x$

    Select the correct answer.

    a.

    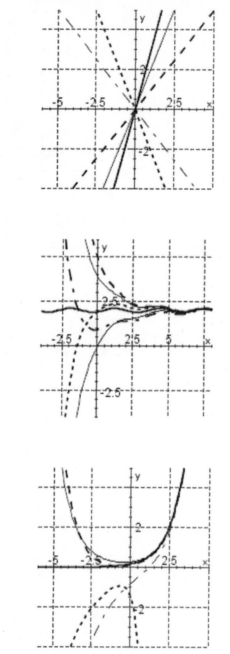

    b.

    c.

10. Solve the differential equation using the method of variation of parameters.

$$y'' + y = \sec x \ , \quad -\frac{\pi}{2} < x < \frac{\pi}{2}$$

Select the correct answer.

a. $\quad y(x) = \left[-\frac{\pi}{2} + \ln(\cos x) \right] \cos x$

b. $\quad y(x) = (c_1 + x)\sin x + c_2 + \ln(\cos x)$

c. $\quad y(x) = (c_1 + x)\sin x + \left[c_2 + \ln(\cos x) \right]\cos(x)$

d. $\quad y(x) = \frac{\pi}{2}\sin x + \left[\frac{\pi}{2} + \ln(\cos x) \right]\cos(x)$

e. $\quad y(x) = \frac{\pi}{2}\sin x + \frac{\pi}{2}\cos(x)$

11. A spring with a 16-kg mass has natural length 0.8 m and is maintained stretched to a length of 1.2 m by a force of 19.6 N. If the spring is compressed to a length of 0.7 m and then released with zero velocity, find the position x(t) of the mass at any time t.

Select the correct answer.

a. $\quad x(t) = -0.1\cos(1.75t) + 0.8\sin(1.75t)$

b. $\quad x(t) = -0.1\cos(1.75t)$

c. $\quad x(t) = 0.8\sin(1.75t)$

d. $\quad x(t) = -0.1e^{-4t}\cos(1.75t)$

e. $\quad x(t) = -0.1e^{-4t}\cos(0.8t)$

12. A spring has a mass of 1 kg and its damping constant is c = 10. The spring starts from its equilibrium position with a velocity of 1 m/s. Graph the position function for the spring constant k = 20.

Select the correct answer.

a.

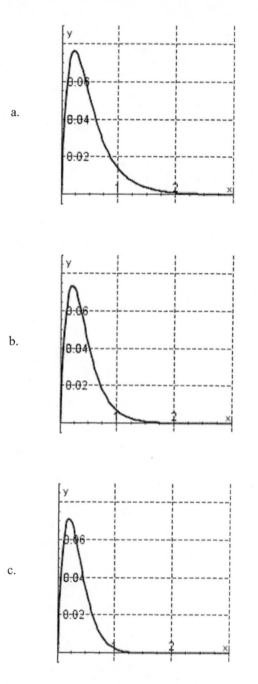

b.

c.

13. A series circuit consists of a resistor $R = 24\ \Omega$, an inductor with $L = 2$ H, a capacitor with $C = 0.005$ F, and a 12-V battery. If the initial charge is 0.0009 C and the initial current is 0, find the current $I(t)$ at time t.

Select the correct answer.

a. $I(t) = \dfrac{e^{-200t}}{200}(0.005\cos(6t) + 8\sin(6t)) - 1$

b. $I(t) = \dfrac{e^{-24t}}{200}$

c. $I(t) = 0.73875e^{-6t}\sin(8t)$

d. $I(t) = \dfrac{e^{-6t}}{200}\cos(8t)$

e. $I(t) = \dfrac{e^{-6t}}{20}\sin(8t)$

14. The solution of the initial-value problem $x^2 y'' + xy' + x^2 y = 0$, $y(0) = 1$, $y'(0) = 0$ is called a Bessel function of order 0. Solve the initial - value problem to find a power series expansion for the Bessel function.

Select the correct answer.

a. $y(x) = x + \displaystyle\sum_{n=0}^{\infty} (-1)^n \frac{x^{2n}}{2^{2n}(n!)^2}$

b. $y(x) = \displaystyle\sum_{n=0}^{\infty} (-1)^{n+1} \frac{nx^{2n-1}}{2^{2n-1}(n!)^2}$

c. $y(x) = \displaystyle\sum_{n=0}^{\infty} (-1)^n \frac{x^{2n}}{2^{2n}(n!)^2}$

d. $y(x) = \displaystyle\sum_{n=0}^{\infty} (-1)^n \frac{x^n}{2^n(2n!)}$

e. $y(x) = 2^x + \displaystyle\sum_{n=0}^{\infty} (-1)^n \frac{x^{2n}}{(n!)^2}$

15. The figure shows a pendulum with length L and the angle θ from the vertical to the pendulum. It can be shown that θ, as a function of time, satisfies the nonlinear differential equation $\dfrac{d^2\theta}{dt^2} + \dfrac{g}{L}\sin\theta = 0$ where g = 9.8 m/s^2 is the acceleration due to gravity. For small values of θ we can use the linear approximation $\sin\theta = \theta$ and then the differential equation becomes linear. Find the equation of motion of a pendulum with length 1 m if θ is initially 0.1 rad and the initial angular velocity is $\dfrac{d\theta}{dt} = 1$ rad/s.

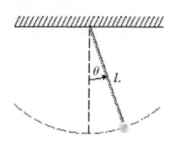

Select the correct answer.

a. $\theta(t) = 0.1\cos(\sqrt{9.8t}) + \dfrac{1}{\sqrt{9.8}}\sin(\sqrt{9.8t})$

b. $\theta(t) = 0.1\sin(\sqrt{9.8t}) + \dfrac{1}{\sqrt{9.8}}\cos(\sqrt{9.8t})$

c. $\theta(t) = 2\cos(9.8t) + \dfrac{1}{9.8}\sin(9.8t)$

d. $\theta(t) = 0.1\cos(\sqrt{9.8t}) + 2\sin(\sqrt{9.8t})$

e. $\theta(t) = \dfrac{1}{9.8}\cos(\sqrt{9.8t}) + 0.1\sin(\sqrt{9.8t})$

16. Use power series to solve the differential equation.

$(x - 6)y' + 2y = 0$

Select the correct answer.

a. $y(x) = c_0 \displaystyle\sum_{n=0}^{\infty} \dfrac{n+1}{6^n} x^n$

b. $y(x) = c_0 \displaystyle\sum_{n=0}^{\infty} \dfrac{x^n}{6^n}$

c. $y(x) = c_0 \displaystyle\sum_{n=0}^{\infty} \dfrac{nx^n}{6^n}$

d. $y(x) = c_0 \displaystyle\sum_{n=0}^{\infty} (n+1)x^n$

e. $y(x) = c_0 \displaystyle\sum_{n=0}^{\infty} \dfrac{(n+1)}{x^n}$

17. Use power series to solve the differential equation.

$$y'' = 16y$$

Select the correct answer.

a. $y(x) = c_1 \cosh 4x + c_2 \sinh 4x + x^2$

b. $y(x) = c_1 \cosh 4x + c_2 \sinh 4x$

c. $y(x) = 4 \cosh x + 4 \sinh x$

d. $y(x) = c_1 \cosh 4x + c_2 \sinh 4x + e^x$

e. $y(x) = c_1 4 \cosh x + c_2 4 \sinh x + e^x$

18. Use power series to solve the differential equation.

$$(x^2 + 1)y'' + xy' - y = 0$$

Select the correct answer.

a. $y(x) = c_0 + c_1 x + c_0 \dfrac{x^2}{2} + c_0 \displaystyle\sum_{n=2}^{\infty} \dfrac{(-1)^{n-1}(2n-3)!}{2^{2n-2} n!(n-2)!} x^{2n+1}$

b. $y(x) = c_0 \displaystyle\sum_{n=2}^{\infty} \dfrac{(-1)^{n-1}(2n-3)!}{2^{2n-2} n!(n-2)!} x^{2n}$

c. $y(x) = c_0 + c_1 x + c_0 \dfrac{x^2}{2} + c_0 \displaystyle\sum_{n=2}^{\infty} \dfrac{(-1)^{n-1}(2n-3)!}{2^{2n-2}(n-2)!} x^{2n}$

d. $y(x) = c_0 + c_1 x + c_0 \dfrac{x^2}{2} + c_0 \displaystyle\sum_{n=2}^{\infty} \dfrac{(-1)^{n-1}(2n-3)!}{2^{2n-2} n!(n-2)!} x^{2n}$

e. $y(x) = c_0 + c_1 x + c_0 \dfrac{x^2}{2} + c_0 \displaystyle\sum_{n=2}^{\infty} \dfrac{(-1)^{n+1}(2n)!}{2^{2n+2} n!(n-2)!} x^{2n+1}$

19. Use power series to solve the differential equation.

$$y'' + x^2 y = 0 \ , \ \ y(0) = 3, \ \ y'(0) = 0$$

Select the correct answer.

a. $\displaystyle y(x) = \sum_{n=1}^{\infty} \frac{(-1)^n 3x^{4n}}{4n(4n-1)...4 \cdot 3}$

b. $\displaystyle y(x) = 3 + \sum_{n=1}^{\infty} \frac{(-1)^n 3x^{4n}}{4n(4n-1)...4 \cdot 3}$

c. $\displaystyle y(x) = 3 - \sum_{n=1}^{\infty} \frac{(-1)^n x^{4n}}{4n(4n-1)...4 \cdot 3}$

d. $\displaystyle y(x) = -3 + \sum_{n=1}^{\infty} \frac{(-1)^n 3x^{4n}}{4n(4n-1)...4 \cdot 3}$

e. $\displaystyle y(x) = -1 + \sum_{n=1}^{\infty} \frac{(-1)^n x^{4n}}{4n(4n-1)...4 \cdot 3}$

20. Solve the differential equation using the method of undetermined coefficients.

$$y'' - 2y' = \sin 6x$$

Select the correct answer.

a. $y(x) = c_1 + c_2 e^{2x} + \dfrac{1}{120}\cos(6x) - \dfrac{1}{40}\sin(6x)$

b. $y(x) = c_1 + c_2 e^{2x} - \dfrac{1}{40}\sin(6x)$

c. $y(x) = \dfrac{1}{120}\cos(6x) - \dfrac{1}{40}\sin(6x)$

d. $y(x) = c_1 e^{2x} + \dfrac{1}{120}\cos(6x) - \dfrac{1}{40}\sin(6x)$

e. $y(x) = c_1 e^{2x} + \dfrac{1}{40}\cos(6x) + \dfrac{1}{120}\sin(6x)$

ANSWER KEY

Stewart - Calculus ET 5e Chapter 17 Form D

1. b

2. a

3. b

4. d

5. c

6. b

7. b

8. c

9. b

10. c

11. b

12. a

13. c

14. c

15. a

16. a

17. b

18. d

19. b

20. a

1. Solve the initial-value problem.

    $$y'' + 16y' + 233y = 0 \ , \quad y(0) = 1, \quad y'(0) = 2$$

2. Solve the initial-value problem.

    $$y'' - 16y' + 64y = 0 \ , \quad y(2) = 0, \quad y'(2) = 1$$

3. Solve the initial-value problem.

    $$y'' + 49y = 0 \ , \quad y\left(\frac{\pi}{7}\right) = 0, \quad y'\left(\frac{\pi}{7}\right) = 1$$

4. Solve the boundary-value problem, if possible.

    $$y'' + 14y' + 49y = 0 \ , \quad y(0) = 0, \quad y(1) = 6$$

    Select the correct answer.

    a. $y(x) = 7xe^{(-6x+6)}$
    b. $y(x) = 6xe^{(-7x+7)}$
    c. $y(x) = 6xe^{(-7x-7)}$
    d. $y(x) = 6e^{(-7x-7)}$
    e. No solution

5. Solve the differential equation using the method of undetermined coefficients.

    $$y'' + 5y' + 4y = x^2$$

    Select the correct answer.

    a. $y(x) = c_1 e^{-4x} + c_2 e^{-x} + \dfrac{21}{32}c_3$
    b. $y(x) = c_1 e^{-4x} + c_2 e^{-x} + \dfrac{1}{4}x^2 - \dfrac{5}{8}x + \dfrac{21}{32}$
    c. $y(x) = \dfrac{1}{4}x^2 - \dfrac{5}{8}x + \dfrac{21}{32}$
    d. $y(x) = c_1 e^{-4x} + c_2 e^{-x}$
    e. $y(x) = c_1 e^{4x} + c_2 e^{x}$

6. Use power series to solve the differential equation.

$$y' = 7x^2 y$$

7. Solve the differential equation.

$$y'' - 14y' + 85y = 0$$

8. Solve the differential equation using the method of variation of parameters.

$$y'' + 9y = x$$

Select the correct answer.

a. $y(x) = Ax$

b. $y(x) = c_1 \cos 3x + c_2 \sin 3x + \dfrac{1}{9}x$

c. $y(x) = c_1 \sin 3x + \dfrac{c_2}{9}x + \cos 3x$

d. $y(x) = c_1 \cos 3x + c_2 \sin 3x + \dfrac{c_3}{9}x$

e. $y(x) = c_1 \cos 3x + c_2 \sin 3x + c_3 x + \dfrac{1}{9}$

9. Solve the differential equation using the method of variation of parameters.

$$y'' - 2y' + y = e^{3x}$$

Select the correct answer.

a. $y(x) = e^x + xe^x$

b. $y(x) = c_1 e^x + c_2 x e^x + \dfrac{1}{4}e^{3x}$

c. $y(x) = c_1 e^x + c_2 e^x + \dfrac{1}{4}e^{3x}$

d. $y(x) = c_1 e^x + \dfrac{1}{4}e^{3x}$

e. $y(x) = c_1 e^x + c_2 e^x + \dfrac{x}{4}e^{3x}$

10. Solve the differential equation using the method of variation of parameters.

$$y'' - 3y' = e^{3x}$$

11. Solve the differential equation using the method of variation of parameters.

$$y'' - 3y' + 2y = \frac{5}{1 + e^{-x}}$$

12. Solve the differential equation using the method of variation of parameters.

$$y'' + 4y' + 4y = \frac{e^{-2x}}{x^3}$$

Select the correct answer.

a. $y(x) = e^{-2x}\left(c_1 + c_2\dfrac{1}{2x}\right)$

b. $y(x) = e^{-2x}\left(c_1 + c_2 x + c_3\dfrac{1}{2x}\right)$

c. $y(x) = e^{-2x}\left(c_1 + c_2 x + \dfrac{1}{2x}\right)$

d. $y(x) = e^{-2x}(c_1 + c_2 x) + \dfrac{1}{2x}$

e. $y(x) = e^{-2x}(c_1 + c_2)$

13. A spring with a 16-kg mass has natural length 0.8 m and is maintained stretched to a length of 1.2 m by a force of 19.6 N. If the spring is compressed to a length of 0.6 m and then released with zero velocity, find the position $x(t)$ of the mass at any time t.

14. A spring with a mass of 2 kg has damping constant 14, and a force of 6 N is required to keep the spring stretched 0.5 m beyond its natural length. The spring is stretched 1m beyond its natural length and then released with zero velocity. Find the position $x(t)$ of the mass at any time t.

Select the correct answer.

a. $x(t) = -6e^{-10t}\sin(0.5t)$

b. $x(t) = -\dfrac{1}{5}e^{-6t} + \dfrac{6}{5}e^{-t}$

c. $x(t) = -\dfrac{1}{5}e^{-2t} - \dfrac{5}{6}e^{-t}$

d. $x(t) = -5\cos(6t)$

e. none of these

15. A spring with a mass of 2 kg has damping constant 14, and a force of 4.8 N is required to keep the spring stretched 0.4 m beyond its natural length. Find the mass that would produce critical damping.

16. A spring with a mass of 3 kg has damping constant 35 and spring constant 129. Find the damping constant that would produce critical damping.

    Select the correct answer.

    a. $c = 6\sqrt{43}$

    b. $c = 6\sqrt{7}$

    c. $c = 9\sqrt{7}$

    d. $c = 9\sqrt{43}$

    e. $c = 43\sqrt{7}$

17. A series circuit consists of a resistor $R = 20\ \Omega$, an inductor with L = 1 H, a capacitor with C = 0.002F, and a generator producing a voltage of $E(t) = 12\cos 10t$.. If the initial charge and current are both 0, find the charge Q(t) at time t.

18. Use power series to solve the differential equation.

    $y'' - xy' - y = 0, \quad y(0) = 4, \quad y'(0) = 0$

19. Use power series to solve the differential equation.

    $y'' + x^2 y = 0, \quad y(0) = 2, \quad y'(0) = 0$

    Select the correct answer.

    a. $y(x) = \sum_{n=1}^{\infty} (-1)^n \dfrac{2x^{4n}}{4n(4n-1)...4 \cdot 3}$

    b. $y(x) = 2 - \sum_{n=1}^{\infty} (-1)^n \dfrac{x^{4n}}{4n(4n-1)...4 \cdot 3}$

    c. $y(x) = -2 + \sum_{n=1}^{\infty} (-1)^n \dfrac{2x^{4n}}{4n(4n-1)...4 \cdot 3}$

    d. $y(x) = 2 + \sum_{n=1}^{\infty} (-1)^n \dfrac{2x^{4n}}{4n(4n-1)...4 \cdot 3}$

    e. $y(x) = 2 - \sum_{n=1}^{\infty} (-1)^n \dfrac{x^n}{4n(4n-1)...4 \cdot 3}$

20. Solve the differential equation.

$$y'' - 11y' + 24y = 0$$

Select the correct answer.

a. $\quad y(x) = c_1 e^{8x} + c_2 x e^{8x}$

b. $\quad y(x) = c_1 e^{3x} + c_2 e^{8x}$

c. $\quad y(x) = c e^{3x}$

d. $\quad y(x) = c_1 e^{3x} + c_2 x e^{3x}$

e. $\quad y(x) = c_1 e^{-3x} + c_2 x e^{-x}$

ANSWER KEY

Stewart - Calculus ET 5e Chapter 17 Form F

1. $e^{-8x}\left(\cos(13x) + \dfrac{10}{13}\sin(13x)\right)$

2. $(x-2)e^{8(x-2)}$

3. $\dfrac{-1}{7}\sin(7x)$

4. b

5. b

6. $y(x) = ce^{\frac{7x^3}{3}}$

7. $e^{7x}\left(c_1\cos(6x) + c_2\sin(6x)\right)$

8. b

9. b

10. $y(x) = c_1 + c_2 e^{3x} + \dfrac{1}{3}xe^{3x}$

11. $y(x) = \left(c_1 + 5\ln(1+e^{-x})\right)e^x + \left(c_2 - 5e^{-x} + 5\ln(1+e^{-x})\right)e^{2x}$

12. c

13. $x(t) = -0.2\cos\left(\dfrac{7}{4}t\right)$

14. b

15. 49/12

16. a

17. $Q(t) = e^{-10t}\left(\dfrac{-3}{125}\cos(20t) - \dfrac{9}{500}\sin(20t)\right) + \dfrac{3}{250}\sin(10t) + \dfrac{3}{125}\cos(10t)$

18. $y(x) = 4e^{\frac{x^2}{2}}$

19. d

20. b

1. Solve the differential equation.

   $y'' - 7y' + 10y = 0$

   Select the correct answer.

   a. $y(x) = ce^{2x}$
   b. $y(x) = c_1e^{2x} + c_2xe^{2x}$
   c. $y(x) = c_1e^{2x} + c_2e^{5x}$
   d. $y(x) = c_1e^{5x} + c_2xe^{5x}$
   e. $y(x) = c_1e^{-x} + c_2xe^{-x}$

2. Solve the differential equation.

   $y'' - 8y' + 41y = 0$

   Select the correct answer.

   a. $y(x) = e^{4x}(c_1\cos(5x) + c_2\sin(5x))$
   b. $y(x) = ce^{4x}\cos(5x)$
   c. $y(x) = e^{5x}(c_1\cos(4x) + c_2\sin(4x))$
   d. $y(x) = e^{4x}(c_1\cos(5x) + c_2x\sin(5x))$
   e. $y(x) = e^{4x}(c_1\cos(4x) + c_2x\sin(4x))$

3. Solve the differential equation.

   $y'' - 14y' + 49y = 0$

4. Solve the differential equation.

   $11y'' = 2y'$

5. Solve the differential equation.

   $9y'' + y = 0$

6. Solve the differential equation.

$$7y'' + y' = 0$$

7. Solve the differential equation.

$$\frac{d^2y}{dt^2} + \frac{dy}{dt} + 10y = 0$$

8. Solve the initial-value problem.

$$2y'' + 19y' + 24y = 0, \quad y(0) = 0, \quad y'(0) = 1$$

9. Solve the initial-value problem.

$$y'' - 16y' + 64y = 0, \quad y(2) = 0, \quad y'(2) = 1$$

Select the correct answer.

a. $y(x) = (x+2)e^{8(x-2)}$
b. $y(x) = (x+2)e^{8(x+2)}$
c. $y(x) = (x-2)e^{8(x-2)}$
d. $y(x) = (x-2)e^{8(x+2)}$
e. $y(x) = (x+1)e^{8(x+1)}$

10. Solve the differential equation using the method of undetermined coefficients.

$$y'' + 4y = e^{2x}$$

11. Solve the differential equation using the method of variation of parameters.

$$y'' - 5y' + 4y = \sin x$$

12. Solve the initial-value problem.

$$y'' + 81y = 0, \quad y\left(\frac{\pi}{9}\right) = 0, \quad y'\left(\frac{\pi}{9}\right) = 1$$

Select the correct answer.

a. $\quad y(x) = \frac{1}{9}x\sin(9x)$

b. $\quad y(x) = -\frac{1}{9}\sin(9x)$

c. $\quad y(x) = \frac{1}{9}\sin(9x)$

d. $\quad y(x) = -\frac{1}{9}x\sin(9x)$

e. $\quad y(x) = -x\sin(9x)$

13. Solve the boundary-value problem, if possible.

$$y'' + 10y' + 25y = 0, \quad y(0) = 0, \quad y(1) = 8$$

14. Solve the boundary-value problem, if possible.

$$y'' + 3y' - 54y = 0, \quad y(0) = 0, \quad y(2) = 1$$

15. Solve the boundary-value problem, if possible.

$$y'' - y' - 2y = 0, \quad y(-1) = 1, \quad y(1) = 0$$

16. Solve the differential equation using the method of undetermined coefficients.

$$y'' - 3y' = \sin 9x$$

17. Solve the differential equation using the method of undetermined coefficients.

$$y'' - 8y' + 17y = e^{-x}$$

18. Graph the particular solution and several other solutions.

$2y'' + 3y' + y = 2 + \cos 2x$

Select the correct answer.

a.

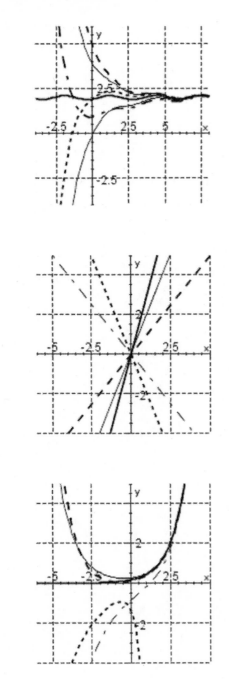

b.

c.

19. Find a trial solution for the method of undetermined coefficients. Do not determine the coefficients.

$$y'' + 3y' + 5y = x^4 e^{2x}$$

Select the correct answer.

a. $\quad y_p(x) = \left(Ax^3 + Bx^2 + Cx + D\right) e^{2x}$

b. $\quad y_p(x) = \left(Ax^4 + B\right) e^{2x}$

c. $\quad y_p(x) = Ax^4$

d. $\quad y_p(x) = \left(Ax^4 + Bx^3 + Cx^2 + Dx + E\right) e^{2x}$

e. $\quad y_p(x) = \left(Ax^4 + Bx^2 + C\right) e^{-2x}$

20. Find a trial solution for the method of undetermined coefficients. Do not determine the coefficients.

$$y'' + 2y' = 1 + xe^{-2x}$$

Select the correct answer.

a. $\quad \begin{aligned} &y_{p1}(x) = A \\ &y_{p2}(x) = x(A+B)e^{-2x} \end{aligned}$

b. $\quad \begin{aligned} &y_{p1}(x) = Ax \\ &y_{p2}(x) = x^2(Ax+B)e^{-2x} \end{aligned}$

c. $\quad \begin{aligned} &y_{p1}(x) = Ax \\ &y_{p2}(x) = x(Ax+B)e^{-2x} \end{aligned}$

d. $\quad \begin{aligned} &y_{p1}(x) = A \\ &y_{p2}(x) = x(A+Bx)e^{-2x} \end{aligned}$

e. $\quad \begin{aligned} &y_{p1}(x) = A \\ &y_{p2}(x) = Bxe^{2x} \end{aligned}$

Stewart - Calculus ET 5e Chapter 17 Form F

1. c

2. a

3. $e^{7x}(c_1 + c_2 x)$

4. $c_1 + c_2 e^{\frac{2x}{11}}$

5. $c_1 \cos\left(\dfrac{x}{3}\right) + c_2 \sin\left(\dfrac{x}{3}\right)$

6. $c_1 + c_2 e^{\frac{-x}{7}}$

7. $e^{\frac{-t}{2}}\left(c_1 \cos\left(\dfrac{\sqrt{39}t}{2}\right) + c_2 \sin\left(\dfrac{\sqrt{39}t}{2}\right)\right)$

8. $\dfrac{2}{13}e^{\frac{-3x}{2}} - \dfrac{2}{13}e^{-8x}$

9. c

10. $y(x) = c_1 \cos(2x) + c_2 \sin(2x) + \dfrac{1}{8}e^{2x}$

11. $y(x) = c_1 e^{4x} + c_2 e^x + \dfrac{5}{34}\cos(x) + \dfrac{3}{34}\sin(x)$

12. b

13. $8xe^{-5x+5}$

14. $\left(e^{12} - e^{-18}\right)^{-1}\left(e^{6x} - e^{-9x}\right)$

15. $\dfrac{1}{e^6 - 1}\left(e^{5-x} - e^{2(x+1)}\right)$

16. $y(x) = c_1 + c_2 e^{3x} + \dfrac{1}{270}\cos(9x) - \dfrac{1}{90}\sin(9x)$

17. $y(x) = e^{4x}\left(c_1 \cos(x) + c_2 \sin(x)\right) + \dfrac{1}{26}e^{-x}$

18. a

19. d

20. c

1. Solve the differential equation.

   $y'' - 17y' + 72y = 0$

2. Solve the differential equation.

   $y'' - 10y' + 25y = 0$

   Select the correct answer.

   a. $y(x) = cxe^{5x}$
   b. $y(x) = ce^{5x}$
   c. $y(x) = e^{5x}(c_1 + c_2 x)$
   d. $y(x) = e^{-5x}(c_1 + c_2 x)$
   e. $y(x) = xe^{-5x}(c_1 + c_2 x)$

3. Solve the initial-value problem.

   $2y'' + 21y' + 27y = 0, \quad y(0) = 0, \quad y'(0) = 1$

4. Solve the initial-value problem.

   $y'' + 8y' + 185y = 0, \quad y(0) = 1, \quad y'(0) = 2$

5. Solve the boundary-value problem, if possible.

   $y'' - y' - 42y = 0, \quad y(-1) = 1, \quad y(1) = 0$

6. Solve the boundary-value problem, if possible.

   $y'' + 2y' + 65y = 0, \quad y(0) = 1, \quad y(\pi) = 2$

7. Solve the differential equation using the method of undetermined coefficients.

   $y'' - 6y' + 10y = e^{-x}$

8. Use power series to solve the differential equation.

   $y' = 9xy$

9. Solve the initial - value problem using the method of undetermined coefficients.

   $y'' - y = xe^{4x}, \quad y(0) = 0, \quad y'(0) = 1$

   Select the correct answer.

   a. $y(x) = -\dfrac{13}{25}e^{-x} + e^{4x}\left(\dfrac{1}{15}x - \dfrac{8}{225}\right)$

   b. $y(x) = \dfrac{5}{9}e^x - \dfrac{13}{25}e^{-x} + e^{4x}\left(\dfrac{1}{15}x - \dfrac{8}{225}\right)$

   c. $y(x) = \dfrac{5}{9}c_1e^x - \dfrac{13}{25}c_2e^{-x} + c_3e^{4x}$

   d. $y(x) = \dfrac{5}{9}c_1e^x - \dfrac{13}{25}c_2e^{-x} + e^{4x}\left(\dfrac{1}{15}x - \dfrac{8}{225}\right)$

   e. $y(x) = \dfrac{13}{25}c_1e^{-x} + e^{4x}\left(\dfrac{1}{15}x - \dfrac{8}{225}\right)$

10. Solve the differential equation using the method of variation of parameters.

    $y'' + 4y = x$

    Select the correct answer.

    a. $y(x) = c_1 \cos 2x + c_2 \sin 2x + \dfrac{1}{4}x$

    b. $y(x) = c_1 \cos 2x + c_2 \sin 2x + \dfrac{c_3}{4}x$

    c. $y(x) = c_1 \sin 2x + \dfrac{c_2}{4}x + \cos 2x$

    d. $y(x) = Ax$

    e. $y(x) = c_1 \sin 2x + \dfrac{c_2}{4}x$

11. Solve the differential equation using the method of variation of parameters.

$$y'' - 2y' + y = e^{3x}$$

Select the correct answer.

a. $y(x) = c_1 e^x + c_2 e^x + \dfrac{1}{4} e^{3x}$

b. $y(x) = c_1 e^x + \dfrac{1}{4} e^{3x}$

c. $y(x) = e^x + xe^x$

d. $y(x) = c_1 e^x + c_2 xe^x + \dfrac{1}{4} e^{3x}$

e. $y(x) = c_1 e^x + c_2 xe^x + e^{3x}$

12. Solve the differential equation using the method of variation of parameters.

$$y'' - 2y' = e^{2x}$$

13. Solve the differential equation using the method of variation of parameters.

$$y'' + 4y' + 4y = \dfrac{e^{-2x}}{x^3}$$

14. A spring with a mass of 2 kg has damping constant 10, and a force of 3.2 N is required to keep the spring stretched 0.4 m beyond its natural length. Find the mass that would produce critical damping.

15. A spring with a mass of 4 kg has damping constant 30 and spring constant 184. Find the damping constant that would produce critical damping.

16. Use power series to solve the differential equation.

$$y'' - xy' - y = 0, \quad y(0) = 8, \quad y'(0) = 0$$

17. A series circuit consists of a resistor $R = 8 \ \Omega$, an inductor with L = 1 H, a capacitor with C = 0.0125 F, and a 28-V battery. If the initial charge and current are both 0, find the charge Q(t) at time t.

18. The figure shows a pendulum with length L and the angle θ from the vertical to the pendulum. It can be shown that θ, as a function of time, satisfies the nonlinear differential equation $\dfrac{d^2\theta}{dt^2} + \dfrac{g}{L}\sin\theta = 0$ where $g = 9.8$ m/s^2 is the acceleration due to gravity. For small values of θ we can use the linear approximation $\sin\theta = \theta$ and then the differential equation becomes linear. Find the equation of motion of a pendulum with length 1 m if θ is initially 0.2 rad and the initial angular velocity is $\dfrac{d\theta}{dt} = 2$ rad/s.

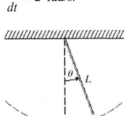

19. Suppose a spring has mass M and spring constant k and let $\omega = \sqrt{k/M}$. Suppose that the damping constant is so small that the damping force is negligible. If an external force $F(t) = F_0\cos(\omega t)$ is applied (the applied frequency equals the natural frequency), use the method of undetermined coefficients to find the equation that describes the motion of the mass.

Select the correct answer.

a. $x(t) = \dfrac{F_0 t}{2M\omega}(c_1\cos(\omega t) + c_2\sin(\omega t))$

b. $x(t) = \dfrac{F_0 t^2}{2M\omega}\cos(\omega t)$

c. $x(t) = c_1\cos(\omega t) + c_2\sin(\omega t) + \dfrac{F_0 e^{-\omega t}}{2M\omega}$

d. $x(t) = c_1\cos(\omega t) + c_2\sin(\omega t) + \dfrac{F_0 t}{2M\omega}\sin(\omega t)$

e. $x(t) = c_1\cos(\omega t) + c_2\sin(\omega t) + \dfrac{F_0 t^{-2}}{2M\omega}\sin(\omega t)$

20. Use power series to solve the differential equation.

$y' = 4x^2 y$

Select the correct answer.

a. $y(x) = ce^{\frac{-4x^3}{3}}$

b. $y(x) = ce^{\frac{4x^3}{3}}$

c. $y(x) = 4e^{\frac{x^3}{3}}$

d. $y(x) = ce^{4x}$

e. $y(x) = 3e^{-4x}$

1. $c_1 e^{8x} + c_2 e^{9x}$

2. c

3. $\dfrac{2}{15} e^{\frac{-3x}{2}} - \dfrac{2}{15} e^{-9x}$

4. $e^{-4x}\left(\cos(13x) + \dfrac{6}{13}\sin(13x)\right)$

5. $\dfrac{1}{e^{26} - 1}\left(e^{20-6x} - e^{7(x+1)}\right)$

6. no solution

7. $y(x) = e^{3x}\left(c_1 \cos(x) + c_2 \sin(x)\right) + \dfrac{1}{17} e^{-x}$

8. $y(x) = ce^{\frac{9x^2}{2}}$

9. b

10. a

11. d

12. $y(x) = c_1 + c_2 e^{2x} + \dfrac{1}{2} xe^{2x}$

13. $y(x) = e^{-2x}\left(c_1 + c_2 x + \dfrac{1}{2x}\right)$

14. 25/8

15. $c = 8\sqrt{46}$

16. $y(x) = 8e^{\frac{x^2}{2}}$

17. $Q(t) = -\dfrac{e^{-4t}}{40}(14\cos(8t) + 7\sin(8t)) + \dfrac{7}{20}$

18. $\theta(t) = 0.2\cos(\sqrt{9.8}t) + \dfrac{2}{\sqrt{9.8}}\sin(\sqrt{9.8}t))$

19. d

20. b

1. Solve the differential equation.

$$y'' - 10y + 25y = 0$$

2. Solve the differential equation.

$$19y'' = 3y'$$

3. Solve the differential equation.

$$81y'' + y = 0$$

4. Solve the differential equation.

$$7y'' + y' = 0$$

5. Solve the initial-value problem.

$$2y'' + 21y' + 27y = 0, \quad y(0) = 0, \quad y'(0) = 1$$

6. Solve the initial-value problem.

$$y'' - 64y = 0, \quad y(0) = 6, \quad y'(0) = 0$$

7. Use power series to solve the differential equation.

$$y'' - xy' - y = 0, \quad y(0) = 2, \quad y'(0) = 0$$

8. Solve the boundary-value problem, if possible.

    $$y'' - y' - 90y = 0, \quad y(-1) = 1, \quad y(1) = 0$$

    Select the correct answer.

    a. $y(x) = \dfrac{1}{e^{38} - 1}\left(e^{29-9x} - e^{10(x+1)}\right)$

    b. $y(x) = \dfrac{1}{e^{38} - 1}\left(e^{29-9x} + e^{10(x+1)}\right)$

    c. $y(x) = \dfrac{1}{e^{38} + 1}\left(e^{29-9x} - e^{10(x+1)}\right)$

    d. $y(x) = \dfrac{e^{10(x+1)}}{e^{38} + 1}$

    e. No solution

9. Solve the differential equation using the method of undetermined coefficients.

    $$y'' + 4y = e^{2x}$$

10. Solve the differential equation using the method of undetermined coefficients.

    $$y'' - 2y' = \sin 6x$$

11. Solve the differential equation using the method of variation of parameters.

    $$y'' - 3y' + 2y = \frac{1}{1 + e^{-x}}$$

    Select the correct answer.

    a. $y(x) = \left(c_1 + \ln(1 + e^{-x})\right)e^{-x}$

    b. $y(x) = \left(c_1 + \ln(1 + e^{-x})\right)e^{-x} + \left(c_2 - e^{-x} + \ln(1 + e^{-x})\right)e^{2x}$

    c. $y(x) = \left(\ln(1 + e^{-x})\right)e^{-x} + \left(c_2 + e^{x} + \ln(1 + e^{x})\right)e^{x}$

    d. $y(x) = \left(c_1 - e^{-x} + \ln(1 + e^{-x})\right)e^{2x}$

    e. $y(x) = \left(c_1 + \ln(1 + e^{-2x})\right)e^{-2x} + \left(c_2 - e^{-2x} + \ln(1 + e^{-2x})\right)e^{-x}$

12. A spring with a mass of 2 kg has damping constant 18, and a force of 8 N is required to keep the spring stretched 0.5 m beyond its natural length. Find the mass that would produce critical damping.

13. A spring with a mass of 2 kg has damping constant 8 and spring constant 80. Graph the position function of the mass at time t if it starts at the equilibrium position with a velocity of 2 m / s.

    Select the correct answer.

    a.

    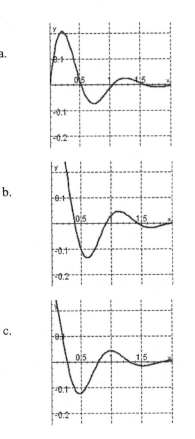

    b.

    c.

14. A spring with a mass of 5 kg has damping constant 31 and spring constant 205. Find the damping constant that would produce critical damping.

    Select the correct answer.

    a. $c = 5\sqrt{7}$
    b. $c = 10\sqrt{7}$
    c. $c = 10\sqrt{41}$
    d. $c = 5\sqrt{41}$
    e. $c = 7\sqrt{41}$

15. A series circuit consists of a resistor $R = 16$ Ω, an inductor with $L = 2$ H, a capacitor with $C = 0.00625$ F, and a 12-V battery. If the initial charge is 0.001 C and the initial current is 0, find the current $I(t)$ at time t.

Select the correct answer.

a. $I(t) = \dfrac{e^{-160t}}{160}(0.00625\cos(4t) + 8\sin(4t)) - \dfrac{1}{2}$

b. $I(t) = 0.74e^{-4t}\sin(8t)$

c. $I(t) = \dfrac{e^{-160t}}{160}\cos(8t)$

d. $I(t) = \dfrac{e^{-16t}}{160}$

e. $I(t) = \dfrac{e^{-16t}}{160}(\cos(8t) + \sin(8t))$

16. Use power series to solve the differential equation.

$y' - y = 0$

17. Use power series to solve the differential equation.

$y' = 7xy$

18. Use power series to solve the differential equation.

$y' = 7x^2 y$

19. Use power series to solve the differential equation.

$y'' = 25y$

20. The figure shows a pendulum with length L and the angle θ from the vertical to the pendulum. It can be shown that θ, as a function of time, satisfies the nonlinear differential equation $\dfrac{d^2\theta}{dt^2} + \dfrac{g}{L}\sin\theta = 0$ where g = 9.8 m/s^2 is the acceleration due to gravity. For small values of θ we can use the linear approximation $\sin\theta = \theta$ and then the differential equation becomes linear. Find the equation of motion of a pendulum with length 1 m if θ is initially 0.3 rad and the initial angular velocity is $\dfrac{d\theta}{dt} = 2$ rad/s.

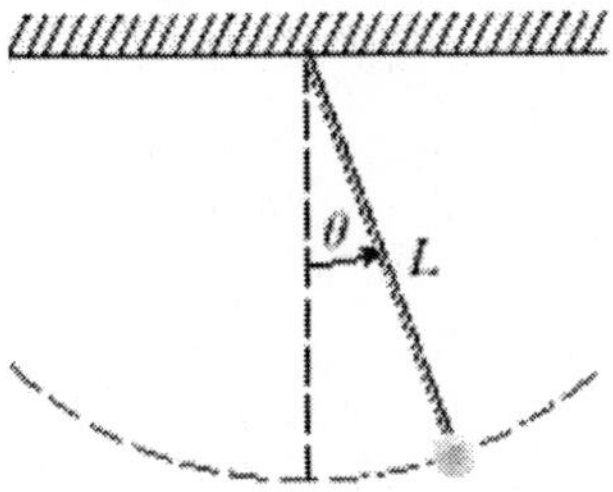

1. $e^{5x}(c_1 + c_2 x)$

2. $c_1 + c_2 e^{\frac{3x}{19}}$

3. $c_1 \cos\left(\dfrac{x}{9}\right) + c_2 \sin\left(\dfrac{x}{9}\right)$

4. $c_1 + c_2 e^{\frac{-x}{7}}$

5. $\dfrac{2}{15} e^{\frac{-3x}{2}} - \dfrac{2}{15} e^{-9x}$

6. $3\left(e^{8x} + e^{-8x}\right)$

7. $y(x) = 2e^{\frac{x^2}{2}}$

8. a

9. $y(x) = c_1 \cos(2x) + c_2 \sin(2x) + \dfrac{1}{8} e^{2x}$

10. $y(x) = c_1 + c_2 e^{2x} + \dfrac{1}{120} \cos(6x) - \dfrac{1}{40} \sin(6x)$

11. b

12. 81/16

13. a

14. c

15. b

16. $y(x) = c e^x$

17. $y(x) = c e^{\frac{7x^2}{2}}$

18. $y(x) = c e^{\frac{7x^3}{3}}$

19. $y(x) = c_1 \cosh(5x) + c_2 \sinh(5x)$

20. $\theta(t) = 0.3 \cos(\sqrt{9.8}\,t) + \dfrac{2}{\sqrt{9.8}} \sin(\sqrt{9.8}\,t)$

1. Estimate the area from 0 to 5 under the graph of $f(x) = 64 - x^2$ using five approximating rectangles and right endpoints.

2. Express the limit as a definite integral on the given interval.

$$\lim_{n \to \infty} \sum_{i=1}^{n} 9w_i \sin(w_i)\Delta w, \quad [9, \ 15]$$

3. Use Part 1 of the Fundamental Theorem of Calculus to find the derivative of the function.

$$g(x) = \int_{10}^{\sqrt{x}} 10\frac{\cos(t)}{t} \, dt$$

4. Evaluate the integral.

$$\int_{0}^{3} (6 + 2y - y^2) \, dy$$

5. The velocity function (in meters per second) is given for a particle moving along a line. Find the distance traveled by the particle during the given time interval.

$$v(t) = 3t - 4, \quad 0 \le t \le 3$$

6. Sketch the region enclosed by $y = 4x^2$ and $y = x^2 + 8$. Decide whether to integrate with respect to x or y. Draw a typical approximating rectangle and label its height and width. Then find the area of the region.

7. The base of S is the parabolic region $\left\{ (x, y) \mid x^2 \le y \le 7 \right\}$. Cross-sections perpendicular to the y-axis are equilateral triangles.

   True or False?

   The volume of S is $49\sqrt{3}$.

8. True or False?

   The volume of a solid torus (the donut-shaped solid shown in the figure) with $r = 3$ and $R = 13$ is $234\pi^2$.

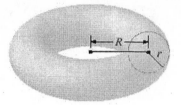

9. True or False?

   If the center of each of two spheres, each having radius $r = 6$, lies on the surface of the other sphere, then the volume common to both spheres is 90π.

10. True or False?

    If a force of 18 lbs is required to hold a spring stretched 4 inches beyond its natural length, then 144 lb-in. of work is done in stretching it from its natural length to 8 in. beyond its natural length.

11. A cable that weighs 4 lb/ft is used to lift 660 lb of coal up a mineshaft 500 ft deep.

    True or False?

    The work required is 830,000 ft-lb.

12. Find $(f^{-1})'(a)$.

    $$f(x) = 2 + x^2 + \tan(\pi x / 2), \ -1 < x < 1, \ a = 2$$

13. Solve the equation for x.

    $$6e^x - e^{2x} = 8$$

14. Find the exact value of the expression.

    $$\log_9 2 + \log_9 40.5$$

15. Differentiate the function

    $$f(t) = \frac{4 + \ln t}{6 - \ln t}$$

16. Find the limit.

$$\lim_{x \to -8} \frac{x^2 + 3x - 40}{x + 8}$$

17. True or False?

An integral for the length of the curve $y = x\sqrt[3]{6 - x}$, $0 \le x \le 2$ is $\displaystyle\int_0^2 \sqrt{1 + \left[\dfrac{18 - 4x}{3(6 - x)^{2/3}} \right]^2}\ dx$.

18. Find the arc length function for the curve $y = 10x^{3/2}$ with starting point $P_o\,(\,1,\,10\,)$.

19. A hawk flying at an altitude of 225 m accidentally drops its prey. The parabolic trajectory of the falling prey is described by the equation $y = 225 - \dfrac{x^2}{36}$ until it hits the ground, where y is its height above the ground and x is the horizontal distance traveled in meters.

True or False?

The distance traveled by the prey from the time it is dropped until the time it hits the ground is approximately 250.27 m.

20. True or False?

If the lamina shown in the figure below has density $\rho = 4$, then its center of mass is $\left(0,\ \dfrac{19}{3} \right)$.

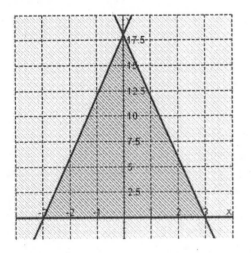

21. A company modeled the demand curve for its product (in dollars) by $p = \dfrac{600{,}000e^{\frac{-x}{4.000}}}{x + 20{,}000}$.

   Use a graph to estimate the sales level when the selling price is $10.96. Then find (approximately, using Simpson's Rule with $n = 10$) the consumer surplus for this sales level.

22. A function $y(t)$ satisfies the differential equation $\dfrac{dy}{dt} = y^4 - 13y^3 + 36y^2$.

   What are the constant solutions of the equation?

23. Use Euler's method with step size 0.25 to estimate $y(0.5)$, where $y(x)$ is the solution of the initial-value problem. Round your answer to two decimal places.

   $y' = 2xy^2, \quad y(0) = 1$

24. Program a calculator to use Euler's method with step size $h = 0.4$ to compute the approximate value of $y(1.8)$ there $y(x)$ is the solution of the initial-value problem

   $y' = x^3 - y^3, \quad y(1) = 1$

25. The table gives estimates of the world population, in millions, from 1750 to 2000:

Year	Population	Year	Population
1750	840	1900	1,510
1800	1,030	1950	2,540
1850	1,200	2000	5,940

   Use the exponential model and the population figures for 1750 and 1800 to predict the world population in 1,900.

26. After 3 days a sample of radon-222 decayed to 58% of its original amount. How long would it take the sample to decay to 64% of its original amount?

27. Scientists can determine the age of ancient objects by a method called *radiocarbon dating*. The bombardment of the upper atmosphere by cosmic rays converts nitrogen to a radioactive isotope of carbon, ^{14}C, with a half-life of about 5730 years. Vegetation absorbs carbon dioxide through the atmosphere and animal life assimilates ^{14}C through food chains. When a plant or animal dies it stops replacing its carbon and the amount of ^{14}C begins to decrease through radioactive decay. Therefore, the level of radioactivity must also decay exponentially.

   A parchment fragment was discovered that had about 56% as much ^{14}C radioactivity as does plant material on Earth today.

   Estimate the age of the parchment.

28. Use either a CAS or a table of integrals to find the exact area of the surface obtained by rotating the given curve about the x-axis.

$$y = \sqrt{x^2 + 1}, \ 0 \le x \le 3$$

29. A thermometer is taken from a room where the temperature is $20°$ C to the outdoors, where the temperature is $2°$ C. After one minute the thermometer reads $13°$ C. Use Newton's Law of Cooling to answer the following question.

When will the thermometer read $5°$ C?

30. Suppose that a population develops according to the logistic equation $\dfrac{dP}{dt} = 0.03P - 0.0003P^2$, where t is measured in weeks.

What is the carrying capacity?

31. One model for the spread of a rumor is that the rate of spread is proportional to the product of the fraction of the population who have heard the rumor and the fraction who have not heard the rumor. Let's assume that the constant of proportionality is $k = 0.01$.

Write a differential equation that is satisfied by y.

32. Biologists stocked a lake with 420 fish and estimated the carrying capacity (the maximal population for the fish of that species in that lake) to be 14,000. The number of fish tripled in the first year. Assuming that the size of the fish population satisfies the logistic equation, find an expression for the size of the population after t years.

33. In a seasonal-growth model, a periodic function of time is introduced to account for seasonal variations in the rate of growth. Such variations could, for example, be caused by seasonal changes in the availability of food.

Find the solution of the seasonal-growth model.

$$\frac{dP}{dt} = kP \cos(rt - \phi) \ \ P(0) = P_0 = 4 \ \text{ for } k = 0.01, \ r = 0.04, \ \phi = 6$$

34. Let $\dfrac{dP}{dt} = kP \cos^2(rt - \phi) \ \ P(0) = P_0 = 9 \ \text{ for } k = 0.07, \ r = 0.49, \ \phi = 7$.

Solve this differential equation with the help of a table of integrals or a CAS.

35. Determine whether the differential equation is linear.

$$y' + y \sin x = x^7 y^7$$

36. Populations of aphids and ladybugs are modeled by the following equations.

$$\frac{dA}{dt} = 5A - 0.01AL, \quad \frac{dL}{dt} = -0.2L + 0.0001AL$$

Find the nonzero equilibrium solutions.

37. How many terms of the series do we need to add in order to find the sum to the indicated accuracy?

$$\sum_{n=1}^{\infty} \frac{(-1)^n n}{2^n} \quad (\,|error| < 0.1562\,)$$

38. Approximate the sum of the series to four decimal places.

$$\sum_{n=1}^{\infty} \frac{(-1)^{n-1}}{2(2n-1)!}$$

39. Test the series for convergence or divergence.

$$\sum_{m=6}^{\infty} \frac{m^2 - 36}{m^2 + 6m}$$

40. Test the series for convergence or divergence.

$$\sum_{n=1}^{\infty} \left(\sqrt[n]{7} - 1 \right)^n$$

41. Find the radius of convergence of the series.

$$\sum_{n=1}^{\infty} \frac{n^2 x^n}{7^n}$$

42. The curves $r_1(t) = \langle t,\ t^2,\ t^7 \rangle$ and $r_2(t) = \langle \sin t,\ \sin 4t,\ t \rangle$ intersect at the origin. Find their angle of intersection correct to the nearest degree.

43. The position function of a particle is given by $r(t) = \langle 8t^2,\ t,\ 8t^2 - 192t \rangle$.

When is the speed a minimum?

44. A projectile is fired with an initial speed of 807 m/s and angle of elevation $31°$.

Find the range of the projectile in kilometers.

45. Use polar coordinates to find the volume of the solid under the paraboloid $z = x^2 + y^2$ and above the disk $x^2 + y^2 \le 100$.

46. Use polar coordinates to find the volume of the solid bounded by the paraboloid $z = 5 - 3x^2 - 3y^2$ and the plane $z = 2$.

47. An agricultural sprinkler distributes water in a circular pattern of radius 100 ft. It supplies water to a depth of e^{-r} feet per hour at a distance of r feet from the sprinkler. What is the total amount of water supplied per hour to the region inside the circle of radius 25 feet centered at the sprinkler?

Round the answer to the nearest thousandth.

48. A steady wind blows a kite due west. The kite's height above ground from horizontal position $x = 0$ to $x = 70$ ft is given by $y = 170 - \dfrac{1}{80}(x - 20)^2$.

True or False?

The distance traveled by the kite is approximately 81.78 ft.

49. Find the area of the surface obtained by rotating the curve about the x-axis.

$$x = \frac{1}{2\sqrt{2}}\left(y^2 - \ln y \right), \quad 1 \le y \le 7$$

50. The masses $m_1 = 15$ and $m_2 = 25$ are located at the points $P_1(15,\ 20)$ and $P_2(-2,\ -2)$.

True or False?

The center of mass of the system is $\left(\dfrac{35}{8},\ \dfrac{25}{4} \right)$.

1. 265

2. $\displaystyle\int_{9}^{15} 9w\sin(w)\ dw$

3. $\dfrac{dg(x)}{dx} = \dfrac{5\cos\sqrt{x}}{x}$

4. 18

5. 1.5

6. 17.42

7. F

8. T

9. T

10. T

11. T

12. $\dfrac{2}{\pi}$

13. $x = \ln(2),\ \ x = \ln(4)$

14. 2

15. $\dfrac{10}{t(6 - \ln(t))^2}$

16. -13

17. T

18. $L = \dfrac{2}{675}\left((1 + 225x)^{3/2} - 226\sqrt{226}\right)$

19. F

20. T

21. 26896

22. 4, 9, 0

23. 1.13

24. 1.6976

25. 1549

26. 2.46

27. 4793

28. $3\sqrt{19}\pi + \dfrac{\pi}{\sqrt{2}}\ln(3\sqrt{2} + \sqrt{19})$

29. 3.6

30. 100

31. $\dfrac{dy}{dt} = 0.01y(1 - y)$

32. $P(t) = \dfrac{14000}{1 + 32.33(0.31)^t}$

33. $P(t) = 4e^{1/4(\sin(0.04t - 6) + \sin(6))}$

34. $f(t) = 0.035t + \dfrac{1}{28}(\sin(0.98t - 14) + \sin(14))$

35. no

36. $A = 2000,\ L = 500$

37. 5

38. 0.420736

39. divergent

40. convergent

41. 7

42. 76

43. $t = 6$

44. 29

45. 5000π

46. $\dfrac{3\pi}{2}$

47. 6.283

48. T

49. $\dfrac{\pi}{8}\left(2496 - 98\ln(7) - (\ln(7))^2\right)$

50. T

1. Evaluate the definite integral.

$$\int_{0}^{\pi/4} \sin 4t \ dt$$

Select the correct answer.

a. 3.5
b. 0.5
c. 0
d. 0.6
e. -1.5

2. Evaluate the definite integral.

$$\int_{e^9}^{e^{81}} \frac{dx}{x\sqrt{\ln x}}$$

Select the correct answer.

a. 12
b. 10
c. 13
d. 15
e. 11.5

3. Sketch the region enclosed by $y = 6x^2$ and $y = x^2 + 7$. Decide whether to integrate with respect to x or y. Draw a typical approximating rectangle and label its height and width. Then find the area of the region.

Select the correct answer.

a. 12.043349
b. 22.086698
c. 3.681116
d. 2.20867
e. 11.043349

4. Racing cars driven by Chris and Kelly are side by side at the start of a race. The table shows the velocities of each car (in miles per hour) during the first ten seconds of the race. Use the Midpoint Rule to estimate how much farther Kelly travels than Chris does during the ten seconds.

t	V_C	V_K		t	V_C	V_K
0	0	0		6	72	83
1	25	27		7	75	86
2	33	38		8	85	97
3	42	48		9	89	101
4	53	60		10	90	102
5	62	71				

Select the correct answer.

a. $118\dfrac{1}{3}$ ft

b. $114\dfrac{2}{3}$ ft

c. $117\dfrac{1}{3}$ ft

d. $115\dfrac{1}{3}$ ft

e. $112\dfrac{1}{3}$ ft

5. Find the positive value of c such that the area of the region bounded by the parabolas $y = x^2 - c^2$ and $y = c^2 - x^2$ is 576.

Select the correct answer.

a.   6
b.   5
c.   13
d.   8
e.   4

6. The region bounded by the given curves is rotated about the specified axis. Find the volume of the resulting solid by any method.

$y = 5$, $y = x^2 - 6x + 10$, about the line $x = -1$

Select the correct answer.

a. $V = 90.78\pi$
b. $V = 85.33\pi$
c. $V = 105.67\pi$
d. $V = 82.83\pi$
e. $V = 80.83\pi$

7. Suppose you make napkin rings by drilling holes with different diameters through two wooden balls (which also have different diameters). You discover that both napkin rings have the same height h as shown in the figure.

Use cylindrical shells to compute the volume of a napkin ring created by drilling a hole with radius m through the center of a sphere of radius B and express the answer in terms of h.

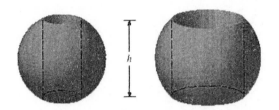

Select the correct answer.

a. $V = \dfrac{1}{6}\pi h^3$

b. $V = \dfrac{1}{3}\pi h^2$

c. $V = \dfrac{1}{4}\pi h^3$

d. $V = \dfrac{1}{6}\pi h^2$

e. $V = \dfrac{1}{6}\pi h$

8. The domain of a one-to-one function f is always equal to the _____.

Choose the answer from the following:

a. domain of f^{-1}
b. range of f^{-1}

9. Find an equation of the plane that passes through the point $(3,\ 0,\ -2)$ and contains the line $x = 10 - 2t,\ y = 7 + 7t,\ z = 2 + 5t$.

Select the correct answer.

a. $7x - 43y + 63z = 0$
b. $7x - 43y + 63z = -105$
c. $7x - 43y + 63z = 105$
d. $7x - 43y + 63z = 15$
e. $7x - 43y + 63z = -15$

10. Use change of base formula to evaluate the logarithm correct to six decimal places $\log_3 13.54$.

Select the correct answer.

    a.   2.372363

    b.   2.371763

    c.   2.374763

    d.   2.371733

    e.   2.371715

11. The region under the curve $y = 7^{-x}$ from $x = 0$ to $x = 1$ is rotated about the x-axis. Find the volume of the resulting solid.

Select the correct answer.

    a. $V = \dfrac{24\pi^2}{49\ln 7}$

    b. $V = \dfrac{24\pi}{49\ln 7}$

    c. $V = \dfrac{24\ln 7}{49\pi^2}$

    d. $V = \dfrac{24\ln 7}{49\pi}$

    e. $V = \dfrac{24\ln 7}{49}$

12. Find the limit.

$$\lim_{x \to 0} \frac{\sin^{-1} 9x}{2x}$$

Select the correct answer.

    a. π

    b. $\dfrac{9}{2}$

    c. ∞

    d. $-\infty$

    e. $\dfrac{1}{2}$

13. Find the limit.

$$\lim_{x \to 6^+} (x-6) \tan \frac{\pi x}{12}$$

Select the correct answer.

a. $-\infty$
b.   0
c. ∞
d. $-\dfrac{12}{\pi}$
e.   1

14. Evaluate the integral.

$$\int_0^1 \frac{x^3}{\sqrt{9-x^2}} \, dx$$

Select the correct answer.

a.   - 0.087
b.   - 6
c.   0.087
d.   6
e.   9

15. Evaluate the integral.

$$\int_{1/3}^{2/3} x^3 \sqrt{4-9x^2} \, dx$$

Select the correct answer.

a. $\dfrac{11}{405}\sqrt{3}$

b. $\dfrac{17}{405}\sqrt{3}$

c. $\dfrac{19}{4320}\sqrt{7}$

d. $\dfrac{1}{15}$

e. $\dfrac{\sqrt{7}}{405}$

16. Evaluate the integral.

$$\int e^t \sqrt{49 - e^{2t}}\ dt$$

Select the correct answer.

a. $\dfrac{49}{2} \arcsin\left(\dfrac{e^t}{7}\right) + \dfrac{1}{2} e^t \sqrt{49 - e^{2t}} + C$

b. $\arcsin\left(\dfrac{e^t}{7}\right) + \dfrac{1}{2} \sqrt{49 - e^{2t}} + C$

c. $\arcsin\left(\dfrac{e^t}{7}\right) + \dfrac{1}{2} e^t \sqrt{49 - e^{2t}} + C$

d. $\dfrac{49}{2} \arcsin\left(\dfrac{e^t}{7}\right) + \dfrac{1}{2} \sqrt{49 - e^{2t}} + C$

e. $\dfrac{7}{2} \arcsin\left(\dfrac{e^t}{49}\right) + \dfrac{1}{2} \sqrt{49 - e^t} + C$

17. Use the substitution to transform the integrand into a rational function and then evaluate the integral.

$$\int \frac{15}{3\sin 15x - 4\cos 15x}\ dx$$

Select the correct answer.

a. $\dfrac{1}{5} \ln\left| \dfrac{2\tan(15x/2) + 2}{\tan(15x/2) - 1} \right| + C$

b. $\dfrac{1}{5} \ln\left| \dfrac{\tan(15x/2) - 1}{\tan(15x/2) + 2} \right| + C$

c. $\dfrac{1}{5} \ln\left| \dfrac{2\tan(15x/2) - 1}{\tan(15x/2) + 2} \right| + C$

d. $\dfrac{1}{5} \ln\left| \dfrac{\tan(15x/2) + 1}{\tan(15x/2) - 2} \right| + C$

e. $\dfrac{1}{5} \ln\left| \dfrac{2\tan(15x/2) + 1}{\tan(15x/2) - 2} \right| + C$

18. Find $8a + 2b$.

$a = 9i - 10k$, $b = 5i - 10j + 4k$

Select the correct answer.

a. $83i - 20j - 70k$
b. $83i - 19j - 71k$
c. $82i + 20j - 72k$
d. $84i + 20j - 70k$
e. $82i - 20j - 72k$

19. Use the Table of Integrals to evaluate the integral.

$$\int \frac{x}{\sqrt{x^2 - 8x}} \, dx$$

Select the correct answer.

a. $\sqrt{x^2 - 8x} + 4\ln\left| x - 4 + \sqrt{x^2 - 8x} \right| + C$

b. $\sqrt{x^2 - 4x} + 4\ln\left| x - 4 + \sqrt{x^2 - 8x} \right| + C$

c. $\sqrt{x^2 - 4x} + 2\ln\left| x - 4 + \sqrt{x^2 - 8x} \right| + C$

d. $\sqrt{x^2 - 2x} + 4\ln\left| x - 4 + \sqrt{x^2 - 2x} \right| + C$

e. $\sqrt{x^2 - 4x} + \ln\left| x - 4 + \sqrt{x^2 - 4x} \right| + C$

20. Let L be the length of the curve $y = f(x)$, $q \le x \le b$, where f is positive and has a continuous derivative. Let S_f be the surface area generated by rotating the curve about the x-axis. If c is a positive constant, define $g(x) = f(x) + c$ and let S_g be the corresponding surface area generated by the curve $y = g(x)$, $q \le x \le b$.

Express S_g in terms of S_f and L.

Select the correct answer.

a. $S_g = S_f + 2\pi bL$
b. $S_g = S_f - 2\pi cL$
c. $S_g = S_f + 2\pi qL$
d. $S_g = S_f + 2\pi cL$
e. $S_g = S_f - 2\pi bL$

21. The demand function for a certain commodity is $p = 6 - \dfrac{x}{12}$.

Find the consumer surplus when the sales level is 30.

Select the correct answer.

    a. $48.75
    b. $41.25
    c. $45.00
    d. $26.25
    e. $37.50

22. A company modeled the demand curve for its product (in dollars) by

$$p = \frac{1,000,000 e^{\frac{-x}{6.000}}}{x + 20,000}$$

Use a graph to estimate the sales level when the selling price is $22.30. Then find (approximately, using Simpson's Rule with $n = 10$) the consumer surplus for this sales level.

Select the correct answer.

    a. $63,410
    b. $36,234
    c. $45,293
    d. $27,176
    e. $49,822

23. A hot, wet summer is causing a mosquito population explosion in a lake resort area. The number of mosquitos is increasing at an estimated rate of $2,500 + 8e^t$ per week (where t is measured in weeks). By how much does the mosquito population increase between the 4th and 8th weeks of summer?

Select the correct answer.

    a.   20,047
    b.   36,752
    c.   33,411
    d.   43,434
    e.   16,705

24. A type of lightbulb is labeled as having an average lifetime of 1,000 hours. It's reasonable to model the probability of failure of these bulbs by an exponential density function with mean $\mu = 1,000$.
Use this model to find the probability that a bulb burns for more than 300 hours.

Select the correct answer.

    a.   0.81
    b.   0.44
    c.   0.37
    d.   0.89
    e.   0.74

25. Eliminate the parameter to find a Cartesian equation of the following curve:

$$x(t) = 4\ln(6t), \quad y(t) = \sqrt{t}$$

Choose the answer from the following:

a. $y = \sqrt{\dfrac{1}{6}e^{x/4}}$

b. $y = \sqrt{\dfrac{1}{6}e^{4/x}}$

c. $y = \sqrt{\dfrac{1}{4}e^{x/6}}$

d. $y = \sqrt{\dfrac{1}{4}e^{6/x}}$

e. $y = \sqrt{\dfrac{1}{6}xe^{4/x}}$

26. Find the area of the shaded region.

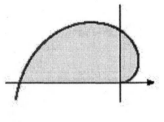

$r = \theta$

Select the correct answer.

a. $A = \dfrac{\pi}{16}$

b. $A = \dfrac{41\pi}{4}$

c. $A = \dfrac{\pi^3}{16}$

d. $A = \dfrac{3\pi}{8} + 1$

e. $A = \dfrac{3\pi^2}{16} + 1$

27. Sketch the parabola.

$$6y + x^2 = 0$$

Select the correct answer.

a.

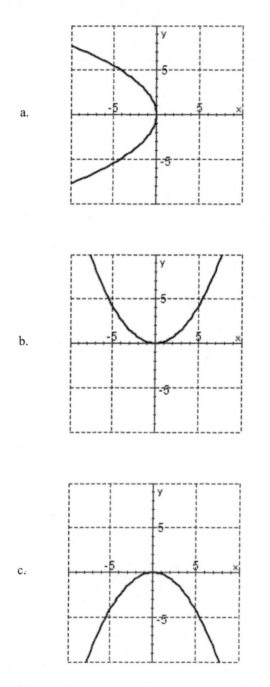

b.

c.

28. Find the vertex, focus, and directrix of the parabola.

$$x^2 + 4x - y + 9 = 0$$

Select the correct answers.

a.   The vertex is $(0, 2)$

b.   The directrix is $y = -\dfrac{19}{2}$

c.   The focus is $\left(-2, \dfrac{21}{4}\right)$

d.   The directrix is $y = \dfrac{19}{4}$

e.   The focus is $\left(0, \dfrac{21}{4}\right)$

f.   The vertex is $(-2, 5)$

29. Find a formula for the general term a_n of the sequence, assuming that the pattern of the first few terms continues.

$$\{2, 9, 16, 23, \ldots\}$$

Select the correct answer.

a. $a_n = 7n + 5$

b. $a_n = 5n - 7$

c. $a_n = 7n - 5$

d. $a_n = 5n + 7$

e. $a_n = 5n + 5$

30. Find the value of the limit for the sequence $\left\{\dfrac{n^3}{n!}\right\}$.

Select the correct answer.

a. 1

b. 3π

c. 0

d. 3

e. π

31. Find parametric equations for the line through the point (1, 7, 2) that is parallel to the plane $x + y + z = 10$ and perpendicular to the line $x = 3 + t, \ y = -18 - t, \ z = 5t$.

Select the correct answer.

    a. $x = 6t - 1, \ y = -4t - 7, \ z = -2t + 2$

    b. $x = 6t + 1, \ y = -4t + 7, \ z = -2t + 2$

    c. $x = 4t + 1, \ y = -6t + 7, \ z = 2t + 2$

    d. $x = 4t + 1, \ y = -6t, \ z = 2t + 2$

    e. $x = 4t, \ y = -6t + 7, \ z = 2t$

32. Use the sum of the first 9 terms to approximate the sum of the following series:

$$\sum_{n=1}^{\infty} \frac{7}{n^7 + n^3}$$

Give your answer to six decimal places.

Select the correct answer.

    a. $s_9 \approx 4.625186$

    b. $s_9 \approx 3.555185$

    c. $s_9 \approx 3.555186$

    d. $s_9 \approx 3.555187$

    e. $s_9 \approx 4.625166$

33. Test the series for convergence or divergence.

$$\sum_{m=4}^{\infty} \frac{4}{m(\ln m)^5}$$

Select the correct answer.

    a.   The series is divergent

    b.   The series is convergent

34. Use series to approximate the definite integral to within the indicated accuracy.

$$\int_{0}^{0.8} x^2 e^{-x^2}\, dx \qquad |\,\text{error}\,| < 0.001$$

Select the correct answer.

a.   0.1051
b.   0.0526
c.   0.1251
d.   0.0951
e.   0.0105

35. Which set of points lies on a straight line?

Select the correct answer.

a. $(-3,\ 6,\ -2),\ (-2,\ -6,\ 6),\ (3,\ -10,\ -2)$
b. $(-2,\ 6,\ 5),\ (-3,\ 7,\ 4),\ (3,\ 1,\ 10)$

36. Find the graph of a silo consisting of a cylinder with radius a and height b surmounted by a hemisphere.

$a = 1, b = 20$

Select the correct answer.

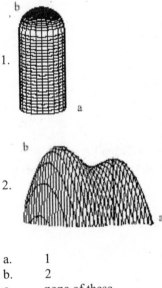

a.   1
b.   2
c.   none of these

37. The *temperature-humidity index I* (or humidex, for short) is the perceived air temperature when the actual temperature is T and the relative humidity is h, so we can write $I = f(t, h)$. The following table of values of I is an excerpt from a table compiled by the National Oceanic and Atmospheric Administration.

For what value of T is $f(T, 50) = 87$?

$T \downarrow$ $h \rightarrow$	20	30	40	50	60	70
80	70	75	79	82	82	85
85	81	84	86	87	88	91
90	86	93	96	96	100	104
95	92	94	101	106	115	118
100	99	104	106	120	134	145

Select the correct answer.

a. $T = 95$
b. $T = 85$
c. $T = 80$
d. $T = 90$
e. $T = 105$

38. Find the limit, if it exists.

$$\lim_{(x,y,z) \to (0,0,0)} \frac{3xy + yz^2 + 4xz^2}{x^2 + y^2 + z^4}$$

Select the correct answer.

a.   3
b.   4
c.   0
d.   1
e.   The limit does not exist

39. The temperature T in a metal ball is inversely proportional to the distance from the center of the ball, which we take to be the origin. The temperature at the point $(1, 2, 2)$ is $150°$. Find the rate of change of T at $(1, 2, 2)$ in the direction toward the point $(2, 6, 1)$.

Select the correct answer.

a.   -27.499
b.   -13.749
c.   -4.481
d.   28.499
e.   20.499

40. Suppose that over a certain region of space the electrical potential V is given by $V(x, y, z) = 7x^2 - 9xy + 3xyz$. Find the rate of change of the potential at (-3, 2, -10) in the direction of the vector $v = 4i + 3j - 5k$.

Select the correct answer.

    a.   84.004286
    b.   -39
    c.   -57
    d.   45
    e.   49

41. At what point is the following function a local maximum?

$$f(x, y) = 3 - 4x + 16y - 2x^2 - 4y^2$$

Select the correct answer.

    a.   (-1, 2)
    b.   (3, 2)
    c.   (2, -1)
    d.   (2, 1)
    e.   (3, 1)

42. Evaluate the integral.

$$\int_1^9 \frac{x^2 + 2}{\sqrt{x}}\, dx$$

Select the correct answer.

    a.   492
    b.   246
    c.   104.8
    d.   113.6
    e.   145.8

43. Use the Midpoint Rule with four squares of equal size to estimate the double integral.

$$\iint_R \cos(x^4 + y^4)\, dA$$

$$R = \left\{ (x, y) \mid 0 \le x \le 1.25,\ 0 \le y \le 1.25 \right\}$$

Select the correct answer.

    a.   0
    b.   3.911443
    c.   1.222326
    d.   1.562216
    e.   1.527908

44. Find the volume of the solid lying under the plane $z = 4x + 5y + 8$ and above the rectangle $R = \left\{ (x,y) \mid -2 \le x \le 0,\ 1 \le y \le 2 \right\}$.

Select the correct answer.

   a. $V = 23$
   b. $V = 39$
   c. $V = 25$
   d. $V = 30$
   e. $V = 35$

45. Find the mass of the lamina that occupies the region D, and has the given density function:

$$D = \left\{ (x,y) \mid 0 \le x \le \frac{\pi}{2},\ 0 \le y \le \cos(x) \right\} \quad \rho(x,y) = 7x$$

Select the correct answer.

   a.   4
   b.   24
   c.   14
   d.   19
   e.   none of these

46. Find the moment of inertia about the x-axis for a cube of constant density 2 and side length 2 if one vertex is located at the origin and three edges lie along the coordinate axes.

Select the correct answer.

   a.   33.3
   b.   128
   c.   10.7
   d.   64
   e.   42.7

47. Use the transformation $x = \sqrt{10}u - \sqrt{\dfrac{10}{3}}v, \; y = \sqrt{10}u + \sqrt{\dfrac{10}{3}}v$ to evaluate the integral

$\displaystyle\iint_R (x^2 - xy + y^2) \; dA$, where R is the region bounded by the ellipse $x^2 - xy + y^2 = 10$.

Select the correct answer.

a. $\dfrac{100\pi}{\sqrt{3}}$

b. $\dfrac{10\pi^2}{\sqrt{3}}$

c. $\dfrac{400\pi}{3^{3/2}}$

d. $\dfrac{100}{\sqrt{3}}$

e. $\dfrac{10}{\sqrt{3}}$

48. Find the area of the region that lies inside the first curve and outside the second curve.

$r = 10\sin\theta, \; r = 5$

Select the correct answer.

a. $A = \dfrac{25\pi}{3} + \dfrac{25\sqrt{3}}{2}$

b. $A = \dfrac{25\sqrt{3}}{2}$

c. $A = \dfrac{25\pi}{3}$

d. $A = \dfrac{25}{3} + \dfrac{25\sqrt{3}}{2}$

e. $A = \dfrac{25}{3} + \dfrac{\sqrt{3}\pi}{2}$

49. Evaluate the integral by interpreting it in terms of areas.

$$\int_{-3}^{3} \sqrt{9 - x^2}\ dx$$

Select the correct answer.

a. 18π
b. 9π
c. 4.5π
d. 5.5π
e. 11.5π

50. Use Part I of the Fundamental Theorem of Calculus to find the derivative of the function.

$$g(x) = \int_{3}^{\sqrt{x}} \frac{5\cos(t)}{t}\ dt$$

Select the correct answer.

a. $\dfrac{dg(x)}{dx} = \dfrac{2.5\cos(\sqrt{x})}{x}$

b. $\dfrac{dg(x)}{dx} = \dfrac{2.5\cos(\sqrt{x})}{\sqrt{x}}$

c. $\dfrac{dg(x)}{dx} = 5\cos(\sqrt{x})$

d. $\dfrac{dg(x)}{dx} = \dfrac{5\cos(\sqrt{x})}{\sqrt{5x}}$

e. $\dfrac{dg(x)}{dx} = \dfrac{2\cos(\sqrt{x})}{5x}$

ANSWER KEY

Stewart - Calculus ET 5e Final Exam Form B

1. b

2. a

3. e

4. c

5. a

6. b

7. a

8. b

9. b

10. b

11. b

12. b

13. d

14. c

15. a

16. a

17. c

18. e

19. a

20. d

21. e

22. c

23. c

24. e

25. a

26. c

27. c

28. c, d, f

29. c

30. c

31. b

32. c

33. b

34. a

35. b

36. a

37. b

38. e

39. a

40. b

41. a

42. c

43. e

44. a

45. a

46. e

47. a

48. a

49. c

50. a

1. Estimate to the hundredth the area from 1 to 5 under the graph of $f(x) = \dfrac{3}{x}$ using four approximating rectangles and right endpoints.

2. Evaluate the integral $\displaystyle\int_0^1 \sqrt{x}\ dx$.

3. If $F(x) = \displaystyle\int_1^x f(t)$, where $f(t) = \displaystyle\int_1^{t^2} \dfrac{\sqrt{9+u^4}}{u}\ du$, find $F''(2)$.

4. Find the general indefinite integral.

$$\int \frac{\sin 16t}{\sin 8t}\ dt$$

5. Use the method of cylindrical shells to find the volume generated by rotating the region bounded by the given curves about the y-axis.

$$y = \frac{1}{x},\ \ y = 0,\ \ x = 1,\ \ x = 3$$

6. Use the method of cylindrical shells to find the volume of solid obtained by rotating the region bounded by the given curves about the x-axis.

$$y^2 - 12y + x = 0,\ \ x = 0$$

Select the correct answer.

a. $V = 6{,}912\pi$
b. $V = 3{,}456\pi$
c. $V = 3{,}506\pi$
d. $V = 3{,}436\pi$
e. $V = 3{,}420\pi$

7. Find the area of the surface obtained by rotating the curve about the x-axis.

$$x = \frac{1}{3}\left(y^2 + 2 \right)^{3/2},\ 0 \le y \le 1$$

8. Sketch a graph to estimate the x-coordinates of the points of intersection of the given curves. Then use this information to estimate the volume of the solid obtained by rotating about the y-axis the region enclosed by these curves.

    $$y = 0, \quad -x^4 + 4x^3 - x^2 + 4x$$

    Select the correct answer.

    a. $V = 315.73\pi$
    b. $V = 336.29\pi$
    c. $V = 313.21\pi$
    d. $V = 320.96\pi$
    e. $V = 396.96\pi$

9. The region bounded by the given curves is rotated about the specified axis. Find the volume of the resulting solid by any method.

    $$y = 5, \quad y = x^2 - 8x + 20; \quad \text{about the line } x = -1$$

10. A particle is moved along the x-axis by a force that measures $\dfrac{3}{(1+x)^2}$ pounds at a point x feet from the origin. Find the work done in moving the particle from the origin to a distance of 2 ft.

11. Suppose g is the inverse function of a differentiable function f and $G(x) = 1/g(x)$. If $f(4) = 2$ and $f'(4) = \dfrac{1}{16}$, find $G'(2)$.

12. Sketch the region bounded by the curves $y = x^2$, $x = 0$, and $y = 1$.

    True or False?

    The centroid of this region is $\left(\dfrac{3}{4}, \dfrac{3}{10} \right)$.

13. If $f(x) = \dfrac{x}{\ln x}$, find $f'(e^3)$.

Select the correct answer.

a. $-\dfrac{2}{9}$

b. $-\dfrac{2}{3}$

c. $\dfrac{2}{9}$

d. $\dfrac{2}{3}$

e. $\dfrac{5}{3}$

14. Find b from the following graph of $f(x) = b + 5(1 - 2^{-x})$.

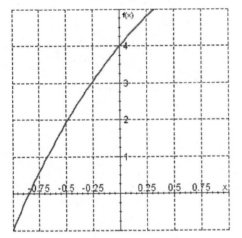

15. Find the centroid of the region bounded by the curves.

$$y = \sin 5x, \quad y = 0, \quad x = 0, \quad x = \dfrac{\pi}{5}$$

16. Evaluate the integral.

$$\int_0^1 xe^{-x^2}\, dx$$

Select the correct answer.

a. $\dfrac{1}{3}(1-e)$

b. $\dfrac{1}{2}(e^{-1}-1)$

c. $\dfrac{1}{2}(1-e^{-1})$

d. $2(1-e^{-1})$

e. $3(1-e^{-1})$

17. Solve the equation for x.

$$e^x = 12$$

18. Differentiate the function.

$$f(x) = \cos(\ln(2x))$$

19. Find the limit.

$$\lim_{x\to 0}(1-6x)^{1/x}$$

20. Use l'Hospital's Rule to calculate the exact value of the limit $\dfrac{f(x)}{g(x)}$ as $x \to 0$.

$$f(x) = e^x - 1 \quad \text{and} \quad g(x) = x^5 + 4x$$

21. Suppose that X and Y are independent random variables, where X is normally distributed with mean 30 and standard deviation 0.1 and Y is normally distributed with mean 35 and standard deviation 0.1. Find the probability.

$$P(30 \le X \le 50,\ 15 \le Y \le 50)$$

22. Evaluate the integral using integration by parts with the indicated choices of u and dv.

$$\int 18\theta \cos(\theta) \ d\theta, \quad u = 18\theta, \quad dv = \cos(\theta) \ d\theta$$

Select the correct answer.

a. $18\theta \cos(\theta) + 18 \sin(\theta) + C$
b. $18\theta \sin(\theta) - 18 \cos(\theta) + C$
c. $18\theta \sin(\theta) + 18 \cos(\theta) + C$
d. $18 \sin(\theta) - 18 \cos(\theta) + C$
e.   none of these

23. Evaluate the integral.

$$\int e^{7x} \cos(4x) \ dx$$

Select the correct answer.

a. $\dfrac{e^{7x}(7\cos(4x) + 4\sin(4x))}{65}$

b. $\dfrac{e^{7x}(7\sin(4x) + 4\cos(4x))}{65}$

c. $\dfrac{e^{7x}(7\sin(4x) - 4\cos(4x))}{65}$

d. $\dfrac{e^{7x}(7\cos(4x) + 4\sin(4x))}{11}$

e.   none of these

24. Evaluate the integral.

$$\int_{1}^{36} \sqrt{t} \ln t \ dt$$

25. Evaluate the indefinite integral.

$$\int x\cos(3x)\ dx$$

Select the correct answer.

a. $\dfrac{1}{3}\cos(3x)+\dfrac{x}{3}\sin(3x)+C$

b. $\dfrac{1}{9}\sin(3x)+\dfrac{x}{3}\cos(3x)+C$

c. $\dfrac{x}{9}\cos(3x)+\dfrac{x}{3}\sin(3x)+C$

d. $\dfrac{1}{9}\cos(3x)+\dfrac{x}{3}\sin(3x)+C$

e. none of these

26. A particle moves on a straight line with velocity function $v(t)=\sin wt\cos^2 wt$.

Find its position function $s=f(t)$ if $f(0)=0$.

27. Find the area of the region bounded by the hyperbola $9x^2-4y^2=36$ and the line $x=10$.

28. Make a substitution to express the integrand as a rational function and then evaluate the integral.

$$\int_4^9 \frac{\sqrt{x}}{x-16}\ dx$$

Round to four decimal places.

29. Find the volume of the resulting solid if the region under the curve $y=1/(x^2+3x+2)$ from $x=0$ to $x=1$ is rotated about the x-axis.

Round your answer to four decimal places.

30. Evaluate the integral.

$$\int_{-1/2}^{\sqrt{2}/2} \frac{x^2}{\sqrt{1-x^2}}\, dx$$

Select the correct answer.

a. $\dfrac{5}{12}\pi - \dfrac{\sqrt{3}+2}{4}$

b. $-\dfrac{5}{24}\pi + \dfrac{\sqrt{3}+2}{8}$

c. $\dfrac{5}{12}\pi + \dfrac{\sqrt{3}+2}{4}$

d. $\dfrac{5}{24}\pi - \dfrac{\sqrt{3}+2}{8}$

e. $\dfrac{5}{24}\pi + \dfrac{\sqrt{3}-2}{8}$

31. Use the Table of Integrals to evaluate the integral.

$$\int 5\sqrt{e^{2x}-1}\, dx$$

32. Use the Table of Integrals to evaluate the integral.

$$\int \frac{x^3}{\sqrt{x^8-2}}\, dx$$

33. Find the area under the curve $y(x) = \dfrac{105}{x^4}$ from $x = 1$ to $x = t$. Evaluate it for $t = 10$, 100, and 1000 in order to find the total area under the curve for $x \geq 1$.

Round to three decimal places.

34. The joint density function for random variables X, Y and Z is $f(x, y, z) = Cxyz$ for $0 \leq x \leq 3$, $0 \leq y \leq 3$, $0 \leq z \leq 1$ and $f(x, y, z) = 0$ otherwise. Find the value of the constant C.

Round the answer to the nearest thousandth.

35. Find the length of the curve for the interval $e \leq t \leq f$.

$$y = \ln\left(\frac{e^t + 1}{e^t - 1}\right)$$

Select the correct answer.

a. $L = \ln\left(\dfrac{e^f + e^{-f}}{e^e + e^{-e}}\right)$

b. $L = \ln\left(\dfrac{e^e - e^{-e}}{e^f - e^{-f}}\right)$

c. $L = \ln\left(\dfrac{e^f + e^{-f}}{e^e - e^{-e}}\right)$

d. $L = \ln\left(\dfrac{e^f - e^{-f}}{e^e - e^{-e}}\right)$

e. none of these

36. True or False?

An integral for the length of the curve $y = x\sqrt[3]{5 - x}$, $0 \leq x \leq 5$ is $\displaystyle\int_0^5 \sqrt{1 + \left[\frac{15 - 4x}{3(5 - x)^{2/3}}\right]^2}\, dx$.

37. A steady wind blows a kite due west. The kite's height above ground from horizontal position $x = 0$ to $x = 80$ ft is given by $y = 180 - \dfrac{1}{60}(x - 30)^2$.

Find the distance traveled by the kite.

38. True or False?

If the lamina shown in the figure below has density $\rho = 10$, then its center of mass is $\left(0, \dfrac{13}{3}\right)$.

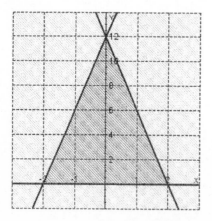

39. True or False?

The center of mass of a lamina with density $\rho = 5$ in the shape of a circle with radius 15 as shown below is $\left(\dfrac{20}{\pi}, \dfrac{20}{\pi} \right)$.

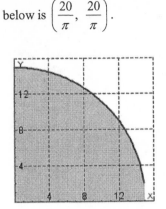

40. A movie theater has been charging $7.50 per person and selling about 400 tickets on a typical weeknight. After surveying their customers, the theater estimates that for every $1.50 that they lower the price, the number of moviegoers will increase by 20 per night. Find the demand function and calculate the consumer surplus when the tickets are priced at $5.

41. The manager of a fast-food restaurant determines that the average time that her customers wait for service is 4 minutes.

The manager wants to advertise that anybody who isn't served within a certain number of minutes gets a free hamburger. But she doesn't want to give away free hamburgers to more than 3% of her customers. What value of x must she use in the advertisement "If you aren't served within x minutes, you get a free hamburger"?

42. For what nonzero values of k does the function $y = A \sin kt + B \cos kt$ satisfy the differential equation $y'' + 16y = 0$ for all values of A and B?

43. A population is modeled by the differential equation $\dfrac{dP}{dt} = 1.6P\left(1 - \dfrac{P}{4,700}\right)$.

For what values of P is the population increasing?

Select the correct answer.

    a. $0 < P < 4,700$
    b. $P > 1.6$
    c. $P > 4,700$
    d. $0 < P < 1.6$
    e.   none of these

44. Program a calculator to use Euler's method with step size $h = 0.8$ to compute the approximate value of $y(0.8)$ where $y(x)$ is the solution of the initial-value problem.

$$\frac{dy}{dx} + 7x^2 y = 4x^2 \quad y(0) = 3$$

45. Solve the differential equation.

$$y' = \frac{7x^6 y}{\ln y}$$

46. Determine whether the differential equation is linear.

$$xy' + \cos x - x^4 y = 0$$

47. Populations of aphids and ladybugs are modeled by the equations

$$\frac{dA}{dt} = 8A - 0.01AL, \quad \frac{dL}{dt} = -0.2L + 0.0001AL.$$

Find the nonzero equilibrium solutions.

48. Find the mass of the lamina that occupies the region D and has the given density function.

$$D = \left\{ (x, y) \mid 0 \le x \le \frac{\pi}{2}, \ 0 \le y \le \cos(x) \right\} \quad \rho(x, y) = 8x$$

Round the answer to the nearest hundredth.

49. Evaluate the integral by reversing the order of integration.

$$\int_0^1 \int_{\arcsin y}^{\pi/2} \cos x \sqrt{4 + \cos^2 x} \ dxdy$$

Select the correct answer.

a. $\dfrac{5^{1/2} - 4^{1/2}}{3}$

b. 0

c. $\dfrac{4^{3/2} - 5^{3/2}}{3}$

d. $\dfrac{4^{1/2} - 5^{1/2}}{3}$

e. $\dfrac{5^{3/2} - 4^{3/2}}{3}$

50. Evaluate the integral by changing to polar coordinates.

$$\iint\limits_{D} e^{-x^2-y^2}\, dA$$

D is the region bounded by the semicircle $x = \sqrt{64-y^2}$ and the y-axis.

1. 3.85

2. 0.666667

3. $\sqrt{265}$

4. $\dfrac{2\sin(8t)}{8} + C$

5. 4π

6. b

7. $\dfrac{3\pi}{2}$

8. a

9. $\dfrac{40}{3\pi}$

10. 2

11. -1

12. T

13. c

14. 4

15. $\left(\dfrac{\pi}{10}, \dfrac{\pi}{8}\right)$

16. c

17. $x = \ln(12)$

18. $\dfrac{-\sin(\ln(2x))}{x}$

19. e^{-6}

20. $\dfrac{1}{4}$

21. $\dfrac{1}{0.02\pi} \displaystyle\int_{30}^{50} \int_{15}^{50} e^{\frac{-(x-30)^2}{0.02}} e^{\frac{-(y-35)^2}{0.02}} \, dy \, dx$

22. c

23. a

24. $\dfrac{432\ln(36)}{3} - \dfrac{860}{9}$

25. d

26. $\dfrac{1-\cos^3(\omega t)}{3\omega}$

27. $6\left(\dfrac{5\sqrt{96}}{2} - \ln\left(\left|\,5+\dfrac{\sqrt{96}}{2}\,\right|\right)\right)$

28. 6.528

29. 0.286835

30. d

31. $5\sqrt{e^{2x}-1} - 5\arccos e^{-x} + C$

32. $\dfrac{1}{4}\ln\left|x^4 + \sqrt{x^8-2}\right| + C$

33. 35

34. 0.099

35. d

36. F

37. 102.28

38. T

39. T

40. 7041.67

41. 14

42. 4, -4

43. a

44. 3

45. $y = e^{\pm\sqrt{2x^7 + C}}$

46. yes

47. $A = 2000, \ L = 800$

48. 4.57

49. e

50. $\dfrac{\left(1 - e^{-64}\right)\pi}{2}$